European Environmental Law

European Environmental Law is a critical, comprehensive and engaging account of the essential and emerging issues in European environmental law and regulation today.

Suitable for advanced undergraduate and postgraduate students, *European Environmental Law* delivers a thematic and contextual treatment of the subject for those taking courses in environmental law, environmental studies, regulation and public policy, and government and international relations.

Placing the key issues in context, *European Environmental Law* takes an interdisciplinary approach to help readers better to understand the implementation and enforcement of environmental law and policy across Europe. It offers an accessible overview and links theory with practical application that will allow students to contextualise the outcomes of legal rules and their impact on public and private behaviours. It provides a definitive account of the subject, examining traditional topics such as nature conservation law, waste law and water law alongside increasingly important fields such as the law of climate change, environmental human rights law and regulation of GMOs and nanotechnology.

Suzanne Kingston is Professor of Law at UCD and Barrister-at-Law practising at the Irish bar, appearing regularly before the Irish and European courts. Suzanne served as a *référendaire* (legal adviser) in the cabinet of Advocate General Geelhoed at the European Court of Justice, Luxembourg from 2004 to 2006, and has been international visiting professor of law at Columbia Law School, New York.

Veerle Heyvaert is Associate Professor of Law (Reader) at LSE where she teaches and publishes on environmental law. Founding Editor-in-Chief of *Transnational Environmental Law*, she has worked as an attorney in Brussels and was Moragoda Professor of Public International Law (Sri Lanka 2015), Sir Peter North Fellow at the Oxford Centre for Socio-Legal Studies and Keble College, and a UNITAR Special Fellow.

Aleksandra Čavoški is a senior lecturer at the School of Law, University of Birmingham. She has over ten years of academic experience in civil and common law jurisdictions and was a key contributor to the development of EU legal studies in Serbia, in particular EU environmental studies. Her publications include research on environmental law in both English and Serbian. She was a visiting professor at Washington and Lee University School of Law (USA 2011).

European Environmental Law

SUZANNE KINGSTON
University College Dublin

VEERLE HEYVAERT
London School of Economics and Political Science

ALEKSANDRA ČAVOŠKI
University of Birmingham

Shaftesbury Road, Cambridge CB2 8EA, United Kingdom

One Liberty Plaza, 20th Floor, New York, NY 10006, USA

477 Williamstown Road, Port Melbourne, VIC 3207, Australia

314–321, 3rd Floor, Plot 3, Splendor Forum, Jasola District Centre, New Delhi – 110025, India

103 Penang Road, #05–06/07, Visioncrest Commercial, Singapore 238467

Cambridge University Press is part of Cambridge University Press & Assessment, a department of the University of Cambridge.

We share the University's mission to contribute to society through the pursuit of education, learning and research at the highest international levels of excellence.

www.cambridge.org
Information on this title: www.cambridge.org/9781107014701

DOI: 10.1017/9781139044202

© Suzanne Kingston, Veerle Heyvaert and Aleksandra Čavoški 2017

This publication is in copyright. Subject to statutory exception and to the provisions of relevant collective licensing agreements, no reproduction of any part may take place without the written permission of Cambridge University Press & Assessment.

First published 2017

A catalogue record for this publication is available from the British Library

Library of Congress Cataloging-in-Publication data
Names: Kingston, Suzanne, 1977– author. | Heyvaert, Veerle, author. | Čavoški, Aleksandra, author.
Title: European environmental law / Suzanne Kingston, Veerle Heyvaert, Aleksandra Čavoški.
Other titles: European Union environmental law
Description: New York : Cambridge University Press, 2017. | Includes bibliographical references and index.
Identifiers: LCCN 2017012395 | ISBN 9781107014701 (hardback)
Subjects: LCSH: Environmental law – European Union countries. | BISAC: LAW / Environmental.
Classification: LCC KJE6242 .K56 2017 | DDC 344.2404/6–dc23
LC record available at https://lccn.loc.gov/2017012395

ISBN 978-1-107-01470-1 Hardback
ISBN 978-1-107-64044-3 Paperback

Cambridge University Press & Assessment has no responsibility for the persistence or accuracy of URLs for external or third-party internet websites referred to in this publication and does not guarantee that any content on such websites is, or will remain, accurate or appropriate.

SK – To Andrew, Saoirse, Róisín, and Cillian
VH – To Jonathan, Jacob, Lia Rose, and the 48%
AC – To my parents, Conor, Niamh and Luka

Contents

List of Figures	xvii
List of Tables	xviii
List of Cases	xix
Preface and Acknowledgements	xxxiii

1 The Foundations of EU Environmental Law: History, Aims and Context   1

History and Development of the European Union's Environmental Policy	1
Aims of EU Environmental Policy	8
A 'High Level of Environmental Protection Taking into Account the Diversity of Situations in the Various Regions of the Union'	9
Sustainable Development	12
Legal Bases and Environmental Guarantee Provisions	16
General Legal Bases	17
Environmental Guarantee Provisions and Minimum Harmonisation	18
The Nature of the European Union's Environmental Competences	22
Understanding EU Environmental Law and Policy in Context	25
Environment, Risk and Science	26
Risk and Risk Regulation	26
Risk Regulation in the European Union	27
Risk Regulation and Critique	29
Science and Expertise in EU Law and Policy	31
Science, Precaution and Discretion	33
Environment and Governance	36
From Pollution Control to Strategic Environmental Governance	37
Multi-level and Transnational Governance	39
Flexible and Decentred Governance	40
Good Governance	41
Environment, Philosophy and Ethics	43
Environment and Geography: The Challenges of Enlargement	47

2 Actors and Instruments   54

Actors	54
The European Commission	54
The Council of the EU	60
The European Parliament	62
The European Council	65

    The Court of Justice of the European Union (CJEU) and the
        General Court   67
   Other Bodies and Actors   68
    The Economic and Social Committee   68
    The Committee of the Regions (CoR)   69
    The European Environment Agency   70
    The European Investment Bank (EIB)   72
    The European Union Network for the Implementation and Enforcement
       of Environmental Law (IMPEL)   73
    Interest Groups   74
       Public Interest Groups   74
       Business Interest Groups   76
   Instruments   76
    Regulations   77
    Directives   78
    Decisions   80
    Environmental Action Programmes   82
    Recommendations and other Soft Law Instruments   83
    Financial Instruments   84
       LIFE (the Financial Instrument for the Environment Regulation)   84
       EU Structural and Investment Funds   86

3 Principles in EU Environmental Law   90
   Introduction   90
   Legal Status and Effect of (Environmental) Principles in EU Law   92
   The Precautionary Principle   94
   The Preventive Principle   99
   The Rectification at Source Principle   100
   The Polluter Pays Principle   100
   The Environmental Integration Principle   103
   Focus on the Integration of EU Economic and Environmental
      Law and Policy   105
    Overview   105
    Environmental Considerations and the Treaty Internal Market Provisions   109
    Environmental Considerations and Article 110 TFEU   109
    Environmental Considerations and Articles 34–36 TFEU   110
    Article 34 TFEU and National Measures Promoting Green Energy   112
    Green Public Procurement   116

4 Techniques of Regulating the Environment   120
   Introduction: The EU's Changing Regulatory Toolbox   120
   Understanding Regulatory Choices: Factors and Philosophies
      Underlying EU Decisions as to Environmental Regulatory
      Technique   123

	Environmental Effectiveness	123
	Economic Efficiency	124
	Political and Administrative Feasibility	125
	Flexibility	126
	Compatibility with Existing EU and National Institutional Frameworks	126
	Compatibility with Beliefs and 'Ideas'	127
	Surveying the EU's Environmental Regulatory Techniques	129
	Hierarchy: Direct or 'Command and Control' Techniques	129
	Overview	129
	Flexible Direct Regulation: Framework Directives	132
	Proceduralised Direct Regulation	133
	The Pros and Cons of Direct Environmental Regulation in the EU	133
	Market-Based Instruments	135
	Overview	135
	Tradable Permit Schemes	139
	Other Examples of the EU's Embrace of Market-Based Instruments	142
	Network-Based Approaches: Voluntary Techniques and Corporate Social Responsibility	143
	Overview	143
	Enabling Corporations	145
	Enabling Consumers and Civil Society	148
5	**Environmental Rights in Europe**	**150**
	Introduction: Why Environmental (Human) Rights?	150
	Rights Originating from the Council of Europe	153
	The 1950 European Convention for the Protection of Human Rights and Fundamental Freedoms (the 'ECHR')	153
	No Right to a Decent Environment	153
	Article 8 ECHR: Right to Respect for Private and Family Life	154
	Article 6(1) ECHR: Right to a Fair Trial	161
	Article 1 of Protocol No. 1: The Right to Property	162
	The 1961 European Social Charter (the 'ESC')	163
	The Charter of Fundamental Rights of the EU (the 'Charter')	165
	The Aarhus Convention on Access to Information, Public Participation in Decision-Making and Access to Justice in Environmental Matters	168
	The Aarhus Convention's Approach to Environmental Rights	169
	Signatories, Ratification and Compliance	170
	Aarhus's Three Substantive Pillars	171
	Access to Information	172
	Public Participation	173
	Access to Justice	176
	Implementation of the Aarhus Convention in EU Law	179
	Other Relevant Sources of International Human Rights Law	182

6 Public Enforcement of EU Environmental Law — 184
Introduction: The Enforcement Deficit in EU Environmental Law — 184
Public Enforcement of EU Environmental Law: Enforcement by the European Commission — 186
  Article 258 TFEU — 186
    Overview — 187
    The Administrative Phase — 188
    The Litigation Phase — 192
  'General and Persistent' Breaches of EU Law — 192
  Defences — 193
    Interim Measures — 194
  Article 260 TFEU — 195
  Broader Commission Initiatives to Improve Enforcement of EU Environmental Law — 199
Public Enforcement of EU Environmental Law: Enforcement by National Authorities — 200
  Principles — 200
  The European Union Network for the Implementation and Enforcement of Environmental Law (IMPEL) Network — 203
  The Environmental Liability Directive — 204
    Overview — 204
    Scope of Application — 205
    Causation — 207
    Duties Imposed on Operators — 209
    Powers and Duties of Competent Authorities — 211
    Observations and Requests for Action — 212
    Transboundary Damage — 212
  Criminal Penalties — 213

7 Private Enforcement of EU Environmental Law — 217
Private Enforcement of EU Environmental Law at National Level — 217
  Direct Effect of EU Environmental Law — 217
    Overview — 217
    Must a Directly Effective Provision Confer a Right on an Individual? — 219
    Which Bodies Must Apply Directly Effective Provisions? — 222
  Other Means of Relying on EU Law before National Courts — 230
    The Duty of Consistent Interpretation ('Indirect Effect') — 230
    'Triangular' Cases — 233
    'Incidental' Horizontal Direct Effect — 234
    Horizontal Direct Effect of a 'General Principle' of EU Law — 235
    State Liability in Damages for Breach of EU Law — 236
  EU Legislation on Access to Justice at National Level and the Role of the Aarhus Convention — 237
    The Provisions of the Aarhus Convention on Access to Justice — 238

Implementation of Article 9 of the Aarhus Convention in EU Law	240
Private Enforcement of EU Law at EU Level	246
Access to Justice before the EU Courts	246
Access to Justice by Means of Internal Review under Regulation 1367/2006	251
Other Means of Accessing Justice at EU Level	254

8 Climate Change 257
Introduction 257
Mandate of the European Union with Regard to Climate Change 258
High Stakes: The Challenge of Climate Change Leadership 260
The External Dimension of Climate Change Leadership 262
The Internal Dimension of Climate Change Leadership 266
The Challenge of Leadership Exemplified: The Case of Aviation 269
The Scope of the Climate Change Challenge 273
Climate Change as a Multi-Level Governance Challenge: The Example of Renewable Energy 275
Renewable Energy Policy in the EU: Reconciling European Ambition with National Differentiation through Multi-Level Governance 275
The 2009 Renewable Energy Directive (RED) 278
   National Action Plans 280
   Cooperation between Member States 281
   Access to the Grid and Guarantees of Origin 282
   The Difficult Question of Biofuels 283
   National Support Schemes 286
Free Movement of Renewable Energy: Navigating between the Goals of Trade Liberalisation, Environmental Protection and National Control over Energy Policy 287
The Challenge of a Regulation-Based Market 289
The ETS as Market-Based Regulation 290
Gauging the Effectiveness of Market-Based Regulation 292
Managing a Regulation-Based Market 293
   The Allocation of Allowances 293
   Recession and Transnational Offsetting 294
   Addressing the Burden of the Past: Backloading and the Market Stability Reserve 296
Concluding Remarks 296

9 Air Pollution and Industrial Emissions 298
Introduction: Key Themes of EU Air Pollution and Industrial Emissions Law 299
Ozone-Depleting Substances 301

Ambient Air Quality	306
Approaches to Standardisation	309
The EU Legal Framework	312
The 2001 NECD	312
The 2008 AQFD	313
Member State Implementation of EU Ambient Air Legislation	315
Regulating Industrial Emissions	321
Integrated Pollution Prevention and Control within the IED	323
'Best Available Techniques' (BAT)	325
Standardisation in the IPPC Framework: The Anchoring Function of BAT	328
The Evolution of BREFs: A Hardening Attitude towards EU Soft Law	330
Flexibility in the IED: An Assessment	333
Coherence in Air Pollution Law	335
Conclusion	336
10 EU Water Law	**338**
Introduction	338
Europe's Waters Interconnected	338
The History of EU Water Law	339
The Inter-Related Threads of EU and International Water Law	340
The 2000 Water Framework Directive	341
History of the Water Framework Directive (WFD)	341
Overview	342
River Basin Management and the 'Programme of Measures'	343
The 'Environmental Objectives'	344
Surface Water	345
Groundwater	348
The Water Framework Directive's Derogations from the Environmental Objectives	352
Combined Approach	353
Priority Substances	354
Economic Analysis	355
Public Involvement	357
Governance	357
Assessment	360
Drinking Water	360
History and Overview	360
Ensuring that Drinking Water is 'Wholesome and Clean'	361
Providing for Hard Cases: Lead and Pesticides	362
Monitoring and Compliance	363
Assessment	364
Bathing Water	365
Defining Bathing Waters	365

From Emissions Limit Values to Classification	366
Monitoring and Assessment	367
Public Participation	367
Assessment	368
Regulation of Dangerous Substances	368
Dangerous Substances in Water Directives	368
Priority Substances Directive	369
Directive 2008/105/EC	369
Listing Substances and Review of Adopted List of Priority Substances	369
Assessment	370
Nitrates	371
Regulating Non-Point Source Pollution	371
'Nitrogen Zones'	371
Improving Environmental Quality	372
Additional Measures and Derogations	372
Assessment	373
Urban and Industrial Waste Water	373
Collection, Treatment and Disposal	374
Sensitive Areas	374
Identifying Eutrophication	375
Less-Sensitive Areas	376
Industrial Waste Water	377
Institutional Framework	377

11 Impact Assessment — 379

History and International Context	379
The 1991 UNECE Espoo Convention on Transboundary Environmental Impact Assessment	382
Overview	382
Obligations	383
The EIA Directive	385
Scope and Purpose	386
What is an EIA?	387
The 'Competent Authority'	389
Projects Subject to EIA	390
Annex I Projects: Mandatory EIA	390
Annex II Projects: The Screening Process	391
Exemptions from the EIA Requirement	393
The EIA Procedure	394
The Developer's EIA Report	394
Consultation and Public Participation	395
Transboundary Projects	396
The Decision to Grant or Refuse Development Consent	396

Relationship with other Assessment Procedures	397
Communication of the Competent Authority's Decision	398
Remedies and Access to Justice	398
The Strategic Environmental Assessment Directive	402
Scope and Purpose of the SEA Directive	403
The Obligation to Carry Out an SEA	403
Plans and Programmes Subject to Mandatory SEA	403
Screening of other Projects	404
Exemptions	404
The SEA Procedure	405
Environmental Report	405
Consultation of Designated Authorities and of the Public Likely to be Affected	405
Transboundary Consultation	406
Relationship with other Assessment Procedures	407
The Decision	407
Remedies	407

12 Nature and Biodiversity Protection — 410

Introduction	410
Changing Narratives: Nature Conservation, Biodiversity Protection and the Safeguarding of Natural Capital	412
The Birds Directive and Habitats Directive: The Twin Pillars of Natura 2000	416
The Birds Directive	416
The Habitats Directive	417
Designation and its Consequences: The Legal Status of SPAS and SACS	419
The Designation Process	420
The Consequences of Designation	421
Designation and its Discontents	422
Biodiversity and Sustainability: The Role of Economic Considerations in Natura 2000	423
Protecting SCIs and the Role of the Precautionary Principle	428
Protective Regimes: The Relation between the Birds and Habitats Directives	429
Timing of Member State Obligations	431
The Management of Protected Sites: Article 6(1) Habitats Directive	432
Avoiding Deterioration and Disturbance: Article 6(2) Habitats Directive	434
Assessing Development: Article 6(3) Habitats Directive	434
Declassification	440
Compensating Biodiversity Losses	441
The Effectiveness of the Birds and Habitats Directives	443
Other Measures	444

Conclusion: Overcoming Institutional and Systemic
   Dichotomy   445

13 Technological Risk Regulation: Chemicals, Genetically Modified Organisms and Nanotechnology   447
Introduction   447
Dual-Purpose Regulation: Reconciling Market Harmonisation
   with Health and Environmental Protection   450
EU Chemicals Regulation as a Network   453
   The REACH Regulation   454
   The CLP Regulation   457
   Further Measures   459
Chemicals, GMO and Nano Regulation as Technological Risk
   Regulation   460
   Information Production   460
   Risk Management   461
   Legitimacy and Effectiveness Challenges of Data-Driven Regimes   463
Regulating Uncertainty   465
   *Legal Principles: The Requirement to Pursue a High Level of
      Environmental Protection (HLP) and the Precautionary
      Principle*   466
   Claims to Legitimacy: Expertise, Transparency and Participation   468
   Claims to Legitimacy: Updating, Review and Monitoring   470
GMO Regulation: A Fraught State of Coexistence   471
   The Regulatory Framework   474
   Scope for Post-Authorisation Differentiation   475
      Coexistence Measures   476
      Safeguard Clauses   477
      Derogation or 'Opt-Ups' under Article 114(4)–(6) TFEU   480
      Article 26(b) DRD: Farewell Internal Market?   480
Nanotechnology: New Rules for New Tools?   483
Conclusion   487

14 Waste   489
EU Waste Policy   489
Waste Framework Directive (WFD)   494
   Overview of the WFD   494
   What is Waste?   498
      By-Product   502
      End-of-Waste   504
      Hazardous Waste   505
   Shipment of Waste   506
   Waste Operations   508
      Landfills   508

Incineration of Waste 510
Waste Streams 512
Packaging 513
Batteries and Accumulators 514
End-of-Life Vehicles 515
Waste Electrical and Electronic Equipment (WEEE) 516
Future Challenges 517

Index 518

Figures

2.1	Percentage of ENVI Co-Decision Files Agreed per Reading in the Last Parliamentary Mandate	65
4.1	Actors in EU Environmental Governance, and Examples of the Associated Regulatory Techniques	122
6.1	Open DG Environment Infringements	187
6.2	Infringements by Environmental Sector (2015)	188
6.3	Article 260(2) TFEU Actions per Member State as at End 2015	198
8.1	Renewable Energy Production 2005 and 2020 Targets	279
14.1	Infringements by Environmental Sector, 2007–2015	493
14.2	EU Waste Hierarchy	495

Tables

2.1 Allocation of Portfolios and Supporting Services in the
Environmental Policy Area 56
2.2 Breakdown of the Available Structural Funds by Theme for
the EU as a Whole 87
12.1 Habitats Non-Deterioration and Non-Disturbance Strategies 435

List of Cases

International Court of Justice

Pulp Mills in the River Uruguay (Argentina v. Uruguay), ICJ Reports 2010,14   381

WTO

EC – Biotech, WT/DS291, WT/DS292, WT/DS293 European Communities – Measures Affecting the Approval and Marketing of Biotech Products   97, 473

US – Gasoline, WT/DS2/AB/R United States – Standards for Reformulated and Conventional Gasoline   286

US – Shrimp WT/DS558/AB/R United States – Import Prohibition of Certain Shrimp and Shrimp Products   286

Court of Justice of the European Union

Abraham and Others, Case C-2/07 ECLI:EU:C:2008:133   386, 387, 388, 390, 391

Acino v. Commission, Case C-269/13P ECLI:EU:C:2014:255   95

ADBHU, Case 240/3, ECLI:EU:C:1985:59   3, 248

Afton Chemical, Case C-343/09 ECLI:EU:C:2010:419   95

Agrarproduktion Staebelow, Case C-504/04 ECLI:EU:C:2006:30   95

Air Transport Association of America and Others v. Secretary of State for Energy and Climate Change, Case C-366/10 [2001] ECR I-13755, ECLI:EU:C:2011:864   10, 68, 270–271

Ålands Vindkraft v. Energimyndigheten, Case C-573/12 ECLI:EU:C:2014:2037   92, 113–116, 119, 283, 288–289

Alpharma v. Council, Case T-70/99 ECLI:EU:T:2002:210   95

Altrip, Case C-72/12 ECLI:EU:C:2013:712   243, 245, 400

AMS, Case C-176/12 ECLI:EU:C:2014:2   235

Antonio Niselli, Case 457/02 ECLI:EU:C:2004:707   501

Arcaro, Case C-168/95 ECLI:EU:C:1996:363   230–232

Arcelor v. Parliament and Council, Case T-16/04 ECLI:EU:T:2010:54   251

ARCO Chemie, Joined Cases C-418/97 and C-419/97 ECLI:EU:C:2000:318   499, 500, 501–502, 504, 505

Artegodan v. Commission, Joined Cases T-74/00, 76/00, 83/00, 84/00, 85/00, 132/00, 137/00 and 141/00 [2002] ECR II-4945; ECLI:EU:T:2002:283   36, 91, 94, 105, 462

Asda Stores, Case C-372/06 ECLI:EU:C:2007:787   224
Association nationale pour la protection des eaux et rivières-TOS, Association OABA v. Ministère de l'Écologie, du développement et de l'Aménagement durables, Case C-473/07 ECLI:EU:C:2009:30   333
Austria v. Commission, Joined Cases C-439/05 P and C-454/05 P ECLI:EU:C:20007:510   18, 21, 451–452, 480
Austria v. Parliament and Council, Case C-161/04 ECLI:EU:C:2006:66   93, 105
Avesta Polarit Chrome, Case C-114/01 ECLI:EU:C:2003:448   501, 504
Azienda Agro-Zootecnica Franchini, Case C-2/10 ECLI:EU:C:2011:502   18, 19
Barker, Case C-290/03 ECLI:EU:C:2006:286   387
Basses Corbières (Commission v. France) Case C-374/98 ECLI:EU:C:2000:670   431
Bathing Waters (Commission v. Spain), Case C-278/01 ECLI:EU:C:2003:635   197, 198
Becker, Case C-8/81 ECLI:EU:C:1982:7   219, 227
Beer Purity (Commission v. Germany), Case 178/84 [1987] ECR 1227   33
Belgian Shell NV, Case C-241/12 ECLI:EU:C:2013:821   500, 501
Bernaldez, Case C-129/94 ECLI:EU:C:1996:143   235
Bettati v. Safety Hi-Tech SRL, Case C-341/95 ECLI:EU:C:1998:353   8, 93, 95
Bluhme (Criminal Proceedings against Ditlev Bluhme), Case C-67/97 ECLI:EU:C:1998:584   111, 112
Boxus, Joined Cases C-128/09 to 131/09, C-134/09 and 135/09 ECLI:EU:C:2011:667   246, 394, 400
Brady v. EPA, Case C-113/12 ECLI:EU:C:2013:627   499, 503
Brasserie du Pêcheur, Case C-46/93 ECLI:EU:C:1996:79   236
British Telecommunications plc Case C-392/93 ECLI:EU:C:1996:131   236
Brussels Hoofdstedlijk Gewest, Case C-275/09 ECLI:EU:C:2011:154   386, 390, 391
Bund für Umwelt und Naturschutz Deutschland v. Germany, Case C-461/13 ECLI:EU:C:2015:433   345, 353, 359
Bund Naturschutz in Bayern and Others, Case C-244/05 ECLI:EU:C:2006:579   432
Busseni, Case C-221/88 [1990] ECR I-495   234
Buzzi Unicem and Others, Joined Cases C-478/08 and C-479/08 ECLI:EU:C:2010:129   206, 207, 208
Campus Oil, Case C-72/83 ECLI:EU:C:1984:256   287–288
Cartagena Protocol, Opinion 2/00 ECLI:EU:C:2001:664   17, 23
Cassis de Dijon (Rewe), Case 120/78 [1979] ECR-659, ECLI:EU:C:1979:42   111, 472, 487
Centrosteel, Case C-456/98 ECLI:EU:C:2000:402   231
CIA Security International, Case C-194/94 [1996] ECR I-2201   234, 235
ClientEarth v. Secretary of State for the Environment, Food and Rural Affairs, Case C-404/13 ECLI:EU:C:2013:805   312, 315, 320–321, 427

List of Cases   xxi

Codomiu, Case C-309/89 ECLI:EU:C:1994:197   249
Commission v. Austria, Case C-320/03 (Inntalautobahn I) [2005] ECR I-987, ECLI:EU:C:2005:684   336, 483
Commission v. Austria, Case C-507/04 ECLI:EU:C:2007:427   78
Commission v. Austria, Case C-508/04 ECLI:EU:C:2007:274   433
Commission v. Austria, Case C-422/08 ECLI:EU:C:2009:385   205
Commission v. Austria, Case C-28/09 (Inn Valley) (Inntalautobahn II) ECLI:EU:C:2011:854   112, 336, 483
Commission v. Belgium, Case C-77/69 ECLI:EU:C:1970:34   194
Commission v. Belgium, Case C-239/85 ECLI:EU:C:1986:457   78, 79
Commission v. Belgium, Case C-247/85 ECLI:EU:C:1987:436   423
Commission v. Belgium, Case C-12/89 ECLI:EU:C:1990:285   361
Commission v. Belgium, Case C-2/90 (Walloon Waste) ECLI:EU:C:1992:310   92, 100, 110–111, 112, 501
Commission v Belgium, Case C-307/98 ECLI:EU:C:2000:284   366
Commission v Belgium, Case C-122/02 ECLI:EU:C:2003:39   365
Commission v Belgium, Case C-435/09 ECLI:EU:C:2011:176   390, 391, 396, 397
Commission v Belgium, Case C-395/13 ECLI:EU:C:2014:2347   377
Commission v Council, Case C-300/89 (Titanium Dioxide) ECLI:EU:C:1991:244   4–5, 17
Commission v Council, Case C-155/91 (Waste Directive) ECLI:EU:C:1993:98   92
Commission v Council, Case C-281/01 (Energy Star) ECLI:EU:C:2002:761   23
Commission v Council, Case C-170/03 (Environmental Criminal Penalties) ECLI:EU:C:2005:176   186
Commission v Council, Case C-176/03 ECLI:EU:C:2005:542   201, 213
Commission v Council, Case C-440/05 (Ship Source Pollution) ECLI:EU:C:2007:625   201, 214, 215
Commission v Council, Case C-378/08 (Raffinerie Méditerranée) [2010] ECR I-919 ECLI:EU:C:2010:126   93, 99, 102–103, 206, 207, 208, 211
Commission v. Denmark, Case C-302/86 (Danish Bottles) ECLI:EU:C:1988:421   111, 112
Commission v. Denmark, Case C-52/90 ECLI:EU:C:1992:151   189
Commission v. Estonia, Case C-505/09 P ECLI:EU:C:2012:178   294
Commission v. Finland, Case C-335/07 ECLI:EU:C:2009:612   375–376
Commission v. Finland, Case C-328/08 ECLI:EU:C:2008:775   205
Commission v. France, Case C-232/78 ECLI:EU:C:1979:215   194
Commission v. France, Case C-252/85 ECLI:EU:C:1988/202   78
Commission v. France, Case C-374/98 (Basses Corbières) ECLI:EU:C:2000:670   431
Commission v. France, Case C-38/99 ECLI:EU:C:2000:674   79
Commission v. France, Case C-220/99 ECLI:EU:C:2001:434   421

Commission v. France, Case C-280/02 [2004] ECR I-8573   375
Commission v. France, Case C-304/02 (French Fisheries) ECLI:EU:
  C:2005:444   196–197
Commission v. France, Case C-147/07 ECLI:EU:C:2008:67   365
Commission v. France, Case C-241/08 [2010] ECR I-1697   435
Commission v. France, Case C-330/08 ECLI:EU:C:2008:720   205
Commission v. France, Case C-333/08 ECLI:EU:C:2010:44   95
Commission v. France, Case C-64/09 ECLI:EU:C:2010:197   79
Commission v. France, Case C-23/13 ECLI:EU:C:2013:723   377
Commission v. Germany, Case C-29/84 ECLI:EU:C:1985:229   79
Commission v. Germany, Case C-178/84 (Beer Purity) [1987] ECR 1227   33
Commission v. Germany, Case C-217/88 ECLI:EU:C:1990:290   189
Commission v. Germany, Case C-57/89 (Leybucht) ECLI:EU:
  C:1991:89   423–425, 430–431, 440
Commission v. Germany, Case C-431/92 ECLI:EU:C:1995:260   219–220
Commission v. Germany, Case C-184/97 ECLI:EU:C:1999:546   353–354
Commission v. Germany, Case C-217/97 ECLI:EU:C:1999:395   182
Commission v. Germany, Case C-71/99 ECLI:EU:C:2001:434   421
Commission v. Germany, Case C-137/14 ECLI:EU:C:2015:683   245, 400, 401
Commission v. Greece, Case C-68/88 ECLI:EU:C:1989:339   200
Commission v. Greece, Case C-68/04 ECLI:EU:C:2005:347   317
Commission v. Greece, Case C-293/07 [2008] ECR I-182   435
Commission v. Greece, Case C-368/08 ECLI:EU:C:2009:326   205
Commission v. Greece, Case C-407/09 ECLI:EU:C:2011:196   199
Commission v. Ireland, Case C-74/82 [1984] ECR 317   33
Commission v. Ireland, Case C-392/96 ECLI:EU:C:1999:431   391, 392
Commission v. Ireland, Case C-67/99 ECLI:EU:C:2001:432   421
Commission v. Ireland, Case C-354/99 ECLI:EU:C:2001:550   201
Commission v. Ireland, Case C-316/00 ECLI:EU:C:2002:657   361
Commission v. Ireland, Case C-494/01 ECLI:EU:C:2004:546   192
Commission v. Ireland, Case C-494/01 ECLI:EU:C:2005:250   193, 493
Commission v. Ireland, Case C-459/03 (Mox Plant) ECLI:EU:C:2006:345   24–25
Commission v. Ireland, Case C-418/04 [2007] ECR I-10947, ECLI:EU:
  C:2007:780   426, 435
Commission v. Ireland, Case C-216/05 ECLI:EU:C:706   396
Commission v. Ireland, Case C-66/06 ECLI:EU:C:2008:637   391
Commission v. Ireland, Case C-215/06 ECLI:EU:C:2008:380   386, 387, 399
Commission v. Ireland, Case C-427/07 ECLI:EU:C:2009:457   79, 178, 240, 244,
  245–246, 386, 400, 401
Commission v. Ireland, Case C-50/09 ECLI:EU:C:2011:109   79, 388, 389,
  390, 397
Commission v. Ireland, Case C-374/11 (Septic Tanks) ECLI:EU:
  C:2012:827   197, 198

Commission v. Italy, Case C-39/72 ECLI:EU:C:1973:13   77
Commission v. Italy, Case C-52/75 ECLI:EU:C:1976:29   79
Commission v. Italy, Case C-92/79 ECLI:EU:C:1980:1   3
Commission v. Italy, Case C-262/85 ECLI:EU:C:1987:340   78, 423
Commission v. Italy, Case C-363/85 ECLI:EU:C:1987:196   78
Commission v. Italy, Case C-365/97 ECLI:EU:C:1999:544   194, 201
Commission v. Italy, Case C-87/02 ECLI:EU:C:2004:363   393
Commission v. Italy, Case C-119/04 ECLI:EU:C:2006:489   197
Commission v. Italy, Case C-486/04 ECLI:EU:C:2006:732   386
Commission v. Italy, Case C-135/05 ECLI:EU:C:2007:250   193
Commission v. Italy, Case C-503/06 R ECLI:EU:C:2007:120   195
Commission v. Italy, Case C-297/08 ECLI:EU:C:2010:115   93
Commission v. Italy, Case C-573/08 ECLI:EU:C:2009:775   195
Commission v. Italy, Case C-565/10 ECLI:EU:C:2012:476   377
Commission v. Italy, Case C-68/11 ECLI:EU:C:2012:815   316, 317–318
Commission v. Italy, Case C-85/13 ECLI:EU:C:2014:251   377
Commission v. Latvia, Case C-267/11 P ECLI:EU:C:2013:624   294
Commission v. Luxembourg, Case C-75/01 [2003] ECR I-1585   435
Commission v. Luxembourg, Case C-273/08 [2008] ECR I-194   317
Commission v. Luxembourg, Case C-331/08 ECLI:EU:C:2009:185   205
Commission v. Malta, Case C-76/08 ECLI:EU:C:2009:535   195
Commission v. Malta, Case C-76/08 R ECLI:EU:C:2008:252   195
Commission v. Netherlands, Case C-96/81 ECLI:EU:C:192   194
Commission v. Netherlands, Case C-236/85 ECLI:EU:C:1987:436   78
Commission v. Netherlands, Case C-247/85 ECLI:EU:C:1987:339   78
Commission v. Netherlands, Case C-3/96 [1998] ECR I-3031   425
Commission v. Netherlands, Case C-146/04 ECLI:EU:C:2005:236   317
Commission v. Netherlands, Case C-368/10 (Dutch Coffee) (Max Havelaar) ECLI:
   EU:C:2012 284   117, 118
Commission v. Poland, Case C-193/07 R ECLI:EU:C:2009:495   195
Commission v. Poland, Case C-165/08 ECLI:EU:C:2009:473   483
Commission v. Poland, Case C-48/12 ECLI:EU:C:2013:3   317
Commission v. Portugal, Case C-233/07 ECLI:EU:C:2008:271   377
Commission v. Portugal, Case C-526/09 ECLI:EU:C:2010:734   377
Commission v. Slovenia, Case C-402/08 ECLI:EU:C:2009:157   205
Commission v. Spain, Case C-355/90 (Santoña Marshes) ECLI:EU:
   C:1993:331   425–426, 435
Commission v. Spain, Case C-278/01 (Bathing Waters) ECLI:EU:C:635   197, 198
Commission v Spain, Case C-29/02 ECLI:EU:C:2003:37   365
Commission v Spain, Case C-416/02 ECLI:EU:C:2005:511   372
Commission v Spain, Case C-332/04 ECLI:EU:C:2006:180   388, 391, 395, 398
Commission v Spain, Case C-189/07 ECLI:EU:C:2008:760   193
Commission v Spain, Case C-560/08 ECLI:EU:C:2011:835   388

Commission v. Spain, Case C-404/09 ECLI:EU:C:2011:768   388
Commission v. Spain, Case C-90/10 ECLI:EU:C:2011:606   433
Commission v. Spain, Case C-343/10 ECLI:EU:C:2011:260   377
Commission v. Sweden, Case C-246/07 (PFOS) ECLI:EU:C:2010:203   25
Commission v. Sweden, Case C-438/07 ECLI:EU:C:2009:613   377
Commission v. UK, Case C-142/89 ECLI:EU:C:1989:528   194
Commission v. UK, Case C-337/89 ECLI:EU:C:1992:456   194, 362
Commission v. UK, Case C-56/90 ECLI:EU:C:1993:307   194, 366
Commission v. UK, Case C-39/99 ECLI:EU:C:1999:326   78
Commission v. UK, Case C-63/02 ECLI:EU:C:2003:38   365
Commission v. UK, Case C-508/03 ECLI:EU:C:2006:287   387
Commission v. UK, Case 6/04 [2005] ECR I-9017   435
Commission v. UK, Case C-390/07 ECLI:EU:C:2009:765   375–376, 377
Commission v. UK, Case C-346/08 ECLI:EU:C:2010:213   79
Commission v. UK, Case C-417/08 ECLI:EU:C:2009:384   205
Commission v. UK, Case C-301/10 ECLI:EU:C:2012:633   377
Commission v. UK, Case C-530/11 ECLI:EU:C:2014:67   79, 245, 401
Commune de Mesquer v. Total France SA and Total International Ltd, Case C-188/07 ECLI:EU:C:2008:359   207, 500, 503
Concordia Bus Finland, Case C-513/99 ECLI:EU:C:2002:495   105, 117
Costa v. ENEL, Case 6/64 ECLI:EU:C:1964:66   218
Council and Commission v. Stichting Natuur en Milieu and Pesticide Action Network Europe, Case T-338/08 ECLI:EU:T:2012:300   253
Council and Commission v. Stichting Natuur en Milieu and Pesticide Action Network Europe, Joined Cases C-404/12 P and C-405/12 P ECLI:EU:C:2015:5   226, 253
Council v. Vereniging Milieudefensie Stichting Stop Luchtverontreiniging Utrecht, Joined Cases C-401/12 P ECLI:EU:C:2015:4   253
Daihatsu Deutschland, Case C-97/96 [1997] ECR I-6843   234
Danielsson, Case T-219/95 ECLI:EU:T:1995:219   248
Danish Bottles (Commission v. Denmark), Case C-302/86 ECLI:EU:C:1988:421   111, 112
Dassonville, Case C-8/74 ECLI:EU:C:1974:82   111
Denmark v. Commission, Case C-3/00 ECLI:EU:C:2003:167   21
Department of the Environment for Northern Ireland v. Seaport, Case C-474/10 ECLI:EU:C:2011:681   406
Deponiezweckverband Eiterköpfe v.Land Rheinland-Pflaz, Case C-6/03 ECLI:EU:C:2005:655   18, 19
Deutsche Unwelthilfe eV v. Germany, Case C-515/11 ECLI:EU:C:2013:523   181
Di Pinto (Criminal Proceedings against Patrice Di Pinto), Case C-361/89 ECLI:EU:C:1991:118   79
Difesa della Cava, Case C-236/92 ECLI:EU:C:1994:60   219, 227–228
Dimos Kropias, Case C-473/14 ECLI:EU:C:2015:582   404

Djurgården, Case C-263/08 ECLI:EU:C:2009:631   243, 395, 400, 401
Dragaggi a.o., Case C-117/03 ECLI:EU:C:2005:16   432
Dusseldorp (Chemische Afvalstoffen Dusseldorp BV and Others v. Minister van Volkshuisvesting, Ruimtelijke Ordening en Milieubeheer), Case C-203/96 ECLI:EU:C:1998:316   111, 112
Dutch Coffee (Commission v. Netherlands) (Max Havelaar), Case C-368/10 ECLI:EU:C:2012:284   117, 118
Ecologistas en Acción-CODA, Case C-142/07 ECLI:EU:C:2008:445   386, 388, 390
Edwards, Case C-260/11 ECLI:EU:C:2013/321   244–245, 401
EEB and Stichting Natuur en Milieu v. Commission, Joined Cases T-236/04 and T-241/04 ECLI:EU:T:2005:426   248, 249
Energy Star (Commission v. Council), Case C-281/01 ECLI:EU:C:2002:761   23
Enichem Base, Case C-380/87 ECLI:EU:C:1989:318   227, 234–235
Environmental Criminal Penalties (Commission v. Council), Case C-170/03 ECLI:EU:C:2005:176   186
ERTA, Case 22/70 ECLI:EU:C:1971:32   23
Essent Belgium, Joined Cases C-204/12 and C-208/12 ECLI:EU:C:2013:294, ECLI:EU:C:2014:2192   116, 283, 288–289
Etimine, Case C-15/10 ECLI:EU:C:2011:504   95
Evropaïki Dynamiki v. European Environment Agency, Case T-33/06, ECLI:EU:T:2010:292   118
Fedesa, Case C-331/88 ECLI:EU:C:1990:391   35
Fediol v. Commission, Case C-70/87 ECLI:EU:C:1989:254   253
Fipa Group Srl and Others, Case C-534/13 ECLI:EU:C:2015:140   208, 211–212
First Corporate Shipping (FCS), Case C-371/98 ECLI:EU:C:2000:600   427–428
Fish Legal, Emily Shirley v. Information Commissioner, United Utilities, Yorkshire Water and Southern Water, Case C-279/12 ECLI:EU:C:2013:853   181
Flachglas Torgau GmbH v. Germany, Case C-204/09 ECLI:EU:C:2012:71   181
Foster v. British Gas, Case C-188/89 ECLI:EU:C:1990:313   228
Foto-Frost v. Hauptzollamt Lübeck-Ost, Case C-314/85 ECLI:EU:C:1987:452   318
Francovich, Joined Cases C-6/90 and 9/90 ECLI:EU:C:1991:428   236, 237
Fratelli Costanzo, Case 103/88 [1989] ECR 1839, ECLI:EU:C:1989:256   220, 222, 234
Fratelli Variola Spa v. Amministrazione delle finanze dello Stato, Case C-34/73 ECLI:EU:C:1973:101   77
French Fisheries (Commission v. France), Case C-304/02 ECLI:EU:C:2005:444   196–197
Gaston Schul Douane-expediteur, Case C-461/03 ECLI:EU:C:2005:742   318
GEMO, Case C-126/01 ECLI:EU:C:2003:622   102
Germany v. Parliament and Council, Case C-233/94 ECLI:EU:C:2000:544   10
Germany v. Parliament and Council, Case C-380/03 [2006] ECR I-11573   452

Google Spain, Case C-131/12 ECLI:EU:C:2014:317   166
Gowan, Case C-77/09 [2010] ECR I-13533, ECLI:EU:C:2010:803   35–36, 92, 93, 94, 95, 462
Green Network, Case C-66/13 ECLI:EU:C:2014:2399   24
Greenpeace, Case C-321/95 P ECLI:EU:C:1997:421   105
Greenpeace, Case C-321/95 P ECLI:EU:C:1998:153   75, 248, 249
Greenpeace and Others v. Commission Case T-585/93 ECLI:EU:C:1995:147   75
Gruber, Case C-570/13 ECLI:EU:C:2015:231   393
Guimont, Case C-448/98 [2000] ECR I-10663   487
Hansa Fleisch, Case C-156/91 ECLI:EU:C:1992:423   223
Hedley Lomas, Case C-5/94 ECLI:EU:C:1996:205   236
Hungary v. Commission, Case T-240/10 ECLI:EU:T:2013:645   473
Industrie du Bois, Case C-195/12 ECLI:EU:C:2014:2192   116
Inn Valley (Commission v. Austria) (Inntalautobahn II), Case C-28/09 ECLI:EU:C:2011:854   112, 336, 483
Inntalautobahn I (Commission v. Austria), Case C-320/03 [2005] ECR I-987, ECLI:EU:C:2005:684   336, 483
Inntalautobahn II (Commission v. Austria) (Inn Valley), Case C-28/09 ECLI:EU:C:2011:854   112, 336, 483
Inter-Environnement Bruxelles, Case C-567/10 ECLI:EU:C:2012:159   403
Inter-Environnement Wallonie, Case C-41/11 ECLI:EU:C:2012:103   408–409
Inter-Environnement Wallonie ASBL v. Région wallonie, Case C-129/96 ECLI:EU:C:1997:628   228–229, 407–408, 500, 501
Inter-Huiles, Case C-172/82 ECLI:EU:C:1983:69   111
International Cadmium Association v. Commission, Case T-456/11 ECLI:EU:T:2013:594   95, 96, 98, 456
Inuit Tapiriit Kanatami and Others v. Parliament and Council, Case T-18/10 ECLI:EU:T:2011:419   250–251
Inuit Tapiriit Kanatami and Others v. Parliament and Council, Case C-583/11 ECLI:EU:C:2013:625   250
Janecek (Dieter Janecek v. Freistaat Bayern), Case C-237/07 [2008] ECR I-6221, ECLI:EU:C:2008:447   222, 312, 316, 319–320, 427
Kraaijeveld Case C-72/95 ECLI:EU:C:1996:404   220–221, 222, 236, 386, 399, 408, 427
Kramer, Joined Cases 3/76, 4/76 and 6/76 ECLI:EU:C:1976:114   23
Križan and Others v. Slovenská inšpekia životného prostredia, Case C-416/10 ECLI:EU:C:2013:8   182, 243, 246, 401
Kücükdeveci, Case C-555/07 ECLI:EU:C:2010:21   235
L v. M, Case C-463/11 ECLI:EU:C:2013:247   404
Land Oberösterreich and Austria v. Commission, Joined Cases T-366/03 and T-235/04 ECLI:EU:T:2005:347   451–452
Land Oberösterreich and Austria v. Commission, Joined Cases C-439/05 P and C-454/05 P ECLI:EU:C:20007:510   18, 21, 451–452, 480

Lapin elinkeino-, liikenne-ja ympäristökeskuksen liikenne ja infrastruktuuri-
vastuualue v. Lapin luonnonsuojelupiiri ry, Case C-358/11 ECLI:EU:
C:2013:142   464, 505
Lappel Bank (R v. Secretary of State for the Environment, ex parte Royal Society for
the Protection of Birds), Case C-44/95 ECLI:EU:C:1996:297   426–427, 446
Leonosio, Case 93/71 ECLI:EU:C:1972:39   223
Lesoochranárske zoskupenie VLK (Slovak Brown Bear) v. Ministerstvo životného
prostredia Slovenskej republiky, Case C-240/09 ECLI:EU:C:2011:125   68,
224–226, 231, 233, 241
Leth, Case C-420/11 ECLI:EU:C:2013:166   236, 379, 386, 388, 399
Leybucht (Commission v. Germany), Case C-57/89 ECLI:EU:
C:1991:89   423–425, 430–431, 440
Linster, Case C-287/98 ECLI:EU:C:2000:468   393, 394, 399
Malagutti-Vezinhet v. Commission, Case T-177/02 ECLI:EU:C:2004:72   95
Mangold, Case C-144/04 ECLI:EU:C:2005:709   223, 235
Marcuccio v. Commission, Case C-1/11 ECLI:EU:C:2012:194   508
Marketgemeinde Straßwalchen, Case C-531/13 ECLI:EU:C:2015:79   391
Marleasing, Case C-106/89 ECLI:EU:C:2004:584   230
Marshall I, Case C-152/84 [1986] ECR 723, ECLI:EU:C:1986:84   229, 233
Max Havelaar (Commission v. Netherlands) (Dutch Coffee) Case C-368/10 ECLI:
EU:C:2012:284   117, 118
Mayer Parry, Case C-444/00   501
McB v. L.E., Case C-400/10 PPU ECLI:EU:C:2010:582   166
Mellor, Case C-75/08 ECLI:EU:C:2009:279   391, 393
Microban, Case C-262/10 ECLI:EU:C:2011:623   247
Ministère Public v. Müller and Others, Case 304/84 [1986] ECR 1511   33
Monsanto, Case C-58/10 [2011] ECR I-17765   462
Monsanto Agricoltura Italia and Others, Case C-236/01 ECLI:EU:C:2003:431   22,
94, 95, 96, 479
Morellato, Case C-416/00 ECLI:EU:C:2003:475   400
Motte, Case 247/84 [1985] ECR 3887   33
Mox Plant (Commission v. Ireland), Case C-459/03 ECLI:EU:C:2006:345   24–25
Nakajima v. Council, Case C-69/89 ECLI:EU:C:1991:186   253
National Farmers' Union, Case C-157/96 ECLI:EU:C:1998:191   94, 99
Netherlands v. Commission, Case C-405/07 P ECLI:EU:C:2008:613   21
Normarchiaki, Case C-43/10 ECLI:EU:C:2012:560   394, 403
N.S. v. Secretary of State for the Home Department, Case C-411/10 ECLI:EU:
C:2011:865   165
Office of Communications v. Information Commissioner, Case C-71/10 ECLI:EU:
C:2011:525   182
Omni Metal Service, Case C-259/05 ECLI:EU:C:2007:363   508
Opinion 2/13 ECLI:EU:C:2014:2454   153
Outokumpu, Case C-213/96 ECLI:EU:C:1998:155   110

Palin Granit, Case C-9/00 ECLI:EU:C:2002:232   501, 502, 503
Panagis Pafitis, Case C-441/93 ECLI:EU:C:1996:92   235
Pedersen, Case C-215/04 ECLI:EU:C:2006:108   508
Pesce v. Prezidenza del Consiglio dei Ministri, Joined Cases C-78/16 and C-79/16 ECLI:EU:C:2016:428   95, 96
Pfeiffer, Joined Cases C-397/01 and 403/01 ECLI:EU:C:2004:584   230
Pfizer Animal Health v. Council, Case T-13/99 ECLI:EU:C:2002:209   30, 95, 96, 469
PFOS (Commission v. Sweden), Case C-246/07 ECLI:EU:C:2010:203   25
Pioneer Hi Bred Italia, Case C-36//11 ECLI:EU:C:2012:534   477
Piraiki-Patraiki, Case C-11/82 ECLI:EU:C:1985:18   249
Plaumann v. Commission, Case 25/62 ECLI:EU:C:1963:17   75, 248, 249, 250
Poumon vert de la Hulpe, Case C-177/09 ECLI:EU:C:2011:738   394
Pretore di Salò, Case C-14/86 ECLI:EU:C:1987:275   229
PreussenElektra, Case C-379/98 ECLI:EU:C:2001:160   92, 111, 112, 114, 115, 116, 288–289
Pro-Braine, Case C-121/11 ECLI:EU:C:2012:225   390
Pupino, Case C-105/03 ECLI:EU:C:2005:386   230
R v. Secretary of State for the Environment, ex parte: Royal Society for the Protection of Birds (Lappel Bank), Case C-44/95 ECLI:EU:C:1996:297   426–427, 446
Raffinerie Méditerranée (Commission v. Council), Case C-378/08 [2010] ECR I-919, ECLI:EU:C:2010:126   93, 99, 102–103, 206, 207, 208, 211
Ragn-Sells, Case C-292/12 ECLI:EU:C:2013:820   100
Ratti, Case 148/78 ECLI:EU:C:1979:110   226, 228
Região autónoma dos Açores, Case C-444/08 P ECLI:EU:C:2009:733   249
Rewe (Cassis de Dijon), Case 120/78 [1979] ECR-659, ECLI:EU:C:1979:42   111, 472, 487
Romonta v. Commission, Case T-614/13 ECLI:EU:T:2014:835   168
Rotterdam Convention case, Case C-94/03 ECLI:EU:C:2006:2   23
Saetti and Frediani, Case C-235/02 [2004] ECR I-1005, ECLI:EU:C:2004:26   333, 501, 502
Salzburger Flughafen, Case C-244/12 ECLI:EU:C:2013:203   391
Sandoz BV, Case 174/82 [1983] ECR 2445   33
Santoña Marshes (Commission v. Spain), Case C-355/90 ECLI:EU:C:1993:331   425–426, 435
Savia, Case C-287/08 ECLI:EU:C:2008:539   386
Seaport (Department of the Environment for Northern Ireland v.), Case C-474/10 ECLI:EU:C:2011:681   406
Septic Tanks (Commission v. Ireland), Case C-374/11 ECLI:EU:C:2012:827   197, 198
Ship Source Pollution (Commission v. Council), Case C-440/05 ECLI:EU:C:2007:625   201, 214, 215

Simmenthal, Case 106/77 ECLI:EU:C:1978:49   222
Simutenkov, Case C-265/03 ECLI:EU:C:2005:213   224, 232
Slovak Brown Bear (Lesoochranárske zoskupenie), Case C-240/09 ECLI:EU:C:2011:125   68, 224–226, 231, 233, 241
Smith & Nephew v. Primecrown, Case C-201/94 ECR [1996] ECR I-5819   234
Société Neptune Distribution v. Ministre de l'Économie et des Finances, Case C-157/14 ECLI:EU:C:2015:823   95
Solgar Vitamins France, Case C-446/08 ECLI:EU:C:2010:233   34–35
Solway, Case C-182/10 ECLI:EU:C:2012 82   246, 394, 398
Solway Pharmaceuticals BV v. Council, Case T-392/02 [2004] ECR II-4055   36, 96
Spain v. Commission, Case C-304/01 ECLI:EU:C:2003:619   105
S.P.C.M. and Others, Case C-558/07 ECLI:EU:C:2009:430   98, 464
Stadt Papenburg, Case C-226/08 ECLI:EU:C:2010:10   428
Standley and Others, Case C-293/97 ECLI:EU:C:1999:215   372
Star Fruit v. Commission, Case C-247/87 ECLI:EU:C:1989:58   189
Stichting Greenpeace International v. Commission Case C-321/95 P ECLI:EU:C:1998:153   75, 248, 249
Stichting Natuur en Milieu and Others v. College van Gedeputeerde Staten van Groningen and College van Gedeputeerde Staten van Zuid-Holland, Joined Cases C-165/09 to 167/09 ECLI:EU:C:2011:348   313, 316, 317, 319
Stichting Natuur en Milieu and Others v. College voor de toelating van gewabeshermingsmiddelen en biociden, Case C-266/09 ECLI:EU:C:2010:779   181
Stichting Natuur en Milieu and Pesticide Action Network Europe (Council and Commission v.), Case T-338/08 ECLI:EU:T:2012:300   253
Stichting Natuur en Milieu and Pesticide Action Network Europe (Council and Commission v.), Joined Cases C-404/12 P and C-405/12 P ECLI:EU:C:2015:5   226, 253
Sweden v. Commission, Case T-229/04 ECLI:EU:T:2007:217   96
Sweetman v. An Bord Pleanála, Case C-258/11 ECLI:EU:C:2013:220   98, 431, 436, 437, 438–439
Sydhavnens, Case C-209/98 ECLI:EU:C:2000:279   100
Syllogos Ellinon Poleodomon, Case C-177/11 ECLI:EU:C:2012:378   407
Syndicat professionnel coordination des pêcheurs de l'étang de Berre et de la région v. Électricité de France (EDF), Case C-213/03 ECLI:EU:C:2004:464   224
Terre wallone and Inter-environnement Wallonie, Case C-105/09 ECLI:EU:C:2010:355   403
Titanium Dioxide (Commission v. Council), Case C-300/89 ECLI:EU:C:1991:244   4–5, 17
Tombesi and Others, Case C-304/94 ECLI:EU:C:1997:314   500
Traen, Joined Cases 372/85, 373/85 and 374/85 [1987] ECR 2141, ECLI:EU:C:1987:222   228, 229

Tre Pini (Cascina Tre Pini Ss v. Ministero dell'Ambiente e della Tutela del Territorio e del Mare and Others), Case C-301/12 ECLI:EU:C:2014:214   440
Trianel (Bund für Umwelt und Naturschutz Deutschland, Landesverband Nordrhein-Westfalen), Case C-115/09 ECLI:EU:C:2011:289   241, 243, 400, 401
TU München v. Haupzollamt München Mitte, Case C-269/90 ECLI:EU:C:1991:438   469
Umweltanwalt von Kärnten, Case C-205/08 ECLI:EU:C:2009:767   396
Unilever Italia, Case C-443/98 [2000] ECR I-7535, ECLI:EU:C:2000:496   234, 235
United Kingdom v. Commission, Case C-180/96 ECLI:EU:C:1998:192   94, 95, 99
UPA, Case C-50/00 P ECLI:EU:C:2002:462   249–250
Valčiukiené, Case C-295/10 ECLI:EU:C:2011:608   404, 407
Van Duyn, Case 41/74 ECLI:EU:C:1974:133   226
Van Gend en Loos, Case 26/62 ECLI:EU:C:1963:1   218–219, 222–223
Van Schijndel, Joined Cases C-430/93 and 431/93 ECLI:EU:C:1995:441   240
Vereniging Dorpsbelang Hees, Case C-419/97 ECLI:EU:C:2000:318   501
Vessoso, Case C-206/88 ECLI:EU:C:1990:145   500
Ville de Lyon v. Caisse des dépots et consignations, Case C-524/09 ECLI:EU:C:2010:822   181
Von Colson, Case C-14/83 ECLI:EU:C:1984:153   200, 230
Waddenzee, Case C-127/02 [2004] ECR I-7405, ECLI:EU:C:2004:482   92, 98, 221–222, 433, 435, 436–438, 439, 441
Walloon Waste (Commission v. Belgium), Case C-2/90 ECLI:EU:C:1992:310   92, 100, 110–111, 112, 501
Waste Directive (Commission v. Council), Case C-155/91 ECLI:EU:C:1993:98   92
Wells, Case C-201/02 [2004] ECR I-723, ECLI:EU:C:2004:12   233–234, 236, 387, 394, 399, 408
Wienstrom, Case C-448/01 ECLI:EU:C:2003:651   117
WWF (Bolzano), Case C-435/97 ECLI:EU:C:1999:418   221, 234, 391, 393, 399, 408
WWF v. Regione Veneto, Case C-118/94 ECLI:EU:C:1996:86   220
WWF-UK, Case C-355/08P ECLI:EU:C:2009:286   249, 251

European Court of Human Rights

Atanasov v. Bulgaria, 2 December 2010 (Appl. no. 12853/03)   156
Balmer-Schafroth v. Switzerland, 26 August 1997 (Appl. no. 22110/93)   161–162
Bor v. Hungary, 18 September 2013 (Appl. no. 50474/08)   160
Deés v. Hungary, 9 November 2010 (Appl. no. 2345/06)   160
Fadeyeva v. Russia, 9 June 2005 (Appl. no. 55723/00)   156

Fägerskiöld v. Sweden, 26 February 2008 (Appl. no. 37664/04)   160
Guerra v. Italy, 19 February 1998 (Appl. no. 14967/89)   157, 159
Hamer v. Belgium, 27 November 2007 (Appl. no. 21861/03)   162–163
Hardy and Maile v. UK, 14 February 2012 (Appl. no. 31965/07)   156, 159–160
Hatton v. UK, 8 July 2003 (Appl. no. 36022/97)   154, 158, 159
Hermann v. Germany, 26 June 2012 (Appl. no. 9300/07)   163
Huoltoasema Matti Eurén v. Finland, 19 January 2010 (Appl. no. 26654/08)   163
Kolyadenko v. Russia, 28 February 2012 (Appl. no. 17423/05)   160–161
Kyrtatos v. Greece, 22 May 2003 (Appl. no. 41666/98)   153, 154, 158, 162
L'Erablière v. Belgium, 24 February 2009 (Appl. no. 49230/07)   162
Lizarraja v. Spain, 27 April 2004 (Appl. no. 62543/00)   162
López Ostra v Spain, 9 December 1994 (Appl. no. 16798/90)   154, 155, 159
Martinez and Manzano v. Spain, 3 July 2012 (Appl. no. 61654/08)   160
Moreno Gómez v. Spain, 16 November 2004 (Appl. no. 4143/02)   160
Öneryilditz v. Turkey, 30 November 2014 (Appl. no. 48939/99)   153
Orlikowscy v. Poland, 4 October 2011 (Appl. no. 7153/07)   156
Pine Valley Development v. Ireland, 29 November 1991 (Appl. no. 12742/87)   162
Powell and Rayner v. UK, 21 February 1990 (Appl. no. 9310/81)   154–155
Taşkin v. Turkey, 10 November 2004 (Appl. no. 46117/99)   157–158, 162
Tätar v. Romania, 27 January 2009 (Appl. no. 67021/01)   158

European Committee of Social Rights

FIDH (International Federation of Human Rights) v. Greece, 23 January 2013, Complaint No. 72/2011   164–165
Marangopoulos Foundation for Human Rights v. Greece, 6 December 2006 (Merits), Complaint No. 30/2005   164

UK

Cambridge Water Co. v. Eastern Counties Leather plc [1994] 2 AC 264   130
R (Rockware Glass Ltd) v. Chester City Council [2006] EWCA Civ 992   311
Rylands v. Fletcher (1868) LR 3 HL 330 [1861– 73] All ER   130

Preface and Acknowledgements

This book was conceived of some five years ago, with the aim of providing a user-friendly, comprehensive and contextual account of an area of law which could not be more critically important, but which is often discounted as technical and dense. Our objective, therefore, was to communicate this vital area of law in a way that was comprehensible, without losing too many of its nuances or ignoring fundamental complexities.

One of the challenges of this field is, of course, its fast-moving nature. Since we first started this book, a great many events have intervened which are of tremendous significance to this area. Some of these have been specifically environmental developments, such as the conclusion of the Paris Agreement at the COP 21 United Nations Climate Change Conference in 2015 (see Chapter 8), the conclusion of the EU's Seventh Environmental Action Programme in 2013 (see Chapter 2), the continued rise in prominence of the Aarhus Convention on Access to Environmental Information, Public Participation and Access to Justice in Environmental Matters, including in the case law of the Court of Justice of the European Union (see Chapters 5 and 7). Other developments have not been environment-specific, but have nevertheless had momentous effects on European environmental law and policy, including the entry into office of the Juncker Commission in 2014, bringing with it different political priorities (see Chapter 2); the ongoing Regulatory Fitness and Performance programme (REFIT) of the European Commission, which has included review of the Habitats and Birds Directives (see Chapters 4 and 12); and, of course, the EU's response to the global financial crisis of 2007–2008 and the subsequent European sovereign debt crisis, which has seen an overwhelming pressure to prioritise economic goals (jobs and growth) and economic governance (see Chapters 1, 3 and 6). The most recent such momentous development has been the June 2016 vote of almost 52 per cent of the British people to 'Brexit', the implications of which – including for the effective protection of the environment in the UK and EU – will certainly be profound, but are as yet unclear.

The title of the book reflects the fact that it aims to cover not only EU environmental law, but also the increasing body of European environmental law that does not originate in the EU, including the law of the ECHR and the Aarhus Convention.

Of the chapters herein, Suzanne Kingston was primarily responsible for Chapters 1 (aside from the sections on the broader context), 3–7 and 11. Veerle Heyvaert was primarily responsible for the sections on Environment, Risk and Science and Environment and Governance in Chapter 1 and

Chapters 8, 9, 12 and 13. Aleksandra Čavoški was primarily responsible for the sections on Environment, Philosophy and Ethics and Environment, Geography and Enlargement in Chapter 1, and Chapters 2, 10 and 14. Siobhán Power and, latterly, Hugh McDowell provided excellent research assistance, for which we are extremely grateful. Sincere thanks also to Professor Antonia Layard of Bristol University, who contributed to Chapter 10, and to Marta Walkowiak and Valerie Appleby at Cambridge University Press, who were unfailingly patient in allowing us time to finish this project.

We have endeavoured to state the law as at 1 July 2016.

1

The Foundations of EU Environmental Law: History, Aims and Context

> Economic expansion is not an end in itself: its first aim should be to enable disparities in living conditions to be reduced ... It should result in an improvement in the quality of life as well as in standards of living. As befits the genius of Europe, particular attention will be given to intangible values and to protecting the environment so that progress may really be put at the service of mankind.
>
> Paris Declaration of the Heads of State or Government
> of the EEC Member States, 20 October 1972

History and Development of the European Union's Environmental Policy

The original EEC Treaty contained no express mention of environmental policy, in part due to the essentially economic aims of that Treaty, and in part because, when the Treaty was drawn up in the late 1950s, the field of 'environmental' law, in the sense of a discrete body of rules governing the way that we interrelate with our natural surroundings, barely existed in the signatory Member States (though national laws had long existed governing certain aspects of the current field, in the form of rules on private property and public health).[1] At international level, a collection of rules was just beginning to emerge in discrete environment-related areas, a process which had begun with the bilateral fisheries treaties of the mid-nineteenth century and in which the 1949 United Nations Conference on the Conservation and Utilisation of Resources (UNCCUR) was a landmark event. These developments undoubtedly contributed to the subsequent emergence of Community environmental law.

While environmental discourse became increasingly prevalent in the late 1950s and in the 1960s at international level,[2] there was little appetite for Community activity in the environmental field, as the institutions and Member States alike were immersed in the task of defining the Community legal and political order in this period. Nonetheless, a small amount of Community legislation was adopted in these years on what would now be considered to be environmental matters. In this period, and up to the entry into force of the Single European Act in 1987, two legal bases were used for such legislation, each requiring unanimity of voting

---

[1] See Richard Lazarus, *The Making of Environmental Law* (University of Chicago Press, 2004). See e.g. in the UK, which joined the Community in 1973, Sections 101–107 of the Public Health Act 1936, which were replaced by the Clean Air Act 1956.

[2] See Philippe Sands and Jacqueline Peel, *Principles of International Environmental Law* (3rd edn., Cambridge University Press, 2012), chapter 2.

in the Council. The first was Article 100 (now, in amended form, Article 115 TFEU). The second was Article 235 (now, in amended form, Article 352 TFEU). The Community's first legislative attempt to address environment-related issues was the 1967 adoption of a Directive on the classification, packaging and labelling of dangerous substances:[3] as it was based on Article 100, however, it was expressed to be aimed at removing the hindrances to trade caused by differing national legislation on the matter, rather than at environmental protection *per se*.[4] This early legislation, therefore, was premised on economic, rather than environmental, reasoning — any achievement of environmental improvement by Community legislation was, in principle, a side effect.

The first real sign of a distinct Community environmental policy came in the run-up to the landmark 1972 United Nations Conference on the Human Environment in Stockholm, convened in 1968 by the United Nations General Assembly.[5] In this way, the birth of Community environmental law occurred simultaneously with the beginning of a new period in international environmental law: as concern mounted for the 'continuing and accelerating impairment of the quality of the human environment',[6] the impetus for international and regional environmental action grew. Thus, while Article 2 of the Treaty of Rome, which set out the EEC's aims, had listed among these aims 'a harmonious development of economic activities, a continuous and balanced expansion, an increase in stability, and accelerated raising of the standard of living', the 1972 Paris Summit of the European Council made clear, as the quote at the start of this chapter indicates, that to focus solely on economic growth was wrong-headed, and that particular attention would be given within the EEC to 'protecting the environment so that progress may really be put to the service of mankind'.[7]

The Commission had already, however, got the ball rolling: the Paris Declaration followed the Commission's 1970 announcement that it would draw up a Community action programme on the environment and the 1971 Commission Communication on Community environmental policy, in which it proposed using Article 235 (now, in amended form, Article 352 TFEU) as a legal basis for potential Community environmental measures.[8] In 1973, the first Action Programme for the Environment was adopted, in the form of a political declaration by the Council and the representatives of Member States' governments meeting in the Council, sparked by France's concern that the Treaty provisions were, in their then form, not an appropriate basis for a European environmental

---

[3] Directive 67/548, OJ 1967 L 196/1 (subsequently amended).
[4] However, protection of public health was mentioned as an aim in the preamble.
[5] UNGA Res. 2398 (XXIII) (1968).
[6] Resolution adopted in July 1968 and a precursor to the convening of the Stockholm Conference: ECOSOC Res. 1346 (XLV) (1968).
[7] Paris Declaration of the European Council, cited in the preamble to the First Action Programme on the Environment, OJ 1973 C 112/1.
[8] Commission Communication on a Community policy for the environment SEC(71)2616 (22 July 1971).

policy.[9] In setting out the Community's environmental programme for the next four years, the First Action programme specified that the Community's Article 2 task of promoting throughout the Community a harmonious development of economic activities and a continuous and balanced expansion 'cannot now be imagined in the absence of an effective campaign to combat pollution and nuisances or of an improvement in the quality of life and the protection of the environment'.[10]

By thus reading in environmental protection as a necessary component of the aim of achieving economic growth, despite the fact that it was not expressly mentioned as an Article 2 aim of the Community, the programme opened the way for the adoption of Community environmental legislation.

Following the first Action programme, three further Action programmes were adopted between 1972 and 1987.[11] More than 150 pieces of Community environmental legislation were passed between 1972 and 1987, covering such diverse areas as environmental impact assessments, waste control, the protection of flora and fauna, and water and air quality.[12] In addition, the Community signed its first international environmental treaties in this period.[13] Such legislation was, by necessity, based on either Article 100 (where it could be argued that the legislation aimed to help achieve the common market)[14] or Article 235 (where no common market rationale could reasonably be found, but there were non-economic reasons for action at Community level);[15] indeed, most legislation was based on both articles.[16] In 1985, the Court of Justice of the European Union (CJEU) in the landmark *ADBHU* case confirmed the validity of using Article 235 EC as a legal basis for environmental legislation on the basis that environmental protection was 'one of the Community's essential objectives' justifying certain limits on the principle of freedom of trade.[17]

---

[9] See Ludwig Krämer, *EU Environmental Law* (8th edn., Sweet & Maxwell, 2015), chapter 1.
[10] Preamble to the First Action Programme on the Environment, OJ 1973 C 112/1.
[11] Second Programme (1977–1981), OJ 1977 C 399/1, Third Programme (1982–1986), OJ 1983 C 46/1, Fourth Programme (1987–1992), OJ 1987 C 328/1.
[12] See e.g. Directive 85/337 on environmental impact assessments, OJ 1985 L 175/40; Directive 75/442 on waste, OJ 1975 L 194/23; Directive 79/409 on the conservation of wild birds, OJ 1979 L 103/1; Directive 75/440 on surface water, OJ 1975 L 194/26; Directive 84/360 on the combating of air pollution from industrial plants, OJ 1984 L 188/20.
[13] See e.g. the Paris Convention for the Prevention of Marine Pollution from Land-Based Sources, Decision 75/437, OJ 1975 L 194/5.
[14] For example, Directive 80/778 on drinking water, OJ 1980 L 229/11; and Directive 73/404 on detergents, OJ 1973 L 347/51. The practice of basing such legislation on Art. 100 was in principle confirmed as compatible with the Treaty by the ECJ in Case 92/79 *Commission* v. *Italy* ECLI:EU:C:1980:1.
[15] See e.g. Directive 79/409 on the conservation of wild birds, OJ 1979 L 103/1.
[16] See e.g. Directive 85/337 on environmental impact assessments, OJ 1985 L 175/40, Directive 84/360 on combating air pollution from industrial plants, OJ 1984 L 188/20, and Directive 78/319 on toxic and dangerous waste, OJ 1978 L 84/43.
[17] Case 240/83 *ADBHU* ECLI:EU:C:1985:59, para. 13.

The rather uncertain status of Community environmental policy was formalised by Article 25 of the Single European Act (SEA) 1986, which inserted a new Title VII on the Environment into the Treaty,[18] making environmental protection an express objective of the Community. While it was clear that this remained an ancillary flanking policy to the primary Community aim of achieving the internal market, the Title nonetheless contained a specific legal basis for environmental legislation (Article 130s), making it unnecessary to find an economic justification for the legislation or to use the 'catch-all' Article 235 provision. Voting remained, however, subject to unanimity under Article 130s, though Member States could maintain or introduce more stringent protective measures than those passed on the basis of Article 130s, if compatible with the Treaty and notified to the Commission (under Article 130t, one of the so-called 'environmental guarantee' or safeguard provisions).

Crucially, however, the SEA introduced a new Article 100a allowing internal market legislation (with some exceptions) to be passed by qualified majority. Environmental measures based on internal market objectives were therefore subject to qualified majority voting in the Council and thus could be adopted with more ease. Moreover, environmental measures passed under this provision had to take 'as a base a high level of environmental protection'[19] and Member States had the possibility of notifying the Commission if they deemed it necessary to 'apply' national provisions in order to protect the environment despite the adoption of Community harmonising legislation (another environmental guarantee provision).[20]

The insertion of Article 100a led to a myriad of legal basis disputes before the CJEU on the question whether a given piece of environmental legislation ought to have been passed on the basis of Article 130s (unanimous voting, consultation of the Parliament) or Article 100a (qualified majority voting, cooperation procedure with the Parliament).

In *Commission v. Council (Titanium Dioxide)*, for instance, the CJEU annulled Directive 89/428/EEC on titanium dioxide waste, which had been based on Article 130s.[21] In holding that the Directive should have been based on Article 100a, the CJEU noted that, while the aim and content of the measure displayed features relating to the protection of the environment as well as achievement of the internal market, a joint legal basis was not possible due, in particular, to the different Council voting rules and the differing role of the European Parliament

---

[18] Arts. 130r–t; in amended form, present Arts. 191–193 TFEU.   [19] Art. 100a(3).
[20] See Art. 100a(4), 'If, after the adoption of a harmonization measure by the Council acting by a qualified majority, a Member State deems it necessary to apply national provisions on grounds of major needs referred to in Art. 36, or relating to protection of the environment or the working environment, it shall notify the Commission of these provisions. The Commission shall confirm the provisions involved after having verified that they are not a means of arbitrary discrimination or a disguised restriction on trade between Member States.'
[21] Case C-300/89 *Commission v. Council (Titanium Dioxide)* ECLI:EU:C:1991:244.

entailed by the Article 100a and Article 130s procedures. The CJEU went on to observe that (at paras. 22–24):

- Article 130 r(2) of the Treaty (the precursor to present Article 11 TFEU, discussed in Chapter 3) provided that 'environmental protection requirements shall be a component of the Community's other policies';
- As national environmental rules may place a burden on industry, 'action intended to approximate national rules concerning production conditions in a given industrial sector with the aim of eliminating distortions of competition in that sector is conducive to the attainment of the internal market'; and
- The Commission was itself obliged by then Article 100a(3) to take as a base a 'high level of protection in matters of environmental protection' in bringing forward legislative proposals based on Article 100a (now Article 115 TFEU).

Titanium Dioxide, therefore, was based on a strongly integrationist approach which expressly recognised the close interface between the EEC's economic and environmental goals.

The SEA expressly set out the objectives of the newly formalised Community environment policy in Article 130 r(1), namely, preserving, protecting and improving the quality of the environment, contributing towards protecting human health, and ensuring a prudent and rational utilisation of natural resources. Importantly, it also set out a number of what it termed 'principles', which were to form a foundation of the Community's environmental policy (Article 130 r(2)), namely: the preventive principle, the source principle, and the polluter pays principle, each discussed below. The SEA also included a type of integration principle requiring that environmental considerations be 'a component of the Community's other policies', which was the first formalisation of the obligation of environmental policy integration, discussed further below, at Treaty level. Although not forming part of Article 130 r(2), another *de facto* 'principle' of environmental law formalised by the SEA was that of subsidiarity (Article 130 r(4)).[22] The SEA also made express provision for the Community to participate in international environmental agreements (Article 130 r(4)).

These developments had a momentous effect on the development and formalisation of the Community's environmental policy. The changes led, amongst other things, to a steady increase in the amount and scope of Community environmental legislation, and to the creation of a separate

---

[22] Art. 130r(4) provided that, 'The Community shall take action relating to the environment to the extent to which the objectives [of Community environmental policy, set out above] can be attained better at Community level than at the level of the individual Member States.' The notion of subsidiarity had been present from the beginning in the Community's environment policy, featuring prominently in the Community's First Environment Programme.

Directorate-General for the Environment (DG XI) in the Commission.[23] This was followed by the creation of the European Environment Agency (EEA), which is tasked with gathering data on the state of the EU's environment.[24]

The entry into force of the Maastricht Treaty brought with it a subtle upgrade in the perceived importance of the Community's environmental policy compared to other policies. The most significant (at least politically) was the first insertion into Article 2 EC, i.e. the fundamental objectives of the Community, of an express reference to environmental protection, including as one of the objectives of the Community 'the promotion, throughout the Community, of a harmonious and balanced development of economic activities, sustainable and non-inflationary growth respecting the environment'. Maastricht also introduced substantial, more practical, changes for the Community's environmental policy – most notably, the introduction of qualified majority voting for the environment legal basis (Article 130s EC, subject to certain express exceptions);[25] the formalisation of the status of the environmental action programme; and the addition of the precautionary principle to the principles of the Community's environmental policy. The principle of subsidiarity, which had been inserted by the SEA into the title on the environment, was elevated to Part One of the Treaty, on the fundamental *Principles* of the Community (Article 3b). In addition, Community financial support for environmental projects was bolstered by the insertion of Article 130d(2) (present Article 177(2) TFEU), providing for a Cohesion Fund to be set up in the field of the environment.

The Treaty of Amsterdam marked a further promotion and concretisation of the Community's environmental aims. Specifically, it introduced the promotion of a 'high level of protection and improvement of the quality of the environment' as an Article 2 EC objective of the Community, and modified the wording of Article 2 EC to refer to the aim of promoting a 'harmonious, balanced and sustainable development of economic activities' (in place of the SEA's reference to 'balanced development' and 'sustainable growth'). The Treaty on European Union was amended to include among its objectives the promotion of 'economic and social progress and [of achieving] balanced

---

[23] Significant legislation passed included legislation creating the European Environment Agency and legislation introducing an eco-label for environmentally friendly products (Regulation 1210/90 on the Establishment of the European Environment Agency and the European Environment Information and Observation Network, OJ 1990 L 120/1, Regulation 880/92 on a Community eco-label award scheme, OJ 1992 L 99/1).

[24] Council Regulation (EEC) No. 1210/90 of 7 May 1990 on the establishment of the European Environment Agency and the European Environment Information and Observation Network, OJ 1990 L 120/1. In contrast to typical national environmental agencies, Member States have never been willing to give the EEA inspection or enforcement powers.

[25] Namely, fiscal measures and measures concerning town and country planning, land use other than waste management, and management of water resources remained subject to unanimity of voting.

and sustainable development'.[26] Further, the integration principle followed subsidiarity in being upgraded from its position in the Environment Title (former Article 130 r EC) to be included in Part One of the Treaty on the 'Principles' of the Community (what was then Article 6 EC).

No significant change was made to the environmental provisions by the Treaty of Nice. The Lisbon Treaty, however, made some changes deserving mention. Environmental values do not feature in the Article 2 TEU list of values upon which the Union is 'founded'. However, Article 3(3) TEU repeats the Treaty of Amsterdam's formulation of the balance between the EU's environmental, social and economic aims,[27] and it is for the first time specified that one of the goals of the Union's external relations policy is the 'sustainable development of the Earth' (Article 3(5) TEU). This is confirmed, and more detail added, by Article 21(2) TEU.[28] In the TFEU, Article 191(1) added the aim of combating climate change to the EU's environmental policy aims, and added a *passerelle* clause in the environmental legal basis provision, discussed further below.[29] Further, the newly inserted Title on Energy Policy includes 'the development of new and renewable forms of energy' within the aims of the EU's policy in this field (Article 194(1) TFEU).

Finally, Article 37 of the Charter of Fundamental Rights of the EU effectively repeats the integration requirement of Article 11 TFEU (previously Article 6 EC), providing that, 'A high level of environmental protection and the improvement of the quality of the environment must be integrated into the policies of the Union and ensured in accordance with the principle of sustainable development.'

---

[26] Art. 2, TEU, from the Maastricht version of promotion of 'economic and social progress which is balanced and sustainable'. Further important environmental changes brought about by Amsterdam were: (1) the 'environmental guarantee' provisions of what is now Art. 114 TFEU were expanded to specify that Member States could, despite the passing of Community harmonisation measures, maintain in force existing environmental measures *or* introduce new environmental measures, as long as the conditions set out therein were satisfied; and (2) the switch in decision-making procedures for (as it then was) Art. 130s EC (present Art. 192 TFEU) from the cooperation procedure to the co-decision procedure.

[27] The relevant extract provides that the Union 'shall work for the sustainable development of Europe based on balanced economic growth and price stability, a highly competitive social market economy, aiming at full employment and social progress, and a high level of protection and improvement of the quality of the environment'.

[28] Art. 21(2) TEU includes within the aims of the EU's external action fostering the 'sustainable economic, social and environmental development of developing countries' (though this is explicitly 'with the primary aim of eradicating poverty') and helping to develop 'international measures to preserve and improve the quality of the environment and the sustainable management of global natural resources, in order to ensure sustainable development'.

[29] The *passerelle* clause of Art. 192(2) TFEU enables the Council, acting unanimously upon a proposal of the Commission and after consulting the European Parliament, the Economic and Social Committee and the Committee of the Regions, to make the ordinary legislative procedure (entailing QMV) applicable to provisions 'primarily of a fiscal nature' (Art. 192(2)(a) TFEU). At present, a special legislative procedure entailing unanimity of voting in the Council applies to environmental fiscal measures.

Aims of EU Environmental Policy

Article 3(3) TEU

The Union shall establish an internal market. It shall work for the sustainable development of Europe based on balanced economic growth and price stability, a highly competitive social market economy, aiming at full employment and social progress, and a high level of protection and improvement of the quality of the environment. It shall promote scientific and technological advance.

The overarching aim of the Union's environmental policy is set out in Article 3(3) TEU, as further specified in Article 191(2) TFEU, which states that, 'Union policy on the environment shall aim at a high level of protection taking into account the diversity of situations in the various regions of the Union'.[30] This aim effectively subsumes the four further aims set out in Article 191(1) TFEU, which provides as follows.

Article 191(1) TFEU

Union policy on the environment shall contribute to pursuit of the following objectives:

– preserving, protecting and improving the quality of the environment,
– protecting human health,
– prudent and rational utilisation of natural resources,
– promoting measures at international level to deal with regional or worldwide environmental problems, and in particular combating climate change.

As already mentioned, the fourth aim in this list was added by the Treaty of Lisbon.

In terms of the EU's external aims, Article 3(5) TEU, inserted by the Treaty of Lisbon, includes within the EU's fundamental foreign policy aims that of contributing to the 'sustainable development of the earth'. Article 21 TEU, also inserted by the Treaty of Lisbon, adds further detail to this, specifying that the EU's external aims include 'the sustainable economic social and environmental development of developing countries, with the primary aim of

---

[30] See, similarly, Art. 114(3) TFEU. On the obligation to take into account 'the diversity of situations in the various regions of the Union', see the discussion of the environmental guarantee provisions below. The aim of achieving a high level of protection does not require an EU measure to aim for the highest level of protection that is technically possible: see Case C-341/95 *Bettati* v. *Safety Hi-Tech SRL* ECLI:EU:C:1998:353, para. 47.

eradicating poverty'.[31] Also included is the aim of helping to develop 'international measures to preserve and improve the quality of the environment and the sustainable management of global natural resources, in order to ensure sustainable development'.[32]

A 'High Level of Environmental Protection Taking into Account the Diversity of Situations in the Various Regions of the Union'

The aim of achieving a 'high level of environmental protection' was introduced into the Treaties by the Single European Act. Initially, it referred only to the Commission's internal market proposals concerning health, safety, environmental and consumer protection which took 'as a base a high level of protection'.[33] As noted above, Article 191(2) TFEU now guarantees that the Union policy on the environment aims at a high level of protection taking into account the diversity of situations in the various regions of the Union.[34] The aim is also embodied in Article 3(3) TEU, including within the general goals of the Union the achievement of a 'high level of protection and improvement of the quality of the environment'.[35]

Article 37 of the EU's Charter of Fundamental Rights, given binding force by the Treaty of Lisbon, further provides that,

> A high level of environmental protection and the improvement of the quality of the environment must be integrated into the policies of the Union and ensured in accordance with the principle of sustainable development.[36]

The objective is also present in the principal legal basis provision for legislation aimed at achieving the internal market, Article 114 TFEU. Specifically, in putting forward legislative proposals pursuant to Article 114(1) TFEU concerning 'health, safety, environmental protection and consumer protection', the Commission is obliged to take 'as a base a high level of protection, taking account in particular of any new development based on scientific facts'.

Consistent with this importance given to the aim in the Treaty, it is frequently visible as an express aim of much of the EU's environmental legislation. The Industrial Emissions Directive, for instance, defines its subject matter as including 'rules designed to prevent or, where that is not practicable, to reduce emissions into air, water and land and to prevent the generation of waste, in order to achieve a high level of protection of the environment taken as a whole'.[37] Similarly, the Strategic Environmental Assessment Directive defines its objective as providing for 'a high level of protection of the environment and to contribute to the integration of environmental considerations into the preparation and

---

[31] Art. 21(2)(d) TEU. [32] Art. 21(2)(f) TEU. [33] Art. 100a(3) SEA.
[34] Art. 191(2) TFEU. [35] Art. 3(3) TEU.
[36] On the environmental integration principle, see, further, Chapter 3.
[37] Directive 75/2010, OJ 2010 L 334/17, Art. 1. See, further, Chapter 9.

adoption of plans and programmes with a view to promoting sustainable development, by ensuring that an environmental assessment is carried out of certain plans and programmes which are likely to have significant effects on the environment.'[38]

The aim has also been taken into account by the CJEU in certain cases. In *ATAA*[39] (discussed further in Chapter 8), for instance, the Grand Chamber of the CJEU held that the application of the EU Emissions Trading Scheme (ETS) to third country airlines was compatible with international law and, in particular, with the principle of territoriality, given that the scheme only applies to commercial aircraft that arrive at or depart from a Member State airport.[40] Nor did the fact that the ETS applied to the whole of the aircraft's journey (not just that which occurred over EU territory) affect this conclusion, given the EU's objective under Article 191(2) TFEU of achieving a high level of environmental protection and its status as a party to the UNFCCC.[41]

Despite its frequent appearance throughout the text of the TEU, TFEU and Charter, the aim of achieving a 'high level of environmental protection' remains profoundly ambiguous in character. Indeed, as with many of the broad aims of the Union, this is perhaps the key to its success as an aim with which all Member States can agree, despite significant ongoing differences in opinion as to the relative importance of environmental policy as compared to, say, economic policy. It is clear, for instance, that the aim does not require Member States to strive for the 'highest' level of environmental protection.[42] Nevertheless, it underlies the Treaties' acceptance that Member States may, subject to certain conditions, be permitted to go beyond the environmental standards agreed upon at EU level, in order to achieve a higher level of environmental protection. These provisions, known as the environmental 'guarantee' provisions, are discussed further below. The need for a certain 'flexibility' of environmental aims is also inherent in the wording of Article 191(2) TFEU itself: the aim is to achieve a high level of protection 'taking into account the diversity of situations in the various regions of the Union'.

This is not a new phenomenon: flexibility has been embedded in the EU's environmental law and policy from its very beginnings. Indeed, the Commission's proposal for the EEC's very first Environmental Action Programme shows that Brussels considered from the outset that, whatever kind

---

[38] SEA Directive 2001/42, OJ 2001 L 197/30, Art. 1. See, further, Chapter 11.
[39] Case C-366/10 *ATAA* ECLI:EU:C:2011:864.   [40] *Ibid.*, para. 127.
[41] *Ibid.*, para. 128.
[42] Case C-233/94 *Germany v. Parliament and Council* ECLI:EU:C:2000:544, para. 48, where, concerning the analogous aim for consumer protection, the CJEU held that 'although consumer protection is one of the objectives of the Community, it is clearly not the sole objective ... Admittedly, there must be a high level of consumer protection ... however, no provision of the Treaty obliges the Community legislature to adopt the highest level of protection which can be found in a particular Member State.' It followed that, although the Directive at issue may result in a lower level of investor protection in certain cases (in particular, compared to the protection available under Germany law), this did not call into question the overall result which it tried to achieve.

of environmental policy the Community would eventually end up with, it could not be a 'one-size-fits-all' policy.

> [T]he EC must take care to leave national, regional and local bodies as much freedom of discretion as possible. Harmonisation must be aimed at only to the extent necessary for a minimum level of protection of the whole EC and for the free circulation of goods as well as undistorted competition ...
>
> The diversity in geographical and natural situations, and between the tasks of the different regions, may sometimes require the application of different standards.
>
> European Commission, Proposal for an EEC Environmental Action Programme (SEC (72)666), p. 6.

In this vein, as the scope and volume of EU environmental legislation has grown vastly (such that, on average, 80 per cent of all national environmental law is now derived from EU law),[43] so too has the reliance on flexibility mechanisms in EU environmental policy. It is not difficult to identify a variety of features suggesting that, by its very nature, EU environmental policy is a prime candidate for flexibility-based approaches. Some of these are obvious. Geographies and environmental conditions differ tremendously across the EU's territory, which comprises more than 10 million km^2, and with population densities ranging from over 1,300/km^2 in Malta to only 18/km^2 in Finland.[44] Each Member State (and region) has its own particular environmental challenges, in part dictated by physical geographies and in part by varying pressure on natural resources placed by human populations. Added to this are important differences in what are often termed 'environmental philosophies' within the EU.

Clearly, Member States' differences in preferences as to environmental protection levels reflect some fundamental differences as to where environmental values and priorities should stand in comparison to other social and economic priorities, as well as differences in economic prosperity.[45] These differences are reflected not only in mechanisms enabling a *higher* level of environmental protection (as with the environmental guarantee provisions), but also in mechanisms enabling a *lower* level of environmental protection. Thus, the EU's flagship legislative instrument for dealing with climate change, the Emissions Trading Scheme Directive,

---

[43] See e.g. Commissioner Dimas, in European Environment Bureau, EU Environmental Policy Handbook (Brussels, 2005), at p. 3; Government of the Netherlands, 'EU legislation': www.government.nl/issues/environment/roles-and-responsibilities-of-central-government/eu-legislation.
[44] Source: Eurostat, Population Density (Inhabitants per km^2), 2012 figures.
[45] See, generally, John Dryzek, *The Politics of the Earth: Environmental Discourses* (2nd edn., Oxford University Press, 2005) and Duncan Liefferink, Bas Arts, Jelmer Kamstra and Jeroen Ooijevaar, 'Leaders and Laggards in Environmental Policy: A Quantitative Analysis of Domestic Policy Outputs' (2009) 16 *Journal of European Public Policy* 677–700. See, further, the discussion below of environment and ethics.

contains multiple derogations for Member States as well as for particular industries which, it is argued, might be particularly heavily hit by the economic consequences of putting a price on carbon, or (in the case of industries) where there is a risk that the companies at issue might decide to leave the EU (the so-called 'carbon leakage' scenario).[46] Similarly, the Water Framework Directive, discussed in Chapter 10, permits Member States to adopt less stringent measures for specific bodies of water where they are (Article 4(5)):

> so affected by human activity ... or their natural condition is such that the achievement of these objectives would be infeasible or disproportionately expensive

and where certain conditions are met, including that the 'environmental and socioeconomic needs served by such human activity cannot be achieved by other means, which are a significantly better environmental option not entailing disproportionate costs'; that the best environmental outcome 'possible' is achieved; and that no further deterioration occurs, subject to periodic review of compliance with these conditions.

These cases of 'downward' flexibility have generally very little to do with achieving effective environmental protection, but are rather typically aimed at protecting the effectiveness of other EU policies (for instance, in the ETS carbon leakage example, the EU's economic competitiveness policy). In other cases, they are merely added for reasons of political expediency to get the measure through (as, for instance, with the manifold derogations from the EU's Energy Taxation Directive).[47]

Sustainable Development

While not expressly an aim of the EU's environmental policy pursuant to Article 191 TFEU, the aim of sustainable development is, as noted in Article 3(3) TEU, a fundamental aim of the EU. Its origin may be traced to the 1972 UN Stockholm Declaration which noted the need to reconcile the environmental protection with economic development.[48] This uneasy relationship

---

[46] Directive 2009/29/EC of the European Parliament and of the Council of 23 April 2009 amending Directive 2003/87/EC so as to improve and extend the greenhouse gas emissions allowance trading scheme of the Community, OJ 2009 L 140/63. See the discussion in Suzanne Kingston, 'Surveying the State of EU Environmental Law' (2013) 62 *International & Comparative Law Quarterly* 965–982 and see, further, Chapter 8.

[47] Council Directive 2003/96/EC of 27 October 2003 restructuring the Community framework for the taxation of energy products and electricity, OJ 2003 L 283/51.

[48] See Principle 11 of the Declaration of the United Nations Conference on the Human Environment 1972: 'The environmental policies of all States should enhance and not adversely affect the present or future development potential of developing countries, nor should they hamper the attainment of better living conditions for all, and appropriate steps should be taken by States and international organizations with a view to reaching agreement on meeting the possible national and international economic consequences resulting from the application of environmental measures.'

between environmental protection and economic development was further addressed by the World Commission on Environment and Development which, in the Brundtland Report, defined sustainable development as 'development that meets the needs of the present without compromising the ability of future generations to meet their own needs'.[49] This definition has been endorsed by the European Council.[50] As the Brundtland Report expressly recognised, this constitutes an essentially anthropocentric definition that focuses on 'satisfaction of human needs and aspirations as the major objective of development'.[51] Again, this anthropocentrism was already clearly present in the 1972 Stockholm Declaration.[52]

As discussed above, the introduction of the sustainable development aim in the EU dates back to the Single European Act calling for the 'prudent and rational utilisation of natural resources'.[53] The Maastricht Treaty used the term sustainable growth[54] for the first time, while the Amsterdam Treaty included within the Community's tasks the promotion of a 'harmonious, balanced and sustainable development of economic activities'.[55]

The Community (in conjunction with the Member States) issued a first Community sustainable development programme in 1993,[56] in the wake of the 1992 UN Conference on Environment and Development in Rio. Following the inclusion of sustainable development in the EU's aims with the Treaty of Amsterdam, the Gothenburg strategy adopted by the European Council in 2001 adopted a Sustainable Development Strategy (SDS) in 2001, declaring that it was adding a third, environmental, limb to the EU's Lisbon Strategy for socio-economic progress, in addition to its social and economic limbs.[57] The EU SDS was reviewed in 2005, renewed in 2006, and reviewed again in 2009.[58] At the legislative level, there are liberal references throughout

---

[49] Gro Harlem Brundtland et al., *Our Common Future* (Oxford University Press, 1987) ('Bruntland Report').
[50] Conclusions of the Gothenburg European Council, 15 and 16 June 2001, SN 200/1/01.
[51] Brundtland Report, chapter 2.IV, para. 4.
[52] See the Stockholm Declaration, principle 1: 'Man has the fundamental right to freedom, equality and adequate conditions of life, in an environment of a quality that permits a life of dignity and well-being, and he bears a solemn responsibility to protect and improve the environment for present and future generations.'
[53] Art. 130r (1) of the Treaty.   [54] Art. 2 of the EC Treaty.
[55] See Recital 7 and Art. B TEU and Art. 2 EC Treaty.
[56] See the Resolution of the Council and the Representatives of the Governments of the Member States on a Community programme of policy and action in relation to the environment and sustainable development, OJ 1993 C 138/1. Sustainable development formed a limb of the Community's Fifth Environmental Action Programme. Commission, 'A Sustainable Europe for a Better World: A European Union Strategy for Sustainable Development', COM(2001)264 final and Fifth Environmental Action Programme, 'Towards Sustainable Development', OJ 1993 C 138/1.
[57] Conclusions of the Gothenburg European Council, 15 and 16 June 2001, SN 200/1/01.
[58] 'The 2005 Review of the EU sustainable development strategy: initial stocktaking and future orientations', COM(2005)37; Council Doc. 10117/06 of 9 June 2006; 'Mainstreaming Sustainable Development into EU Policies: 2009 Review of the

EU environmental secondary legislation to sustainable development as an underlying aim.[59]

Despite all this policy activity, the precise benefits of the sustainable development aim from the environmental protection perspective remain largely unclear. The main practical import of sustainable development in the EU is a procedural one, namely, an *ex ante* impact assessment must be undertaken by the Commission when proposing initiatives expected to have significant direct economic, social or environmental impacts.[60] The substantive aspect of the environmental pillar of sustainable development is given greater specification in the Article 11 TFEU integration requirement, which provides that,

> Environmental protection requirements must be integrated into the definition and implementation of the Union policies and activities, in particular with a view to promoting sustainable development.

As noted above, Article 37 of the EU's Charter of Fundamental Rights similarly provides,

> A high level of environmental protection and the improvement of the quality of the environment must be integrated into the policies of the Union and ensured in accordance with the principle of sustainable development.

It is notable that Article 37 expressly describes 'sustainable development' as not only an aim, but a 'principle'.

The significance and status of the integration requirement is discussed further in Chapter 3.

It is clear therefore that, as a matter of primary EU law, those drawing up and implementing EU economic *and* environmental policies have a legal duty to balance the EU's environmental and economic aims, with the ultimate objective of achieving a highly competitive social market economy at the same time as a high level of environmental protection.[61] Moreover, while the meaning of the concept of sustainable development is highly

---

European Union Strategy for Sustainable Development', COM(2009)400; and Presidency Report on the 2009 Review of the EU Sustainable Development Strategy, Council of the EU, 1 December 2009, 16818/09.

[59] See, for instance, the Water Framework Directive, discussed in Chapter 10, and the Strategic Environmental Assessment Directive, discussed in Chapter 11.

[60] See the Commission's Impact Assessment Guidelines, SEC(2009)92; Commission Communication on impact assessment, COM(2002)276.

[61] For an analysis of the legal implications of Art. 11 TFEU, see Suzanne Kingston, *Greening EU Competition Law and Policy* (Cambridge University Press, 2012), chapter 3 and Beate Sjåfjell, 'The Legal Significance of Article 11 TFEU for EU Institutions and Member States' in Beate Sjåfjell and Anje Wiesbrock, *The Greening of European Business under EU Law: Taking Article 11 TFEU Seriously* (Routledge, 2014).

contested,[62] the constitutionalisation of this concept in each of Article 3(3) TEU, Article 11 TFEU and Article 37 of the Charter may reasonably be understood as demonstrating a belief, at the highest political level within the EU, that it is *actually possible* to achieve economic, social and environmental goals at the same time. This is, in itself, by no means an ideologically neutral position. One might contrast, for instance, the influential 'limits to growth' movement (also variously described as a deep green or ecological position) which rejects the goal of constantly seeking economic growth as fundamentally in conflict with a high level of environmental protection.[63]

At a constitutional level, therefore, the EU not only acknowledges the important relationship between its economic and environmental policies, but proposes and indeed mandates a balance. As one would expect, this position as a matter of law can also be discerned in the EU's policy positions on sustainable development, discussed above.

Nevertheless, the precise requirements of the sustainable development goal remain extremely open-textured and, as with the aim of a 'high level of protection of the environment', leave room for a wide spectrum of Member State views as to the relative importance of environmental protection compared to, for instance, economic goals or social protection. As already noted, these views might legitimately differ, for instance, depending on the relative level of economic prosperity of the Member State at issue (as, for instance, the lower standard for certain Member States permitted by the EU Emissions Trading Scheme Directive, discussed above, recognises).[64] Similarly, views differ markedly between (and within) Member States on such basic issues as the extent to which environmental goods and bads can be monetised or economised and, linked to this, the extent to which cost–benefit analysis is acceptable in the case of sensitive areas of environmental regulation such as nature conservation, as discussed further below.[65]

Clearly, these are fundamental issues in decisions on the future direction of EU environmental policy. The EU's Seventh, current, Environmental Action Programme (EAP) has confirmed the persistence of unsustainable trends in the four priority areas identified in its previous EAP, including in the fields of climate change; nature and biodiversity; environment and health and quality of life; and

---

[62] See Michael Jacobs, 'Sustainable Development as a Contested Concept' in Andrew Dobson, *Fairness and Futurity: Essays on Environmental Sustainability and Social Justice* (Oxford University Press, 1999).
[63] See, notably, Donella Meadows et al., *The Limits to Growth: 30 Years Update* (Taylor & Francis, 2005) and Tim Jackson, *Prosperity without Growth: Economics for a Finite Planet* (Earthscan/Routledge, 2009).
[64] This reason for diverse obligations is also present in international environmental law in the form of the principle of Common but Differentiated Responsibilities (CBDR). See, further, Sands and Peel, *Principles of International Environmental Law* (3rd edn., Cambridge University Press, 2012), chapter 6.
[65] For instance, the UK has embraced the notion of (putting a price on) ecosystem services, but this has not been done to the same extent in other Member States. See UNEP-WCMC *UK National Ecosystem Assessment*, June 2011.

natural resources and wastes.[66] The same conclusion was reached at the international level during the Rio+20 in 2012 which acknowledged that since 1992 there are 'areas of insufficient progress and setbacks in the integration of the three dimensions of sustainable development'.[67]

Legal Bases and Environmental Guarantee Provisions

Article 192 TFEU

1. The European Parliament and the Council, acting in accordance with the ordinary legislative procedure and after consulting the Economic and Social Committee and the Committee of the Regions, shall decide what action is to be taken by the Union in order to achieve the objectives referred to in Article 191.
2. By way of derogation from the decision-making procedure provided for in paragraph 1 and without prejudice to Article 114, the Council acting unanimously in accordance with a special legislative procedure and after consulting the European Parliament, the Economic and Social Committee and the Committee of the Regions, shall adopt:
   (a) provisions primarily of a fiscal nature;
   (b) measures affecting:
      – town and country planning,
      – quantitative management of water resources or affecting, directly or indirectly, the availability of those resources,
      – land use, with the exception of waste management;
   (c) measures significantly affecting a Member State's choice between different energy sources and the general structure of its energy supply.
   The Council, acting unanimously on a proposal from the Commission and after consulting the European Parliament, the Economic and Social Committee and the Committee of the Regions, may make the ordinary legislative procedure applicable to the matters referred to in the first subparagraph.
3. General action programmes setting out priority objectives to be attained shall be adopted by the European Parliament and the Council, acting in accordance with the ordinary legislative procedure and after consulting the Economic and Social Committee and the Committee of the Regions.
   The measures necessary for the implementation of these programmes shall be adopted under the terms of paragraph 1 or 2, as the case may be.

---

[66] Seventh Environmental Action Programme, 'Living Well, Within the Limits of Our Planet', OJ 2013 L 354/171.
[67] UN A/RES/66/288, para. 20.

4. Without prejudice to certain measures adopted by the Union, the Member States shall finance and implement the environment policy.
5. Without prejudice to the principle that the polluter should pay, if a measure based on the provisions of paragraph 1 involves costs deemed disproportionate for the public authorities of a Member State, such measure shall lay down appropriate provisions in the form of:
   – temporary derogations, and/or
   – financial support from the Cohesion Fund set up pursuant to Article 177.

General Legal Bases

As noted above, in the past, environmental measures frequently gave rise to legal basis disputes before the ECJ, particularly when what is now Article 114 TFEU (entailing qualified majority voting in the Council) was used instead of what is now Article 192(1) TFEU (which originally required unanimity).[68] With the move to qualified majority voting in Article 192(1) TFEU accomplished by the Treaty of Maastricht, however, legal basis disputes are less frequent in this field, although disputes between the use of Article 192(1) and Article 352 TFEU still occur.[69] Post-Lisbon, Article 192(1) TFEU remains the key legal basis for environmental provisions, and provides for the ordinary legislative procedure after consultation with ECOSOC and the Committee of the Regions.

By way of derogation, however, Article 192(2) TFEU provides that a special legislative procedure requiring unanimity of voting in the Council, and consultation of the European Parliament, ECOSOC and the Committee of the Regions, applies in the case of (a) provisions 'primarily of a fiscal nature'; (b) measures affecting town and country planning, the quantitative management of water resources or affecting, directly or indirectly, the availability of those resources, and land use, with the exception of waste management; and (c) measures significantly affecting a Member State's choice between different energy sources and the general structure of its energy supply. This provision applies 'without prejudice to Article 114', i.e. in the case of legislation that falls within these categories, but also falls within the scope of Article 114 TFEU, precedence should be given to the latter legal basis.

The Lisbon Treaty added a *passerelle* clause to Article 192(2) TFEU, whereby the areas listed may be made subject to qualified majority voting following a unanimous decision of the Council and after consultation of the European Parliament, ECOSOC and the Committee of the Regions, without the necessity for Treaty amendment.

Article 192(3) TFEU contains a legal basis provision for the adoption of the EU's multiannual Environmental Action Programmes, discussed above, to which the ordinary legislative procedure applies.

---

[68] See, for instance, Case C-300/89 *Commission v. Council (Titanium Dioxide)*, cited above.
[69] See, for instance, Opinion 2/00, *Cartagena Protocol* ECLI:EU:C:2001:664.

Environmental Guarantee Provisions and Minimum Harmonisation

Where environmental legislation is passed on the basis of Article 192 TFEU or Article 114 TFEU, the Treaty expressly allows Member States, subject to compliance with certain conditions, to prefer a higher level of environmental protection via national measures. As noted above, these provisions are consistent with the EU's stated aim of promoting a 'high level of protection taking into account the diversity of situations in the various regions of the Union' (Article 191(2) TFEU).

First, Article 191(2) TFEU provides that harmonisation measures 'answering environmental protection requirements' shall include, 'where appropriate', a safeguard clause allowing Member States to take provisional measures, for non-economic environmental reasons, subject to a procedure of inspection by the Union.

Secondly, Article 193 TFEU provides that the protective measures adopted pursuant to Article 192 shall not prevent any Member State from 'maintaining or introducing more stringent protective measures', as long as they are compatible with the Treaties and notified to the Commission. The CJEU has held that the principle of proportionality does not apply to measures falling within this provision.[70]

It is clear that the test set out in Article 193 TFEU for the introduction of new, greener national provisions is far less prescriptive than Article 114(5) TFEU, discussed below, and, therefore, one might reasonably suppose, far easier for Member States to satisfy. By contrast to Article 114(5), there is no requirement for new scientific evidence; there is no requirement to demonstrate a problem specific to one Member State. Further, as the CJEU has held, failure to notify the Commission of the relevant measures, or to obtain the Commission's agreement to them, does not render such measures invalid.[71] However, as with the other conditions for these safeguard clauses, the burden of proving this lies on the Member State.[72]

> **The Article 193 TFEU Environmental Safeguard Provision**
>
> Up until recent years, Article 193 had been dealt with relatively rarely by the CJEU, suggesting that Member States may not be relying on it (in comparison, for instance, with the quite frequent reliance on the internal market safeguard clauses). Recently, however, the CJEU has dealt with a number of cases clarifying the scope of this provision and its use where there is relevant EU environmental legislation. Many of these cases have focused on the question whether the relevant existing EU environmental legislation can be interpreted to allow a higher level of environmental protection on the part of Member States. This will be so where, as properly interpreted, the legislation achieves minimum but not exhaustive harmonisation.

---

[70] Case C-6/03 *Deponiezweckverband Eiterköpfe* ECLI:EU:C:2005:655.
[71] See Case C-2/10 *Azienda Agro-Zootecnica Franchini* ECLI:EU:C:2011:502, para. 53.
[72] See e.g. Joined Cases C-439/05 P and C-454/05 P *Land Oberösterreich* v. *Commission* ECLI:EU:C:2007:510.

To date, these cases show that the CJEU has typically interpreted the level of harmonisation achieved by a given environmental Directive to be minimum in nature, relying on the terms of the Directive as well as Article 193 TFEU to conclude that Member States are in principle free to enact more stringent measures in furtherance of the overall aim of a high level of protection of the environment. In *Fornasor*, the CJEU held that the EU hazardous waste Directive 91/689 did not preclude Member States from unilaterally classifying additional categories of waste as hazardous, reasoning that (para. 46):

> the Community rules do not seek to effect complete harmonisation in the area of the environment. Even though [present Article 191] of the Treaty refers to certain Community objectives to be attained, both [present Article 193 TFEU] and Directive 91/689 allow the Member States to introduce more stringent protective measures. Under [present Article 191] of the Treaty, Community policy on the environment is to aim at a high level of protection, taking into account the diversity of situations in the various regions of the Community.

Similarly, in *Deponiezweckverband Eiterköpfe*,[73] the CJEU interpreted the Landfill Directive in the light of the principles of the EU's environmental policy set out in what is now Article 191(2) TFEU, to conclude that the Directive did not achieve complete harmonisation, but permitted Member States to adopt stricter landfill rules in compliance with Article 193 TFEU (citing *Fornasor*). The CJEU also rejected the contention that Article 193 TFEU in itself included any proportionality test, emphasising that it 'falls to the Member States to define the extent of the protection to be achieved' in cases falling under this Article (para. 61). By contrast, the proportionality principle would be applicable insofar as Article 193 TFEU was being used to assess whether the national measures complied with other Treaty provisions, as is required by Article 193 TFEU. For instance, proportionality is evidently highly relevant when assessing compatibility of *prima facie* restrictive measures under Article 34 TFEU on the free movement of goods, considered in Chapter 3.

Most recently, in *Azienda Agro-Zootecnica Franchini*,[74] the CJEU considered the question of the circumstances in which Member States were entitled to take more protective measures as compared to the EU's nature conservation legislation (namely, the Habitats and Birds Directives).[75] That case concerned Italian measures which restricted a priori the building of wind turbines on land situated within protected areas to cases where those turbines were intended for self-consumption only. Wind turbines intended for other use were refused authorisation, even without carrying out any appropriate assessment of the

---

[73] Case C-6/03 *Deponiezweckverband Eiterköpfe* v. *Land Rheinland-Pflaz* ECLI:EU:C:2005:655.
[74] Cited above.
[75] Council Directive 92/43/EEC of 21 May 1992 on the conservation of natural habitats and of wild fauna and flora, OJ 1992 L 206/7 and Council Directive 79/409/EEC of 2 April 1979 on the conservation of wild birds, OJ 1979 L 103/1.

> project's environmental impacts as is provided for in the Habitats and Birds Directives. In holding that such measures were compatible with the Directives, the CJEU noted that, contrary to the Birds Directive, the Habitats Directive did not contain any express provision authorising more stringent measures. However, Article 193 TFEU could be relied upon, despite the fact that the Italian measures had not been notified to or approved by the Commission in advance.
>
> The CJEU went on to consider whether, as required by Article 193 TFEU, the Italian measures complied with other TFEU provisions. On that point, the applicants had submitted in this regard that the objective of developing new and renewable forms of energy, as established for European Union policy by Article 194(1)(c) TFEU, should take precedence over the environmental protection objectives pursued by the Habitats and Birds Directives. The CJEU's response was clear (§§56–57):
>
>> Suffice it to observe in that connection that Article 194(1) TFEU states that European Union policy on energy must have regard for the need to preserve and improve the environment.
>>
>> Moreover, a measure such as that at issue in the main proceedings, which prohibits only the location of new wind turbines not intended for self-consumption on sites forming part of the Natura 2000 network, with the possibility of exemption for wind turbines intended for self-consumption with a capacity not exceeding 20 kW, is not, in view of its limited scope, liable to jeopardise the European Union objective of developing new and renewable forms of energy.
>
> It is evident, however, that the CJEU's review would be far more intensive in case of alleged incompatibility with the free movement provisions, for instance, where the Treaty's rules are much more precise, and do not have the same commonality of purpose as the TFEU's energy and environment provisions.

Thirdly, Article 114(4) TFEU provides that if, after the adoption of a harmonisation measure by the European Parliament and the Council, by the Council or by the Commission, a Member State deems it necessary to maintain national provisions on *inter alia* grounds 'relating to the protection of the environment or the working environment', it shall notify the Commission of these provisions as well as the grounds for maintaining them.[76]

Fourthly, without prejudice to Article 114(4) TFEU, Article 114(5) TFEU provides that if, after such a harmonisation measure, a Member State deems it

---

[76] Contrast the version of this provision as originally introduced by the Single European Act, as Art. 100a(4), discussed above: 'If, after the adoption of a harmonization measure by the Council acting by a qualified majority, a Member State deems it necessary to *apply* national provisions on grounds of major needs referred to in Art. 36, or relating to protection of the environment or the working environment, it shall notify the Commission of these provisions. The Commission shall confirm the provisions involved after having verified that they are not a means of arbitrary discrimination or a disguised restriction on trade between Member States' (emphasis added).

necessary to introduce national provisions based on new scientific evidence relating to *inter alia* the protection of the environment 'on grounds of a problem specific to that Member State arising after the adoption of the harmonisation measure', it shall notify the Commission of the envisaged provisions as well as the grounds for introducing them.

Both Article 114(4) and (5) are subject to the procedural provisions contained in Articles 114(6)–(9) (as inserted by the Treaty of Amsterdam), which set a period of six months for the Commission to approve or reject the measure and, where a measure has been authorised, oblige the Commission to consider proposing an adaptation to the relevant EU legislation.

It is clear from the above that the conditions for introducing new national measures (Article 114(4) TFEU) are stricter than those for maintaining existing measures (Article 114(5) TFEU). In contrast to the far more permissive notion for legacy environmental provisions that the Member State must 'deem it necessary' to maintain such provisions on grounds 'relating' to the environment (Article 114(4)),[77] for new provisions Member States must prove that:

- there is 'new scientific evidence' relating to the protection of the environment (i.e. since the adoption of the EU harmonising measure) which justifies the measure; and
- the problem is 'specific to that Member State'.

For instance, the CJEU has affirmed that a ban on the use of genetically modified organisms in Upper Austria did not fall under Article 114(5) TFEU, because it did not raise any issues specific to that Member State.[78] In *Denmark v. Commission*, in holding that Article 114(5) will be narrowly interpreted, the CJEU noted that, in contrast to Article 114(4), the Community legislature by definition could not have taken the national measures at issue into account when passing the relevant harmonising legislation.[79] In *Netherlands v. Commission*, the CJEU emphasised that, although the Commission enjoyed a wide discretion in assessing whether the conditions of Article 114(5) are made out, this does not exclude a relatively intensive judicial review of the Commission's decision, particularly as the administrative procedure of Article 114(5) does not include a right to be heard as such.[80] This judgment also highlights the fact that the problem giving rise to the proposed more stringent national measure need not have occurred *exclusively* in that Member State to qualify for the Article 114(5) derogation. Rather, the specificity of the problem to the local area need only be such that harmonisation measures would not be adequate on their own to mitigate it.

---

[77] Or other relevant objective of public interest; note the narrower scope of justifications permitted for Art. 114(5) as compared to Art. 114(4).
[78] Joined Cases C-439/05 P and C-454/05 P *Land Oberösterreich and Austria v. Commission* ECLI:EU:C:2007:510.
[79] Case C-3/00 *Denmark v. Commission* ECLI:EU:C:2003:167, para. 58.
[80] Case C-405/07P *Netherlands v. Commission* ECLI:EU:C:2008:613, paras. 54–56.

It is also worth observing that, in contrast to Article 193 TFEU considered above, Article 114(5) does not specify that the national provisions envisaged must result in more stringent (as opposed to merely different) levels of environmental protection, as long as such difference is justified by new scientific evidence and meets the specificity criterion. This raises the possibility that Article 114(5) could extend not only to environmental safeguard measures, but also potentially to derogation measures.

Aside from Article 114(4)/(5) and Article 193 TFEU, which enshrine (in principle pro-environmental) flexibility tests in the Treaty, it is important to note the separate phenomenon whereby, in the case of certain EU environmental legislation, the legislation itself provides for or permits different standards for different States or actors (sub-constitutional flexibility). In the case of legislation based on Article 114(1) TFEU, this possibility is expressly provided for in Article 114(10) TFEU, which provides,

> The harmonisation measures [adopted on the basis of Article 114(1) TFEU] shall, in appropriate cases, include a safeguard clause authorising the Member States to take, for one or more of the non-economic reasons referred to in Article 36, provisional measures subject to a Union control procedure.

Perhaps the best-known examples of express safeguard clauses in EU environmental legislation are those contained in EU legislation regulating genetically modified organisms (GMOs). As discussed further in Chapter 3, the CJEU has held these safeguard clauses to be an expression of the precautionary principle, and therefore they must be interpreted in the light of this principle.[81]

The Nature of the European Union's Environmental Competences

As Article 4(2) TFEU, inserted by the Treaty of Lisbon, now expressly clarifies, environmental policy constitutes an express shared competence between the Union and its Member States. This means, pursuant to Article 2(2) TFEU, that,

> the Union and the Member States may legislate and adopt legally binding acts in that area. The Member States shall exercise their competence to the extent that the Union has not exercised its competence. The Member States shall again exercise their competence to the extent that the Union has decided to cease exercising its competence.

The exception to the above is the conservation of marine biological resources under the common fisheries policy, which Article 3(1)(d) TFEU clarifies is an

---

[81] Case C-236/01 *Monsanto* ECLI:EU:C:2003:431.

exclusive competence of the Union.[82] In this field, therefore, 'only the Union may legislate and adopt legally binding acts, the Member States being able to do so themselves only if so empowered by the Union or for the implementation of Union acts'.[83]

In terms of the EU's external competences, the *existence* of the EU's competence to conclude international environmental agreements is, therefore, not in dispute.[84] The *nature* of the EU's external environmental competence – and, in particular, the extent to which it has exclusive external environmental competence – has been more controversial.

A first divisive question has been the extent to which an environmental agreement may be considered to fall within the *express* exclusive external competences of the EU and, in particular, the Common Commercial Policy defined in Article 207 TFEU. In Opinion 2/00 (Cartagena Protocol), the CJEU held that the legal basis for the conclusion of the Cartagena Protocol on Biosafety to the Convention on Biological Diversity must be what is now Article 192 TFEU (the environmental legal basis, discussed above), and not Article 207 TFEU on the Common Commercial Policy. This meant that the Protocol must be concluded as a so-called 'mixed' agreement, by the Union (at the time, the Community) *and* its Member States, and not exclusively by the Union.[85] In so holding, the CJEU rejected the Commission's argument that the mere fact that a Union action was liable to have repercussions on trade was enough for the agreement to fall within the scope of the Common Commercial Policy.[86] Rather, the centre of gravity of the Protocol's objectives was environmental, rather than trade-related: effects on trade were indirect.[87]

A second question is the extent to which, even if an international environmental agreement does not fall within the express exclusive competences of the Union, it may nevertheless be considered to fall within the Union's *implied* exclusive competences. Article 3(2) TFEU, inserted by the Treaty of Lisbon, was intended essentially to codify the CJEU's rather complex *ERTA* jurisprudence[88] on the circumstances in which the EU could be considered to have implied exclusive external competence to act in a field, and provides:

---

[82] In the context of external competences, this had already been held by the CJEU in Joined Cases 3/76, 4/76 and 6/76 *Kramer* ECLI:EU:C:1976:114.
[83] Art. 2(1) TFEU.   [84] See, further, Art. 216(1) TFEU.
[85] See, generally, the discussion at Piet Eeckhout, *EU External Relations Law* (2nd edn., Oxford University Press, 2011), 42 onwards.
[86] See, further, Case C-281/01 *Commission* v. *Council (Energy Star)* ECLI:EU:C:2002:761.
[87] By contrast, in the *Rotterdam Convention* case, the CJEU held that the Rotterdam Convention on the Prior Informed Consent procedure for hazardous chemicals and pesticides in international trade must be based on two legal bases, present Art. 192 TFEU and Art. 207 TFEU on the Common Commercial Policy, Case C-94/03 ECLI:EU:C:2006:2. Applying its reasoning on a legal basis, discussed above, the CJEU held that the aims of trade and environmental protection were indissociably linked in that case, and neither could be considered to constitute a secondary aim.
[88] Case 22/70 *ERTA* ECLI:EU:C:1971:32 and see the discussion in Eeckhout, *EU External Relations Law*.

> The Union shall ... have exclusive competence for the conclusion of an international agreement when its conclusion is provided for in a legislative act of the Union or is necessary to enable the Union to exercise its internal competence, or in so far as its conclusion may affect common rules or alter their scope.

Given the large body of internal harmonising legislation that now exists in the environmental context, this offers considerable scope for arguments that specific international environmental agreements now fall within the implied external exclusive competence of the Union. Whether this is indeed the case can ultimately only be determined by the CJEU, after examining the provisions of the particular international agreement and the relevant provisions of the EU internal environmental legislation. In *Green Network*, the CJEU considered the extent to which the 2009 Renewable Energy Directive, discussed further in Chapter 3, had harmonised the regulation of green electricity to such an extent as to mean that the Union had acquired implied exclusive external competence to act in this field. That case concerned an Italian law enabling Italy to exempt from its green certificates scheme green electricity produced in a third State (in that case, Switzerland) where an agreement between Italy and Switzerland had been signed to provide for such an exemption. The Italian agreement with Switzerland was held to be contrary to the EU Treaty. Specifically, applying Article 3(2) TFEU, the CJEU held that the EU provisions on guarantees of origin (in that case, applying the prior RES Directive, Directive 2001/77) had been harmonised such that, if Italy were to sign an agreement on the topic with Switzerland, this would be liable to 'alter the scope of common rules' within the meaning of the CJEU's case law on the EU's exclusive competence.[89]

A final important restriction on Member States' competence to act in the international environmental sphere is the CJEU's case law on the implications of the Article 4(3) TEU duty of loyal or sincere cooperation. Article 4(3) TEU provides,

> Pursuant to the principle of sincere cooperation, the Union and the Member States shall, in full mutual respect, assist each other in carrying out tasks which flow from the Treaties.
>
> The Member States shall take any appropriate measure, general or particular, to ensure fulfilment of the obligations arising out of the Treaties or resulting from the acts of the institutions of the Union.
>
> The Member States shall facilitate the achievement of the Union's tasks and refrain from any measure which could jeopardise the attainment of the Union's objectives.

In the CJEU's *MOX Plant* judgment, Ireland was held to have breached the duty of loyal cooperation by suing the UK before the International Tribunal of the

---

[89] Case C-66/13 *Green Network* ECLI:EU:C:2014:2399, para. 49.

Law of the Sea for breach of the provisions of the UN Convention of the Law of the Sea in relation to pollution of the Irish Sea with radioactive waste from the Sellafield nuclear reprocessing plant.[90]

Further, in its controversial perfluorooctane sulfonate (*PFOS*) judgment, the CJEU ruled that Sweden had breached its duty of loyal cooperation by unilaterally proposing to list a substance in an Annex to the Stockholm Convention on Persistent Organic Pollutants, in circumstances where the EU had delayed in taking any action (due, *inter alia*, to a conflict of views) and Sweden had decided to take matters into its own hands.[91] In the external context, this broad interpretation of the implications of Article 4(3) TEU places important limitations on the ability of Member States to strive for a higher level of environmental protection where no consensus can be reached in the EU institutions.

Understanding EU Environmental Law and Policy in Context

As will be evident throughout this book, EU environmental law and policy cannot properly be understood in isolation from the broader context in which environmental problems arise, and the insights of other disciplines, including science, economics, philosophy and politics. This is consistent with the approach taken in the scientific literature, where the environment is viewed as a classic example of a complex system, in the sense of a system composed of many interacting variables, where it is not possible to distinguish simple causal links between these variables.[92] This polycentric nature of environmental problems means that, using Fuller's metaphor of a spider's web, 'a pull on one strand will distribute tensions after a complicated pattern throughout the web as a whole'.[93] The final section of this chapter highlights four aspects of this context, namely:[94]

- environment, science and risk;
- environment and governance;
- environment, philosophy and ethics; and
- environment and geography, and the challenges of enlargement.

The environment/economics interface, another key theme within EU environmental policy, is considered in the above discussion of sustainable development, and is focused on in the discussion of the integration principle in Chapter 3.

---

[90] Case C-459/03 *Commission v. Ireland* ECLI:EU:C:2006:345.
[91] Case C-246/07 *Commission v. Sweden* ECLI:EU:C:2010:203.
[92] See James Ladyman, James Lambert and Karoline Wiesner, 'What is a Complex System?' (2013) 3 *European Journal of Philosophy of Science* 33; Simon A. Levin, 'Ecosystems and the Biosphere as Complex Adaptive Systems' (1998) 1 *Ecosystems* 431–436.
[93] Lon L. Fuller and Kenneth I. Winston, 'The Forms and Limits of Adjudication' (1978) 92 *Harvard Law Review* 353, at 395.
[94] This is in no sense intended to be an exhaustive list of cross-cutting themes in EU environmental law and policy, but rather a selection of certain aspects of the context of particular importance and/or interest.

Environment, Risk and Science

Any conversation on EU environmental law must engage with the concept of risk and with the role of science in decision-making. EU environmental law overwhelmingly relies on risk regulation strategies to pursue its mandate of guaranteeing a high level of environmental protection.[95] And the way we understand risk, for the purposes of legal decision-making, is to a large extent shaped by scientific modes of reasoning and scientific expertise. The paragraphs below explore the key characteristics of EU risk regulation as an environmental governance strategy and highlight its most prominent strengths and weaknesses. We then examine the position and treatment of scientific expertise within the EU regulatory and judicial sphere. The tale that emerges from the discussion is one of complexity and subtly shifting relationships. The adoption of the risk regulation paradigm has helped to impart structure and a degree of rationality to the otherwise quite disorganised field of EU regulation, but it also constrains the extent to which the EU can be a genuinely responsive regulator. Science, in turn, is a necessary but insufficient basis for environmental policy and law. In itself, this is not necessarily problematic, but strategies that effectively and legitimately balance the scientific and the 'alternative' aspects of decision-making prove hard to find.

Risk and Risk Regulation

Risk regulation strategies espouse the view that the fundamental mission of regulation is to facilitate economic and social progress by managing and controlling its potential negative consequences.[96] To this end, risk regulation regimes perform four tasks:

Risk regulation structures decision-making in the following way:

Risk identification	Identifying the possible hazards associated with a particular event, activity or entity
Risk assessment	Weighing the likelihood and seriousness of identified hazards materialising
Risk management	Formulating a response to the assessed risks
Risk communication	Conveying risk management decisions (communication)[97]

---

[95] Veerle Heyvaert, 'Governing Climate Change: Towards a New Paradigm for Risk Regulation' (2011) 74(6) *Modern Law Review* 817–844, at 822–823.

[96] Julia Black, 'The Role of Risk in Regulatory Processes' in Robert Baldwin, Martin Cave and Martin Lodge (eds.), *Oxford Handbook of Regulation* (Oxford University Press, 2010), 302; Marjolein B. A. van Asselt and Ortwinn Renn, 'Risk Governance' (2011) 14(4) *Journal of Risk Research* 431–449.

[97] Laura Drott, Lukas Jochum, Frederik Lange, Isabel Skierka, Jonas Vach and Marjolein B. A. van Asselt, 'Accountability and Risk Governance: A Scenario-Informed Reflection on European Regulation of GMOs' (2013) 16(9), *Journal of Risk Research* 1123–1140, at 1124.

It goes without saying that the workability of risk regulation frameworks is heavily premised on a shared understanding of what 'risks' are. In the context of EU environmental law, risks are typically interpreted to comprise the array of possible negative impacts of technologies and their applications on human health, on environmental media (air, water, soil), on the health of living organisms and, in some instances, on the resilience of natural habitats. It is moreover useful at this point to reflect on some obvious but important attributes of risk within a regulatory context. Risks are *anticipated* impacts: based on information and indications in our possession today, we make predictions about future consequences. This information may be more or less abundant and reliable, but as risks inevitably engage with the future, there is an equally inevitable degree of fallibility in determinations of risk. Moreover, risk management is informed not only by the likelihood of negative impacts occurring, but also by their magnitude. Even when a broad consensus exists on how *likely* the occurrence is of a particular environmental harm, people can reasonably disagree about how *serious* this harm is. Bird watchers may perceive the risks of pesticides to non-target species very differently from stockholders in agro-chemical companies. The inescapably predictive and evaluative nature of risk means that the management of risk is an exercise of discretion: risk regulators must choose which predictions and whose perceptions carry weight in formulating a response. This exposes the regulator, which in the EU context is frequently the European Commission, to intense scrutiny.

Risk Regulation in the European Union
EU environmental law is rich in 'technological risk regulation', which refers to regimes that govern particular industrial processes (such as the cultivation of genetically modified produce, or the deployment of carbon capture and storage technology) and products (for instance, chemicals, passenger cars, cosmetics). The full reach of risk regulation, however, stretches well beyond technological risk regulation: it is possible to discern risk-based strategies in most EU environmental legal instruments, covering policies from habitats protection to water quality.[98] Moreover, risk regulation is far from unique to environmental governance: instruments in fields ranging from EU financial regulation to data protection are said to embrace a risk-based perspective.[99] The lessons drawn from the analysis of environmental risk regulation therefore resonate far beyond the thematic confines of this book.

A high proportion of EU risk regulation is 'dual purpose regulation', designed both to protect human health and the environment and to facilitate intra-EU trade. In fact, the early adoption of harmonised health, safety and environmental

---

[98] Heyvaert, 'Governing Climate Change', 822–823.
[99] Joana Gray and Jenny Hamilton, *Implementing Financial Regulation: Theory and Practice* (Wiley & Sons, 2006), 25–54; Niel Van Dijk, Raphael Gellert and Kjetil Rommetveit, 'A Risk to a Right? Beyond Data Protection Risk Assessments' (2016) 32(2) *Computer Law and Security Review* 286–306.

standards was typically done precisely in order to foster the free movement of goods across national borders. This prominent trade–risk nexus has had a defining impact on the identity of EU risk regulation. First, a large proportion of the information that goes into the risk identification, assessment and management process comes from the sphere of trade; it is produced and supplied by manufacturers or importers who seek to market their goods across the EU. In many cases, the very production of risk information will be a precondition for (continued) access to the market. Furthermore, determinations regarding the seriousness of risk, and the corresponding desirability of regulatory intervention, are invariably taken against a backdrop of trade and economic competitiveness considerations.[100]

A second prominent feature of EU risk regulation is its heavy reliance on compartmentalisation as a problem-solving strategy.[101] The object of EU risk regulation is not to generate answers to the big, existential questions society faces with regard to techno-scientific developments, such as 'should we aspire towards a society in which driverless cars are the primary mode of transport?' Rather, EU risk regulation breaks the issue down into a wealth of smaller, more technical questions, the answers to which aim to ensure that, if driverless cars are indeed the wave of the future, we are ready to respond to and control the range of new safety, health and environmental impacts that their introduction entails. EU risk regulation, thus, tends to operate in a rather micro-managerial manner: it 'reviews identified risks substance-by-substance, technological application-by-application, product-by-product and, within the wider field of EU environmental regulation, installation-by-installation and/or project-by-project'.[102]

A third and, for the purposes of this brief discussion, final key feature of EU risk regulation is that it maintains a strict formal divide between the different stages of the risk regulation process, particularly between the stages of risk assessment and risk management. The assessment stage is cast as a predominantly fact-based exercise conducted by independent techno-scientific experts. Risk management, in turn, is considered to be rooted in policy. Management decisions involve the exercise of discretion, and are therefore within the purview of EU policy-makers and administrative authorities.[103] The institutional arrangements that characterise the vast proportion of EU risk regulation mirror this divide: the task of assessing risk is typically bestowed upon an Agency (for example, the European Chemicals Agency or the European Food Safety Authority) or an expert advisory body. These entities assess the risks (or, more frequently, peer review risk assessments submitted by the private sector) and formulate management opinions or

---

[100] Heyvaert, 'Governing Climate Change', 822–824.   [101] Ibid., 824–825.
[102] Ibid., 825. See also Elizabeth Fisher's analysis of the 'rationalist-instrumental' approach to risk regulation in Elizabeth Fisher, *Risk Regulation and Administrative Constitutionalism* (Hart Publishing, 2007).
[103] Michelle Everson and Ellen Vos, 'European Risk Governance in a Global Context' in Ellen Vos (ed.), *European Risk Governance: Its Science, its Inclusiveness and its Effectiveness*, Connex Report Series No. 6 (2008), 10–15, at 11.

recommendations, which are forwarded to the EU decision-maker. In many cases, this will be the European Commission, acting either in its capacity as delegated lawmaker (under Art. 291 TFEU) or under comitology rules.[104]

Risk Regulation and Critique

Risk-based strategies are deeply entrenched in EU environmental regulation. Their appeal is strong as risk regulation infuses structure into decision-making and enables problem solving by breaking down larger market trends into discrete sets of predictable and manageable impacts. The focus on risks, rather than on proven instances of harm, enables the regulator to engage with new technologies and practices at an early stage of their development, to pursue preventive rather than remedial policies, and to shape trade flows in a way that harnesses competitiveness while taking into account the potential consequences for health and the environment. Moreover, risk regulation is at the same time inclusive and selective: it engages with all (known) health and environmental risks at the stage of risk identification, but zeroes in on a smaller set of significant risks at the stage of risk management, an approach that is expressly legitimised by the risk regulation ethos of tailoring responses to not just the likelihood, but also the magnitude of adverse effects. The systematic appearance of the risk identification process, the focus on managing the impacts of trade rather than prescribing or prohibiting particular forms of entrepreneurship, and the selectiveness of the risk-management process, all help to consolidate the image of the EU as an informed, neutral and rational regulator.

Yet risk regulation, and its practice in the European Union, has not been spared criticism. Some of its alleged virtues, it has been claimed, are considerably overstated. Moreover, regulatory experience has revealed a number of limitations, even dysfunctions, within EU risk regulation, to the extent that some commentators have referred to the 'pathology' of EU risk regulation.[105] A first and pragmatic critique relates to the cost of the approach. The kind of data that informs risk assessment is usually expensive to produce and undersupplied by the market, which implies that it must be custom-made for the purpose of regulation. As Maria Lee observes: 'A vast amount of work lies behind risk assessment, which may depend for example on laboratory experiments, field work, or epidemiological studies. Risk assessment may involve complex modelling, from computer simulations of the entire climate system, to relatively simpler modelling of smaller systems, such as water quality in a particular river.'[106] It is customary in EU risk regulation to place the burden of production on the regulated parties (typically, manufacturers, importers, downstream users or service providers), which accords with the polluter pays principle. It does, however, stir concerns among the private

---

[104] Regulation (EU) No. 182/2011 laying down the rules and general principles concerning mechanisms for control by Member States of the Commission's exercise of implementing powers, OJ 2011 L 55/13.
[105] Heyvaert, 'Governing Climate Change', 824.
[106] Maria Lee, *EU Environmental Law, Governance and Decision-Making* (2nd edn., Hart Publishing, 2014), 30.

sector about regulatory burdens eroding profitability and weakening the position of European business on the global market.

Arguably, the expense of risk regulation might be more easily justified if broad agreement existed that the information generated in the process is, indeed, comprehensive, reliable and a sound basis for the development of effective risk management. Yet this has been called into question. In the first place, risk regulation focuses on impacts that are *predictable* and does not necessarily include provisions to stimulate the identification of thus far unknown consequences. Secondly, the suggestion that risk regulation identifies *every single known risk*, too, is an overstatement. Risks 'count' if they jeopardise values we care about, a view reflected in the CJEU's Pfizer ruling which defines risk as 'a function of the probability that the use of a product or a procedure will adversely affect the *interests safeguarded by the legal order*'.[107] Chemicals regulation pursues protection of human health and the environment generally, but its data and testing requirements are geared towards uncovering short-term human and animal toxicity. Adverse effects on inanimate natural organisms, long-term effects and impacts on 'quality of life' values such as animal behaviour, to name but a few alternative risks, fall outside the risk regulatory remit. The narrowness of risk identification is further exacerbated by risk regulation's reliance on compartmentalisation, which leaves little scope for the examination of combined impacts and synergy.

The third and most persistent stream of criticism relates to the claims of objectivity and neutrality that surround the risk regulation process and, particularly, the risk assessment / risk management divide. The representation of risk assessment as fact-based has been strongly challenged, since pronouncements on the seriousness of adverse effects necessarily involve the exercise of judgment.[108] From the perspective of a bio-conservationist, a shift in bird migration patterns due to land use changes may not constitute a serious risk if it does not threaten the resilience of the bird population. Local bird-watching societies, though, might view the matter differently. The discretionary elements within the assessment process also beg the question why the views of experts should be privileged over public risk perception. This critique has given rise to a call for public participation in risk decision-making.[109] A number of EU environmental regulatory frameworks respond to this call, but coherently integrating expert and public perceptions of risk within one decision-making framework has proved fraught with difficulty.[110] Finally, the meaningfulness of the institutional separation between the Agencies, advisory bodies and committees that supply the opinions, and the EU authorities which take the decisions, can be questioned. In most instances, expert opinions will include risk management recommendations, and

---

[107] Case T-13/99 *Pfizer Animal Health* v. *Council* ECLI:EU:T:2002:209, para. 13.
[108] Alberto Alemanno, 'EU Risk Regulation and Science: The Role of Experts in Decision-Making and Judicial Review' in Vos, *European Risk Governance*, 37–88, at 47.
[109] Emily Hammond, 'Public Participation in Risk Regulation: The Flaws of Formality' (2016) 1 *Utah Law Review* 169–192, at 177.
[110] Maria Lee, 'Risk and Beyond: EU Regulation of Nanotechnology' (2011) 35(6) *European Law Review* 799–821.

regulators will follow expert advice. As will be explored in the next section, this pattern has been further entrenched by CJEU case law which constrains the conditions under which EU public authorities can disregard or act counter to expert advice. On the one hand, these arrangements may allay worries about undue 'politicking' within administration, and about the Commission using its decision-making powers for strategic instead of public interest purposes. On the other hand, they do little to appease concerns about government by an elite, expert community which is neither representative of nor accountable to the interests it subsumes.

The discussion above only scratches the surface of the many and complex challenges that accompany the implementation of risk regulation strategies, and hardly does justice to the richness and range of the scholarly debate on this issue. However, it does convey some of the core dynamics and attributes of EU environmental legal frameworks. Chief among these is the pivotal role of scientific evidence in decision-making. It is to this aspect that we now turn.

Science and Expertise in EU Law and Policy

The importance of scientific evidence for decision-making is threaded through EU environmental law and policy, as affirmed in sources ranging from Treaty articles to informal Commission press releases.

Treaty Provisions on Scientific Evidence for Environmental Policy

Article 191(3) TFEU

In preparing its policy on the environment, the Union shall take account of ... available scientific and technical data ...

Article 114(3) TFEU

The Commission, in its proposals envisaged in paragraph 1 [proposals for internal market legislation] concerning health, safety, environmental protection and consumer protection, will take as a base a high level of protection, taking account in particular of any new development based on scientific facts. Within their respective powers, the European Parliament and the Council will also seek to achieve this objective.

Article 114(5) TFEU

[I]f, after the adoption of a harmonisation measure by the European Parliament and the Council, by the Council or by the Commission, a Member State deems it necessary to introduce national provisions based on new scientific evidence relating to the protection of the environment or the working environment on grounds of a problem specific to that Member State arising after the adoption of the harmonisation measure, it shall notify the Commission of the envisaged provisions as well as the grounds for introducing them.

EU Treaty provisions establish a firm expectation that environmental decision-making, whether at the EU or the Member State level, will be grounded in scientific evidence. This expectation also resonates in many environmental regulations and directives. For example, the 2009 Renewable Energy Directive underlines that Commission reports on sustainability criteria for energy uses of biomass, and any accompanying proposals, must be 'based on the best available scientific evidence, taking into account new developments in innovative processes'.[111] Similarly, Article 6(2)(b) of the Restriction of Hazardous Substances (ROHS) Directive requires that Commission proposals to review and amend the list of substances that should be restricted for use in electrical and electronic equipment contain 'references and scientific evidence for the restriction'.[112] Moreover, the requirement of scientific evidence-based decision-making extends to both the EU and the national levels. Thus, Annex II of Directive 1999/94/EC stipulates that, in organising the availability of consumer information on the fuel economy and CO_2 emissions of new passenger cars, Member States must ensure that guidebooks as a minimum contain 'an explanation of the effects of greenhouse gas emissions, potential climate change and the relevance of motor cars as well as a reference to the different fuel options available to the consumer and their environmental implications based on the latest scientific evidence and legislative requirements'.[113]

At the EU policy level, the Juncker Commission (2014–2019) has shown itself particularly keen to present evidence-based policy-making as one of the keystones of its administration. Its 2015 position paper, 'Strengthening Evidence-Based Policy-Making through Scientific Advice'[114] declares an aspiration to streamline and strengthen the extensive but scattered network of EU advisory bodies, which includes the Joint Research Centre or JRC (the Commission's in-house expert service), specialised scientific committees established by the Commission,[115] advisory bodies within different Commission

---

[111] Directive 2009/28/EC on the promotion of the use of energy from renewable sources and amending and subsequently repealing Directives 2001/77/EC and 2003/30/EC, OJ 2009 L 140/16, Art. 17.

[112] Directive 2011/65/EU on the restriction of the use of certain hazardous substances in electrical and electronic equipment, OJ 2011 L 174/88 (ROHS Directive).

[113] Directive 1999/94/EC relating to the availability of consumer information on fuel economy and CO_2 emissions in respect of the marketing of new passenger cars, OJ 2000 L 12/16.

[114] European Commission, 'Strengthening Evidence-Based Policy-Making through Scientific Advice: Reviewing Existing Practice and Setting up a European Science' (15 May 2015), available at: https://ec.europa.eu/research/sam/pdf/strengthening_evidence_based_policy_making.pdf.

[115] Two specialised committees in the field of environmental policy are the Scientific Committee on Health and Environmental Risks (SCHER), which provides opinions of the risks of environmental pollution, and the Scientific Committee on Emerging and Newly Identified Health Risks (SCENIHR). The latter gives opinions on emerging or newly identified health and environmental risks and on broad, complex or multidisciplinary issues, such as nanotechnology, fertility reduction and cloning.

Departments, external expert groups, standing advisory committees, commissioned study networks and consultancy outfits. To this end, the Commission has set up a new Scientific Advice Mechanism (SAM), spearheaded by a High-Level Group of seven independent scientific advisers, drawn from different Member States and different scientific disciplines.[116]

The focus on streamlining channels for scientific advice, and the renewed insistence on the importance of evidence-based policy, fit well with the Better Regulation ethos that currently informs the Commission's approach to governance.[117] Whether it still allows much scope for precautionary thinking, however, is more questionable. The Commission's 2015 position paper refers to scientific uncertainty and advocates that, correspondingly, scientific advisers should exercise their role with humility and 'acknowledge the inherent limits and biases of science and appropriately frame uncertainty'.[118] However, it does not indicate that scientific advisers should take into account that, pursuant to EU law, the policy-makers whom they are advising must respect the precautionary principle. In fact, the term 'precautionary' does not feature anywhere in the 28-page document.

Finally, given the Treaty-, law- and policy-based endorsements of scientific evidence as an essential basis for environmental decision-making, it would be plausible to expect the CJEU, too, to fall in line and enforce expectations of scientific evidence-based decision-making on public authorities. To a degree, such expectations are met. Yet CJEU rulings on the role of scientific expertise in decision-making, and on the extent to which legality hinges on scientific support for a measure, are both more nuanced and complex than a straightforward endorsement of the importance of scientific expertise. The various considerations that inform CJEU judgments are briefly explored in the next paragraphs.

Science, Precaution and Discretion

The vast majority of Court opinions on the use of scientific expertise stem from two sources: case law on the permissibility of national trade barriers examined with reference to internal market legislation or Articles 34 to 36 TFEU; and decisions on judicial review of EU legal acts. The first line of cases, in which the CJEU scrutinises regulatory and administrative decision-making at the Member State level, clearly affirms that, in principle, Member States must justify any decision to derogate from market harmonisation measures, or from free movement provisions, on the basis of scientific research that is internationally recognised.[119] In cases of scientific uncertainty, Member States may take

---

[116] Commission Decision on the setting up of the High Level Group of Scientific Advisors, COM(2015)6946 final, 16 October 2015.
[117] See Chapter 3.   [118] Commission, 'Strengthening Evidence-Based Policy-Making', 15.
[119] Case 178/84 *Commission* v. *Germany* [1987] ECR 1227 (*Beer Purity*); Case 174/82 *Sandoz BV* [1983] ECR 2445; Case 247/84 *Motte* [1985] ECR 3887; Case 304/84 *Ministère Publique* v. *Müller and others* [1986] ECR 1511; Case 74/82 *Commission* v. *Ireland* [1984] ECR 317.

precautionary action, but even in those circumstances they must, at least, show that a genuine risk exists. Moreover, uncertainty does not absolve Member States from using the best available evidence. The CJEU stance on scientific evidence at the Member State level is effectively encapsulated in the 2008 *Solgar* ruling, which examines the legality of French rules that set maximum amounts of vitamins and minerals to be used in the manufacture of food supplements. In so doing, France went beyond the requirements for vitamins and minerals contained in Directive 2002/46 on the approximation of the laws of the Member States relating to food supplements.[120]

> Case C-446/08, *Solgar Vitamins France*[121]
>
> 48. Directive 2002/46 must be interpreted as meaning that in a situation such as that in the main proceedings where, when setting the maximum amount of a mineral which may be used in the manufacture of food supplements, it is impossible to calculate precisely the intake of that mineral from other dietary sources, and so long as the Commission has not laid down the maximum amounts of vitamins and minerals which may be used in the manufacture of food supplements in accordance with Article 5(4) of that directive, a Member State may, if there is a genuine risk that that intake will exceed the upper safe limit established for the mineral in question, and provided that [Article 34 and 36 TFEU] are respected, set the maximum amount at a zero level ...
> 54. In exercising their discretion relating to the protection of public health, the Member States must comply with the principle of proportionality. The means which they choose must therefore be confined to what is actually necessary to ensure the safeguarding of public health or to satisfy overriding requirements regarding, for example, consumer protection. They must be proportional to the objective thus pursued, which could not have been attained by measures which are less restrictive of trade within the European Union ...
> 55. Furthermore, it is for the national authorities to show in each case, in the light of national nutritional habits and in the light of the results of international scientific research, that their rules are necessary to give effective protection to the interests referred to in [Article 36 TFEU] and, in particular, that the marketing of the products in question poses a real risk to public health ...
> 56. It must therefore be established that, in the light of national nutritional habits and taking account of the results of international scientific research, a measure which applies to the entire population a maximum amount appropriate for a group of sensitive consumers, such as children, is necessary in order to ensure the protection of the health of the persons

---

[120] OJ 2002 L 183, at 51.   [121] ECLI:EU:C:2010:233.

belonging to that group, since the marketing of food supplements whose content in nutrients exceed that maximum amount poses a real risk to public health, and that that objective cannot be attained by measures which are less restrictive of trade within the European Union.

65. It is clear that setting [maximum amounts of vitamins and minerals for use in food supplements] must in particular be based on consideration of the upper safe limits established, for the vitamins and minerals concerned, following a scientific assessment of the risks to human health based on the relevant scientific data and not on purely hypothetical considerations.

67. That being the case, although, in the absence of such a risk ... a scientific risk assessment could reveal that scientific uncertainty persists as regards the existence or extent of real risks to human health. In such circumstances, it must be accepted that a Member State may, in accordance with the precautionary principle, take protective measures without having to wait until the reality and seriousness of those risks are fully demonstrated. However, the risk assessment cannot be based on purely hypothetical considerations ...

In sum, Member State authorities are required to back up health and environmental decisions that affect the internal market with scientific evidence. In the case of scientific uncertainty, Member States may take precautionary measures, but the precautionary principle should not be used as a carte blanche for discretionary decision-making: at least enough indications must be available to corroborate the existence of a genuine risk, and Member States must still deploy the best available evidence in decision-making.

The same basic conditions for legality resonate in the CJEU case law regarding the use of scientific expertise by EU authorities. Additionally, this second line of Court judgments displays a few distinctive features. First, more so than in its pronouncements regarding decision-making at the Member State level, the CJEU has had to reconcile a demand for science-based decisions with a strong tradition of judicial deference towards EU regulators and, to a slightly lesser degree, administrators.[122] CJEU rulings in this field tend to insist on scientific evidence but at the same time afford a broad margin of discretion to EU authorities to determine which evidence should be relied on and how it should be interpreted. At times, this imparts a certain 'see-saw' quality to CJEU judgments, with the Court seemingly vacillating between the importance of expertise on the one hand, and discretion on the other.[123]

Secondly, CJEU decisions on the judicial review of EU legal acts have explained in greater depth the impact of the precautionary principle on science-based decision-making. Following the *Gowan* judgment,

---

[122] Case C-331/88 *Fedesa* ECLI:EU:C:1990:391.
[123] Veerle Heyvaert, 'Facing the Consequences of the Precautionary Principle in European Community Law' (2006) 31(2) *European Law Review* 185–207, at 198–199.

precautionary decisions must be preceded by a two-step analysis: first, to identify potentially negative consequences for the environment or health and, secondly, to make a 'comprehensive assessment of the risk' to the environment or health, 'based on the most reliable scientific data available and the most recent results of international research'.[124] Finally, while the cut-off point between hypothetical and genuine risks remains subject to case-by-case determination, application over time makes decision-making more predictable. For example, in the *Solvay* ruling the Court made clear that the sheer structural similarity at the molecular level between a substance under review, and one concerning which more risk data is available, would not be enough to warrant regulatory action.[125] The *Artegodan* decision, in turn, affirmed that an alleged change in consensus on the efficacy of a certain product type (in the case at issue, the efficacy of diet pills) is not a firm enough basis to withdraw the product from the market.[126]

CJEU rulings thus aim to affirm expectations of evidence-based decision-making without leaving EU public authorities hamstrung under conditions of scientific uncertainty. It is a difficult balance to achieve, and questions have been raised about effectiveness of CJEU rulings in this regard.[127] Ultimately, the proof is arguably in the pudding: instances when the CJEU annuls an EU legal act for not being scientifically justified remain extremely rare. This suggests that, Treaty provisions notwithstanding, the evidence-based nature of EU regulation will in the first place be determined by political willingness rather than legal requirement.

Environment and Governance

The collectivity of EU initiatives and responsibilities with regard to the environment is increasingly expressed in terms of 'environmental governance'. The proliferation of 'governance' as a term of art is not restricted to the environmental field. Indeed, in the past decade it has become the dominant way of referring to the organisation of institutions, ideas and practices in the pursuit of public interest goals within academic and professional circles.

There is, undeniably, a fashionable aspect to contemporary enthusiasm for governance. Like popular tunes, terms catch on, spread rapidly, and occasionally outstay their welcome. To push the comparison further, catchy terminology may have a broad appeal because its meaning is flexible, often fairly generic and open to individual interpretation. Definitions of governance are, indeed, numerous

---

[124] Case C-77/09 *Gowan* ECLI:EU:C:2010:803, paras. 75–78. The role of the precautionary principle is further discussed in Chapter 3.
[125] Case T-392/02 *Solvay Pharmaceuticals BV* v. *Council* [2004] ECR II-4055, para. 135.
[126] Joined Cases T-74/00, 76/00, 83/00, 84/00, 85/00, 132/00, 137/00 and 141/00, *Artegodan GmbH* v. *Commission* [2002] ECR II-4945.
[127] Heyvaert, 'Facing the Consequences', 202.

and varied, and tend to have an inherent flexibility in meaning. Douglas Kysar, for example, uses governance to denote 'all processes and institutions, both formal and informal, that guide and restrain the collective activities of a group'.[128] Aynsley Kellow and Anthony Zito deploy a narrower definition of governance, one that emphasises a less direct, more steering-oriented mode of engagement but still assumes the central position of a public authority: 'Governance is the capacity of governments or designated public actors to steer their economy and society in a goal-oriented way that differs from what the spontaneous cooperation of actors in the markets and society might achieve.'[129] Christoph Möllers, in turn, treats 'governance' as the institutional perspective on the conduct of public institutions that focuses particularly on their externality from the State,[130] whereas Joost Pauwelyn, Ramses Wessel and Jan Wouters relate 'governance' particularly to policy coordination between public and private actors.[131]

Yet while definitions differ, they also reveal a shared preoccupation with understanding the exercise of authority in the public interest as something that is more complex, more nuanced, and more expansive, than a State office ordering a private entity to do X or to refrain from Y. Fashion notwithstanding, the ascendance of governance signals a paradigmatic shift in the conceptualisation of society's relation to the environment. To document this shift and its significance fully exceeds the confines of this discussion, but the following paragraphs offer a brief overview of four key aspects of governance that are particularly relevant in the context of EU environmental law and policy. The four aspects, or 'faces', of environmental governance are listed below.

The four faces of EU environmental governance

1. Strategic governance
2. Multi-level governance
3. Decentred governance
4. Good governance

From Pollution Control to Strategic Environmental Governance
The concept of environmental governance reflects an awareness of the maturing of environmental decision-making from a mostly incidental, short-term and reactive enterprise to one that is cross-sectorally and cross-temporally conceived,

---

[128] Douglas Kysar, 'Sustainable Development and Private Global Governance' (2005) 83 *Texas Law Review* 2109–2166, at 2145.
[129] Aynsley Kellow and Anthony R. Zito, 'Steering through Complexity: EU Environmental Regulation in the International Context' (2002) 50 *Political Studies* 43–60, at 43.
[130] Christoph Möllers, 'European Governance: Meaning and Value of a Concept' (2006) 43 (2) *Common Market Law Review* 313–336, at 314–318.
[131] Joost Pauwelyn, Ramses A. Wessel and Jan Wouters, *Informal International Lawmaking* (Oxford University Press, 2012), at 2.

and proactively implemented. In discussions of the evolution of environmental law and policy, commentators tend to distinguish different stages.[132] These typically include: an early industrial stage during which environmental concerns were legally relevant only if they engaged property rights or public sanitation orders; a nature conservation era during which the legal awareness regarding the environment was mostly restricted to the protection of fauna and flora; and a pollution control era during which preventive and managerial permitting approaches blossomed and which was marked by a stronger understanding of displacement problems and the corresponding need to regulate across environmental media. The last stage, which in the EU region characterised much of environmental law and policy from the 1970s to the early 2000s, displays a comparatively stronger sensibility to the need for integrated thinking and advance planning to deliver effective environmental outcomes. However, environmental pollution was typically still approached as a side-effect; a consequence of choices that, themselves, were not part of the decision-making equation.

The global, cross-generational and intensely disruptive nature of the environmental challenges that characterise the first decades of the twenty-first century, with climate change in pole position, have underscored the need to move beyond a consequence-focused approach to environmental protection and weave environmental considerations into knowledge production, education, public policy and international relations. This reflects environmental governance in its strategic incarnation.[133] The slightly longer established concept of sustainable development partially reflects this ethos as it focuses on the interplay of environment, economy and society. It also shares with environmental governance a long-term perspective which, in the case of sustainable development, is closely bound up with the pursuit of intergenerational equity. Arguably, one reason why environmental governance tends to eclipse sustainable development in scholarly and professional writing today is because the latter is more narrowly associated with the late 1980s context of bridging the environment/development tensions between the global North and South in international environmental negotiations. Environmental governance, by contrast, refers to strategy development in a largely post-MEA world, where international agreements are but one of a wealth of behaviour-influencing tools. Moreover, like pollution control, sustainable development is an outcome-oriented notion, whereas environmental governance draws the attention towards modes of interaction and the actors who deploy them. Finally, notwithstanding the emphasis on integrated decision-making, writings on sustainable development tend to take the spheres of environment,

---

[132] See Daniel Bodansky, *The Art and Craft of International Environmental Law* (Harvard University Press, 2010), 21–35; Louis Kotzé, *Global Environmental Governance: Law and Regulation for the 21st Century* (Edward Elgar, 2012), 3–6; Neil Gunningham, 'Environmental Law, Regulation and Governance: Shifting Architectures' (2009) 21(2) *Journal of Environmental Law* 179–212.

[133] Maria Carmen Lemos and Arun Agrawal, 'Environmental Governance' (2006) 31 *Annual Review of Environment and Resources* 297–325, at 298, 301.

economy and society as a given and focus on achieving balanced outcomes.[134] Environmental governance arguably accommodates a stronger conceptual awareness of environment, economy and society as co-constitutive.

Multi-level and Transnational Governance

Compared to 'rules', or even 'regulation' more generally, 'governance' is typically conceived of as involving multiple actors operating at various levels of government. This multiplicity is expressed in the notion of 'multi-level governance'. Liesbeth Hooghe and Gary Marks define multi-level governance as a 'system of continuous negotiation among nested governments at several territorial tiers' and argue that, in order to understand how public authority works, it is vital to see governance as essentially interconnected instead of hierarchically ranked.[135] For instance, subnational authorities may formally resort under the State or federal level, but they also engage directly with the supranational level. National governments, in turn, 'share, rather than monopolize, control over many activities that take place in their respective territories'.[136]

As an analytic approach, multi-level governance directs students of regulation to take into account the multiple layers of frameworks, laws, rules and guidance that bear down on regulatory addressees in order to obtain better insight into how regulation works and why it may falter. This perspective has proven uniquely resonant within the European Union context: to understand European environmental governance, we need to analyse across levels, or scales, of government.[137] In this endeavour, it is important not to reduce our understanding of the EU–Member State relationship to a hierarchical, single-direction exchange, but instead be attuned to the interactive nature of the EU/Member State/local authority dynamic.[138] Moreover, it is an increasingly widely held view that a full understanding of governance must also engage with the role of private authority, and private actors, within governance networks. The term most frequently used to denote the involvement of private as well as public actors within a governance network is 'transnational' governance.[139] There exists, hence, a strong affinity between multi-level and transnational perspectives, but the former is more focused on the multiplicity

---

[134] OECD, *Policies to Enhance Sustainable Development* (OECD Publishing, 2001).
[135] Gary Marks, Liesbeth Hooghe and Kermit Blank, 'European Integration from the 1980s: State-Centric v. Multi-level Governance' (1996) 34(3) *Journal of Common Market Studies* 341–378; Liesbeth Hooghe and Gary Marks, *Multi-level Governance and European Integration* (Rowan & Littlefield, 2001).
[136] Hooghe and Marks, *Multi-Level Governance*, 4.
[137] Beate Kohler Koch and Berthold Rittberger, 'The "Governance Turn" in EU Studies' (2006) 44 *Journal of Common Market Studies Annual Review* 27–49, at 43.
[138] Veerle Heyvaert, 'What's in a Name? The Covenant of Mayors as Transnational Environmental Regulation' (2013) 21(1) *Review of European Community & International Environmental Law* 78–90, at 80–81.
[139] Veerle Heyvaert and Thijs Etty, 'Introducing Transnational Environmental Law' (2012) 1(1) *Transnational Environmental Law* 1–11, at 6.

of levels of government, whereas the latter engages primarily with the multiplicity of actors.

As a normative theory, multi-level governance posits that regulatory networks are better equipped to tackle the transboundary and complex environmental problems facing the world today than national authorities acting as sole regulator. Correspondingly, the normative stream in transnational studies considers that multi-actor governance networks are relatively more resilient and effective. In the words of Maria Carmen Lemos and Arun Agrawal: 'The fragmentary nature of the sources of complex environmental problems, such as global climate change, and the reluctance or inability of nation states to regulate the sources of these problems, means that nonstate actors and organizations may be able to play an essential role in mobilizing public opinion and generating innovative solutions.'[140] Evidently, multi-level and transnational governance regimes also introduce a range of new challenges. The multiple interactions between levels and actors within environmental governance networks represent just as many instances for communication and coordination problems to occur. In the transnational context, the involvement of non-State actors may be seen as desirable, but it is difficult to engineer. In its discussion of EU environmental law and policy, this book offers many opportunities to appreciate both the promises and the challenges of multi-level and transnational environmental governance.

Flexible and Decentred Governance

A third and very prominent aspect of the turn to governance in environmental policy is the much stronger reliance on flexible and decentred modes of steering.[141] In their pursuit of environmental targets, public authorities now often start by investigating whether it is necessary to adopt and impose mandatory standards or whether, instead, regulatory addressees might be moved to change their environmental behaviour by alternative means. The most frequently deployed alternative strategies are economic incentive-based strategies. The best-known example of an EU framework that espouses an incentive-based approach, in turn, is the EU Emissions Trading System (EU ETS) for greenhouse gases (GHGs), which is a pivotal axis of the EU's climate change mitigation strategy. Approaches such as the ETS are called 'flexible' because they arguably leave regulatory addressees a broader range of choice in how to respond to the regulatory stimulus. For example, a tax on non-recyclable waste might spur company A to review its production processes and increase reliance on recyclable materials; company B to downscale over time the production lines that generate a higher level of non-recyclable waste and upscale those that have fewer taxable by-products; and company C to pay more taxes.

Many flexible instruments essentially push the addressees to perform an economic cost–benefit analysis, and still rely quite heavily on the mandatory trappings of regulation. EU steel producers may decide whether to buy or sell

---

[140] Lemos and Agrawal, 'Environmental Governance', 301.
[141] *Ibid.*, 305; Gunningham, 'Shifting Architectures'.

emissions allowances on the market, but their participation in the ETS scheme is mandatory. Some frameworks, however, operate on a voluntary basis. The EU Eco-Management and Audit Scheme (EMAS), for example, invites but does not compel enterprises to sign up. In this case, the EU relies predominantly on decentred market forces to incentivise behavioural change. In the case of EMAS, such decentred market forces might be channelled through consumer feedback, or through the actions of civil society organisations. Or, enterprises may sign up in order to achieve efficiency gains, if they espouse the view that cleaner and greener operating processes are also less wasteful.

The ETS, EMAS and other flexible approaches in EU environmental regulation are richly reviewed in Chapter 4, which also offers a comparative assessment of strengths and weaknesses of command-based or 'direct' regulatory approaches versus flexible alternatives. For the purpose of this discussion, the key message is that the adoption of a governance perspective significantly extends demands on regulatory expertise. In addition to understanding how direct regulation works, the EU as an environmental regulator must now grapple with a host of flexible instruments and anticipate their impact and pitfalls. As illustrated in the discussions of the EU ETS in Chapters 4 and 8, building up such expertise can be a process of painful trial and frequent error.

Good Governance

A fourth aspect of governance relates to the expectation that the exercise of authority in the pursuit of public interest goals meets a number of qualitative benchmarks. Views on what it takes for environmental governance to constitute 'good governance' may differ, but there is broad consensus that adherence to procedural requirements, including transparency, openness to public participation and the availability of accountability mechanisms, is an essential aspect of good governance.[142]

The EU administrative position on good governance is set out in a 2001 Commission White Paper on governance.[143] The White Paper embraces flexible approaches and explicitly calls for the EU to rely on a combination of binding and non-legislative instruments in the pursuit of policy goals. Additionally, it identifies five principles for good governance that EU policy must respect.

The White Paper's Five Principles of Good Governance

* **Openness**. The Institutions should work in a more open manner. Together with the Member States, they should actively communicate about what the EU does and the decisions it takes. They should use language that is

---

[142] Robert Baldwin, Martin Cave and Martin Lodge, *Understanding Regulation: Theory, Strategy and Practice* (2nd edn., Oxford University Press, 2012), 25–31.
[143] Commission, 'White Paper on European Governance', COM(2001)428 final, OJ 2001 C287/1.

accessible and understandable for the general public. This is of particular importance in order to improve the confidence in complex institutions.
* **Participation**. The quality, relevance and effectiveness of EU policies depend on ensuring wide participation throughout the policy chain – from conception to implementation. Improved participation is likely to create more confidence in the end result and in the Institutions which deliver policies. Participation crucially depends on central governments following an inclusive approach when developing and implementing EU policies.
* **Accountability**. Roles in the legislative and executive processes need to be clearer. Each of the EU Institutions must explain and take responsibility for what it does in Europe. But there is also a need for greater clarity and responsibility from Member States and all those involved in developing and implementing EU policy at whatever level.
* **Effectiveness**. Policies must be effective and timely, delivering what is needed on the basis of clear objectives, an evaluation of future impact and, where available, of past experience. Effectiveness also depends on implementing EU policies in a proportionate manner and on taking decisions at the most appropriate level.
* **Coherence**. Policies and action must be coherent and easily understood. The need for coherence in the Union is increasing: the range of tasks has grown; enlargement will increase diversity; challenges such as climate and demographic change cross the boundaries of the sectoral policies on which the Union has been built; regional and local authorities are increasingly involved in EU policies. Coherence requires political leadership and a strong responsibility on the part of the Institutions to ensure a consistent approach within a complex system.

In the area of environmental governance, the force of the White Paper principles is further harnessed by the EU's membership of the Aarhus Convention, which demands access to environmental information, participation in decision-making and access to justice in environmental matters. The Convention and its impact are analysed in detail in Chapters 5 and 7 of this book.

There is a strong synergy between the rise of multi-level and flexible environmental governance and the growing importance of the procedural virtues of openness, participation and accountability. The proliferation of non-traditional regulators in the governance network – be they the European Commission or standardisation bodies or civil society organisations – creates significant legitimacy challenges. Within the national context, regulatory bodies typically vest their authority in their legal mandate and their accountability vis-à-vis a democratically elected parliament. The connection between supranational or decentred regulators and representative democracy is much more tenuous. Procedural guarantees can help to bridge the legitimacy gap.[144] However, as will be amply illustrated, their successful fulfilment is not unproblematic and should not be taken for granted in EU environmental governance.

Environment, Philosophy and Ethics

At a time when the world faces serious global environmental problems such as the depletion of natural resources, climate change and diminished biological diversity, questions of environmental philosophy and ethics have become increasingly salient. It is clear that human activity has had an adverse impact on the environment and on natural ecosystems, especially over the last two centuries. To advocate that the Earth is a self-regulating system or that it is instrumental for man's use is no longer a sustainable approach. The perspectives offered by environmental philosophy and ethics provide the moral context in which to examine the policy discourse and legal regulation of the environment, including that of the EU.

While environmental ethics is a recently established discipline, the question of man's relationship with nature has a much longer lineage. In the Western tradition, there has been very little focus on the environment as a good in itself. The preservation of the environment as a moral value is not deeply rooted in Western philosophical or religious traditions. Even Aristotle did not regard the protection of nature as worthwhile, but viewed nature in a purely instrumental way.[145] In *Pol'tics*, he advocated an explicitly anthropocentric view that 'nature has made all things specifically for the sake of man'.[146]

Judeo-Christian thought advocated the belief that nature was created by God for use by mankind.[147] Human beings were given a dominion over nature which entailed an absolute power over it.[148] Nature is seen as having instrumental value only for human benefit. However, there is another interpretation of the Old Testament which advocates human stewardship over nature where human beings are selected to preserve nature:[149] thus, 'the earth is the Lord's, and everything in it, the world, and all who live in it; for he founded it on the seas and established it on the waters'.[150] In this conception, human beings do not own the Earth, but hold it on trust.[151] This belief clearly entails human responsibility to cherish nature and let it flourish as God's creation. Stewardship does not necessarily conflict with dominion, as the Christian tradition stipulates clear ethical conditions for dominion over nature.[152] This anthropocentric view in Western philosophy continued into the Middle Ages.

---

[144] Heyvaert, 'What's in a Name?', 87–88.
[145] See more in Robin Attfield, *Environmental Philosophy: Principles and Prospects* (Avebury, 1994), 79.
[146] Aristotle, *Politics*, Book 1, chapter 8.   [147] Genesis 1:26.
[148] Attfield, *Environmental Philosophy*, 41.
[149] See more in Robin Attfield, *Environmental Ethics: An Overview for the Twenty-First Century* (Polity, 2003), 21–23.
[150] Psalms 24; see also Psalms 104.   [151] Attfield, *Environmental Ethics*, 21.   [152] *Ibid.*, 22.

Thomas Aquinas, the most influential philosopher of the period, reconciled Aristotle with Christian philosophy and argued that non-human animals were 'ordered to man's use'.[153]

As Western philosophy entered the modern era, the Aristotelian and Christian view of man's dominion over the environment changed little. The only alteration was to incorporate the development of new tools of science, which rendered the Earth more amenable to man. This idea was explored and advocated by Francis Bacon in his plea to 'let the human race recover that right over nature which belongs to it by divine bequest, and let power be given it'.[154] However, this may only be achieved by interpreting nature through a 'collection of facts and their methodical investigation'.[155] Bacon was an empiricist and viewed science as a means of extending man's dominion over nature. Although a range of modern philosophers such as Locke, Hume and Bentham were concerned with issues of animal welfare, man's relationship with the environment was not a central question of modern philosophy until very recently.[156]

Environmental ethics emerged as a distinct discipline in the 1970s.[157] This was concurrent with the development of an environmental consciousness after incidents such as the Cuyahoga river fire in the USA in 1969 sparked widespread outrage at environmental degradation caused by industry and agriculture. The focus of environmental ethics at the time was a move away from the traditionally held view that nature had been created for use by humans. It was argued at the time that that morality should be extended to include the relationship between humans and nature.[158] Philosophers began to distinguish various theories of value focusing on the human relationship to the environment. One of these theories of value is anthropocentrism, a theory that places humans as the most important species on the planet and gives humans the right to change and shape the environment.[159] In anthropocentric value theory, only humans have moral standing: human goals and interests are central, and nature has only instrumental value as a means to further human interest and well-being.[160] As discussed above, this theory of value has been deeply embedded in Western thought, culture and, subsequently, Western law and policy-making. These theories advocate the preservation of nature in the form of incidental protection 'only insofar as it advances

---

[153] Thomas Aquinas, *Summa Contra Gentiles*, Book 3, Pt 2, Ch. 112.
[154] Francis Bacon, *Novum Organon*, Book 1, Aph. 59.
[155] Jürgen Klein, 'Francis Bacon', in E. N. Zalta (ed.), *The Stanford Encyclopaedia of Philosophy* (winter 2015 edn.): http://plato.stanford.edu/archives/win2015/entries/francis-bacon/.
[156] Attfield, *Environmental Philosophy*, 49.
[157] See more in Attfield, *Environmental Ethics*, 37–58.
[158] Katherine V. Kortenkamp and Colleen F. Moore, 'Ecocentrism and Anthropocentrism: Moral Reasoning about Ecological Commons Dilemmas' (2001) 21 *Journal of Environmental Psychology* 261–272.
[159] Ibid.
[160] See Andrew Brennan and Yeuk-Sze Lo, 'Environmental Ethics', in E. N. Zalta (ed.), *The Stanford Encyclopaedia of Philosophy* (winter 2015 edn.): http://plato.stanford.edu/archives/win2015/entries/ethics-environmental/.

human interests or value'.[161] The logical corollary is that environmental regulation should concern itself only with problems affecting humans.

A contrary value theory is sentientism, which holds that all sentient (conscious) creatures have moral standing.[162] This theory maintains that all sentient animals' welfare has independent moral value, and that this is important regardless of human needs and goals. While this rejects the anthropocentric view that only human interests matter and broadens the theory of value, it is still too limited to allow for a comprehensive theory of value that would allow for environmental protection of non-sentient creatures.

Biocentrism is a more expansive theory and holds that 'all living creatures have a good of their own, and have moral standing as such, and their flourishing or attaining their good is intrinsically valuable'.[163] This places the value or moral good not on consciousness, but rather on the fact that creatures are living and, according to biocentrists, this fact allows for the consideration of ecosystems comprised of many living creatures. While biocentrists place the greatest value on plants and animals, ecocentrists go further and argue that ecosystems have a moral value beyond that of their constituent individuals.[164] Ecocentrists place a greater emphasis on the ecosystems themselves rather than living creatures. Thus, for an ecocentrist, the obligation of humans is to maintain and preserve the integrity of ecosystems as the highest moral good. An ecocentrist would also stress the interconnectedness between the ecosystems and humans, as the well-being of humans depends on ecological stability. In terms of approaches to policy-making, an ecocentric approach is clearly challenging insofar as its ecosystems are, by their nature, highly complex and subject to constant change.

These theories of value are not merely intellectual constructs, but also inform policy choices and political decisions regarding the environment. As public attitudes in the 1970s changed towards the environment, so too did political articulation of environmental issues, such as the rise of Green Parties and the passing of significant environmental legislation. To a certain extent, this reflected a move away from a primarily anthropocentric outlook, towards a more ecocentric view. An example at international level is the Convention on Biological Diversity[165] where the preamble of the Convention underlines the 'intrinsic value of biological diversity and of the ecological, genetic, social, economic, scientific, educational, cultural, recreational and aesthetic values of biological diversity and its components'.[166] The importance of marine environmental protection is also recognised in the OSPAR Convention[167] which represents a shift from the anthropocentric approach to the environment insofar as it guarantees the protection of the marine environment both to safeguard human

---

[161] Alyson C. Flournoy, 'In Search of an Environmental Ethic' (2003) 28 *Columbia Journal of Environmental Law* 63, at 80.
[162] Attfield, *Environmental Ethics*, 10.   [163] *Ibid.*   [164] *Ibid.*, 11.
[165] Convention on Biological Diversity (CBD), 5 June 1992, 31 ILM 818.   [166] *Ibid.*
[167] Convention for the Protection of the Marine Environment of the North-East Atlantic (OSPAR Convention), 22 September 1992, 32 ILM.

health and to conserve marine ecosystems.[168] Biocentric views are fully embodied in the World Charter for Nature which advocates that 'every form of life is unique, warranting respect regardless of its worth to man, and, to accord other organisms such recognition, man must be guided by a moral code of action'.[169]

Nevertheless, an anthropocentric position still remains prevalent in environmental law. Both the UN Stockholm Declaration on Human Environment[170] and the Rio Declaration,[171] two major soft law international documents, advocate the anthropocentric approach to the environment. Principle 2 of the Stockholm Declaration emphasises the importance of the environment in a purely instrumental way for human benefit.[172] The Rio Declaration represents an even more radical shift to anthropocentrism where the 'human beings are at the centre of concerns for sustainable development'.[173]

The objective of sustainable development, discussed earlier in this chapter, also promotes the anthropocentric view in its focus on the needs of present (human) generations without compromising the ability of future (human) generations to meet their own needs. The concept is based on human development being sustainable without mentioning the intrinsic value of nature.[174] As discussed in Chapter 5, an anthropocentric approach is also inherent in most environmental rights approaches, which are becoming more popular within Europe and internationally. The same conclusion applies to national pollution prevention laws, which may be considered to be excellent examples of anthropocentrism insofar as their key objective is essentially to prevent the adverse impact of pollution on humans.[175]

Despite the extensive EU environmental *acquis* and the EU's commitment to the preservation of natural eco-systems, the anthropocentric approach is evident in much of the EU's environmental legislation, although there is little public

---

[168] Art. 2 (1)(a): 'The Contracting Parties shall, in accordance with the provisions of the Convention, take all possible steps to prevent and eliminate pollution and shall take the necessary measures to protect the maritime area against the adverse effects of human activities so as to safeguard human health and to conserve marine ecosystems and, when practicable, restore marine areas which have been adversely affected.'
[169] UNGA Res. 37/7, 28 October 1982.
[170] Stockholm Declaration of the United Nations Conference on the Environment (Stockholm Declaration) 16 June 1972, 11 ILM.
[171] Rio Declaration on Environment and Development, 13 June 1992, 31 ILM.
[172] Principle 2, Declaration of the United Nations Conference on the Human Environment: 'Both aspects of man's environment, the natural and the man-made, are essential to his well-being and to the enjoyment of basic human rights the right to life itself'. See, further, Chapter 5.
[173] Principle 1, Rio Declaration. [174] See Attfield, *Environmental Ethics*, 126–137.
[175] Joshua J. Bruckerhoff, 'Giving Nature Constitutional Protection: A Less Anthropocentric Interpretation of Environmental Rights' (2007–2008) 86 *Texas Law Review* 615, at 618.

discourse concerning the ethical values that inform environmental policy choices.[176] Even in its protection of biodiversity, perhaps the least anthropocentric of the EU's environmental policy fields, the Birds Directive recognises the need for conservation of species of wild birds as natural resources which form an 'integral part of the heritage of the peoples of Europe', rather than a part of the natural eco-system.[177] Sustainable development is also perceived as an underlying goal of the Habitats Directive.[178] The current (seventh) Environmental Action Programme emphasises the implications of biodiversity loss and the degradation of ecosystems in the Union not 'only for the environment and human well-being, but also for future generations'.[179] As discussed further in Chapter 3, this Programme focuses on the significance of natural ecosystems for further economic development of humans, without emphasising its intrinsic value.[180] The Programme's emphasis on an ecosystem services approach, and its claim that environmental degradation will have particular impact on 'economic actors in sectors that depend directly on ecosystem services', offer further examples of an unabashedly anthropocentric approach to EU environmental regulation.[181]

Environment and Geography: The Challenges of Enlargement

As discussed above, it is inherent in the fundamental aims of the EU's environmental policy as defined by Article 192(2) TFEU that recognition must be given to diversity, including geographic and economic diversity, between Member States. The challenges posed by the enlargement process offer an excellent illustration.

In 2013, the EU completed its most recent enlargement, with Croatia's accession. It now faces further challenges with other Western Balkan countries which are next in line to accede to the EU.[182] As with all previous enlargements, each accession country has to undergo unprecedented reforms in all policy areas, including environmental policy. Most accessions to the EU have generated

---

[176] See more in Flournoy, 'In Search of an Environmental Ethic', 63.
[177] Directive 2009/147/EC of the European Parliament and of the Council on the conservation of wild birds, OJ 2010 L 20/7.
[178] 'Whereas, the main aim of this Directive being to promote the maintenance of biodiversity, taking account of economic, social, cultural and regional requirements, this Directive makes a contribution to the general objective of sustainable development; whereas the maintenance of such biodiversity may in certain cases require the maintenance, or indeed the encouragement, of human activities.' Council Directive 92/43/EEC on the conservation of natural habitats and of wild fauna and flora, OJ 1992 L 206/7.
[179] General Union Environment Action Programme to 2020, 'Living well, within the limits of our planet', OJ 2013 L 354/171.
[180] Ibid.   [181] Ibid.
[182] The list of countries preparing to join is available at: http://ec.europa.eu/enlargement/countries/check-current-status/index_en.htm.

concerns about the impact of the process on both current and prospective Member States, as well as fears that the enlargement process would adversely affect the development of EU environmental policy.[183] This policy area was not of great importance during the accession of Denmark, Ireland and the UK since, at the time of their accession in 1973, no formal EEC environmental policy existed, and there were only initial attempts to take action in that field, as discussed earlier in this chapter. However, this has changed with later accessions, as certain countries had weak environmental policies and a legacy of serious environmental pollution. There was particular apprehension with the accessions of Greece (1981) Spain and Portugal (1986) as their environmental standards were lower than in the rest of the EEC at that time, and these countries encountered challenges in implementing the Community's environmental *acquis*.[184] The accession of Finland, Austria and Sweden in 1995 was very different: here, States with very high standards of environmental protection acceded to the EU.[185]

The greatest challenge to date has been the accession of the central and eastern European countries in 2004 and 2007, when gloomy scenarios about the effects of their membership on EU environmental policy were put forward.[186] It was well known at the time that most of those countries inherited serious environmental problems, especially in relation to air and water pollution.[187] Likewise, they shared common problems with

---

[183] See more in Joann Carmin and Stacy D. Vandeveer, 'Enlarging EU Environments: Central and Eastern Europe from Transition to Accession' (2004) 13(1) *Environmental Politics* 3–24; Maria Lee, *EU Environmental Law: Challenges, Change and Decision-Making* (Hart Publishing, 2005).

[184] See the history of EU environmental policy in Miranda Schreurs, 'Environmental Protection in an Expanding European Community: Lessons from Past Accessions' (2004) 13(1) *Environmental Politics* 27, at 38.

[185] The acceding countries negotiated a four-year transitional period during which they could apply higher environmental standards and opt out from applying certain EC environmental measures. See Arts. 69, 84 and 112 of the Act concerning the conditions of accession of the Kingdom of Norway, the Republic of Austria, the Republic of Finland and the Kingdom of Sweden and the adjustments to the Treaties on which the European Union is founded, OJ 1994 C 241/9.

[186] See more about the effects of enlargement on EU environmental law and policy in Petr Jehlička and Andrew Tickle, 'Environmental Implications of Eastern Enlargement: The End of Progressive EU Environmental Policy?' (2004) 13(1) *Environmental Politics* 77–95; Gerda Falkner and Oliver Treib, 'Three Worlds of Compliance or Four? The EU-15 Compared to New Member States' (2008) 46(2) *Journal of Common Market Studies*; Jon Birger Skjærseth and Jørgen Wettestad, 'Is EU Enlargement Bad for Environmental Policy? Confronting Gloomy Expectations with Evidence' (2007) 7 *International Environmental Agreements* 263–280.

[187] See David Turnock, 'Environmental Problems and Policies in East Central Europe: A Changing Agenda' (2001) 54 *GeoJournal* 485–505, at 485; Petr Pavlínek and John Pickles, 'Environmental Pasts/Environmental Futures in Post-Socialist Europe' (2004) 13(1) *Environmental Politics* 237–265; Dušan Plut, 'Environmental Challenges of Europe: The State of Environment and Environmental Trends in the EU (EU15) and the Accession Countries (AC10)' (2000) 52(2) *GeoJournal* 149–155.

inefficient and overly bureaucratic institutions which, due to the lack of expertise and insufficient capacities, struggled with the implementation of the EU environmental *acquis*. Yet despite the apprehension of accession, the EU did not slow the development of its environmental policies and both new and old Member States benefited greatly from enlargement. Naturally, advantages for newly acceded countries were more extensive. The accession process created a momentous development and improvement of environmental protection laws and policies, modern and professional administrative and judicial capacities, environmental remediation, availability of various environmental or related funds, development of environmental civil society and participation of citizens in decision-making processes. The European Commission at the time estimated that the total value of the benefits from the implementation of EU environmental Directives for the ten candidate countries ranged from €134 billion to €681 billion.[188]

The EU also benefits environmentally from the accession process. A key advantage is that the new export markets for products must attain compliance with the existing EU environmental standards. In addition, the prevention and control of cross-border pollution is also an important advantage given that the protection of the environment is a global concern. Another advantage is 'a more "pluralistic" approach to environmental decision-making' which brings together countries with different approaches and outcomes in ensuring environmental protection.[189] Furthermore, the success of previous enlargements also confirmed the EU's role as an international environmental leader, a label which the EU has welcomed.[190] This is evidenced by the fact that the EU has succeeded in providing a regulatory framework for the environment to a geographically and economically varied group of accession countries.

Although each accession country has its own specific environmental problems and challenges in the accession process, past and current experiences demonstrate some common difficulties shared by all accession countries.[191] The environmental chapter is generally considered to be one of the most complex chapters for negotiations, both for the candidate countries and for

---

[188] Guide for Negotiations: http://ec.europa.eu/enlargement/archives/enlargement_process/future_prospects/negotiations/eu10_bulgaria_romania/chapters/chap_22_en.htm (p. 67).

[189] Schreurs, 'Environmental Protection in an Expanding European Community', 29.

[190] See more about the early developments of the EU as an international actor in Charlotte Bretherton and John Vogler, *The European as a Global Actor* (Routledge, 2006) and John McCormick, *Environmental Policy in the EU* (Palgrave Macmillan, 2001). For more recent developments, see Tom Delreux and Sander Happaerts, *Environmental Policy and Politics in the European Union* (Palgrave Macmillan, 2016).

[191] See more in John M. Kramer, 'EU Enlargement and the Environment: Six Challenges' (2004) 13(1) *Environmental Politics* 290–311.

the Commission.[192] Croatia, which acceded to the EU in 2013, identified this chapter as the most demanding policy area.[193]

Why has it been so difficult for accession countries to implement the EU environmental *acquis*? Legal adjustments are one of the most common challenges in the implementation process as the EU environmental *acquis* encompasses various different policies ranging from general environmental protection laws to very specific policy areas and it is subject to frequent amendments resulting from scientific and technological developments. Challenges in legal adjustments may also be explained by different legal cultures in accession countries. These can lead to distinctive legal approaches in regulating the environment, mechanisms and practices,[194] or indeed a lack thereof.[195]

In the implementation process, national authorities in accession countries particularly struggle with the transposition of environmental Directives, as some leave wide discretion in the choice of national measure implemented to reflect the objective of a Directive, while others tend to be highly technical. National authorities in accession countries also find it difficult to understand the objective of a Directive and due to this they prefer to copy the entire text of the Directive in order to avoid incorrect transposition.[196] This often leads to the adoption of a piece of legislation which is not in compliance with other legislation in force or is challenging to apply. No less important is the interpretation of vague provisions or definitions. This also may be the case with certain technical and legal terms and concepts in the environmental policy area which have specific meaning within the EU context that differs from the meaning of the same term in national law.

Similarly, all accession countries are required to make institutional adjustments, including administrative, judicial and enforcement capacities. Western Balkan countries, for instance, are generally accepted to have weak institutions and poorly developed networks of State and non-State actors in the environmental

---

[192] The EU *acquis* is divided into 35 chapters and the environment is placed in chapter 27, including 200 major legal acts. Diahanna Lynch, 'Closing the Deception Gap: Accession to the European Union and Environmental Standards in East Central Europe' (2000) 9(4) *Journal of Environment and Development* 426–437.

[193] Ivana Vlašić and Mirna Vlašić Feketija, 2006, *The Importance of Environmental Protection: Croatia in The European Union Accession Process* at 328: www.ssoar.info/handle/documents/6135.

[194] See about Czech experience in Eva Kružíková, 'EU Accession and Legal Change: Accomplishments and Challenges in the Czech Case' (2004) 13(1) *Environmental Politics* 99–113.

[195] See more about early experiences in the UK in Peter Bird, 'Applying EC Environmental Law on the Ground' in Han Somsen (ed.), *Protecting the European Environment: Enforcing Environmental Law* (Blackstone Press, 1996).

[196] As this problem persisted with all Central and Eastern European countries, the Commission made it clear in the Guide for Approximation that 'a word for word' transposition is not required, although the national law must reflect the directive; Guide to the Approximation of European Union Environmental Legislation, 21–22: http://ec.europa.eu/environment/archives/guide/contents.htm.

policy area.[197] They often lack experts with appropriate training and experience, especially for climate change law[198] as well as judges and prosecutors with expert knowledge of environmental matters. Equally important is for those countries to improve administrative capacities to monitor and enforce laws[199] and develop environmental, operational and financing strategies at an early stage of the accession process.[200] Clear delineation of powers between line ministries but also between central and regional or local government as well as coordination of actions at different levels of government are particular challenges for national authorities in accession countries.[201] In addition to this institutional challenge there is also the issue of high costs and investments required for the implementation of environmental legislation.[202] Although certain EU funds are available to accession countries for this purpose, the primary responsibility for financing the implementation of the

---

[197] See more in Tanja A. Börzel and Adam Fagan, 'Environmental Governance in South East Europe/Western Balkans: Reassessing the Transformative Power of Europe', *Environment and Planning C: Government and Policy* (2015) 33(5) 885–900; see more about experiences in individual accession countries in A. Taylor, 'Environmental Governance in Croatia and Macedonia: Institutional Creation and Evolution', *Environment and Planning C: Government and Policy* (2015) 33(5) 969–985; Adam Fagan and Indraneel Sircar, 'Europeanisation and Multi-Level Environmental Governance in a Post-Conflict Context: The Gradual Development of Environmental Impact Assessment Processes in Bosnia-Herzegovina', *Environment and Planning C: Government and Policy* (2015) 33(5) 919–934.

[198] A good illustration is the 2014 Commission's Report for Bosnia and Herzegovina SWD (2014) 305 in regard to climate change at 46: 'The country's capacities for monitoring, reporting and verification in this area remain weak and should be considerably strengthened. Significant efforts are still needed to raise awareness at all levels of society, and to promote cooperation between all relevant stakeholders ... Administrative capacity in the environment and climate sectors remains weak.'

[199] See also the 2014 Progress Report for Macedonia SWD (2014) 303, at 55: 'Negligible efforts were made to strengthen the administrative capacity for implementation and enforcement of legislation, which thus continues to be largely insufficient, both at national and local level. Coordination between the relevant bodies remains ineffective. Stakeholders are still not sufficiently involved in decision-making. Enforcement of legislation is not yet efficient.'

[200] See e.g. the findings in the 2014 Progress Report for Serbia SWD (2014) 302, at 58: 'Strategic planning, greater administrative capacity and substantial investments linked to strategic priorities are needed to further align with EU policies in areas of environment, climate action and civil protection.'

[201] A good illustration is the Commission Opinion on Serbia's application for membership of the European Union, COM(2011)668 final, at 120: 'Significant efforts are needed at all levels of the country to promote cooperation and coordination between the different ministries and authorities involved.'

[202] In terms of costs for implementing environmental *acquis* in former central and eastern European countries it was estimated that 'compliance with the environmental *acquis* required investment of around €80 to €120 billion for the ten Central and Eastern European Countries alone'. See Guide for Negotiations: http://ec.europa.eu/enlargement/archives/enlargement_process/future_prospects/negotiations/eu10_bulgaria_romania/chapters/chap_22_en.htm. See also Christophe Hillion, *EU Enlargement: A Legal Approach* (Hart Publishing, 2004).

environmental *acquis* is with the accession countries themselves. This often imposes significant obstacles for those countries.[203]

Accession countries also confront political constraints affecting the implementation process. In almost all former central and eastern European countries and in most Western Balkan countries, governments tend not to consider the environment as a priority policy area.[204] Additionally, the pressure from various industrial and commercial interest groups and lobbies on the environmental policy-making process may also negatively affect the implementation of the environmental *acquis*.[205] Unlike in many western European countries, environmental interest groups often do not provide a countervailing force. At the same time, high levels of clientelism and corruption in environmental matters may significantly slow down the implementation process, as was the case in Portugal, Spain, Greece and Italy.[206]

In order to facilitate the implementation process, the EU negotiates transitional periods with the accession countries which are limited in time and scope. It is not an easy task for national authorities to identify the need for transitional measures in the adoption phase, and to provide detailed implementation plans clearly indicating the timeline of future implementation. Transitional measures are most numerous for the environmental *acquis* and all countries that recently joined from 2004 in 2007 requested a wide range of transitional measures; some of these were requested and incorporated in the accession treaties.[207] Croatia had exactly the same experience in the accession process.[208]

The EU also provides assistance through various funds which have changed as the enlargement process has evolved.[209] In recent years, current candidate and

---

[203] The financial challenges in implementing the environmental *acquis* in Croatia were already identified in the Screening Report for chapter 27, at 2: http://ec.europa.eu/enlargement/pdf/croatia/screening_reports/screening_report_27_hr_internet_en.pdf. In Croatia's 2011 Opinion on Membership, the Commission stated that 'investment in environmental infrastructure in Croatia is low. Significant investments need to be secured to ensure implementation of the environmental *acquis*.'

[204] John Kramer argues that the approximation process requires the existence of a 'political will to enact requisite policies to fulfil the environmental *acquis* that are inevitably controversial, fiscally onerous and disadvantageous to key groups in society': Kramer, 'EU Enlargement and the Environment', 306.

[205] See more about Hungarian experience in Sándor Kerekes and Károly Kiss, 'Hungary's Accession to the EU: Environmental Requirements and Strategies' (1998) 8(5) *European Environment* 161–170.

[206] Tanja A. Börzel, Ana Fernandez and Nuria Font, 'Coping with Accession to the EC: New Modes of Environmental Governance', paper presented at the Annual Convention of the American Political Science Association, Washington, DC, 1–5 September 2010, at 6.

[207] Annexes V, VI, VII, VIII, IX, X, XI, XII, XIII and XIV of the Treaty of Accession of the Czech Republic, Estonia, Cyprus, Latvia, Lithuania, Hungary, Malta, Poland, Slovenia and Slovakia, OJ 2003 L 236/17; Annexes VI and VII of the Treaty of Accession of the Republic of Bulgaria and Romania, OJ 2005 L 157/11.

[208] Annex V of the Treaty of Accession of Croatia, OJ 2012 L 112/21.

[209] The main financial instrument was the Phare Programme, OJ 1989 L 375/17; see also SAPARD (Special accession programme for agriculture and rural development).

potential candidate countries benefited from the programme of Community Assistance for Reconstruction, Development and Stabilisation (CARDS).[210] Currently, assistance is provided through the Instrument for Pre-Accession Assistance (IPA) funds[211] together with technical assistance through Technical Assistance and Information Exchange (TAIEX) and Twinning programmes. However, even with these funds, accession countries still struggle with implementation costs as those countries are expected to spend on average between 2 per cent and 3 per cent of GDP to ensure full implementation of the EU environmental *acquis*.[212] Serbia, with the biggest population of all Western Balkan countries, allocates only 0.3 per cent from the budget to environmental protection which still is far from this target.[213]

In sum, accession countries face a complex and long process which places stringent requirements on all candidates in the environmental policy area. Moreover, as accession is a two-way process it also places significant demands on the EU institutions and individual Member States. At a time when the EU has been under significant institutional pressure due to various crises, the appetite for current EU Member States to accept new members may be considered low. This will certainly affect the willingness of the accession countries to make changes in this demanding policy area, if the accession process becomes prolonged.

---

[210] It was the EU's main instrument of financial assistance to the Western Balkans from 2000 to 2006.
[211] The IPA is made up of five different components, where only candidate countries can use all components; see more at: http://ec.europa.eu/regional_policy/thefunds/ipa/index_en.cfm.
[212] COM(2001)304.
[213] Environment: analysis and recommendations, National Convention on the European Union, Belgrade 2014 (Nacionalni konvent o Evropskoj uniji 2012/2014): www.emins.org/uploads/useruploads/publikacije/Nacionalni-konvent-o-EU-Zivotna-sredinu-web.pdf (p. 23).

2

Actors and Instruments

This chapter discusses the role of the key institutions and actors involved in formulating EU environmental law and policy, focusing on:

- The European Commission;
- The Council of the EU;
- The European Parliament;
- The Court of Justice of the European Union; and
- The European Council.[1]

Beside these five main EU institutions, no study of this field would be complete without an examination of some of the other main actors involved, namely:

- The Economic and Social Committee;
- The Committee of the Regions;
- The European Environment Agency;
- The European Investment Bank;
- The European Union Network for the Implementation and Enforcement of Environmental Law (IMPEL); and
- other interest groups.

The chapter will conclude by examining the key instruments used in the field of EU environmental policy.

Actors

The European Commission

The European Commission is often regarded as the institution that underpins the EU environmental policy and has made significant contributions in developing this area.[2] Despite concerns about internal coordination and implementation of the EU environmental *acquis*, the Commission remains a key actor in this policy area.[3] The Commission is headed by the College of Commissioners composed of

---

[1] The role of other European institutions such as the European Court of Human Rights and the European Committee on Social Rights, which do not form part of the EU institutional framework, is discussed in Chapter 5.
[2] See more about the development, operation and functions of the European Commission in Neil Nugent and Mark Rhinard, *The European Commission* (Palgrave Macmillan, 2015).
[3] See Emmanuelle Schön-Quinlivan, 'The European Commission' in Andrew Jordan and Camilla Adelle (eds.), *Environmental Policy in the EU: Actors, Institutions and Processes* (3rd edn., Routledge, 2012), 96.

one commissioner per Member State, appointed for five years. Commissioners each have a *cabinet* composed of political advisers. Each Commissioner is allocated a portfolio, some of which enjoy greater prestige than others. The environmental portfolio was regarded for a long time as a middle-ranking portfolio[4], which was changed with the creation of a separate climate change portfolio in 2010. Though this immediately raised the profile of the environment at the EU level, the 2014 decision that the fisheries and maritime portfolios would be dealt with by the same Commissioner who is responsible for the environment portfolio signals a relegation in the importance of the environment. Similarly, the merger of the climate change and energy portfolios in the same year raises the risk that environmental policy in the Commission will be subordinated to energy policy. Equally disappointing is the lack of reference to the environmental agenda in the mandate of the High Representative, even though one of the objectives of the EU external action programme is 'to help develop international measures to preserve and improve the quality of the environment and the sustainable management of global natural resources, in order to ensure sustainable development'.[5]

The size of the Commission is a constant topic of debate. Its current formation of one commissioner per Member State was to have been changed by the Lisbon Treaty so as to form a new and significantly smaller Commission, corresponding to two thirds of the number of Member States.[6] Alterations to the size of the Commission seem highly unlikely in the near future, since the commitment to maintain the current size of the Commission was one of the deals brokered with the Irish after the first unsuccessful referendum on the Lisbon Treaty in 2008.[7] The incumbent Juncker Commission advocates a 'new collaborative way of working', entailing a strong team cooperating across portfolios to develop more integrated and coordinated policies. For this purpose, Juncker has entrusted several policy areas to vice-presidents whose responsibility is to direct and coordinate work across the Commission in those key areas. Environment has been placed in the 'project team' Energy Union, under the responsibility of Vice-President Maroš Šefčovič from Slovakia. The new Commission's institutional structure means there is potentially an extra layer through which environmental policy and legislation will have to pass. In the previous structure, the environment portfolio was represented directly in the College of Commissioners. However, the environment portfolio is now represented by a vice-president who is responsible for a much broader and potentially conflicting portfolio.[8]

The same concern exists for the large number of directorates general which 'makes effective internal coordination more difficult'.[9] At the moment the

---

[4] McCormick, *Environmental Policy in the European Union*, 99. [5] Art. 21 TEU.
[6] Art. 17(5) TEU. [7] Brussels European Council, Conclusions of 18/19 June 2009.
[8] See more about the new Commission in Aleksandra Čavoški, 'A Post-Austerity European Commission: No Role for Environmental Policy?' 2015 24(3) *Environmental Politics* 501.
[9] 'Shifting EU Institutional Reform into High Gear', Report of the CEPS High-Level Group (2014), Centre for European Policy Studies Brussels, 4.

Table 2.1 Allocation of Portfolios and Supporting Services in the Environmental Policy Area

Portfolios	Name	Services
First Vice-President, in charge of Better Regulation, Inter-Institutional Relations, the Rule of Law and the Charter of Fundamental Rights	Frans Timmermans	Horizontal responsibility for sustainable development
Vice-President for Energy Union	Maroš Šefčovič	The Vice-President for Energy Union steers and coordinates the work of several Commissioners, in particular the Commissioners for Climate Action and Energy; Transport; Internal Market, Industry, Entrepreneurship and SMEs; Environment, Maritime Affairs and Fisheries; Regional Policy; Agriculture and Rural Development; and Research, Science and Innovation.
Climate Action and Energy	Miguel Arias Cañete	DG Energy (ENER); DG Climate Action (CLIMA); The Euratom Supply Agency (ESA); The relevant parts of the Executive Agency for Small and Medium-Sized Enterprises (EASME); The relevant parts of the Innovation and Networks Executive Agency (INEA) responsible for relations with the Agency for the Cooperation of Energy Regulators (ACER)
Environment, Maritime Affairs and Fisheries	Karmenu Vella	DG Environment (ENV); DG Maritime Affairs and Fisheries (MARE); The relevant parts of the Executive Agency for Small and Medium-Sized Enterprises (EASME) responsible for relations with the European Fisheries Control Agency (EFCA) and the European Environment Agency (EEA)

Source: European Commission. See http://ec.europa.eu/info/sites/info/files/commissioners-college-structure-annex_en.pdf.

Commission consists of thirty-three directorates general (DGs), covering major policy areas and several services. DG Environment is primarily responsible for environmental issues and its work is often described as highly technical.[10] There are also a number of DGs dealing with issues closely related to the environment, such as DG Climate Change, DG Energy, DG Agriculture and Rural Development, DG Maritime Affairs and Fisheries, DG Health and Food Safety, DG Internal Market, Industry, Entrepreneurship and SMEs and DG International Cooperation and Development (Table 2.1).

---

[10] Schön-Quinlivan, 'The European Commission', 101.

DG Environment was initially set up in 1973 as a team of five people in a branch of DG Industry.[11] It became a separate DG in 1981, called DG XI, and was subsequently renamed as DG Environment after the Amsterdam Treaty.[12] Until 2010, it also covered climate change but a separate DG was created to address this issue more effectively.[13] At the moment, DG Environment employs around 500 staff and receives about €400 million annually from the EU budget.[14] DG Climate Action has a staff of around 160 civil servants[15] and the EU agreed that at least 20 per cent of the EU budget for 2014–2020 should be allocated to climate change issues, amounting to €180 billion.[16] In line with the EU's Environmental Action Programme[17] and the political priorities of the Commission, DG Environment periodically sets out its objectives in its Strategic Plans which are further developed in annual management plans.[18] The 2016 Management Plan clearly reflects the emphasis of the new Commission on the green economy; however, it is questionable whether the Commission is able to find a balance between Europe's economic growth and social and environmental stability.[19]

The Commission enjoys wide competences as prescribed by the Treaty on European Union.[20] The most significant is the Commission's exclusive power to make legislative proposals in the environmental field.[21] At the moment, the environmental *acquis* comprises around 200 legal acts, which undoubtedly reflects the legislative activism of the Commission in this policy area.[22] DG Environment plays a major role in formulating all the Commission's environmental proposals and ensuring the application of the EU environmental *acquis* in Member States. As a majority of proposals are highly technical or require specific scientific knowledge, DG Environment relies to a great extent on the input of external expert groups.[23] Together with the DG Research and DG Enterprise, these three

---

[11] DG Environment: http://ec.europa.eu/environment/pubs/pdf/factsheets/dg_environment.pdf.
[12] The number of DGs does not correspond to the number of commissioners, which means a commissioner may be responsible for more than one DG.
[13] DG Environment is divided into smaller directorates following several thematic areas – Directorate A: Policy; Directorate B: Natural Circular Economy and Green Growth; Directorate C: Quality of Life; Directorate D: Natural Capital; Directorate E: Implementation and Support to Member States; Directorate F: Global Sustainable Development.
[14] 2014 Annual Activity Report: http://ec.europa.eu/atwork/synthesis/aar/doc/env_aar_2014.pdf. In 2014 it had 588 staff members including external personnel (pp. 35–36).
[15] See http://ec.europa.eu/clima/about-us/mission/index_en.htm.
[16] See http://ec.europa.eu/clima/policies/budget/index_en.htm.
[17] Discussed further below.
[18] Strategic Plan for 2016–2020 and 2016 Management Plan available at: http://ec.europa.eu/dgs/environment/index_en.htm.
[19] See Management Plan 2016, and see, further, the discussion in Chapter 3.
[20] Art. 17 TFEU. [21] Art. 17(2) TFEU.
[22] See http://ec.europa.eu/environment/pubs/pdf/factsheets/dg_environment.pdf.
[23] The list of all expert groups used by the DG environment is available at: http://ec.europa.eu/transparency/regexpert/index.cfm.

DGs are 'super users' of expert groups.[24] They represent various groups of participants comprising diverse social interests including scientists, academics, industry and non-governmental organisations (NGOs), whose involvement to some extent may also be justified by a lack of sufficient resources or specialised expertise within the Commission.[25] DG Environment also works closely with the Joint Research Centre, the in-house science service of the European Commission, which provides scientific expertise necessary for legislative drafting. Likewise, the European Environment Agency provides significant expertise to the Commission, and delivers relevant data and other useful information in drafting proposals.[26]

Before submitting a document to the Commission, the DG Environment must consult other departments whose scope of work relates to the environmental issue under consideration.[27] It must also consult the Legal Service on all drafts or proposals for legal instruments and on all documents which may have legal implications.[28] The Directorates-General responsible for the budget, personnel and administration have to be consulted on all proposals which may have implications concerning the budget and finances or personnel and administration respectively.[29] Due to the technical nature of the environmental proposals and complex procedure, the legal drafting of environmental proposals is time consuming and it is a lengthy process. Once the proposal is drafted within DG Environment, it is circulated to other DGs. If other DGs expressed opposing views during the consultation, their differing views must be attached to the proposal.[30] If there are no objections the proposal is adopted by the College of Commissioners. Decisions are in principle adopted by consensus in a collegiate way. If a member requests a vote, the proposal is adopted if a majority of the Members vote in favour.[31] Meetings of the Commission are not public.[32] All members have collective responsibility which means that they cannot disclose how they voted and they are bound by the decision regardless of their vote.

The introduction of the 'citizens' initiative' mechanism may even further the Commission's legislative role in this policy area.[33] This mechanism allows no

---

[24] Åse Gornitzka and Ulf Sverdrup, 'Access of Experts: Information and EU Decision-Making' (2011) 34(1) *West European Politics* 62. See more recent studies on the role of expert groups in Åse Gornitzka and Ulf Sverdrup, 'Societal Inclusion in Expert Venues: Participation of Interest Groups and Business in the European Commission Expert Groups' (2015) 3(1) *Politics and Governance* 151–165.

[25] See about the impact of scientists on policy-making in the Commission in Dovile Rimkutė and Markus Haverland, 'How Does the European Commission Use Scientific Expertise? Results from a Survey of Scientific Members of the Commission's Expert Committees' (2015) 13 *Comparative European Politics* 430–449 and Åse Gornitzka and U. Sverdrup, 'Who Consults? The Configuration of Expert Groups in the European Union' (2008) 31(4) *West European Politics* 725–750.

[26] See more about the role of the EU agencies in the decision-making process in Lee, *EU Environmental Law, Governance and Decision-Making*, 44–47.

[27] Rules of Procedure of the European Commission, Art. 21. [28] Ibid. [29] Ibid., para. 2.

[30] Ibid., para. 3. [31] Ibid., Art. 8. [32] Ibid., Art. 9. [33] See, further, Chapter 7.

fewer than one million citizens who are nationals of a significant number of Member States to take the initiative by calling the Commission to submit any appropriate proposal on matters where citizens consider a legal act of the Union is required for the purpose of implementing the Treaties.[34]

Likewise, the Commission has the competence to propose environmental action programmes (EAPs) which provide a list of actions and objectives the EU must achieve in a certain time frame. The Commission also influences the development of the environmental policy area by initiating the adoption of various soft law instruments, such as white and green papers; and inter-institutional communications. In addition, the Commission is responsible for setting the legislative programme for each year which determines measures to be taken in each policy area.[35]

Despite a long history of implementation deficit in the area of environmental policy, the Commission, with its limited resources, has exercised its supervisory powers entrusted to it by the Treaty.[36] To that effect, the Commission developed some management tools including the collection of national reports sent by Member States to fulfil reporting obligations as part of the transposition process and database management systems for monitoring the transposition of directives.[37] The Commission also compiles reports and prepares comprehensive statistical data on the implementation of the EU environmental *acquis* which is available on the DG Environment website.[38] Furthermore the Commission has frequently used the infringement procedure set out in the TFEU in order to achieve compliance with the EU environmental *acquis* (see further, Chapter 6).[39]

The Commission may also represent the EU's interests or negotiate the Union's position in various international forums.[40] Equally, the Commission uses its 'soft power' by working closely with other environmental actors, thus influencing the development of international environmental law. This is best illustrated through its work in negotiating international environmental

---

[34] Art. 11(4) TEU. The European Citizens' Initiative 'Right2Water' was the very first successful example. See Commission Communication on the European Citizens' Initiative, 'Water and Sanitation are a Human Right! Water is a Public Good, Not a Commodity!', COM(2014)177 final.
[35] The latest one is COM(2015)610 final.   [36] Art. 17(1) TEU. See, further, Chapter 6.
[37] See Melanie Smith, *Centralised Enforcement, Legitimacy and Good Governance in the EU* (Routledge, 2009), 113.
[38] See http://ec.europa.eu/environment/legal/law/statistics.htm.
[39] See more in Aleksandra Čavoški, 'An Assessment of Compliance Strategies in the Environmental Policy Area' (2016) 41(2) *European Law Review* 252–274.
[40] Art. 17(1) TFEU: With the exception of the common foreign and security policy, and other cases provided for in the Treaties, it shall ensure the Union's external representation. The Commission's position in policy formulation and negotiation will depend on the subject matter and the Union's competences in the specific policy area. The Commission's mandate to negotiate must be approved by the Council of the EU (Art. 218 TFEU).

agreements where Commission makes a significant impact in shaping the EU's policy response.[41]

The Council of the EU

The Council of the EU is the institution that represents the interests of EU Member States. It exercises legislative and budgetary functions and it is composed of a representative of each Member State at ministerial level.[42] The Council works in ten different configurations,[43] with the Environment Council being composed of ministers responsible for environmental matters. The Environment Council was established in 1973 as a result of a growing awareness about the importance of environmental protection. It reflects differences of policy preferences when it comes to the environment.[44] It is often said that there is a well-known division between the leaders and laggards of EU environmental policy; the leaders being Demark, Germany, Netherlands, Austria, Finland and Sweden while Spain, Italy and Greece are amongst those considered laggards.[45] However, this cleavage does not take into account different environmental problems, priorities and regulatory styles that affect a Member State's approach to the environment.[46]

The number of sessions of the Environment Council has grown steadily over the years, now meeting about four times a year. This clearly demonstrates the increasing workload of the Environment Council, especially after the Single European Act, which gave a significant impetus for the adoption of the most extensive corpus of the EU environmental *acquis*. In general, Member States send only one minister responsible for the environment, although the practice of sending two ministers to the session regarding environment was also common for some States.[47] It is also not unusual for the Council to hold joint Council

---

[41] See more in Schön-Quinlivan, 'The European Commission' and Tom Delreux, 'The EU as an Actor in Global Environmental Politics' in Jordan and Adelle, *Environmental Policy in the EU*. The Commission also cooperated with the United Nations Environment Programme (UNEP) and its engagement in reforming the role and mandate of the UN regarding environmental matters. See 'The 2005 UN Summit – Addressing the Global Challenges and Making a Success of the Reformed UN', COM(2005)259 final.

[42] Art. 16(2) TEU.

[43] Before the Treaty of Lisbon there were nine configurations. The former General and Foreign Affairs Council is now divided into two separate configurations.

[44] See more in Albert Weale, Geoffrey Pridham, Michelle Cini, Dimitrios Konstadakopulos, Martin Porter and Brendan Flynn, *Environmental Governance in Europe* (Oxford University Press, 2005), 93–100.

[45] See more about early environmental compliance in Member States in Tanja A. Borzel, 'Why There is No "Southern Problem": On Environmental Leaders and Laggards in the European Union' (2000) 7(1) *Journal of European Public Policy* 141–162.

[46] Andrea Lenschow, 'Environmental Policy' in Helen S. Wallace, Mark A. Pollack and Alasdair R. Young (eds.), *Policy-Making in the European Union* (6th edn., Oxford University Press, 2010), 315.

[47] This was the case for Spain; see Philippa Sherrington, *The Council of Ministers* (Pinter, 2000), 115.

meetings with other relevant Council configurations such as the council for transport, industry or health, as environment touches upon various other policy areas.[48]

The Council meetings are chaired by the respective minister of the Member State holding the Council presidency for six months, which means that the Environment Council sessions are chaired by the minister of the presidency Member State responsible for the environment.[49] The presidency of the Council is an ideal opportunity for a Member State to pursue its own policy objectives for its six month term, although this may go against the obligation of the presidency to be neutral and impartial in its role. Every eighteen months, the pre-established group of three Member States holding the presidency of the Council for that period prepares a draft programme of Council activities, which ensures some consistency in pursuing environmental policy in the three consecutive rotations of the presidency.[50] Moreover, the programme provides the context for the agenda of each of the Council meetings during a six-month term. This may somewhat limit the agenda-setting scope of the incumbent President of the Council to frame its own policy objectives. Previous presidencies have shown that the traditional 'green' countries, such as Germany and Sweden, are more likely to push for the further development of the environmental law and policy during their term of office.[51] However, the extent to which green Member States are successful in imposing a particular environmental agenda often does not depend on their commitment, but on the overall interests of all Member States. A recent example was during the Swedish Presidency in 2009, which had high hopes about reaching an international agreement at the Copenhagen Summit of the United Nations Framework Convention on Climate Change. However, Sweden spent most of the presidency lowering any expectations on reaching a legally binding agreement, which was a great disappointment for green Member States and environmental interest groups.[52]

The successful passage of an environmental agenda will depend on the negotiation skills of the Presidency and its interaction with the Commission as the main initiator of environmental proposals, but also on 'the negotiating styles of the representatives of each state'.[53] However, with the appointment of the President of the European Council, the rotating presidency's political leadership has been effectively reduced to a management and coordination

---

[48] Weale et al., *Environmental Governance in Europe* (2005), 100; see more in Rudiger K. W. Wurzel, 'Member States and the Council', in Jordan and Adelle, *Environmental Policy in the EU*, 87

[49] European Council Decision on the exercise of the Presidency of the Council, 2009/881/EU, OJ 2009 L 315/50.

[50] Art. 2 (6) Rules of Procedure of the Council of the European Union, Council Decision 2009/937/EU, OJ 2009 L 325, 35–61.

[51] See Jonas Tallberg, 'The Agenda-Shaping Powers of the EU Council Presidency' (2003) 10 (1) *Journal of European Public Policy* 9.

[52] Lee Miles, 'The Swedish Presidency' (2010) 48 *JCMS Annual Review* 81–93.

[53] McCormick, *Environmental Policy in the European Union*, 128.

role.[54] This is especially apparent in relation to foreign policy, as the Council presidency's external role in relation to environmental issues has been diminished.[55]

In its work, the Council is assisted by the General Secretariat and a Committee of Permanent Representatives (COREPER). The General Secretariat primarily provides technical and logistical assistance to the Council and ensures the smooth functioning of the Presidency of the Council. It provides the same services to COREPER and the working groups.[56] In order to provide better services there has been increased specialisation in the General Secretariat which resulted in the establishment of the Directorate-General 'Environment, Education, Transport and Energy'.[57]

COREPER has a central role in preparing the work for all the Council meetings.[58] It examines all the proposals on the Council's agenda and tries to reach an agreement before the proposals are submitted to the Council for adoption.[59] Its work is highly dependent on the discussions held in the working groups which precede the discussion on the proposal within COREPER. The working groups are composed of representatives from Member States who have specialised expert knowledge in particular policy areas. Two working groups are especially important in the environmental policy area – the Working Party on Environment, which is responsible for environmental matters within the EU, and the Working Party on International Environmental Issues, which is responsible for negotiating and coordinating international environmental issues.[60] Working groups responsible for Environment also represent a link with the Commission since the relevant working groups were already involved in the Commission's work on any environmental proposal.[61]

The European Parliament

The European Parliament exercises legislative, budgetary and supervisory functions and has experienced a momentous widening of its legislative powers with every

---

[54] Simone Bunse and Christopher Klein, 'What's Left of Rotating Presidency' in François Foret and Yann-Sven Rittelmeyer (eds.), *The European Council and European Governance: The Commanding Heights of the EU* (Routledge, 2014), 81.
[55] Ibid., 80
[56] See more about the history of COREPER in Sherrington, *The Council of Ministers*, 49–53.
[57] See www.consilium.europa.eu/en/general-secretariat/staff-budget/.
[58] Art. 240 TFEU.
[59] It works in two configurations: COREPER I, consisting of the deputy permanent representatives, which is responsible for technical matters, and COREPER II, consisting of the ambassadors responsible for political, commercial, economic or institutional matters. Environmental issues fall within the scope of COREPER I, together with some related issues such as transport, fisheries, social issues and industrial issues.
[60] See www.consilium.europa.eu/en/meetings/working-parties.
[61] See McCormick, *Environmental Policy in the European Union* and Krämer, *EU Environmental Law*.

Treaty amendment.[62] Members of the European Parliament are directly elected from EU Member States for a five-year term.[63] The Parliament has an important institutional function in increasing the EU's democratic legitimacy. The environment is a transnational issue that affects all Member States and thus should be of particular importance to the Parliament. However, in most Member States, elections to the Parliament are 'second order national elections'[64] rather than reflecting issues that affect all of Europe. As a result, the significance of the environment as a transnational issue for the European Union may not be fully expressed. Likewise, the Parliament's interaction with the Commission and the Council of the EU determines its role in the development of environmental policy.

A crucial role in the legislative process lies within the Parliament's committees, which are responsible for scrutinising legislative proposals and preparing reports on the Commission's proposal. The Environment, Public Health and Food Safety Committee (the Environment Committee), established in 1973, has a broad agenda which also includes the environment. It is one of the largest committees in the Parliament, with 69 members. In relation to the environment, the committee is responsible for numerous environmental issues, including the air, soil and water pollution, waste management, chemicals, noise protection, climate change and protection of biodiversity.[65] Climate change and cultivation of GMOs and their use in Member States are two priority areas at the early stages of the current parliamentary term.[66] The Environment Committee of the Parliament monitors the work of several EU agencies, most notably the European Environment Agency and the European Chemicals Agency.[67]

The major impetus to reinforce the role of the Environment Committee and to ensure an improved position for the European Parliament came with the co-decision procedure (renamed after the Lisbon Treaty to become the ordinary legislative procedure), which dramatically changed the balance of powers within the EU. The European Parliament truly became an equal legislative partner with the Council. Likewise, the Parliament is empowered to, under Article 225 TFEU, request the Commission to submit 'any appropriate proposal on matters on which it considers a Union act is required for the purpose of implementing the Treaties.' By introducing the consent procedure for ratifying international agreements, the Treaty of Lisbon furthermore strengthened the EP's role in international governance,

---

[62] Art. 14(1) TEU.
[63] Art. 14 (2) TEU: The Treaty of Lisbon prescribes a cap on the number of members; which cannot exceed 750 in number, plus the President.
[64] Simon Hix and Christopher Lord, *Political Parties in the European Union* (Palgrave Macmillan, 1997), 87–90.
[65] Not less important are sustainable development, civil protection, restoration of environmental damage, and international and regional measures and agreements aimed at protecting the environment; see ANNEX VI: Powers and responsibilities of standing committees of the Rules of Procedure of the European Parliament.
[66] See www.europarl.europa.eu/committees/en/envi/home.html.   [67] Ibid.

which may be valuable in furthering the EU's climate change agenda.[68] In addition, any general Environmental Action Programme (EAP) has to be adopted by the European Parliament and the Council, acting in accordance with the ordinary legislative procedure, which shall apply to any future EAP.[69] The presence of the Green party in the European Parliament further contributes to the greening of the Parliament's agenda.[70]

Still, the extent to which these procedural changes positively impacted the Parliament's pro-environmental agenda remains unclear. There is a general consensus that the Parliament is more powerful in the environmental policy area than in many other policy areas, but it is not as environmentally radical as could be expected.[71] There are several reasons for this. The Environment Committee, which has a pivotal role in the Parliament, lacks the expert and scientific knowledge required for the investigation of the Commission's draft proposals.[72] Changes in the membership of the Environment Committee over successive parliamentary terms have also affected the passage of environmental legislation.[73] During the 7th parliamentary term (2009–2014) the Environment Committee was responsible for 61 new legislative acts, demonstrating its impressive activism.[74] Finally, the Environment Committee ultimately has to ensure the support of a majority of MEPs in plenary session in order to have amendments adopted, which may prove difficult.

Nonetheless, the Parliament has improved its interaction with other actors in the legislative process. The Commission is active in the meetings of the Environment Committee and it encourages consultations with MEPs at an earlier stage of the procedure.[75] In terms of the Parliament's relationship with the Council, there is

---

[68] Art. 36 TEU and Art. 218 (TFEU). See Katja Biedenkopf, 'The European Parliament in EU External Climate Governance' in Stelios Stavridis and Daniela Irrera (eds.), *The European Parliament and its International Relations* (Routledge, 2015), 94–96.

[69] Art. 192(3) TFEU.

[70] See more about the evolution and impact of the Green Party in the European Parliament in Nathalie Brack and Camille Kelbel, 'The Greens in the European Parliament' in Emilie van Haute (ed.), *Green Parties in Europe* (Taylor & Francis, 2016).

[71] See more in Elizabeth Bomberg and Charlotte Burns, 'The Environment Committee of the European Parliament: New Powers, Old Problems' (1999) 8(4) *Environmental Politics* 174–179; see Charlotte Burns, 'The European Parliament' in Jordan and Adelle, *Environmental Policy in the EU*.

[72] McCormick, *Environmental Policy in the European Union*, 130. This was recently confirmed in 'Shifting EU Institutional Reform into High Gear'.

[73] The empirical study showed that the Parliament's behaviour changed over time, which can be seen from the sixth parliamentary term when the 'Parliament proposed fewer environmentally important amendments but it became more successful in getting amendments into legislation'. See more in Bomberg and Burns, 'The Environment Committee of the European Parliament', 174–179.

[74] Committee on the Environment, Public Health and Food Safety (ENVI): Activity report for the 7th parliamentary term 2009–2014.

[75] Bomberg and Burns, 'The Environment Committee of the European Parliament', 174–179.

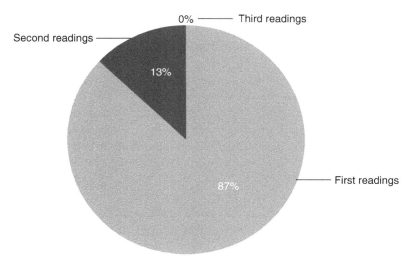

Figure 2.1 Percentage of ENVI Co-Decision Files Agreed per Reading in the Last Parliamentary Mandate
Source: ENVI Activity Report on the 7th parliamentary term. See www.europarl.europa.eu/document/activities/cont/201405/20140527ATT84522/20140527ATT84522EN.pdf.

a culture of informal negotiation, and this is reflected in the number of proposals agreed during the first reading.[76] During the last parliamentary mandate, agreement was reached on the first reading in 87 per cent of cases.[77] Avoiding conciliation is another incentive for the two institutions to reach an agreement at an earlier stage. The Parliament also maintains regular contacts with national parliaments regarding the implementation of EU environmental *acquis*, and tries to engage more citizens in its work, albeit not always successfully (Figure 2.1).

The European Council

The European Council brings together the Heads of State or Government of the Member States, and its role is usually associated with the common foreign and security policy (CFSP) and the economic and monetary policy of the EU. However, the development of any EU policy would be unthinkable without the European Council's approval, as it provides the Union with the necessary impetus for its development, and defines general political directions and

---

[76] See more in Charlotte Burns, Neil Carter, Graeme A. M. Davies and Nicholas Worsfold, 'Still Saving the Earth? The European Parliament's Record' (2013) 22(6) *Environmental Politics* 1–20.
[77] Activity report for the 7th parliamentary term 2009–2014.

priorities.[78] It was the European Council which called on the Community to develop a blueprint for a formal environmental policy by July 1973, which led to the publication of the First Environmental Action Programme.[79] The European Council was especially active in the 1980s and 1990s and several important European Council meetings contributed to the further development of environmental law and policy.[80] The Dublin European Council in 1990 was especially important, as the European Council underlined the need for a more systematic approach in environmental protection and the improvement of environmental monitoring and research.[81] In recent years the focus of the European Council agenda has shifted to pressing issues such as global warming and climate change.[82] This was also the result of growing international efforts to regulate this area and the aspiration of the EU to position itself as a major global actor in relation to climate change. In March 2007, the European Council underlined the EU's leading role in international climate protection and stressed the need for collective action.[83] In October 2014 the European Council agreed to the world's most ambitious 2030 climate energy policy and called other countries to follow this ambitious target in advance of the 2015 Conference of the Parties in Paris.[84] The frequency of European Council meetings has also increased significantly in recent years, which is another indicator of its more prominent role.[85] Although the creation of the new office of the elected President of the European Council with the Treaty of Lisbon was expected to ensure cohesion and continuity in the work of this institution, there are concerns that this new role together with the role of the High Representative of the Union for Foreign Affairs have complicated the EU's representation in international environmental negotiations.[86]

Besides its role in shaping the environmental agenda, the European Council also facilitates the legislative process by interacting with all other institutions, notably the Commission and the Council of the EU. The relationship with the Commission as the main driving force of environmental policy was improved through the participation of the President of the Commission at meetings of the European Council.[87] Likewise, consistency in the work of the European Council and the Council of the EU is ensured through the General Affairs Council which

---

[78] Art. 15(1) TEU.
[79] See, further, Chapter 1 and McCormick, *Environmental Policy in the European Union*, 97.
[80] McCormick, *Environmental Policy in the European Union*, 97–98.
[81] Presidency Conclusions, 1990, Annex II.
[82] The European Council also played a crucial role in the development of the EU Sustainable Development Strategy. See Göteborg European Council, June 2001 and, further, Chapter 3. See more in Uwe Puetter, 'The European Council: The New Centre of EU Politics' (October 2013) 16 *European Policy Analysis* 1.
[83] Brussels European Council Conclusions of 8/9 March 2007, para. 29.
[84] Brussels European Council Conclusions of 23–24 October 2014.
[85] See more in Puetter, 'The European Council: The New Centre of EU Politics', 1–16.
[86] See more in Wurzel, 'Member States and the Council', 88.   [87] Art. 15(2) TEU.

prepares the follow-up to meetings of the European Council, in liaison with the President of the European Council and the Commission.[88] However, there are some recent criticisms that in practice the General Affairs Council has lost some importance.[89]

The Court of Justice of the European Union (CJEU) and the General Court

The Court of Justice of the European Union has played a pivotal role in ensuring the interpretation and application of EU law in all policy areas.[90] The Court consists of one judge from each Member State. The Treaty of Lisbon changed the appointment procedure, whereby judges are appointed by common accord of the governments of the Member States for six years, after consultation with the Article 255 TFEU panel which provides an opinion on candidates' suitability to perform the duties of Judge.[91] Judges are chosen from persons meeting moral and professional appointment criteria,[92] and are assisted by Advocates-General, who must satisfy the same appointment criteria.[93] Besides the CJEU, the General Court and the national courts are also integral to the system of EU judicial protection tasked with interpreting and applying EU law, including EU environmental law. The General Court was recently reformed by increasing the number of judges with the aim of addressing its growing workload. The number of judges will be gradually increased so as to have two judges per Member State from 1 September 2019.[94] There are no permanent Advocates-General in the General Court.[95] Its primary jurisdiction is to hear cases at first instance, provided that they are not referred directly to the Court of Justice.[96] The Treaty provides that the General Court may in the future be given jurisdiction to rule on questions referred for a preliminary ruling in specific areas laid down by the Treaties.[97]

One of the most important achievements of the CJEU in the environmental policy area was the interpretation and clarification of EU environmental *acquis*.

---

[88] Its competences are defined in Art. 16(6) TEU.
[89] 'Shifting EU Institutional Reform into High Gear', 19.
[90] Art. 19(1) TEU. On the development of the fundamental constitutional principles of direct effect and supremacy, see Chapter 6.
[91] Art. 255 TFEU.
[92] Art. 253 TFEU: 'whose independence is beyond doubt, who possess the qualifications required for appointment to the highest judicial offices in their respective countries or who are jurisconsults of recognised competence'.
[93] As from 1 July 2013 there are 9 Advocates-General and their number rose to 11 from 7 October 2015. See Council Decision 2013/336/EU of 25 June 2013 increasing the number of Advocates-General of the Court of Justice of the European Union, OJ L 179/92 (2013).
[94] Regulation 2015/2422 amending Protocol No. 3 on the Statute of the Court of Justice of the European Union, OJ 2015 L341/14.
[95] A judge may be appointed as an Advocate-General.   [96] Art. 256 TFEU, para. 1.
[97] *Ibid.*, para. 2 and para. 3.

A perfect tool for that was the preliminary ruling procedure under Article 267 TFEU,[98] although some interpretations were provided by the infringement procedure. Bearing in mind the specific meanings of some EU environmental concepts and the potential danger in having divergent interpretations in Member States, the Court has been careful to safeguard the consistency of EU environmental law. One of the best illustrations is the interpretation of the concept of waste as an autonomous concept of EU law.[99] No less significant is the Court's role in clarifying the EU's external environmental competences by interpreting the obligations deriving from international environmental law.[100]

The CJEU also plays an important role in enforcing EU environmental law by ruling in infringement procedures, as the implementation gap in Member States represents the weakest link of the integration process (see more in Chapter 6). The environmental policy area was always identified as one of the most challenging areas for the implementation of the EU *acquis* as it encompasses a wide range of issues, such as air and water quality, water protection, waste management, climate change, GMOs, soil protection, nature and biodiversity, chemicals and environmental impact assessments. This is reflected in the number of infringement cases: as discussed in Chapter 6, the environment features as one of the areas with the highest number of infringements.[101] The CJEU has also endeavoured to strike a balance between market integration and environmental protection through its case law.[102]

Other Bodies and Actors

The Economic and Social Committee

The European Economic and Social Committee (EESC) is the Union's advisory body representing the interests of three main groups: employers, workers and various interests. It was set up in 1957 by the Treaty on the European Economic Community with the objective of expressing views of various social and economic interest groups. It has 350 members and this number is capped by

---

[98] A national court may refer a question regarding the interpretation of the treaties or the validity of acts of the institutions, bodies, offices or agencies of the Union to the ECJ, if it believes that the ECJ's ruling is necessary to enable it to give judgment. The court or tribunal against whose decisions there is no judicial remedy under national law is obliged to refer the matter to the ECJ.

[99] See, further, Chapter 14 and Eloise Scotford, 'The New Waste Directive – Trying to Do it All ... An Early Assessment' (2009) 11(2) *Environmental Law Review* 75–96; Robert Lee and Elen Stokes, 'Rehabilitating the Definition of Waste: Is it Fully Recovered?' in T. Etty and H. Somson (eds.), (2008) 8 *Yearbook of European Environmental Law* 162.

[100] See Case C-240/09 *Lesoochranárske zoskupenie VLK v. Ministerstvo životného prostredia Slovenskej republiky* ECLI:EU:C:2011:125 and Case C-366/10, *Air Transport Association of America and Others* ECLI:EU:C:2011:864, discussed in Chapters 1 and 7.

[101] See the latest report, COM(2015)329, final.

[102] See, further, Chapter 3 and Francis Jacobs, 'The Role of the European Court of Justice in the Protection of the Environment' (2006) 18(2) *Journal of Environmental Law* 185–205.

the Treaty of Lisbon.[103] The EESC must be consulted prior to the adoption of legislation based on the environmental legal basis of the Treaty, Article 192 TFEU. Besides this mandatory consultation, the Committee may give opinions on certain issues of its own initiative.

The Committee operates through six specialised sections, each responsible for a certain policy area. The Agriculture, Rural Development and the Environment section (NAT) is responsible for environmental issues, especially climate change, renewable energy, energy efficiency and biodiversity. Although the organisation of the EESC may not specifically imply the environmental mandate of this institution, the EESC is becoming more involved with environmental problems. In its 2014 Action Plan for Europe, the EESC recognises the overarching principle of sustainable development 'at the heart of the Union's policies for the environment, the economy and, above all, energy'.[104] Through its specialised section on environment, the EESC attempts to bring together relevant NGOs and national and European authorities in order to ensure a diversity of opinions. In recent years, there was a clear rise in the number of environment-related opinions delivered by the EESC, especially in relation to climate change issues.[105] However, there are still concerns that it has very little influence and its opinions do not carry great weight.[106]

The Committee of the Regions (CoR)

The Committee of the Regions is another advisory body of the EU consisting of representatives of regional and local bodies who either hold a regional or local authority electoral mandate or are politically accountable to an elected assembly.[107] It was introduced by the Maastricht Treaty in order to reflect the importance of the regional dimension in the integration process.[108] At the moment there are 350 members from twenty-eight Member States. The cap

---

[103] Art. 301 TFEU.
[104] See www.eesc.europa.eu/?i=portal.en.publications&itemCode=32017 (p. 11).
[105] See www.eesc.europa.eu/?i=portal.en.nat-section. See more about the influence of the EESC on EU policy-making in Christoph Hönnige and Diana Panke, 'The Committee of the Regions and the European Economic and Social Committee: How Influential are Consultative Committees in the European Union?' (2013) 51 *Journal of Common Market Studies* 452–471.
[106] The recent study suggests that its opinions are often not even read. The same applies to the opinion of the Committee of the Regions. See Christoph Hönnige and Diana Panke, 'Is Anybody Listening? The Committee of the Regions and the European Economic and Social Committee and their Quest for Awareness' (2015) 23(4) *Journal of European Public Policy* 624–642.
[107] Art. 300 (3) TFEU. The members and an equal number of alternative members are appointed by the Council for a renewable term of five years.
[108] The TEU initially prescribed that the CoR should be composed of 'representatives of regional and local bodies'. This was amended by the Treaty of Nice which introduced the existing provision. See William E. Carroll, 'The Committee of the Regions: A Functional Analysis of the CoR's Institutional Capacity' (2011) 21(3) *Regional and Federal Studies* 341–354.

limit of a maximum of 350 members also applies to the Committee of the Regions.[109] In environmental matters, the European Parliament and the Council must consult the CoR when passing legislation on the basis of Article 192 TFEU.[110] The Treaty of Lisbon empowers the Committee of the Regions to bring actions to protect its prerogatives when other institutions fail to consult it.[111]

The Committee operates through six commissions. The Commission for the Environment, Climate Change and Energy Commission (ENVE) is responsible for the environmental portfolio. The main task of those commissions is to participate in the preparation of opinions submitted as a response to a legislative proposal. The ENVE commission should have an important role in the environmental policy area as the local and regional authorities are often responsible for the implementation of the EU environmental *acquis*. One of the ENVE commission's recent opinions on the role of local and regional authorities in environmental policy-making emphasised the necessity of their greater involvement in the formulation and implementation of EU policy.[112] Besides the core environmental issues, the commission addresses the issue of climate change adaptation and mitigation, renewable energy, trans-European networks in the energy sector, new energy policies and space policy.[113]

The European Environment Agency

The European Environment Agency is considered to be one of the most significant EU agencies in this policy area.[114] It was Jacques Delors who suggested the establishment of the Agency in his speech to the European Parliament in 1989.[115] The Member States were quite divided over this issue. Environmental 'leaders' such as Germany, Netherlands, Belgium and Luxembourg favoured the proposal, while the Southern 'laggards' were opposed to it.[116] Despite strong opposition, the French Presidency succeeded in getting countries on board and the Regulation setting up the agency was quickly adopted.[117] The European Environment Information and Observation Network (Eionet) was also created by this Regulation. However, the agency only became operational in 1994

---

[109] Art. 305(1) TFEU. [110] Art. 192(1) TFEU. [111] Art. 263 TFEU.
[112] CdR 164/2010 final. The Committee also produced another opinion in 2015 (ENVE-VI /008) calling for a European Commission to work closely with the Committee of the Regions concerning 'any future initiatives that aim at improving environmental implementation and governance'.
[113] See http://cor.europa.eu/en/activities/commissions/enve/Pages/role.aspx.
[114] See more about the role of agencies in the environmental policy area in Lee, *EU Environmental Law, Governance and Decision-Making*, 44–47.
[115] Sherrington, *The Council of Ministers*, 115–116. [116] *Ibid.*
[117] Council Regulation (EEC) No. 1210/90 on the establishment of the European Environment Agency and the European Environment Information and Observation Network, OJ 1990 L 120/01-06. As this Regulation was amended several times, it was codified by the adoption of the Regulation (EC) No. 401/2009 of the European Parliament and of the Council.

as a result of disagreements between Member States over the location of its official seat.[118]

The Agency is not a regulatory agency, although there were proposals to broaden its scope of work. The European Parliament always supported the EEA to become a regulatory agency.[119] There were even suggestions of vesting the Agency with more extensive supervisory powers over the implementation of EU environmental law by Member States.[120] Its primary responsibility is to gather and disseminate information about the state of the environment to EU institutions and Member States.[121] To that effect, it works closely with Eurostat. It also aims to assess adopted measures based on information gathered and to disseminate environmental information more effectively. Priority areas of work at present include air quality and atmospheric emissions; water quality, pollutants and water resources; the state of the soil, of the fauna and flora, and of biotopes; land use and natural resources; waste management; noise emissions; chemical substances which are hazardous for the environment; and coastal protection.[122] The information is provided in the form of reports which may be general or thematic.

Besides providing information which is often significant in formulating environmental proposals, the Agency has an impact on the environmental policy process by providing specific support to DG Environment.[123] However, this close relationship with the European Commission and in particular DG Environment only developed in recent years as a result of a 'learning process' on the part of both institutions.[124] It also works closely with the DG Climate Action, DG for Research and Innovation, DG Transport and Mobility, DG Energy, DG Agriculture and Rural Development, DG for Regional and Urban Policy and the Joint Research Centre. The relationship with the Council and the European Parliament is less intensive, even though those two institutions approve the Agency's budget. The European Parliament also has a say in the appointment of EEA members which is an incentive for the EEA to maintain close ties with the Parliament.[125]

The Eionet network, consisting of the main component elements of the national information networks, the national focal points and the topic centres, plays an important role in gathering information.[126] It has proved to be a valuable asset both for the Agency and for DG Environment in establishing close links

---

[118] The Agency is now based in Copenhagen.
[119] David A. Westbrook, 'Environmental Policy in the European Community: Observations on the European Environment Agency' (1991) 15 *Harvard Environmental Law Review* 257, at 262. See, further, Chapter 6.
[120] Westbrook, 'Environmental Policy in the European Community', 267–268.
[121] Art. 2(a) of the Regulation (EC) No. 401/2009.   [122] *Ibid.*, Art. 3(2).
[123] Maria Martens, 'Voice or Loyalty? The Evolution of the European Environment Agency (EEA)' (2010) 48(4) *Journal of Common Market Studies* 894.
[124] *Ibid.*, 883.   [125] Art. 8 of the Regulation (EC) No. 401/2009.
[126] *Ibid.*, Art. 4 (1). Currently 300 institutions are part of the network.

with national environmental agencies, both within EU Member States and in accession or partner States.

The European Investment Bank (EIB)

The European Investment Bank is not an institution usually associated directly with environmental protection. Nevertheless, it has a twofold role with regard to EU environmental policy.[127] First, it assists the EU in implementing the EU environmental policy by financing diverse environmental projects. Secondly, it promotes environmental sustainability by ensuring that all projects fulfil the objective of protecting and improving the natural and urban environment. In its most recent Environmental and Social Handbook, 'the promotion of sustainable development – in particular the protection and enhancement of biodiversity, the fight against climate change and the respect of human rights', are recognised as goals underpinning the EIB's lending strategy and objectives.[128] The EIB finances projects not only in the EU but also covers other regions, including accession countries, EFTA members, the Mediterranean region, EU Eastern Neighbours, Central Asia, South Africa, Sub-Saharan Africa, the Caribbean and Pacific and Asia and Latin America.

The EIB has financed a range of environmental projects, particularly projects related to urban and natural environment and climate change. In terms of climate change projects alone, in 2014, the EIB invested more than €19 billion in climate action, which accounted for around 20 per cent of its overall climate change lending for 2010–2014.[129] Applicants for each project must submit technical and environmental data in order to demonstrate that the project will not have an adverse effect on the environment.[130] That will include an environmental impact assessment, where appropriate, as well as reference to 'relevant laws, mitigating measures to protect the environment, [and] specific studies'.[131] However, there has been much criticism that these requirements are merely dead letters, that many projects have had damaging effects on the environment and that there is no transparency in decision-making, which are criticisms often also targeted at other major lending institutions such as the World Bank or the European Bank of

---

[127] Art. 309 TFEU.
[128] See www.eib.org/attachments/strategies/environmental_and_social_practices_handbook_en.pdf. Its commitment to sustainable development also stems from the Corporate Responsibility Report 2012: www.eib.org/attachments/general/reports/crr2012en.pdf. See more about the impact of soft power in Joseph S. Nye, *Soft Power: The Means to Success in World Politics* (Public Affairs, 2004).
[129] See more at www.eib.org/infocentre/publications/all/promoting-climate-action.html. 'In 2015, the EIB financed EUR 19.6 billion in projects enhancing environmental protection': www.eib.org/projects/priorities/urban/index.htm.
[130] For more on the EIB's Environmental and Social Principles and Standards in lending, see www.eib.org/infocentre/publications/all/environmental-and-social-principles-and-standards.htm.
[131] See www.eib.europa.eu/attachments/application_documents_en.pdf.

Reconstruction and Development.[132] As a response, the EIB has adopted a revised set of criteria for energy projects, but it remains to be seen whether this will improve the environmental consequences of approved loans.[133]

The European Union Network for the Implementation and Enforcement of Environmental Law (IMPEL)

As further discussed in Chapter 6, IMPEL was set up in 1992 by Member States as a response to growing concerns about poor implementation of the EU environmental *acquis*. The idea was to set up an environmental enforcement network within Member States which would not be part of the formal Treaty enforcement structure.[134] IMPEL's role in enhancing the effectiveness of cooperation between the authorities in the Member States responsible for implementation and enforcement of EU environmental legislation was recognised in the 5th Environmental Action Programme (EAP).[135] IMPEL's role in improving implementation records was again confirmed in the 7th EAP[136] and this was subsequently defined as IMPEL's first priority in its 2016–2020 Strategic Work Programme.[137] This is primarily achieved through the exchange of information and experiences on the application and enforcement of the EU environmental *acquis* between environmental authorities in Member States, accession countries and EEA countries as well as establishing links between these institutions.[138] As their missions overlap, the Commission and IMPEL are regarded as natural partners which has resulted in the Commission engaging in IMPEL's work from 1994 onwards. IMPEL has proved to be useful as a source of information for the Commission, which is highly dependent on external resources when it comes to the implementation of the environmental *acquis*.[139]

---

[132] Environmental NGOs were most vocal in criticism of the EIB's lending practices. CEE Bankwatch Network especially criticised negative practices on climate change in energy and transport lending. See http://bankwatch.org/our-work/who-we-monitor/eib/eib-negative-impacts.
[133] Available at: www.eib.org/infocentre/publications/all/eib-energy-lending-criteria.htm.
[134] See more at http://impel.eu/about/history/.
[135] Art. 4 of the Decision No. 2179/98/EC of the European Parliament and of the Council on the review of the European Community programme of policy and action in relation to the environment and sustainable development 'Towards sustainability', OJ 1998 L 275/01-13.
[136] 5.2 of 5th EAP and para. 65(iii) of 7th EAP.
[137] IMPEL's Strategic Work Programme 2016–2020: www.impel.eu/publications/multi-annual-strategic-programme-2016-2020/.
[138] See more in Statutes – European Union Network for the Implementation and Enforcement of Environmental Law (IMPEL): http://impel.eu/wp-content/uploads/2013/02/IMPEL-Statute-web-version-06-Dec-2012.pdf.
[139] See more about the role and impact of IMPEL in providing information on challenges of implementing EU environmental law and the practical issues faced by national enforcement bodies, in Richard Macrory, 'Environmental Sanctions – Challenges and Opportunities' (2015) 45(6) *Environmental Policy and Law* 276–281; Christoph Knill

Although not formally involved in the legislative process, IMPEL has succeeded in making some impact. IMPEL's work on minimum criteria for inspections from 1997 was used as a starting point in drafting the Recommendation on minimum criteria for environmental inspections in the Member States, discussed further in Chapter 6.[140] After the adoption of the act, IMPEL was prominent in promoting the application of these minimum requirements in Member States.

Interest Groups

In the last 20 years, there has been considerable growth in environmental interest groups at the EU level capable of influencing the EU decision-making process.[141] They vary in the interests they represent, size and level of organisation. However, several types of interest groups play a meaningful role in relation to the development of EU environmental policy.

Public Interest Groups

Environmental NGOs and other public interest groups have a long history in the EU policy-making process.[142] Public interest groups represent a variety of broad and diverse interests. Their impact on policy-making depends on several factors, including available resources at the EU level, organisational structure and the level of specialised expertise. Some of the problems may be overcome by joining interests and forces under 'federal' organisational structures such as the European Environmental Bureau[143] or establishing networks with other large environmental organisations. A most influential network at the moment is Green 10 which was very vocal in expressing its concerns at the absence of a clear environmental agenda in the Juncker Commission.[144] In response to pressure from Green 10 and other environmental NGOs, Vice-President Frans Timmermans was

---

and Andrea Lenschow, *Implementing EU Environmental Policy: New Directions and Old Problems* (Manchester University Press, 2000), 42.

[140] Recommendation of the European Parliament and of the Council of 4 April 2001 providing for minimum criteria for environmental inspections in the Member States (2001/331/EC).

[141] See more about the role of interest groups in Heike Klüver, *Lobbying in the European Union: Interest Groups, Lobbying Coalitions and Policy Change* (Oxford University Press, 2013).

[142] The participatory role of NGOs and individuals was recognised in the 5th EAP, which called for their 'greater public involvement in the implementation and enforcement of environmental policies'; see Camilla Adelle and Jason Anderson, 'Lobby Groups' in Jordan and Adelle, *Environmental Policy in the EU* and Lars K. Hallstrom, 'Eurocratising Enlargement? EU Elites and NGO Participation in European Environmental Policy' (2004) 13(1) *Environmental Politics* 175–193.

[143] The European Environmental Bureau is one of the oldest and largest umbrella organisations that brings together 150 member organisations. Its main objective is to make coalitions with other environmental organisations and liaise with national governments in order to voice collective interests more effectively.

[144] See www.green10.org/; Green 10.

entrusted with, among other responsibilities, coordinating Commission policy in line with sustainable development.

The lack of resources for NGOs is partly resolved through the funding provided directly to certain NGOs by the European Commission as an attempt to initiate a dialogue with all stakeholders.[145] Under the Life Regulation, the non-profit-making entities which are primarily active in the field of environment or climate action and are involved in the development, implementation and enforcement of Union policy and legislation are entitled to apply for operating grants supporting some of their operational and administrative costs.[146]

Over time, public interest groups have succeeded in becoming a part of the decision-making process. NGOs have effectively interacted with the main EU institutions and improved the legitimacy of decision-making. As Hix points out, the European Environmental Bureau had the opportunity to attend the meetings of the Environment Council and to become a member of the Commission's delegation to the Earth Summits.[147] Environmental NGOs have also proven to be a valuable source of information on the implementation of the environmental *acquis* in Member States, which may lead to the launch of the infringement proceeding by the European Commission.[148] NGOs may also voice their concerns by using the preliminary reference procedure and direct actions to challenge the validity of a Union act. However, in cases of direct actions, their standing is extremely limited (see further, Chapter 7).[149]

The European Parliament has also recognised the importance of environmental NGOs and other interest groups. Rapporteurs, via Secretariat officials, receive expert policy advice required to draft reports on the Commission's proposals.[150] Besides providing credible expertise and advice, environmental public interest groups are useful in mobilising national governments and citizens through

---

[145] See http://ec.europa.eu/environment/life/funding/ngos.
[146] Art. 21 of Regulation (EU) No. 1293/2013.
[147] Simon Hix and Bjørn Høyland, *The Political System of the European Union* (3rd edn., Palgrave, 2011), 173.
[148] Andonova gives an example of Romanian and Bulgarian NGOs which identified cases of non-implementation of nature and biodiversity *acquis* in respective Member States: Lilianna B. Andonova and Iona A. Tuta, 'Transnational Networks and Paths to EU Environmental Compliance: Evidence from New Member States' (2014) 52 *Journal of Common Market Studies* 775–793; see Commission reports on monitoring the application of EU law at http://ec.europa.eu/atwork/applying-eu-law/infringements-proceedings/annual-reports/index_en.htm.
[149] See Case C-25/62 *Plaumann* v. *Commission* ECLI:EU:C:1963:17 and T-585/93 *Greenpeace and Ors* v. *Commission* ECLI:EU:T:1995:147 and Case C-321/95 P *Stichting Greenpeace International* v. *Commission* ECLI:EU:C:1998:153.
[150] David Marshall, 'Do Rapporteurs Receive Independent Expert Policy Advice? Indirect Lobbying Via the European Parliament's Committee Secretariat' (2012) 19(9) *Journal of European Public Policy* 1377–1395.

their national branches and in generating media interest on issues which have significant transnational impact.

Business Interest Groups

Unlike environmental organisations, business interest groups are regarded as highly organised with very narrow technical expertise. As the EU institutions often face resource constraints, such groups may provide them with expert advice and opinion.[151] They are well positioned within the EU institutional system and have a long lineage in the EU.[152] Besides their expert knowledge expertise, business groups have more specific interests which are easier to relate to particular Commission proposals. Studies have shown that business groups tend to be more successful in lobbying the Commission than public interest groups, as they represent concentrated interests.[153]

As is the case with environmental NGOs, business groups also tend to join together within umbrella organisations which may either represent broader business interests or more specific sectoral interests. The European Chemical Industry Council,[154] the European Crop Protection Association[155] and the European Round Table of Industrialists[156] are very successful industry interest groups at the EU level. The European Chemical Industry Council, for example, not only successfully participated in the passage of the REACH Directive,[157] but is also involved in its implementation through the preparation of guidance documents and tools to support companies in the implementation of REACH, in cooperation with the Commission and the European Chemicals Agency.[158] Another example is the European Automobile Manufacturers Association, which has successfully represented the car industry over the years. In 1998, it concluded voluntary agreements with the European Commission with the aim of reducing CO_2 emissions from cars.[159]

Instruments

A range of legal and non-legal instruments have been deployed in EU environmental policy. Regulations, Directives and Decisions, as legally binding acts within the meaning of Article 288 TFEU, have retained a central role. The choice of instrument is left to the EU institutions, unless otherwise specified

---

[151] See Hix and Høyland, *The Political System of the European Union*, 165–169; W. Grant, 'Business' in Jordan and Adelle, *Environmental Policy in the EU*, 176–177.
[152] See the history of BusinessEurope at: www.businesseurope.eu/Content/Default.asp.
[153] Adriana Bunea, 'Issues, Preferences and Ties: Determinants of Interest Groups' Preference Attainment in the EU Environmental Policy' (2013) 20(4) *Journal of European Public Policy* 567.
[154] See www.cefic.org/. [155] See www.ecpa.eu/. [156] See www.ert.eu/.
[157] The Registration, Evaluation, Authorisation and Restriction of Chemicals Directive 2006/121/EC, OJ 2006 L 396/850.
[158] See, further, Chapter 13.
[159] ACEA agreement, COM(1998) 495, final. See, further, Chapter 4.

by the Treaties.[160] This flexibility is most appreciated in the passage of environmental *acquis*, which is reflected in the frequent use of Directives as they leave a certain level of discretion to Member States.

Regulations

Regulations are legally binding acts applicable to all Member States. They are binding in their entirety and cannot be applied 'in an incomplete or selective manner'.[161] Regulations are self-executing in all Member States, which means that they are directly applicable in Member States without the need to transpose them within the national legal system.

Member States are prohibited from using any 'methods of implementation that are contrary to the Treaty which would have the result of creating an obstacle to the direct effect of Community Regulations and of jeopardizing their simultaneous and uniform application in the whole of the Community'.[162] However, this does not prevent Member States from amending national law or passing additional measures to ensure compliance with a Regulation. In the environmental policy area, Member States must often pass a national measure, as this is necessary to apply certain Regulations which may require different legal and institutional adjustments.[163] For example, the Regulation on the EU Ecolabel requires Member States to designate one or more bodies responsible for the labelling process at the national level, which would involve in most civil law countries the passage of some legal act allocating this competence to a governmental department or agency.[164] Still, this does not change the legal effect of a Regulation, though it may be argued that the difference between Regulations and Directives may seem blurred at times.[165]

Although not used as frequently as Directives, Regulations ensure the uniform application of EU environmental law in the entire Union. This is often the case with putting in place certain institutional, administrative or financial frameworks which are aimed at uniformity in all Member States. A prime example is Regulation 691/2011 on European environmental economic accounts which is aimed at setting up a common legal framework for compiling harmonised accounts across the EU.[166] Regulations are more often used to lay down uniform

---

[160] Art. 296 TFEU.　[161] Case C-39/72 *Commission* v. *Italy* ECLI:EU:C:1973:13, para. 20.
[162] *Ibid.*
[163] See, for instance, the case of nature protection and chemicals, discussed in Chapters 12 and 13.
[164] Regulation (EC) No. 66/2010 of the European Parliament and of the Council on the EU Ecolabel, OJ 2010 L 27/01–19.
[165] Case C-34/73 *Fratelli Variola Spa* v. *Amministrazione delle finanze dello Stato* ECLI:EU:C:1973:101; see more in P. Craig and G. de Búrca, *EU Law: Text, Cases, and Materials* (Oxford University Press, 2011), 105.
[166] Reg (EU) 691/2011 of the European Parliament and of the Council of 6 July 2011 on European environmental economic accounts, OJ 2011 L 192/1. Another example is Reg (EC) 166/2006 of the European Parliament and of the Council concerning the

technical standards. For instance, a Regulation was ultimately used to deal with air pollution from motor vehicles by the introduction of uniform technical emissions requirements and specific emissions targets.[167] Regulations in the environmental policy area are also used to transpose obligations of international environmental conventions into EU law.[168]

Directives

The Directive is the most frequently used instrument in environmental policy, due to its legal nature. It is binding as to the result to be achieved, but leaves discretion to Member States as to the choice of forms and methods of implementation.[169] It is addressed to the Member States. This flexibility is appealing for Member States which are often faced with costly and demanding EU environmental legislation. However, this discretion is not always exercised by all Member States as some national authorities tend to transpose the Directive into the national legal system 'formally and *verbatim* in express specific legislation'.[170] Directives must be implemented in a manner which fully meets the requirement of legal certainty.[171] In the case of certain Directives, however, the CJEU encourages 'faithful transposition', as in the case of the Birds Directive, discussed

---

establishment of a European Pollutant Release and Transfer Register and amending Council Directives 91/689/EEC and 96/61/EC.

[167] Reg (EU) No. 510/2011 of the European Parliament and of the Council setting emissions performance standards for new light commercial vehicles as part of the Union's integrated approach to reduce CO_2 emissions from light-duty vehicles; Regulation (EC) No. 443/2009 of the European Parliament and of the Council setting emissions performance standards for new passenger cars as part of the Community's integrated approach to reduce CO_2 emissions from light-duty vehicles (Text with EEA relevance); Reg (EC) No. 595/2009 of the European Parliament and of the Council on type-approval of motor vehicles and engines with respect to emissions from heavy duty vehicles (Euro VI) and on access to vehicle repair and maintenance information and amending Reg (EC) No. 715/2007 and Directive 2007/46/EC and repealing Directives 80/1269/EEC, 2005/55/EC and 2005/78/EC (Text with EEA relevance).

[168] See e.g. the Reg (EC) No. 1005/2009 of the European Parliament and of the Council on substances that deplete the ozone layer (Text with EEA relevance), OJ 2009 L 286/1–30.

[169] Art. 288 TFEU.

[170] See Case C-363/85 *Commission* v. *Italy* ECLI:EU:C:1987:196, para. 7.

[171] Case C-239/85 *Commission* v. *Belgium* ECLI:EU:C:1986:457, para. 7. In Case C-252/85 *Commission* v. *France* ECLI:EU:C:1988:202, the Court ruled that 'a general legal context may be sufficient if it actually ensures the full application of the directive in a sufficiently clear and precise manner'. There are a great number of cases dealing with the transposition of directives – C-262/85 *Commission* v. *Italy* ECLI:EU:C:1987:340, Case C-339/87 *Commission* v. *Netherlands* ECLI:EU:C:1990:119, Case C-236/85 *Commission* v. *Netherlands* ECLI:EU:C:1987:436, Case C-507/04 *Commission* v. *Austria* ECLI:EU:C:2007:427. See more about the history of environmental directives in Ralf Wägenbaur, 'The European Community's Policy on Implementation of Environmental Directives' (1990) 14 *Fordham International Law Journal* 458–460.

in Chapter 12.[172] As a part of reforms in the choice of proposed policy instruments, discussed in Chapter 4, the Commission has stated that it favours the use of environmental Framework Directives, with open textured, broad norms representing a move from 'gold plating' in some Member States.[173] This is prominent in the waste, water and air sectors.

A Directive must be transposed into a national legal system within the time limit prescribed therein. The time limit for transposition will usually depend on the complexity of the Directive, and the costs and investment involved. National authorities must adopt or amend national laws and regulations in order to incorporate EU law into their national legal orders. A directive may be transposed through one or more national measures, depending on the assessment made by national authorities. In exercising its discretion, a national authority is limited by the fact that it should adopt a legally binding national provision, unless there are 'general principles of constitutional or administrative law that may render implementation by specific legislation superfluous'.[174]

Member States have experienced many problems in implementing EU environmental Directives[175] despite the fact that they are regarded as a preferred tool by Member States.[176] Occasional vagueness of Directives and their legal concepts may lead to divergent interpretations of the text of the Directive or different approaches to implementation, and ultimately may lead to non-compliance.[177] Likewise, the implementation of a Directive may prove challenging, as national legal systems may already have developed practices, procedures or instruments that are not easy to change, as is the case with some key Directives such as the

---

[172] See Case C-38/99 *Commission v. France* ECLI:EU:C:2000:674. See also Case C-262/85 *Commission v. Italy* ECLI:EU:C:1987:340.

[173] Rob Van Gestel, 'The "Deparliamentarisation" of Legislation: Framework Laws and the Primacy of the Legislature' (2013) 106(9) *Utrecht Law Review* 115. See also Helen S. Wallace, Mark A. Pollack and Alasdair R. Young (eds.), *Policy-Making in the European Union* (7th edn., Oxford University Press, 2014), 323–326.

[174] See Case C-29/84 *Commission v. Germany* ECLI:EU:C:1985:229, para. 23. See also Case C-52/75 *Commission v. Italy* ECLI:EU:C:1976:29, Case C-239/85 *Commission v. Belgium* ECLI:EU:C:1986:457.

[175] Here implementation involves both transposition and practical implementation.

[176] See more about experiences in the past in Andrew Jordan, 'The Implementation of EU Environmental Policy: A Policy Problem without a Political Solution?', *Environment and Planning C: Government and Policy* (1999) 17 69–90, at 78.

[177] An example is the Environmental Liability Directive. See Isabel Rodriguez Valero, 'The Environmental Liability Directive: Practical Impact and Implementation' (2005) 2 JEEPL 342–346; for example, what falls within the definition of a combustion plant in Case C-346/08 *Commission v. UK* ECLI:EU:C:2010:213; the interpretation of 'dismantling information' and 'stripping' under Directive 2000/53/EC in Case C-64/09 *Commission v. France* ECLI:EU:C:2010:197; the term 'the public concerned' in Directive 2003/35 in Case C-427/07 *Commission v. Ireland* ECLI:EU:C:2009:457. One interesting question that arose in regard to implementation of the *acquis* in the UK and Ireland was the extent to which environmental Directives may be transposed by case law in common law systems, the Commission opposing the idea that this would be an acceptable form of transposition. See Case C-50/09 *Commission v. Ireland* ECLI:EU:C:2011:109 and Case C-530/11 *Commission v. UK* ECLI:EU:C:2014:67.

Environmental Liability Directive, the Habitats Directive and the WEEE Directive.[178]

Equally important is the designation of national authorities responsible for the implementation of a respective law or regulation, which will often depend on the territorial organisation within the Member States. Member States are sometimes successful in preserving existing institutional and procedural structures intact.[179] This may prove more challenging with the implementation of Directives which require an integrated management approach and cross-sectoral coordination and communication, as was the case in some Member States in implementing the Noise Directive and the Water Framework Directive.[180] Sometimes, environmental Directives implemented in several phases represent a learning experience for national authorities, which have been able to improve subsequent implementation.[181] Lack of technical and scientific expertise or high implementation costs are often regarded as additional difficulties for certain Member States.[182]

Decisions

A Decision is binding in its entirety and specifies to whom it is addressed.[183] Only the addressee of the Decision shall be bound by it. It represents an important

---

[178] See Chapters 6 and 12 and see, further, Gerd Winter, Jan H. Hans, Richard Macrory and Ludwig Krämer, 'Weighing up the EC Environmental Liability Directive' (2008) 20(2) *Journal of Environmental Law* 163–191; Jenni Ylä-Mella, Kari Poikela, Ulla Lehtinen, Ritta Keiski and Eva Pongrácz, 'Implementation of Waste Electrical and Electronic Equipment Directive in Finland: Evaluation of the Collection Network and Challenges of the Effective WEEE Management' (2014) 86 *Resources, Conservation and Recycling* 38–46; Lars Borrass, 'Varying Practices of Implementing the Habitats Directive in German and British Forests' (2014) 38 *Forest Policy and Economics* 151–160; Knill and Lenschow argue that transposition will be less successful if it does not correspond to national regulatory traditions in C. Knill and A. Lenschow, 'Compliance, Communication and Competition: Patterns of EU Environmental Policy Making and their Impact on Policy Convergence' (2005) 15 *European Environment* 114–128.

[179] See Borrass, 'Varying Practices of Implementing the Habitats Directive', 151–160. The Netherlands was fortunate to keep as much as possible of the existing legal, financial and institutional framework intact in implementation of the Water Framework Directive. See S. J. Junier and E. Mostert, 'The Implementation of the Water Framework Directive in The Netherlands: Does it Promote Integrated Management?' (2012) 47–48, *Physics and Chemistry of the Earth* 2–10.

[180] Junier and Mostert, 'The Implementation of the Water Framework Directive in The Netherlands', 2–10; E. A. King, E. Murphy and H. J. Rice, 'Implementation of the EU Environmental Noise Directive: Lessons from the First Phase of Strategic Noise Mapping and Action Planning in Ireland', *Journal of Environmental Management* 92 (2011) 756–764.

[181] King, Murphy and Rice, 'Implementation of the EU Environmental Noise Directive'.

[182] This was often the case with the Urban Waste Water Treatment Directive (COM/2013/0574) and the Habitats Directive. See more in Raoul Beunen, Wim G. M. van der Knaap and G. Robbert Biesbroek, 'Implementation and Integration of EU Environmental Directives: Experiences from Netherlands' (2009) 19(1) *Environmental Policy and Governance* 57–69.

[183] Art. 288 TFEU.

source of EU environmental law and it is used quite frequently. In the past they have often accompanied Directives, and have, for instance, contained questionnaires for notifying the Commission on the transposition of Directives.[184] While Regulations are used for integrating international treaty provisions into EU law, Decisions are used as an instrument of ratification.[185] This instrument was also used to set up a new mechanism for monitoring and reporting greenhouse gas emissions in order to ensure the compliance with the United Nations Framework Convention on Climate Change (UNFCCC) and the Kyoto Protocol.[186] As Decisions may refer to natural and legal persons, they are also widely used to regulate the behaviour of companies via application of the EU competition rules and/or State aid rules.[187] The enforcement powers of the Commission to impose fines and refer a matter to the CJEU constitute special powers conferred on the Commission in the field of competition and State aid.

---

[184] 2001/753/EC: Commission Decision of 17 October 2001 concerning a questionnaire for Member States' reports on the implementation of Directive 2000/53/EC of the European Parliament and of the Council on end-of-life vehicles (notified under document number C 2001/3096), OJ 2001 L 282/77–80; 98/184/EC: Commission Decision concerning a questionnaire for Member States' reports on the implementation of Council Directive 94/67/EC on the incineration of hazardous waste (implementation of Council Directive 91/692/EEC) OJ 1998 L 67/48–50; 97/622/EC: Commission Decision concerning questionnaires for Member States' reports on the implementation of certain Directives in the waste sector (implementation of Council Directive 91/692/EEC), OJ 1997 L 256/13–19.

[185] Council Decision 93/98/EEC on the conclusion, on behalf of the Community, of the Convention on the control of transboundary movements of hazardous wastes and their disposal (Basel Convention); Council Decision 97/640/EC on the approval, on behalf of the Community, of the amendment to the Convention on the control of transboundary movements of hazardous wastes and their disposal (Basel Convention), as laid down in Decision III/1 of the Conference of the Parties; Council Decision 2006/507/EC concerning the conclusion, on behalf of the European Community, of the Stockholm Convention on Persistent Organic Pollutants; Council Decision 2005/370/EC on the conclusion, on behalf of the European Community, of the Convention on access to information, public participation in decision-making and access to justice in environmental matters; Council Decision 81/462/EEC on the conclusion of the Convention on long-range transboundary air pollution; Council Decision 81/462/EEC on the conclusion of the Convention on long-range transboundary air pollution; Council Decision 82/461/EEC on the conclusion of the Convention on the conservation of migratory species of wild animals (Bonn Convention).

[186] See, further, Chapter 8. Decision 280/2004/EC of the European Parliament and of the Council concerning a mechanism for monitoring Community greenhouse gas emissions and for implementing the Kyoto Protocol. Similarly, it was used for setting up the Scientific Committees and experts in the field of consumer safety, public health and the environment – Commission Decision 2008/721/EC setting up an advisory structure of Scientific Committees and experts in the field of consumer safety, public health and the environment and repealing Decision 2004/210/EC.

[187] Kingston, *Greening EU Competition Law and Policy*.

Environmental Action Programmes

Environmental action programmes (EAPs) have a long history in this policy area, going back to the first EAP in 1973. EAPs are adopted jointly by the European Parliament and the Council of the EU via the ordinary legislative procedure and following consultation with the Economic and Social Committee and the Committee of the Regions.[188] They set the general context for legislative activity as they outline the priority objectives to be achieved by the EU and guide the development of environmental policy area over the covered years. Each programme reflects the environmental concerns existing at the time of its adoption, but also the general regulatory approach in tackling environmental problems at the time. EAPs should also provide continuity and consistency in addressing environmental concerns. Six action programmes have been adopted since 1973, and the European Parliament and the Council adopted the 7th (current) EAP in November 2013, covering the period up to 2020.[189]

The origin of the First EAP dates back to 1972, when Heads of State of the Member States invited the Commission to establish a programme of action.[190] It was underlined that 'economic expansion is not an end in itself' and 'particular attention will be given to intangible values and to protecting the environment so that progress may really be put at the service of mankind'.[191] As a result the First EAP (1973–1982) was adopted in 1973, just after the first UN Conference on the Environment in Stockholm in 1972. It was a sign of a more engaged Community role in developing what would become Community environmental policy, and its commitment to stronger international cooperation. Together with the Second EAP, the First EAP was often characterised as a reactive programme as both programmes were an initial response to growing environmental problems, especially water, air and waste pollution.[192]

The Third EAP (1982–1986)[193] and the Fourth EAP (1987–1992)[194] took a significant departure from the previous programmes, as they set a more ambitious approach to environmental protection, which took into account the

---

[188] Art. 192 (3). [189] OJ 2013 L 354/171.
[190] Declaration of the Council of the European Communities and of the representatives of the Governments of the Member States meeting in the Council on the programme of action of the European Communities on the environment, OJ 1973 C 112/1. See, further, Chapter 1.
[191] OJ 1973 C 112/1.
[192] OJ 1977 C 139/1; see Albert Weale et al., *Environmental Governance in Europe* and J. H. Jans, *European Environmental Law* (Europa Law Publishing, 2000). The First Action Programme set out three main objectives which included the prevention, reduction and as far as possible the elimination of pollution and nuisances, the maintenance of a satisfactory ecological balance and the protection of the biosphere. It also called for the safeguarding and sound management of, and the avoidance of exploitation of, resources or of nature, which might cause significant damage to the ecological balance. It especially focused on the need to encourage further scientific and technological progress as an instrument in conserving and improving the environment. Those objectives were further developed in the Second EAP (1977–1981), with the additional focus on nature protection.
[193] OJ 1983 C 46/1. [194] OJ 1987 C 328/1.

objective of completing the internal market. Unlike previous programmes, the third programme enhanced the preventive character of Community environmental policy and the integration of environmental protection in other policy areas, notably agriculture, energy, industry, transport and tourism. This was reaffirmed in the Fourth EAP, which made a breakthrough by calling for the development of economic instruments for environmental protection, discussed further in Chapter 4.

The Fifth EAP (1992–1999) is best known for giving greater impetus to sustainable development through improving shared action and partnership approaches.[195] It developed further the idea of creating new instruments, especially market-oriented principles and called for measures to improve the implementation and enforcement of the environmental *acquis*, as well as the concept of environmental liability at the Member State level. A more strategic approach to meeting future environmental challenges was recognised in the Sixth EAP (2002–2012) which called for such an approach as the best way to meet the challenges of today's environmental problems.[196] The programme envisaged the adoption of seven thematic strategies covering air pollution, the marine environment, sustainable use of resources, prevention and recycling of waste, sustainable use of pesticides, soil protection and urban environment.

The most recent Seventh EAP, 'Living Well, within the Limits of Our Planet',[197] comes at a difficult time for all Member States struggling to cope with the effects of a prolonged economic crisis. It sets a very ambitious programme which is to guide the EU towards a resource-efficient, green and competitive low-carbon economy while preserving at the same time the EU's natural capital and ensuring the health and well-being of EU citizens. It seems uncertain how the EU will be able to reach the targets set, as it is becoming more difficult to reconcile the economic goals and environmental standards. Likewise, the EU needs to reaffirm its political leadership at both the EU and international levels, which may be challenging in the current political and economic climate.

Recommendations and other Soft Law Instruments

While there is a growing tendency and incentive to use 'soft' (non-binding) environmental instruments, the full potential of recommendations is not recognised at the EU level. It seems that they are used even less frequently than in the past.[198] Recommendations have in some cases shown themselves to be a useful

---

[195] OJ C 1993 138/I. It was reviewed in 1998 – OJ 1998 L275/I. [196] OJ 2002 L 242/1.
[197] OJ 2013 L 354/171.
[198] Some of the recommendations adopted in the past: Commission Recommendation on the protection of the public against exposure to radon in drinking water supplies (notified under document number C(2001) 4580), OJ 2001 L 344/85–88; 90/143/Euratom: Commission Recommendation on the protection of the public against indoor exposure to radon, OJ 1990 L 080/26–28; Commission Recommendation on the results of the risk

instrument to bridge different legal traditions and practices in regulating various environmental issues in Member States. A good example is the Recommendation on environmental inspections which lays down criteria and minimum guidelines for inspections performed in Member States.[199] Likewise, Recommendations may also prove useful to keep up with scientific and technological development, when there is insufficient scientific evidence to act with a legally binding instrument.

Besides Recommendations, the use of a wide range of other soft law instruments is quite characteristic for the environmental policy area, including Guidelines, Communications and Resolutions. The use of Guidelines in all environmental sectors aims to clarify and interpret environmental concepts which may be different from those in national jurisdictions, or may be at times highly technical.[200] Likewise, the Commission frequently deploys Communications which may be entitled variously strategies, green and white papers, reports and communications.[201]

Financial Instruments

LIFE (the Financial Instrument for the Environment Regulation)

Bearing in mind the variety of financial instruments at the EU level covering a wide range of policy areas, none of the big five EU funds is specifically designed for the environment.[202] The EU recently launched the EU Solidarity

---

evaluation and the risk reduction strategies for the substances: diphenylether/pentabromo derivative and cumene (Text with EEA relevance) (notified under document number C (2001) 439), OJ 2001 L 69/30–36; 98/480/EC: Commission Recommendation concerning good environmental practice for household laundry detergents (notified under document number C(1998) 2163), OJ 1998 L 215/73–75.

[199] Recommendation 2001/331/EC of the European Parliament and of the Council providing for minimum criteria for environmental inspections in the Member States, OJ 2001 L 118/41. See, further, Chapter 6.

[200] Some of the examples are the Guidelines drafted for specific environmental sectors: Guidance document on the Waste Framework Directive (see Chapter 14); Handbook for Implementation of EU Environmental Legislation – Air Quality (see Chapter 9); Guidelines for the establishment of the Natura 2000 network in the marine environment (see Chapter 12).

[201] See, for instance, Communication from the Commission to the Council, the European Parliament, the European Economic and Social Committee and the Committee of the Regions, entitled: 'Small, clean and competitive – A programme to help small and medium-sized enterprises comply with environmental legislation', COM(2007)379, final; Commission Communication to the European Parliament, the Council, the European Economic and Social Committee and the Committee of the Regions: 'A Blueprint to Safeguard Europe's Water Resources', COM(2012)673, final; Commission Communication, 'Our Life Insurance, Our Natural Capital: An EU Biodiversity Strategy to 2020', COM(2011)244, final.

[202] European Regional Development Fund, European Social Fund, Cohesion Fund, European Agricultural Fund for Rural Development and European Maritime and Fisheries Fund.

Fund,[203] which is not as such an environmental fund, but an aim of which is improving the state of the environment. This, however, is a response to more frequent environmental disasters prompted by climate change and the effects of global warming. The lack of any proper environment fund may raise concerns about the application of the Article 11 TFEU principle of integration, discussed in Chapter 3, with regard to the financing of EU projects. Nevertheless, LIFE is regarded as a central EU financial instrument covering environmental, nature conservation and climate action projects in the EU.[204] It was launched in 1992 and has been implemented through four cycles so far.[205] Several funding programmes such as the *Action Communautaire pour l'Environnement* preceded LIFE, but they had much more limited funding.[206]

To date, it is estimated that around 4,171 projects have been financed through the LIFE programme, amounting to approximately €3.4 billion funding devoted to the protection of the environment.[207] The focus of each LIFE funding has changed through the four phases of the programme. During the first phase the emphasis was on the promotion of sustainable development and the quality of the environment, nature conservation, improvement of administrative structures and education, while the second and third phases were predominantly devoted to nature conservation. The current LIFE was launched in 2014 to cover the period until 2020 with a budget of €3.46 billion.[208] It is divided into two main components, environment and climate change, with each component subsequently divided into three priority areas.[209] The priorities set out in the EAP and thematic strategies are reflected in each LIFE programme phase, and the Commission ensures that elected projects are in line with the EAP's objectives. LIFE is regarded as the main financial instrument in supporting key environment initiatives such as the NATURA 2000 network.

Irrespective of its unique focus on environment and financing of large environmental projects there are some concerns regarding the synergy and coherence of LIFE with national, regional and local programmes.[210] Moreover, the method of national allocations within the LIFE Regulation has been subject to criticism from Member States.[211] Before the launch of the most recent LIFE programme,

---

[203] Council Regulation (EC) No. 2012/2002 establishing the European Union Solidarity Fund, OJ 2002 L 311/3.
[204] See more at http://ec.europa.eu/environment/life/index.htm.
[205] LIFE I: 1992–1995, LIFE II: 1996–1999 and LIFE III: 2000–2006; LIFE+ IV: 2007–2013.
[206] See http://ec.europa.eu/environment/life/about/index.htm#background.
[207] See http://ec.europa.eu/environment/life/index.htm.
[208] The LIFE 2014–2020 Regulation (EC) No. 1293/2013 was published in the OJ 2013 L 347/185.
[209] *Ibid.*, Art. 9.
[210] Final Evaluation of LIFE+: http://ec.europa.eu/environment/life/about/documents/12 1214_conclusions.pdf.
[211] See Art. 19 of the LIFE Regulation: The Commission shall, for the duration of the first multiannual work programme, ensure geographical balance for projects other than

there were suggestions of outsourcing the operating of the scheme to an agency, which would have raised controversies about the ongoing trend of agency proliferation at the EU level, especially at the time of budgetary constraints. However, such outsourcing never in fact took place.

EU Structural and Investment Funds

Five main financial instruments operate as structural and investment funds, including the European Regional Development Fund, the European Structural Fund, the Cohesion Fund, the European Agricultural Fund for Rural Development and the European Maritime and Fisheries Fund. The first three funds have been developed under the umbrella of regional policy, and have important environmental implications. EU regional policy has its origin in the Treaty of Rome, although its introduction was agreed during the first enlargement in 1973.[212] Structural and Cohesion funds are the most relevant for the environment. Between 2007 and 2013, the total amount of Structural and Cohesion Funds allocated to environmental programmes has doubled since the previous period to around €100 billion, and now constitutes 30 per cent of the total.[213]

Amongst the aims of the European Social Fund is the promotion of projects focusing on green skills and green jobs, which will aim to become more prominent as the EU moves towards a resource-efficient, green and competitive low-carbon economy as declared in the 7th EAP. Of the various funds, the Cohesion Fund is more directly connected to the protection of the environment. Article 177 TFEU stipulates that the Cohesion Fund provides a 'financial contribution to projects in the fields of environment and trans-European networks in the area of transport infrastructure'. The main aim of the Cohesion Fund is the strengthening of the economic and social cohesion of the Union in the interests of promoting sustainable development.[214] Assistance is provided to environmental projects 'within the priorities assigned to the Community environmental protection policy under the policy and action programme on the environment',[215] which provides a very broad scope for funding in this field. This fund may also provide

---

integrated projects submitted under the sub-programme for Environment, by proportionately distributing funds among all Member States according to indicative national allocations established in accordance with the criteria set out in Annex I. Where indicative national allocations are not applicable, projects shall be selected exclusively on the basis of merit.

[212] See more on the history of cohesion policy and reform efforts in Iain Begg, 'Cohesion or Confusion: A Policy Searching for Objectives' (2010) 32(1) *Journal of European Integration* 77–96.

[213] 'Working for the Regions' EU Regional Policy 2007–2013, EU Commission DG Regional Policy, January 2008, at 16: http://ec.europa.eu/regional_policy/sources/doc gener/presenta/working2008/work_en.pdf.

[214] Art. 1 of Council Regulation (EC) No. 1084/2006 establishing a Cohesion Fund and repealing Regulation (EC) No. 1164/94, OJ 2006 L 210/79–81.

[215] *Ibid.*, Art. 2(1)(b).

Table 2.2 Breakdown of the Available Structural Funds by Theme for the EU as a Whole

Regional policy funding	Priority areas
European Regional Development Fund	• Innovation and research • The digital agenda • Support for small and medium-sized enterprises (SMEs) • The low-carbon economy
Cohesion Fund	• Trans-European transport networks, in particular priority projects of European interest • The environment: projects related to energy or transport, as long as they clearly benefit the environment in terms of energy efficiency, use of renewable energy, developing rail transport, supporting intermodality, strengthening public transport, etc.
European Social Fund	• Promoting employment and supporting labour mobility • Promoting social inclusion and combating poverty • Investing in education, skills and lifelong learning • Enhancing institutional capacity and an efficient public administration
Agricultural Fund for Rural Development	• Improving the competitiveness of the agricultural and forestry sector • Improving the environment and the countryside • Improving the quality of life in rural areas and encouraging diversification of the rural economy
European Maritime and Fisheries Fund	• Helps fishermen in the transition to sustainable fishing • Supports coastal communities in diversifying their economies • Finances projects that create new jobs and improve quality of life along European coasts • Makes it easier for applicants to access financing

Source: European Commission. See http://ec.europa.eu/regional_policy/en/funding/ and http://ec.europa.eu/agriculture/cap-funding/funding-opportunities/index_en.htm.

assistance to other areas such as 'energy efficiency and renewable energy and, in the transport sector outside the trans-European networks, rail, river and sea transport, intermodal transport systems and their interoperability, management of road, sea and air traffic, clean urban transport and public transport'.[216] These areas are regarded to be directly in line with the sustainable development which is, as discussed in Chapters 1 and 3, one of the major aims underpinning the EU environmental policy.

However, cohesion policy still remains a very controversial policy, with important concerns remaining such as the lack of strategic planning, lack of

[216] *Ibid.*

focus on priorities and a lack of political and policy debate on results.[217] Moreover, many other EU objectives beyond regional disparities are associated with structural funds over time comprising 'economic growth, competitiveness, employment, sustainable development, subsidiarity, regionalism and good governance including participation of civil society as well as with bringing the EU "closer to citizens"'.[218] Hence, there is a question of multiplicity of policy goals, compromised policy effectiveness and the ability to deliver results. Similarly, regional policy is associated with a great number of objectives, only one of which is environmental protection.

In the same vein, agricultural policy has undergone several reforms, as it had become unsustainable in its original form.[219] As was the case with other policy areas, the Common Agricultural Policy (CAP) did not originally take environmental protection into consideration, but has gradually become greener. In addition, the issue of GMOs brings a dilemma of whether the EU 'should relax' the precautionary principle in relation to the CAP.[220] One of the recent CAP reforms was the introduction of the Single Farm Payment System, whereby direct support to farmers is subject to the principle of cross-compliance, meaning that farmers must comply with public health, animal and plant health standards, environmental standards and animal welfare standards in order to receive payments under the CAP.[221]

Finally, the European Maritime and Fisheries Fund, with a budget of €5.7 billion, encourages sustainable fishing and sustainable aquaculture.[222] Some of the funding opportunities for the protection of the environment include the support of low impact equipment; management, restoration

---

[217] 'An Agenda for a Reformed Cohesion Policy: A place-based approach to meeting European Union challenges and expectations', Independent Report prepared at the request of Danuta Hübner, Commissioner for Regional Policy, by Fabrizio Barca: http://admin.interact-eu.net/downloads/1224/Agenda_Reformed_Cohesion_Policy_04_2009.pdf. See also John Bachtler and Ivan Turok, *The Coherence of EU Regional Policy: Contrasting Perspectives on the Structural Funds* (Routledge, 2013) and John Bachtler and Colin Wren, 'Evaluation of European Union Cohesion Policy: Research Questions and Policy Challenges' (2006) 40(2) *Regional Studies* 143–153.

[218] David Allen, 'Cohesion and Structural Funds' in Wallace et al., *Policy-Making in the European Union*, 6th edn., 230.

[219] See more in Hix and Høyland, *The Political System of the European Union*, 224–229.

[220] Christilla Roederer-Rynning, 'The Common Agricultural Policy: The Fortress Challenged' in Wallace et al., *Policy-Making in the European Union*, 6th edn., 198.

[221] Arts. 4 and 5 Council Regulation (EC) No 73/2009 establishing common rules for direct support schemes for farmers under the common agricultural policy and establishing certain support schemes for farmers, amending Regulations (EC) No 1290/2005, (EC) No 247/2006, (EC) No 378/2007 and repealing Regulation (EC) No 1782/2003, OJ 2009 L 30.

[222] Art. 1 Regulation (EU) No. 508/2014 of the European Parliament and of the Council on the European Maritime and Fisheries Fund and repealing Council Regulations (EC) No. 2328/2003, (EC) No. 861/2006, (EC) No. 1198/2006, and (EC) No. 791/2007 and Regulation (EU) No. 1255/2011 of the European Parliament and of the Council, OJ L 149.

and monitoring of Natura 2000 sites and of other marine protected areas; permanent cessation of fishing activities to reduce the fishing pressure from fleet segments in overcapacity, and climate change mitigation measures in particular through energy audits and changes of fishing vessel engines to increase energy efficiency and to reduce emissions.[223]

---

[223] 'Questions and Answers on the new European Maritime and Fisheries Fund (EMFF)': europa.eu/rapid/press-release_MEMO-14-311_en.doc.

3

Principles in EU Environmental Law

Introduction

One of the characteristic features of environmental law is the importance it attaches to principles. As de Sadeleer argues, environmental law is 'a goal oriented discipline, marked by the presence of an array of principles'.[1] This begs, of course, the question as to what precisely is meant by a legal 'principle'. In distinguishing between rules and principles in his classic work, *Taking Rights Seriously*, Dworkin notes that, while both principles and rules point to particular decisions about legal obligations, they differ in the character of the directions that they give.[2] While rules stipulate answers, due to their specificity and their concrete nature, principles state reasons giving arguments in one direction, but do not necessitate a particular result.[3]

Within EU law, a distinction should be made between what are termed 'general' principles of EU law, on the one hand, and principles specific to EU environmental law, on the other. The precise meaning of a 'principle', or indeed a 'general principle', of EU law is a matter of some controversy. Summing up the academic commentary on the issue, Tridimas suggests a distinction between two types of 'general principle' of EU law:

(a) Principles which 'derive from the rule of law', such as the public law principles of the protection of fundamental rights, equality, proportionality, legal certainty, the protection of legitimate expectations and the rights of defence; and
(b) 'Systemic principles' which underlie the constitutional structure of the Union, such as the principles of supremacy of EU law, direct effect, attribution of competences, subsidiarity and the Article 4(3) TEU duty of loyal or sincere cooperation.[4]

In many, but not all,[5] cases, the existence of these principles as fundamental constitutional principles of the EU legal order was 'discovered' first by the CJEU, on the basis that they were inherent, albeit not explicit, in the Community legal

---

[1] Nicolas de Sadeleer, 'Environmental Principles, Modern and Post-Modern Law' in Richard Macrory, Ian Havercroft and Ray Purdy (eds.), *Principles of European Environmental Law* (Europa Law Publishing, 2004), 231.
[2] Ronald Dworkin, *Taking Rights Seriously* (Gerald Duckworth & Co, 1997), 24.
[3] *Ibid.*, 26.
[4] Takis Tridimas, *The General Principles of EU Law* (2nd edn., Oxford University Press, 2007), 4.
[5] For instance, the principle of attribution of competences and the principle of loyal cooperation were present from the Treaty of Rome.

order.[6] In some (but not all)[7] cases, they have subsequently been written in to the Treaty expressly.[8]

Distinct from these fundamental constitutional principles applicable across EU law generally stand the discrete principles of particular substantive areas of EU law, including those of EU environmental law.

Article 191(2) TFEU

Union policy on the environment shall aim at a high level of protection taking into account the diversity of situations in the various regions of the Union. It shall be based on the precautionary principle and on the principles that preventive action should be taken, that environmental damage should as a priority be rectified at source and that the polluter should pay.

As is evident from the above, Article 191(2) TFEU provides for four principles on which the Union's environmental policy 'shall be based': the precautionary principle, the principle that preventive action should be taken (the 'preventive principle'), the principle that environmental damage should as a priority be rectified at source (the 'rectification at source principle') and the principle that the polluter should pay (the 'polluter pays principle'). To these must be added the Article 11 TFEU requirement to integrate environmental protection requirements into the definition and implementation of all Union policies and activities (the 'integration principle').

Again, it is a point of some debate whether these principles might aptly be described as 'general' principles of EU law.[9] In an obvious sense, they are not general, in the sense that they are expressly stated to be the basis of only one field of EU law, namely, EU environmental law. In another sense, however, the very essence of the Article 11 TFEU environmental integration principle, also reflected in Article 37 of the Charter of Fundamental Rights of the EU, is that principles of EU environmental policy should also be integrated into all other EU policy areas. In that vein, it is notable that the environmental integration principle was originally located in the environmental title of what is now the TFEU (formerly at Article 130 r), but was subsequently 'promoted' into the general provisions of the Treaty with the Treaty of Amsterdam (to become what was then Article 6 EC). Similarly, the principle of subsidiarity was originally located in the environmental title, but subsequently moved to the general provisions of what is now the TEU.[10] The CJEU has itself described the precautionary principle as a 'general principle' of EU law.[11]

---

[6] On supremacy, direct effect and national procedural autonomy, see, further, Chapter 7.
[7] For instance, the principles of supremacy and direct effect still do not appear expressly in the Treaties.
[8] For instance, the principle of respect for fundamental rights.
[9] See, for instance, Tridimas, as above, 5, who describes them as such.
[10] See Art. 5(3) TEU.
[11] Joined Cases T-74/00 etc. *Artegodan* ECLI:EU:T:2002:283, para. 184.

In reality, the critical question from a legal perspective is perhaps not whether the label 'general principle' can or should be placed on an individual principle, but rather as to the legal status and effect of the particular principle at issue, which ultimately can only be determined by the CJEU.

Legal Status and Effect of (Environmental) Principles in EU Law

As mentioned above, in the case of the four principles set out in Article 191(2) TFEU, the Treaty states that the Union's 'policy on the environment' 'shall be based' on these principles. Thus, for instance, the EU's current Environmental Action Programme expressly states that the Article 191(2) TFEU principles form the basis for that programme.[12] This mandatory directive to EU policy-makers leaves open, however, the question of the legal status of the principles of the Union's environmental policy. Here again, the CJEU's approach to the different individual principles has varied, and generalisations are therefore dangerous. The specific case law on each individual principle is considered further below.

Nevertheless, the status of the principles as interpretative aids for the CJEU (and, when acting within the scope of EU law, national courts) is clear: the CJEU has frequently made use of the principles to interpret provisions of EU law.[13] Due in particular to the Article 11 TFEU integration principle, this includes measures going outside the realms of EU environmental law in the sense of measures based on Article 192 TFEU.[14]

The CJEU has also, for instance, relied on environmental principles in legal basis disputes as to whether EU legislation was properly adopted on the environmental legal basis contained in what is now Article 192 TFEU. In *Commission v. Council (Waste Directive)*, for instance, the CJEU reasoned that, as a key aim of the Waste Directive was to implement the rectification at source principle, the Directive had properly been adopted on the basis of what is now Article 192 TFEU, rather than what is now Article 114 TFEU on achieving the internal market.[15]

A further question is the extent to which these principles may constitute a self-standing ground of review of legality of EU law and/or of Member State action falling within the scope of EU law. It would seem from the CJEU's case law to date (insofar as it has considered the matter) that this will only be possible in case

---

[12] Seventh Environmental Action Programme, OJ 2013 L 354/171, Art. 2(2).
[13] See, for instance, Case C-2/90 *Commission v. Belgium* ECLI:EU:C:1992:310 ('*Walloon Waste*'); Case C-379/98 *PreussenElektra* ECLI:EU:C:2001:160; Case C-127/02 *Landelijke Vereniging tot Behoud van de Waddenzee* ECLI:EU:C:2004:482; Case C-573/12 *Ålands Vindkraft* v. *Energimyndigheten* ECLI:EU:C:2014:2037.
[14] See the CJEU in Case C-77/09 *Gowan* ECLI:EU:C:2010:803, at para. 71, using this reasoning.
[15] Case C-155/91 ECLI:EU:C:1993:98, para. 14.

of a manifest failure to respect the principle at issue.[16] This is consistent with the notion that policy-makers enjoy a wide discretion in deciding how best to implement the principles at issue in practice. Again, following the logic of Article 11 TFEU, such a legality review would not be restricted to a review of EU measures passed on the basis of Article 192 TFEU. Nevertheless, in *Raffinerie Méditerranée*, the CJEU held that the polluter pays principle did not apply to national legislation which fell outside the scope of EU environmental legislation adopted on the basis of Article 192 TFEU (in that case, the Environmental Liability Directive).[17] The CJEU reasoned that what is now Article 191 TFEU, which establishes the polluter pays principle, is directed at action at EU level, and 'cannot be relied on as such by individuals in order to exclude the application of national legislation ... in an area covered by environmental policy for which there is no [EU] legislation adopted on the basis of Article [192] TFEU that specifically covers the situation in question.'

An important distinction should be drawn between 'principles' and 'aims' of EU environmental law. As discussed in Chapter 1, within the latter category fall the Article 3 TEU aims of, for instance, sustainable development and a high level of protection of the environment, as well as the aims of EU environmental policy set out in Article 191(1) TFEU. Such aims are often considered to be principally aspirational or directive in nature. Nevertheless, one sees in a variety of judgments the CJEU drawing on these aims in interpreting a provision of EU law, in a manner not unlike its use of 'principles'. Again, therefore, the distinction between the legal status of a 'principle' and an 'aim' can, in practice, be a fine one. This was the case, for instance, in *Commission v. Italy* where Italy's disrespect of the Article 191(1) TFEU aim of protecting human health and the quality of the environment in waste management was regarded as an indication that it had exceeded the discretion conferred by Directive 2006/12.[18]

In addition to the above-mentioned principles and aims of Union environmental policy, Article 191(3) TFEU provides that, in preparing its policy on the environment, the Union 'shall take account' of available scientific and technical data, environmental conditions in the various regions of the Union, the potential benefits and costs of action or lack of action, the economic and social development of the Union as a whole and the balanced development of its regions. Clearly, respect for this provision constitutes a procedural requirement rather than an obligation to respect any substantive principle. Article 191(3) TFEU does, however, provide an insight into the EU's regulatory philosophy in this field which, as discussed in Chapter 1, has veered towards economisation of environmental costs and benefits in recent years.

---

[16] See, for instance, *Bettati*, cited; *Gowan*, *ibid.*; Opinion of A. G. Geelhoed in Case C-161/04 *Austria* v. *Parliament and Council* ECLI:EU:C:2006:66, paras. 59–60.
[17] Case C-378/08 *Commission* v. *Council* ECLI:EU:C:2010:126, para. 46. See, further, Chapter 6.
[18] C-297/08 *Commission* v. *Italy* ECLI:EU:C:2010:115.

The Precautionary Principle

The precautionary principle was inserted into what is now Article 191 TFEU by the Treaty of Maastricht, and was originally derived from the Vorsorgeprinzip principle of German environmental law.[19] Although it is not defined anywhere in the Treaty, the CJEU has held that, as a matter of EU law, the precautionary principle requires that, 'where there is uncertainty as to the existence or extent of risks to the health of consumers, the institutions may take protective measures without having to wait until the reality and the seriousness of those risks become fully apparent'.[20]

In its 2000 Communication on the Precautionary Principle, the Commission defined the principle as a risk management strategy to be employed,

> where scientific evidence is insufficient, inconclusive or uncertain and there are indications through preliminary objective scientific evaluation that there are reasonable grounds for concern that the potential dangerous effects on the environment, human, animal or plant health may be inconsistent with the chosen level of protection.[21]

It is well-established that, although the principle appears in Title XX TFEU on environmental policy, it is also a vital principle in the fields of public health and the common agricultural policy.[22] Indeed, as aforementioned, the General Court has held that the principle constitutes a general principle of EU law.[23] This strong espousal of the legal status of the precautionary principle as a matter of EU law may be contrasted with its rather more controversial status in international environmental law.[24] The 1992 Rio Declaration, for instance, speaks of a precautionary 'approach', rather than a 'principle', although there is support in certain quarters for its recognition as a principle of international environmental law.[25]

---

[19] See Konrad von Moltke, *The* Vorsorgeprinzip *in West German Environmental Policy* (Institute for European Environmental Policy, 1987).

[20] *Gowan*, as above, para. 73; Case C-157/96 *National Farmers' Union* ECLI:EU:C:1998:191, para. 63; Case C-180/96 *United Kingdom* v. *Commission* ECLI:EU:C:1998:192, para. 99; Case C-236/01 *Monsanto Agricoltura Italia* ECLI:EU:C:2003:431, para. 111.

[21] Communication on the Precautionary Principle (COM(2000)1 final), at 9–10.

[22] See, for instance, *National Farmers' Union*, cited above, para. 64.

[23] Joined Cases T-74/00, T-76/00 et al. *Artegodan* v. *Commission* ECLI:EU:T:2002:283.

[24] See, for trenchant criticism of the precautionary principle, for instance, Cass Sunstein, *Laws of Fear: Beyond the Precautionary Principle* (Cambridge University Press, 2005).

[25] Rio Declaration on Environment and Development of 1992, Principle 15 ('In order to protect the environment, the precautionary approach shall be widely applied by States according to their capabilities. Where there are threats of serious or irreversible damage, lack of full scientific certainty shall not be used as a reason for postponing cost-effective measures to prevent environmental degradation'). See the dissenting judgment of Judge Weearmantry in Nuclear Tests (New Zealand request) (1995) ICJ Reports at 342.

According to the CJEU, the precautionary principle requires a two-stage analysis.[26] First, the potentially negative consequences for the environment or health (as the case may be) must be identified. Secondly, it requires a 'comprehensive assessment of the risk' to the environment or health, 'based on the most reliable scientific data available and the most recent results of international research'.[27]

If, following this analysis, it proves 'impossible to determine with certainty the existence or extent of the alleged risk because of the insufficiency, inconclusiveness or imprecision of the results of studies conducted', but there remains a 'likelihood of real harm' to the environment or public health if the risk materialises, the precautionary principle will apply to justify objective and non-discriminatory measures that would otherwise be prima facie precluded due to their restrictive nature.[28] Specifically, protective measures will be justified (whether by a Member State or EU institution) 'without having to wait until the reality and seriousness of those risks become fully apparent'.[29]

In terms of the legal effects of the principle, the CJEU has held that it will only annul a decision to apply the precautionary principle in this manner in case of manifest error.[30] This is consistent with the CJEU's position that, in areas of 'evolving and complex technology' requiring the assessment of 'highly complex scientific and technical facts', the EU Courts will be reluctant to substitute their view for those of the first instance expert decision-maker formed after an appropriate risk assessment.[31]

---

[26] *Gowan*, cited above, paras. 75–78; Case C-333/08 *Commission* v. *France* ECLI:EU:C:2010:44, paras. 92–93. See also Case T-13/99 *Pfizer Animal Health* v. *Council* ECLI:EU:T:2002:209, paras. 142–144 and 149–162. Compare the Commission's description of the principle in its Communication on the Precautionary Principle (COM(2000)1) ('where there are reasonable grounds for concern that potential hazards may affect the environment or human, animal or plant health, and when at the same time the available data preclude a detailed risk evaluation, the precautionary principle has been politically accepted as a risk management strategy').

[27] *Gowan*, cited above, paras. 75–78.

[28] *Ibid.*; Case C-269/13 P *Acino* v. *Commission* ECLI:EU:C:2014:255, para. 58; Case C-157/14 *Société Neptune Distribution* v. *Ministre de l'Économie et des Finances* ECLI:EU:C:2015:823, para. 82.

[29] Case C-157/14 *Société Neptune Distribution* v. *Ministre de l'Économie et des Finances*, *ibid.*, para. 81; Case C-269/13 P *Acino* v. *Commission*, *ibid.*, para. 57; Case T13/99 *Pfizer Animal Health* v. *Council* ECLI:EU:T:2002:209, para. 139. See, further, Case T70/99 *Alpharma* v. *Council* ECLI:EU:T:2002:210, paras. 152 and 154; Case C180/96 *United Kingdom* v. *Commission* ECLI:EU:C:1998:192, para. 99; Case C236/01 *Monsanto Agricoltura Italia and Others* ECLI:EU:C:2003:431, para. 111; Case C504/04 *Agrarproduktion Staebelow* ECLI:EU:C:2006:30, para. 39; and Case T177/02 *Malagutti-Vezinhet* v. *Commission* ECLI:EU:T:2004:72, para. 54.

[30] *Gowan*, para. 79; *Bettati*, cited above, para. 35; Joined Cases C-78/16 and Case C-79/16 *Pesce* v. *Presidenza del Consiglio dei Ministri* ECLI:EU:C:2016:428, para. 49.

[31] See, for instance, Case C343/09 *Afton Chemical* ECLI:EU:C:2010:419, para. 28, and Case C15/10 *Etimine* ECLI:EU:C:2011:504, paras. 59 and 60; Case T-456/11 *International Cadmium Association* v. *Commission* ECLI:EU:T:2013:594, para. 45.

By contrast, the precautionary principle will not justify action taken where the evidence shows that the risks to the environment or human health are merely hypothetical.[32] Further, the principle must be applied in a manner consistent with the principle of proportionality.[33] In addition, it is not enough for a decision-maker simply to rely on the fact that an expert scientific risk evaluation has been carried out: rather, the ultimate decision-maker must be given sufficiently reliable and cogent information to allow it to understand the ramifications of the scientific question raised and to decide on a policy in 'full knowledge of the facts'.[34] A decision-maker cannot, therefore, merely delegate the risk assessment to scientists and avoid taking a view itself: its decisions must, in order not to be considered arbitrary, be based on as 'thorough a scientific evaluation of the risks as possible, account being taken of the particular circumstances of the case at issue'.[35] In *International Cadmium Association* v. *Commission*, for instance, the General Court annulled a Commission Regulation adding certain cadmium pigments to Annex VII of the REACH Regulation, thus restricting their use, on the basis that the Commission had not adequately evaluated all of the relevant factors and circumstances and had, therefore, manifestly erred in concluding, albeit on the basis of scientific evidence, that there was a risk to human health and the environment.[36]

Within the environmental context, the principle has been particularly important in interpreting the environmental guarantee and safeguard clauses, discussed in Chapter 1. These clauses – namely, Articles 114(4), (5) and (10), and 193 TFEU – permit Member States under certain conditions to prefer a higher level of environmental protection. The CJEU has held, for instance, that the safeguard clauses adopted pursuant to Article 114(10) TFEU contained in EU environmental legislation regulating genetically modified organisms (GMOs) are an expression of the precautionary principle, and that they therefore must be interpreted in the light of this principle.[37]

An example of such a safeguard clause is Article 23 of Directive 2001/18 on the deliberate release of GMOs into the environment,[38] which provides that,

---

[32] See, for instance, *Pfizer*, para. 143; Case T-229/04 *Sweden* v. *Commission* ECLI:EU:T:2007:217, para. 161; Case T-392/02 Solvay ECLI:EU:T:2003:277, para. 129.
[33] Joined Cases C-78/16 and C-79/16 *Pesce* v. *Presidenza del Consiglio dei Ministri* ECLI:EU:C:2016:428, para. 48.
[34] Case T-456/11 *International Cadmium Association* v. *Commission* ECLI:EU:T:2013:594, para. 52.
[35] Case T13/99 *Pfizer Animal Health* v. *Council* ECLI:EU:T:2002:209, para. 162; Case T-456/11 *International Cadmium Association* v. *Commission, ibid.*, para. 52.
[36] Case T-456/11 *International Cadmium Association* v. *Commission, ibid.*
[37] Case C-236/01 *Monsanto* ECLI:EU:C:2003:431. On the regulation of GMOs, see, further, Chapter 13.
[38] Directive 2001/18/EC of the European Parliament and of the Council of 12 March 2001 on the deliberate release into the environment of genetically modified organisms and repealing Council Directive 90/220/EEC, OJ 2001 L 106/1.

> Where a Member State, as a result of new or additional information made available since the date of the consent and affecting the environmental risk assessment or reassessment of existing information on the basis of new or additional scientific knowledge, has detailed grounds for considering that a GMO as or in a product which has been properly notified and has received written consent under this Directive constitutes a risk to human health or the environment, that Member State may provisionally restrict or prohibit the use and/or sale of that GMO as or in a product on its territory.
>
> The Member State shall ensure that in the event of a severe risk, emergency measures, such as suspension or termination of the placing on the market, shall be applied, including information to the public ...

In such cases, Member States have an obligation to inform the Commission and other Member States immediately, providing *inter alia* reasons and the environmental risk assessment, with the Commission to take a decision on the matter within 60 days, to which time period is added, for instance, the time necessary to consult the Scientific Committee as provided for in Article 30(2) of that Directive.

It is unsurprising that, given the wide divergence of views at political but also citizen level on GMOs and their safety within the EU, numerous Member States have chosen to make use of this safeguard clause to ban the use and/or sale of certain GMO products within their territory (at the time of writing, Austria, France, Greece, Hungary, Germany and Luxembourg apply the clause).

While the reasons for such flexibility as to GMOs may be clear on an internal EU level, it has caused major problems for the EU on the world stage, most notably in the context of the WTO, where the EU's GMO system has been found to contravene WTO rules and to be unjustified by the precautionary principle. In *EC-Biotech*, the WTO Panel found that the EC's application of its GMO rules, including Member States' actions in taking safeguard measures prohibiting the import and marketing of specific GMO products within their territory, contravened the WTO's SPS Agreement.[39] In particular, the WTO Panel held that no adequate scientific risk assessment had been carried out for the purposes of Article 5.1 of the SPS Agreement in taking the impugned safeguard measures. In June 2014, political agreement was reached within the EU to replace the EU's current GMO legislation with a new settlement which increases flexibility for Member States to ban cultivation of certain GMO products on their territory, which has led to a 2015 amendment to Directive 2001/18 to allow greater scope for Member States to restrict or prohibit the cultivation of GMOs in their territory,[40] and a 2015

---

[39] DS291 European Communities – Measures Affecting the Approval and Marketing of Biotech Products.

[40] Directive 2015/412 of the European Parliament and of the Council of 11 March 2015 amending Directive 2001/18/EC as regards the possibility for the Member States to restrict

Proposal amending Regulation 1829/2003 on genetically modified food and feed.[41]

The precautionary principle has also been crucial in the field of habitat protection. In *Waddenzee*, the CJEU interpreted Article 6(3) of the Habitats Directive[42] in light of the precautionary principle to hold that an appropriate assessment of the implications of a plan or project for a protected site's conservation objectives must be carried out if it 'cannot be excluded, on the basis of objective information, that it will have a significant effect on that site, either individually or in combination with other plans or projects'.[43] Following such assessment, the activity could be authorised only if the national authorities 'have made certain that it will not adversely affect the integrity of the site', meaning that 'no reasonable scientific doubt remains as to the absence of such effects'.[44] Where a Member State can show that their plan or project is necessary for imperative requirements of public interest, however, Article 6(4) permits them to go ahead as long as they take 'compensatory measures' to ensure that the overall coherence of Natura 2000 is protected.[45] It is evident that the duty which this places on national authorities is particularly exacting: it will often be very difficult to be 'certain' that a plan/project will have no adverse effects on a site's integrity, and scientists will often disagree in their predictions of what precisely those effects may be.

A final field where the precautionary principle has been particularly influential is that of EU chemicals regulation. The EU's flagship REACH Regulation, discussed in detail in Chapter 13, is expressly based on the principle, in the context of the broader aim of ensuring a high level of protection of human health and the environment.[46] Nevertheless, as the *International Cadmium Association* judgment discussed above illustrates, the EU courts have demonstrated their willingness to exercise robust judicial review of the limits of the precautionary principle even in the context of legislation explicitly based on this principle.[47]

---

or prohibit the cultivation of genetically modified organisms (GMOs) in their territory, OJ 2015 L68/1. See recital (2) to the Preamble which provides that 'The precautionary principle should always be taken into account in the framework of Directive 2001/18/EC and its subsequent implementation.'

[41] COM(2015)177.

[42] Directive 92/43 of 21 May 1992 on the conservation of natural habitats and of wild fauna and flora, OJ 1992 L 206/7. See, further, Chapter 12.

[43] *Waddenzee*, cited above, para. 45.

[44] Ibid., para. 61. In *Sweetman* v. *An Bord Pleanála*, the ECJ interpreted the requirement not adversely to affect the 'integrity of the site' as requiring 'the lasting preservation of the constitutive characteristics of the site concerned that are connected to the presence of [the] natural habitat type' being protected: Case C-258/11 ECLI:EU:C:2013:220.

[45] In the case of priority species, the permissible justifications are more narrowly defined: see Art. 6(4).

[46] Regulation 1907/2006 REF, recital (69) of the Preamble. See Case C558/07 *S.P.C.M. and Others* ECLI:EU:C:2009:430, para. 45, and the discussion in Chapter 13.

[47] Case T-456/11 *International Cadmium Association* v. *Commission*, cited above.

The Preventive Principle

The principle that 'preventive action should be taken' has been present in what is now Article 191 TFEU since the environmental title was first inserted into the Treaty with the Single European Act. The idea behind the preventive principle is the simple adage that prevention is better than cure, i.e. it is simpler, and probably cheaper and more effective, to avoid pollution in the first place than to try and clean it up afterwards. This philosophy can be seen underlying a great many of the EU's environmental laws and policies, particularly those involving pollution control such as the Industrial Emissions Directive, the Environmental Liability Directive and the Waste Directive.[48] A version thereof is also to be found in international environmental law, as expressed in Principle 21 of the Stockholm Declaration on the Human Environment 1972, which provides that States have 'the responsibility to ensure that activities within their jurisdiction or control do not cause damage to the environment of other States or of areas beyond the limits of national jurisdiction'.

The prevention principle is often discussed together with the precautionary principle, as both principles may be viewed as having a similar objective, namely, the elimination or prevention of environmental harm or damage. The close relationship between the two principles has led some to argue that, in fact, they may be used interchangeably.[49] Others contend that the prevention principle applies in situations when the relevant risk is 'quantifiable'[50] or 'known'[51] and there is a certainty that the damage will occur. The lack of a clear distinction between the two principles has, indeed, resulted in difficulties in legal translation of CJEU judgments in the field. Good examples are the CJEU's judgments on measures adopted in the BSE crisis, *National Farmers' Union*[52] and *UK v. Commission*[53] where the English version of the judgments refers to the prevention principle only, while the German[54] and other language versions[55] use a phrase meaning 'precautionary and prevention principle'.[56] Nevertheless, it is undoubtedly the case that the rich CJEU jurisprudence discussed above has evolved specifically in the context of the

---

[48] Directive 2010/75 on industrial emissions (integrated pollution prevention and control), OJ 2010 L334/17; Directive 2004/35 on environmental liability regarding the prevention and remedying of environmental damage, OJ 2004 L 143/56; and Directive 2008/89 on waste (Waste Framework Directive), OJ 2008 L 312/3. See e.g. Opinion of A. G. Kokott, Case 378/08 *Raffinerie Méditerranée* [2010] ECR I-919, paras. 54–76.

[49] See Krämer, *EU Environmental Law*, 24.

[50] Wybe T. Douma, 'The Precautionary Principle in the European Union' (2000) 9(2) *Review of European Community & International Environmental Law* 132.

[51] Elizabeth Fisher, 'Environmental Principles and Environmental Justice', 318.

[52] C-157/96 ECLI:EU:C:1998:191.   [53] Case C-180/96 ECLI:EU:C:1998:192.

[54] 'Grundsätzen der Vorsorge und Vorbeugung'.

[55] ES: 'principios de cautela y de acción preventiva', DA: 'forsigtighedsprincippet og princippet om forebyggende indsats', FR: 'principes de précaution et d'action preventive'.

[56] 'Studies on translation and multilingualism, Language and Translation in International Law and EU Law', European Commission, 6/2012, 113.

precautionary principle, and the prevention principle has been the subject of far less jurisprudence to date.

The Rectification at Source Principle

The principle that environmental damage should 'as a priority be rectified at source' has, like the preventive principle, been in the Treaty since the Single European Act, but has never been the subject of much jurisprudence or debate. Again, this is in large part because it is rather ambiguous by nature. One can extract from this principle, for instance, that a polluter should bear responsibility for cleaning up its own pollution, and that a polluting region should bear responsibility for cleaning up pollution coming from within its jurisdiction. The latter point is present in what remains the leading CJEU judgment on the topic, *Walloon Waste*. In this judgment, the CJEU held that, while a regional ban on imports of hazardous waste amounted to a restriction on free movement of goods that was *prima facie* contrary to what is now Article 34 TFEU, interpreting this Article in light of the rectification at source principle, the ban should not be considered to be discriminatory, and could be justified on environmental protection grounds.[57] In contrast, in *Sydhavnens*, the rectification at source principle did not justify a restriction on export of non-hazardous waste, where such waste was destined for recovery.[58]

The rectification at source principle is implicit in much of the EU's legislation on waste (including, for instance, the Waste Framework Directive, discussed in Chapter 14) and the Environmental Liability Directive (discussed in Chapter 6).[59] By contrast, it is clear that the principle does not impose any absolute obligation for legislators to seek to ensure that polluters 'rectify' pollution in any normal sense of the term. As discussed in Chapter 4, for instance, the regulatory philosophy underlying the EU's flagship market-based environmental regulatory instruments (such as the EU's Emissions Trading Scheme) is not to rectify pollution at source but simply to place a price on it which, if paid by the polluter, will render the polluting activity perfectly legal.

The Polluter Pays Principle

Prior to its insertion into the Treaty with the Single European Act, the polluter pays principle was already well established as a principle of international environmental law and indeed as a first principle of environmental economics, insofar as it

---

[57] *Walloon Waste*, paras. 34–35.
[58] Case C-209/98 *Sydhavnens* ECLI:EU:C:2000:279. See also Case C-292/12 *Ragn-Sells* ECLI:EU:C:2013:820.
[59] Directive 2004/35/CE of the European Parliament and of the Council of 21 April 2004 on environmental liability with regard to the prevention and remedying of environmental damage, OJ 2004 L 143/56.

requires those who cause environmental damage to pay for it.[60] It had also been embraced by the Commission as early as its first Environmental Action Programme of 1973.[61] This led to a Commission Communication on the matter subsequently endorsed by the Council in a 1975 Recommendation. The Communication defined the polluter pays principle as meaning that,

> natural or legal persons governed by public or private law who are responsible for pollution must pay the costs of such measures as are necessary to eliminate that pollution or to reduce it so as to comply with the standards or equivalent measures which enable quality objectives to be met or, where there are no such objectives, so as to comply with the standards or equivalent measures laid down by the public authorities.
>
> Consequently, environmental protection should not in principle depend on policies which rely on grants of aid and place the burden of combating pollution on the Community.[62]

Of further relevance here is Article 192(4) TFEU, which provides that, 'without prejudice to certain measures adopted by the Union', the Member States shall finance and implement the EU's environmental policy. An important caveat to this principle is added by Article 192(5) TFEU, enabling derogation from Member States' Article 192(4) TFEU obligations, and/or financial support from the EU's Cohesion Fund, if national authorities are faced with costs 'deemed disproportionate'. While this provision is expressed to be 'without prejudice to' the polluter pays principle, it effectively implies that, as a matter of EU constitutional law, Member States will not be responsible for the costs of cleaning up pollution in their own jurisdiction where such costs are 'deemed' disproportionate.

In practice, EU environmental law as it stands implements the polluter pays principle only imperfectly, and there are many exceptions where society at large ends up bearing the cost of pollution caused by a subsection of the population. A good example is the EU's State aid policy, where a polluter pays approach is evident in some of the Commission and CJEU case law (especially on the definition of aid),[63] but is notably absent

---

[60] See the 1972 OECD Council Recommendation on Guiding Principles Concerning the International Economic Aspects of Environmental Policies, the 1974 OECD Council Recommendation on the Implementation of the Polluter Pays Principle and the discussion in Sands and Peel, *Principles of International Environmental Law*. See, subsequently, Principle 16 of the 1992 Rio Declaration on Environment and Development.

[61] OJ 1973 C 112/1.

[62] Annex to Council Recommendation 75/436/Euratom, ECSC, EEC regarding cost allocation and action by public authorities on environmental matters, OJ 1975 L 194/1, point 2.

[63] For instance, where an undertaking has polluted a particular site, a grant by the State to clean up the pollution will, in compliance with the polluter pays principle, constitute aid unless the clean-up costs are subsequently recovered from the polluter. In Commission Decision 1999/272/EC *Kiener Deponie Bachmanning*, OJ 1999 L 109/51, for example, the Commission held that the owner of a contaminated site was responsible for

in other areas.[64] Thus, under the EU's Guidelines on State aid for environmental protection and energy, it is still permissible for the State to subsidise a company's own waste management, and even for the State to grant subsidies to environmentally damaging activities, as long as the conditions set out in Article 107 TFEU are otherwise met.[65] More broadly, however, the effect of a polluter pays approach can be seen clearly in the EU's waste policy, which requires the cost of disposing of waste to be borne by the waste producer or by the current or previous waste holders,[66] and in certain elements of its water policy.[67] A polluter pays approach is also evident in the EU's embrace of market-based instruments (such as emissions trading) in environmental policy, which instruments aim to factor in the cost of environmental damage within the market's price mechanism. Market-based instruments of environmental regulation are discussed further in Chapter 4.

The polluter pays principle also expressly underpins the Environmental Liability Directive, discussed further in Chapter 6, and has frequently been considered by the CJEU in the context of that Directive. In *Raffinerie Méditerranée*, the CJEU applied

decontamination costs. As the Austrian authorities had financed the clean-up operation, the Commission decided that no State aid would be involved as long as the costs were recovered from the owner. In contrast, in Commission Decision N 856/97 *Schmid Schraubenwerke*, OJ 1998 C 409/5 the Commission decided that a grant for the decontamination of an industrial site, which had suffered past environmental damage as a result of the operation of a chemical plant, did not confer any advantage on the present owner, who was not responsible for the pollution and who had not been aware that he would have been responsible for it when he purchased the site. XXVIIIth Report on Competition Policy (1998) at 256. See Kingston, *Greening EU Competition Law and Policy*, chapter 12.

[64] See, further, the observations of A. G. Jacobs in Case C-126/01 *GEMO* ECLI:EU:C:2003:622 on the significance of the polluter pays principle for Art. 107(1): 'the principle is used as an analytical tool to allocate responsibility according to economic criteria for the costs entailed by the pollution in question. A given measure will constitute State aid where it relieves those liable under the polluter pays principle from their primary responsibility to bear the costs.' He contrasts this with the significance of the polluter pays principle in Art. 107(3), where it 'is used by contrast in a prescriptive way as a policy criterion. It is relied on to argue that the costs of environmental protection should as a matter of sound environmental and State aid policy ultimately be borne by the polluters themselves rather than by States' (paras. 68–70).

[65] Commission Communication, Guidelines on State aid for environmental protection and energy 2014–2020, OJ 2014, C 200/1, paras. 6 and 158–159 (namely para. 156, noting the polluter pays principle).

[66] See the Waste Framework Directive 2008/98/EC Directive 2008/98/EC of the European Parliament and of the Council of 19 November 2008 on waste and repealing certain Directives, OJ 2008 L 312/3, Art. 14, and see, further, Chapter 14. Member States are, however, left with considerable discretion as to how to measure the costs of waste disposal: see Case C-254/08 Futura Immobiliare ECLI:EU:C:2009:479.

[67] See Art. 9 of the Water Framework Directive which outlines full-cost pricing for water in accordance with the polluter pays principle: Directive 2000/60/EC of the European Parliament and of the Council establishing a framework for the Community action in the field of water policy, OJ 2000 L 327/1, discussed in Chapter 10.

the polluter pays principle to hold that a competent authority must have 'plausible evidence' capable of justifying a presumption that a particular operator had in fact caused the pollution at issue.[68]

The Environmental Integration Principle

Article 11 TFEU

Environmental protection requirements must be integrated into the definition and implementation of the Union's policies and activities, in particular with a view to promoting sustainable development.

The environmental integration principle, in its current form, has been present in what is now the TFEU since the Treaty of Amsterdam. A weaker version of this provision, requiring only that environmental considerations be a 'component' of other Community policies, was inserted by the Single European Act into the environmental title of the Treaty. The Treaty of Amsterdam, however, elevated the principle to Part One of the Treaty, as one of the generally applicable principles in the EU's legal order. Its position has been further strengthened by its inclusion, in largely identical terms, in the Charter of Fundamental Rights of the European Union, Article 37 of which provides that, 'A high level of environmental protection and the improvement of the quality of the environment must be integrated into the policies of the Union and ensured in accordance with the principle of sustainable development.'

Aside from its position in the Treaty and the Charter, the language of Article 11 TFEU makes clear that it is of a different nature to the Article 191(2) TFEU principles. Rather than simply stating that EU 'policy' must be 'based on' the principle, it goes much further, mandating that environmental protection requirements be integrated into the 'definition and implementation' of the EU's 'policies and activities' (emphasis added). It is evident, therefore, that this is not just a high-level directive to policy-makers, but is a mandatory requirement for all decisions taken by EU bodies. The distinctive strength of the provision is further highlighted by comparison with the 'integration' clauses inserted by the Treaty of Lisbon for other policy areas such as consumer protection, discrimination and social protection, which are phrased in weaker terms.[69] Indeed, it may be argued that the very inclusion of the integration obligation within the EUCFR, and its consequent characterisation as a fundamental human right within the EU, denotes a recognition that environmental protection constitutes one of the core values upon which the Union is founded, within

---

[68] See, further, Chapter 6.
[69] Arts. 8–10 and 12–13 TFEU. See *contra*, however, Jan H. Jans, 'Stop the Integration Principle?' (2011) 33 *Fordham International Law Journal* 1533.

the meaning of Article 2 TEU.[70] The concept of a *value* of the Union is, it is reasonable to conclude from the post-Lisbon structure of the TEU, something distinct from (and perhaps even more fundamental than) an *aim* or *task* of the Union.

Despite the strength of the legal provision, the practical implementation of the integration principle has been rather disappointing to date from the environmental protection perspective. In 1998, the European Council launched the Cardiff process, by which different formations of the Council of Ministers were requested to develop strategies to achieve environmental integration, starting with energy, transport and agriculture.[71] This led, at the Council of Ministers level, to the development of bilateral integration strategies and programmes for a wide number of Council formations, including the internal market (which encompasses competition policy),[72] industry,[73] development,[74] fisheries,[75] general affairs and external relations[76] and economic and financial affairs[77] formations, in addition to the energy,[78] transport[79] and agriculture[80] formations. At the Commission level, a variety of bilateral sectoral environmental integration strategies have been developed in a wide range of policy areas, mirroring the Council's sectoral strategies.[81] In 2004, the Commission undertook to carry out

---

[70] See Art. 2 TEU, 'The Union is founded on the values of respect for human dignity, freedom, democracy, equality, the rule of law and respect for human rights, including the rights of persons belonging to minorities.' Environmental protection is not otherwise mentioned as one of the fundamental values of the Union within this Article, but by virtue of the EUCFR the environmental integration obligation may be included within the concept of respect for human rights. On the history of the drafting of what is now the Art. 11 TFEU integration obligation, see Julian Nowag, 'The Sky is the Limit: On the Drafting of Art. 11 TFEU's Integration Obligation and its Intended Reach' in Beate Sjåfjell and Anja Wiesbrock (eds.), *The Greening of European Business under EU Law: Taking Article 11 TFEU Seriously* (Routledge, 2014).

[71] The Cardiff Summit followed a Commission Communication, 'Partnership for Integration' (COM(98) 333), which identified a variety of necessary steps to translate what is now Art. 11 TFEU into concrete results.

[72] See the Council's report to the Helsinki European Council, November 1999, doc. No. 13622/99.

[73] *Ibid.*   [74] *Ibid.*

[75] See the Council Conclusions on integration of environment and sustainable development into the Common Fisheries Policy, 26 April 2001, doc. No. 7885/01.

[76] See the COREPER Report 7791/01 of 4 April 2001, adopted at the General Affairs Council of 10 April 2001.

[77] See the Council's Report to the Nice European Council of 27 November 2000, doc. No. 13054/1/00.

[78] See the Council's adoption of an energy integration strategy, November 1999, doc. No. 9994/99.

[79] See e.g. Council Resolution, 'Follow-up to the Cardiff/Helsinki Summit on the integration of environment and sustainable development into the transport policy', doc. No. 7329/01.

[80] See the Council's adoption of an agriculture integration strategy, 15 November 1999, doc. No. 13078/99.

[81] Commission Communication, 'Partnership for Integration', COM(98) 333 final.

an annual stocktaking of the progress of the Cardiff process, but this was never followed up.[82] The main cross-cutting practical effort to implement Article 11 TFEU, however, is again the procedural requirement that the Commission must undertake an impact assessment when proposing all major policy measures, discussed above as a component of the EU's Sustainable Development Strategy (SDS).

At the CJEU level, the integration principle has been relied upon in cases on the relationship between EU free movement of goods law and environmental protection, discussed further below. More broadly, an integration approach is evident in fields such as public procurement and State aid.[83] The CJEU has also relied on the integration principle in a number of legal basis judgments, and has used it as an aid to the interpretation of secondary legislation,[84] including when deciding how to apply the Article 191(2) TFEU principles of EU environmental policy.[85] To date, however, the CJEU has stopped short of pronouncing the integration principle to form a self-standing ground of annulment of EU legislation, though some of its Advocates General would have gone this far.[86]

Focus on the Integration of EU Economic and Environmental Law and Policy

Overview

In terms of integrating economic concerns into EU environmental policy,[87] a decided turn towards emphasising the 'win–win' potential synergies between EU environmental and economic policies, and incorporating economic approaches into EU environmental policy, has been evident for some time. We see this, for instance, in the major shift towards use of (more economically efficient) market-based instruments, whether by their creation at EU level (e.g. emissions trading) or their promotion at national level (e.g. via the environmental

---

[82] See 'Integration of Environmental Considerations into other Policy Areas – A Stocktaking of the Cardiff Process', COM(2004)394 final, and Kingston, *Greening EU Competition Law and Policy*, chapter 3.
[83] See e.g. Case C-513/99 *Concordia Bus* ECLI:EU:C:2002:495.
[84] See e.g. the Opinion of A. G. Kokott, Case C-304/01 *Spain* v. *Commission* ECLI:EU:C:2003:619 (interpretation of fisheries legislation).
[85] See e.g. *Artegodan*, cited above.
[86] See e.g. A. G. Cosmas in Case C-321/95P *Greenpeace* ECLI:EU:C:1997:421, stating that the integration principle should be capable of direct effect; A. G. Geelhoed in Case C-161/04 *Austria* v. *Parliament and Council* ECLI:EU:C:2006:66, stating that review should be on the basis of manifest error. In the latter case, the Court never had an opportunity to rule on the matter, as Austria withdrew its action prior to judgment.
[87] Due to limitations of space, the present section takes only the examples of free movement of goods law and green public procurement. For detailed discussion of the interface between EU competition law and environmental considerations, see Kingston, *Greening EU Competition Law and Policy*, chapter 2.

State aid guidelines), discussed further in Chapter 4.[88] The encouragement of eco-innovation by promoting green public procurement within Member States, most recently in the 2014 legislative package on public procurement, also fits this paradigm.[89] However, perhaps the *pièce de résistance* of new environmentalism in this sense is the EU's Seventh Environment Action Programme (EAP), on which political agreement was reached in June 2013. The Seventh EAP sets out the nine overarching priority objectives of the EU's environmental policy up to 2020.[90] The intense effort to repackage environmental aims as, at the same time, economic aims is striking throughout this document, particularly when contrasted with previous EAPs. Indeed, the very first recital of this, the EU's key environmental policy road map for seven years, leads not with the EU's environmental aims *per se*, but rather with the starting point that the 'Union has set itself the objective of becoming a smart, sustainable and inclusive economy by 2020'. Even the EU's goals in biodiversity and nature conservation, a policy area which has not traditionally lent itself to an economic philosophy, has been rebranded in economic terms as the thematic priority of 'protecting, conserving and enhancing the Union's natural capital',[91] emphasising the role of biodiversity and ecosystems as a necessary input into the Union's economy. In fields as diverse as habitats protection to enforcement, the need for increased EU activity is now argued for by DG environment, therefore, on the basis of the economic benefits that such activity can bring, quantified in cash terms, with the intrinsic environmental value of the action typically relegated to a secondary line of argument.

This is not to say that the Seventh EAP necessarily in itself suggests a watered-down, 'paler green' environmental policy. Indeed, certain of the Seventh EAP's goals are unquestionably ambitious and, if followed through on, would revolutionise our relationship with the environment within Europe. These include the vision of a circular economy, meaning an economy where 'nothing is wasted and where natural resources are managed sustainably, and biodiversity is protected, valued and restored in ways that enhanced our society's resilience',[92] and the goal of 'an absolute decoupling of economic growth and environmental protection'.[93] Rather, what is remarkable about the Seventh EAP in this regard is its virtually wholesale repackaging of environmental goals in economic, or partially economic, terms. While this

---

[88] For an early policy document, see the Commission's 'Green Paper on Market-Based Instruments for Environment and Related Policy Purposes', COM(2007)140. See, generally, Kingston, *Greening EU Competition Law and Policy*, chapter 2.

[89] Namely, Directive 2014/24/EU on public procurement, OJ 2014 L 94/65, Directive 2014/25/EU on procurement by entities operating in the water, energy, transport and postal services sectors, OJ 2014 L94/243, Directive 2014/23/EU on the award of concession contracts, OJ 2014 L94/1.

[90] Decision 1386/2013/EU on a General Union Environment Action Programme to 2020 'Living well, within the limits of our planet', OJ 2013 L 354/171.

[91] Ibid., 178.   [92] Ibid., 176.   [93] Ibid., recital 18.

may be anathema to more traditional ecological political movements,[94] it is also couched in realism in view of the overwhelming concentration on economic goals in recent years in the EU.

In this regard, the commitment to integration of environmental and economic goals displayed in the EU's environmental policy in recent years has, in certain economically crucial EU policy areas, not been met with any serious reciprocal commitment to integration. Foremost amongst these areas is the EU's macro-economic policy. While the EU for many years had its own overarching Sustainable Development Strategy (the EU SDS), this has not been renewed since 2009, and has, according to the Commission, now been subsumed into the EU's general macroeconomic strategy, known as 'Europe 2020'.[95] Upon closer examination, however, the only elements of EU environmental policy meaningfully incorporated as part of the Europe 2020 Strategy are the EU's climate and energy goals.[96] At this, the highest policy level, therefore, the meaning of sustainable development, EU-style, does not extend to large tranches of traditional EU environmental policy.

Even more notable, from a practical perspective, is the lack of governance structures put in place to operationalise the environmental pillar of the EU's sustainability strategy, as contained in Europe 2020. As is well known, in the wake of the financial and subsequent economic crisis within Europe and beyond, the EU engaged in a large-scale reform of its economic governance model in the form of the European Semester process, entailing, *inter alia*, close monitoring of economic performance by means of the Annual Growth Survey, detailed reviews of Member States experiencing macro-economic imbalances, reports on Member States' excessive deficits, and Country Specific Recommendations.[97] In the case of the environmental aspects of sustainable development, while Eurostat continues to produce biennial reports on the EU's achievements in relation to the (more than 130) Sustainable Development Indicators set out in the EU SDS (which are divided into economic, social and environmental indicators), there is no specific follow-up to these reports. Similarly, while the European Environment Agency monitors over 200 environmental indicators, its four-yearly State of the European Environment and Outlook Report does not lead to any specific consequences or follow-up from EU institutions. Specifically, the advanced governance framework of the European Semester process does not apply to the non-economic elements of sustainability (although the Seventh EAP tentatively raises this possibility, by setting the goal by 2020 of 'assessing the

---

[94] See, generally, Andrew Dobson, *Green Political Thought* (4th edn., Routledge, 2007).
[95] 'Europe 2020: A strategy for smart, sustainable and inclusive growth', COM(2010)2020. See, stating that the Commission will implement its Rio +20 sustainable development goals through *Europe 2020*, European Commission, 'A Decent Life for All: Ending Poverty and Giving the World a Sustainable Future', COM(2013)92, 6. See also the discussion in Lee, *EU Environmental Law, Governance and Decision-Making*, chapter 3.
[96] Europe 2020, 14–16.
[97] These documents are available per Member State and per year at: http://ec.europa.eu/europe2020/index_en.htm.

appropriateness of the inclusion of a lead indicator and target in the European Semester'.[98] As Lee has aptly commented, 'Almost by accident, monitoring and review of the environmental and the economic seem to have been separated, with all of the emphasis on the economic.'[99]

The Commission's May 2016 Communication on an Environmental Implementation Review, proposing a cycle of country-specific reports to be prepared every two years, represents an effort to correct this governance deficit, and is discussed further in Chapter 6.

Against this, it must be recognised that, in certain policy fields, a greater effort at genuine substantive integration between the EU's environmental and economic fields is evident. The EU's trade policy, for instance, has long accommodated environmental protection concerns,[100] and indeed the EU has used its external trade policy as an instrument to achieve its environmental sustainability goals, as illustrated by the EU's published negotiated position on the EU–US Transatlantic Trade and Investment Partnership, which includes a position paper devoted to sustainable development.[101] Nevertheless, even in the case of the EU's climate and energy policies, commonly vaunted as the greatest example of substantive environment/economic policy integration, the tension between these aims has been apparent in the context of the recent economic turndown, as evidenced by the removal of binding renewable energy targets for individual Member States in favour of an EU-level target in the EU's 2030 Climate and Energy Policy Framework, on which agreement was reached in 2014.[102] It is striking that the very Council conclusions containing this Framework, which is the EU's central climate/energy strategy for the next 15 years, follows on by stating that, 'The economic and employment situation remains our highest priority'.

The EU's Better Regulation agenda has, through the Regulatory Fitness and Performance Programme (REFIT), also led the EU to map the entire EU legislative stock to identify burdens, gaps and inefficient or ineffective measures and identify possibilities for simplification or repeal. As part of this exercise, the costs of the environmental acquis were estimated at €1.18 billion per annum, or around 1 per cent of the total for all EU legislation.[103] In response to this, in 2012, the Commission released an action plan to reduce the costs for the seven most

---

[98] Seventh EAP, 186.
[99] Lee, *EU Environmental Law, Governance and Decision-Making*, 76.
[100] See, generally, Nicolas de Sadeleer, *EU Environmental Law and the Internal Market* (Oxford University Press, 2014).
[101] TTIP EU Position Paper on Trade and Sustainable Development, published on 7 January 2015, available at: www.trade.ec.europa.eu.
[102] Conclusions of the European Council of 24 October 2014, EUCO 169/14. See e.g. the comment of the Polish Prime Minister Kopacz at the conclusion of the negotiations: 'I said that we will not return from this summit with new [financial] burdens, and indeed there are no new burdens', Euractiv, 'EU leaders adopt "flexible" energy and climate targets for 2030', 24 October 2014.
[103] European Commission, Regulatory Fitness and Performance Programme (REFIT): Initial Results of the Mapping of the Acquis SWD (2013) 401, p. 59.

burdensome pieces of environmental legislation for business by around €300 million per annum.[104] From the outset, the Juncker Commission indicated its intention to continue as a priority an 'in-depth' review of the legislative cornerstones of EU nature conservation policy, the Birds and Habitats Directives, again in the interests of the Better Regulation agenda.[105] Again, the economic lens through which any redrafting of these Directives would be done is apparent, as is clear from the narrative coming from DG Environment on this issue that 'Protecting nature and maintaining Europe's competitiveness must go hand-in-hand as nature and biodiversity policy can play a key role in creating jobs and stimulating investment.'[106]

Against this, the CJEU has demonstrated leadership in taking the EU's environmental objectives seriously, and in integrating them into the EU's economic policies. The following section considers, by way of illustration, the CJEU's case law on the approach to environmental considerations in applying the Treaty internal market provisions.

Environmental Considerations and the Treaty Internal Market Provisions

In a variety of cases, the CJEU has demonstrated that it is willing to apply the integration principle in EU internal market law, by taking environmental considerations into account.[107]

Environmental Considerations and Article 110 TFEU

A first category of case concerns the application of Article 110 TFEU.

Article 110 TFEU

No Member State shall impose, directly or indirectly, on the products of other Member States any internal taxation of any kind in excess of that imposed directly or indirectly on similar domestic products.

Furthermore, no Member State shall impose on the products of other Member States any internal taxation of such a nature as to afford indirect protection to other products.

---

[104] Action Programme for Reducing Administrative Burdens in the EU – Final Report, SWD (2012) 422. Specific burdens were identified in the fields of waste and chemicals, particularly REACH.
[105] Letter from Commission President Juncker to Commissioner for Environment, Maritime Affairs and Fisheries Vella, 1 November 2014, p. 4.
[106] This is the chosen topic of Commissioner Vella's speech at the EU's Green Week 2015: see www.greenweek2015.eu/.
[107] This section discussed the judgments specific to environmental considerations only. For an overview of case law more generally in this area, see Catherine Barnard, *The Substantive Law of the European Union* (5th edn., Oxford University Press, 2016).

In *Outokumpu*, the CJEU considered the question whether it was permissible for Member States to apply different rates of internal taxation to electricity according to the manner of its production.[108] In that case, Finland imposed lower taxation on electricity produced from greener sources within Finland. However, imported electricity was subject to flat rate taxation irrespective of its source and method of production. The CJEU held that the Finnish taxation system contravened Article 110(1) TFEU, despite the environmental aims underlying the system. In particular, the CJEU rejected the Finnish Government's argument that, because the method of production of electricity could not be determined once it had been imported and entered the Finnish electricity network, the differential treatment of imported and domestically produced electricity was justified.

The largest category of environment-related free movement of goods cases, however, has concerned the CJEU's interpretation of Article 34 TFEU on non-fiscal restrictions on free movement of goods.

Environmental Considerations and Articles 34–36 TFEU

Article 34 TFEU

Quantitative restrictions on imports and all measures having equivalent effect shall be prohibited between Member States.

Article 35 TFEU

Quantitative restrictions on exports, and all measures having equivalent effect, shall be prohibited between Member States.

Article 36 TFEU

The provisions of Articles 34 and 35 shall not preclude prohibitions or restrictions on imports, exports or goods in transit justified on grounds of public morality, public policy or public security; the protection of health and life of humans, animals or plants; the protection of national treasures possessing artistic, historic or archaeological value; or the protection of industrial and commercial property. Such prohibitions or restrictions shall not, however, constitute a means of arbitrary discrimination or a disguised restriction on trade between Member States.

In *Walloon Waste*, the CJEU rejected the argument that waste did not comprise a 'good' within the meaning of what is now Article 34 TFEU, on the basis that 'objects which are transported over a frontier in order to give rise to commercial transactions are subject to [Article 34 TFEU], irrespective of the nature of those

---

[108] Case C-213/96 ECLI:EU:C:1998:155.

transactions'. This reasoning applied even, it held, to waste that could not be recycled or reused.[109]

As the CJEU has consistently held, Article 34 TFEU applies not only to measures which distinguish between imports and domestic products (distinctly applicable measures), but also to measures which apply without distinction to imports and domestic products but which are 'capable of hindering, directly or indirectly, actually or potentially, intra-[EU] trade' (indistinctly applicable measures).[110] In a wide range of cases, environmental measures have been considered to constitute 'measures having equivalent effect' to a quantitative restriction in this sense. In *Danish Bottles*, for instance, the Danish system obliging both domestic manufacturers and importers of beer and soft drinks to sell them in approved reusable containers was held to constitute a measure having equivalent effect to a quantitative restriction.[111] In *Bluhme*, Danish laws prohibiting keeping a particular (non-native) bee species on a particular Danish island constituted a quantitative restriction under Article 34 TFEU.[112] In *Preussen Elektra*, a German feed-in tariff which obliged electricity supply undertakings to purchase electricity produced in their area of supply from renewable sources, and specified the price to be paid for this electricity, was held to constitute a measure having effect to a quantitative restriction.

Conversely, in *Inter-Huiles*, the CJEU held that French rules requiring waste oils to be delivered to approved disposal undertakings, which effectively prevented the export of such oils outside France, contravened what is now Article 35 TFEU.[113] Similarly, in *Dusseldorp*, Dutch rules prohibiting the export of oil filters for processing outside the Netherlands – unless the quality of such processing was superior and there was insufficient capacity in the Netherlands – were held to infringe Article 35 TFEU.[114]

National measures which in principle fall within the scope of, and infringe, Articles 34 and 35 TFEU, may be justified under Article 36 TFEU, whether they are distinctly or indistinctly applicable. In the case of indistinctly applicable measures, they may also be justified on the basis of the CJEU's own additional justifications developed on a case-by-case basis pursuant to what is known as the 'rule of reason' doctrine first established in *Cassis de Dijon*, where the measure is necessary and proportionate to satisfy a 'mandatory requirement' in the public interest identified as such by the Court.[115]

While Article 36 TFEU specifically includes the 'protection of the health and life of humans, animals or plants', the CJEU has seemed to interpret this rather narrowly to date. In particular, in a number of cases, it has held that the

---

[109] Case C-2/90 *Commission v. Belgium (Walloon Waste)* ECLI:EU:C:1992:310.
[110] Case C-8/74 *Dassonville* ECLI:EU:C:1974:82.
[111] Case C-302/86 *Commission v. Denmark (Danish Bottles)* ECLI:EU:C:1988:421.
[112] Case C-67/97 *Bluhme* ECLI:EU:C:1998:584.
[113] Case C-172/82 *Inter-Huiles* ECLI:EU:C:1983:69.
[114] Case C-203/96 *Dusseldorp* ECLI:EU:C:1998:316.
[115] Case C-120/78 *Rewe (Cassis de Dijon)* ECLI:EU:C:1979:42.

protection of the environment as such does not fall within the meaning of this phrase.[116]

By contrast, the CJEU has confirmed that environmental protection as such constitutes a valid 'mandatory requirement' in the public interest, within the meaning of the rule of reason doctrine. This was first accepted in the *Danish Bottles* judgment, where the CJEU held that, 'the protection of the environment is one of the [EU's] essential objectives, which may as such justify certain limitations of the principles of free movement of goods'.[117]

This principle was subsequently confirmed in, for instance, *Walloon Waste*, despite the fact that it would seem that the national measure at issue in that case was distinctly applicable, and therefore only susceptible to justification on the grounds set out in Article 36 TFEU.[118]

Where a Member State can, therefore, demonstrate that an indistinctly applicable national measure is: (a) necessary to achieve the 'mandatory requirement' of environmental protection; and (b) proportionate to that aim (in the sense that it is suitable to achieve such an aim and cannot be achieved by less restrictive means), it will be justified under the 'rule of reason' doctrine. Where, however, the field has in fact been harmonised by EU legislation, it will not be open to justification on the basis of a mandatory requirement.

Article 34 TFEU and National Measures Promoting Green Energy

In *PreussenElektra*, the CJEU relied on the integration principle to support its conclusion that the German rules favouring locally generated renewable electricity fell within the scope of, but did not breach, what is now Article 34 TFEU.[119] As noted above, the German feed-in tariff scheme obliged electricity supply undertakings to purchase electricity produced in their area of supply from renewable sources, and specified the price to be paid for this electricity. The CJEU held this to be compatible with what is now Article 34 TFEU, on the ground that the discrimination against imported renewable energy inherent in the German scheme was justified and proportionate given that, because the internal renewable energy market had not yet been fully achieved, the environmental objectives of the scheme could not be achieved in a less restrictive manner.[120]

---

[116] See, for instance, Case C-2/90 *Commission v. Belgium (Walloon Waste)* ECLI:EU:C:1992:310; Case C-203/96 *Chemische Afvalstoffen Dusseldorp BV and Others v. Minister van Volkshuisvesting, Ruimtelijke Ordening en Milieubeheer* ECLI:EU:C:1998:316. See *contra*, however, Case C-67/97 *Criminal proceedings against Ditlev Bluhme* ECLI:EU:C:1998:584, where the CJEU considered that the protection of a distinct species of bee qualified as an aim of protecting the life of such animals.

[117] Case 302/86 *Commission v. Denmark* ECLI:EU:C:1988:421.

[118] Case C-2/90 *Walloon Waste* ECLI:EU:C:1992:310.

[119] Cited above. An integration approach is also evident in, for instance, Case 302/86 *Commission v. Denmark* ECLI:EU:C:1988:421; Case C-2/90 *Commission v. Belgium* ECLI:EU:C:1992:310 (*Walloon Waste*); Case C-203/96 *Dusseldorp* ECLI:EU:C:1998:316; and Case C-28/09 *Commission v. Austria (Inn Valley)* ECLI:EU:C:2011:854.

[120] *Ibid.*, paras. 68–81.

This approach has been further vindicated in the CJEU's judgment in *Ålands Vindkraft*. This case concerned the compatibility with the Treaty free movement of goods provisions of the way in which Sweden chose to transpose part of the EU's 2009 renewable energy (RES) directive.[121]

The Renewable Energy Directive at Issue in *Vindkraft*

The RES Directive formed a key plank of the 2009 climate and energy package, setting mandatory individual national targets for Member States with the aim of reaching a 20 per cent EU-wide share of energy from renewable sources by 2020 overall, and a mandatory 10 per cent target for each Member State in the transport sector.[122] Under the RES Directive, this was to be done, *inter alia*, via the adoption of national renewable energy action plans to cover the period to 2020, which were to be notified to the Commission by June 2010. In contrast to the position in relation to ETS national allocation plans in Phases I/II, however, the Commission was only granted the power to issue a recommendation by reason of an evaluation of national renewable energy action plans – and not the power of approval *per se*.[123] The RES Directive also contained various innovative methods of encouraging cooperation between Member States in meeting their targets, via statistical transfers of renewable energy between Member States,[124] joint projects between Member States and between Member States and third countries,[125] and joint national (financial) support schemes.[126] These methods must be viewed in the context of the broader efforts to achieve an EU internal market in electricity, in line with the EU's three successive legislative packages to achieve a single market for gas and electricity in the EU.[127]

In the situation considered in *Vindkraft*, Sweden had chosen to implement the RES Directive by *inter alia* passing legislation on electricity certificates in 2011, by which approved producers are awarded an electricity certificate for each megawatt-hour (MWh) of green electricity produced. These certificates are tradable on an open competitive market. Electricity suppliers, and some users, are legally obliged to hold, and to surrender to the Swedish State in April each year, a certain quota of certificates corresponding to a proportion of their

---

[121] Directive 2009/28/EC on the promotion of the use of energy from renewable sources, OJ 2009 L 140/16.
[122] RES Directive, *ibid.*, Art. 3. See, further, Chapter 8. See also Art. 7d(6) of the Fuel Quality Directive, Directive 2009/30/EC, OJ 2009 L 140/88, which introduced the mandatory target of achieving by 2020 a 6 per cent reduction in the greenhouse gas intensity of fuels used in road transport and non-road mobile machinery.
[123] RES Directive, Art. 3(5). [124] *Ibid.*, Art. 6. [125] *Ibid.*, Arts. 7–10.
[126] *Ibid.*, Art. 11.
[127] See, in relation to electricity, the most recent Directive, Directive 2009/72/EC of the European Parliament and of the Council of 13 July 2009 concerning common rules for the internal market in electricity and repealing Directive 2003/54/EC, OJ 2009 L 211/55.

total quantity of electricity supplied or consumed in the previous year (failing which surrender a penalty was payable). Importantly, while the Swedish legislation did not say so expressly, the referring court stated that in fact approval for the award of green electricity certificates was reserved to green electricity production installations located in Sweden. Further, while in principle other States' green electricity certificates could be used to fulfil a producer/consumer's quota where an international agreement was in place with that State, no such agreement existed at the relevant time with Finland.

In *Vindkraft*, the plaintiff (Vindkraft), a wind farm located in Finland, sought and was refused approval from the Swedish Energy Agency to be awarded green electricity certificates for the energy that it produced, and challenged this refusal in the Swedish courts on grounds *inter alia* of infringement of Article 34 TFEU on free movement of goods, arguing that the effect of the Swedish scheme was to reserve around 18 per cent of the Swedish electricity market (i.e. the portion subject to the quota) to Swedish electricity producers. The referring court was unsure how to proceed, given that, in particular, the RES Directive provides that Member States may meet their binding renewables obligations by applying 'support schemes' (Article 3(3) RES Directive), defined to include any instrument that promotes the use of renewable energy, including green certificate schemes, and expressly provides that, 'Without prejudice to Articles [107 TFEU and 108 TFEU], Member States shall have the right to decide, in accordance with Articles 5 to 11 of this Directive, to which extent they support energy from renewable sources which is produced in a different Member State.'

Further, Article 15 of the RES Directive requires Member States to ensure that proof of the renewable source of energy in an energy supplier's energy mix must be proven by guarantees of origin, 'in accordance with objective, transparent, and non-discriminatory criteria'.

Vindkraft, therefore, raised the important question whether the CJEU's position on the role of environmental factors in EU internal market law had changed since *PreussenElektra*, in circumstances where the internal market had been further harmonised in the interim by, amongst other things, the RES Directive.

The CJEU ruled that a national renewable energy support scheme was compatible with Article 34 TFEU even where the green energy certificates at issue were only awarded for the production of renewable energy within the territory of that Member State, and not for renewable energy produced in other EU Member States.[128] It noted first that, while the RES Directive clarified that Member States have the right to decide to what extent they support green energy produced in another Member State, it did not fully

---

[128] *Ålands Vindkraft*, cited above. See Suzanne Kingston, 'The Uneasy Relationship between the EU's Economic and Environmental Policies: The Role of the Court of Justice' in Beate Sjåfjell and Anja Wiesbrock (eds.), *Sustainable Public Procurement in EU Law: New Perspectives on the State as Stakeholder* (Cambridge University Press, 2015).

harmonise national support schemes such as to exclude the application of Article 34 TFEU.[129] Next, the CJEU held that, while the Swedish rules constituted a measure having equivalent effect to a quantitative restriction and, as such, were *prima facie* contrary to Article 34 TFEU, promoting the use of renewable energy sources for the production of electricity constituted a legitimate objective which was in principle capable of justifying barriers to the free movement of goods.[130]

The CJEU went on to consider the proportionality of the territorial restriction, reasoning that, while the internal market in renewable energy had moved on since *PreussenElektra*, the Swedish scheme at issue was nevertheless proportionate 'as EU law currently stands'.[131] In particular, despite the fact that the RES Directive provided for guarantees of origin of renewable energy (Article 15), the 'systematic identification' of green electricity was still 'difficult to put into practice' at the distribution and consumption stages,[132] and national support schemes for green electricity had not yet been fully harmonised,[133] with different Member States having different RES targets and different renewable energy potentials (and costs).

Finally, the CJEU considered the proportionality of the Swedish legislation as a whole, and specifically of its use of a market mechanism to achieve Sweden's environmental/energy goals. Here, the CJEU noted that, in designing its national support scheme so that consumers bear the additional cost of producing renewable energy, Sweden was validly exercising its discretion in pursuit of the legitimate aim of increasing green electricity production; further, the ability of the scheme to achieve that aim was proven.[134] Nevertheless, in order to be proportionate, such a market must be proven to function effectively and fairly such that traders subject to renewables obligations can in fact 'obtain certificates effectively and under fair terms'.[135] To this end, it was 'important that mechanisms be established which ensure the creation of a genuine market for certificates in which supply can match demand, reaching some kind of balance, so that it is actually possible for the relevant suppliers and users to obtain certificates under fair terms'.

Further, the CJEU added, the method for determining the penalty for non-compliance with the quota and the amount of that penalty must not go beyond what is necessary to provide an incentive to comply, and must not be 'excessive'.[136] This aspect of the judgment is fascinating in that it shows the CJEU's willingness to embrace a Member State's effort to use a market-based approach in achieving its environmental/energy goals, but only if the Member State proves that the market is actually functioning the way that *the CJEU considers* it should.

---

[129] *Vindkraft*, paras. 61–63.
[130] Citing *PreussenElektra*, the Kyoto Protocol and Art. 194(1)(c), inserted by the Treaty of Lisbon.
[131] *Ibid.*, para. 105. [132] *Ibid.*, paras. 90, 96. [133] *Ibid.*, para. 94.
[134] *Ibid.*, paras. 109–112. [135] *Ibid.*, para. 113. [136] *Ibid.*, para. 116.

Some months later, the CJEU effectively repeated its *Vindkraft* position in *Essent Belgium*, this time in the context of the previous RES Directive,[137] and concerning the Belgian scheme whereby only Belgian-produced renewable energy could be taken into account in determining whether Belgian electricity producers had satisfied their renewable obligations. The CJEU declined to follow the Opinion of Advocate General Bot,[138] who had concluded that the Belgian scheme breached EU internal market law, as the EU internal electricity market had now developed far enough to make it possible to verify whether electricity produced in other Member States comes from renewable sources, and that *PreussenElektra* was no longer good law.[139]

Aside from territoriality restrictions on the grant of green electricity certificates, the CJEU has also considered the compatibility of other limitations on the grant of such certificates by Member States. In its 2013 judgment in *Industrie du Bois*, the plaintiff challenged the compatibility of the restrictions placed by the Walloon region of Belgium on the grant of green certificates to co-generation plants powered by wood (as opposed to, in particular, biomass), on the ground that these restrictions breached the principle of equal treatment and the EU Charter of Fundamental Rights. The CJEU was not convinced by this argument, holding that, in the present state of EU law, Member States were entitled, when introducing national support schemes for cogenerations and renewable energy production, to provide for enhanced support measures of particular benefit to cogeneration plants principally using biomass.[140]

Green Public Procurement

The EU's 2014 public procurement legislative package is a further example of the encouragement of a 'win–win' approach to economic and environmental objectives and, specifically, the encouragement of eco-innovation by promoting green public procurement within Member States.[141] As such, it represents definite progress in integrating environmental considerations within procurement procedures. In particular, the horizontal clause of Article 18(2) now means that Member States must ensure that, in the performance of public contracts, economic operators comply with, *inter alia*, EU environmental law; enterprises which do not respect environmental law may be excluded from the tender

---

[137] Directive 2001/77 on the promotion of electricity produced from renewable energy sources in the internal electricity market, OJ 2001 L 283/33.
[138] Opinion of AG Bot ECLI:EU:C:2013:294.   [139] Opinion, paras. 100 *et seq.*
[140] *Industrie du Bois*, paras. 53 *et seq.*
[141] Namely, Directive 2014/24/EU on public procurement, OJ 2014 L 94/65, Directive 2014/25/EU on procurement by entities operating in the water, energy, transport and postal services sectors, OJ 2014 L94/243, Directive 2014/23/EU on the award of concession contracts, OJ 2014 L94/1.

procedure,[142] or not awarded the contract, or their tender rejected where it is abnormally low due to lack of compliance with these obligations. Member States have also gained clarity on the conditions in which they can legitimately require products/services to have a specific eco-label (Article 43),[143] and on the conditions in which they can legitimately set criteria relating to the production process (Article 67(3)) and use life-cycle costing (Article 68).

However, the 2014 Public Procurement Directive still leaves the choice to contracting authorities whether or not they wish to include environmental considerations in their public procurement procedures. In particular, Recital (91) of the Directive, citing Article 11 TFEU, notes the Directive's aim of clarifying how the contracting authorities '*can* contribute to the protection of the environment and the promotion of sustainable development, whilst ensuring that they can obtain the best value for money for their contracts'. The Directive expressly declines to make green public procurement (GPP) mandatory, however, on the ground that, given 'the important differences between individual sectors and markets, it would ... not be appropriate to set general mandatory requirements for environmental, social and innovation procurement'.[144] This mirrors the weak language on this issue in the Seventh EAP, which noted only that Member States 'should take further steps' to applying GPP standards to 50 per cent of their tenders.[145] The result is that the areas in which GPP is, as a matter of EU law, mandatory remain limited to office equipment and road transport vehicles.[146]

The CJEU has considered national green public procurement measures in a number of cases. In *Max Havelaar*, the CJEU held that the way in which the province of North Holland had included an eco-label requirement in its technical specifications for a tender for the supply and management of automatic coffee machines breached the 2004 Public Procurement Directive.[147] Specifically, the province had referred to two particular eco-labels in the award criteria, the EKO label (an organic produce label) and the MAX HAVELAAR label (a fair trade label). Drawing on its jurisprudence in *Concordia Bus* and *Wienstrom*,[148] the CJEU recalled that the contracting authority's decision to award a contract to the tenderer who submits the most economically advantageous tender must be based on criteria which are in compliance with the requirements of the

---

[142] Note, however, that failure to comply with EU environmental law is not a mandatory ground for exclusion from the tender process (in contrast, for instance, with failure to comply with national social security law): see Art. 57(1)–(2) of the 2014 Directive.

[143] Contrast the situation under the previous Directive, Directive 2004/18/EC, OJ 2004 L 134/14: see Case C-368/10 *Commission* v. *Netherlands* ECLI:EU:C:2012:284 (Max Havelaar).

[144] Directive 2014/24, recital (95).   [145] Seventh EAP, 184.

[146] See Regulation 106/2008 on a Community energy-efficiency labelling programme for office equipment, OJ 2008 L 39/1 and Directive 2009/33/EC on the promotion of clean and energy-efficient road transport vehicles, OJ 2009 L 120/5.

[147] OJ 2004 L 134/114.

[148] Case C-513/99 *Concordia Bus Finland* ECLI:EU:C:2002:495, Case C-448/01 *Wienstrom* ECLI:EU:C:2003:651.

Directive, which award criteria may in principle be not only economic but also qualitative, including environmental characteristics (Article 53(1) of the 2004 Directive).[149] The CJEU also recalled, however, that the award criteria must be linked to the subject-matter of the contract, and must be objective, with the award procedure in compliance with the principles of equality, non-discrimination and transparency. In the present case, the award criteria at issue concerned environmental and social characteristics within the meaning of the Directive, and related to products to be supplied as part of the subject-matter of the contract. Further, as regards the fair trade criterion, there is no requirement that an award criterion relates to an 'intrinsic characteristic of a product' as opposed to the way in which the product was produced.[150] Nevertheless, the Directive did not entitle a contracting authority to make the use of a specific eco-label a technical specification of the tender. Rather, use of such a label was allowed only to create a presumption that the products bearing the label comply with the characteristics defined, but other appropriate means of proof must also be allowed.[151]

In *Evropaïki Dynamiki*, the General Court rejected the plaintiff's argument that the European Environment Agency (EEA) had, in the context of an award criterion referring to the 'general environmental policy of the company', wrongly awarded a tender to the only tenderer which had submitted a certified environmental management scheme. Pursuant to the relevant rules for the award of contracts for Community institutions in force at the time, which were in turn based on the 2004 Public Procurement Directive, the criteria justified by the subject of the contract included the environmental characteristics of the product. It will be recalled that, in contrast to the general rule under that Directive excluding criteria or conditions relating to a general corporate policy, proof of the environmental policy of the company constitutes a legitimate way of adducing evidence as to the environmental characteristics of the product. The plaintiff argued that, rather than relying on the certificate, the EEA should have had regard to the actual environmental performance of the company. Rejecting this argument, the General Court held that the general wording of the award criterion enabled tenderers to present their environmental policy as they wish and to supply the evidence they consider to be appropriate. Submission of an environmental management certificate was 'one of a number of conventional ways of providing' such evidence.[152] Importantly, the evidence showed that, in that case, the evaluation committee had actually made a comparative assessment of the tenders and had evaluated whether the environmental policies submitted by the tenderers were 'genuine', and had not simply accepted the environmental management certificate without more evidence.[153]

---

[149] *Dutch Coffee*, as above, para. 85.   [150] *Ibid.*, para. 91.   [151] *Ibid.*, para. 94.
[152] As above, para. 75.   [153] *Ibid.*, para. 76.

In effect, therefore, the CJEU's reasoning in the context of public procurement mirrors, albeit applied in a partially codified legislative context, the proportionality-based approach evident in free movement of goods cases such as *Vindkraft*: the means used to achieve the environmental/social goal at issue must not be more restrictive than actually necessary to achieve those goals.

4

Techniques of Regulating the Environment

Introduction: The EU's Changing Regulatory Toolbox

The techniques that the EU uses to regulate for environmental issues have changed dramatically over the past 40 years. For around the first 20 years of its existence, Community environmental policy relied almost exclusively on what we might call 'traditional' regulatory techniques, relying primarily on hierarchical proscriptions by lawmakers (e.g. the imposition of environmental standards, or the banning of environmental hazardous substances) to be enforced by public authorities (e.g. agencies or courts).

These techniques, often called 'hierarchical', 'direct' or 'command-and-control' regulation, were supplemented in the 1990s by an increasing reliance upon market mechanisms to achieve environmental aims. Such 'market-based' instruments, such as emissions trading and environmental taxes and charges, now play a vital role in the EU's regulatory mix.[1] At its heart, this change reflects the ideological shift that had taken place under Reagan in the USA, and Thatcher in the UK, towards neo-liberalism and belief that free-market values should apply throughout not only economic, but also social, political and environmental life.[2] While traditional direct regulation remains important within the EU, the use of market-based instruments is being considered in increasingly wide areas of EU environmental policy, including areas such as habitat conservation where it was formerly thought inappropriate.[3]

A third important part of the regulatory mix in contemporary EU environmental policy is the increasing use of instruments aimed at encouraging individuals and organisations (voluntarily) to get involved in achieving the EU's environmental policy goals. These instruments may be viewed as forming part of the development of 'network-based' governance, i.e. reliance on non-hierarchical, societal-driven methods of achieving policy aims.[4] In the case of

---

[1] This Chapter draws in part on Suzanne Kingston, *Greening EU Competition Law and Policy*, chapter 2. See, generally, Suzanne Kingston, 'Developments in EU Law: Environment' (2010) 59 *International and Comparative Law Quarterly* 1129.
[2] See, generally, Neil Gunningham, 'Environmental Law, Regulation and Governance: Shifting Architectures' (2009) 21(2) *Journal of Environmental Law* 179.
[3] See EFTEC, 'The Use of Market-Based Instruments for Biodiversity Protection – The Case of Habitat Banking', Report of February 2010 for the European Commission, available at: http://ec.europa.eu/environment; and the Commission's 'Green Paper on Market-Based Instruments for Environment and Related Policy Purposes', COM(2007)140 final.
[4] See Andrew Jordan and Adriaan Schout, *The Coordination of the European Union: Exploring the Capacities of Network Governance* (Oxford University Press, 2006).

corporations, one example is the emphasis on 'corporate social responsibility', a trend generally embraced by the EU and Member State governments, but regarded with deep suspicion by some environmentalists. More broadly, the emphasis on improving environmental governance in Europe, in particular by means of the principles of access to information, participation and access to justice in environmental matters, provided for in the Aarhus Convention of 1998, can also be viewed as part of the effort to get non-governmental individuals and organisations involved in environmental protection. This 'enabling' of civil society, through the increased recognition of environmental rights, now forms an important part of the regulatory toolkit for improving environmental protection within the EU and Europe more broadly. Viewed together with the EU's embrace of market-based instruments, it represents a change in the architecture of EU environmental governance, from a State-centred approach to a more pluralist harnessing of business and society in pursuit of the EU's environmental aims.[5]

Of course, a vibrant scholarly debate has raged for years on how best to classify regulatory instruments, going far beyond the environmental sphere.[6] This trifold division of regulatory instruments is, therefore, not set in stone, and the boundaries between these categories are not watertight: important overlaps exist between the categories. Thus, many market-based and network-based instruments rely, for instance, on a legal framework that, in itself, is hierarchical in nature (i.e. created and enforced by the State). The EU's Emissions Trading Scheme, for instance, is the product of EU Directives (plus other legal measures), implemented and enforced by the European Commission, EU Courts and Member State authorities. Similarly, EU Regulations form the legal framework for the EU's eco-label. In this sense, such instruments may be viewed as 'hybrid' animals drawing on two or even three of our families of techniques. Nonetheless, these instruments seek to achieve discrete environmental policy goals (mitigation of climate change, greener consumption) in a manner distinctively different from typical direct regulatory techniques.

Broadly speaking, this trifold distinction in regulatory technique mirrors the three sectors of society involved in environmental governance, as mapped out in Chapter 1: namely, the public sector, the private sector and civil society. The overlaps between these sectors, and the resultant hybridity of the regulatory instrument, can usefully be represented by Figure 4.1.

---

[5] See, further, Andrew Jordan, Rüdiger Wurzel and Anthony Zito, 'Policy Instrument Innovation in the European Union: A Realistic Model for International Environmental Governance?' in Gerd Winter (ed.), *Multilevel Governance of Global Environmental Change* (Cambridge University Press, 2011), 470.

[6] For an excellent overview of the literature on policy instrument typologies, see Rüdiger Wurzel, Anthony Zito and Andrew Jordan, *Environmental Governance in Europe: A Comparative Analysis of New Environmental Policy Instruments* (Edward Elgar, 2013), 14.

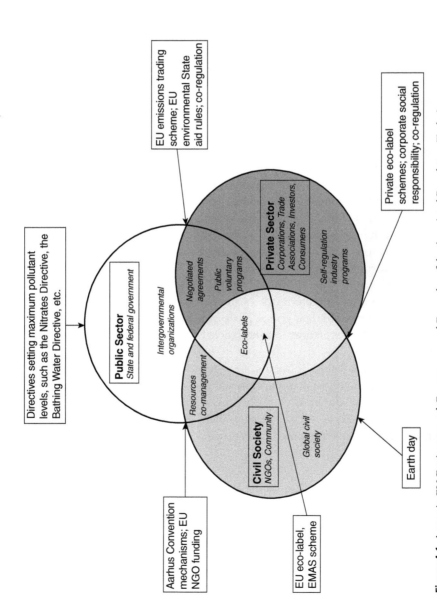

Figure 4.1 Actors in EU Environmental Governance, and Examples of the Associated Regulatory Techniques

Source: Adapted from Magali Delmas and Oran Young, 'Introduction: New Perspectives on Governance for Sustainable Development' in Magali Delmas and Oran Young (eds.), *Governance for the Environment: New Perspectives* (Cambridge University Press, 2009), 8.

As discussed further below, the EU has, over the years, expanded its regulatory mix to include elements of all three families of instruments, and intends to do so further, as this extract from the EU's current, Seventh, Environmental Action Programme (2013–2020) illustrates:[7]

> An appropriate mix of policy instruments would enable businesses and consumers to improve their understanding of the impact of their activities on the environment and to manage that impact. Such policy instruments include economic incentives, market-based instruments, information requirements as well as voluntary tools and measures to complement legislative frameworks and to engage stakeholders at different levels.

This chapter discusses the three groups of European environmental regulatory technique – hierarchy, market and network – in turn. It begins by placing these trends in context, by considering briefly what kinds of factors might influence choices of (environmental) regulatory instrument in the EU.

Understanding Regulatory Choices: Factors and Philosophies Underlying EU Decisions as to Environmental Regulatory Technique

Of course, decisions as to environmental regulatory technique at EU level do not take place in a vacuum, but are a product of the specific institutional, political and cultural contexts in which they are made. Within the regulatory literature, a wide variety of reasons for environmental regulatory instrument choice have been identified, which may be broadly distilled as follows (in no particular order).[8] It is immediately clear from this overview that the process of choosing regulatory form and instrument is inherently value-laden and, in many respects, a political one entailing difficult choices between competing regulatory objectives.

Environmental Effectiveness

How well will the instrument achieve the environmental policy goal at issue? Clearly, there are potentially serious limits to how accurately this criterion can be assessed, depending on the accuracy of the scientific evidence available. Particular

---

[7] Decision No. 1386/2013/EU of the European Parliament and of the Council of 20 November 2013 on a General Union Environment Action Programme to 2020 'Living well, within the limits of our planet', OJ 2013 L 354/171, Preamble, recital 33.

[8] See, especially, Giandomenico Majone, 'Choice among Policy Instruments for Pollution Control' (1976) 2 *Policy Analysis* 589-613; Peter Hall, 'Policy Paradigms, Social Learning and the State' (1993) 25(3) *Comparative Politics* 275–296; and, generally, Wurzel, Zito and Jordan, *Environmental Governance in Europe*, chapter 2. These reasons are not mutually exclusive, and there is a degree of overlap between some of them (e.g. the question of flexibility is governed in part by the legal principle of subsidiarity, which as a general principle of EU law is part of the institutional framework of the EU).

difficulties arise in the case of novel regulatory instruments, where the science rests by definition on projections, as is illustrated by the example of the regulatory experiment of emissions trading in the EU, discussed below and in Chapter 7. Such difficulties are, however, endemic in the case of environmental regulation, where scientific uncertainty, risk and rapidly changing underlying variables form an inevitable part of the regulatory context (see further, Chapter 1).

Economic Efficiency

How do the projected economic costs of the instrument compare to its projected economic benefits? The relative importance of cost–benefit analysis (CBA) in regulatory instrument decisions may vary quite significantly per jurisdiction. In part, this is because the process of trying to quantify a 'cost' for certain environmental damage may be highly contested. How much, for instance, is it worth to the EU to prevent the freshwater pearl mussel from going extinct? This difficulty has been noted by the European Commission.

> In the environment policy area, differences of perception can arise about the costs and benefits of regulation. For example, the Polluter Pays Principle means that there is often a difference between those who face the costs of abatement, and those who benefit from a cleaner environment. These differences can generate a public expression from the 'payers' that environmental regulation is burdensome. In some cases, people and businesses accept making an extra effort because they support the environmental benefits whilst others can be irritated by having to do tasks which, although less burdensome, are perceived to bring little useful result. European Commission, Regulatory Fitness and Performance Programme (REFIT): Initial Results of the Mapping of the Acquis SWD (2013) 401, p. 58.

Despite these difficulties, CBA has become an increasingly important part of EU environmental regulation. This is particularly true in light of the EU's Better or Smart Regulation strategy, which requires, amongst other things, regulatory impact assessments to be carried out on all EU initiatives expected to have significant direct economic, social or environmental impacts.[9] The strategy also requires, through the Regulatory Fitness and Performance Programme (REFIT), the EU to map the entire EU legislative stock to identify burdens, gaps and inefficient or ineffective measures and identify possibilities for simplification or repeal. As part of this exercise, the costs of the environmental *acquis* were estimated at €1.18 billion per annum, or around 1 per cent of the total for all EU

---

[9] See the EU's Impact Assessment Guidelines, 15 January 2009, SEC(2009)92, and the Seventh EAP, OJ 2013 L 354/171, Preamble, recital 34 and Article 2(4): 'All measures, actions and targets set out in the 7th EAP shall be proposed and implemented in accordance with the principles of smart regulation and, where appropriate, subject to a comprehensive impact assessment.'

legislation.[10] In response to this, in 2012, the Commission released an action plan to reduce the costs for the seven most burdensome pieces of environmental legislation for business by around €300 million per annum.[11] Notably, this part of the Better Regulatory Strategy followed extensive consultation with business leaders and small and medium-sized enterprises, and is largely viewed by environmentalists to be aimed at fulfilling business, rather than environmental, needs.

As a further part of the Better Regulation Strategy, the EU has also committed to 'better lawmaking' by means of the 2003 Interinstitutional Agreement between the European Parliament, Council and Commission, which agrees, amongst other things, to make greater use of 'alternative methods of regulation, particularly co- and self-regulation', 'in suitable cases or where the Treaty does not specifically require the use of a legal instrument'.[12] This is discussed further below.

Political and Administrative Feasibility

Will the Member State's politicians be able to sell the EU measure 'back home'? How easy will it be to administer or operationalise the measure? These factors, which are closely linked, are in practice of course critical to EU regulatory decisions. Member States' preferences and priorities differ, and this adds an extra layer of complication to the process of agreeing on EU regulatory forms and methods which does not exist (or at least not to the same degree) in a purely national context. In this sense, the EU's model of multi-level governance discussed in Chapter 1, above, is highly relevant to understanding its regulatory choices. Such differences may extend to diverging views on the priority to be given to environmental objectives as compared with other social aims, as well as to diverging views on the appropriateness of market-based instruments to achieve environmental aims. For instance, post-unification Germany has typically opted for a regulatory model with a large number of command-and-control regulations based on the best available technology technique, but the UK has traditionally been viewed as preferring a pragmatic regulatory approach with an emphasis on cost-effectiveness and practicability.[13]

---

[10] European Commission, Regulatory Fitness and Performance Programme (REFIT): Initial Results of the Mapping of the Acquis SWD (2013) 401, 59.

[11] Action Programme for Reducing Administrative Burdens in the EU – Final Report, SWD (2012) 422. Specific burdens were identified in the fields of waste and chemicals, particularly REACH.

[12] Interinstitutional Agreement of the European Parliament, Council and Commission on better law-making (2003) C321/01, at para. 16. See also the Annual Reports on Better Lawmaking, and latterly Subsidiarity and Proportionality, available at: http://ec.europa.eu/smart-regulation/better_regulation/reports_en.htm.

[13] See, further, Andrew Jordan and Duncan Liefferink (eds.), *Environmental Policy in Europe: The Europeanisation of National Environmental Policy* (Routledge, 2004).

Flexibility

Can the measure be adjusted to fit the demands of a specific situation, or the differing conditions of a particular Member State or region? This regulatory concern is perhaps particularly prevalent in the environmental context: clearly, environmental conditions vary tremendously across the EU's territory, which comprises more than 10 million km², and with population densities ranging from over 1,300/km² in Malta to only 18/km² in Finland.[14] Similarly, uneven distribution of pollutant industries across the EU contributes to an uneven distribution of environmental problems. For these reasons, it is no coincidence that the principle of subsidiarity, which is now found in Article 5(3) TEU, began its life as a principle of EU law within the environmental chapter of the Treaty, before being promoted to the general, cross-cutting Treaty provisions with the Treaty of Maastricht in 1992 (see Chapter 1, above). This principle requires that,

> in areas which do not fall within its exclusive competence, the Union shall act only if and in so far as the objectives of the proposed action cannot be sufficiently achieved by the Member States, either at central level or at regional and local level, but can rather, by reason of the scale or effects of the proposed action, be better achieved at Union level.

The principle has been given more teeth by, amongst other things, the institution of the red card/yellow card system by the Treaty of Lisbon, giving national parliaments the power to supervise the legislative initiatives proposed by the European Commission for compliance with the subsidiarity and proportionality principles, as well as the EU's Annual Reports on Subsidiarity and Proportionality forming part of the EU's Better Regulation Strategy, discussed above.

Compatibility with Existing EU and National Institutional Frameworks

Theoretical explanations for policy choice and instrument selection often focus on the importance of 'institutions'. Institutions, in the sense of this strand of political science literature, however (sometimes termed 'new institutional' theories), extend far beyond the narrow concept of, for instance, institutions as defined in Article 13 TEU (e.g. the European Commission), or organisations, to a far wider category, encompassing any

> relatively stable collection of practices and rules defining appropriate behaviour for specific groups of actors in specific situations.[15]

---

[14] Source: Eurostat, Population Density (Inhabitants per km²), 2012 figures. See, generally, on the notion of flexibility applied to EU environmental policy, Chapter 1.

[15] James March and Johan Olsen, 'The Institutional Dynamics of International Political Orders' (1998) 52(4) *International Organisation* 943–969.

'Institutions' in this sense should be understood as including law and legal principles, as well as socially constructed rules, norms and cultures.[16] In the context of the EU's environmental policy, the institutional context includes not only general principles of EU law such as subsidiarity, but also legal principles that perhaps do not (as yet) have the formal status as general principles of EU law, such as the legally binding Article 11 TFEU principle, requiring that 'Environmental protection requirements must be integrated into the definition and implementation of the Union policies and activities' (discussed in Chapter 3, above). The institutional context also, of course, includes non-legal rules and practices developed at EU and national levels.

One of the particular insights of new institutional literature is that institutions are particularly relevant in understanding how, and why, policy and policy instrument preferences change over time. Specifically, institutions, in this wide meaning, are 'sticky', in the sense that they tend to change not immediately but incrementally, and policy change is path-dependent. As a result, institutions make the process of policy change slower than it might otherwise be, because policy must fit to the institutional context.[17] In the EU context, again, this is further complicated by the fact that policy direction and instruments must fit not only to the EU's institutional context, but also to Member States' varying national institutional contexts. As a result, policy change in EU environmental policy tends to be gradual. As Rüdiger Wurzel, Anthony Zito and Andrew Jordan write,[18]

> 'Revolutionary policy learning' ... is rare, usually occurring in the environmental policy field after an ecological catastrophe or spectacular policy failure. When confronted with challenges (such as the selection of the most appropriate policy instruments), actors prefer to refine what they have already before searching for novel approaches.

This insight is particularly relevant when considering the EU's decision to embrace market-based and voluntary instruments of environmental regulation, and the limited success of certain of these instruments in some jurisdictions, discussed below.

Compatibility with Beliefs and 'Ideas'

A final important factor in the EU's environmental regulatory technique decisions is the question of the higher-level set of beliefs, ideas or 'world view' about the nature of the issue being regulated and its interrelation with other policy issues. These ideas may change over time, and are formed in a dynamic

---

[16] See, generally, Fritz Scharpf, *Games Real Actors Play: Actor-Centred Institutionalism in Policy Research* (Westview Press, 1997).
[17] See, for instance, March and Olsen, 'The Institutional Dynamics of International Political Orders'.
[18] Wurzel, Zito and Jordan, *Environmental Governance in Europe*, 34.

learning process involving not just the EU and Member States, but also society at large, interest groups, policy networks and the media. As Peter Hall writes,

> Politicians, officials, the spokesmen for social interests, and policy experts all operate within the terms of political discourse that are current in the nation at a given time, and the terms of political discourse generally have a specific configuration that lends representative legitimacy to some social interests more than others, delineates the accepted boundaries of state action, associates contemporary political developments with particular interpretations of national history, and defines the context in which many issues will be understood.[19]

In this way, Hall argues, 'policy paradigms' develop over time, which influence policy alongside but independently of institutions.[20]

While Hall was writing about the shift in economic policy in the 1970s under Thatcher in the UK, the point is highly relevant in understanding the current mix of regulatory techniques in use in the EU. Stepping back from the detail of EU environmental law and policy, it is not difficult to discern a battle of ideas or philosophies underlying the EU's regulatory choices in the environmental sphere. Many of these battles have at their heart the distinction between an ecocentric, as opposed to anthropogenic, environmental policy, discussed in Chapter 1, above. As John Dryzek writes,

> Industrial societies have of course featured many competing ideologies, such as liberalism, conservatism, socialism, Marxism, and fascism. But whatever their differences, all these ideologies are committed to industrialism. From an environmental perspective they can all look like variations on this theme ... If what we now call environmental issues were thought about at all, it was generally in terms of inputs to industrial processes.[21]

Regulatory decisions also reflect fundamental choices about the hierarchy, and balance, between the EU's many and varied competing policy goals. On that point, it is fair to say that the idea (or ideology?) of sustainable development is presently winning the battle of policy paradigms within the EU, i.e. the notion that the goals of economic growth and environmental and social protection can, at the same time, be pursued. This can be seen from the text of Article 3(3) TEU, setting out the EU's aims in this regard as the

> sustainable development of Europe based on balanced economic growth and price stability, a highly competitive social market economy, aiming at full employment and social progress, and a high level of protection and improvement of the quality of the environment.

---

[19] Peter Hall, 'Policy Paradigms, Social Learning and the State' (1993) 25(3) *Comparative Politics* 275–296, at 289.
[20] Ibid., 290.   [21] Dryzek, *The Politics of the Earth: Environmental Discourses*, 13–14.

As discussed in Chapter 1, however, it is inherent in that notion that (economic) development and economic growth is a non-negotiable precondition to EU action in the environmental (and social) spheres. In this sense, the EU's environmental policy is premised upon the belief system of economic growth. Indeed, the language of the EU's Seventh Environmental Action Programme illustrates the centrality of economic approaches to the EU's current environmental policy and, indeed, the essential anthropocentrism of this policy:[22]

> To live well in the future, urgent, concerted action should be taken now to improve ecological resilience and maximise the benefits environment policy can deliver for the economy and society, while respecting the planet's ecological limits. The 7th EAP reflects the Union's commitment to transforming itself into an inclusive green economy that secures growth and development, safeguards human health and well-being, provides decent jobs, reduces inequalities and invests in, and preserves biodiversity, including the ecosystem services it provides (natural capital), for its intrinsic value and for its essential contribution to human well-being and economic prosperity.

Similarly, as discussed below, environmental regulatory instrument choices reflect deep-seated beliefs about the proper role of the EU, the private sector, and civil society in achieving the EU's environmental goals.

It is clear from the above, therefore, that regulatory instrument choice is an inherently value-laden and political matter at EU level, just as it is at State level. Indeed, it is difficult to disagree with the conclusion that 'EU environmental regulations often resemble a patchwork which reflects different member state preferences and regulatory philosophies'.[23] The following analysis of the EU's environmental regulatory mix should be viewed in that context.[24]

Surveying the EU's Environmental Regulatory Techniques

Hierarchy: Direct or 'Command and Control' Techniques

Overview

For centuries, environmental law did not exist as a discrete body of regulation in most present EU Member States. Rather, issues which would now be viewed as environmental were left to be dealt with by private law alone, primarily via tort

---

[22] Seventh EAP, Decision No. 1386/2013/EU of the European Parliament and of the Council of 20 November 2013 on a General Union Environment Action Programme to 2020 'Living well, within the limits of our planet', OJ 2013 L 354/171, Annex, para. 10; see also Article 2(1)(a).
[23] Wurzel, Zito and Jordan, *Environmental Regulatory Techniques*, 202.
[24] The following section draws on Kingston, *Greening EU Competition Law and Policy*, chapter 2.

and property law.[25] By the 1970s, separate bodies of regulatory rules began to emerge in Member States, laying down public law standards of environmental protection to be observed by citizens and to be enforced by public authorities. As discussed in Chapter 1, these changes were mirrored at (what was then) Community level by the gradual development of Community environmental law, beginning in the 1960s with the regulation of hazardous substances, and followed in the 1970s with legislation regulating a wide range of environmental issues using directly regulatory techniques.[26]

Direct regulation, which is sometimes (rather pejoratively) termed 'command and control' regulation, remains the primary regulatory tool of EU environmental policy, although it is often now combined with market-based and/or voluntary approaches.[27] Indeed, Giandomenico Majone has famously termed the EU a 'regulatory state' due to its traditional reliance on hierarchy and direct regulation.[28] Direct regulation is characterised by what John Dryzek has termed 'administrative rationalism':[29] a reliance on the (presumed) good sense and good information of bureaucrats to set the right environmental standards, and on public resources to enforce them.[30]

---

[25] A classic example in UK tort law is the rule of private nuisance in *Rylands* v. *Fletcher* (1868), LR 3 HL 330 [1861–73] All ER, laying down the rule that 'the person who for his own purpose brings on his lands [...] anything likely to do mischief if it escapes, must keep it at his peril and is prima facie answerable for all the damage which is the natural consequence of its escape'. Per Blackburn J. See also *Cambridge Water Co. Ltd* v. *Eastern Counties Leather plc* [1994] 2 AC 264.

[26] See e.g. Council Directive 75/442/EEC of 15 July 1975 on waste, OJ 1975 L 194/23 and Council Directive 79/409/EEC of 2 April 1979 on the conservation of wild birds, OJ 1979 L 103/1.

[27] Classic forms of EU environmental direct regulation include: the establishment of environmental quality standards setting down (maximum) permitted levels of pollution or environmental interference, whether for a given environment (e.g. a habitat designated as a Special Area of Conservation under the Habitats Directive, Council Directive 92/43/EEC of 21 May 1992 on the conservation of natural habitats and of wild fauna and flora, OJ 1992 L 206/07) or environmental medium (e.g. water, air); the establishment of product-specific standards (e.g. Council Directive 67/548/EEC of 27 June 1967 on the approximation of laws, regulations and administrative provisions relating to the classification, packaging and labelling of dangerous substances, OJ 1967 L 196/1); the establishment of emissions standards, setting maximum levels for pollutants emitted from installations, activities or products (e.g. Directive 2008/1/EC of the European Parliament and of the Council of 15 January 2008 concerning integrated pollution prevention and control, OJ 2008 L 24/8); and the use of process standards, requiring the use of a particular technology, technique, or practice in carrying out an activity or in the design of an installation (e.g. Directive 2006/12/EC of the European Parliament and of the Council of 5 April 2006 on waste, OJ 2006 L114/9).

[28] See e.g. Giandomenico Majone, 'The Rise of the Regulatory State in Europe' (1994) 17(3) *West European Politics* 77–101.

[29] Dryzek, *The Politics of the Earth: Environmental Discourses*, 76.

[30] See e.g. Carolyn Abbot, 'Environmental Command Regulation' in Benjamin Richardson and Stepan Wood (eds.), *Environmental Law for Sustainability* (Hart Publishing, 2006), 63–64, contrasting direct regulation with private 'substantive' law and reflexive law, drawing on

Direct regulation typically involves a State-prescribed command backed by the State's authority to impose a negative sanction, the control.

In the environmental sphere, command and control regulation normally entails the adoption of standards by the State or its environmental protection bodies, which standards are enforced by public authorities and/or private persons via the courts. In this regulatory scenario, public authorities play a central role – setting the standards and enforcing them. Direct regulation is often characterised by the use of permits (otherwise known as licensing or authorisation) systems, or (exceptionally) complete prohibition (for example, of an activity or substance).[31] Enforcement techniques differ by jurisdiction, but may involve national courts, via the imposition of civil or criminal penalties, and/or non-judicial public enforcement agencies, via the imposition of civil or administrative penalties or the revocation of licences granted.

Historically, the EU has traditionally relied on environmental standards arrived at using the 'best available techniques' (BAT) method, whereby pollution limits are imposed based on the 'best available' technology in the particular sector. This drew considerably on the German model of environmental regulation, which has traditionally relied heavily on direct regulation combined with BAT techniques, inspired by the precautionary principle. This approach may be contrasted, for instance, with the traditional UK approach to environmental standard-setting, which has typically focused more on practicability, cost-effectiveness, and on achieving environmental quality obligations rather than (uniform) emissions limits.[32]

'Best available techniques' mean the most effective and advanced stage in the development of activities and their methods of operation which indicates the practical suitability of particular techniques for providing the basis for emissions limit values and other permit conditions designed to prevent and, where that is not practicable, to reduce emissions and the impact on the environment as a whole ...

---

the work of Gunther Teubner, 'Substantive and Reflexive Elements in Modern Law' (1983) 17 *Law and Society Review* 239.

[31] For instance, particularly ecologically important sites may need to be kept free from interference, or endangered species may need absolute protection by the law. In EU law, examples include the Annex A species of the EU's Regulation on trade in endangered species, trade in which is only authorised in exceptional circumstances (Council Regulation (EC) No. 338/97 of 9 December 1996 on the protection of species of wild fauna and flora by regulating trade therein, OJ 1997 L 61/1).

[32] See Rüdiger Wurzel, *Environmental Policy-Making in Britain, Germany and the European Union* (Manchester University Press, 2002); Wurzel, Zito and Jordan, *Environmental Regulatory Techniques*, 191–205.

Unsurprisingly, the current EU approach to emissions standard-setting reflects elements of these and other regulatory approaches, as can be seen from the definition of BAT in the current Industrial Emissions Directive.[33]

As discussed further in Chapter 7, the BAT for each industry is arrived at by a consultative process whereby BAT reference documents (BREFs) are drawn up through an exchange of information, organised by the European Commission, between Member States, the industries concerned, NGOs promoting environmental protection and the Commission.[34]

The BAT principle has, in some instances, been coupled with the principle of the best available technique not entailing excessive costs (BATNEEC), which has traditionally been preferred by the UK.[35]

The EU's typical traditional model of direct regulation has, since the 1990s, been modified by two important trends in regulatory technique at EU level.

Flexible Direct Regulation: Framework Directives

The first is the trend towards flexibility in direct regulation: that is to say, the use of broad, framework-style Directives, which typically set out the essential principles and regulatory architecture for the field covered, but leave it to 'daughter' Directives to flesh out the detail for particular sub-fields, leaving Member States with a significant degree of discretion on how to implement the objectives of the Directive in a manner appropriate to the specific environmental conditions of their State, or to select regulatory instruments within the policy area as appropriate to that State's regulatory culture. This contrasts with the tendency in the 1970s and 1980s for EU legislation to impose fixed minimum standards for the Community as a whole, leaving little discretion to Member States to take local environmental conditions into account, or to use different instruments, in implementation. Two of the most important examples of this regulatory technique are found in the Waste Framework Directive, discussed in Chapter 13, and the Water Framework Directive, discussed in Chapter 9.

The movement, which was particularly evident in the Community's Fifth Environmental Action Programme (1992),[36] resulted from a drive towards more effective environmental legislation, as well as from concerns about the EU's international competitiveness.[37] As has been seen above, this emphasis on cost-effectiveness and on minimising unnecessary regulatory burdens for business

---

[33] Industrial Emissions Directive, Article 3(10).
[34] Article 13, Industrial Emissions Directive.
[35] See, for instance, Article 4, Council Directive 84/360/EEC of 28 June 1984 on the combating of air pollution from industrial plants, OJ 1984 L 188/200.
[36] Resolution of the Council and the Representatives of the Governments of the Member States, meeting within the Council of 1 February 1993 on a Community programme of policy and action in relation to the environment and sustainable development – A European Community programme of policy and action in relation to the environment and sustainable development, OJ 1993 C 138/1.
[37] See e.g. Richard Macrory and Sharon Turner, 'Participatory Rights, Transboundary Environmental Governance and the Law' (2002) 39 *Common Market Law Review* 489–522.

has been a key part of the European Commission's current Better Regulation Strategy.

Proceduralised Direct Regulation
A second important regulatory trend is the trend towards proceduralisation of direct regulation: that is to say, the use of direct regulation not to set down substantive standards *per se*, but rather to establish procedures aimed at evaluating the effects of regulatory or administrative action on the environment. One example is the requirement for the Commission to carry out regulatory impact assessments of its proposals, discussed above. A further obvious example is the Environmental Impact Assessment (EIA) Directive which, as discussed in Chapter 11, requires that projects likely to have significant effects on the environment must, before being given development consent, undergo an assessment of environmental impacts.[38] Such EIAs are carried out on the basis of an environmental report or statement prepared by the developer, and following consultation of the public concerned. A similar principle is inherent in the Strategic Environmental Assessment Directive, which requires environmental impact assessment of public plans and programmes.[39]

More broadly, the trend towards proceduralisation, public participation and consultation is evident in the 1998 UNECE Aarhus Convention and EU laws passed to implement the principles of that Convention, discussed in Chapter 5. Proceduralisation in this sense achieves a dual aim: demonstrating expressly to the public that the final decision represents the culmination of a thorough reasoning process, in which the regulator has taken all relevant environmental factors into account, as well as increasing the democratic credentials of the ultimate decision taken. However, it is vital to note that procedural techniques do not necessarily ensure a particular environmental outcome, or standard of environmental protection, but may (as in the case of the EIA Directive) simply provide for a mandatory process to be followed in taking decisions with potential environmental impacts. This can be contrasted with the proceduralisation contained in Article 6(3) of the Habitats Directive, which specifically requires that the decision taken following an 'appropriate assessment' must not adversely affect the integrity of the site (see Chapter 12).

The Pros and Cons of Direct Environmental Regulation in the EU
Direct regulation is well-suited to certain areas of environmental regulation: in particular, setting pollution limits for specific installations (e.g. large industrial

---

[38] Article 2(1), Environmental Impact Assessment Directive, Directive 2011/92/EU of the European Parliament and of the Council of 13 December 2011 on the assessment of the effect of certain public and private projects on the environment, OJ 2012 L 26/1, as amended by Directive 2014/52/EU of the European Parliament and of the Council of 16 April 2004, OJ 2014 L124/1.

[39] Directive 2001/42/EC of the European Parliament and of the Council of 27 June 2001 on the assessment of the effects of certain plans and programmes on the environment, OJ 2001 L 197/30.

installations as covered by the Industrial Emissions Directive). It is ideally suited to regulating point-source pollution, enabling specific limits to be prescribed per industry, while still leaving some scope for flexibility via the adaptation of regulatory requirements to local conditions. Further, it has generally been viewed as the only acceptable way of protecting certain especially precious natural resources, such as preserving biodiversity, endangered species or special habitats. In these fields, market mechanisms and private law rights have traditionally been regarded (at least in the EU) as insufficient to achieve such protection: as the beneficiaries of such resources (humanity as a whole) cannot easily be charged with the cost of protecting them, insufficient market incentives exist for the owners or managers of these resources to preserve them.[40] Direct regulation also has legal certainty and transparency advantages, both from the perspective of those regulated, and the perspective of the general public.[41]

Nonetheless, direct regulatory techniques suffer from a range of drawbacks, as identified in the regulatory literature. First, there is a problem of time lag: with traditional direct regulation, standards are fixed by the regulator at given points in time. Though more or less frequent revisions to the standards may be built into the system, even the most ambitious revision programme will probably fail to keep up with technical innovations in the industry, or indeed to changes in environmental or economic conditions. As a result, direct regulation may sometimes disincentivise innovation: industry has little incentive to develop more cost-effective, efficient methods of reducing pollution if this would mean going beyond their legal obligations under the applicable standard set down by law. A further problem is regulatory information deficit: regulators may lack accurate, up-to-date information as to what type of regulation, or which standards, are best for an industry, which may lead to over- or under-regulation. In addition, whatever information that regulators can obtain is costly to gather, making standard-setting a relatively costly means of regulating.[42] The drive towards flexibility and consultation, mentioned above, is an attempt to remedy each of these problems.

Perhaps the core disadvantage of direct environmental regulation is, however, that it is dependent on effective public enforcement, which in turn depends on the level of public resources available, and on enforcement policy of the day. In the EU context, as discussed in Chapter 6, it is fair to say that (lack of) enforcement of environmental law is the Achilles heel of contemporary EU environmental policy (though, of course, it is not a problem specific to EU or environmental law).

---

[40] See, however, the discussion of habitat banking as a potential policy instrument within the EU, below.
[41] See John Harman, 'Environmental Regulation in the 21st Century' (2004) 6 *Environmental Law Review* 145–146.
[42] This may to some extent be remedied by the use of bespoke permits, the conditions of which are tailored to the individual operator. The downside of such permits is, however, that costs to the regulator are increased by the cost of negotiating the bespoke permit.

Of course, the EU has no environmental enforcement agency – proposals to this effect made by some commentators have been vociferously rejected by Member States.[43] This means that EU direct regulation is dependent for effectiveness on (1) Member States' enforcement authorities' taking action against individual non-complying operators, which is dependent on the financial resources allocated by the State; (2) the enforcement of EU law (or an implementing national law) by private parties through their national courts, which is dependent on robust access to justice rules and favourable funding conditions; and (3) the direct enforcement actions taken by the European Commission pursuant to Articles 258 and 260 TFEU against Member States before the Court of Justice of the EU, which again are dependent on finite Commission resources and priorities. The limitations on each of these enforcement methods mean that, at present, standards set by direct EU regulation will often not be enforced in reality.

In sum, while direct regulation has, in many respects, treated the EU very well as a regulatory technique for environmental problems, it has clear limits in terms of effectiveness. The EU has reached a plateau in the effectiveness of direct regulatory techniques in its environmental policy. While landmark EU legislation has, from the 1970s onwards, been passed in those areas that lend themselves naturally to this form of regulation – such as biodiversity regulation, the regulation of waste and the regulation of particular dangerous substances – the pace of such legislative activity began to slow in the early 1990s. With most of the obvious candidates for direct regulation covered, and some of the disadvantages of direct regulation becoming evident, the EU began in earnest to look for alternative, more efficient regulatory tools.[44] It is in this context that the emergence of market-based instruments within the EU must be viewed.

Market-Based Instruments

Overview

Economic environmental regulatory instruments, otherwise known as incentive- or market-based instruments, came into vogue in EU environmental policy in the 1990s sparked by a similar rise in interest in the USA.[45]

---

[43] The Commission, however, has mooted the setting up of an enforcement agency for waste policy. See Milieu Ltd, AmbienDura and FFact, 'Study on the Feasibility of the Establishment of a Waste Implementation Agency', Revised Final Report of 7 December 2009 for the Commission, available at: http://ec.europa.eu/environment/waste/studies/pdf/report_waste_dec09.pdf.

[44] Charlotte Halpern, 'Governing Despite its Instruments? Instrumentation in EU Environmental Policy' (2010) 33(1) *West European Politics* 39.

[45] See, generally, Bruce Ackerman and Richard Stewart, 'Reforming Environmental Law' (1985) 37 *Stanford Law Review* 1333; Richard Stewart, 'The Importance of Law and Economics for European Environmental Law' (2002) 2 *Yearbook of European Environmental Law* 1.

> The essential feature of market-based instruments is that market mechanisms are used to provide incentives to guide behaviour towards an environmentally favourable outcome.

The origins of this wave can be traced back to the Law and Economics movement[46] and, more broadly, the rise in popularity of neo-liberal ideology which had taken place by the 1980s in a number of countries, including the USA under Reagan and the UK under Thatcher. In the environmental context, this movement has found expression in instruments and principles which seek to adopt an economic solution to the problem, discussed in Chapter 1, above, that many environmental resources amount to public goods in the economic sense. Garrett Hardin's celebrated tragedy of the commons scenario, discussed in Chapter 1, posits that, where environmental resources are public goods, this leads to overexploitation of the resource.[47] In economic terms, therefore, environmental damage is traditionally viewed as a *negative externality*.

> In economics, a negative externality is a situation where one actor's production or consumption decisions have an unintentional negative impact on another's utility or profit, for which no compensation is made.

In other words, absent corrective regulation, I will not have to pay (enough) if I cause environmental damage that negatively affects others. As a result, economic theory holds that, without corrective regulation, the operation of the market will result in more pollution being produced than efficiency requires (i.e. market failure), because market actors do not have to pay for the cost to society of their pollution.

Environmental economic instruments aim to tackle this problem by internalising negative environmental externalities into market actors' decision-making processes, i.e, bringing the environment 'into the boardroom'. Consistently with the polluter pays principle of Article 191(2) TFEU, discussed in Chapter 3, this is normally achieved by placing a price on pollution – whether this price is decided upon by the State (in the case of environmental charges and taxes) or by market operators themselves (in the case of tradable permit systems). In a 2007 Green Paper, the European Commission set out the case for using market-based environmental regulation as follows:

---

[46] Though tracing its roots back to Jeremy Bentham, this movement has since flourished particularly in the US, and is epitomised by the writings of academics such as Ronald Coase, Guido Calabresi, Richard Posner and, in the environmental field, Richard Revesz and Richard Stewart. For an overview of law and economics thinking in the environmental context, see above, Stewart, 'The Importance of Law and Economics', 1.

[47] Garrett Hardin, 'The Tragedy of the Commons' (1968) 162 *Science* 1243, taking its name from the fact that, historically, resources such as pastureland and fisheries were owned in common.

The Case for Using Market-Based Instruments as Policy Tools

The economic rationale for using market-based instruments lies in their ability to correct market failures in a cost-effective way. Market failure refers to a situation in which markets are either entirely lacking (e.g. environmental assets having the nature of public goods) or do not sufficiently account for the 'true' or social cost of economic activity. Public intervention is then justified to correct these failures and, unlike regulatory or administrative approaches, MBIs have the advantage of using market signals to address the market failures.

Whether by influencing prices (through taxation or incentives), or setting absolute quantities (emissions trading), or quantities per unit of output, MBI implicitly acknowledge that firms differ from each other and therefore provide flexibility that can substantially reduce the costs of environmental improvements. MBI are not a panacea for all problems. They need a clear regulatory framework in which to operate and will often be used in a policy mix with other instruments. But if the right instrument is chosen and appropriately designed, MBI carry certain advantages over regulatory instruments:

- They improve price signals, by giving a value to the external costs and benefits of economic activities, so that economic actors take them into account and change their behaviour to reduce negative – and increase positive – environmental and other impacts.
- They allow industry greater flexibility in meeting objectives and thus lower overall compliance costs.
- They give firms an incentive, in the longer term, to pursue technological innovation to further reduce adverse impacts on the environment ('dynamic efficiency').
- They support employment when used in the context of environmental tax or fiscal reform.

At the international level, the use of economic instruments has been officially championed since the 1990s. An example is Principle 16 of the Declaration of the 1992 UN Rio Conference, which proclaimed,[48]

---

[48] See also the UN Framework Convention on Climate Change, 9 May 1992 (1992) 31 ILM 849, Article 4(2)(e) of which requires developed country contracting parties to 'coordinate as appropriate with other such Parties, relevant economic and administrative instruments developed to achieve the objective of the Convention'. Article 4(2)(e) in turn laid the foundation for the 1997 Kyoto Protocol (Protocol to the UN Framework Convention on Climate Change, 11 December 1997 (1998) 37 ILM 22), which, in authorising certain greenhouse gas emissions trading arrangements, set the scene at international level for one of the most important economic instruments in use today – tradable permit systems, discussed in Chapter 7.

> National authorities should endeavour to promote the internalisation of environmental costs and the use of economic instruments, taking into account the approach that the polluter should, in principle, bear the cost of pollution with due regard to the public interest and without distorting international trade and investment.

Within the EU, the Fifth Environmental Action Programme (1992–2002), 'Towards Sustainability', saw economic regulatory instruments shift firmly into the regulatory spotlight. One of the principal themes of this EAP was broadening the range of instruments used in EU environmental law.[49] It identified five particular types of economic instrument on which the Community would focus: charges and levies, fiscal incentives, State aids, environmental auditing and environmental liability.[50] Tradable permits were mentioned as an 'alternative' to these instruments, to be studied in further depth.[51] This approach was combined with accentuation of the environmental integration principle (present Article 11 TFEU), discussed in Chapter 3. In practice, however, differences between Member States meant that operationalising the Community's ambitions proved difficult. In 1992, for instance, the European Commission proposed the first international environmental tax, which would have levied a tax on certain fossil fuel products on the basis of carbon dioxide emissions and energy content.[52] However, it was never approved by the Council.

The EU's Sixth Environmental Action Programme (2002–2012) continued the emphasis on a market-based approach to environmental regulation, including the need for policy integration in pursuit of sustainability as one of its 'strategic approaches'.[53] This was followed by the European Commission's 2007 Green Paper on market-based instruments in environmental policy, mentioned above, where the Commission stated that:

---

[49] See chapter 7 of the Fifth EAP, which states that, 'In order to bring about substantial changes in current trends and practices and to involve all sectors of society, in a spirit of shared responsibility, a broader mix of "instruments" needs to be developed and applied. Environmental policy will rest on four main sets of instruments: regulatory instruments, market-based instruments (including economic and fiscal instruments and voluntary agreements), horizontal supporting instruments (research, information, education etc.) and financial support mechanisms.' Fifth Environmental Action Programme, A European Community programme of policy and action in relation to the environment and sustainable development, OJ 1993 C 138/1, 68. Article 3 of the 1998 Review of the Fifth EAP confirmed this general focus. On the status of EAPs as a policy instrument, see Chapter 2.

[50] OJ 1993 C 138/1, 71–72.   [51] *Ibid.*, 71.

[52] Commission Proposal for a Council Directive Introducing a Tax on Carbon Dioxide Emissions and Energy, COM(92) 226 final.

[53] Decision No. 1600/2002/EC of the European Parliament and of the Council of 22 July 2002 laying down the Sixth Community Environment Action Programme, OJ 2002 L 242/1, Preamble, recitals 13–14 and Article 2(3) and Article 3(5).

market-based instruments and fiscal policies in general will play a decisive role in delivering the EU's policy objectives. 'Green Paper on Market-Based Instruments for Environment and Related Policy Purposes', COM(2007)140 final, 2.

The Green Paper was followed by a resolution of the European Parliament which was generally supportive of an increase in the use of market-based instruments in EU environmental policy.[54] The Commission strongly reaffirmed its commitment to market-based instruments in its 2010 Europe 2020 strategy.[55] The EU's current, Seventh, Environmental Action Programme (2013–2020) continues to emphasise the importance of market-based instruments in the EU's environmental policy mix, including in fields such as biodiversity where they are still not widely accepted in the EU (in contrast, for instance, to the USA).[56] As part of this, a major emphasis has been placed on developing programmes of payments for 'ecosystem services' at EU and national levels. This move to 'economise', or place a value on, natural resources is discussed in Chapter 3.

To date, however, the main examples of market-based instruments in EU environmental policy have been its use of a tradable permit scheme to help achieve its climate objectives, and the development of a policy on environmental State subsidies and taxes.

Tradable Permit Schemes

As Chapter 7 discusses, in its simplest meaning, a tradable permit scheme is a regime whereby polluters are granted (or sold) a limited number of pollution rights (in the case of emissions trading schemes, rights to emit).[57] Should they pollute less than allowed by their permit, they may sell the excess to other polluters. In this way, tradable permit schemes can minimise costs, by encouraging firms that would find it costly to reduce their emissions to purchase the right

---

[54] European Parliament resolution of 24 April 2008 on the 'Green Paper on Market-Based Instruments for Environment and Related Policy Purposes' (2007/2203(INI)), OJ 2009 C 259/86.
[55] Commission communication 'Europe 2020: a strategy for smart, sustainable and inclusive growth', COM(2010)2020, at 13.
[56] Seventh EAP, Decision No. 1386/2013/EU of the European Parliament and of the Council of 20 November 2013 on a General Union Environment Action Programme to 2020 'Living well, within the limits of our planet', OJ 2013 L354/171, Preamble, recital 33. See also Article 2(1)(g) (listing addressing environmental externalities as a priority objective) and Annex, para. 9 ('Addressing some of those complex issues requires tapping into the full potential of existing environmental technology and ensuring the continuous development and uptake by industry of the best available techniques and emerging innovations, as well as increased use of market-based instruments') and para. 76 (specifying biodiversity policy).
[57] As trading takes place in the right to pollute, emissions trading schemes are distinct from, though similar in some respects to, the concept of green electricity certificate trading. In the latter case, electricity suppliers are given a target for supplying renewable energy; to prove conformity with this target, they may purchase certificates attesting to the generation of a unit of renewable energy.

to pollute from firms for which this cost is lower. In principle, such schemes can allow for economic development to be reconciled with environmental protection, by allowing new industrial activities in the area covered by the scheme without necessarily increasing the total volume of emissions from that area.[58] One of the first emissions trading schemes widely recognised as successful was the US sulphur dioxide emissions trading scheme, brought in by the 1990 amendments to the Clean Air Act and which subsequently inspired the Kyoto Protocol and the EU's ETS.[59] The USA's switch to a tradable permit scheme for sulphur dioxide emissions reduced such emissions by 50 per cent over ten years, achieving an estimated accumulated capital saving of $10 billion on the costs of complying with the Clean Air Act.[60]

Emission trading schemes may broadly be divided into two categories: cap and trade (absolute regimes)[61] or baseline and credit systems (relative regimes).[62]

Cap and trade versus baseline and credit schemes

Cap and trade regimes generally set a total cap, or absolute maximum quantity of emissions (measured over a specified period of time), on all emissions from the sources covered by the regime. This quantity is then allocated as individual allowances, either free of charge or by auction – a process which, in effect, creates new transferable property rights. After the allocation, sources can either choose to reduce their emissions and sell the excess, or increase their emissions and buy others' excess allowances. These choices are made on the basis of the market price of the allowances and the marginal costs of the emissions reductions for that source. Sources have the possibility, therefore, of acting in the most cost-effective manner. Such trading systems have a fixed compliance period, at the end of which sources must be able to show that they

---

[58] Note, however, that the term 'emissions trading scheme' is misleading, as trading takes place not in the emissions themselves, but in the allowances to emit the pollutant(s) covered by the scheme.

[59] See, Tom Tietenberg, *Emissions Trading: Principles and Practice* (2nd edn., Resources for the Future, 2006).

[60] Tom Tietenberg, 'Economic Instruments for Environmental Regulation' in Anil Markandya and Julie Richardson (eds.), *The Earthscan Reader in Environmental Economics* (Earthscan, 1992), 267–286.

[61] A number of Member States – including Germany, the Netherlands and the UK – had, prior to the EU ETS, negotiated relative (voluntary) target emissions agreements with industry. See Regine Barth and Birgid Dette, 'The Integration of Voluntary Agreements into Existing Legal Systems' (2001) 1 *Environmental Law Network International Review* 20. Likewise, the Netherlands' domestic nitrous oxide trading scheme is also a relative scheme, setting a relative target in amounts of nitrogen oxide emissions per unit of energy consumed. See also Markus Gehring and Charlotte Streck, 'Emissions Trading: Lessons from SOx and NOx Emissions Allowance and Credit Systems: Legal Nature, Title, Transfer and Taxation of Emission Allowances and Credits (2005) 35 *Environmental Law Reporter* 10219.

[62] The baseline is usually expressed in terms of the source's emissions efficiency compared to its activity. Unlike cap and trade regimes, however, allowances are not allocated up-front, but when a source demonstrates that it is performing better than its baseline.

have sufficient allowances to cover their actual emissions. In addition, the cap may be reduced over time, to improve environmental quality. Examples of current cap and trade systems are the scheme envisaged by the Kyoto Protocol and the EU's Emissions Trading Scheme (ETS), both of which are discussed in further detail in Chapter 7.

In contrast, baseline and credit systems have relative targets: no total cap of emissions is fixed; rather, a relative target is set by defining a baseline. However, due to the relative nature of these targets, they do not give the same certainty of environmental outcome which cap and trade systems have in principle.

Overall, typical components of a tradable permit scheme are, therefore: a binding (absolute or relative) target; a unit of trade (for emissions trading, normally one tonne of carbon dioxide equivalent); a system for distributing allowances to participants; and a compliance period, at the end of which participants must have enough allowances to cover their emissions, failing which they are subject to a penalty.

The creation of the EU ETS by Directive of 2003, discussed further in Chapter 8, represents the greatest regulatory experiment the EU has ever undertaken in environmental policy. The 2003 ETS Directive created the world's first international ETS covering, at least in its initial incarnation, carbon dioxide emissions from around 11,000 large industrial installations (essentially, those covered by the EU's Integrated Pollution Prevention and Control (IPPC) Directive),[63] amounting to around 40 per cent of the EU's total GHG emissions. In its initial two phases, however, the EU's carbon market has suffered what many perceived merely to be teething problems, including a persistently low carbon price due in part to overallocation of allowances by Member States (which, under the original Directive, had been competent for allowance allocation). This led to a revision of the 2003 Directive in 2009.

However, the ETS has continued to be plagued with difficulties, which have lasted into Phase III of the scheme thus far. Foremost amongst these difficulties has been the continued descent of the EU carbon price, which plummeted to under €3 in the early months of 2013, in circumstances where it became evident that, in the context of a serious economic recession, the supply of allowances allocated to installations far exceeded demand. Aside from the pricing/oversupply issue, the ETS has also suffered from serious difficulties relating to fraud which, while not directly undermining the environmental integrity of the scheme in terms of oversupply of allowances, have raised major question marks against the credibility of the EU's carbon market more generally. In particular, the EU ETS

---

[63] Directive 2008/1/EC of the European Parliament and of the Council of 15 January 2008 concerning integrated pollution prevention and control, OJ 2008 L 24/8 (now replaced by Directive 2010/75/EU of the European Parliament and of the Council of 24 November 2010 on industrial emissions (integrated pollution prevention and control), OJ 2010 L 334/17).

has been used for wide-scale VAT fraud, in the form of bogus 'carousel' schemes peaking in 2009 and made possible by the divergent VAT treatment of EU allowances across Member States (estimated to have cost EU governments around €5 billion in total), giving rise to a concerted police response across the EU and internationally involving thousands of officers.[64] Separately, large volumes of ETS allowances have been stolen from the registry accounts in which they are kept, peaking at the end of 2010 and beginning of 2011, when allowances to a value of over €30 million were stolen. These persistent difficulties with the EU's flagship environmental market-based instrument illustrate well that bringing the 'market' into environmental policy does not remove difficulties of regulatory design.

Other Examples of the EU's Embrace of Market-Based Instruments
In a further confirmation of the central role that the EU sees for market-based environmental policy instruments in Europe, the 2012 Energy Efficiency Directive[65] contains an innovative provision obliging Member States to create national energy efficiency obligation schemes, but expressly allowing them to employ a variety of market-based measures (such as transferable certified energy savings, energy and carbon taxes and voluntary environmental agreements) in implementation of, or as an alternative to, such schemes.[66] However, in spite of this support for national energy taxes, the EU continues to have difficulty in progressing proposals in relation to a harmonised EU-level energy tax, due to the need for unanimity within the Council in order for such a measure to pass. Following an unsuccessful 1992 Commission proposal on the matter,[67] and a 2003 Directive leaving much leeway to Member States in the field,[68] the Commission's newest (2011) Proposal[69] is currently stalled in the Council.[70] Aside from the 2003 Directive, there are few examples of environmental charges, and taxes currently in use at the EU level are few,[71] due mainly to the reluctance of Member States to allow the EU to legislate on fiscal matters, which is still subject to unanimity of voting under the legal bases for indirect taxation[72] and direct taxation.[73] By contrast, the EU plays an

---

[64] See Europol Press Release, 'Further investigations into VAT fraud linked to the carbon emissions trading system', 28 December 2010.
[65] Directive 2012/27/EU of the European Parliament and of the Council of 25 October 2012 on energy efficiency, amending Directives 2009/125/EC and 2010/30/EU and repealing Directives 2004/8/EC and 2006/32/EC, OJ 2012 L 315/1.
[66] Article 7. [67] COM(1992)226.
[68] Council Directive 2003/96/EC of 27 October 2003 restructuring the Community framework for the taxation of energy products and electricity, OJ 2003 L 283/51.
[69] COM(2011)169.
[70] See Council of the EU, Irish Presidency Note, 'Energy Taxation Directive – State of Play', 12 June 2013, 10825/13.
[71] See, generally, Commission Communication, 'Environmental taxes and charges in the Single Market', COM(97) 9 final.
[72] Article 113 TFEU – i.e. taxation not collected directly from the taxpayer, such as VAT.
[73] Article 115 TFEU – i.e. taxation collected directly from the taxpayer, such as income tax.

important role in regulating environmental subsidies and taxation in Europe via its State aid policy.[74]

Network-Based Approaches: Voluntary Techniques and Corporate Social Responsibility

Overview

In addition to hierarchy and market-based instruments, our final family of regulatory instruments involves voluntary instruments, whereby the regulator's role is essentially to enable and incentivise a network of corporate and social actors to contribute to achieving environmental objectives. Where the actor at issue is a corporation, such regulatory techniques fall under the broad-umbrella phenomenon of Corporate Social Responsibility (CSR).

In the environmental context, network-based, CSR-inspired regulatory techniques have led to the incentivisation of voluntary agreements and covenants, environmental codes and charters, voluntary environmental management systems and voluntary eco-labels. The CSR concept has awakened massive interest in policy-makers at national, EU and international levels, who have latched onto it eagerly as fitting perfectly with the goals of sustainable development and environmental integration – once again, as a way of combining growth and enterprise with environmental protection.[75] The difficulty from a regulatory perspective, of course, is that the regulator is tasked with creating an architecture or regulatory climate that is favourable to voluntary pro-environmental activity, without crossing over into actually mandating such activity. This demands a subtle and sophisticated understanding of the interrelation between regulation and individual/corporate autonomous decision-making or, as Tanja Börzel has termed it, the 'shadow of a hierarchy'.[76] This rather delicate balance between intervention and laissez-faire has been characterised by Richard Thaler and Cass Sunstein, in their book *Nudge*, as 'libertarian paternalism' or 'choice architecture'.[77]

As with the EU's Sustainable Development Strategy, a win–win discourse is employed in EU CSR policy, arguing that greener behaviour can give firms a market advantage (consumers, investors and employees may prefer greener firms; early development of greener technologies will give a first-mover

---

[74] See, further, Kingston, *Greening EU Competition Law and Policy*.
[75] See, generally, Thomas Lyon and John Maxwell, *Corporate Environmentalism and Public Policy* (Cambridge University Press, 2004) (who describe corporate environmentalism as 'the most notable trend in environmental policy since the 1990s') and Olivier De Schutter, 'Corporate Social Responsibility European Style' (2008) 14(2) *European Law Journal* 203.
[76] Tanja A. Börzel, 'European Governance: Negotiation and Competition in the Shadow of Hierarchy' (2010) 48(2) *Journal of Common Market Studies* 191–219.
[77] Richard Thaler and Cass Sunstein, *Nudge* (Yale University Press, 2008).

advantage) or reduce environmental costs (energy costs, the costs of cleaning up pollution). From an environmental democracy perspective, by providing consumers with additional information on environmental performance in taking purchase decisions, market transparency can be increased.

At worst, however, voluntary environmental initiatives may be employed tactically by undertakings to avoid being regulated – and the concomitant costs of compliance, potential inefficiency and loss of control over the applicable standard and regime – or to postpone it for as long as possible.[78] Moreover, empirical economic research suggests that this may be a tactic that works.[79] A high-profile illustration within the EU was the choice of the EU car industry to enter into agreements on emissions standards, essentially in order to avoid being regulated. After unsatisfactory environmental performance, this ended in failure in 2010 when the EU lost patience, passing a Regulation on passenger car emissions.[80]

Overall, many view CSR as little more than a cosmetic exercise, with no assurance that environmental objectives will be attained, little accountability on the part of undertakings, and little ultimate practical effect on the behaviour of businesses.[81] Such criticism comes not only from the environmental camp, but also from the corporate governance perspective: in the capitalist corporate model, managers are accountable to shareholders for profits, and any attempts to achieve other goals at the same time are illegitimate. The 'triple bottom line' which the UN and the Commission advocate – aiming not just to make money, but also to protect the environment and to improve social justice – distracts attention from ultimate managerial duties.

In sum, as with market-based approaches, voluntary initiatives have in some circumstances certain clear advantages in comparison to direct regulation. In the right context, they may offer an important contribution to achieving a higher level of environmental protection by complementing, though not replacing, direct regulation. Their principal disadvantage lies in their very nature: they are not compulsory, and therefore inappropriate for use alone to deal with immediately serious environmental risks. Even where their use is in principle appropriate, their success in achieving environmental protection goals (and, where relevant, environmental governance goals) depends on how the initiative is constructed and functions in practice.

---

[78] In this way, CSR can become 'a codeword for abandoning to market mechanisms certain questions which might otherwise be the target of regulatory approaches': De Schutter, 'Corporate Social Responsibility European Style', 204.
[79] See Christopher Decker, 'Corporate Environmentalism and Environmental Statutory Permitting' (2003) 46 *Journal of Law and Economics* 103.
[80] Regulation 443/2009 of the European Parliament and of the Council of 23 April 2009 setting emissions performance standards for new passenger cars as part of the Community's integrated approach to reduce CO_2 emissions from light-duty vehicles, OJ 2009 L 140/1.
[81] See Anthony Ogus, 'Rethinking Self-Regulation' (1995) 15 *Oxford Journal of Legal Studies* 97.

Enabling Corporations

The European Commission defines CSR as:[82]

> the responsibility of enterprises for their impacts on society. Respect for applicable legislation, and for collective agreements between social partners, is a prerequisite for meeting that responsibility. To fully meet their corporate social responsibility, enterprises should have in place a process to integrate social, environmental, ethical, human rights and consumer concerns into their business operations and core strategy in close collaboration with their stakeholders, with the aim of:
> – maximising the creation of shared value for their owners/shareholders and for their other stakeholders and society at large;
> – identifying, preventing and mitigating their possible adverse impacts.

Clearly, therefore, the CSR concept goes well beyond environmental issues, to human rights and other social concerns. The concept does not, however, dictate which of these concerns the corporation at issue should prioritise.

At the EU level, the European Commission has developed a CSR 'agenda', which is largely based on soft-law, non-binding efforts such as enhancing the visibility of CSR and disseminating good practices. However, it has also led to measures with more teeth, including a 2014 Directive on disclosure of non-financial and diversity information by large companies (with more than 500 employees) and groups.[83] This will oblige companies falling within its scope to disclose information on policies, risks and outcomes as regards, amongst other things, environmental matters. However, companies are left with significant flexibility as to the manner in which they choose to disclose relevant information (for instance, they may follow UN, European or national guidelines, depending on their preference).

A further outcome of the current EU CSR agenda has been an emphasis on improving self- and co-regulation processes. In the environmental context, an important technique for achieving this has been the use of voluntary environmental agreements, i.e. agreements entered into by private parties aimed at achieving environmental objectives.[84] These may include

---

[82] Commission Communication, 'Implementing the Partnership for Growth and Jobs: Making Europe a pole of excellence on CSR', COM(2006)136 final, restated in Commission Communication, 'A Renewed EU Strategy 2011–2014 for Corporate Social Responsibility', COM(2011)681 final.

[83] Directive 2014/95/EU of the European Parliament and of the Council of 22 October 2014 amending Directive 2013/34/EU as regards disclosure of non-financial and diversity information by certain large undertakings and groups, OJ 2014 L 330/1.

[84] Communication on Environmental Agreements, Commission Communication to the European Parliament, the Council, the Economic and Social Committee and the Committee of the Regions, COM(2002)412 final.

self-regulatory arrangements, where the agreement is put in place solely by market actors, on a voluntary basis, whether in the form of binding agreements or gentlemen's agreements. Alternatively, co-regulation may be used, i.e. where a legislative or regulatory act entrusts attainment of environmental aims to non-State actors.[85]

In some cases, such as in the USA's public voluntary programme, the legislator or regulator establishes the key elements of the regulation – which may, for instance, include the regulatory objectives, the deadlines and mechanisms relating to implementation, methods of monitoring the application of the legislation and any sanctions which are necessary to guarantee the legal certainty of the legislation – and the firms subsequently agree on the means of implementing it.[86] In other cases, as is popular within many EU States, the regulator and industry may arrive at a negotiated agreement, which includes environmental obligations.[87] Voluntary agreements have traditionally been particularly popular as part of the regulatory mix in the Netherlands, Germany and Denmark.

The European Commission has signalled its cautious approval and encouragement of the use of environmental agreements in Communications of 1996 and 2002, and has formally recognised voluntary agreements on a number of occasions, normally by adopting a Recommendation confirming the content of the industry's engagement, or simply acknowledging the environmental agreement by exchange of letters. The Commission has stressed, however, that such action can 'never' mean that it forgoes its right of initiative.[88]

A further type of corporate voluntary environmental initiative is the use of eco-management standards in undertakings' internal processes and planning, in

---

[85] See the EU's definition included in the *Interinstitutional Agreement on better law making*, OJ 2003 C 321/4, at para. 18.

[86] An example is the US EPA's 33/50 Programme, which invited firms to commit to reducing 17 priority chemicals and set as its goal a 33 per cent reduction in releases and transfers of these chemicals by 1992 and a 50 per cent reduction by 1995, measured against a 1988 baseline. See Gunningham, 'Environmental Law, Regulation and Governance: Shifting Architectures', 186.

[87] For example, the Federated Association of German Industry in 1995 agreed to propose a reduction of carbon dioxide emissions by up to 20 per cent by 2005, in exchange for which the federal government announced the withdrawal of plans to introduce a waste heat ordinance and promised an exemption from a possible energy tax.

[88] Communication on Environmental Agreements, COM(2002)412 final, p. 5. See e.g. the recommendations issued acknowledging a voluntary agreement on the labelling of detergents in 1989 (Commission Recommendation 89/542/EEC, OJ 1989 L 291/55), and the recommendations acknowledging voluntary agreements between associations of European, Japanese and Korean car manufacturers on the reduction of carbon dioxide emissions from passenger cars (Commission Recommendation 1999/125, OJ 1999 L 40/49, Commission Recommendation 2000/303, OJ 2000 L 100/45 and Commission Recommendation 2000/304, OJ 2000 L 100/57).

order to achieve environmental aims. While some environmental management standards are mandatory, a substantial number are voluntary, with firms choosing to sign up to eco-management systems in order to enjoy regulatory rewards and/or enhanced consumer reputation. In terms of public perception, the success of the publication of an environmental report by undertakings ultimately depends on the reliability of the information and whether consumers and/or shareholders will find it convincing. Adherence to credible, recognised environmental initiatives, such as environmental management systems and ecolabels, discussed further below, increases the credibility of such reports.

At an international level, eco-management standards have been formalised in the ISO 14001 environmental management systems standard of the International Organization for Standardization.[89] A further relatively successful framework for environmental reporting has developed in the form of non-binding guidelines issued by the Global Reporting Initiative (GRI), a multi-stakeholder network launched in 1997 by the Ceres group of investors and environmental organisations.[90]

In 1993, the EU passed a Regulation creating its own voluntary Eco-Management and Audit Scheme (EMAS), now covered by Regulation 1221/2009.[91] With disappointing uptake in the 1990s and 2000s, one of the principal aims of the 2009 Regulation was to increase participation by (EU and non-EU)[92] undertakings. Essentially, in order to participate in EMAS, an undertaking must conduct an environmental review and audit of its activities, products and services, have these documents verified by an '*environmental verifier*',[93] then prepare an environmental statement as set out in Annex IV of the Regulation. These documents are submitted to the competent authority in the relevant Member State for a decision on registration.[94] Databases detailing EMAS-registered organisations, environmental statements, and environmental verifiers are made publicly available by the Commission.[95] A key feature of the 2009 Regulation is the EU's desire to avoid duplication of effort by undertakings. Thus, the substantive requirements of EMAS mirror to some extent the ISO 14001 standard,[96] and Member States may request the Commission to recognise

---

[89] The International Organization for Standardization is a non-governmental organisation comprised of national standards agencies of 162 countries. See www.iso.org.
[90] By the end of the decade, 35 per cent of the world's 250 largest companies voluntarily produced formal corporate environmental reports, many of them based on GRI guidelines. *Ibid.*, 389.
[91] Regulation (EC) No. 1221/2009 of the European Parliament and of the Council of 25 November 2009 on the voluntary participation by organisations in a Community eco-management and audit scheme (EMAS), repealing Regulation (EC) No. 761/2001 and Commission Decisions 2001/681/EC and 2006/193/EC, OJ 2009 L 342/1 (the 'EMAS Regulation').
[92] EMAS Regulation, Article 1.
[93] *Ibid.* Chapter 5 sets out the requirement for environmental verifiers.
[94] *Ibid.*, Article 3 and chapter 4.   [95] *Ibid.*, Article 42.   [96] *Ibid.*, Annex II.

national environmental management standards as fulfilling part or all of the EMAS requirements.[97]

Enabling Consumers and Civil Society

The key legal method of enabling individuals and civil society to become involved in environmental regulation and decision-making is clearly the Aarhus Convention, which is based on the principles of access to information, public participation and access to justice in environmental matters. This is discussed in Chapter 5. Aside from this, the EU's ecolabel regulation is perhaps its leading instrument aimed at nudging European consumers towards environmentally friendlier behaviour. This voluntary scheme was established in 1992, leading to the award of the EU flower logo. Applicant manufacturers must apply to the relevant national competent authority to be awarded the EU's flower eco-label. Although the Eco-Label Regulation sets out broad criteria for the award, detailed requirements are developed through the EU's Eco-Labelling Board, composed of national competent authorities and a 'consultation forum' comprising a 'balanced participation of all relevant interested parties concerned with that product group'.[98] In 2010, a new ecolabel Regulation was passed,[99] aimed in large part at increasing the label's effectiveness, including by streamlining the award process.

A variety of other EU labelling measures coexist with the Flower label, some of which are mandatory, some voluntary. Examples of mandatory measures include the EU's organic farming Regulation, which sets down requirements for organic production,[100] and the energy class rating system, which identifies refrigerators, freezers and other household equipment which are particularly economical in terms of electricity consumption.[101] Similar initiatives have been undertaken for buildings, where participation is on a voluntary basis, with energy efficiency

---

[97] Ibid., Article 45.
[98] Ibid., Article 15. Grant of the eco-label can have further consequences: for example, when granted to an energy-using product, the eco-label means that the product is considered to comply with Directive 2009/125/EC of the European Parliament and of the Council of 21 October 2009 establishing a framework for the setting of ecodesign requirements for energy related products, OJ 2010 L 285/10.
[99] Regulation (EC) No. 66/2010 of the European Parliament and of the Council of 25 November 2009 on the EU Ecolabel, OJ 2010 L 27/1. Medicinal products and certain hazardous chemicals are excluded from the system.
[100] Council Regulation (EC) No. 834/2007 of 28 June 2007 on organic production and labelling of organic products and repealing Regulation (EEC) No. 2092/91, OJ 2007 L 189/1. A new regulation has been proposed by the European Commission: COM(2014) 180 final.
[101] Ratings range from A++ rating to G. See Directive 2010/30/EU of the European Parliament and of the Council of 19 May 2010 on the indication by labelling and standard product information of the consumption of energy and other resources by energy-related products, OJ 2010 L 153/1. See also Regulation (EC) No. 106/2008 of the European Parliament and of the Council of 15 January 2008 on a Community energy-efficiency labelling programme for office equipment, OJ 2008 L 39/1.

certificates being awarded for energy-efficient structures.[102] Further, the Commission has indicated its willingness to recognise voluntary schemes set up by operators to demonstrate their compliance with biofuels or bioliquids requirements set out in EU legislation.[103]

---

[102] For a list, see the Commission Communication, 'Action Plan for Energy Efficiency: Realising the Potential', COM(2006)545 final, p. 9.
[103] Commission Communication on voluntary schemes and default values in the EU biofuels and bioliquids sustainability scheme, OJ 2010 C 160/1.

5

Environmental Rights in Europe

Introduction: Why Environmental (Human) Rights?

> Man has the fundamental right to freedom, equality and adequate conditions of life, in an environment of a quality that permits a life of dignity and well-being, and he bears a solemn responsibility to protect and improve the environment for present and future generations.
>
> Principle 1, Report of the UN Conference on the Human Environment, Declaration of the UN Conference on the Human Environment, UN Doc. A/CONF.48.14/Rev.1, p. 3 (5–16 June 1972) (the 'Stockholm Declaration')

In addition to the regulatory techniques discussed in the previous Chapter – hierarchical, market-based and network-based – a further important means of achieving environmental protection in Europe is by recognising environmental rights. While environmental rights discourse has become more prevalent in Europe in recent years, there are many different understandings of what precisely is meant by an environmental right, and what the consequences of breach of such a right might be. This chapter discusses these understandings, their development before the European courts and other institutions, and the implications of such development.

As the above extract from the Stockholm Declaration illustrates, conceptualising environmental protection in terms of a human right to an environment of a decent quality is nothing new.

Yet, over 30 years after this Declaration, the application of human rights principles to environmental issues remains contested. Central questions of controversy include the following:

- Who should have standing to enforce environmental human rights? Should standing be limited to the victims of breaches of rights, as is traditional in many human rights regimes, or should those acting in the public interest have standing to bring environmental rights claims?
- How can we ensure that the interests of future generations, who may be severely affected by environmental degradation occurring now, are represented?
- Does a human rights-based approach to environmental protection risk prioritising anthropocentric, human-focused concerns over other environmental concerns?

- Does a human rights-based approach to environmental protection mean applying existing general human rights law to environment-related issues (i.e. 'greening' existing human rights)? Or should we recognise a self-standing right to a decent environment?[1]
- Alternatively, should we focus on embedding procedural rights such as those ensuring that the public is informed of, and can participate in and challenge, environmental decisions, rather than trying to define a substantive right to a decent environment?

Underpinning these questions is the broader debate about *why* environmental protection should be treated as a human rights issue (or why not). While there are many views on this debate, it is clear that a human rights-based approach enables the effects of environmental damage on the lives and property of individuals to be directly addressed in a way that may not be possible using environmental regulation focused on protecting the environment as such. Human rights approaches might also increase environmental protection, in that many States have signed up to far-reaching human rights obligations, and have given human rights a pre-eminent status within their legal order, in a way which they have not done for environmental concerns more generally.[2]

Against this, however, some have argued that human rights approaches to environmental protection are based on an unacceptably reductivist philosophy of environmental law, whereby the environment is valued largely because of its utility to humans. Further, certain human rights commentators have argued that extending human rights discourses to environmental protection risks diluting the force of the classic, traditional civil and political rights catalogue such as, in the European instance, that contained in the European Convention on Human Rights.[3] The better view is perhaps the *via media* summarised by Dinah Shelton whereby:

> human rights and environmental protection [are seen] as each representing different, but overlapping, societal values. The two fields share a core of common interests and objectives, although obviously not all human rights violations are necessarily linked to environmental degradation. Likewise, environmental issues cannot always be addressed effectively within the human rights framework, and any attempt to force all such issues into a human rights rubric may fundamentally distort the concept of human rights. This approach recognizes the potential conflicts between environmental

---

[1] For a summary of the EU States which currently recognise some kind of substantive constitutional environmental right, see the discussion in Gracia Marín Durán and Elisa Morgera, 'Article 37' in Steve Peers, Tamara Hervey, Jeff Kenner and Angela Ward (eds.), *The EU Charter of Fundamental Rights: A Commentary* (Hart Publishing, 2014). See also Article 24 of the African Charter on Human and Peoples' Rights, and Article 11 of the Additional Protocol to the American Convention on Human Rights (1969).
[2] See the discussion in Alan Boyle, 'Human Rights and the Environment: Where Next?' (2012) 23(3) *European Journal of International Law* 613.
[3] See the discussion in Donald Anton and Dinah Shelton, *Environmental Protection and Human Rights* (Cambridge University Press, 2011), 119.

> protection and human rights, but also the contribution each field can make to achieving their common objectives.[4]

Prior to discussing the remainder of the questions posed above, it is useful to examine what the current approach to environmental human rights is within Europe. One of the striking features of human rights protection within Europe is the variety of different sources of such protection. The relationship between these sources is at times complex, not only because of differences in the substantive definitions of rights protected by each regime, but also because of institutional differences between the regimes, as well as potential differences in the legal status accorded by signatory States to rights protected by these regimes. While a detailed discussion of European human rights law is outside the scope of this book, an understanding of these differences is nevertheless important in appreciating the variations in approach to environmental human rights within Europe at present.[5] This chapter discusses the following sources of environmental rights protection within Europe:

- rights originating from the Council of Europe, in particular the 1950 European Convention for the Protection of Human Rights and Fundamental Freedoms (the 'ECHR') and the 1961 European Social Charter (the 'ESC');
- rights originating from EU law, in particular the Charter of Fundamental Rights of the EU (the 'EU Charter');
- rights contained in the 1998 Convention on Access to Information, Public Participation in Decision-Making and Access to Justice in Environmental Matters (the 'Aarhus Convention').

The chapter concludes with a brief discussion of other sources of environmental rights, namely, relevant international human rights law applicable to European States.

It is fair to say that, internationally, environmental rights have progressed the most in the field of civil and political rights, especially in the area of procedural rights and the right to respect for family and private life. Nevertheless, as the discussion below indicates, progress has been made in certain jurisdictions in recent years in recognising and, perhaps more importantly, enforcing certain economic and social rights of direct environmental relevance including, in some cases, a right to a decent/healthy environment.

---

[4] Dinah Shelton, 'Human Rights, Environmental Rights, and the Right to Environment' (1991) 28 *Stanford Journal of International Law* 103, at 105.
[5] See, on ECHR law, David Harris, Michael O'Boyle, Ed Bates and Carla Buckley, *Law of the European Convention on Human Rights* (3rd edn., Oxford University Press, 2014); on the EU Charter of Fundamental Rights, Peers et al., *The EU Charter of Fundamental Rights: A Commentary*. For an overview of the interaction between international human rights law and environmental protection, see Sands and Peel, *Principles of International Environmental Law*, 775–789 and, for a fuller discussion, Anna Grear and Louis Kotzé (eds.), *Research Handbook on Human Rights and the Environment* (Edward Elgar, 2015).

Rights Originating from the Council of Europe

The 1950 European Convention for the Protection of Human Rights and Fundamental Freedoms (the 'ECHR')

The ECHR was concluded under the auspices of the Council of Europe, and has been ratified to date by 47 States. Dealing essentially with civil and political rights, it falls under the ultimate jurisdiction of the European Court of Human Rights (ECtHR) in Strasbourg, which consists of 47 permanent, full-time judges, that is, one per Contracting State. While all EU Member States have ratified the ECHR in their own right, the EU is not currently a party. The Treaty of Lisbon expressly enabled the EU to accede to the ECHR, although the CJEU rejected the draft accession agreement put before it in Opinion 2/13 on grounds that it was incompatible with the TEU.[6]

The ECHR does not contain any express provision concerning the environment. Nevertheless, the ECtHR's jurisprudence applying ECHR rights to environmental issues is, by now, considerable. These cases largely concern Article 8 ECHR, which protects the right of an individual to respect for his or her private and family life, home and correspondence, but have also involved Article 2 ECHR protecting the right to life,[7] Article 6 ECHR protecting the right to a fair hearing in the determination of civil rights and obligations, Article 10 ECHR on freedom of expression,[8] and Article 1 of Protocol No. 1 to the ECHR on the right to property. The Council of Europe has produced a Manual on Human Rights and the Environment giving an overview of the case law of the ECtHR and the decisions of the European Committee of Social Rights in this area.[9]

No Right to a Decent Environment

The ECtHR has consistently refused to recognise any right to a healthy or decent environment as such in the ECHR. In *Kyrtatos* v. *Greece*, the ECtHR addressed this issue head on, in refusing to extend the scope of Article 8 ECHR to the protection of the environment as such, in the absence of proof of interference with the applicant's private or family life.

That case concerned a challenge to the Greek authorities' decision to zone and grant a building permit for an area of swampland adjacent to the applicants' home. One of the arguments raised by the applicants was that the urban development had destroyed the swamp at issue, damaging the habitats of birds and other protected species, and destroying the area's scenic beauty.

---

[6] *Opinion 2/13* ECLI:EU:C:2014:2454.
[7] See, for instance, ECtHR, *Öneryildiz* v. *Turkey*, 30 November 2014 (Appl. no. 48939/99) (illegal landfill resulted in methane explosion and a landslide of refuse, covering adjacent slum dwellings and killing 39 people).
[8] Particularly in relation to access to information on the environment.
[9] *Manual on Human Rights and the Environment* (2nd edn., Council of Europe Publishing, 2012).

Rejecting this argument, the ECtHR held that, while severe environmental pollution may affect individuals' well-being and prevent them from enjoying their homes in such a way as to affect their private and family life adversely, without seriously endangering their health (see *López Ostra*, discussed below), the crucial element in order for Article 8 to be applicable was the existence of a harmful effect on a person's private or family sphere and not simply the general deterioration of the environment. Neither Article 8 nor any of the other Articles of the Convention is specifically designed to provide general protection of the environment as such; to that effect, other international instruments and domestic legislation are more pertinent in dealing with this particular aspect.[10]

Notably, however, numerous efforts have been made over the years to insert a right to a decent environment into the ECHR, beginning with a German proposal of 1973 which was rejected by the Committee of Ministers on the basis that there was no need for such a provision.[11] The Parliamentary Assembly of the Council of Europe has, more recently, called for the addition of a protocol to the ECHR on the right to a healthy and viable environment.[12] No action has yet been taken on this issue by the Committee of Ministers.

Article 8 ECHR: Right to Respect for Private and Family Life

Development of the ECtHR's Approach

The ECtHR's approach to Article 8 in the environmental context was broadly summarised by the Grand Chamber in *Hatton v. United Kingdom* as follows,

> There is no explicit right in the Convention to a clean and quiet environment, but where an individual is directly and seriously affected by noise or other pollution, an issue may arise under Article 8.[13]

The groundwork for this approach was laid in a number of important judgments in the 1990s. In *Powell and Rayner v. the United Kingdom*, the applicants complained about disturbance from daytime aircraft noise from Heathrow airport. The ECtHR applied a two-stage reasoning which remains characteristic of its analysis in these cases:

---

[10] ECtHR, *Kyrtatos v. Greece*, 22 May 2003 (Appl. no. 41666/98), para. 52.
[11] See Jonathan Verschuuren, 'Contribution of the Case Law of the European Court of Human Rights to Sustainable Development in Europe' in Werner Scholtz and Jonathan Verschuuren (eds.), *Regional Integration and Sustainable Development in a Globalised World* (Edward Elgar, 2015).
[12] See, most recently, Recommendation 1885 of 30 September 2009 of the Parliamentary Assembly.
[13] ECtHR, *Hatton v. UK*, 8 July 2003 (Appl. no. 36022/97), para. 96.

First, are the applicants' right to private and family life sufficiently affected by the environmental degradation (in that case, noise pollution) to mean that Article 8 is applicable? In *Powell and Rayner*, this was indeed the case, as 'the quality of [each] applicant's private life and the scope for enjoying the amenities of his home [had] been adversely affected by the noise generated by aircraft using Heathrow Airport'.[14]

Secondly, if Article 8 is applicable, has it been violated? In *Powell and Rayner*, the ECtHR held that, in assessing breach, regard must be had to the fair balance that has to be struck between the competing interests of the individual and of the community as a whole; and in both contexts the State enjoys a certain margin of appreciation in determining the steps to be taken to ensure compliance with the Convention.[15]

Applying this test, the ECtHR took into account the measures which had been introduced by the competent authorities to control the levels of aircraft noise, such as aircraft noise certification, night flight restrictions, and runway alternation, noting that these measures had been, 'adopted progressively as a result of consultation of the different interests and people concerned, have taken due account of international standards established, developments in aircraft technology, and the varying levels of disturbance suffered by those living around Heathrow Airport'.[16] It followed that no violation of Article 8 had been established.

In its seminal judgment in *López Ostra* v. *Spain*, however, the ECtHR took the principles set down in *Powell and Rayner* further by finding a violation of Article 8 ECHR in the case of a complaint about a liquid and solid waste management plant operated by a group of tanneries some 12 metres from the applicant's home. The applicant claimed that the fumes, repetitive noise and strong smells caused her and her family serious health problems. Despite the conflicting evidence about the seriousness of the health problems caused in that case, the ECtHR held that Article 8 was applicable, as severe environmental pollution could 'affect individuals' well-being and prevent them from enjoying their homes in such a way as to affect their private and family life adversely, without, however, seriously endangering their health'.[17]

As to the question of violation, the ECtHR noted that, in this case, as soon as it started up, the plant caused nuisance and health problems for the locals. Further, while the plant was not run by the State, the Spanish authorities bore some direct responsibility in that the town where the plant was located allowed it to be built on its land, and the State subsidised the plant's construction. Further, while the town had subsequently rehoused the family in the centre of town, this had only been done after 3 years had elapsed. The ECtHR concluded that Spain had not implemented the measures necessary for protecting the applicant's right to respect for her home and for her private and family life under Article 8.

[14] ECtHR, 21 February 1990 (Appl. no. 9310/81), para. 40.   [15] *Ibid.*, para. 41.
[16] *Ibid.*, para. 43.   [17] ECtHR, 9 December 1994 (Appl. no. 16798/90), para. 51.

More recently, in *Hardy and Maile* v. *UK*, the ECtHR further clarified its approach to the applicability of Article 8 ECHR, holding that,

> In cases concerning environmental pollution, the pollution must attain a certain minimum level if the complaints are to fall within the scope of Article 8 ... The assessment of that minimum is relative and depends on all the circumstances of the case, such as the intensity and duration of the nuisance and its physical or mental effects. The general context of the environment should also be taken into account. There would be no arguable claim under Article 8 if the detriment complained of was negligible in comparison to the environmental hazards inherent to life in every modern city.[18]

In that case, Article 8 ECHR was held to be applicable to a challenge to the construction and operation of two liquefied natural gas (LNG) terminals in a harbour, despite the fact that there was no suggestion that the normal operation of the terminals posed any risk to the applicants or to the environment, and there was no allegation that the terminals caused continued pollution of the harbour. However, the evidence showed that there was a risk of collision in the harbour, which could lead to the escape of a large quantity of LNG and the potential for an explosion or a fire as a result of such (hypothetical) accident. The ECtHR relied, in reaching this conclusion, on the facts that the project was such as to necessitate environmental impact assessments pursuant to the EU EIA Directive, and that the terminals fell within the scope of the UK's laws controlling major accident hazards.[19] Nevertheless, there had been no violation of Article 8 ECHR in that case, as the evidence showed that the domestic UK authorities had carried out a detailed risk assessment, which the applicants had not countered with their own expert evidence, and there was a 'coherent and comprehensive legislative and regulatory framework governing the activities in question'.[20] This element of the case is discussed further below.

The Relevance of Adequate Procedures to the Article 8 Assessment
In a number of judgments, the ECtHR has focused on the extent to which adequate procedures were followed, including the public availability of relevant information, in assessing whether Article 8 ECHR was violated in environmental cases.

---

[18] ECtHR, *Hardy and Maile* v. *UK*, 14 February 2012 (Appl. no. 31965/07), para. 188. See also ECtHR, *Fadeyeva* v. *Russia*, 9 June 2005 (Appl. no. 55723/00).

[19] ECtHR, *Hardy and Maile* v. *UK*, 14 February 2012 (Appl. no. 31965/07), paras. 190–191. Contrast, for instance, ECtHR, *Atanasov* v. *Bulgaria* [2010] 2 December 2010 (Appl. no. 12853/03), where Article 8 was held to be inapplicable because the applicant, who complained about the reclamation of a pond near his home, had not 'apparently suffered any actual harm to date': para. 78. See, similarly, ECtHR, *Orlikowscy* v. *Poland*, 4 October 2011 (Appl. no. 7153/07).

[20] ECtHR, *Hardy and Maile* v. *UK*, 14 February 2012 (Appl. no. 31965/07), para. 231.

In *Guerra* v. *Italy*, the ECtHR found a violation of Article 8 ECHR where the applicants lived around one kilometre away from a chemical factory which produced fertiliser and other chemical compounds, and claimed (without being contradicted by the State) that in the course of its production cycle the factory released large quantities of inflammable gas, which could potentially cause explosive chemical reactions, as well as sulphur dioxide, nitric oxide, sodium, ammonia, metal hydrides, benzoic acid and arsenic trioxide. It was accepted that accidents had occurred in the past, including one which resulted in an explosion following which 150 people were admitted to hospital for acute arsenic poisoning.

The ECtHR reasoned that, first, Article 8 was applicable, due to the direct effect of the toxic emissions on the applicants' right to respect for their private and family life.[21] Secondly, as to violation of Article 8 ECHR, the ECtHR concluded that the State had failed in its positive obligation to take the necessary steps to ensure effective protection of this right, in that the residents had not received essential information that would have enabled them to assess the risks they and their families might run if they continued to live in the town at highest risk from the effects of a potential accident. In so holding, the ECtHR effectively incorporated procedural rights of access to information into its substantive analysis of whether Article 8 had been violated. By contrast, the ECtHR rejected in that case the argument that Article 10 ECHR imposed a positive obligation to collect, process and disseminate information in order to prevent any violation of rights occurring.[22]

The relevance of adequate procedures and information in analysing Article 8 ECHR violations was also evident in *Taşkin* v. *Turkey*, in which the applicants appealed against the Turkish authorities' decision to issue a permit for an operating process using sodium cyanide in a gold mine. Expanding upon the *López Ostra* principles, the ECtHR placed great weight on the fact that an environmental impact assessment had been carried out, holding that Article 8 was applicable where the dangerous effects of an activity to which the individuals concerned are likely to be exposed have been determined as part of an environmental impact assessment procedure in such a way as to establish a sufficiently close link with private and family life for the purposes of Article 8 of the Convention.[23]

In assessing whether a violation of Article 8 had occurred, the ECtHR recalled its case law outside the environmental context holding that whilst Article 8 contains no explicit procedural requirements, 'the decision-making process leading to measures of interference must be fair and such as to afford due respect for the interests of the individual as safeguarded by Article 8'.[24]

---

[21] ECtHR, 19 February 1998 (Appl. no. 14967/89), para. 57.   [22] *Ibid.*, para. 53.
[23] ECtHR, *Taşkin* v. *Turkey*, 10 November 2004 (Appl. no. 46117/99), para. 113.
[24] *Ibid.*, para. 118.

Drawing on its prior case law, the ECtHR summarised the procedural requirements imposed by Article 8 ECHR as follows,

> Where a State must determine complex issues of environmental and economic policy, the decision-making process must firstly involve appropriate investigations and studies in order to allow them to predict and evaluate in advance the effects of those activities which might damage the environment and infringe individuals' rights and to enable them to strike a fair balance between the various conflicting interests at stake (see *Hatton* [...]). The importance of public access to the conclusions of such studies and to information which would enable members of the public to assess the danger to which they are exposed is beyond question (see, [*Guerra* v. *Italy*]). Lastly, the individuals concerned must also be able to appeal to the courts against any decision, act or omission where they consider that their interests or their comments have not been given sufficient weight in the decision-making process (see [*Hatton*]).[25]

In that case, while the original permit for the gold mine had been granted following appropriate consultation and studies, a subsequent judgment of the Turkish Supreme Administrative Court holding the mine to have breached the right to life and a healthy environment in the Turkish Constitution had effectively been ignored, and a new authorisation had subsequently been granted.[26] As a result, Article 8 had been violated.

In *Tätar* v. *Romania*, the ECtHR further developed these principles in holding that Article 8 ECHR was applicable in a case also concerning the risk posed by the use of sodium cyanide at a gold mine, but where there was no contemporaneous domestic report indicating the degree of danger posed by the mining in a sufficiently clear manner.[27] Nevertheless, the ECtHR held that the environmental impacts were evident in that case, particularly as there had been an accident involving chemical spillage during the relevant period. Further, Article 8 had been violated in circumstances where, despite the fact that Romania had ratified the Aarhus Convention, in contrast to *Hatton* and *Taşkin*, the applicants had not had the opportunity to see the results of studies carried out on the mine.[28] In so holding, it is significant that the ECtHR again placed weight on the existence of a right to a healthy environment in Romanian constitutional law, as well as the precautionary principle of international environmental law.[29] *Tätar*, therefore, represents a fascinating example of cross-fertilisation between different strands of international and domestic law (Aarhus Convention, precautionary principle, national constitutional law) in determining the limits of environmental human rights in Europe.

The Margin of Appreciation

The limits of Article 8 ECHR in the environmental context are clear from *Kyrtatos* v. *Greece*, discussed above, where ECtHR refused to extend the scope

---

[25] *Ibid.*, para. 119. [26] *Ibid.*, paras. 122–125.
[27] ECtHR, *Tätar* v. *Romania*, 27 January 2009 (Appl. no. 67021/01), para. 93.
[28] *Ibid.*, paras. 116–118. [29] *Ibid.*, para. 109.

of Article 8 ECHR to the protection of the environment as such, in the absence of proof of interference with the applicant's private or family life. The ECtHR has also, in cases involving balancing of competing interests, consistently allowed States a wide margin of appreciation. This approach is perhaps epitomised by the ECtHR's judgment in *Hatton* v. *UK*; the applicants alleged that the UK government's policy on night flights from Heathrow airport was in violation of Article 8 ECHR, as well as Article 13 ECHR on the right to an effective domestic remedy. Overturning the Chamber judgment on the matter, the Grand Chamber found that there had been no violation of Article 8 ECHR. In relation to the substantive merits of the UK government's night flights policy, the Grand Chamber recalled that States enjoyed a wide margin of appreciation in implementing social and economic policies, due to the direct democratic legitimation of national authorities. It followed that, 'in matters of general policy, on which opinions within a democratic society may reasonably differ widely, the role of the domestic policy-maker should be given special weight'.[30]

In such areas, therefore, the ECHR's role was 'fundamentally subsidiary'.[31] Applying this to the facts of the case, the ECtHR distinguished cases like *López Ostra* and *Guerra* on the basis that these cases had, in some sense, concerned a situation that was illegal or irregular as a matter of national law. By contrast, the UK's policy on night flights had been held by the UK courts to be compatible with domestic law and, according to the UK government, was necessary in the economic interest not just of airline operators and passengers, but of the country as a whole. *Hatton*, therefore, shows clearly that States may legitimately take into account negative economic effects and balance economic interests against the interests of individuals (in this case, those residents affected by noise pollution).[32] The ECtHR specifically declined to adopt a special approach to environmental protection by reference to a 'special status of environmental human rights'.[33] While a narrower approach to the margin of appreciation in assessing general policy measures might be warranted in extreme circumstances of intrusion into private life, these circumstances did not include the sleep deprivation relied upon by the applicants.[34] Nor had the applicants demonstrated any relevant procedural irregularities: while it was impossible to be certain that all relevant scientific data had been available to the UK prior to drawing up its policy, the applicants had been given the opportunity to make representations prior to the decision.

After *Hatton*, therefore, it is fair to conclude that general policy decisions involving balancing economic and environmental interests are unlikely to breach Article 8 ECHR save in exceptionally serious cases, or where adequate procedures have not been followed.

A similarly wide margin of appreciation in assessing breach is evident in *Hardy and Maile*, discussed above, where (following Hatton), the ECtHR rejected the contention that Article 8 was violated because the UK authorities allegedly had

---

[30] ECtHR, *Hatton* v. *UK*, 8 July 2003 (Appl. no. 36022/97), para. 97.   [31] *Ibid.*
[32] *Ibid.*, paras. 121–122.   [33] *Ibid.*, para. 122.   [34] *Ibid.*, para. 123.

not sufficiently considered the risks resulting from a potential port collision in proximity to LNG terminals. The ECtHR recalled that the protection afforded by Article 8 in this area does not mean that decisions can only be taken if comprehensive and measurable data are available in relation to each and every aspect of the matter to be decided. In the present case, there was a coherent and comprehensive legislative and regulatory framework governing the activities in question. It is clear that extensive reports and studies were carried out in respect of the proposed LNG terminals ... The planning and hazardous substances authorities as well as the domestic courts were satisfied with the advice provided by the relevant authorities.[35]

It followed that there had been no manifest error of appreciation by the national authorities in striking a fair balance between the competing interests in the case.

Similarly, in *Fägerskiöld v. Sweden*, the ECtHR rejected a claim that the Swedish authorities' decision to grant a permit for construction of a wind turbine violated the applicants' Article 8 ECHR rights. Aside from the fact that the applicants had not shown that the noise was sufficiently great as to constitute an interference with their private and family life, the ECtHR held that any interference was proportionate with the clear public interest in operating the wind turbine (i.e. the promotion of renewable energy), particularly as the applicants had the ongoing opportunity to request measures restricting the turbine's activity.[36]

By contrast, where the national authorities have not followed their own procedures, the ECtHR will be more ready to find an Article 8 ECHR violation. In *Moreno Gómez v. Spain*, for instance, a failure by the Spanish authorities effectively to police noise nuisance from nightclubs and bars was held to violate Article 8 ECHR; a vital factor here was that the establishments were operating in breach of their licence.[37] Similarly, in *Bor v. Hungary*, the applicant lived opposite a train station where, once the switch to diesel trains was made, noise levels breached the relevant statutory requirements. The ECtHR held that Hungary had violated Article 8 by failing to protect the applicant from this serious noise disturbance, such as by requiring a noise-proof wall to be erected.[38]

One of the most interesting recent judgments on this issue is *Kolyadenko v. Russia*, in which the ECtHR held Russia to have violated Article 8 ECHR, as well as Article 2 ECHR and Article 1 of Protocol No. 1 of the ECHR, following the

---

[35] ECtHR, *Hardy and Maile v. UK*, 14 February 2012 (Appl. no. 31965/07), para. 231.
[36] ECtHR, *Fägerskiöld v. Sweden*, 26 February 2008 (Appl. no. 37664/04). See also ECtHR, *Martinez and Manzano v. Spain*, 3 July 2012 (Appl. no. 61654/08) (no violation of Article 8 ECHR where applicants were living in an industrial zone not meant for residential use, and where the pollution from an active stone quarry was tolerable).
[37] ECtHR, *Moreno Gómez v. Spain*, 16 November 2004 (Appl. no. 4143/02). See also ECtHR, *Deés v. Hungary*, 9 November 2010 (Appl. no. 2345/06).
[38] ECtHR, *Bor v. Hungary*, 18 September 2013 (Appl. no. 50474/08).

release of large volumes of water by a Russian dam operator necessitated by particularly heavy rainfall.[39] The release flooded large areas including the applicants' homes. In that case, the evidence showed that, despite the fact that the flood was foreseeable, the residents had not been informed or warned of the flood risk or the potential consequences of a flood. Further, the authorities had failed to keep the relevant river channel clear of debris before and after the incident. Given the increased risk of flooding predicted as a result of climate change, the significance of this judgment is evident.

Article 6(1) ECHR: Right to a Fair Trial

Environmental issues have also arisen in the context of Article 6(1) ECHR, which provides for the right, in the determination of civil rights and obligations or of any criminal charge, to a fair and public hearing within a reasonable time by an independent and impartial tribunal established by law.

In many instances, these cases have concerned challenges to limits set by national procedural law on the ability to obtain effective access to justice in national courts. In *Balmer-Schafroth* v. *Switzerland*, the applicants resided in villages between four and five kilometres from a nuclear power station and claimed that their right to a fair trial had been violated by their inability to bring any judicial challenge to a decision to grant the power station's operator an indefinite extension to its permit and permission to expand its operations. In a controversial 12–8 judgment, the ECtHR held that Article 6(1) was not applicable. It reasoned that was what at issue was of a technical, not legal nature and, even supposing that the courts had the necessary knowledge and time to hear the case, the moral and political responsibility for the decision nonetheless lay with the political authorities ... If, on the other hand, every decision capable of affecting a person's pecuniary interests had, in the last instance, to be taken by a court, democratic political debate would become meaningless.[40]

The ECtHR also stated that the decision at issue, which had been taken by the Swiss Federal Council (i.e. the government executive), involved the review of whether the statutory requirements for extension of a permit had been complied with, and was therefore 'more akin to a judicial act than to a general policy decision'.[41] In any event, the ECtHR held, the applicants had not established a direct link between their complaints and their right to protection of their physical integrity, insofar as they had not shown that the dangers of injury were serious, specific and imminent. This judgment is highly problematic in many aspects, not least because all access to an independent court was denied despite the fact that the applicants claimed construction defects and safety issues with the nuclear power station. The judgment has been heavily criticised.[42]

---

[39] ECtHR, *Kolyadenko* v. *Russia*, 28 February 2012 (Appl. no. 17423/05).
[40] ECtHR, *Balmer-Schafroth* v. *Switzerland*, 26 August 1997 (Appl. no. 22110/93), para. 35.
[41] *Ibid.*, para. 37.
[42] See Nicolas de Sadeleer, *Environmental Principles: From Political Slogans to Legal Rules* (Oxford University Press, 2002), 103.

Balmer-Schafroth may be contrasted, however, with *Taşkin* v. *Turkey*, where the ECtHR held Article 6(1) to be violated in circumstances where Turkey had failed to enforce a judgment of the Turkish Supreme Administrative Court finding that the gold mine at issue breached the Turkish right to live in a healthy and balanced environment, provided by the Turkish Constitution.[43] Of course, in *Balmer-Schafroth*, the applicants had no such domestic judgment to rely on, precisely because they had been denied access to a court.

Limitations on access to justice of ENGOs can also fall under Article 6(1) ECHR. In *L'Erablière* v. *Belgium*, for instance, the ECtHR held that Belgium had violated Article 6(1) by failing to allow an NGO standing to challenge a planning permission for extension of a landfill, where the NGO had direct links to the municipality concerned.[44]

Article 1 of Protocol No. 1: The Right to Property
The right to property has also been raised in environmental cases, often raised by landowners refusing to comply with the requirements of environmental regulation. The ECtHR has largely rejected such efforts. In *Hamer* v. *Belgium*, it gave one of its strongest affirmations of the public interest in environmental protection, and the legitimacy of prioritising environmental over (individual) economic interests:

> while none of the Articles of the Convention is specifically designed to provide general protection of the environment as such (see *Kyrtatos* v. *Greece*, 22 May 2003 [Appl. no. 41666/98]), in today's society the protection of the environment is an increasingly important consideration … The environment is a cause whose defence arouses the constant and sustained interest of the public, and consequently the public authorities. Financial imperatives and even certain fundamental rights, such as ownership, should not be afforded priority over environmental protection considerations, in particular when the State has legislated in this regard. The public authorities therefore assume a responsibility which should in practice result in their intervention at the appropriate time in order to ensure that the statutory provisions enacted with the purpose of protecting the environment are not entirely ineffective.

Thus, restrictions on property rights may be allowed on condition, naturally, that a fair balance is maintained between the individual and collective interests concerned.[45]

In that case, the ECtHR held that the Belgian authorities had respected this balance in making a demolition order for the applicant's holiday home, which

---

[43] ECtHR, *Taşkin* v. *Turkey*, 10 November 2004 (Appl. no. 46117/99).
[44] Judgment of ECtHR, *L'Erablière* v. *Belgium*, 24 February 2009 (Appl. no. 49230/07). See also ECtHR, *Lizarraja* v. *Spain*, 27 April 2004 (Appl. no. 62543/00).
[45] ECtHR, *Hamer* v. *Belgium*, 27 November 2007 (Appl. no. 21861/03), paras. 79–80. See also ECtHR, *Pine Valley Development* v. *Ireland*, 29 November 1991 (Appl. no. 12742/87).

had been built without planning permission in a forested area, despite the fact that the house had been built 27 years previously.[46]

Conversely, in *Herrmann v. Germany*, the ECtHR confirmed that the imposition of an obligation to tolerate hunting on their property imposes a disproportionate burden on landowners who are opposed to hunting for ethical reasons. By imposing such an obligation, therefore, Germany had violated Article 1 of Protocol No. 1.[47]

The 1961 European Social Charter (the 'ESC')

Like the ECHR, the ESC was concluded under the auspices of the Council of Europe; it has to date been ratified by 27 States. The ESC is monitored by the European Committee of Social Rights (ECSR), a quasi-judicial body which consists of 15 (part-time) members, and who have the power to issue conclusions in respect of national annual reports submitted to it, and decisions on collective complaints submitted by eligible NGOs, trade unions and employers' organisations, where the State at issue has signed up to this mechanism.[48]

The ESC is divided into Parts, which have different functions. Part I contains a list of rights the attainment of which the parties accept 'as the aim of their policy, to be pursued by all appropriate means both national and international in character'. While many of the rights concern social and employment rights, also included is, at Article 11, the right to the protection of health, 'Everyone has the right to benefit from any measures enabling him or her to enjoy the highest possible standard of health attainable.'

Part II of the ESC specifies the obligations by which the parties undertake to 'consider themselves bound', subject to Part III. In relation to Article 11, these obligations are specified in the following terms,

> With a view to ensuring the effective exercise of the right to protection of health, the Parties undertake, either directly or in cooperation with public or private organisations, to take appropriate measures designed *inter alia*:

- to remove as far as possible the causes of ill-health;
- to provide advisory and educational facilities for the promotion of health and the encouragement of individual responsibility in matters of health;
- to prevent as far as possible epidemic, endemic and other diseases, as well as accidents.

---

[46] See also, for instance, ECtHR, *Huoltoasema Matti Eurén v. Finland*, 19 January 2010 (Appl. no. 26654/03) (requirement to apply for environmental permit compatible with Article 1 of Protocol No. 1).

[47] ECtHR, *Herrmann v. Germany*, 26 June 2012 [2012] (Appl. no. 9300/07).

[48] A list of organisations eligible to submit complaints is available at: www.coe.int/t/dghl/monitoring/socialcharter/OrganisationsEntitled/OrganisationsIndex_en.asp.

The ECSR has interpreted Article 11 as including the right to a healthy environment. In *Marangopoulos Foundation for Human Rights* v. *Greece*,[49] the applicant NGO lodged a complaint that Greece had failed to comply with Article 11 of the ESC as it had failed to take sufficient account of the environmental effects of lignite mining, or to develop an appropriate strategy to prevent and combat public health risks. The ECSR upheld the complaint. In recognising that the right to protection of health included the right to a healthy environment, the ECSR considered that it was interpreting Article 11 in the light of current conditions, and explicitly drew on a variety of other sources of international law including international environmental law, as well as the case law of the ECtHR, the Inter-American Court of Human Rights, CJEU judgments, and decisions of other international tribunals.[50] It was not decisive for this purpose that it was a company, not the State itself, which carried out the mining activities. Noting that sulphur dioxide and nitrogen oxide levels had surpassed EU law requirements in some of the areas affected by the lignite mines, the ECSR ruled that, 'Measures required under Article 11 should be designed, in the light of current knowledge, to remove the causes of ill-health resulting from environmental threats such as pollution.'[51]

While overcoming pollution was an objective that could only be achieved 'gradually', 'the states party must strive to attain this objective within a reasonable time, by showing measurable progress and making best possible use of the resources at their disposal'.

These efforts would be assessed with reference to the State's national legislation and regulations and undertakings entered into with regard to the European Union and the United Nations, as well as how the relevant law is applied in practice.[52] Applying this test, the ECSR found that, while Greece had a significant body of relevant environmental law, there were significant gaps in implementation, information was at times not passed on, and very little had been done to organise monitoring of environmental and health effects. It followed that the margin of discretion granted to the Greek authorities had been exceeded, and that Greece had 'not managed to strike a reasonable balance between the interests of persons living in the lignite mining areas and the general interest'.[53] Further, the ECSR rejected the argument that it had no jurisdiction *ratione temporis* because the pollution had been taking place for many years, finding that the obligation to prevent pollution existed in cases of continuing breach.

In *FIDH* v. *Greece*, the ECSR confirmed the approach taken in *Marangopoulos*, finding that, in failing to take enough steps to eliminate or reduce the harmful impact of the dumping of waste in the River Asopos,

---

[49] *Marangopoulos Foundation for Human Rights* v. *Greece*, Decision of 6 December 2006 (Merits), Complaint No. 30/2005.
[50] *Ibid.*, para. 195.　[51] *Ibid.*, para. 202.　[52] *Ibid.*, para. 204.　[53] *Ibid.*, para. 221.

Greece had violated Article 11.[54] While recognising that this was a 'complex situation', the ECSR noted that the situation had been unresolved for over 40 years, that the Greek authorities had delayed in taking initiatives to remedy the problems, and that those efforts which had been made had largely not helped the matter, as shown, amongst other things, by the CJEU's judgments against Greece for non-compliance with EU water law.[55] Nor had Greece provided adequate information to the persons affected by the pollution, in breach of Article 11(2) of the ESC.

The ECSR has also specified obligations to reduce environmental risk in its conclusions on certain national State reports, including concerning risks from nuclear power[56] and from asbestos.[57]

The Charter of Fundamental Rights of the EU (the 'Charter')

The Charter was solemnly proclaimed by the European Parliament, the Council of the EU and the European Commission in 2000, and became legally binding on all EU Member States with the entry into force of the Treaty of Lisbon on 1 December 2009 (the 'Charter').[58] The Charter is under the ultimate jurisdiction of the Court of Justice of the European Union in Luxembourg. The provisions of the Charter should be read alongside its Explanations which, as provided by Article 52(7) of the Charter, must be given 'due regard' by the EU and national courts.

While EU courts had, of course, recognised and developed a general principle of respect for fundamental rights in their case law long before the Charter was drafted, a key aim of the Charter was, as its Preamble states, to 'strengthen the protection of fundamental rights in the light of changes in society, social progress

---

[54] *International Federation for Human Rights (FIDH)* v. *Greece*, decision of 23 January 2013, Complaint No. 72/2011.

[55] *Ibid.*, para. 127 *et seq.*

[56] Conclusions XV-2, vol. 1, Denmark, Article 11(3), 'Reduction of environmental risks'; Conclusions XV-2, vol. 1, France, Article 11(3), 'Reduction of environmental risks'.

[57] Conclusions XVII-2, vol. 2, Portugal, Article 11(3), 'Reduction of environmental risks'; Conclusions XVII-2, vol. 2, Latvia, Article 11(3), 'Reduction of environmental risks'.

[58] At the time of negotiation of the Treaty of Lisbon, the UK and Poland negotiated a Protocol which was hailed at the time as achieving a limited 'opt-out' from the binding effect of the Charter in these Member States. Article 1(1) of the Protocol on the Application of the Charter of Fundamental Rights of the European Union to Poland and to the United Kingdom, annexed to the Treaty of Lisbon, provides, 'The Charter does not extend the ability of the Court of Justice of the European Union, or any court or tribunal of Poland or of the United Kingdom, to find that the laws, regulations or administrative provisions, practices or action of Poland or of the United Kingdom are inconsistent with the fundamental rights, freedoms and principles that it reaffirms.' However, it is now reasonably clear that this Protocol does not achieve anything other than confirmation of what is contained in the text of the Charter itself. See the judgment of the CJEU in Case C-411/10 *NS* ECLI: EU:C:2011:865 and Steve Peers, 'The Opt Out that Fell to Earth: The British and Polish Protocol Concerning the EU Charter of Fundamental Rights' (2012) 12(2) *European Human Rights Law Review* 375.

and scientific and technological developments by making those rights more visible in a Charter'. Nevertheless, the interpretation of Charter rights in certain of the CJEU's case law has demonstrated that the Charter has not only increased visibility of the rights contained therein, but has certainly in some cases led to a strengthening of the substance of these rights.[59] However, case law on the application of the Charter, before the EU and national courts, is developing rapidly.[60]

By Article 51(1) of the Charter, its provisions are addressed to 'the institutions, bodies, offices and agencies of the Union with due regard for the principle of subsidiarity and to the Member States only when they are implementing Union law'. The interpretation of this provision has given rise to much controversy,[61] although it is of perhaps less relevance in the environmental sphere, where so much of the field is occupied by EU legislation in any event and therefore clearly falls within the scope of EU law.

As with the ECHR, the Charter does not contain any right to a decent or healthy environment. However, Article 7 of the Charter, within Title II on 'Freedoms', provides for the right to respect for private and family life, home and communications.[62] The Explanations make clear that the rights conferred by Article 7 of the Charter 'correspond to those guaranteed by Article 8 of the ECHR', and this has also been confirmed by the CJEU.[63] Nevertheless, as Article 52(3) read with Article 53 of the Charter confirm, in principle, the ECHR represents the minimum, but not the maximum, level of protection for corresponding rights contained in the Charter, including Article 7. Applying this logic, the CJEU would be obliged, applying Article 7 of the Charter, to grant at least the same level of protection in cases of environmental degradation as the ECtHR has done for Article 8 ECHR, discussed above. Moreover, the CJEU could go further (Article 52(3)), although none of its judgments to date indicates a willingness to do so. Other Charter provisions of environmental relevance which broadly correspond to ECHR provisions include Article 2 on the right to life (corresponding to Article 2 ECHR), Article 11 on freedom of information (corresponding to Article 10 ECHR)[64] and Article 17 of the Charter on the right to property (corresponding to Article 1 of Protocol No. 1 to the ECHR).

[59] An example is the Article 8 right to data protection: see, for instance, Case C-131/12 *Google Spain* ECLI:EU:C:2014:317.
[60] See, generally, Peers, Hervey, Kenner and Ward, *Commentary on the EU Charter of Fundamental Rights*.
[61] Koen Lenaerts, 'Exploring the Limits of the EU Charter of Fundamental Rights' (2012) 8(3) *European Constitutional Law Review* 375.
[62] The term communications, rather than correspondence (as in Article 8 ECHR), was used to take account of developments in technology; see the Explanations to Article 7.
[63] Case C-400/10 PPU *McB* ECLI:EU:C:2010:582.
[64] See also more specifically on access to (environmental) information, Article 42 of the Charter, which provides that, 'Any citizen of the Union, and any natural or legal person residing or having its registered office in a Member State, has a right of access to documents of the institutions, bodies, offices and agencies of the Union, whatever their medium.'

Notably, the Preamble to the Charter indicates a definite environmental sensibility in its aims, recalling the EU aim of promoting 'balanced and sustainable development' and, perhaps more significantly, that enjoyment of its rights 'entails responsibilities and duties with regard to other persons, to the human community and to future generations' (emphasis added).

Clearly, this represents an anthropocentric philosophy of rights. However, the reference to the duties owed to future generations raises interesting questions, for instance, as to whether a broader right of standing might apply to environment-related breaches (of Article 7, for instance) than a more traditional victim-based approach.

A further significant environmental provision is Article 37 of the Charter, found within Title IV on 'Solidarity', which provides, 'A high level of environmental protection and the improvement of the quality of the environment must be integrated into the policies of the Union and assured in accordance with the principle of sustainable development.'

As will be evident, this provision is similar in its terms to Article 11 TFEU, discussed in Chapter 3;[65] both essentially mandate environmental policy integration.[66] However, the text of Article 37, which specifies that a 'high level' of environmental protection 'must be ... assured', is, on balance, stronger than that of Article 11 TFEU, and draws on the text of Article 3 TEU, as the Explanations confirm. The effect of this stronger language, however, must be appreciated in light of the distinction made between 'rights' and 'principles' in the Charter (see Article 51(1) and Article 52(5)). As the Explanations specify, Article 37 should be considered as a principle, rather than a right. This means, according to the Explanations, that while the Member States are bound to 'observe' such principles, they do not 'give rise to direct claims for positive action by the Union's institutions or Member States authorities'. Further, many of the key concepts contained in Article 37 are, at best, inherently ambiguous in their definition — how high a level of environmental protection? Which version of sustainable development?[67] This has given rise to vociferous debate on the precise legal significance of Article 37 of the Charter, mirroring a similar debate on the significance of the Article 11 TFEU integration obligation, which is discussed in Chapter 3. The upshot of this debate is essentially that it is clear that Article 37 of the Charter (and Article 11 TFEU) imposes legal environmental integration obligations on those drawing

---

[65] Article 11 TFEU provides, 'Environmental protection requirements must be integrated into the definition and implementation of the Union's policies and activities, in particular with a view to promoting sustainable development.'

[66] The Explanations to the Charter specify that the principles set out in Article 37 'have been based on Articles 2, 6 and 174 of the EC Treaty, which have now been replaced by Article 3(3) of the Treaty on European Union and Articles 11 and 191 of the Treaty on the Functioning of the European Union. It also draws on the provisions of some national constitutions.'

[67] See the discussion in Chapter 1.

up and implementing EU policy, mandating integration not just on a procedural, but also on a substantive, level. However, it is less clear that a court would find a breach of Article 37 of the Charter/Article 11 TFEU to constitute, for instance, a self-standing ground of invalidity of an EU measure.[68]

Nevertheless, references to Article 37 of the Charter are increasing in the CJEU's case law, although in the vast majority of cases to date this has been in the Advocate General's Opinion rather than the CJEU's judgment. An exception is the General Court's judgment in *Romonta v. Commission*, where, in dismissing arguments that the absence of a hardship clause in the rules on free allocation of allowances in the EU Emissions Trading Scheme was disproportionate, the Court noted that the Commission had to balance the operator's individual rights against environmental protection as provided in, *inter alia*, Article 37 of the Charter.[69] *Romonta*, therefore, illustrates the potential significance of elevating the integration obligation to the Charter, adding weight to the environmental protection imperative when balanced against other (individual) human rights.

The Aarhus Convention on Access to Information, Public Participation in Decision-Making and Access to Justice in Environmental Matters

Aside from these sources of European human rights law, no discussion of environmental rights within Europe can be complete without treatment of the 1998 Aarhus Convention on Access to Information, Public Participation in Decision-Making and Access to Justice in Environmental Matters.[70] Together with the 1991 Espoo Convention on Environmental Impact Assessment in a Transboundary Context,[71] the Aarhus Convention forms one of the two key environmental Conventions negotiated under the auspices of the UN Economic Commission for Europe (UNECE), which is one of five regional commissions of the United Nations. UNECE has 56 Member States ranging across the European Union, non-EU Western and Eastern Europe, South-East Europe, the Commonwealth of Independent States (CIS) and North America. The Aarhus and Espoo Conventions therefore constitute regional instruments of international law which are specific to

---

[68] See the discussion in Suzanne Kingston, 'Integrating Environmental Protection and EU Competition Law: Why Competition isn't Special' (2010) 16(6) *European Law Journal* 780 and Marín Durán and Morgera, 'Article 37' in Peers et al., *Commentary on the EU Charter of Fundamental Rights*.
[69] Case T-614/13 *Romonta v. Commission* ECLI:EU:T:2014:835.
[70] United Nations, Treaty Series, vol. 2161, p. 447.
[71] United Nations, Treaty Series, vol. 1989, p. 309.

Europe.[72] While the Espoo Convention confers rights and obligations on contracting States, as is typical for international treaties, the approach of the Aarhus Convention is inherently rights-based.

The Aarhus Convention's Approach to Environmental Rights

The Convention has been hailed by the Secretary-General of the United Nations, Ban-Ki Moon, as 'the most ambitious venture in the field of environmental democracy under the auspices of the United Nations'.[73] As the reference to environmental democracy suggests, the approach of the Aarhus Convention is firmly aimed at increasing citizens' involvement in achieving environmental protection, following on from Principle 10 of the Rio Declaration adopted by the 1992 Rio Conference on Environment and Development (UNCED), which provides,

> Environmental issues are best handled with participation of all concerned citizens, at the relevant level. At the national level, each individual shall have appropriate access to information concerning the environment that is held by public authorities, including information on hazardous materials and activities in their communities, and the opportunity to participate in decision-making processes. States shall facilitate and encourage public awareness and participation by making information widely available. Effective access to judicial and administrative proceedings, including redress and remedy, shall be provided.

The three 'pillars' of the Convention – access to information, public participation and access to justice – have, at their core, the aims of improving transparency, democracy and accountability in decisions affecting the environment. Central to this approach is the idea that, by enabling citizens to access information on their environment, to participate in environmental decision-making and to challenge environmental decisions before courts/tribunals, this will in itself contribute to achieving a higher level of environmental protection. While the Convention adopts an essentially procedural approach to environmental rights, the Preamble to the Convention makes it clear that its authors envisaged these procedural rights not as an end in themselves but as a means of achieving what they recognised as a universal right, 'to live in an environment adequate to his or her health and well-being, and the duty, both individually and in association with others, to

---

[72] However, non-UNECE States may choose to become parties to each of these Conventions. See the Meeting of the Parties to the Aarhus Convention, 'Decision IV/5 on Accession to the Convention by non-United Nations Economic Commission for Europe Member States' (ECE/MP.PP/2011/CRP.3, 1 June 2011) and the first amendment to the Espoo Convention, which entered into force in 2014. Cameroon and Mongolia have formally expressed an interest in acceding to the Aarhus Convention.
[73] *The Aarhus Convention: An Implementation Guide* (2nd edn., UNECE, 2014), 3.

protect and improve the environment for the benefit of present and future generations'.

Similarly, Article 1 of the Convention provides,

> In order to contribute to the protection of the right of every person of present and future generations to live in an environment adequate to his or her health and well-being, each Party shall guarantee the rights of access to information, public participation in decision-making, and access to justice in environmental matters in accordance with the provisions of this Convention.

The link to, and implicit recognition of, a substantive right to an 'adequate' environment was not overlooked by the signatory States, with the UK in particular lodging an express reservation noting its view that the rights conferred by the Convention were exclusively procedural.[74] Nevertheless, the assumption that enhanced procedural rights will necessarily lead to substantive environmental improvements has been challenged by some authors:[75]

> Aarhus environmental rights straddle uneasily between, on the one hand, their embodiment as procedural entitlements and, on the other, the social welfare aspiration, expressed in Article 1 [of the Convention], to provide environmental quality adequate to the human health and well-being of all persons. The UNECE assumption that the former necessarily promotes the latter is asserted rather than substantiated.
>
> Michael Mason, 'Information Disclosure and Environmental Rights: The Aarhus Convention' (2010) 10(3) *Global Environmental Politics* 10–31, at 17.

Signatories, Ratification and Compliance

The Aarhus Convention was signed in 1998 by 35 of the UNECE Member States, and by the European Community in its own right, and entered into force in October 2001 following ratification by 16 States.[76] As of May 2016, there were

---

[74] The UK Reservation reads, 'The United Kingdom understands the references in article 1 and the seventh preambular paragraph of this Convention to the "right" of every person "to live in an environment adequate to his or her health and well-being" to express an aspiration which motivated the negotiation of this Convention and which is shared fully by the United Kingdom. The legal rights which each Party undertakes to guarantee under article 1 are limited to the rights of access to information, public participation in decision-making and access to justice in environmental matters in accordance with the provisions of this Convention.'

[75] See, further, Maria Lee and Carolyn Abbot, 'The Usual Suspects? Public Participation Under the Aarhus Convention' (2003) 66 *Modern Law Review* 80.

[76] As required by Article 20(1) of the Convention.

47 Parties to the Convention (46 States, plus the European Union), with Ireland and Switzerland the most recent European States to ratify, in 2012 and 2014 respectively. A Protocol to the Convention on Pollutant Release and Transfer Registers (PRTRs) was signed in 2003,[77] and entered into force in 2009. To date, the PRTR protocol has been ratified by 34 UNECE States.[78] While the USA and Canada are UNECE members, they elected not to participate in the negotiation of the Convention and have remained outside the Convention since then.

Implementation of the Aarhus Convention is monitored by the Aarhus Convention Compliance Committee (the 'Compliance Committee'), composed of 9 part-time members. The Compliance Committee can consider submissions on compliance made by other States, referred by its own secretariat, or by members of the public (termed 'communications'), and can examine compliance issues on its own initiative and draw up a report and recommendations thereon, which are subsequently considered and decided upon by the Meeting of the Parties.[79] The Compliance Committee cannot, therefore, take binding decisions in its own capacity, and is non-judicial in nature. Nevertheless, the Aarhus Convention compliance procedure can, in line with the Convention's ethos, certainly be considered to be far more open, transparent and in line with the values of environmental democracy than typical compliance procedures for international environmental treaties, not least because:

(a) as aforementioned, the Compliance Committee is empowered to receive complaints directly from the public, rather than only from contracting States Parties;
(b) the cost of making a complaint is free; and
(c) with certain exceptions, all communications, submissions and other documentation in relation to cases are published on the Compliance Committee's website (in contrast, for instance, to the practice of the CJEU, where pleadings and submission are not published).

Aarhus's Three Substantive Pillars

As its full title suggests, the Aarhus Convention confers rights falling into three broad 'pillars': access to information, public participation and access to justice in environmental matters. These pillars are flanked by general provisions obliging,

---

[77] UN Doc. MP.PP/2003/1.
[78] An amendment to the Convention, on public participation in decisions on the deliberate release into the environment and placing on the market of genetically modified organisms (GMOs), was signed in 2005 but has not yet been ratified by a sufficient number of parties to enter into force.
[79] See the Report of the First Meeting of the Parties to the Aarhus Convention, Decision I/7 Review of Compliance, October 2002 (ECE/MP.PP/2/Add. 8), establishing the Compliance Committee. For a very helpful overview of the key findings of the Compliance Committee, see the UNECE Implementation Guide (*The Aarhus Convention: An Implementation Guide*; as above).

for instance, each party to take the necessary legislative, regulatory and other measures to establish and maintain a 'clear, transparent and consistent framework' to implement the Convention.[80]

Access to Information

Article 4(1) of the Aarhus Convention states,

> Each Party shall ensure that, subject to the following paragraphs of this article, public authorities, in response to a request for environmental information, make such information available to the public, within the framework of national legislation, including, where requested and subject to sub-paragraph (b) below, copies of the actual documentation containing or comprising such information:
>
> (a) Without an interest having to be stated;
> (b) In the form requested unless
>   i. It is reasonable for the public authority to make it available in another form, in which case reasons shall be given for making it available in that form; or
>   ii. The information is already publicly available in another form.

Article 4 goes on to further specify the nature of the right of access to information under the Convention, including:

- the time period for providing the information (one month maximum, unless the volume and complexity of information justify an extension to two months);[81]
- the grounds on which a request for information may be refused (which include cases where the request is manifestly unreasonable, and where refusal would adversely affect public security, the course of justice, intellectual property rights or confidential personal data;[82]
- the fee that may be charged for supplying the information, which 'shall not exceed a reasonable amount'.[83]

Four features of the Convention's right of access to information should be emphasised.

---

[80] Article 3, Aarhus Convention.
[81] Article 4(2), Aarhus Convention. On this, see the Findings and Recommendations of the Compliance Committee on Communication ACCC/C/2008/24 (Spain).
[82] Article 4(3) and (4), Aarhus Convention. However, the volume of information requested does not in itself justify a refusal to provide it: see the Findings and Recommendations of the Compliance Committee on Communication ACCC/C/2004/3 (Ukraine). The scope of the exceptions must be restrictively interpreted: see the Findings of the Compliance Committee on Communication ACCC/C/2007/21 (European Community).
[83] Article 4(8), Aarhus Convention.

First, it applies only to requests made to 'public authorities'. This term is defined to include, for instance, persons providing public services in relation to the environment 'under the control' of a government or public administrative body, but excludes 'bodies or institutions acting in a judicial or legislative capacity'.[84]

Secondly, the concept of 'environmental information' is defined in broad terms to include 'any information in written, visual, aural, electronic or any other material form' on not just the state of the environment as such, but also, for instance, 'factors ... affecting or likely to affect the environment' as well as 'cost-benefit and other economic analyses and assumptions used in environmental decision-making'.[85]

Thirdly, the beneficiary of the right is also defined in broad terms as the 'public', meaning 'one or more natural or legal persons and, in accordance with national legislation or practice, their associations, organizations or groups'. This may be contrasted with the narrower concept of the 'public concerned' applicable to the right of public participation, discussed below.

Finally, the specific right set down in Article 4 of the Convention is buttressed by the more general obligations incumbent on Contracting States Parties set out in Article 5 thereof, which oblige States to ensure, amongst other things, that public authorities possess and update environmental information which is relevant to their functions and, in the event of any imminent threat to human health or the environment, take positive steps to disseminate information to members of the public who may be affected.[86] States are also obliged to ensure that environmental information is made available to the public in a transparent and accessible manner, and progressively to ensure its availability in electronic form.[87]

Public Participation
The Aarhus Convention contains three types of public participation right.[88]

Public Participation in Decisions on 'Specific Activities'
The first is the right of public participation in decisions on 'specific activities', namely, those activities listed in Annex I of the Convention and other activities which 'may have a significant effect on the environment'.[89] This right may, on

---

[84] Article 2(2), Aarhus Convention. [85] Article 2(3), Aarhus Convention.
[86] Article 5(1), Aarhus Convention. [87] Article 5(2) and (3), Aarhus Convention.
[88] On the interrelationship between the public participation provisions of the Aarhus and Espoo Conventions, see the Implementation Guide to the Aarhus Convention as above, p. 121 (explaining that the Aarhus Convention is broader in scope than Espoo and that, while public participation is a mandatory part of environmental impact assessment, environmental impact assessment is not a mandatory part of public participation). On environmental impact assessment, see Chapter 10.
[89] Article 6(1), Aarhus Convention. States may decide on the extent to which decisions on whether to permit the deliberate release of genetically modified organisms into the environment are covered by Article 6: see Article 6(11), Aarhus Convention.

a case-by-case basis, be restricted in the case of activities serving national defence purposes.[90] Annex I contains a list of 19 activities including activities within the energy, metal, mineral, chemical, waste management, waste-water and transport sectors. There is an overlap between this list and the list set out in EU law of projects for which an environmental impact assessment is mandatory,[91] but the two lists are not identical. In addition, paragraph 20 of Annex I includes within the scope of Article 6 any activity not expressly listed in the annex but where 'public participation is provided for under an environmental impact assessment procedure in accordance with national legislation'. In this way, the public participation standards of the Aarhus Convention are extended to situations where national legislation considers that an EIA is necessary.

Article 6(2) of the Convention provides that the 'public concerned shall be informed … early in an environmental decision-making procedure, and in an adequate, timely and effective manner' of, amongst other things, the features of the activity and the envisaged procedure for decision-making.[92] Further, all information relevant to the decision-making available at the time of the public participation procedure must be given, upon request, to the public concerned.[93] The 'public concerned', for this purpose, is defined as the public 'affected or likely to be affected by, or having an interest in, the environmental decision-making', with environmental NGOs 'meeting any requirements under national law' deemed to have such an interest.[94] While contracting States Parties need only inform and provide information to the 'public concerned', they must allow any member of the 'public' to participate in the decision-making process by making observations.[95] As to the outcome of the participation process, each State is to 'ensure that in the decision due account is taken of the outcome of the public participation.'[96]

---

[90] Article 6(1)(c), Aarhus Convention.
[91] Namely, the list set out at Annex I of the EU's Environmental Impact Assessment Directive (Directive 2011/92/EU of the European Parliament and of the Council of 13 December 2011 on the assessment of the effects of certain public and private projects on the environment, OJ 2012 L26/1). See, further, Chapter 10.
[92] Article 6(2), Aarhus Convention. The function of informing the public concerned may be delegated to, for instance, a private operator. See the Findings of the Compliance Committee on Communication ACCC/C/2009/37 (Belarus). However, States may not rely solely on the developer to ensure public participation: see the Findings of the Compliance Committee on Communication ACCC/C/2006/16 (Lithuania).
[93] Article 6(6), Aarhus Convention.   [94] Article 2(5), Aarhus Convention.
[95] Article 6(7), Aarhus Convention. Where States have limited the right to participate to the public concerned, this will not comply with the Convention: see the Findings of the Compliance Committee on Communication ACCC/C/2006/16 (Lithuania).
[96] Article 6(8) Aarhus Convention. The effect is, therefore, very similar to that set out in the EU's EIA Directive, which requires that the results of consultations and the information gathered pursuant to that Directive 'shall be taken into consideration in the development consent procedure'. EIA Directive, Article 8. See Chapter 10. However, the public participation obligation under the Aarhus Convention does not, as such, require an EIA to be carried out. See, further, the *Aarhus Convention: An Implementation Guide*, 127.

Clearly, therefore, there is no obligation to reach a specific (greener) substantive outcome as a result of the public participation process,[97] although States must include in the written reasoned decision discussion how the public participation procedure was taken into account.[98]

> In many national laws, the question of whether an application for a permit concerning an activity that is potentially harmful to the environment should be approved may, at least in part, depend on the usefulness of the project, this is not a requirement of the Convention. The Convention Parties may apply different criteria for approving and dismissing an application for authorisation, for instance with regard to the standard of technology, the effects on health and the environment, and the usefulness of the activity in question. However, these issues are not addressed by the Convention.
> Findings of the Compliance Committee in Communication ACCC/C/2007/22 (France).

Public Participation in Plans, Programmes and Policies Relating to the Environment

The second and third categories of public participation right, conferred by Articles 7 and 8 of the Aarhus Convention, may be dealt with more briefly. In comparison with the right of public participation relating to specific activities, the Compliance Committee has rarely made specific findings on the implications and interpretation of these provisions. Article 7 of the Convention provides that, 'Each Party shall make appropriate practical and/or other provisions for the public to participate during the preparation of plans and programmes relating to the environment, within a transparent and fair framework, having provided the necessary information to the public.'

Within this framework, certain features of the public participation obligations concerning activities, discussed above, are to apply.[99] The public which may participate is to be 'identified by the relevant public authority' taking into account the objectives of the Convention. States are to 'endeavour' 'to the

---

[97] See, however, the comments in the Aarhus Convention Implementation Guide, 119–120 ('It must be emphasized that public participation requires more than simply following a set of procedures; it involves public authorities genuinely listening to public input and being open to the possibility of being influenced by it. Ultimately, public participation should result in some increase in the correlation between the views of the participating public and the content of the decision. In other words, the public input should be capable of having a tangible influence on the actual content of the decision. When such influence can be seen in the final decision, it is evident that the public authority has taken due account of public input').

[98] Findings of the Compliance Committee on Communication ACCC/C/2008/24 (Spain).

[99] Namely, the provisions on reasonable time frames, early public participation and the obligation to ensure that due account is taken of the participation: Article 6(3) (4) and (8), Aarhus Convention.

extent appropriate' to provide opportunities for public participation in relation to policies.

The terms 'plans', 'programmes' and 'policies' are not defined in the Convention. Clearly, however, they refer to decisions which concern not just a specific activity within the sense of Article 6 of the Convention, but which are broader and more general in nature (such as, for instance, a development plan for a town or region). In this sense, the legislation giving effect to Article 7 of the Convention will often entail Strategic Environmental Assessment (SEA), although the Article does not as such contain a requirement to perform an SEA. The concept of SEA, and the attendant legislation in EU law, is discussed further in Chapter 11.

Public Participation During the Preparation of Regulations or Legislation

With respect to executive regulations and legislation, the Aarhus Convention's obligations in relation to public participation are notably weak. Article 8 provides, 'Each Party shall strive to promote effective public participation at an appropriate stage, and while options are still open, during the preparation by public authorities of executive regulations and other generally applicable legally binding rules that may have a significant effect on the environment.'

The terms 'strive to promote' and 'appropriate stage' are notably (and deliberately) vague. Nevertheless, Article 8 goes on to specify a number of steps that 'should' be taken, namely, the fixing of time frames sufficient for effective participation; the publication of draft rules; and the opportunity for the public to comment either directly or through representative bodies. The result of the participation is to be taken into account 'as far as possible'.

The Aarhus Convention Implementation Guide notes that many, but not all, contracting States Parties publish draft environmental laws online or elsewhere prior to passing the laws, but draws attention to best practice where draft laws are not only published but specifically circulated to interested parties (such as environmental NGOs) for comment.[100]

Access to Justice

Article 9 of the Aarhus Convention deals with the Convention's third pillar, access to justice in environmental matters. This reflects the increasing recognition that, on the one hand, unless a failure to uphold environmental rights can be legally challenged, such rights will be largely worthless. On the other hand, however, the traditional procedural rules governing legal claims in most States, including rules on standing, legal costs and time limits for bringing a claim, may make it very difficult in practice to bring environmental cases of a public interest nature. For instance, in order to have standing to bring a claim in many jurisdictions, the claimant must demonstrate that he/she is affected in a special way by the case, or has suffered particular damage. In most cases, however, such standards are

---

[100] *Aarhus Convention: An Implementation Guide*, 184.

evidently inappropriate to deal with claims brought by those acting out of pure public interest in protecting the environment which, as a public good,[101] typically affects a large group of people in much the same way.

To this end, one of the signal achievements of the Aarhus Convention was to set out a range of requirements which the contracting Parties must ensure are satisfied by their legal system, in order to enable environmental public interest litigation to be brought in their jurisdiction. Due to the novelty and potentially broad implications of these requirements, it is fair to say that this has proven to be the most controversial of the Aarhus Convention pillars – as witnessed by the fact that it is the only pillar on which the European Commission has, to date, failed to garner sufficient support for a stand-alone Directive.[102]

Article 9 of the Aarhus Convention contains three broad categories of obligation for contracting Parties in relation to access to justice.

Article 9(1) concerns access to justice in relation to decisions on access to environmental information. It provides,

> Each Party shall, within the framework of its national legislation, ensure that any person who considers that his or her request for information under article 4 has been ignored, wrongfully refused, whether in part or in full, inadequately answered, or otherwise not dealt with in accordance with the provisions of that article, has access to a review procedure before a court of law or another independent and impartial body established by law.

A number of features of this right will be noted. First, the beneficiaries of this right include anyone who has made a request for access to environmental information within the meaning of the Convention. Secondly, the review procedure may be, but need not be, judicial in nature: any review procedure by an 'independent and impartial body established by law' will suffice. This may, for instance, include national ombudspersons, where they satisfy these requirements. Thirdly, in accordance with Article 9(4) of the Convention, the procedures covered by Article 9(1) must,

---

[101] For a discussion of the concept of 'public good', see the section on 'Environment and Economics' in Chapter 1.

[102] A proposal was presented by the Commission for such a Directive in 2003, but did not achieve the requisite support (Proposal for a directive of the European Parliament and of the Council 24 October 2003 on access to justice in environmental matters, COM(2003)624. Efforts have since been made to revive interest in general EU level legislation on this topic: see, for instance, the Commission Initiative on a Roadmap on Access to justice in environmental matters at Member State level in the field of EU environment policy, November 2013, available at: http://ec.europa.eu/smart-regulation/impact/planned_ia/docs/2013_env_013_access_to_justice_en.pdf (accessed 20 May 2016).

- Provide 'adequate and effective remedies, including injunctive relief as appropriate, and be fair, equitable, timely and not prohibitively expensive'.
- Be 'given or recorded in writing. Decisions of courts, and whenever possible of other bodies, shall be publicly accessible.'

Article 9(2) of the Aarhus Convention confers a further and more broadly applicable type of access to justice right. It provides,

> Each Party shall, within the framework of its national legislation, ensure that members of the public concerned
>
> (a) Having a sufficient interest
>
> or, alternatively,
>
> (b) Maintaining impairment of a right, where the administrative procedural law of a Party requires this as a precondition,
>
> have access to a review procedure before a court of law and/or another independent and impartial body established by law, to challenge the substantive and procedural legality of any decision, act or omission subject to the provisions of article 6 and, where so provided for under national law and without prejudice to paragraph 3 below, of other relevant provisions of this Convention …

Article 9(2) of the Convention, therefore, obliges Parties to grant a right of review of decisions, acts and omissions insofar as they fall within the scope of Article 6 of the Convention on public participation in relation to specific activities, discussed above.

Of particular note here are, first, that the beneficiaries of the right are expressed to be the 'public concerned' – and not the broader category of the 'public', discussed above. Secondly, the concepts of 'sufficient interest' and 'impairment of a right' are stated to be determined in accordance with national law but 'consistently with the objective of giving the public concerned wide access to justice within the scope of this Convention'. Nevertheless, environmental NGOs 'promoting environmental protection and meeting any requirements under national law' shall be deemed to have a sufficient interest in this sense.[103] Thirdly, the review must be not only of procedural legality, but also the substantive legality, of the decision taken.[104] Fourthly, Article 9(2) is expressly without prejudice to any requirement to exhaust administrative review

---

[103] Article 9(2), read with Article 2(5) of the Convention.

[104] This has raised difficult questions about the compatibility with Article 9(2), and similarly phrased implementing provisions, of national judicial review procedures focusing largely on procedural legality. See, for instance, the argument of the European Commission in Case C-427/07 *Commission* v. *Ireland* ECLI:EU:C:2009:457 (although this point was not decided by the CJEU).

procedures prior to recourse to judicial review procedures insofar as such requirement exists under the relevant national law. Fifthly, as with Article 9(1), the proviso of Article 9(4) applies, i.e. remedies must be 'adequate and effective', must be 'fair, equitable, timely and not prohibitively expensive', and must be in writing and, if a court decision, publicly accessible.

The third and final category of access to justice obligation is set out in Article 9(3), which provides,

> In addition, and without prejudice to the review procedures referred to in paragraphs 1 and 2 above, each Party shall ensure that, where they meet the criteria, if any, laid down in its national law, members of the public have access to administrative or judicial procedures to challenge acts and omissions by private persons and public authorities which contravene provisions of its national law relating to the environment.

As is clear from its terms, while the scope of Article 9(3) is broader than that of Article 9(2) in that it applies to any acts and omissions by private persons and public authorities which breach national environmental law, Article 9(3) does not impose an absolute obligation to ensure access to justice in such cases, but only insofar as a claim meets 'the criteria, if any, laid down in ... national law'. The effect is that the obligations provided by Article 9(3) are relatively minimal (namely, ensuring *some* access to administrative or judicial procedures) and does not in itself require contracting Parties to amend their national law criteria governing access to justice in environmental matters.

Implementation of the Aarhus Convention in EU Law

As noted above, one of the features of the Aarhus Convention is that the EU itself, and not only the EU Member States, has signed and approved the Convention.[105] The Aarhus Convention has been implemented in EU law at two distinct levels.

First, the EU has, via Regulation 1367/2006, sought to apply the Aarhus Convention to the EU's own institutions and bodies.[106] This Regulation covers each of the three pillars of Aarhus and applies to all EU institutions and bodies, with the exception of when they are acting in a judicial or (in the case of the public participation and access to justice elements) legislative capacity.[107]

---

[105] See Council Decision 2005/370/EC on the conclusion, on behalf of the European Community of the Convention on access to information, public participation in decision-making and access to justice in environmental matters, OJ 2005 L 124/1.
[106] Regulation (EC) No. 1367/2006 of the European Parliament and of the Council of 6 September 2006 on the application of the provisions of the Aarhus Convention on Access to Information, Public Participation in Decision-Making and Access to Justice in Environmental Matters to Community institutions and bodies, OJ 2006 L 264/13.
[107] *Ibid.*, Article 2(1)(c).

The Regulation creates a right of access to environmental information building on the more general pre-existing rights of access to information contained in EU law,[108] alongside an obligation to collect and disseminate environmental information that is 'up-to-date, accurate and comparable'.[109] As with the equivalent right in the Aarhus Convention, this right is subject to certain exceptions, although these are stated not to apply in relation to emissions into the environment and must be restrictively interpreted.[110] As regards the second pillar of the Aarhus Convention, the Regulation creates a right of public participation concerning plans and programmes relating to the environment, which includes an obligation for the European Commission to provide for public participation when preparing a proposal for such a plan or programme, and to take due account of the outcome of such participation.[111] Notably, the concept of a 'plan or programme relating to the environment' is defined to include all plans or programmes which 'contribute to, or are likely to have significant effects on' the achievement of the EU's environmental policy, but not financial or budget plans or programmes.[112] In light of the obligation under EU law to integrate environmental protection considerations into all other areas of activity, discussed further in Chapter 3, the scope of the Regulation's access to information obligation is therefore considerable. Finally, in relation to the third pillar of the Aarhus Convention, the Regulation provides for a right for NGOs which meet certain specified criteria to request an internal review of administrative acts or omissions of an EU institution or body.[113]

Secondly, the EU has passed two Directives aimed at imposing, as a matter of EU law, certain obligations relating to the Aarhus Convention on EU Member States. These Directives do not purport to constitute a comprehensive incorporation of the provisions of the Aarhus Convention into EU law. Specifically, their scope is limited to access to information (Directive 2003/4/EC) and public participation and access to justice in the field of environmental impact assessment and industrial emissions (Directive 2003/35/EC).[114] A significant body of case law interpreting each of these Directives has now developed. In interpreting the provisions of these Directives intended to implement the Aarhus Convention, the CJEU has had express regard to the practice of the

---

[108] See Regulation 1049/2001 regarding public access to European Parliament, Council and Commission documents, OJ 2001 L145/53.
[109] Regulation 1367/2006, as above, Articles 3–6.
[110] Regulation 1049/2001, Article 4, read with Regulation 1367/2006, Article 6(1).
[111] Regulation 1367/2006, Article 9.   [112] Ibid., Article 2(1)(e).
[113] Ibid., Articles 10–11.
[114] Directive 2003/4/EC of the European Parliament and of the Council of 28 January 2003 on public access to environmental information and repealing Council Directive 90/313/EEC, OJ 2003 L 41/26; Directive 2003/35/EC of the European Parliament and of the Council of 26 May 2003 providing for public participation in respect of the drawing up of certain plans and programmes relating to the environment and amending with regard to public participation and access to justice Council Directives 85/337/EEC and 96/61/EC, OJ 2003 L 56/17.

Aarhus Convention Compliance Committee and the Aarhus Convention Implementation Guide.[115]

In relation to access to information, Directive 2003/4 replaces a previous weaker access to environmental information regime contained in Directive 90/313/EEC.[116] Directive 2003/4 provides for a right of access to environmental information from public authorities upon request, subject to the exceptions set out in Article 4 of the Directive.[117]

Member States may provide that the definition of public authorities shall not include bodies or institutions when acting in a judicial or legislative capacity.[118] Further, the CJEU has held that, in interpreting the concept of a 'public authority' under the Directive, in the case of privatised companies, it should be examined whether those entities are vested, under the national law which is applicable to them, with special powers beyond those which result from the normal rules applicable in relations between persons governed by private law.[119] In addition, a private company will be considered to be under the 'control' of the government or other public administration, and therefore also to constitute a 'public authority' for the purposes of the Directive, if it does not determine in a 'genuinely autonomous manner' the way in which it provides the services at issue.[120] Such companies will only, however, fall within the scope of the Directive insofar as they carry out 'public services in the environmental field'.[121]

The CJEU has held that the Article 4 exceptions require that the balancing exercise which the Directive prescribes between the public interest served by disclosure of the environmental information, and the specific ground for non-disclosure, be carried out on a case-by-case basis, even where national legislation sets criteria for such exercise.[122] Further, in carrying out this balancing exercise,

---

[115] See, for instance, Case C-279/12 *Fish Legal, Emily Shirley* v. *The Information Commissioner, United Utilities, Yorkshire Water and Southern Water* ECLI:EU:C:2013:853, para. 50.

[116] Council Directive 90/313/EEC of 7 June 1990 on the freedom of access to information on the environment, OJ 1990 L 158/56.

[117] On the scope of application of Directive 2003/4 in the Emissions Trading Scheme context, see Case C-524/09 *Ville de Lyon* v. *Caisse des dépôts et consignations* ECLI:EU:C:2010:822 (holding that Directive 2003/4 did not apply).

[118] On the scope of the concept of legislative capacity, see Case C-204/09 *Flachglas Torgau GmbH* v. *Germany* ECLI:EU:C:2012:71 (holding that this may extend to ministries to the extent that they participate in the legislative procedure, but cannot extend after the legislative process in question has ended) and Case C-515/11 *Deutsche Umwelthilfe eV* v. *Germany* ECLI:EU:C:2013:523 (holding the concept may not be applied to ministries adopting a regulation with a lower rank than a law).

[119] Case C-279/12 *Fish Legal, Emily Shirley* v. *The Information Commissioner, United Utilities, Yorkshire Water and Southern Water* ECLI:EU:C:2013:853.

[120] Ibid., para. 73.   [121] Ibid., para. 83.

[122] See Article 4(2) of Directive 2003/4 and Case C-266/09 *Stichting Natuur en Milieu and Others* v. *College voor de toelating van gewasbeschermingsmiddelen en biociden* ECLI:EU:C:2010:779.

the grounds for refusal may be taken into account cumulatively.[123] While Member States may charge a 'reasonable cost' for accessing the information at issue, the Member State may not pass on the entire cost of collecting the information, including the indirect costs of such collection.[124]

The provisions of the Industrial Emissions and EIA Directives in relation to public participation, and implementing Directive 2003/35, are discussed in Chapters 9 and 11 respectively. More generally, however, it should be noted that the manner in which the Aarhus Convention has been implemented in EU law to date has effectively brought about a 'two-tier' system whereby environmental matters falling within the 2003 Directives (access to information, EIA and Industrial Emissions) benefit from the special status and enforcement mechanisms particular to EU law, but environmental matters falling outside the Directives do not. This means that the effect given to the Aarhus Convention outside the scope of these Directives is essentially a matter of national law, and depends on the manner in which the particular Member State gives force to international law within its domestic legal system. The complexities and inconsistencies to which this gives rise in practice in the field of access to justice will be examined further in Chapter 7.

Other Relevant Sources of International Human Rights Law

Finally, while the above has considered environmental rights obligations particular to States within Europe, it should be remembered that European States are also subject, as with non-European States, to obligations derived from international human rights law. While not the focus of this book,[125] some of these obligations have informed and inspired the European discussion of the environment/rights interface in important ways. Of particular relevance are:

- The 1966 International Covenant on Civil and Political Rights (ICCPR), which to date has 168 States Parties.[126]
- The 1966 International Covenant on Economic, Social and Cultural Rights (ICESCR), which to date has 164 States Parties.[127]

---

[123] Case C-71/10 *Office of Communications* v. *Information Commissioner* ECLI:EU:C:2011:525. On the scope of the exception on grounds of confidential or industrial information, see Case C-416/10 *Križan and Others* v. *Slovenská inšpekcia životného prostredia* ECLI:EU:C:2013:8.
[124] Case C-217/97 *Commission* v. *Germany* ECLI:EU:C:1999:395.
[125] For further discussion, see Sands and Peel, *Principles of International Environmental Law*, 775–789 and, for fuller discussion, Grear and Kotzé (eds.), *Research Handbook on Human Rights and the Environment*.
[126] The ICCPR is monitored by the UN's Human Rights Committee, which is composed of 18 part-time members and examines States Parties' periodic reports and, in the case of States which have signed up to the Optional Protocol, may take decisions on individual complaints.
[127] The ICESCR is monitored by the UN's Committee on Economic, Social and Cultural Rights, which, like the Human Rights Committee, is composed of 18 part-time members and examines State periodic reports and, in the case of States which have signed up to the Optional Protocol, may take decisions on individual complaints.

Also of relevance is the UN's Human Rights Council, an intergovernmental body created by the UN's General Assembly in 2006, which replaced the UN Commission on Human Rights.[128] The Human Rights Council, and its predecessor Commission on Human Rights, have, since the 1990s, appointed a number of Special Rapporteurs who have delivered important reports on the human rights/environment interface. A key example is the 1994 Report of Special Rapporteur Ksentini on Human Rights and the Environment, for instance, who was appointed by the Commission on Human Rights' Sub-Commission on Prevention of Discrimination and Protection of Minorities.[129] In that Report, Ksentini argued strongly that there was a need for human rights to gain an 'extra dimension', making it,

> possible to go beyond reductionist concepts of 'mankind first' or 'ecology first' and achieve a coalescence of the common objectives of development and environmental protection. This would signify a return to the principal objective that inspired the Universal Declaration of Human Rights, whose article 28 states, 'Everyone is entitled to a social and international order in which the rights and freedoms set forth in this Declaration can be fully realized.'[130]

The Report resulted in a draft declaration of principles on human rights and the environment, Article 2 of which recognised a universal right to 'a secure, healthy and ecologically sound environment'.

In March 2012, the Human Rights Council decided to establish a Special Rapporteur on Human Rights and the Environment, whose tasks include studying the human rights obligations relating to the enjoyment of a safe, clean, healthy and sustainable environment, and promoting best practices relating to the use of human rights in environmental policy-making.[131] The Office of the High Commissioner for Human Rights has also emphasised the environment/human rights linkages, particularly in the context of climate change.[132]

---

[128] The Human Rights Council is composed of 47 States, which are elected by majority vote in the UN General Assembly through secret ballot. It has responsibility, amongst other things, for undertaking the Universal Periodic Review of UN States' compliance with their human rights obligations under international law, as well as for considering complaints submitted by individuals, groups or non-governmental organisations that claim to be victims of human rights violations or that have direct, reliable knowledge of such violations.

[129] Final Report of F. Z. Ksentini on Human Rights and the Environment, UN Doc. E/CN.4/Sub.2/1994/9.

[130] *Ibid.*, para. 5.

[131] In addition, the Human Rights Council and its predecessor have issued significant resolutions and decisions underscoring the environment–human rights link. See, for instance, UN Commission on Human Rights, 'Human Rights and the Environment', 6 March 1990, E/CN.4/RES/1990/41, available at: www.refworld.org/docid/3b00f04030.html.

[132] See, generally, the Submission of the Office of the High Commissioner for Human Rights to the 21st Conference of the Parties to the United Nations Framework Convention on Climate Change, 26 November 2015, available at: www.ohchr.org/Documents/Issues/ClimateChange/COP21.pdf.

6

Public Enforcement of EU Environmental Law

Introduction: The Enforcement Deficit in EU Environmental Law

> The foundation for short- and long-term improvements in Europe's environment, people's health and economic prosperity rests on full implementation of policies, and better integration of the environment into the sectoral policies that contribute most to environmental pressures and impacts.
>
> EEA, The European Environment: State and Outlook 2015: Synthesis Report (European Environment Agency, Copenhagen), 15.

It is evident that, without adequate enforcement, EU environmental law will be ineffective. While the scope of substantive EU environmental law continues to expand, we are not witnessing the parallel improvement in the state of the European environment that one might expect.

Unsurprisingly, therefore, the need to improve the governance and enforcement of EU environmental law has been a major theme in recent years. This has focused on efforts to improve the rather poor record of under-enforcement of EU environmental law, and efforts to improve environmental governance by bringing the EU's laws, and those of its Member States, into line with the 1998 Aarhus Convention.[1] In setting out the key elements of the legal regime for enforcing EU environmental law at EU and national levels, this chapter considers each of these trends.

It would be wrong, of course, to blame the failure of the EU to meet its environmental quality aims entirely on under-enforcement of EU environmental law.[2] In many vital areas, agreement has not been reached at EU level on appropriate legislation (as, for instance, in the case of the proposed Soil Framework Directive, the proposal for which was withdrawn in 2014,[3] and in the case of the proposed

---

[1] UNECE *Convention* on Access to Information, Public Participation in Decision-Making and Access to Justice in Environmental Matters, Aarhus, 25 June 1998, in force 30 October 2001, 2161 UNTS 447.

[2] On the current quality of the environment within the EU, see EEA, The European Environment: State and Outlook 2015: Synthesis Report (European Environment Agency, Copenhagen), Table ES.1, which notes that the EU was largely on course to meet its targets in only 3 of 19 areas examined.

[3] See Proposal for a Directive of the European Parliament and of the Council establishing a framework for the protection of soil and amending Directive 2004/35/EC COM(2006) 232 final.

Access to Justice Directive, discussed further below). More broadly, many fundamental problems result not from the content and (lack of) enforcement of EU environmental legislation as such, but from the lack of consideration given to environmental concerns in non-environmental legislation, in the sense of legislation with a legal basis other than Article 192 TFEU, in breach of the integration principle considered in Chapter 3. Nonetheless, a significant improvement in the enforcement of EU environmental law would bring undeniable benefits, not only from an environmental quality perspective, but also in terms of ensuring a basic respect for the rule of law within the EU.

To this end, the EU's Seventh (and current) Environmental Action Programme lists improvement of implementation and enforcement as amongst the key priorities of EU environmental policy to 2020.

> Decision No. 1386/2013/EU of the European Parliament and of the Council of 20 November 2013 on a General Union Environment Action Programme to 2020 'Living well, within the limits of our planet' (OJ 2013 L 354/171).
>
> **THE ENABLING FRAMEWORK**
>
> [...]
>
> Priority objective 4: To maximise the benefits of Union environment legislation by improving implementation
>
> 56. [...] The benefits of ensuring that Union environment legislation is actually implemented are threefold: the creation of a level playing field for economic actors operating in the Internal Market; the stimulation of innovation; and the promotion of first-mover advantages for European companies in many sectors. The costs associated with failure to implement legislation, by contrast, are high, broadly estimated at around €50 billion a year, including costs related to infringement cases. In 2009 alone there were 451 infringement cases related to Union environment legislation, with a further 299 reported in 2011 together with an additional 114 new proceedings being initiated, making the environment acquis the area of Union law with most infringement proceedings. The Commission also receives numerous complaints directly from Union citizens, many of which could be better addressed at Member State or local level.
>
> 57. Improving the implementation of the Union environment acquis at Member State level will therefore be given top priority in the coming years. There are significant differences in implementation between and within Member States. There is a need to equip those involved in implementing environment legislation at Union, national, regional and local levels with the knowledge, tools and capacity to improve the delivery of benefits from that legislation, and to improve the governance of the enforcement process ...

It will not be lost on readers that, in justifying the need to prioritise enforcement of the EU's environmental policy in what is the key document setting out the

EU's environmental priorities to 2020, the principal reasons given are not environmental at all, but economic in nature.

This chapter looks at the legal principles governing enforcement of EU environmental law by public authorities, namely, the European Commission and national authorities. The following chapter turns to the legal regime governing enforcement of EU environmental law by private parties (NGOs, individuals and companies), on which much emphasis has been placed in recent years.

Public Enforcement of EU Environmental Law: Enforcement by the European Commission

Article 17 TEU provides that the Commission,

> shall ensure the application of the Treaties, and of measures adopted by the institutions pursuant to them. It shall oversee the application of Union law under the control of the Court of Justice of the European Union …

As this provision indicates, the role attributed to the Commission has traditionally been considered to be that of 'guardian of the Treaties', tasked with ensuring the application of EU law but subject always to the judgments of the CJEU which, according to Article 19 TEU, enjoys the final word on the interpretation and application of the Treaties.

The principal mechanism by which the Commission carries out this role in the environmental context is the so-called infringement action, set out in Articles 258, 260 and, in relation to interim measures, 279 TFEU. Actions seeking the invalidity of an EU measure, pursuant to Article 263 TFEU, may also be brought by the Commission as of right, as provided by Article 263(2) TFEU which grants the Commission privileged status to bring such actions. However, with some notable exceptions which are considered below,[4] significant environmental cases have rarely arisen in that context. For this reason, Article 263 TFEU will be considered in detail in the section on private enforcement of EU environmental law, below.

Article 258 TFEU

> If the Commission considers that a Member State has failed to fulfil an obligation under the Treaties, it shall deliver a reasoned opinion on the matter after giving the State concerned the opportunity to submit its observations.
>
> If the State concerned does not comply with the opinion within the period laid down by the Commission, the latter may bring the matter before the Court of Justice of the European Union.

---

[4] See, in particular, Case C-170/03 *Commission* v. *Council (Environmental Criminal Penalties)* ECLI:EU:C:2005:176.

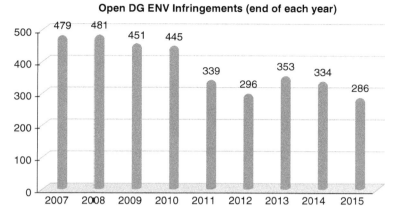

Figure 6.1 Open DG Environment Infringements
Source: European Commission, 'Statistics on Environmental Infringements' (2015). See http://ec.europa.eu/environment/legal/law/statistics.htm.

Overview

As noted in the excerpt from the Seventh Environmental Action Programme cited at the beginning of this chapter, environmental cases have in recent years consistently formed the largest body of open infringement cases as compared to any other area of EU law, again highlighting the serious enforcement problems endemic in this field. It should, however, be noted that the number of open infringement actions in the environmental sector decreased considerably in 2015 (see Figure 6.1). This follows the appointment of the new Commission presided over by Jean-Claude Juncker in November 2014, which has from the outset reduced the number of infringement cases brought by the Commission in the environmental sphere.[5]

Within environmental infringement cases, as Figure 6.2 indicates, infringements in relation to EU water law comprise the largest portion of cases (at 25 per cent), followed closely by EU waste law (at 21 per cent) and nature conservation law (at 17 per cent) in 2015.

The Commission typically distinguishes between three types of infringement of EU law on the part of Member States:[6]

- **non-notification** cases, meaning cases where Member States have failed to notify the Commission of the requisite national implementing measures by the transposition date set in a Directive;

---

[5] In May 2015, the Commission reported, in the context of its Single Market Scoreboard, that 'the number of pending infringements has never been lower' (see http://ec.europa.eu/internal_market/scoreboard/performance_by_governance_tool/infringements/index_en.htm).

[6] See, for instance, European Commission, 'Monitoring the Application of Union Law: 2014 Annual Report', COM(2015)329, p. 6.

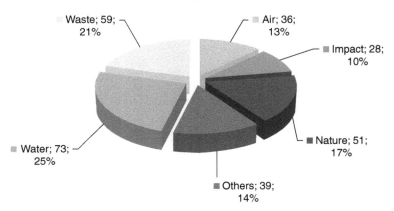

Figure 6.2 Infringements by Environmental Sector (2015)
Source: European Commission, 'Statistics on Environmental Infringements' (2015). See http://ec.europa.eu/environment/legal/law/statistics.htm.

- **non-conformity/non-compliance** cases, meaning cases where the Commission considers that a Member State's legislation is not in line with what EU law requires; and
- **bad application** cases, meaning cases where the Commission considers that EU law is not being applied correctly or at all by the Member State.

The evidence required to prove a case of bad application will normally be far greater than that required to prove a case of non-notification. Since the entry into force of the Lisbon Treaty, the incentive for Member States to notify transposition measures to the Commission on time has further increased, by the insertion of a new Article 260(3) TFEU enabling the Commission to request the CJEU to impose a fine or penalty payment on a Member State in such cases on the first round of infringement proceedings, without needing to obtain a prior judgment of infringement of Article 258 TFEU by that Member State.[7] In all other cases, as discussed below, the Commission may ask for a fine or penalty payment to be imposed on a Member State only after having obtained a first CJEU judgment holding that the Member State is in breach of EU law.

As Article 258 TFEU indicates, the infringement procedure is divided into two main stages: the pre-litigation (administrative) stage and the litigation stage.

The Administrative Phase

The administrative phase of Article 258 TFEU proceedings involves two formal stages. First, a 'formal notice' is issued to the Member State,

---

[7] Article 260(3) TFEU provides for such a possibility in the case of failure to notify measures transposing a 'directive adopted under a legislative procedure'.

outlining the Commission's concerns, to which the Member State is given a chance to respond. If the response is unsatisfactory from the Commission's perspective, it may progress the matter to the second stage, in which a 'reasoned opinion' is issued, to which again the Member State has a chance to respond. The reasoned opinion is an important document if the matter eventually makes it to court as, in order to ensure respect for the Member State's right of defence, the Commission may only raise matters before the CJEU which were contained in the reasoned opinion (and to which the Member State has thus had an opportunity to respond).[8] In 2014, the Commission sent 174 letters of formal notice to Member States in the environmental policy field and 60 reasoned opinions, the most of any policy field.[9]

Cases can come to the Commission's attention in a variety of ways. In the environmental context, the Commission has traditionally received a large volume of complaints from members of the public and other interested parties alerting them to a potential infringement of EU law.[10] From the complainant's perspective, this method has the distinct advantage of being free, and simple to do; the downside is that, unlike a private party in litigation, the complainant plays no official role in the proceedings after alerting the Commission, and indeed cannot force the Commission to act further on its complaint. The Commission may also choose to open infringement proceedings of its own motion (*ex officio*), without any complaint being lodged.

The Commission's Prioritisation of Cases

Clearly, the Commission does not have the resources to investigate all environmental complaints which it receives. For this reason, and for broader reasons of strategy, it may wish to prioritise certain areas of enforcement, and certain cases, over others. The wording of Article 258 TFEU makes clear (and the CJEU has confirmed)[11] that it is within the Commission's discretion to decide its own enforcement priorities, and to select the cases in which it wishes to commence formal infringement proceedings. In recent years, the Commission has issued a number of Communications indicating how it intends to exercise this discretion, including in the environmental context. As a result, the way in which the Commission in practice exercises its function as guardian of the Treaties in this field has changed considerably.

In its 2007 Communication, 'A Europe of Results – Applying Community Law', the Commission indicated its intention to prioritise three categories of cases, namely:

---

[8] Case C-52/90 *Commission* v. *Denmark* ECLI:EU:C:1992:151; Case C-217/88 *Commission* v. *Germany* ECLI:EU:C:1990:290.
[9] European Commission, 'Monitoring the Application of Union Law: 2014 Annual Report', 13.
[10] In 2014, the Commission received 508 environmental complaints, constituting the fourth-largest body of complaints received by the Commission after complaints concerning the employment, internal market and justice fields. *Ibid.*, 8.
[11] Case 247/87 *Star Fruit* v. *Commission* ECLI:EU:C:1989:58.

(a) Non-communication of national measures transposing directives or failure to respect other notification obligations. In a 2011 Communication, the Commission made clear its intention to rely on the new powers set out in Article 260(3) TFEU, discussed above, 'as a matter of principle' in *all* non-communication cases falling within its scope;[12]
(b) Breaches of EU law raising 'issues of principle or having particularly far-reaching negative impact for citizens'; and
(c) Failure to respect Court judgments declaring the existence of infringements (i.e. Article 260(2) TFEU cases, discussed below). In this case, compliance is expected within an average of 12–24 months, subject to the 'specific circumstances of exceptional cases'.[13]

The scope of category (b) in the specific context of the environmental sector was further expanded upon by a 2008 Communication, in which the Commission stated that it considered the following breaches to fall within this category:

- non-conformity of 'key legislation' viewed as presenting a significant risk for correct implementation of environmental rules, which means breaches of (provisions of) directives that 'set the main framework' for environmental protection;[14]
- systematic breaches of environmental quality or other requirements presenting 'serious adverse consequences or risks' for human health or aspects of nature with 'high ecological value' (i.e. contravention 'repeatedly or on a significant scale' of particularly important environmental obligations or key procedural or activity-related obligations, such as those requiring landfills to operate under a waste permit);[15]
- breaches of 'core, strategic obligations on which fulfilment of other obligations depends' (e.g. failure to designate sites under the Habitats Directive, or to come up with appropriate waste management plans);
- breaches concerning large infrastructure projects or projects involving EU funding, particularly in cases where irreversible ecological damage may arise.[16] In such situations, the Commission indicated its intention to seek interim measures, discussed further below, in suitable cases where the (rather strict) conditions for grant of this remedy are made out.

The effect of prioritisation may be that unless an issue falls within one of the prioritised categories set out, the issue will in practice be unlikely to be pursued by the Commission – at least in the short term, and subject perhaps to the possibility of greater resources being made available to the Commission.

---

[12] Commission Communication on implementation of Article 260(3) TFEU, OJ 2011 C 12/1, para. 17.
[13] Commission Communication on implementing European Community Environmental Law, COM(2008)773, p. 8.
[14] *Ibid.*   [15] *Ibid.*, 9.   [16] *Ibid.*

The EU 'Pilot' Scheme and the 'CHAP' Complaint Registry

The way in which complaints are handled has changed significantly in recent years with the institution of the EU Pilot scheme, which has been in operation since 2008 (and is not confined to environmental law).[17] Essentially, the idea of the Pilot scheme is, once a complaint at EU level has been registered, it is transferred to the relevant Member State for their input – whether in the form of clarification, information or potential solutions to the problem. The Member State may communicate directly with the complainant to this end. In the absence of (what the Commission deems to be) a satisfactory solution, the Commission retains the power to commence infringement proceedings in the normal fashion.[18] The EU Pilot scheme complements the CHAP central registry for complaints and enquiries created in September 2009. All complaints and enquiries are first registered in CHAP, and then transferred to EU Pilot if the Commission needs to obtain further factual or legal information, or to provide the Member State in question with an opportunity to propose a solution compliant with EU law. There is a 10-week deadline for Member States to reply to questions put to them in EU Pilot, although the figures show that certain Member States have regularly not respected this deadline.[19]

Since instituting the EU Pilot scheme, the Commission has reaffirmed its intentions further to 'delegate' complaint-handling responsibilities to national authorities in this manner, especially in those fields of environmental enforcement which are not of strategic importance to the Commission.[20] In 2014, the largest proportion of EU Pilot cases opened – 17 per cent – concerned environmental complaints.[21] The scheme can be viewed as a move towards a more network-based style of governance in enforcement,[22] which had been announced in the 2001 'White Paper on European Governance', as well as in the 2007 Communication mentioned above, which set out the overarching principles that the Commission would apply

---

[17] See Commission Communication, 'A Europe of Results: Applying Community Law', COM(2007)502 and Suzanne Kingston, 'Mind the Gap: Difficulties in Enforcement and the Continuing Unfulfilled Promise of EU Environmental Law' in S. Kingston (ed.), *European Perspectives on Environmental Law and Governance* (Routledge, 2013), 147.

[18] The Pilot scheme does not apply to non-communication cases, where infringement actions will be commenced directly. *Ibid.*

[19] See European Commission, 2014 Annual Report on Monitoring the Application of Union Law, 12.

[20] Commission Communication, 'Improving the Delivery of Benefits from EU Environment Measures: Building Confidence through Better Knowledge and Responsiveness', COM (2012)95, p. 8; Commission Communication on implementing environmental law, COM (2008)773.

[21] European Commission (2015), 'Internal Market Scoreboard by Governance Tool', available at: http://ec.europa.eu/internal_market/scoreboard/performance_by_governance_tool/eu_pilot.

[22] See, for instance, Ingmar von Homeyer, 'Emerging Experimentalism in EU Environmental Governance' in Charles Sabel and Jonathan Zeitlin (eds.), *Experimentalist Governance in the European Union* (Oxford University Press, 2010).

to the application of EU environmental law.[23] A cooperative approach also fits with the Article 4(3) TEU principle of sincere cooperation, whereby the 'Union and the Member States shall, in full mutual respect, assist each other in carrying out tasks which flow from the Treaties'. From a resource perspective, this carries the advantage of shifting some of the burden of responding to complaints and comments from the Commission to Member States.

Yet this approach also raises potential issues about the objectivity and reliability of the information received pursuant to this process: at its most basic, Member States are being asked to help inform the Commission about matters which may potentially lead to an infringement action against them. While efforts to improve enforcement are in principle to be welcomed, the increased delegation of enforcement to Member States carried with it evident risks, and it is critical that the Commission supervises Member States carefully in this context.[24] It is striking that, in the vast majority of cases, cases opened in EU Pilot are resolved at that stage and do not go any further.[25]

The Litigation Phase

If the Commission decides that it is not satisfied by the Member State's response to the reasoned opinion, it may choose to institute formal legal proceedings before the CJEU. In practical terms, this is done by lodging an application seeking a declaration of failure to fulfil the relevant EU law obligations (and potentially, in the case of Article 260(3) TFEU cases of non-communication of transposition measures, also seeking a fine and/or penalty payment) on the part of the Member State concerned. The Member State has an opportunity to lodge a defence, which may be followed by a reply from the Commission and a rejoinder from the Member State. The burden of proof in Article 258 TFEU cases rests on the Commission to prove its case.

While environmental cases again represent the largest proportion of Article 258 TFEU judgments delivered by the CJEU, only a tiny fraction of cases in which infringement proceedings are opened ever make it to this stage. In 2014, for instance, the CJEU gave judgment in only ten Article 258 TFEU environmental cases.[26]

'General and Persistent' Breaches of EU Law

The legality and consequences of bringing actions for systemic, rather than individual, breaches of EU law were considered by the Court of Justice in

---

[23] COM(2007)502 final, p. 7.
[24] See, further, Kingston, 'Surveying the State of EU Environmental Law: Much Bark with Little Bite?', 965.
[25] In 2014, 75 per cent of all EU Pilot cases opened were resolved without the need to escalate the matter further. European Commission (2015), 'Internal Market Scoreboard by Governance Tool', available at: http://ec.europa.eu/internal_market/scoreboard/performance_by_governance_tool/eu_pilot.
[26] European Commission, 2014 Annual Report on Monitoring the Application of Union Law, 16.

Commission v. *Ireland* (Case C-494/01), in which the Commission argued that the situations raised in twelve separate complaints with regard to illegal waste activities constituted evidence not only of the twelve separate infringements, but also of a general and persistent, or systemic, breach of Ireland's obligations under the Waste Directive.[27] The Court came down strongly on the Commission's side, following Advocate General Geelhoed, who had argued forcefully that this was necessary in order to increase the effectiveness of EU environmental law, in view in particular of the relative scarcity of resources on the part of the Commission to investigate complaints, and in the interests of efficiency in grouping complaints together.[28] Importantly, the Court ruled that the consequences of a plea of systemic breach were that, in respect of that plea, the normal rule that all arguments and evidence to be relied upon against the Member State must be contained in the Reasoned Opinion did not apply. Rather, 'the production of additional evidence intended, at the stage of proceedings before the Court, to support the proposition that the failure thus alleged is general and consistent cannot be ruled out in principle'.[29]

In such cases, therefore, the Commission's hand is strengthened considerably, not least in that, once the Court has found a systemic breach to exist, the Commission can continue to gather evidence from environmental NGOs and other sources in any follow-on Article 260 TFEU proceedings. Further, in relation to the burden of proof, the Court noted that it was enough for the Commission to adduce 'sufficient' evidence to show that a Member State's authorities had developed a repeated and persistent practice contrary to the Directive; once this threshold had been reached, the burden shifted to the Member State to challenge the information produced and consequences flowing therefrom.[30] The Court has since confirmed the validity of the systemic breach approach in a number of other judgments.[31]

Defences

Amongst the defences most commonly relied upon by Member States in Article 258 TFEU proceedings is that of fair procedures and the right of defence. As explained above, it is critical to the Article 258 TEU procedure that Member States should have had the opportunity properly to exercise their rights of defence and that, following on from that, the Commission cannot include in the judicial stage of the procedure any concerns which were not expressly put to the Member State in the Reasoned Opinion. Given the length of time which it

---

[27] The relevant directive in force at the time was Council Directive 75/442/EEC of 15 July 1975 on waste, OJ 1975 L 194/39, as amended. See, further, Pal Wennerås, 'A New Dawn for Commission Enforcement under Articles 226 and 228 EC' (2006) 43 *Common Market Law Review* 31.
[28] Opinion in Case C-494/01 *Commission* v. *Ireland* [2005] ECLI:EU:C:2004:546.
[29] C-494/01 *Commission* v. *Ireland* ECLI:EU:C:2005:250, para. 37.   [30] *Ibid.*, para. 47.
[31] See, for instance, Case C-135/05 *Commission* v. *Italy* [2007] ECLI:EU:C:2007:250; Case C-189/07 *Commission* v. *Spain* [2008] ECLI:EU:C:2008:760.

may take for judicial proceedings to come before the CJEU, in practice this may significantly limit the Commission's ability to update its claim to take into account deteriorating environmental conditions. Nevertheless, as set out above, in cases where the Commission relies on the doctrine of general and persistent breach, the effect of such limitation is mitigated.

While breach of the right of defence has successfully been argued in numerous cases, defences that the CJEU has rejected include:

- The presence of internal circumstances within the Member State concerned which are preventing compliance. The CJEU has typically dismissed such arguments, including those based on economic difficulties,[32] constitutional issues[33] and delays in the domestic legislative process.[34]
- The argument that the Member State has taken all reasonably practicable measures to achieve the required environmental outcome (but has not in fact achieved it). This defence was famously rejected by the CJEU in a case brought against the UK for failure to achieve the requisite bathing water standards as set out in the Bathing Water Directive around the Blackpool region.[35] Similarly, the CJEU has rejected arguments that, in case of pollution in contravention of EU law within the territory of a Member State, that pollution was caused by unknown third parties and not by the State itself.[36]
- The fact that other Member States may also be in breach of the relevant EU law, again deemed irrelevant by the CJEU.[37]
- The fact that Member States have administrative measures in place to transpose a Directive, even though no sufficient legal measures exist. This has been rejected by the CJEU on grounds that 'mere administrative practices which by their nature may be altered at the whim of the administration' do not fulfil obligations arising from a Directive.[38]

Interim Measures

Article 279 TFEU provides that the CJEU is entitled to prescribe 'in any cases before it any necessary interim measures'. This includes Article 258 and 260 TFEU cases. Given that it may take over two years from when an infringement action is lodged before the CJEU and delivery of the judgment, the importance of interim measures in certain environmental cases, and in particular those where environmental conditions may be rapidly deteriorating, is obvious. It is unsurprising, therefore, that the Commission has indicated its intention to pursue interim measures in such cases, and has done so successfully

---

[32] See, for instance, Case 232/78 *Commission* v. *France* ECLI:EU:C:1979:215.
[33] See, for instance, Case C-337/89 *Commission* v. *UK* ECLI:EU:C:1992:456.
[34] See, for instance, Case 77/69 *Commission* v. *Belgium* ECLI:EU:C:1970:34.
[35] Case C-56/90 *Commission* v. *UK* ECLI:EU:C:1993:307.
[36] See, for instance, Case C-365/97 *Commission* v. *Italy* ECLI:EU:C:1999:544.
[37] See, for instance, Case C-142/89 *Commission* v. *UK* ECLI:EU:C:1989:528.
[38] Case 96/81 *Commission* v. *Netherlands* ECLI:EU:C:1982:192.

in a number of cases in situations where natural resources could have been irreversibly damaged by the time the Court delivered a judgment in the main action.[39] Evidently, however, in cases where interim measures are obtained, their effectiveness is dependent on the Member State's respect for the Court's judgment.

The Case of Maltese Bird-Hunting

A case in point is Malta's breach of the Birds Directive in relation to bird-hunting. While the Commission successfully obtained interim measures against Malta pending the outcome of Article 258 TFEU infringement proceedings,[40] followed by judgment against Malta in those proceedings,[41] it subsequently brought Article 260(2) TFEU proceedings against Malta for failure to comply with that judgment.[42] In April 2015, a referendum proposing to retain the spring hunting of migratory birds claimed a narrow victory in Malta, and as a result such hunting still continues.

Article 260 TFEU

1. If the Court of Justice of the European Union finds that a Member State has failed to fulfil an obligation under the Treaties, the State shall be required to take the necessary measures to comply with the judgment of the Court.
2. If the Commission considers that the Member State concerned has not taken the necessary measures to comply with the judgment of the Court, it may bring the case before the Court after giving that State the opportunity to submit its observations. It shall specify the amount of the lump sum or penalty payment to be paid by the Member State concerned which it considers appropriate in the circumstances.

---

[39] See, for instance, the Orders of the President in Case C-193/07 R *Commission* v. *Poland* ECLI:EU:C:2009:495 and also Case C-503/06 R *Commission* v. *Italy*, Order of the President of 27 February 2007 ECLI:EU:C:2007:120, Case C-76/08 R *Commission* v. *Malta*, Order of the President of 24 April 2008 ECLI:EU:C:2008:252, Case C-573/08 *Commission* v. *Italy*, Order of the President of 10 December 2009 ECLI:EU:C:2009:775. See, generally, Martin Hedemann-Robinson, 'Enforcement of EU Environmental Law and the Role of Interim Measures' (2010) 19(5) *European Energy and Environmental Law Review* 204.

[40] Case C-76/08 R. *Commission* v. *Malta*, Order of the President of 24 April 2008 ECLI:EU:C:2008:252.

[41] Case C-76/08 *Commission* v. *Malta* ECLI:EU:C:2009:535.

[42] See Commission Press Release of 28 October 2010, 'Commission Requests Malta to Comply with Court Ruling on Bird Hunting' IP/10/1409.

> If the Court finds that the Member State concerned has not complied with its judgment it may impose a lump sum or penalty payment on it. This procedure shall be without prejudice to Article 259.[43]
>
> 3. When the Commission brings a case before the Court pursuant to Article 258 on the grounds that the Member State concerned has failed to fulfil its obligation to notify measures transposing a directive adopted under a legislative procedure, it may, when it deems appropriate, specify the amount of the lump sum or penalty payment to be paid by the Member State concerned which it considers appropriate in the circumstances.
>
> If the Court finds that there is an infringement it may impose a lump sum or penalty payment on the Member State concerned not exceeding the amount specified by the Commission. The payment obligation shall take effect on the date set by the Court in its judgment.

Article 260(2) TFEU and, since its insertion by the Lisbon Treaty, Article 260(3) TFEU, constitute crucial means by which the Commission, and in turn the CJEU, may seek to give the CJEU's judgments real teeth. The original version of the EEC Treaty contained no possibility for the CJEU to impose monetary penalties on a Member State which failed to comply with an Article 258 TFEU judgment declaring that it had breached EU law. This changed with the insertion of what is now Article 260(2) TFEU into the Treaty, with the Treaty of Maastricht in 1992. As discussed above, Article 260(3) TFEU, inserted by the Lisbon Treaty, now enables the CJEU to impose monetary penalties directly in Article 258 TFEU proceedings, without needing to wait for a second round of follow-on proceedings, in cases where a Member State has failed to notify transposition measures required by a Directive to the Commission.

The CJEU has held that the concept of a fine refers to a single lump sum aimed at retrospectively assessing the effects of non-compliance with the first round judgment, while the concept of a penalty payment is a payment imposed periodically and aimed at bringing to an end the breach as soon as possible:[44]

> While the imposition of a penalty payment seems particularly suited to inducing a Member State to put an end as soon as possible to a breach of obligations which, in the absence of such a measure, would tend to persist, the imposition of a lump sum is based more on assessment of the effects on public and private interests of the failure of the Member State concerned to comply with its obligations, in particular where the breach has persisted for a long period since the judgment which initially established it.

---

[43] Note: Article 259 TFEU is the procedure whereby a Member State may bring an action against another Member State for failure to fulfil a Treaty obligation (a procedure rarely invoked in practice).
[44] Case C-304/02 *Commission* v. *France (French Fisheries)* ECLI:EU:C:2005:444, paras. 81–82.

The text of Article 260 TFEU refers to the possibility of imposing a 'fine or penalty payment'. However, the CJEU in *Commission* v. *France (French Fisheries)* interpreted this as enabling the imposition of a fine and/or a penalty payment, given the different purposes of each of these concepts.[45] The Commission has produced guidance on the criteria which it will take into account in deciding on the level of fine and/or penalty payment which it proposes to the CJEU in Article 260 TFEU proceedings.[46] In the case of lump sum payments pursuant to Article 260(2) TFEU, the Commission will calculate its proposal by multiplying a daily lump sum figure (calculated on the basis of a flat rate per day multiplied by coefficients depending on the seriousness of the infringement and the Member State at issue) by the number of days that the infringement persists between the date of the first judgment and the date that it comes to an end or the date of delivery of the Article 260(2) TFEU judgment. A similar technique is used for calculating the proposal to be made in relation to penalty payments. In the case of fines/penalty payments proposed under Article 260(3) TFEU, the Commission has issued a separate Communication specifying a slightly different calculation method for such proceedings.[47] Nevertheless, as the text of Article 260 TFEU makes clear, it is ultimately up to the CJEU to set the level of fine/penalty payment to be imposed, although the Court has indicated that it views the Commission's guidelines as a 'useful point of reference'.[48] For its part, the CJEU has indicated that it will exercise its discretion in setting the level of fine/penalty payment in a way that is appropriate to the circumstances, and in a manner proportionate to the nature of the breach and the ability of the Member State to pay.[49]

The Article 260(2) TFEU procedure has been used by the Commission relatively frequently in environmental cases, as indicated by Figure 6.3, which sets out the number of open Article 260(2) TFEU actions per Member State as at end 2015.

Procedurally, the Commission must go through the same stages (letter of formal notice, reasoned opinion) prior to instituting Article 260(2) TFEU proceedings as it must do for Article 258 TFEU proceedings. As with Article 258 TFEU proceedings, the burden of proof rests on the Commission to make out its case.[50]

---

[45] *Ibid.*
[46] Commission Communication, 'Application of Article 228 of the Treaty', SEC(2005)1658. This Communication has been regularly updated to take account of inflation. See most recently Commission Communication, 'Updating of Data Used to Calculate Lump Sum and Penalty Payments to be Proposed by the Commission to the Court of Justice in Infringement Proceedings', C (2015) 5511.
[47] Commission Communication on implementation of Article 260(3) of the Treaty, SEC (2010)1371.
[48] Case C-278/01 *Commission* v. *Spain* ECLI:EU:C:2003:635, para. 41.
[49] See, for instance, Case C-374/11 *Commission* v. *Ireland* ECLI:EU:C:2012:827, paras. 36 and 50.
[50] See, for instance, Case C-119/04 *Commission* v. *Italy* ECLI:EU:C:2006:489.

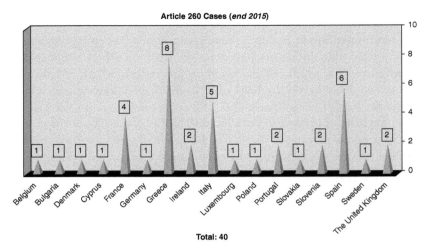

Figure 6.3 Article 260(2) TFEU Actions per Member State as at End 2015
Source: European Commission, 'Statistics on Environmental Infringements' (2015).
See http://ec.europa.eu/environment/legal/law/statistics.htm.

An argument which Member States have often made before the CJEU is that, in cases of bad application in the environmental field (as opposed to non-transposition or non-conformity), they need more time to ensure that a first round Article 258 TFEU is complied with in practice, due to the complexity of the environmental issue at stake. This argument was made, and rejected, in *Commission* v. *Ireland (Septic Tanks)*, where Ireland had contended that the period of 21 months between the first round Article 258 TFEU judgment and the second round referral to the CJEU was insufficient, as the judgment required the creation of a new monitoring and inspection system for septic tanks and other on-site systems for the treatment of waste water and drains resulting from the discharge of domestic waste water, and required owners of such systems to ensure that they were registered with the competent water services authority. The CJEU, however, rejected the argument that the Commission's Article 260(2) TFEU application had been made prematurely, holding that 'the importance of immediate and uniform application of European Union law means that the process of compliance must be initiated at once and completed as soon as possible'.[51]

This approach was also taken in *Commission* v. *Spain (Bathing Waters)* where, in contrast to its Advocate General, the CJEU rejected Spain's arguments that it had been given insufficient time to deal with the technical difficulties raised by the first round judgment.[52] The CJEU adopted a strict approach, holding that the determinative factor was whether the Member State was in compliance at the expiry of the deadline for response to the Commission's reasoned opinion.

---

[51] Case C-374/11 *Commission* v. *Ireland (Septic Tanks)* ECLI:EU:C:2012:827, para. 21.
[52] Case C-278/01 *Commission* v. *Spain (Bathing Waters)* ECLI:EU:C:2003:635.

In other cases, however, the CJEU has taken the fact that the Member State has belatedly complied with the first round judgment into account in setting the level of fine/penalty payment imposed.[53]

Broader Commission Initiatives to Improve Enforcement of EU Environmental Law

As the Seventh Environmental Action Programme reflects, improvement of enforcement remains one of the key priorities of the Commission. In 2012, the Commission issued a Communication entitled 'Improving the Delivery of Benefits from EU Environment Measures',[54] in which the Commission stressed the need to improve knowledge about implementation (meaning knowledge about the state of the environment and the measures intended to protect it), and emphasised that the 'chief responsibility for implementation lies within Member States'.[55] It identified a number of distinct sub-aims in achieving this goal, including making it easier to access environmental information at Member State level, improving the environmental information available at EU level, and improving confidence in the environmental information available. Secondly, the Commission emphasised the need to improve responsiveness at national, regional and local levels, including by improving inspections and surveillance, improving complaint handling, and improving access to justice. The Commission also proposed concluding what it called 'partnership implementation agreements' between the Commission and Member States, setting out national commitments to put in place specific measures, 'with benchmarks and timelines, to deliver the required results'.[56] This aspect of the Communication was followed up with a 2016 Communication setting out the Commission's intention to undertake regular 'Environmental Implementation Reviews' (EIRs) tailored to each Member State. The idea behind such reviews is in many respects similar to the annual cycle of the European Semester process adopted in 2011 following the financial crisis, with the aim of ensuring that Member States implement the EU's macroeconomic policies. The EIR cycle will, the Commission intends, entail country-specific reports being drafted every two years, focusing on the key topics in the area of environmental legislation and policy in each Member State, and highlighting the main challenges and successes of each Member State in the implementation of the EU environmental acquis. The findings of these country-specific reports will in turn form the basis for 'issue papers' dealing with all Member States, prepared by the Commission to be submitted to the Council and European Parliament for discussion. The Commission was, however, careful

---

[53] See, for instance, Case C-407/09 *Commission* v. *Greece* ECLI:EU:C:2011:196 (where no fine/penalty payment was ultimately imposed as a result).
[54] Commission Communication, 'Improving the Delivery of Benefits from EU Environment Measures: Building Confidence through Better Knowledge and Responsiveness', COM (2012)95. See also the 2008 Communication on improving implementation of EU environmental law, COM(2008)773.
[55] *Ibid.*, 4.   [56] *Ibid.*, 10.

to emphasise that preparing the country-specific reports 'will not entail an additional burden for the Member States and there will be no new reporting obligations'.[57] As such, the added value of the EIR process remains to be seen, and will depend on Member States themselves.

Public Enforcement of EU Environmental Law: Enforcement by National Authorities

Principles

It is clear that, even viewed merely in terms of resources, the Commission cannot be the sole or even the primary public enforcer of EU environmental law. This role falls, as mentioned above, to national authorities, including central government, national environmental protection agencies and, in the case of environmental offences which have been criminalised, national police forces and prosecutors.

As a matter of EU law, all national authorities are of course subject to the Article 4(3) TEU principle of sincere cooperation, which obliges Member States to take 'any appropriate measure' to ensure fulfilment of their Treaty obligations, and to 'facilitate the achievement of the Union's tasks'. In principle, therefore, national authorities play the crucial role of ensuring on-the-ground enforcement in circumstances where the Commission has neither the resources nor the competence to do so. The importance of implementation at national level, and the interest of the EU in facilitating this, is further emphasised in Article 197 TFEU, which provides, 'Effective implementation of Union law by the Member States, which is essential for the proper functioning of the Union, shall be regarded as a matter of common interest.'

The CJEU has held that the duties of implementation imposed by what is now Article 4(3) TEU bind not only Member States' central government, but also all national authorities (both judicial and administrative), including those responsible for supervising the implementation of policy in national law.[58] Pursuant to the principle of national procedural autonomy, in principle, it is for Member States to decide on and implement the appropriate remedial regime to deal with infringements of EU law within their territory. However, the CJEU has held that Article 4(3) TEU implies two important limitations on this principle. First, Member States have a duty to ensure that they prosecute and pursue infringements of EU (environmental) law as assiduously as they do so for infringements of equivalent national law provisions (a principle sometimes known as the principle of 'equivalence' of remedies for breach of EU law and national law).[59] Secondly, Member States have a duty to ensure that infringements of EU law are punished by effective, proportionate and dissuasive

---

[57] Commission Communication, 'Delivering the Benefits of EU Environmental Policies through a Regular Environmental Implementation Review', COM(2016)316.
[58] See, for instance, Case 14/83 *Von Colson* ECLI:EU:C:1984:153, para. 26.
[59] See, for instance, Case 68/88 *Commission* v. *Greece* ECLI:EU:C:1989:339.

sanctions.[60] The CJEU has also held that Member States have a duty to help the Commission gather information so as to allow it to form a view on a complaint of infringement of EU law made to it.[61] In cases where an EU Directive has not been (adequately) transposed, however, the extent of Member States' obligations to enforce the Directive will be subject to the limitations of the doctrine of direct effect, discussed further below.

While in principle it is for Member States to decide precisely how they wish to organise their own environmental enforcement systems (national procedural autonomy), a battle has been ongoing over the limits of this discretion, and the extent to which harmonisation of enforcement techniques at EU level is legitimate and necessary. This is nothing new, being at the heart, for instance, of the dispute over whether the European Environment Agency should have the competence to monitor the application of environmental law, a position supported by the European Parliament,[62] but ultimately rejected at the behest of a number of Member States.[63] More recently, the battle was particularly evident in the hotly contested criminal sanctions saga where, following the ECJ's determination that Article 192 TFEU constituted the proper legal basis for criminal penalties that were essential for combating serious environmental offences, the Directive on the Protection of the Environment through Criminal Law was passed in 2008.[64] Nonetheless, in *Ship Source Pollution*, the Court emphasised that determination of the 'type and level of the criminal penalties to be applied' did not fall within the Community's sphere of competence.[65] Article 83(2)(1) TFEU, inserted by the Lisbon Treaty, not only codifies, but also expands, the Court's jurisprudence in this regard, in providing that directives may establish minimum rules with regard to the definition of criminal offences *and sanctions* where this is 'essential to ensure the effective implementation of a Union policy' in an area which has already been subject to harmonisation measures. The Directive on the Protection of the Environment through Criminal Law, along with the Environmental Liability Directive in the sphere of civil liability, represent the most advanced examples of positive harmonisation of EU environmental sanctions to date, and are discussed further below.

A first stage in the national enforcement process is, as underlined by the Commission's 2012 Communication on 'Improving the Delivery of Benefits from EU Environment Measures', discussed above, the process of gathering information on the state of the environment, and detecting potential regulatory

---

[60] See, for instance, Case C-354/99 *Commission* v. *Ireland* ECLI:EU:C:2001:550.
[61] See, for instance, Case C-365/97 *Commission* v. *Italy* ECLI:EU:C:1999:544.
[62] See OJ 1990 C 96/114.
[63] See Ludwig Krämer, 'The Environmental Complaint in EU Law' (2009) 6(1) *Journal for European Environmental and Planning Law* 13.
[64] Case C-176/03 *Commission* v. *Council* [2005] ECLI:EU:C:2005:542, Directive 2008/99/EC of the European Parliament and of the Council of 19 November 2008 on the protection of the environment through criminal law, OJ 2008 L 328/28.
[65] Case C-440/05 *Commission* v. *Council* [2007] ECLI:EU:C:2007:625, para. 70.

breaches, naturally must take place primarily at national level. As the 2012 Communication makes clear, a key aim at present is that of improving knowledge of what is going on 'on the ground', by putting more effective information systems in place at EU and national levels, and improving national inspections aimed at enforcing EU environmental law. Such inspections have traditionally remained within the competence of Member States,[66] but the EU's current Environmental Action Plan envisages greater use of binding inspection requirements.

To date, while binding inspections provisions have existed for some time in rare sectoral directives,[67] the principal instrument on the matter at EU level has been the 2001 Recommendation on minimum criteria for environmental inspections (RMCEI), a non-binding document arrived at in a victory for the Council, which preferred a non-binding recommendation, over the European Parliament, which preferred a binding directive on inspections.[68] However, in an excellent illustration of the 'hardening' of soft law, the RMCEI principles have recently been transposed into binding law in the form of Article 23 of the Industrial Emissions Directive, which recasts the IPPC Directive[69] and is discussed further in Chapter 9.[70] This provision obliges Member States, within the field of IPPC installations, to set up a system of environmental inspections to examine the 'full range' of relevant environmental effects, to draw up an environmental inspection plan that addresses a range of specified matters, and 'regularly' to draw up programmes for routine environmental inspections, as well as carrying out non-routine inspections to investigate serious environmental complaints. Such 'hardening' is also evident in a number of other sectoral environmental Directives, including Directive 2012/18/EU on the control of major accident hazards involving dangerous substances,[71] Directive 2012/19/EU on waste electrical and electronic equipment (WEEE)[72] and Directive 2010/63/EU on the protection of animals used for scientific purposes.[73]

---

[66] Subject only to a non-binding measure, Recommendation 2001/331/EC providing for minimum criteria for environmental inspections in Member States, OJ L 118/41.

[67] See, for instance, Council Directive 96/82/EC of 9 December 1996 on the control of major-accident hazards involving dangerous substances, OJ 1997 L 10/13 ('Seveso II'), as amended, Article 18.

[68] OJ 2001 L 118/41.

[69] See Directive 2008/1/EC of the European Parliament and of the Council of 15 January 2008 concerning integrated pollution prevention and control, OJ 2008 L 24/8.

[70] Directive 2010/75/EU of the European Parliament and of the Council of 24 November 2010 on industrial emissions (integrated pollution prevention and control), OJ 2010 L 334/17.

[71] Directive 2012/18/EU of the European Parliament and of the Council of 4 July 2012 on the control of major-accident hazards involving dangerous substances, OJ 2012 L 197/1, Article 20.

[72] Directive 2012/19/EU of the European Parliament and of the Council of 4 July 2012 on waste electrical and electronic equipment (WEEE), OJ 2012 L 197/38, Article 23.

[73] Directive 2010/63/EU of the European Parliament and of the Council of 22 September 2010 on the protection of animals used for scientific purposes, OJ 2010 L 276/33, Articles 34 and 35.

In line with the indications in the Seventh Environmental Action Plan, the Commission is currently considering revising the EU legal framework on environmental inspections, and has held a public consultation on this. While the Commission had indicated that it was considering adopting a Proposal for a horizontal directive replacing RMCEI,[74] no such Proposal has yet issued. As evident since the aforementioned debate about the role of the EEA, the issue of greater EU involvement in or harmonisation of environmental inspections remains controversial.

The European Union Network for the Implementation and Enforcement of Environmental Law (IMPEL) Network

While, as mentioned above, Member States have to date resisted the idea of a supranational EU environmental regulator tasked with inspections and enforcement other than the Commission itself, a network has emerged in this field since 1992, aimed at fostering cooperation between competent Member State authorities and information exchange (IMPEL).[75] While it originated as an informal network, the status of IMPEL has now been formalised as an international non-profit association of the environmental authorities of EU Member States, acceding and candidate countries of the EU, EEA and EFTA countries, formed under Belgian law and based in Brussels.

> **IMPEL's Aims**
>
> to create the necessary impetus in the European Union to make progress on ensuring a more effective application of environmental legislation. The core of IMPEL's activities take place within a project structure and concern awareness raising, capacity building, peer review, exchange of information and experiences on implementation, international enforcement collaboration as well as promoting and supporting the practicability and enforceability of European environmental legislation.[76]

In 2009, a Memorandum of Understanding was signed between IMPEL and the Commission recognising IMPEL's role with regard to improving the implementation and enforcement of EU environmental law and setting out the parameters of cooperation between the Commission and IMPEL. IMPEL has been supported by the Commission financially via the LIFE+ programme since 2008. IMPEL has been recognised in the EU's Environmental Action

---

[74] See the Commission's roadmap, 'Communication on Implementing EU Environmental Law and Policy: A Common Challenge', available at: http://ec.europa.eu/governance/impact/planned_ia/docs/2011_env_007_common_challenge_en.pdf.
[75] See, further, the discussion in Chapter 2.
[76] See, further, IMPEL's statute available at: www.impel.eu.

Programmes as playing an important supportive role in attaining the EU's aim of improving enforcement and implementation.[77]

> **The EU's Seventh Environmental Action Programme, para. 61**
>
> The general standard of environmental governance throughout the Union will be further improved by enhancing cooperation at Union level, as well as at international level, between professionals working on environmental protection, including government lawyers, prosecutors, ombudsmen, judges and inspectors, such as the European Union Network for the Implementation of Environmental Law (IMPEL), and encouraging such professionals to share good practices.

While the Seventh EAP therefore expressly endorses IMPEL as a forum for improving EU environmental governance, at the same time its affirmation of the need to increase use of binding inspections standards in EU environmental law, discussed above, reflects a clear acknowledgement of the limits of 'soft' networks such as IMPEL in improving compliance on the ground.

The Environmental Liability Directive

Overview

As mentioned above, the 2004 Environmental Liability Directive,[78] together with the 2008 Directive on the Protection of the Environment through Criminal Law,[79] to date represent the most advanced forms of positive harmonisation (i.e. legislation) of sanctions in EU environmental law.

The Environmental Liability Directive (ELD) places national public authorities at the centre of enforcing civil sanctions for breach of EU environmental law, and must be viewed alongside the developments encouraging the role of private parties in civil litigation, discussed further below. While discussions on an EU environmental civil liability regime had taken place since the 1970s at EU (then EEC) level, these discussions only began to gain serious momentum with the catastrophic industrial accident which occurred at the Sandoz chemical plant in Switzerland in 1986, and which caused major environmental damage to the Rhine. After a long and rather fraught gestation, the ELD was finally passed in 2004, and has since been amended three times.[80] The difficulty which many Member States had with transposing the ELD is illustrated by the fact that the

---

[77] See, for instance, the Seventh Environmental Programme, OJ 2013 L 354/171, para. 63.
[78] Directive 2004/35/CE of the European Parliament and of the Council of 21 April 2004 on environmental liability with regard to the prevention and remedying of environmental damage, OJ 2004 L 143/56.
[79] Directive 2008/99/EC of the European Parliament and of the Council of 19 November 2008 on the protection of the environment through criminal law.
[80] By Directive 2006/21/EC on the management of waste from extractive industries, OJ 2006 L 102/15, Directive 2009/31/EC on the geological storage of carbon dioxide,

Commission was forced to bring no fewer than seven Article 258 TFEU enforcement actions for failure to transpose on time.[81]

The broad aim of the Directive is encapsulated in its second recital.

Recital 2, Environmental Liability Directive

The prevention and remedying of environmental damage should be implemented through the furtherance of the polluter pays principle, as indicated in the Treaty and in line with the principle of sustainable development. The fundamental principle of this Directive should therefore be that an operator whose activity has caused the environmental damage or the imminent threat of such damage is to be held financially liable, in order to induce operators to adopt measures and develop practices to minimise the risks of environmental damage so that their exposure to financial liabilities is reduced.

The basic strategy of the ELD is to adopt a public law approach to preventing and remedying environmental damage. Competent national authorities are essentially placed in charge of ensuring that the operators covered by the ELD prevent or, as the case may be, remedy relevant environmental damage. The Directive does not adopt the approach of providing for a private law remedy whereby an individual or company can sue for environmental damage caused or about to be caused, although private citizens may make a complaint to the appropriate competent authority. In this, the ELD is similar in approach to federal US legislation adopted in the 1980s such as the Comprehensive Environmental Response, Compensation and Liability Act (CERCLA, or Superfund), which enables the US Environmental Protection Agency to compel site clean-up or to undertake the clean-up itself using, *inter alia*, the Superfund trust fund.

Scope of Application

The principal legal responsibility for preventing and remedying damage caused lies, under the ELD, with the 'operator', meaning the person who operates or controls the relevant occupational activity (or, where national legislation so provides, enjoys decisive economic power over the technical functioning of such activity).[82] 'Occupational activity' is defined to mean 'any activity carried out in

---

OJ 2009 L 140/114, and Directive 2013/30/EU on the safety of offshore oil and gas operations, OJ 2013 L 178/66.

[81] Case C-417/08 *Commission v. UK* ECLI:EU:C:2009:384; Case C-422/08 *Commission v. Austria* ECLI:EU:C:2009:385; Case C-368/08 *Commission v. Greece* ECLI:EU:C:2009:326; Case C-331/08 *Commission v. Luxembourg* ECLI:EU:C:2009:185; Case C-402/08 *Commission v. Slovenia* ECLI:EU:C:2009:157; Case C-328/08 *Commission v. Finland* ECLI:EU:C:2008:775; Case C-330/08 *Commission v. France* ECLI:EU:C:2008:720.

[82] Art. 2(6), ELD.

the course of an economic activity, a business or an undertaking, irrespective of its private or public, profit or non-profit character'.[83] As such, the scope of the ELD's obligations does not extend to those who may cause environmental damage, no matter how serious, in the course of activities which are considered to be non-economic in nature.[84] Further, the ELD does not apply to activities which have national defence or international security as their main purpose, or the protection from natural disasters as their sole purpose.[85]

Article 3 ELD further specifies that the scope of the ELD only extends to:

- environmental damage caused by (or the imminent threat of such damage being caused by) certain occupational activities, namely, those listed in Annex III of the Directive. This Annex largely cross-refers to activities falling within the scope of other EU environmental legislation, including the operation of installations subject to the IPPC Directive,[86] waste management operations covered by the Waste Framework Directive,[87] and discharges into inland surface and ground water covered by the relevant EU water Directives;[88] and
- damage to protected species and natural habitats caused by (or the imminent threat of such damage being caused by) any occupational activities other than those listed in Annex III. While this category of damage goes beyond the terms of Annex III, it is subject to the significant qualification that it will fall within the ELD's scope only when the operator has been 'at fault or negligent'. By contrast, the liability of operators of Annex III occupational activities, discussed above, is not restricted to situations of fault or negligence, and strict liability therefore applies.[89]

Certain restricted categories of environmental damage are, however, in all cases excluded from the scope of the ELD, including damage caused by armed conflict or a 'natural phenomenon of exceptional, inevitable and irresistible character' and damage covered by other international conventions or falling under the Euratom Treaty.[90]

As the above extract makes clear, the ELD focuses specifically on 'environmental' damage as defined therein, to the exclusion of harm such as damage to persons, including personal injury, economic loss and/or damage to private property.[91] Article 3(3) ELD expressly states that it does not give private parties any right of compensation as a result of environmental damage or of an imminent threat of such damage. The Directive similarly expressly does not affect rights of compensation for damage available under certain pre-existing international

---

[83] Art. 2(7), ELD.
[84] See, by analogy, the scope of application of the EU competition rules and the concept of an undertaking under Articles 101–107 TFEU.
[85] Art. 4(6) ELD.   [86] See Chapter 9.   [87] See Chapter 14.   [88] See Chapter 10.
[89] See, confirming this, Case C-378/08 *Raffinerie Méditerranée* ECLI:EU:C:2010:126, para. 65 and Joined Cases C-478 and C-479/08 *Buzzi Unicem and Others*, EU:C:2010:129, para. 45.
[90] Art. 4(1)–(4), ELD.   [91] Recital 14, ELD.

agreements on civil liability.[92] The ELD further acknowledges that national civil law may apply to some of the situations covered therein, and specifies that Member States are free to maintain or adopt more stringent provisions concerning the prevention and remedying of environmental damage, and to adopt appropriate measures where double recovery of costs could occur in circumstances where action is taken under the Directive by a competent authority and a concurrent action is taken by a person under national civil law whose property is affected by the environmental damage in question.[93]

Not all environmental damage is covered by the Directive. Article 2(1) ELD defines 'environmental damage' for the purposes of the Directive to mean:

- Damage to protected species and natural habitats, but only where this has 'significant adverse effects on reaching or maintaining the favourable conservations status of such habitats or species' and where this does not result from an act expressly authorised under the Habitats/Birds Directives or equivalent provisions of national law on nature conservation;[94]
- Water damage, but only where this 'significantly adversely affects' the ecological, chemical or quantitative status or the ecological potential (as defined in the Water Framework Directive) of the waters concerned, or the environmental status of marine waters (as defined in the Marine Strategy Framework Directive);[95]
- Land damage, but only in cases of 'land contamination that creates a significant risk of human health being adversely affected as a result of the direct or indirect introduction, in, on or under land, of substances, preparations, organisms or micro-organisms'.

In terms of its temporal scope, the ELD does not apply to damage caused by emissions, events or incidents which took place prior to the transposition date of 30 April 2007, or when damage derives from an activity which finished before that date, or from an emission, event or incident occurring more than 30 years ago.[96]

Causation

Environmental damage (or the imminent threat thereof) is only covered where a causal link can be established between the damage and the activities of individual operators, including in the case of diffuse-source pollution.[97] The CJEU has

---

[92] Recitals 11–12 and Art. 4(2), ELD. The list of relevant international conventions is contained in Annex IV ELD (including, for instance, the 1992 International Convention on Civil Liability for Oil Pollution Damage). Contrast the Waste Framework Directive, which makes no such exclusion: see Case C-188/07 *Commune de Mesquer* ECLI:EU:C:2008:359, para. 87.
[93] Art. 16, ELD. [94] See, further, Chapter 12. [95] See, further, Chapter 10.
[96] Art. 17, ELD. On this, see Case C-378/08 *Raffinerie Méditerranée (ERG) SpA, Polimeri Europa SpA and Syndial SpA v. Ministero dello Sviluppo economico* ECLI:EU:C:2010:126, paras. 40–41 (confirming that the ELD does apply where the activity was commenced but not completed by the transposition date) and Joined Cases C-478 and C-479/08 *Buzzi Unicem and Others*, EU:C:2010:129.
[97] Art. 4(5) ELD.

confirmed that the duty to establish causation, in accordance with the national rules of evidence, rests on the competent authority, even in cases where strict liability applies (i.e. operators of Annex III activities).[98] Further, cases of multiple party causation continue to be covered by the rules of national law on apportionment of liability and cost allocation.[99]

The CJEU has handed down a number of judgments further refining the concept of causation under the ELD, and applying the polluter pays principle. In particular, the CJEU has held that the competent authority must establish a causal link 'between the activity of one or more identifiable operators and concrete and quantifiable damage, irrespective of the type of pollution at issue'.[100] In *Raffinerie Méditerranée*, the CJEU held that it is compatible with the ELD for the competent authority to operate on the presumption that there is a causal link between operators and the pollution found on account of the fact that the operators' installations are located close to the polluted area (including in cases involving diffuse pollution). The CJEU applied the polluter pays principle to hold, however, that in order for such a causal link thus to be presumed, that authority must have 'plausible evidence' capable of justifying its presumption. The CJEU noted that this might include, for instance, the fact that the operator's installation is located close to the pollution found and that there is a correlation between the pollutants identified and the substances used by the operator in connection with his activities.[101] In so holding, the CJEU further noted that operators must, pursuant to Article 11(4) ELD, have legal remedies available to them to challenge findings of a causal link and, pursuant to Article 8(3) ELD, operators need not bear the costs of remedial actions where they can prove that the damage was caused by a third party and occurred despite the fact that appropriate safety measures were in place. The CJEU also relied on Article 16 ELD in so concluding, which permits Member States to take more stringent measures than those set out in the Directive in relation to environmental damage.[102]

Where no causal link can be established between the environmental damage and the activity of the operator, the CJEU has held that the situation is governed by national law, subject to observance of the EU Treaties and without prejudice to other EU secondary legislation.[103]

---

[98] Case C-378/08 *Raffinerie Méditerranée*, as above, paras. 54 and 64.   [99] Art. 9, ELD.

[100] See C-534/13 *Ministero dell'Ambiente e della Tutela del Territorio e del Mare and Others* v. *Fipa Group Srl and Others* ECLI:EU:C:2015:140, para. 54 and, to that effect, Case C-378/08 *Raffinerie Méditerranée*, EU:C:2010:126, paras. 52 and 53, and Joined Cases C-478 and C-479/08 *Buzzi Unicem and Others*, EU:C:2010:129, para. 39.

[101] Cases C-378/08 *Raffinerie Méditerranée*, paras. 52–70. See similarly, Joined Cases C-478 and C-479/08 *Buzzi Unicem and Others*.

[102] *Ibid.*, paras. 67–68.

[103] C-534/13 *Fipa Group Srl and Others* ECLI:EU:C:2015:140, para. 46; Case C-378/08 *Raffinerie Méditerranée* para. 44; Joined Cases C-478 and C-479/08 *Buzzi Unicem*, as above, para. 34.

Duties Imposed on Operators

The duties imposed by the ELD on operators are essentially as follows.

First, the operator is obliged to take the 'necessary preventive measures' without delay in cases where environmental damage has not yet occurred but there is an 'imminent threat' thereof.[104] In such cases, it is incumbent on the operator to inform the competent national authority, which may require the operator to provide further information or take the necessary preventive measures, give instructions to the operator on what needs to be done, or indeed take the necessary preventive measures itself.[105]

Secondly, where environmental damage has occurred, the operator is obliged to inform the competent national authority without delay of 'all relevant aspects of the situation', to take all 'practicable steps' to immediately control the situation, and to take the necessary remedial measures.[106] Pursuant to Article 7 ELD, the operator is obliged to identify potential remedial measures and get approval on what needs to be done in advance from the competent authority. The competent authority must take its decision on the necessary remedial measures after inviting observations from anyone who has lodged a request for action or the relevant landowner where the measures are proposed to be carried out.[107] Again, the competent authority may require the operator to provide further information or take the necessary measures, give instructions to the operator on what needs to be done, or take the necessary measures itself.[108]

Thirdly, pursuant to Article 8 ELD, the operator must bear the costs for the preventive and remedial actions taken pursuant to the Directive, in accordance with the polluter pays principle. The competent authority must recover any costs it has incurred in taking preventive/remedial action from the operator, unless the cost of so recovering would exceed the recoverable sum, or the operator cannot be identified.[109] In 2016, the Commission reported that the average cost of remedial action taken pursuant to the ELD was around €42,000.[110]

However, an operator can successfully avoid paying such costs where he can prove that the damage was caused by a third party and occurred despite the existence of appropriate safety measures, or was the result of complying with an order of a public authority.[111] Article 8(4) contains a further possibility for Member States, if they wish, to absolve operators from their obligation to pay the costs:

---

[104] Art. 5(1), *ibid*. [105] Art. 5(3), *ibid*. [106] Art. 6, *ibid*. [107] Art. 7(4), *ibid*.
[108] Art. 6(2), *ibid*. [109] Art. 8(2), *ibid*.
[110] Report from the Commission to the Council and the European Parliament under Article 18(2) of Directive 2004/35/EC on environmental liability with regard to the prevention and remedying of environmental damage, COM(2016)204, at para. 3.3.
[111] Art. 8(3), *ibid*.

> **Article 8(4) ELD**
>
> The Member States may allow the operator not to bear the cost of remedial actions taken pursuant to this Directive where he demonstrates that he was not at fault or negligent and that the environmental damage was caused by:
>
> (a) an emission or event expressly authorised by, and fully in accordance with the conditions of, an authorisation conferred by or given under applicable national laws and regulations which implement those legislative measures adopted by the Community specified in Annex III, as applied at the date of the emission or event;
>
> (b) an emission or activity or any manner of using a product in the course of an activity which the operator demonstrates was not considered likely to cause environmental damage according to the state of scientific and technical knowledge at the time when the emission was released or the activity took place.

The latter exception, known as the 'state-of-the-art' defence, was particularly controversial when passed as, it was argued, it allowed Member States to flout the polluter pays principle in a particularly egregious manner. A 2010 Commission report on the implementation of the ELD showed that fewer than half of Member States chose to implement both discretionary defences contained in Article 8(4) ELD.[112]

An obvious weakness of the ELD is that it does not provide for a solution in cases where an operator becomes insolvent, leaving in its wake unremediated environmental damage. The ELD does not require, at present, any guarantee, security or insurance to be taken out by operators such as would deal with this possibility. The issue is dealt with only weakly by Article 14(1) ELD, which requires Member States to take measures to 'encourage' the development of such mechanisms.[113] Instead, it is the competent authority (i.e. the taxpayer) which will have to meet the costs of clean-up in such circumstances. This is in contrast to the CERCLA/Superfund regime in the USA, where the Superfund trust fund was created *inter alia* to deal with such eventualities.

---

[112] COM(2010)581. See, generally, Lucas Bergkamp and Barbara Goldsmith (eds.), *The EU Environmental Liability Directive: A Commentary* (Oxford University Press, 2013), at 4.38.

[113] A 2010 Commission Report on the matter concluded that there was no sufficient justification for introducing a harmonised system of mandatory security (COM(2010) 581). In the wake of the 2010 Hungarian 'red sludge' disaster at the Ajka alumina plant, however, a further report was prepared for the Commission in 2013 to examine the feasibility of creating a fund to cover environmental liability and losses occurring from industrial accidents (see http://ec.europa.eu/environment/archives/liability/eld/eld fund/index.html). No action has been taken to date by reason of this report.

Powers and Duties of Competent Authorities

Pursuant to Article 11 ELD, it is for Member States to designate the competent authority for their own jurisdiction. As set out above, the competent authority has the power in the case of preventive and remedial actions to require the operator to provide further information or take the necessary measures, give instructions to the operator on what needs to be done, or take the necessary measures itself. It may also institute proceedings for recovery of any costs it has incurred in taking preventive or remedial action within five years of the later of (a) completion of the measures or (b) identification of the operator.[114] As set out above, the duty to establish which operator has caused the relevant damage or imminent threat thereof, and to determine which remedial measures are appropriate, lies with the competent authority.[115]

The CJEU has interpreted the powers and duties of competent authorities in a number of preliminary references from the Italian courts raising the legality of the Italian legislation implementing the ELD. In *Raffinerie Méditerranée*, the CJEU held that a competent authority may alter environmental remedial measures previously adopted, and may do so on its own initiative, even without an initial proposal by the operator.[116] However, in such circumstances, the operator, and the persons on whose land the remedial measures are to be carried out, must have an opportunity to be heard.[117] Further, if the competent authority decides substantially to change remedial measures adopted after the requisite consultation, it must explain its actions and undertake a cost–benefit analysis ensuring 'that it is in fact possible, as a result of the option finally chosen, to achieve the best results from an environmental point of view, without thereby causing the operators concerned to incur manifestly disproportionate costs by comparison with those they had or would have had to incur in connection with the first option chosen by that authority'.[118]

Importantly, the CJEU further held that it was permissible for national legislation to permit the competent authority to make the use of operators' land conditional on carrying out remedial works required by the authority, even where the land at issue was not affected by those measures.[119] However, in order to do this, the competent authority must show that the measure is justified by the aim of preventing environmental deterioration or further occurrence of damage in the area where it is implemented.[120]

More recently, in *Fipa Group*, the CJEU considered the legality of national legislation which aimed to tackle the situation where no polluter can be identified or pursued. In that case, the CJEU held that it was compatible with the polluter pays principle for national legislation, in cases where it is impossible to identify who the polluter of a plot of land is or to have that person adopt remedial measures, to prohibit the competent authority from making the landowner (who did not

---

[114] Art. 10, *ibid*.
[115] Art. 11(2), *ibid*., and see Case C-378/08 *Raffinerie Méditerranée*, paras. 54 and 64.
[116] Case C-379/08 *Raffinerie Méditerranée*, para. 51.   [117] *Ibid*., para. 56.
[118] *Ibid*., para. 64.   [119] *Ibid*., para. 92.   [120] *Ibid*.

cause the pollution) adopt preventive and remedial measures. However, national legislation may allow the competent authority in such circumstances to require the landowner to reimburse the costs of measures undertaken by the authority 'within the market value of the site'.[121]

Observations and Requests for Action

The role of private parties under the ELD is, as set out above, tightly circumscribed. However, Article 12 ELD provides for the possibility for natural and legal persons to lodge observations or a 'request for action' with the competent authority if they can demonstrate that they are affected (or likely to be affected) by the damage concerned, have a sufficient interest in environmental decision-making relating to the damage, or (where required by national law) allege the impairment of a right.[122] As with the amendments to the EIA and IPPC Directives made with a view to implementing the Aarhus Convention,[123] environmental NGOs recognised as such under national law are automatically considered to have a sufficient interest for this purpose.[124] Crucially, the competent authority is not obliged to take action by reason of a request for action or observations made, but need only 'consider' them after giving the relevant operator a chance to respond, and notify the complainant of its decision 'as soon as possible' and in accordance with relevant national law provisions.[125] Pursuant to Article 13 ELD, the complainant must have access to a 'court or other independent and impartial public body' to review the 'procedural and substantive legality' of the decisions, acts or failure to act of the competent authority under the ELD. Again, this is couched in similar terms to the amendments to the IPPC and EIA Directives made in implementation of the access to justice provisions of the Aarhus Convention.[126] However, national law on access to justice expressly continues to apply: the ELD is stated to be 'without prejudice to' national law regulating access to justice and those requiring that administrative review procedures be exhausted prior to recourse to judicial procedures.[127]

Transboundary Damage

Article 15 ELD expressly deals with situations where environmental damage affects or is likely to affect several Member States. In such circumstances, Member States have an obligation to cooperate, including via information exchange, with a view to ensuring that preventive and, where necessary, remedial action is taken in respect of such damage. A crucial question arises, of course, as to which Member State is obliged to pay for clean-up in such circumstances. On this, Article 15(3) ELD provides that, where a Member State identifies damage in its territory which has not been caused there, it may report the matter

---

[121] Case C-534/13 *Ministero dell'Ambiente e della Tutela del Territorio e del Mare and Others* v. *Fipa Group Srl and Others* ECLI:EU:C:2015:140, para. 63.
[122] Art. 12, *ibid*. [123] See, further, Chapters 9 and 11. [124] Art. 12(1), ELD.
[125] Art. 12(3), ELD. [126] See, further, Chapters 9 and 11. [127] Art. 13(2), ELD.

to the Commission and to the other Member State(s) concerned, recommend preventive or remedial measures, and 'seek, in accordance with this Directive, to recover the costs it has incurred' in relation to such measures.

Criminal Penalties

As discussed above, pursuant to the principle of national procedural autonomy, it is for Member States to design the remedial system available for breaches of EU environmental law, as long as such remedies are effective and equivalent to those available for similar breaches of national law. In this context, harmonisation of criminal law has long represented an area of particular political sensitivity for Member States, and is widely considered to be an area at the heart of national sovereignty and in which real differences of approach remain between Member States, particularly between those with common law systems and civil law systems. For this reason, the field of police and judicial cooperation in criminal law matters was dealt with under separate (intergovernmental) constitutional rules to the 'first pillar' of (supranational) Community law when first included in the EU Treaties as part of the so-called 'third pillar' under the Treaty of Maastricht, and until the entry into force of the Lisbon Treaty in 2009.[128] After a failed Commission proposal for a (first pillar) Directive dealing with serious environmental crime,[129] a (third pillar) Framework Decision was passed by the Council in 2003.[130] In a controversial judgment, however, the CJEU in 2005 held that, despite this, Article 192 TFEU constituted the proper legal basis for criminal penalties that were essential for combating serious environmental offences.[131] The CJEU reasoned that, while as a general rule, neither criminal law nor the rules of criminal procedure fell at that time within the Community's competence, this did not prevent the Community legislature, when the application of effective, proportionate and dissuasive criminal penalties by the competent national authorities is an essential measure for combating serious environmental offences, from taking measures which relate to the criminal law of the Member States which it considers necessary in order to ensure that the rules which it lays down on environmental protection are fully effective.[132]

---

[128] The Treaty of Amsterdam restructured the third pillar to remove the civil law aspects of the area of freedom, security and justice (incorporating these into the Community pillar), leaving only the provisions on Police and Judicial Cooperation in Criminal Matters (PJCCM) in the third pillar. On the concepts of supranationalism and intergovernmentalism, see e.g. Helen Wallace et al., *Policy-Making in the European Union* (7th edn., Oxford University Press, 2015), chapter 2.

[129] COM(2001)139.

[130] Framework Decision 2003/80/JHA of 27 January 2003 on the protection of the environment through criminal law, OJ 2003 L 29/55.

[131] Case C-176/03 *Commission v. Council* [2005] ECLI:EU:C:2005:542; Directive 2008/99/EC of the European Parliament and of the Council of 19 November 2008 on the protection of the environment through criminal law, OJ 2008 L 328/28.

[132] Case C-176/03 *ibid.*, para. 48.

In its subsequent judgment in *Ship Source Pollution*, the CJEU followed this by emphasising that determination of the 'type and level of the criminal penalties to be applied' did not fall within the Community's sphere of competence.[133] As the Commission had, when that judgment was delivered, already proposed a Directive containing detailed provisions on precisely that,[134] it was forced to remove these provisions from the Proposal.

In 2008, partially harmonising EU legislation on environmental criminal law was finally passed in the form of Directive 2008/99 on the Protection of the Environment through Criminal Law (the 'PECL Directive').[135] The PECL Directive obliges Member States to criminalise a number of specified serious environmental offences as follows:

> **Article 3 PECL Directive**
>
> Member States shall ensure that the following conduct constitutes a criminal offence, when unlawful and committed intentionally or with at least serious negligence:
>
> (a) the discharge, emission or introduction of a quantity of materials or ionising radiation into air, soil or water, which causes or is likely to cause death or serious injury to any person or substantial damage to the quality of air, the quality of soil or the quality of water, or to animals or plants;
>
> (b) the collection, transport, recovery or disposal of waste, including the supervision of such operations and the after-care of disposal sites, and including action taken as a dealer or a broker (waste management), which causes or is likely to cause death or serious injury to any person or substantial damage to the quality of air, the quality of soil or the quality of water, or to animals or plants;
>
> (c) the shipment of waste, where this activity falls within the scope of Article 2(35) of Regulation (EC) No. 1013/2006 of the European Parliament and of the Council of 14 June 2006 on shipments of waste and is undertaken in a non-negligible quantity, whether executed in a single shipment or in several shipments which appear to be linked;

---

[133] Case C-440/05 *Commission* v. *Council* [2007] ECLI:EU:C:2007:625, para. 70 (concerning the legal basis of Framework Decision 2005/667/JHA of 12 July 2005 to strengthen the criminal-law framework for the enforcement of the law against ship-source pollution, OJ 2005 L 255/164).

[134] COM(2007)51.

[135] Directive 2008/99/EC of the European Parliament and of the Council of 19 November 2008 on the protection of the environment through criminal law, OJ 2008 L 328/28. At Council of Europe level, the 1998 Council of Europe Convention on the Protection of the Environment through Criminal Law pre-dated the EU's harmonisation of the area, but this has not yet received enough ratifications in order to enter into force.

(d) the operation of a plant in which a dangerous activity is carried out or in which dangerous substances or preparations are stored or used and which, outside the plant, causes or is likely to cause death or serious injury to any person or substantial damage to the quality of air, the quality of soil or the quality of water, or to animals or plants;
  (e) the production, processing, handling, use, holding, storage, transport, import, export or disposal of nuclear materials or other hazardous radioactive substances which causes or is likely to cause death or serious injury to any person or substantial damage to the quality of air, the quality of soil or the quality of water, or to animals or plants;
  (f) the killing, destruction, possession or taking of specimens of protected wild fauna or flora species, except for cases where the conduct concerns a negligible quantity of such specimens and has a negligible impact on the conservation status of the species;
  (g) trading in specimens of protected wild fauna or flora species or parts or derivatives thereof, except for cases where the conduct concerns a negligible quantity of such specimens and has a negligible impact on the conservation status of the species;
  (h) any conduct which causes the significant deterioration of a habitat within a protected site;
  (i) the production, importation, exportation, placing on the market or use of ozone-depleting substances.

Evidently, the PECL Directive does not harmonise environmental criminal law as such, but only those types of environmental offences which are deemed to be the most serious in nature. Inciting, aiding and abetting the above offences must also be criminalised.[136]

As mentioned above, it was clear following the CJEU's *Ship-Source Pollution* judgment that the Commission's original proposal to include considerable detail on the levels of penalties which may be imposed for the above offences needed to be amended. Article 5 of the PECL Directive as passed merely states, therefore, that Member States 'shall take the necessary measures to ensure that the offences referred to in Articles 3 and 4 are punishable by effective, proportionate and dissuasive criminal penalties'.

The Directive specifies that Member States must ensure that not only natural persons, but also legal persons (i.e. companies) can be held liable for the offences covered thereby. However, Article 6 of the Directive states that such liability need only exist where the offence has been committed for the benefit of the legal person 'by any person who has a leading position within the legal person', based on a power of representation of the legal person, or authority to take decisions on behalf of or to exercise control within that person. Article 6(2) covers the scenario

---

[136] PECL Directive, Art. 4.

of liability by omission, providing that Member States shall ensure that legal persons can be held liable where the lack of supervision or control by a person with a leading position within the company has 'made possible' the commission of a relevant offence.

With the abolition of the pillar structure brought about by the 2007 Treaty of Lisbon, the separate constitutional status of the area of freedom, security and justice has disappeared, and the rules on cooperation in criminal matters are to be found under Title V TFEU on the Area of Freedom, Security and Justice, at Articles 82–89 TFEU.[137] Article 83(2) TFEU, inserted by the Treaty of Lisbon, provides as follows.

> **Article 83(2) TFEU**
>
> If the approximation of criminal laws and regulations of the Member States proves essential to ensure the effective implementation of a Union policy in an area which has been subject to harmonisation measures, directives may establish minimum rules with regard to the definition of criminal offences and sanctions in the area concerned. Such directives shall be adopted by the same ordinary or special legislative procedure as was followed for the adoption of the harmonisation measures in question, without prejudice to Article 76.

Nevertheless, this provision is subject to the 'emergency brake' procedure set out in Article 83(3) TFEU, which enables a Member State to request that a draft directive be referred to the European Council if it considers that it would affect 'fundamental aspects of its criminal justice system'. In that event, the ordinary legislative procedure is suspended for discussions. It may, in the case of consensus, be restarted; where there is no consensus, a smaller group of Member States may decide to invoke the Treaties' provisions on enhanced cooperation, where the conditions for this are fulfilled.

---

[137] The UK (pending its exit from the EU), Ireland and Denmark have retained their opt-outs from the area of freedom, security and justice. See Protocol (No. 21) on the Position of the United Kingdom and Ireland in respect of the Area of Freedom, Security and Justice, OJ 2012 C 326/295 and Protocol (No. 22) on the Position of Denmark, OJ 2012 C 326/299 in the Consolidated Version of the Treaty of the Functioning of the European Union, OJ 2012 C 326/47.

7

Private Enforcement of EU Environmental law

The increasing involvement of private and civil society actors in European environmental governance is a constant theme of this book.[1] As discussed there, European environmental governance has become a classic instance of what is often termed 'networked' governance, whereby centralised bodies 'have become increasingly dependent upon the cooperation and joint resource mobilization of policy actors outside their hierarchical control'.[2] This chapter considers the extent to which private actors play a role in the enforcement of EU environmental law, as a counterpart to the public enforcement of EU environmental law by the European Commission and Member State national authorities discussed in Chapter 6.

Private Enforcement of EU Environmental Law at National Level

Direct Effect of EU Environmental Law

Overview

The force of international law in a given national legal system is, according to traditional conceptions, decided upon according to the principles of that legal system. Certain States may choose to adopt the position that international law effectively forms part of the same legal system as domestic law, such that norms passed at international level which the State is bound by may also be relied upon directly before national courts (an approach typically known as the 'monist' approach to international law).[3] Other States may choose to view the domestic legal system and international legal system as distinct, such that international norms – even those ratified by the State in question – only become part of the domestic legal system if a domestic law is passed transposing or incorporating that norm which achieves this (an approach typically known as the 'dualist' approach to international law).[4]

---

[1] See, in particular, Chapters 1, 4 and 5.
[2] See Andrew Jordan and Adriaan Schout, *The Coordination of the European Union* (Oxford University Press, 2006), 6.
[3] The Netherlands, for instance, is typically viewed as having a partly monist system, based on Arts. 93 and 94 of the Dutch Constitution. It is generally agreed that there is in fact a spectrum of monism and dualism, rather than one single definition of each: in reality, many States have their own distinct approach to international law which may display features of each doctrine. See, further, the detailed discussion in Mario Mendez, *The Legal Effects of EU Agreements* (Oxford University Press, 2013), 37–47.
[4] The UK and Ireland, for instance, are typically viewed as having dualist systems. See Art. 29.6 of the Irish Constitution.

The CJEU, however, has since the outset famously developed its own constitutional principles governing the force which, in its view, must be accorded to (what is now)[5] EU law within national legal orders. In its seminal 1964 judgment in *Costa* v. *ENEL*, the CJEU established the principle of supremacy of EU law over national law, meaning that, in the event of a conflict between a provision of national law and a provision of EU law, a national court must give precedence to the latter.[6] This was directly preceded by the establishment, in the CJEU's 1963 judgment in *Van Gend en Loos*, of the principle of direct effect of EU law, meaning that, where the conditions of direct effect are made out, private parties must have the possibility of relying on EU law directly before their national courts.[7] The revolutionary nature of these judgments has been well canvassed: in so holding, the CJEU radically deviated from the traditional approach whereby the force of international law is determined by national legal systems, and chose *as a matter of EU law* to establish its own constitutional principles governing the force of EU law at domestic level.[8]

In *Van Gend en Loos*, the CJEU reached its groundbreaking ruling that EU law is directly effective – as long as the conditions for direct effect are satisfied by the particular provision at issue – by examining the 'spirit, the general scheme and the wording' of the Treaty of Rome (including, in particular, the aim of establishing a common market, the reference to 'peoples' and not just governments in the Treaty, the establishment of institutions with 'sovereign rights', and the presence of the preliminary reference procedure in the Treaty). In what is perhaps the most famous of all the CJEU's pronouncements, it concluded as follows.

Van Gend en Loos, at pp. 12–13

the Community constitutes a new legal order of international law for the benefit of which the States have limited their sovereign rights, albeit within limited fields, and the subjects of which comprise not only Member States but also their nationals. Independently of the legislation of Member States, Community law therefore not only imposes obligations on individuals but is also intended to confer upon them rights which become part of their legal heritage.

---

[5] The CJEU's judgments discussed herein related solely to what was then known as Community law, and the twin constitutional principles of direct effect and supremacy of EU law did not apply to what were, after the Treaty of Maastricht, known as the second and third pillars of EU law (namely, the Common Foreign and Security Policy (CFSP), and the Area of Freedom, Security and Justice, respectively). However, the Treaty of Lisbon abolished the pillar structure, incorporating the former third pillar into general EU law. It also replaced the 'European Community' (and the concept of Community law) with the 'European Union' (and EU law). The only field where the fundamental constitutional principles of supremacy and direct effect of EU law do not apply now is, therefore, the CFSP (the former second pillar). See, generally, for instance, Paul Craig and Gráinne de Búrca, *EU Law: Text, Cases and Materials* (6th edn., Oxford University Press, 2015), chapter 1.

[6] Case 6/64 *Costa* v. *ENEL* ECLI:EU:C:1964:66.

[7] Case 26/62 *Van Gend en Loos* ECLI:EU:C:1963:1.

[8] See, generally, for instance, Craig and de Búrca, *EU Law: Text, Cases and Materials*, chapter 7.

In *Van Gend en Loos* and subsequent judgments,[9] the CJEU has clarified that, in order for an individual provision of EU law to be directly effective, it must be:

- Clear and sufficiently precise, in the sense that the obligation which it imposes must be set out in unequivocal terms;[10] and
- Unconditional, in the sense that its effect is not subject to adoption of any further measure by the Union or its Member States.[11]

Must a Directly Effective Provision Confer a Right on an Individual?

A question of great importance in the environmental context is whether, in order to be directly effective, a provision of EU law must be shown not only to be clear, sufficiently precise and unconditional, but also that it confers rights on individuals. Such a suggestion can be derived from the language used by the CJEU in judgments as far back as *Van Gend en Loos* itself, in which the CJEU held that Article 12 EEC must be interpreted as producing direct effects 'and creating individual rights which national courts must protect'.[12] It is evident, however, that many critical provisions of EU environmental law cannot reasonably be considered to confer substantive rights on any particular individuals.[13] For instance, it is clear that Member States have strict obligations to protect biodiversity imposed by the Habitats and Birds Directives, but it is far less clear that such obligations could reasonably be characterised as giving rise to rights conferred on individuals.[14]

The question of the interrelationship between substantive individual rights and the doctrine of direct effect has yet to be definitively resolved by the CJEU. However, a number of important judgments indicate that it is unnecessary for a provision to confer rights in order to be invoked before national courts.

In *Commission* v. *Germany*,[15] which concerned the question whether Germany had infringed the Environmental Impact Assessment (EIA) Directive by granting development consent for the extension of the Großkrotzenburg thermal power station, the CJEU rejected Germany's argument that the direct effect of Directives exists only where they confer specific rights on individuals. The CJEU noted that, in order for the Commission's (Article 258 TFEU) action to succeed, the question was whether Germany had observed the obligation flowing directly from the Directive to assess the environmental impact of the project concerned. This question was, the CJEU noted, 'quite separate' from the question whether individuals may rely as against the State on provisions of an unimplemented Directive which are unconditional and sufficiently clear and precise.[16] *Commission* v. *Germany*, therefore, confirmed that Member States may be held

---

[9] See, for instance, *Van Gend en Loos* ECLI:EU:C:1963:13; Case C-8/81 *Becker* ECLI:EU:C:1982:7, para. 25.
[10] Case C-236/92 *Difesa della Cava* ECLI:EU:C:1994:60, para. 10.
[11] See, for instance, *ibid.*, para. 9.   [12] *Ibid.*, para. 13.
[13] See, generally, the discussion on environmental rights in Chapter 5.
[14] See, further, Chapter 12.
[15] Case C-431/92 *Commission* v. *Germany* ECLI:EU:C:1995:260.   [16] *Ibid.*, paras. 24–26.

to be in breach of a Directive (in that case, in an Article 258 TFEU infringement action before the CJEU) irrespective of whether or not the Directive's provisions confer rights on individuals.

In *WWF* v. *Regione Veneto*,[17] the CJEU held that the prohibition on hunting of protected species set out in the Birds Directive could be relied upon by a private party (in that case, the Italian branch of the World Wildlife Fund) before its national courts. The CJEU applied its classic direct effect reasoning based on *effet utile* ('useful effect') of EU law:

> **WWF v. Regione Veneto, para. 19**
>
> where by means of a directive the Community authorities have placed Member States under a duty to adopt a certain course of action, the effectiveness of such a measure would be diminished if persons were prevented from relying upon it in proceedings before the courts and national courts were prevented from taking it into consideration as an element of Community law (judgment in Case 8/81 *Becker* v. *Finanzamt Münster-Innenstadt* [1982] ECR 53, para. 23). Consequently, wherever the provisions of a directive appear, as far as their subject-matter is concerned, to be unconditional and sufficiently precise, those provisions may be relied upon by an individual against any authority of a Member State where that State has either failed to implement the directive in national law by the end of the period prescribed or has failed to implement it correctly (judgment in Case 103/88 *Fratelli Costanzo* v. *Comune di Milano* [1989] ECR 1839, paras. 29 and 30).

Importantly, no reference is made to any requirement for a directly effective provision to confer individual rights.

In its judgment in *Kraaijeveld*, the CJEU clarified that, in order for an EU provision to be invoked before a national court, it need not expressly or impliedly confer substantive rights on individuals.[18] That case concerned the question whether Articles 2(1) and 4(2) of the Environmental Impact Assessment (EIA) Directive had direct effect.[19] Article 2(1) of the Directive provides, 'Member States shall adopt all measures necessary to ensure that, before consent is given, projects likely to have significant effects on the environment by virtue *inter alia* of their nature, size or location are made subject to a requirement for development consent, and an assessment with regard to their effects. These projects are defined in Article 4.'

Article 4(2) of the EIA Directive states that Member States are competent to determine whether projects listed in Annex II of the Directive must be subject to an impact assessment.

The CJEU accepted that these provisions contained a discretion for Member States, and did not lay down a right as such. However, the CJEU went on to

---

[17] Case C-118/94 ECLI:EU:C:1996:86.
[18] Case C-72/95 *Kraaijeveld* ECLI:EU:C:1996:404.   [19] See, further, Chapter 11.

recall its classic reasoning as to the *effet utile* of Directives, including the EIA Directive:

> where the Community authorities have, by directive, imposed on Member States the obligation to pursue a particular course of conduct, the useful effect of such an act would be weakened if individuals were prevented from relying on it before their national courts, and if the latter were prevented from taking it into consideration as an element of Community law in order to rule whether the national legislature, in exercising the choice open to it as to the form and methods for implementation, has kept within the limits of its discretion set out in the directive.[20]

On this basis, the CJEU confirmed that the Dutch courts must, by virtue of the doctrine of direct effect, review the question whether or not the Dutch authorities had exceeded their discretion in the manner in which they had implemented the Directive.[21] Further, if that discretion had been exceeded, it was incumbent on Member State authorities to take all necessary measures to ensure that projects are examined to determine whether they are likely to have significant effects on the environment (i.e. the so-called 'screening' obligation) and, if so, to ensure that an impact assessment is carried out.

Kraaijeveld, therefore, confirmed that national courts must review whether national authorities have exceeded the limits of their discretion even in cases where no individual right exists. It is also important confirmation that national authorities are obliged in such cases to give effect to the relevant provision of EU law directly, even where the relevant provisions of national law are inadequate. In *WWF* v. *Bozen*, the CJEU confirmed and expanded upon the *Kraaijeveld* ruling, holding that national authorities' obligation to take all necessary measures to ensure that projects are examined to determine whether they are likely to have significant effects on the environment and, if so, to ensure that they are subject to an impact assessment, also applied in circumstances where an assessment procedure had been carried out, but had been challenged as being inadequate.[22]

In *Waddenzee, Kraaijeveld* was further expanded, this time in the context of the question whether a national court asked to determine the legality of an authorisation for a plan or project within the meaning of Article 6(3) of the Habitats Directive may examine whether the limits of the discretion of the competent national authorities laid down by that provision have been complied with, even though it had not been transposed into the legal order of the relevant Member State at all (the Netherlands).[23] Repeating its ruling in *Kraaijeveld*, the CJEU held that the obligation imposed on national courts also applied to determining whether, where there had been no transposition

---

[20] Ibid., para. 56   [21] Ibid., para. 59.
[22] Case C-435/97 *WWF* v. *Bozen* ECLI:EU:C:1999:418.
[23] On the obligation of appropriate assessment imposed by Art. 6(3) of the Habitats Directive, see Chapter 12.

of Article 6(3), the national authority which adopted the authorisation had kept within the limits of its discretion set by that Article.[24] Applying this principle, the CJEU further held that the Dutch authorities could only authorise the plan/project at issue in that case (mechanical cockle fishing in the Waddenzee protected site of the Netherlands) if they have made 'certain that it will not adversely affect the integrity' of the protected site, taking into account the conclusions of the appropriate assessment of the implications of the project at issue. The national authorities would be in breach of this obligation if they authorised the activity 'in the face of uncertainty as to the absence of adverse effects for the site concerned'.[25] By allowing authorisation only where there is certainty of no negative effects on a site's integrity, Waddenzee undoubtedly represents a challenging precautionary-based standard for national authorities authorising activities covered by the Birds and Habitats Directive.[26]

In *Janecek*, the CJEU further applied the *Kraaijeveld* principle to Article 7(3) of the Air Quality Framework Directive (Directive 96/62 on ambient air quality assessment and management).[27] Article 7(3) required Member States to draw up an action plan indicating the measures to be taken in the shorter term where there was a risk of the limit values and/or alert thresholds set by the Directive being exceeded. Applying *Kraaijeveld*, the CJEU held that, while Member States enjoyed a discretion in drawing up those action plans, Article 7(3) placed limits on that discretion which may be relied upon before national courts, concerning the adequacy of the measures which must be included in the action plan.[28]

Which Bodies Must Apply Directly Effective Provisions?

The doctrine of direct effect was developed by the CJEU in parallel with the doctrine of supremacy of EU law, such that national courts must, where a directly effective provision of EU law is raised before them, disapply a conflicting provision of national law (whether passed prior to or subsequent to the provision of EU law).[29] In *Fratelli Costanzo*, the CJEU held that this obligation applied not just to national courts and tribunals, but also to administrative authorities, including decentralised administrative authorities such as local authorities and municipalities.[30] This includes, therefore, authorities tasked with applying EU environmental law such as environmental protection agencies and other administrative bodies.

Direct Effect of Treaty Provisions, Regulations, Decisions and International Agreements

It was clear from *Van Gend en Loos* that provisions of the EEC Treaty (as it then was) could have direct effect, as long as the individual provision at issue was

---

[24] Case C-127/02 *Waddenzee* ECLI:EU:C:2004:482, para. 66.   [25] *Ibid.*, paras. 67–69.
[26] See, further, the discussion of the precautionary principle in Chapter 3.
[27] Case C-237/07 *Janecek* ECLI:EU:C:2008:447. See, further, Chapter 9.
[28] *Ibid.*, paras. 43–47.   [29] See Case 106/77 *Simmenthal* ECLI:EU:C:1978:49.
[30] Case 103/88 ECLI:EU:C:1989:256.

clear, unconditional and sufficiently precise.[31] In that case, what was then Article 12 EEC (which prohibited the increase in customs duties or charges having equivalent effect) was held to satisfy that test. In the environmental context, the question arises whether any of what is now Title XX on environment, or the other Treaty provisions dealing with the environment, could satisfy those requirements and be held to be directly effective. Upon examining each of these provisions, most of them are unlikely to do so. In particular, many of the key environmental provisions of the Treaty – including Article 3(3) TEU, and much of Article 191 TFEU – are drafted in rather general terms, setting out the broad aims and principles on which EU environmental policy must be based, but without defining these in a manner that would probably be considered to be 'sufficiently precise'. The integration obligation contained in Article 11 TFEU may potentially also fall foul of the same difficulty. Nevertheless, as discussed further in Chapter 3, some aspects of the meaning of Article 11 TFEU are unambiguous – in particular, the obligation to demonstrate that environmental protection requirements have at least been considered where relevant in defining and implementing Union policies and activities. To this extent, the direct effect of this provision cannot be excluded. Similarly, the CJEU has not yet definitively pronounced on whether the principles of EU environmental policy set out in Article 191(2) TFEU – or at least some of them – are directly effective, particularly in light of the clarification given to many of these principles now provided by the case law of the Court.[32] In that context, it is of relevance that the CJEU has held that certain of the so-called 'general principles' of EU law – namely, the fundamental constitutional principles which were at least originally not present in the Treaty but have been developed by the CJEU – are capable of being directly effective.[33]

In the case of Regulations and Decisions,[34] the CJEU similarly confirmed relatively early on in its case law that, in principle, these can be directly effective (in the case of a Decision, against the person to whom they are addressed).[35] Again, the specific provision of the Regulation/Decision at issue must, however, satisfy the conditions of being clear, unconditional and sufficiently precise.

---

[31] The CJEU in *Van Gend en Loos* also included a condition that the provision constitute a negative obligation, but this was dropped in subsequent judgments.

[32] See, further, Chapter 3.

[33] See, for instance, Case C-144/04 *Mangold* ECLI:EU:C:2005:709 (non-discrimination on grounds of age).

[34] See Art. 288 TFEU, which, in defining the types of secondary legislation which may be passed by the Union, states that, 'A regulation shall have general application. It shall be binding in its entirety and directly applicable in all Member States' and that 'A decision shall be binding in its entirety. A decision which specifies those to whom it is addressed shall be binding only on them.'

[35] See, in the case of Regulations, Case 93/71 *Leonosio* ECLI:EU:C:1972:39 and, in the case of Decisions, Case C-156/91 *Hansa Fleisch* ECLI:EU:C:1992:423.

In the case of international environmental agreements, pursuant to Article 216 TFEU, agreements concluded by the Union are binding upon the institutions of the Union and on its Member States. The CJEU has held that,

> a provision in an agreement concluded by the European Union with a non-member country must be regarded as being directly applicable when, regard being had to its wording and to the purpose and nature of the agreement, the provision contains a clear and precise obligation which is not subject, in its implementation or effects, to the adoption of any subsequent measure.[36]

In *Syndicat professionnel coordination des pêcheurs de l'étang de Berre et de la région* v. *Électricité de France* (EDF),[37], the CJEU applied this test to hold that Article 6(3) of the 1980 Protocol for the Protection of the Mediterranean Sea against Pollution from Land-based Sources and Article 6(1) of the amended Protocol of 1996, following its entry into force, have direct effect. In that case, the plaintiff syndicate of fishermen had brought proceedings against the defendant electricity company, concerning discharges from a hydroelectric power station into the Étang de Berre in France. The relevant articles of the protocol and amended protocol essentially made such discharges subject to receipt of prior authorisation by the competent authorities. The CJEU had no hesitation in holding that the wording of the provisions was clear, precise and unconditional.[38] Further, the purpose and nature of the Protocol, which was the prevention of pollution of the Mediterranean Sea caused by discharges from land-based sources, also supported recognition of the direct effect of the provisions in question.[39]

In *Slovak Brown Bear*, the Grand Chamber of the CJEU considered the question whether Article 9(3) of the Aarhus Convention was directly effective.[40] Article 9(3) provides,

> In addition and without prejudice to the review procedures referred to in paragraphs 1 and 2 above [concerning access to justice in relation to access to environmental information and public participation],[41] each Party shall ensure that, where they meet the criteria, if any, laid down in its national law, members of the public have access to administrative or judicial procedures to challenge acts and omissions by private persons and public authorities which contravene provisions of its national law relating to the environment.

The question was whether, as a matter of EU law, Article 9(3) of the Aarhus Convention should be viewed as being directly effective in national legal orders

---

[36] See, for instance, Case C-240/09 *Lesoochranárske zoskupenie* ECLI:EU:C:2011:125, para. 44; Case C-265/03 *Simutenkov* ECLI:EU:C:2005:213, para. 21, and Case C-372/06 *Asda Stores* ECLI:EU:C:2007:787, para. 82.
[37] Case C-213/03 ECLI:EU:C:2004:464.   [38] *Ibid.*, para. 41.   [39] *Ibid.*, para. 45.
[40] Case C-240/09 *Lesoochranárske zoskupenie* ECLI:EU:C:2011:125.
[41] See, further, Chapter 5.

in its own right, even in the absence of any generally applicable Directive on access to environmental justice being passed at EU level.[42] The matter arose in the context of a challenge by a Slovakian environmental NGO to the refusal on the part of the Slovak State to admit the NGO as a party to administrative proceedings concerning the grant, within Slovakia, of derogations to the system of protection, required pursuant to Article 12 of the Habitats Directive, for species such as the brown bear.[43]

Applying the Court's case law on mixed international agreements,[44] Advocate General Sharpston had taken the view that, insofar as the EU had not yet legislated on the implications of Aarhus for national provisions on access to environmental justice, the question of the direct effect of Article 9(3) in the national legal order was a matter solely for the national court. Indeed, this was the conclusion that might have seemed natural to anyone seeking to apply the Court's standard reasoning on how far the scope of EU law (and therefore the scope of the doctrine of direct effect) extends. In a complex and far-reaching judgment, however, the Grand Chamber declined to follow its Advocate General, holding that it did in fact have jurisdiction to rule on whether Article 9(3) of the Convention was directly effective. The Court reached this conclusion by reasoning that, 'a specific issue which has not yet been the subject of EU legislation is part of EU law, where that issue is regulated in agreements concluded by the European Union and the Member State and it concerns a field in large measure covered by it'.[45]

As the dispute at issue concerned the system of species protection required by the Habitats Directive, this test was satisfied and the matter fell within the scope of EU law.[46] The fact that no specific Directive had yet been adopted on access to environmental justice was not, therefore, decisive, as the relevant field was covered 'in large measure' (albeit not exhaustively) by EU law.[47]

This left the Court free to consider the further question whether Article 9(3) of the Convention satisfied the conditions required to be directly effective as a matter of EU law. The CJEU held that Article 9(3) was not directly effective, as it did not contain any clear and precise obligation capable of directly regulating the legal position of individuals. As only members of the public who meet the criteria, if any, laid down by national law are entitled to exercise the rights conferred thereby, Article 9(3) of the Aarhus Convention could not be considered to be unconditional in nature, as it was subject to the adoption of

---

[42] *Ibid.* Namely, the failed Commission Proposal for a Directive on access to justice, COM (2003)624 final. See, further, Chapter 5.

[43] For the conditions of derogation, see Art. 16 of the Habitats Directive (Council Directive 92/43/EEC of 21 May 1992 on the conservation of natural habitats and of wild fauna and flora, OJ 1992 L 206/7, as amended).

[44] Meaning, international agreements which fall partly within the competence of the EU and partly within the competence of the Member States, such that the EU and the Member States must be signatories thereto. See, further, Chapter 2.

[45] para. 36.   [46] paras. 33–38.   [47] para. 40.

a subsequent measure.[48] Nevertheless, as discussed further below, the CJEU went on to apply the duty of consistent interpretation (indirect effect) to mitigate the effect of this finding, holding that national courts were obliged to interpret national law concerning a species protected by EU law in a way which 'to the fullest extent possible' was consistent with the aims of Article 9(3).

Direct Effect of Directives
Relying on Directives against the State and 'Emanations of the State' ('Vertical' Direct Effect) While the fact that Regulations and Decisions are capable of having direct effect was settled relatively early on by the CJEU, uncertainty remained about Directives, most notably because it was unclear how a Directive could be considered to be 'unconditional' in nature. Article 288 TFEU defines a Directive as follows: 'A directive shall be binding, as to the result to be achieved, upon each Member State to which it is addressed, but shall leave to the national authorities the choice of form and methods.'

By its very definition, therefore, a Directive is subject to transposition measures being taken by Member States as a matter of national law, and national authorities are left some discretion as to the choice of form and methods of transposition.

In its 1974 judgment in *Van Duyn*, the CJEU nevertheless confirmed that Directives are capable of having direct effect against the State and public authorities (so-called 'vertical' direct effect).[49] As the vast majority of EU environmental secondary legislation takes the form of Directives, these rulings are crucial for the effectiveness of enforcement of EU environmental law before national courts. In *Van Duyn*, the CJEU relied on a mixture of *effet utile*-based reasoning,

> It would be incompatible with the binding effect attributed to a Directive by Article [288 TFEU] to exclude, in principle, the possibility that the obligation which it imposes may be invoked by those concerned. In particular, where the [Union] authorities have, by Directive, imposed on Member States the obligation to pursue a particular course of conduct, the useful effect of such an act would be weakened if individuals were prevented from relying on it before their national courts and if the latter were prevented from taking it into consideration as an element of [Union] law.[50]

The CJEU subsequently added an estoppel-based argument in judgments such as *Ratti*, in which it has reasoned that a Member State which has not adopted implementing measures required by a Directive within the prescribed period may not plead, as against individuals, its own failure to perform the obligations entailed thereby.[51] Further, it has interpreted the concept of 'unconditionality' in the context of Directives as satisfied where, upon examination of the provision at

---

[48] para. 45. See, similarly, joined Cases C-404/12 P and C-405/12 P *Council and Commission v. Stichting Natuur en Milieu and Pesticide Action Network Europe* ECLI:EU:C:2015:5, para. 47.
[49] Case 41/74 *Van Duyn* ECLI:EU:C:1974:133.   [50] *Ibid.*, para. 12.
[51] Case 148/78 *Ratti* ECLI:EU:C:1979:110, para. 22.

issue, it provides for a minimum guarantee which does not leave any option to the Member State as to the particular result to be achieved.[52]

In the environmental context, difficulties have frequently arisen as to whether the provision at issue is clear, sufficiently precise and unconditional, due to the often open-textured nature of key provisions of certain environmental Directives. In the case of the Waste Framework Directive (WFD),[53] this issue arose in the CJEU's judgment in *Enichem Base*.[54] In that case, the CJEU held that Article 3(2) of the former WFD, Directive 75/442, did not have direct effect. That provision required Member States to inform the Commission in good time of any draft rules regarding waste disposal but, as the CJEU noted, did not lay down any procedure for monitoring of such rules by the Commission, and did not make implementation of the national rules conditional on the Commission's approval.[55] The CJEU held that the wording and the purpose of the provision, which was to ensure that the Commission was informed of any such national measures and to take appropriate measures if necessary, supported the view that failure to observe its requirements rendered the national rules unlawful.[56] As such, the CJEU concluded, Article 3(2) concerned 'relations between the Member States and the Commission and does not give rise to any rights for individuals which might be infringed by a Member State's breach of its obligation to inform the Commission in advance of draft rules'.

The ruling in *Enichem Base* may be contrasted with the CJEU's rulings on so-called 'incidental' horizontal direct effect, considered further below, in which *Enichem* was distinguished. In any event, Article 3(2) has been removed from the WFD in its 2008 revision.[57]

In *Difesa della Casa*,[58] the CJEU considered the question whether Article 4 WFD had direct effect. Article 4 of the WFD provided,

> Member States shall take the necessary measures to ensure that waste is disposed of without endangering human health and without harming the environment, and in particular:
> – without risk to water, air, soil and plants and animals,
> – without causing a nuisance through noise or odours,
> – without adversely affecting the countryside or places of special interest.

The CJEU held that this provision did not satisfy the requirements of sufficient precision and unconditionality. Rather, Article 4 indicated:

> a programme to be followed and sets out the objectives which the Member States must observe in their performance of the more specific obligations imposed on them

---

[52] See, for instance, Case C-8/81 *Becker* ECLI:EU:C:1982:7, para. 40.
[53] See, further, Chapter 14.   [54] Case C-380/87 *Enichem Base* ECLI:EU:C:1989:318.
[55] *Ibid.*, para. 20.   [56] *Ibid.*, para. 22.   [57] See, further, Chapter 14.
[58] Case C-236/92 *Difesa della Casa* ECLI:EU:C:1994:60.

> by Articles 5 to 11 of the directive concerning planning, supervision and monitoring of waste-disposal operations.
>
> 13 It must also be noted that the Court has already held, in relation to the Member States' obligations under Article 10 of the directive, that that provision does not lay down any particular requirement restricting the freedom of the Member States regarding the way in which they organise the supervision of the activities referred to therein but that that freedom must be exercised having due regard to the objectives mentioned in the third recital in the preamble to the directive and Article 4 thereof (see the judgment in Joined Cases 372 to 374/85 Ministère Public v. Traen [1987] ECR 2141).
>
> 14 Thus, the provision at issue must be regarded as defining the framework for the action to be taken by the Member States regarding the treatment of waste and not as requiring, in itself, the adoption of specific measures or a particular method of waste disposal. It is therefore neither unconditional nor sufficiently precise and thus is not capable of conferring rights on which individuals may rely as against the State.[59]

The Concept of the 'State'   The CJEU has held that the concept of the 'State' for the purposes of the doctrine of (vertical) direct effect must be broadly interpreted. The leading case here remains *Foster* v. *British Gas*, which concerned the question whether the privatised British Gas Corporation fell within the concept of an emanation of the State.

> ***Foster* v. *British Gas*, para. 20**
>
> a body, whatever its legal form, which has been made responsible, pursuant to a measure adopted by the State, for providing a public service under the control of the State and has for that purpose special powers beyond those which result from the normal rules applicable in relations between individuals is included in any event among the bodies against which the provisions of a directive capable of having direct effect may be relied upon.[60]

The doctrine of direct effect, therefore, applies not only in proceedings against central government departments, but also local and regional authorities and even privatised bodies which satisfy the test set out in *Foster* v. *British Gas*.

Direct effect of Directives prior to the expiry of the transposition period   A further question arises as to whether Directives may have any effect prior to the expiry of their transposition period. In *Ratti*, the CJEU rejected the argument that an individual could have any legitimate expectation that a Directive would be transposed prior to the transposition date, and therefore that Directives had no direct effect before this date.[61]

In *Inter-Environnement Wallonie*,[62] however, the CJEU expanded on this position, holding that what is now Article 4(3) TEU, the duty of sincere cooperation,

---

[59] *Ibid.*, paras. 12–14.   [60] C-188/89 *Foster* v. *British Gas* ECLI:EU:C:1990:313.
[61] See *Ratti* ECLI:EU:C:1979:110, paras. 39–47.
[62] Case C-129/96 *Inter-Environnement Wallonie* ECLI:EU:C:1997:628.

obliged Member States even prior to the expiry of the transposition period to 'refrain from taking any measures liable seriously to compromise the result prescribed' by the Directive. In assessing whether this standard had been reached, the CJEU held that the questions whether the relevant national provisions purported to constitute full transposition of the Directive, and the effects in practice of applying those incompatible provisions and their duration in time, must be considered. In particular, if the national provisions at issue only purported to constitute transitional measures, and not full transposition, this would not necessarily breach the Member State's obligations.[63]

Relying on Directives against Private Parties ('Horizontal' Direct Effect)   The CJEU has consistently held that Directives cannot be relied upon in themselves before national courts to place obligations upon private parties, i.e. that Directives do not have 'horizontal' direct effect. In *Marshall I*, the CJEU reasoned that,[64]

> With regard to the argument that a Directive may not be relied upon against an individual, it must be emphasised that according to Article [288 TFEU] the binding nature of a Directive, which constitutes the basis for the possibility of relying on the Directive before a national court, exists only in relation to 'each Member State to which it is addressed'. It follows that a Directive may not of itself impose obligations on an individual and that a provision of a Directive may not be relied upon as such against such a person.

This principle has been applied in a variety of environmental cases. In *Pretore di Salò*, the CJEU emphasised that a Directive (in that case, Directive 78/659 on the quality of fresh waters needing protection or improvement in order to support fish life) could not, of itself and independently of a national law adopted by a Member State, have the effect of aggravating the criminal law liability of an individual who had contravened the Directive (i.e. Directives cannot have 'reverse' direct effect relied upon by the State against a private party).[65] Similarly, the CJEU has confirmed that the Waste Framework Directive cannot be relied upon in prosecutions of private parties in and of itself, in the absence of appropriate national implementing measures.[66]

Clearly, the prohibition on horizontal direct effect of Directives significantly diminishes the effectiveness of Directives (including environmental Directives) in cases where a Member State has failed to pass any, or any adequate, transposition measures. The impact of this prohibition has, however, been mitigated by the CJEU in five principal ways: first, via the doctrine of indirect effect; secondly, by its approach to so-called 'triangular' cases; thirdly, by its approach in cases of 'incidental' horizontal direct effect; fourthly, in cases where a so-called 'general principle' of EU law has been held to be horizontally directly effective; and

---

[63] *Ibid.*, paras. 45–50.   [64] See Case C-152/84 *Marshall* I ECLI:EU:C:1986:84, para. 48.
[65] Case C-14/86 ECLI:EU:C:1987:275, para. 20.
[66] Joined Cases C-372–375/85 *Traen* ECLI:EU:C:1987:222, paras. 23–26.

fifthly, via the doctrine of State liability for breach of EU law. These are dealt with in turn below.

Other Means of Relying on EU Law before National Courts

The Duty of Consistent Interpretation ('Indirect Effect')

The duty of consistent interpretation (*interprétation conforme*) was first articulated by the CJEU in its landmark judgment in *Von Colson*,[67] where the CJEU held that, in a case where the relevant national provisions could be interpreted in a manner that was consistent with EU law (in that case, the Directive on equal treatment of men and women), it was incumbent on national courts to adopt such interpretation.

> **Von Colson, para. 26**
>
> the Member States' obligation arising from a Directive to achieve the result envisaged by the Directive and their duty under [Article 4(3) TEU] to take all appropriate measures, whether general or particular, to ensure the fulfilment of that obligation, is binding on all the authorities of Member States including, for matters within their jurisdiction, the courts. It follows that, in applying the national law and in particular the provisions of a national law specifically introduced in order to implement [the Equal Treatment Directive], national courts are required to interpret their national law in the light of the wording and the purpose of the Directive in order to achieve the result referred to in the third paragraph of [Article 288 TFEU].

As noted above, the doctrine of indirect effect is one of the principal ways in which the effectiveness of Directives can be upheld even in proceedings between private parties in national courts, and in this sense mitigates the effects of the prohibition on horizontal direct effect. However, the CJEU has confirmed that the doctrine has its limits: national courts are only obliged to adopt an interpretation consistent with the relevant Directive where, applying the applicable national law rules of legal interpretation, it is possible to do so. This does not, in particular, require a national court to adopt an interpretation *contra legem* (i.e. which contradicts the text of the relevant national law).[68]

In *Arcaro*,[69] the CJEU held that the doctrine of indirect effect could not be applied so as to determine or aggravate the liability in criminal law of persons who act in contravention of a Directive. That case concerned the prosecution of Mr Arcaro by Italian prosecutors for contravening an Italian decree on industrial

---

[67] Case 14/83 ECLI:EU:C:1984:153.
[68] Case C-105/03 *Pupino* ECLI:EU:C:2005:386, paras. 47–48. See also Case C-106/89 *Marleasing* ECLI:EU:C:1990:395; Joined Cases C-397/01–C-403/01 *Pfeiffer* ECLI:EU:C:2004:584.
[69] Case C-168/95 *Arcaro* ECLI:EU:C:1996:363.

discharge of dangerous substances into the aquatic environment. In its Order for Reference, the national court raised the issue that the decree did not seem fully to transpose Directive 76/464/EEC on pollution caused by certain dangerous substances discharged into the aquatic environment and Directive 83/513 on limit values and quality objectives for cadmium discharges. The CJEU held that the doctrine of direct effect could not be relied upon against Mr Arcaro (by virtue of the prohibition on 'reverse' vertical direct effect, discussed above), and the same applied to the doctrine of indirect effect.[70] However, the *Arcaro* limitation is confined to the field of criminal law, and does not prevent reliance on the doctrine of indirect effect in civil proceedings between private parties.[71]

In its 2011 judgment in *Slovak Brown Bear*, discussed above, the CJEU applied the duty of consistent interpretation, together with the general principle of effectiveness of remedies for breach of EU law, in a highly creative manner, this time to use international law (namely, the Aarhus Convention) to interpret EU law. As discussed above, the issue in this case was whether Article 9(3) of the Aarhus Convention should be viewed as being directly effective in national legal orders in its own right, even in the absence of any generally applicable Directive on access to environmental justice being passed at EU level.[72] The matter arose in the context of a challenge by a Slovakian environmental NGO to the refusal on the part of the Slovak State to admit the NGO as a party to administrative proceedings concerning the grant, within Slovakia, of derogations to the system of protection, required pursuant to Article 12 of the Habitats Directive, for species such as the brown bear.[73]

Applying the Court's case law on mixed agreements, Advocate General Sharpston had taken the view that, insofar as the EU had not yet legislated on the implications of Aarhus for national provisions on access to environmental justice, the question of the direct effect of Article 9(3) in the national legal order was a matter solely for the national court. Indeed, this was the conclusion that might have seemed natural to anyone seeking to apply the Court's standard reasoning on how far the scope of EU law (and therefore the scope of the doctrine of direct effect) extends.

In a complex and far-reaching judgment, however, the Grand Chamber declined to follow its Advocate General, holding that it did in fact have jurisdiction to rule on whether Article 9(3) of the Convention was directly effective. The Court reached this conclusion by reasoning that 'a specific issue which has not yet been the subject of EU legislation is part of EU law, where that issue is

---

[70] *Ibid.*, paras. 41–42.
[71] See, for instance, Case C-456/98 *Centrosteel* ECLI:EU:C:2000:402.
[72] See n. 152, below. Namely, the failed Commission Proposal for a Directive on access to justice, COM(2003)624 final, and the discussion of the Aarhus Convention in Chapter 5.
[73] For the conditions of derogation, see Article 16 of the Habitats Directive (Council Directive 92/43/EEC of 21 May 1992 on the conservation of natural habitats and of wild fauna and flora, OJ 1992 L 206/7, as amended).

regulated in agreements concluded by the European Union and the Member State and it concerns a field in large measure covered by it'.[74]

As the dispute at issue concerned the system of species protection required by the Habitats Directive, this test was satisfied and the matter fell within the scope of EU law.[75] The fact that no specific Directive had yet been adopted on access to environmental justice was not, therefore, decisive, as the relevant field was covered 'in large measure' (albeit not exhaustively) by EU law.[76]

This left the Court free to consider the further question whether Article 9(3) of the Convention satisfied the conditions required to be directly effective as a matter of EU law. Here again, the Court demonstrated considerable creativity of approach in concluding that these conditions were indeed met. The Court acknowledged that Article 9(3) of the Aarhus Convention did not contain any clear and precise obligation capable of directly regulating the legal position of individuals without subsequent implementing measures (as would normally have been required for direct effect):[77] the wording of Article 9(3) itself, after all, makes clear that the requirement of access to environmental justice pursuant to that provision is subject to meeting the 'criteria, if any' laid down in national law. Nonetheless, the Court avoided this difficulty by relying instead on the general principle of effectiveness of national procedural remedies, which requires Member States to ensure that rights derived from EU law (in this case, the Habitats Directive) are effectively protected.[78] It followed that national courts were obliged, as regards a species protected by the Habitats Directive, to interpret their national procedural rules 'in a way which, to the fullest extent possible, is consistent with the objectives laid down in Article 9(3) of the Aarhus Convention'.[79]

This judgment is a significant one, demonstrating a willingness on the part of the Grand Chamber to interpret its own jurisprudence creatively with a view to furthering the objectives of access to environmental justice within the EU, even in circumstances where the EU legislator has not been able to achieve this result. In practical terms, the impact of the judgment is potentially very considerable: the Court has created a duty of consistent interpretation for national courts applying national procedural rules to interpret them in conformity with the Aarhus Convention 'to the fullest extent possible'. A comparison with the original (French) version of the text confirms the remarkably strong language employed by the Court in this regard ('*dans toute le mesure du possible*'). Indeed, the Court gave a clear indication as to what it considered the outcome of such interpretation should be in the case at hand, stating that the interpretation should be done 'so as to enable' ('*afin de permettre*') an environmental protection organisation, such as the one at issue, to challenge before a court a decision taken following administrative proceedings liable to be contrary to EU environmental law.[80] This strong version of the duty of consistent interpretation effectively obliges national courts,

---

[74] para. 36. [75] paras. 33–38. [76] para. 40.
[77] See e.g. Case C-265/03 *Simutenkov* ECLI:EU:C:2005:213. [78] paras. 44–48.
[79] para. 50. [80] para. 51.

therefore, to achieve via interpretative means the aims of this aspect of the Aarhus Convention in the absence of applicable EU legislation on access to justice, unless this would require a *contra legem* interpretation of national law.

Moreover, while the *Slovak Brown Bear* case itself involved a question of standing of environmental NGOs, its implications are far broader, extending to *any* national procedural rule which is open to interpretation in conformity with Article 9(3), as long as the case at hand falls within the scope of EU law.[81] This would include, for instance, rules in relation to costs, where such rules make access to environmental justice impossible or excessively difficult. The full significance of the judgment, therefore, remains to be seen. However, it certainly means that EU law may be of some assistance in access to justice cases before national courts even where no harmonising EU legislation yet exists on the matter.[82]

'Triangular' Cases

In a number of environmental cases, the CJEU has faced a situation where the national proceedings in form constitute a challenge by a private party to an authorisation decision of a public authority, but are in substance directed against the actions of the private party who applied for the authorisation. The leading case here is *Wells*,[83] in which the applicant, Mrs Wells, challenged a decision of the UK Secretary of State for Transport, Local Government and the Regions to grant consent for mining operations at Conygar Quarry without first carrying out an environmental impact assessment. Before the CJEU, the UK government argued that, if the applicant were allowed to invoke the relevant provisions of the EIA Directive directly before the national court, this would amount to reverse direct effect which would directly oblige the Member State concerned to deprive another private party (in that case, the owners of Conygar Quarry) of their rights.

The CJEU rejected this argument, drawing a fine distinction between cases where a Directive is relied upon to place obligations on a private party (which is impermissible horizontal direct effect), and cases where a Directive merely results in negative repercussions for a private party:

Wells, paras. 56–57

As to that submission, the principle of legal certainty prevents directives from creating obligations for individuals. For them, the provisions of a directive can only create rights (see Case 152/84 *Marshall* [1986] ECR 723, para. 48).

---

[81] See also Art. 47 of the EU Charter of Fundamental Rights, which guarantees an 'effective remedy', which applies only where the right relied on falls within the scope of EU law.
[82] As discussed below, to date harmonising EU legislation on access to environmental justice only exists in the specific fields of the Environmental Impact Assessment and IPPC/Industrial Emissions Directives, by virtue of Directive 2003/35/EC (as well as in relation to access to environmental information, as provided by Directive 2003/4/EC: see, further, Chapter 5).
[83] Case C-201/02 *Wells* ECLI:EU:C:2004:12.

> Consequently, an individual may not rely on a directive against a Member State where it is a matter of a State obligation directly linked to the performance of another obligation falling, pursuant to that directive, on a third party (see, to this effect, Case C-221/88 *Busseni* [1990] ECR I-495, paras. 23–26, and Case C-97/96 *Daihatsu Deutschland* [1997] ECR I-6843, paras. 24 and 26).
>
> On the other hand, mere adverse repercussions on the rights of third parties, even if the repercussions are certain, do not justify preventing an individual from invoking the provisions of a directive against the Member State concerned (see to this effect, in particular, Case 103/88 *Fratelli Costanzo* [1989] ECR 1839, paras. 28–33, *WWF and Others*, cited above, paras. 69 and 71, Case C-194/94 *CIA Security International* [1996] ECR I-2201, paras. 40–55, Case C-201/94 *Smith & Nephew and Primecrown* [1996] ECR I-5819, paras. 33–39, and Case C-443/98 *Unilever* [2000] ECR I-7535, paras. 45–52).

Wells has been criticised by certain academic commentators as effectively allowing horizontal direct effect by the back door, and relying on an intellectually unconvincing distinction between 'obligations' and 'negative repercussions'.[84] Nevertheless, given the prevalence of the use of authorisation and permitting procedures in EU environmental Directives, the CJEU's judgment was enormously important in confirming the ability of private parties to rely on these Directives before their national courts, and thereby promoting the effectiveness of EU environmental law in national legal systems.

'Incidental' Horizontal Direct Effect

A further way in which the impact of the prohibition on horizontal direct effect of Directives has been reduced in practice has been the development of what has been termed the doctrine of 'incidental' direct effect by the CJEU in a number of judgments. This doctrine has developed in the specific context of the Technical Specifications Directive, which obliges Member States *inter alia* to notify the Commission of draft technical specifications prior to their adoption, and to implement a standstill period prior to adopting such specifications in order to give the Commission and Member States time to comment thereon.[85] In *CIA Security*, the CJEU has held that, where a Member State has failed to notify national technical regulations in a manner contrary to the Directive, this renders those regulations inapplicable so that they may not be enforced against individuals, and must be disapplied by a national court.[86] The CJEU expressly distinguished its judgment in *Enichem Base*, discussed above, on the basis that,

---

[84] See, for instance, the discussion in Martin Hedemann-Robinson, *Enforcement of European Union Environmental Law* (2nd edn., Routledge, 2015), 302–303.

[85] See, previously, Art. 8 of Directive 98/34/EC REF and, for the current version, Directive 2015/1535/EU, OJ 2015 L 241/1.

[86] Case C-194/94 *CIA Security* ECLI:EU:C:1996:172, paras. 48 and 55.

according to the wording and purpose of the Directive at issue in that case, failure of the Member State to notify the relevant national rules did not render them unlawful.[87] The CJEU contrasted this with the situation under the Technical Specifications Directive, where the purpose of the notification obligation was not just to inform the Commission, but to give the Commission and Member States an opportunity to respond if they wished.[88] *CIA Security* concerned national proceedings between private parties in which one party sought to rely on un-notified technical regulations as the basis for its claim against the other party.[89]

In *Unilever Italia*,[90] the CJEU extended this principle to include situations where the impugned national technical regulation was relied on as a defence, rather than a basis for claim, and where the national regulations had been notified but were implemented early, in breach of the standstill provision. The CJEU in *Unilever* specifically dismissed the argument that the rule in *CIA Security* did not contravene the prohibition on horizontal direct effect, because the Technical Specifications Directive did not 'in any way define the substantive scope of the legal rule on the basis of which the national court must decide the case before it', and 'creates neither rights nor obligations for individuals'.[91]

While the principle of incidental horizontal direct effect has been applied in a small number of contexts other than the Technical Specifications Directive,[92] it has not to date been applied to an environmental Directive.

Horizontal Direct Effect of a 'General Principle' of EU Law

In other cases, the CJEU has effectively got around limits on the doctrine of direct effect by invoking a 'general principle' of EU law, i.e. a fundamental principle of EU constitutional law which is, at least in its origins, implied by the CJEU into the Treaty rather than expressly found there. Classic examples are the CJEU's judgments in *Mangold* and *Kücükdeveci*, in which it held that the principle of non-discrimination on grounds of age represented a general principle of EU law which applied in proceedings between private parties (in that case, between an individual and his employer), thus getting around the difficulty that the relevant Directive in that case could not have horizontal direct effect.[93] In *AMS*, however, the CJEU clarified that not all general principles of EU law (and, in particular, not all rights contained in the EU Charter of Fundamental Rights) have direct effect against private parties.[94]

---

[87] *Ibid.*, para. 49.   [88] *Ibid.*, para. 50.
[89] Namely, Signalson and Securitel sought to rely on un-notified Belgian laws as a basis for a counterclaim against CIA.
[90] Case C-443/98 ECLI:EU:C:2000:496.   [91] *Ibid.*, paras. 50–51.
[92] See, in particular, Case C-129/94 *Bernaldez* ECLI:EU:C:1996:143 and Case C-441/93 *Panagis Pafitis* ECLI:EU:C:1996:92.
[93] Case C-144/04 *Mangold* ECLI:EU:C:2005:709; Case C-555/07 *Kücükdeveci* ECLI:EU:C:2010:21.
[94] Case C-176/12 *AMS* ECLI:EU:C:2014:2.

'General principles' of EU law in this sense are, as discussed in Chapter 3, to be distinguished from the specific principles of EU environmental policy, such as the precautionary principle. It is as yet unclear whether the environmental integration obligation contained in Article 11 TFEU and Article 37 of the Charter may be considered to be a general principle of EU law, and whether it may have direct effect in certain circumstances including against private parties.

State Liability in Damages for Breach of EU Law

In *Francovich*, the CJEU held for the first time that individuals must, if certain conditions are fulfilled, have the right to sue the State before their national court for damages for breach of EU law.[95] Again, in coming to this conclusion, the CJEU relied in particular on the principle of *effet utile* of EU law and the duty of sincere cooperation contained in Article 4(3) TEU. In subsequent case law, the CJEU has clarified that the conditions for State liability in damages to be made out are as follows:[96]

- The rule of EU law at issue must be intended to confer rights on individuals.
- The breach of EU law must be 'sufficiently serious'. The CJEU has held this condition to be satisfied, for instance, where no discretion has been left by the relevant EU law to Member States,[97] but not where the EU law is ambiguously phrased.[98]
- The plaintiff must prove a causal link between the breach and the damage.

As discussed in Chapter 5, environmental rules, including EU environmental rules, often do not lend themselves to easy characterisation as conferring substantive individual 'rights'. Nevertheless, it is of note that, in *Wells*, applying the *Kraaijeveld* doctrine discussed above, the CJEU expressly raised the possibility that the national court might award compensation for harm suffered by an individual by virtue of a breach of the Environmental Impact Assessment Directive on the part of the State (in that case, the relevant planning authorities), but left this issue for the national court to determine.[99] This is despite the fact that the EIA Directive does not, in any traditional sense, confer substantive rights on individuals, and may indicate that the CJEU is, as per the above discussion, at times willing to relax requirements as to substantive individual rights in the environmental context. Nevertheless, in *Leth*, the CJEU held that failure to carry out an EIA does not in principle in itself confer a right to compensation on an individual for pecuniary damage caused by a decrease in the value of property due to negative environmental effects.[100] However, it was ultimately for the national court to determine whether the requirements of EU law applicable to the right to compensation, in particular

---

[95] Joined Cases C-6/90 and 9/90 ECLI:EU:C:1991:428.
[96] See, for instance, Case C-46/93 ECLI:EU:C:1996:79.
[97] Case C-5/94 ECLI:EU:C:1996:205.   [98] Case C-392/93 ECLI:EU:C:1996:131.
[99] Case C-201/02 *Wells* ECLI:EU:C:2004:12, para. 49.
[100] Case C-420/11 *Leth* ECLI:EU:C:2013:166.

the existence of a direct causal link between the breach alleged and the damage sustained, had been satisfied.

The requirement of proof of a causal link may cause problems in environment-related *Francovich* damages claims, particularly in cases of environmental damage caused by multiple sources. Indeed, the paradigm of monetary compensation in damages for an individual (or group of individuals) may, in many cases, simply be inappropriate as an adequate remedy for a serious environmental breach, and a remedy such as an injunction may be far more effective in practice.

EU Legislation on Access to Justice at National Level and the Role of the Aarhus Convention

As discussed in Chapter 5, the EU has been striving to improve environmental access to justice in recent years. In part, this has been driven by the 1998 Aarhus Convention of the UN Economic Commission for Europe, which lays down obligations for its signatories to ensure access to information, public participation and access to justice in environmental matters. Since May 2005, the Community (and subsequently the Union) has been a party to the Convention, alongside its Member States,[101] and has implemented it on two levels. First, in terms of measures directed at Member States, it passed two Directives in 2003 implementing the Convention's access to information and public participation principles (Directives 2003/4 and 2003/35, respectively),[102] although the latter applies only in narrowly designated fields of EU environmental law, namely, environmental impact assessment (EIA) and integrated pollution prevention and control (IPPC, now covered by the Industrial Emissions Directive), discussed below.[103] Due to opposition from certain Member States, the Commission's 2003 proposal for a general Directive on access to environmental justice implementing the third pillar of the Convention, access to justice, never passed in the Council.[104] Secondly, in terms of measures directed at EU institutions and bodies, the EU passed a Regulation in 2006 aimed at implementing all of the three pillars of the Convention.[105] These measures are discussed further below.

---

[101] Council Decision of 17 February 2005 on the conclusion, on behalf of the European Community, of the Convention on access to information, public participation in decision-making and access to justice in environmental matters, OJ 2005 L 124/1.

[102] Directive 2003/4/EC of the European Parliament and of the Council of 28 January 2003 on public access to environmental information, OJ 2003 L 41/26; Directive 2003/35/EC of the European Parliament and of the Council of 26 May 2003 providing for public participation in respect of the drawing up of certain plans and programmes relating to the environment, OJ 2003 L 156/17. On Directive 2003/4, see Chapter 5.

[103] See, further, on the EIA Directive, Chapter 11; on IPPC and industrial emissions, Chapter 9.

[104] *Ibid.* Namely the failed Commission Proposal for a Directive on access to justice, COM (2003)624 final. See, further, Chapter 5.

[105] Regulation 1367/2006 of the European Parliament and of the Council on the application of the provisions of the Aarhus Convention on Access to Information, Public Participation

The Provisions of the Aarhus Convention on Access to Justice
Article 9 of the Aarhus Convention deals with access to justice in environmental matters.

Article 9(1) on Access to Justice concerning Environmental Information Decisions

Article 9(1) concerns access to justice regarding decisions on access to environmental information covered by Article 4 of the Convention, discussed further in Chapter 5.

Contracting States are obliged 'within the framework of its national legislation' to ensure that 'any person' who considers that his/her request for information made under Article 4 of the Convention has been ignored or not properly dealt with, have access to a 'review procedure before a court of law or another independent and impartial body established by law'.

Where review is provided by a court, the person must also have access to an 'expeditious procedure established by law that is free of charge or inexpensive' before a public authority or an 'independent and impartial body other than a court of law'. Review decisions must be binding and reasons must be given in writing.

Article 9(2) on Access to Environmental Justice concerning Public Participation

Article 9(2) of the Convention concerns access to justice regarding decisions on public participation covered by Article 6 of the Convention, also discussed further in Chapter 5. It provides as follows.

> **Article 9(2) of the Aarhus Convention**
>
> Each Party shall, within the framework of its national legislation, ensure that members of the public concerned
>
> (a) Having a sufficient interest or, alternatively,
> (b) Maintaining impairment of a right, where the administrative procedural law of a Party requires this as a precondition,
>
> have access to a review procedure before a court of law and/or another independent and impartial body established by law, to challenge the substantive and procedural legality of any decision, act or omission subject to the provisions of article 6 and, where so provided for under national law and without prejudice to paragraph 3 below, of other relevant provisions of this Convention.

in Decision-making and Access to Justice in Environmental Matters to Community institutions and bodies, OJ 2006 L 264/13. The access to environmental information and public participation elements of this Regulation are discussed in Chapter 5.

What constitutes a sufficient interest and impairment of a right shall be determined in accordance with the requirements of national law and consistently with the objective of giving the public concerned wide access to justice within the scope of this Convention. To this end, the interest of any NGO meeting the requirements referred to in Article 2, paragraph 5, shall be deemed sufficient for the purpose of subparagraph (a) above. Such organisations shall also be deemed to have rights capable of being impaired for the purpose of subparagraph (b) above.

The provisions of this paragraph 2 shall not exclude the possibility of a preliminary review procedure before an administrative authority and shall not affect the requirement of exhaustion of administrative review procedures prior to recourse to judicial review procedures, where such a requirement exists under national law.

As discussed below, many of the key concepts included in Article 9(2) have been reflected in the provisions of Directive 2003/35/EC, and have been interpreted as a matter of EU law by the CJEU. It will be noted that, in contrast to Article 9(1), the right of access to justice is provided not to 'any person', but only to the 'public concerned', which is defined by Article 2(5) of the Convention as follows: '"The public concerned" means the public affected or likely to be affected by, or having an interest in, the environmental decision-making; for the purposes of this definition, non-governmental organisations promoting environmental protection and meeting any requirements under national law shall be deemed to have an interest.'

Article 9(3) on Access to Environmental Justice in General

Article 9(3) is broader than Article 9(1) and (2) in scope, in that it applies not only to decisions covered by Article 4 (on access to environmental information) and Article 6 (on public participation) of the Convention, but also to any 'acts and omissions by private persons and public authorities which contravene provisions of its national law relating to the environment'. However, it is far weaker in terms of the obligation imposed on Contracting States, providing only that,

without prejudice to the review procedures referred to in paragraphs 1 and 2 above, each Party shall ensure that, where they meet the criteria, if any, laid down in its national law, members of the public have access to administrative or judicial procedures to challenge acts and omissions by private persons and public authorities which contravene provisions of its national law relating to the environment.

The general right of access to justice is, therefore, made expressly subject to the conditions set out in national law, which may seriously compromise its effectiveness in practice.

Despite the lack of specific EU legislation on access to justice in Member States, a variety of recent ECJ judgments have gone some way to implement the access to justice provisions of the Convention in EU law.

Article 9(4) on Conditions of Access to Justice

Article 9(4) of the Convention provides that,

> without prejudice to paragraph 1 above, the procedures referred to in paragraphs 1, 2 and 3 above shall provide adequate and effective remedies, including injunctive relief as appropriate, and be fair, equitable, timely and not prohibitively expensive. Decisions under this article shall be given or recorded in writing. Decisions of courts, and whenever possible of other bodies, shall be publicly accessible.

This provision, therefore, gives important further clarification on the precise nature of the access to justice obligations set out in Article 9(1)–(3) of the Convention. Again, many of these key concepts have now been interpreted by the CJEU via their incorporation into EU law, as discussed further below.

Article 9(5) on Public Information and Legal Aid

Article 9(5) of the Convention provides that each State shall 'ensure that information is provided to the public on access to administrative and judicial review procedures and shall consider the establishment of appropriate assistance mechanisms to remove or reduce financial and other barriers to access to justice'.

Clearly, there is no obligation as such to provide legal aid in environmental matters. However, the obligation to provide public information on access to justice is couched in robust terms and, again, has been translated into EU law and applied by the CJEU.[106]

Implementation of Article 9 of the Aarhus Convention in EU Law

National Procedural Autonomy, Effectiveness and Equivalence

As discussed in Chapter 6, the CJEU has consistently held that, in the absence of specific EU legislation harmonising national procedures and remedies available for breach of EU law, it is for Member States to organise their national procedures (including rules on standing and legal costs), as long as the principles of effectiveness of remedies for breach of EU law, and equivalence of remedies for breach of EU and national law, are respected.[107]

---

[106] See Case C-427/07 *Commission* v. *Ireland* ECLI:EU:C:2009:457, discussed further below.

[107] See, for instance, Joined Cases C-430/93 and C-431/93 *Van Schijndel* ECLI:EU:C:1995:441, and the discussion in Chapter 6.

The appropriate balance between these principles has been expressed by the CJEU as follows:

Case C-115/09 *Bund für Umwelt und Naturschutz Deutschland, Landesverband Nordrhein-Westfalen (Trianel)*, **para. 43**

in the absence of EU rules governing the matter, it is for the legal system of each Member State to designate the courts and tribunals having jurisdiction and to lay down the detailed procedural rules governing actions for safeguarding rights which individuals derive from EU law, those detailed rules must not be less favourable than those governing similar domestic actions (principle of equivalence) and must not make it in practice impossible or excessively difficult to exercise rights conferred by EU law (principle of effectiveness).

As discussed above, in *Slovak Brown Bear*,[108] a case which fell outside the scope of relevant harmonising legislation on access to justice, the CJEU declined to find Article 9(3) of the Aarhus Convention to be directly effective, but held that, despite the fact that the Habitats Directive does not include any access to justice provisions, it was incumbent on Member States to ensure that the rights provided therein are 'effectively protected in each case'.[109] In practical terms, this meant that the national court had a duty to interpret national law 'in a way which, to the fullest extent possible, is consistent with the objectives laid down in Article 9(3) of the Aarhus Convention' and the objective of effective judicial protection of the relevant EU law rights 'so as to enable' an environmental association such as that at issue to challenge the disputed measure.[110]

Harmonising EU Legislation on Access to Environmental Justice: Directive 2003/4 and Directive 2003/35[111]
Article 9(1)/(4) of the Convention is implemented, in very similar terms, in Article 6 of the EU Directive on access to environmental information (Directive 2003/4/EC), discussed further in Chapter 5. These provisions are considerably stronger than the previous provisions on access to justice regarding information requests, which merely required Member States to provide for 'judicial or administrative review' of decisions of competent authorities concerning information requests.[112]

---

[108] Case C-240/09 *Lesoochranárske zoskupenie* ECLI:EU:C:2011:125.   [109] *Ibid.*, para. 47.
[110] *Ibid.*, paras. 50–51.
[111] Further harmonising provisions on access to justice are found in Articles 12 and 13 of the Environmental Liability Directive 2004/35 (concerning 'requests for action' under that Directive), which are discussed separately in the treatment of that Directive in Chapter 6 on Public Enforcement.
[112] Directive 90/313, OJ 1990 L 158/56, Art. 5.

Article 9(2)/(4) of the Convention is implemented by Directive 2003/35/EC.[113] Present Article 11 (formerly Article 10a) of the EIA Directive, as inserted by Directive 2003/35/EC, provides as follows:

> **Article 11 (previously Article 10a) of the EIA Directive (as amended)**
>
> Member States shall ensure that, in accordance with the relevant national legal system, members of the public concerned:
>
> (a) having a sufficient interest, or alternatively,
> (b) maintaining the impairment of a right, where administrative procedural law of a Member State requires this as a precondition,
>
> have access to a review procedure before a court of law or another independent and impartial body established by law to challenge the substantive or procedural legality of decisions, acts or omissions subject to the public participation provisions of this Directive.
>
> Member States shall determine at what stage the decisions, acts or omissions may be challenged.
>
> What constitutes a sufficient interest and impairment of a right shall be determined by the Member States, consistently with the objective of giving the public concerned wide access to justice. To this end, the interest of any non-governmental organisation meeting the requirements referred to in Article 1(2), shall be deemed sufficient for the purpose of subparagraph (a) of this Article. Such organisations shall also be deemed to have rights capable of being impaired for the purpose of subparagraph (b) of this Article.
>
> The provisions of this Article shall not exclude the possibility of a preliminary review procedure before an administrative authority and shall not affect the requirement of exhaustion of administrative review procedures prior to recourse to judicial review procedures, where such a requirement exists under national law.
>
> Any such procedure shall be fair, equitable, timely and not prohibitively expensive.
>
> In order to further the effectiveness of the provisions of this article, Member States shall ensure that practical information is made available to the public on access to administrative and judicial review procedures.

The relevant amendment to what was then the IPPC Directive, inserting Article 15a, was phrased in similar terms, and this is now present in Article 25 of the Industrial Emissions Directive.[114]

---

[113] See Directive 2003/35/EC, preamble, recital (11), stating that the aim of the amendments to the EIA and IPPC Directives was to 'ensure that they are fully compatible with the provisions of the Aarhus Convention, in particular Article 6 and Article 9(2) and (4) thereof'.

[114] See Chapter 9.

In a number of important judgments, the CJEU has interpreted the access to justice provisions inserted by Directive 2003/35/EC into the IPPC (now Industrial Emissions) Directive and the EIA Directive.

A first group of cases has concerned the conditions required to have standing before national courts and review bodies. In *Trianel*, the CJEU held that a German law restricting *locus standi* in EIA and IPPC matters to those environmental associations who can demonstrate impairment of rights was contrary to the access to justice provisions set out in the EIA and IPPC Directives.[115] Relying on the duty of consistent interpretation, the CJEU held that these provisions must 'be interpreted in the light of, and having regard to, the objectives of the Aarhus Convention, with which – as is stated in recital 5 to Directive 2003/35 – EU law should be "properly aligned"'.[116]

In *Križan*, the CJEU confirmed that the same principle applied in the case of Article 15a of the IPPC Directive (now Article 25 of the Industrial Emissions Directive).[117]

The CJEU further noted that the principle of national procedural autonomy was limited by the terms of the access to justice provisions of Directive 2003/35, including its provisions as to the standing of ENGOs.[118]

In *Djurgården*, the CJEU held that members of the public concerned, within the meaning of Articles 1(2) and 11 of the EIA Directive, must be able to have access to a review procedure to challenge the decision by which a body attached to a court of law of a Member State has given a ruling on a request for development consent, regardless of the role they might have played in the examination of that request by taking part in the procedure before that body and by expressing their views.[119] The CJEU further held that a Swedish rule which limited the definition of ENGOs with a 'sufficient interest' to bring an appeal against decisions on projects falling within the scope of the EIA Directive to those organisations with at least 2,000 members did not satisfy the requirements of what is now Article 11 of that Directive.[120]

In *Altrip*,[121] the CJEU held that, in cases where a national legal system required proof of impairment of a right in order to demonstrate *locus standi*, it was permissible for a Member State (in that case, Germany) to refuse standing if it was conceivable, having regard to the circumstances of the case, that the contested decision would not have been different without the procedural defect alleged by the applicant. However, it was not permissible for a Member State to place the burden of proving that the decision would have been different on the applicant: this was for the court or body hearing the action to determine on the basis of all of the facts before it.[122]

A second group of cases has concerned legal costs and interpretation of the concept of 'not prohibitively expensive'. In *Commission v. Ireland*, the

---

[115] Case C-115/09 ECLI:EU:C:2011:289.   [116] *Ibid.*, para. 41.
[117] Case C-416/10 *Križan* ECLI:EU:C:2013:8, para. 77.   [118] *Ibid.*, para. 43.
[119] Case C-263/08 ECLI:EU:C:2009:631, para. 39.   [120] *Ibid.*, para. 52.
[121] Case C-72/12 ECLI:EU:C:2013:712.   [122] *Ibid.*, paras. 50–57.

CJEU held that a mere judicial discretion not to award costs against an unsuccessful party was not sufficient to satisfy the obligations imposed by Directive 2003/35.[123]

In *Edwards*, the CJEU interpreted the meaning of the obligation to ensure that judicial proceedings should not be 'prohibitively expensive' under the IPPC and EIA Directives as meaning that 'the persons covered by those provisions should not be prevented from seeking, or pursuing a claim for, a review by the courts that falls within the scope of those articles by reason of the financial burden that might arise as a result'.[124] It followed that, where a national court was asked to make an order for costs against a member of the public who is an unsuccessful claimant in an environmental dispute, or where the court is required to state its views, at an earlier stage of the proceedings, on a possible capping of the costs for which the unsuccessful party may be liable, it must 'satisfy itself that that requirement has been complied with, taking into account both the interest of the person wishing to defend his rights and the public interest in the protection of the environment'.[125]

Nevertheless, in terms of the appropriate criteria for deciding whether costs in an individual case were prohibitively expensive, the CJEU emphasised that Member States retained a 'broad discretion' as to the methods of implementing Directive 2003/35, while still ensuring that the Directive is fully effective. The CJEU specifically noted that 'significant differences' remained between national laws in this regard, and that all the provisions of national law, including as to the availability of legal aid and costs protection, must be taken into account.[126] However, such assessment could not be carried out solely on the basis of the estimated financial resources of an 'average' applicant (an 'objective' assessment): the court must also have regard to the particular circumstances of the applicant at hand (a 'subjective' assessment). Further factors which may, the CJEU held, be taken into account were:[127]

- the situation of the parties concerned;
- whether the claimant has a reasonable prospect of success;
- the importance of what is at stake for the claimant and for the protection of the environment;
- the complexity of the relevant law and procedure; and
- the potentially frivolous nature of the claim at its various stages.

In addition, the fact that a claimant had not in practice been deterred from pursuing his claim was not in itself sufficient proof that the costs of so doing were not prohibitively expensive.[128]

The assessment must, the CJEU added, not be different depending on whether the claim is at first instance or on appeal.[129]

---

[123] Case C-427/07 ECLI:EU:C:2009:457, paras. 93–94.
[124] Case C-260/11 *Edwards* ECLI:EU:C:2013:221, para. 35.   [125] *Ibid.*
[126] *Ibid.*, paras. 37–38.   [127] *Ibid.*, para. 42.   [128] *Ibid.*, para. 43.   [129] *Ibid.*, para. 45.

In *Commission* v. *UK*, the CJEU further expanded on *Edwards*, holding that national courts were not precluded from making an order for costs in judicial proceedings as long as they are reasonable in amount and that the costs borne by the party concerned as a whole are not prohibitive.[130] However, the UK system at issue did not, the CJEU held, ensure reasonable predictability as regards whether costs were payable and as to their amount, an issue which was particularly important because of the high legal fees in the UK.[131] The CJEU further held that the requirement to give cross-undertakings as to costs in order to be eligible for interim relief breached Directive 2003/35, as it introduced an additional element of uncertainty and imprecision as to the ultimate level of costs to be awarded.[132]

It is notable that the CJEU's rulings on the UK's system mirror to a significant extent the findings of the Aarhus Convention Compliance Committee on, for instance, the requirement of cross-undertakings in damages for injunctive relief. In this way, as more decisions are handed down by the Committee and as the Aarhus compliance mechanism matures, one may perhaps see the development of a mutually reinforcing and supporting dialectic between the EU and Aarhus jurisdictions, of a similar kind to that which has developed over the years between the EU and Strasbourg courts. In the wake of the CJEU's rulings (and the findings of the Compliance Committee), and following a consultation process and two reports,[133] a new costs regime was introduced for environmental cases in April 2013, amending the Civil Procedure Rules (CPR) applicable in England and Wales (Section VII of Part 45, CPR) to provide for a fixed recoverable costs regime at first instance, whereby the amount recoverable from the claimant is capped at £5,000 where the claimant is an individual, and £10,000 in other cases.[134]

A further question arises as to the scope and nature of review required by Directive 2003/35. In *Altrip*, the CJEU held that it was contrary to what is now Article 11 of the EIA Directive for a Member State (in that case, Germany) to limit the scope of national transposition measures for that provision solely to cases in which the legality of a decision was challenged on the ground that no EIA had been carried out, and excluding cases where an EIA had been carried out but was alleged to be inadequate.[135] In *Commission* v. *Ireland*, the Commission claimed that the remedy of judicial review in Irish law

---

[130] Case C-530/11 ECLI:EU:C:2014:67, para. 44.   [131] *Ibid.*, para. 58.
[132] *Ibid.*, para. 71.
[133] L. J. Sullivan et al., 'Ensuring Access to Environmental Justice in England and Wales', Report of May 2008 and Update Report of August 2010, available at: www.unece.org/env/pp/compliance/C2008-33/correspondence/FrCAJE_updatedSullivanReport_2010.09.14.pdf. See also the Report of L. J. Jackson, 'Review of Civil Litigation Costs', January 2010.
[134] See, further, Andrew Lidbetter and Nehal Depani, 'The Aarhus Convention and Judicial Review' (2014) 19(1) *Judicial Review* 30.
[135] However, restrictions on pleas made abusively or in bad faith are permissible: see Case C-137/14 *Commission* v. *Germany* ECLI:EU:C:2015:683, para. 81.

did not sufficiently allow review of the 'substantive' (as opposed to the procedural) legality. However, the matter was not dealt with by the CJEU due to inadequacies in the manner in which the case had been pleaded.[136] In *Boxus* and *Solvay*, the CJEU held that the fact that approval for a project that would otherwise be subject to EIA was given by legislative measure, cannot in itself exclude the application of the access to justice provisions of the EIA Directive.[137]

The CJEU has also held that effective access to justice under Directive 2003/35 requires that interim measures be available to applicants falling within its scope. In *Križan*, the CJEU held that Article 15a of the IPPC Directive (now Article 25 of the Industrial Emissions Directive) requires that members of the public concerned must be able to ask the court or competent independent and impartial body established by law to order interim measures such as temporary suspension of the application of a permit, pending the final decision.[138]

In terms of the level of court required for the review procedure, in *Križan*, the CJEU further held that the access to justice provisions of the IPPC directive allow Member State discretion as to the level of tribunal competent to regularise a breach of access to information provisions, as long as the principles of effectiveness and equivalence of remedies are respected. Specifically, it was permissible for a Member State to rectify an unjustified refusal to make available an urban planning decision to the public concerned during the first instance administrative procedure, by means of a second instance administrative procedure, provided that 'all options and solutions remain possible and that rectification at that stage of the procedure still allows that public effectively to influence the outcome of the decision-making process'.[139] The CJEU further dismissed the developer's argument that the annulment of a permit pursuant to proceedings brought under Article 15a constituted an unjustified interference with its right to property pursuant to Article 17 of the Charter of Fundamental Rights.[140]

Private Enforcement of EU Law at EU Level

Access to Justice before the EU Courts

The principal means of accessing justice directly before the EU courts is Article 263 TFEU, which enables actions to be brought directly before the EU's General Court to review the legality of, 'legislative acts, of acts of the Council, of the Commission and of the European Central Bank, other than recommendations and opinions, and of acts of the European Parliament and of the European

---

[136] Case C-427/07 ECLI:EU:C:2009:457, para. 89.
[137] Joined Cases C-128/09 to C-131/09, C-134/09 and C-135/09 *Boxus* ECLI:EU:C:2011:667 and Case C-182/10 *Solvay* ECLI:EU:C:2012:82.
[138] Case C-416/10 *Križan* ECLI:EU:C:2013:8, para. 110. [139] *Ibid.*, para. 91.
[140] *Ibid.*, para. 116.

Council intended to produce legal effects vis-à-vis third parties'.[141] The General Court is also empowered to review the acts of 'bodies, offices or agencies of the Union intended to produce legal effects vis-à-vis third parties'. The grounds on which acts can be reviewed are specified by Article 263(2) TFEU to be:

- lack of competence;[142]
- infringement of an essential procedural requirement;
- infringement of the Treaties or of any rule of law relating to their application; and
- misuse of powers.

A small group of applicants are granted automatic right of standing to bring Article 263 TFEU claims by Article 263(2), namely, Member States, the European Parliament, the Council and the Commission (as well as, in claims to protect their prerogatives, the Court of Auditors, the European Central Bank and the Committee of the Regions). The right of private parties is dealt with in Article 263(4) TFEU, which provides as follows.

> Any natural or legal person may, under the conditions laid down in the first and second paragraphs, institute proceedings against an act addressed to that person or which is of direct and individual concern to them, and against a regulatory act which is of direct concern to them and does not entail implementing measures.

The CJEU's interpretation of the requirement of 'direct and individual' concern has been highly controversial, particularly in the context of environmental challenges.

As regards 'direct concern', the CJEU has interpreted this requirement as requiring that the EU measure must directly affect the legal situation of the individual, and must leave no discretion to its addressees, with implementation being 'purely automatic and resulting from [EU] rules without the application of other intermediate rules'.[143] In draft findings of 2016, the Aarhus Convention Compliance Committee noted that the requirement that a measure 'directly affect' an individual's legal situation in principle excludes, for instance, actions brought by ENGOs acting purely out of environmental protection interests.[144]

---

[141] Other direct actions before the EU courts (General Court) include: (1) Article 265 TFEU (proceedings in respect of failure to act), which is broadly similar to Article 263 TFEU in terms of the difficulties arising in environmental cases, and will not be discussed separately here; and (2) Articles 268 and 340(2) TFEU on the non-contractual liability of the EU, which, again, will not be discussed separately here. See, generally, Craig and de Búrca, *EU Law: Text, Cases and Materials*, chapter 16.

[142] This includes arguments as to incorrect legal basis used for an EU measure. See, generally, Craig and de Búrca, *EU Law: Text, Cases and Materials*, chapter 15.

[143] See, for instance, Case T-262/10 *Microban* ECLI:EU:T:2011:623, para. 27.

[144] Draft findings in ACCC/C/2008/32, part II, at paras. 68–71.

It is, however, the CJEU's interpretation of the requirement of 'individual' concern which has been the focus of most criticism, as this interpretation renders it virtually impossible in many cases for private parties to gain access to justice before the EU courts to challenge the legality of an EU measure other than an EU decision specifically addressed to them.

In particular, in cases where a measure other than an EU decision addressed to the applicant is being challenged, the CJEU in its 1963 judgment in *Plaumann* famously interpreted individual concern in a manner that effectively requires the applicant to demonstrate that it is affected by the EU measure in a different manner from any other person.[145]

The specific difficulties to which application of such a test in environmental cases gives rise have been flagged before the EU courts, but to no avail. In *Greenpeace*, the applicant organisation argued that the application of the standard *Plaumann* test to an environmental challenge would create a 'legal vacuum in ensuring compliance with Community environmental legislation, since in this area the interests are, by their very nature, common and shared'.[146] This situation, combined with the Court's affirmation in cases like *ADBHU* that environmental protection constituted one of the 'Community's essential objectives', meant in the applicants' view that a different interpretation of Article 263(4) TFEU must be adopted for environmental challenges. The Court rejected this argument, confirming the application of *Plaumann* and holding that effective judicial protection could be ensured by national courts (in that case, by a challenge to the national decision authorising the construction of power plants allegedly in breach of the EIA Directive).[147]

In *EEB*, the General Court was asked to reconsider the matter in the context of a challenge to a Commission decision on plant protection products by two prominent environmental NGOs, the Brussels-based European Environmental Bureau and the Dutch *Stichting Natuur en Milieu*, which had special consultative status at EU and Dutch levels respectively.[148] While the applicants argued that the right to effective judicial protection in environmental matters would be breached by application of the strict *Plaumann* test, they did not explicitly rely on the Aarhus Convention, which was approved by the EU by Decision in 2005.[149] The Court rejected the applicants' arguments and held that the standard *Plaumann* test applied in this case: despite the applicants' special status as consultative bodies at EU and national levels, respectively, they did not benefit from any specific

---

[145] Case 25/62 *Plaumann* ECLI:EU:C:1963:17.
[146] Case C-321/95 P *Greenpeace* ECLI:EU:C:1998:153, para. 18. See also Case T-219/95 *Danielsson* ECLI:EU:T:1995:219.
[147] *Greenpeace* ECLI:EU:C:1998:153, paras. 27–35.
[148] Joined Cases T-236/04 and T-241/04 *EEA and Stichting Natuur en Milieu* v. *Commission* ECLI:EU:T:2005:426.
[149] Council Decision 2005/370 of 17 February 2005 on the conclusion, on behalf of the European Community, of the Convention on access to information, public participation in decision-making and access to justice in environmental matters, OJ 2005 L 124/3.

'procedural guarantees' in the EU decision-making process in the way, for instance, complainants in competition proceedings do.[150]

In *WWF-UK*, the Court of Justice confirmed this approach in an action brought by an environmental NGO for the partial annulment of a Regulation fixing the total allowable catches in respect of cod fishing for the year 2007 in areas covered by a previous Regulation establishing measures for the recovery of cod stocks.[151] Despite the fact that WWF-UK was a member of the regional advisory council for the North Sea, which has consultative status in fisheries matters within that area and has the right to submit recommendations on such matters, this did not amount to a sufficient procedural guarantee for WWF-UK to be individually concerned.[152]

The effect of the Court's decisions in cases such as *Greenpeace, EEB* and *WWF-UK* is that the test of 'individual concern' is effectively impossible to satisfy in cases of challenges to EU measures on environmental grounds (other than challenges to decisions addressed to the applicant).[153]

The final clause of Article 263(4) TFEU ('and against a regulatory act which is of direct concern to them and does not entail implementing measures') was inserted by the Treaty of Lisbon, in the wake of severe criticism of the lacuna in judicial protection to which the CJEU's *Plaumann* doctrine gave rise. It fell to the EU courts to determine, however, what precisely was meant by this phrase.

Many commentators considered that the amendment should be viewed in the context of the debate about the deficiencies of *Plaumann* in the (non-environmental) *UPA* case, in which Advocate General Jacobs had sharply criticised *Plaumann* for failing to provide effective judicial protection, in potential breach, *inter alia*, of the requirements of the fundamental right to a fair trial under Article 6 of the European Convention of Human Rights.[154] This was in particular so in the case of a challenge to an EU Regulation, where there would be no

---

[150] *Ibid.*, para. 62.
[151] Council Regulation (EC) No. 41/2007 of 21 December 2006 fixing for 2007 the fishing opportunities and associated conditions for certain fish stocks and groups of fish stocks, applicable in Community waters and, for Community vessels, in waters where catch limitations are required, OJ 2007 L 15/1; Council Regulation (EC) No. 423/2004 of 26 February 2004 establishing measures for the recovery of cod stocks, OJ 2004 L 70/8.
[152] Order of the Court of 5 May 2009 in Case C-355/08 P *WWF-UK* ECLI:EU:C:2009:286. See also Order of the Court of 26 November 2009 in Case C-444/08 P *Região autónoma dos Açores* ECLI:EU:C:2009:733 (Autonomous Region of the Azores did not have standing to challenge an EU fisheries regulation on the ground that the regulation, by opening up its territory to non-Portuguese vessels, would damage its marine environment).
[153] The lines of jurisprudence in which the Court has adopted a more relaxed approach to standing – for instance, where an applicant has a specific right to be involved in the administrative procedure which gave rise to the decision under challenge (see e.g. Case C-309/89 *Codorniu* ECLI:EU:C:1994:197); or where the applicant can demonstrate that it belongs to a closed class of applicants whose interests the EU is bound to take into account (see e.g. Case 11/82 *Piraiki-Patraiki* ECLI:EU:C:1985:18) – do not generally apply to environmental challenges.
[154] Case C-50/00 P *UPA* ECLI:EU:C:2002:462.

national implementing measures to seek to challenge in national courts. While recognising this gap, the Court in *UPA* declined to follow its Advocate General, effectively attributing a constitutional status to *Plaumann* by holding that the test could only be altered by Treaty amendment.[155] Viewed in this light, it might have seemed logical to interpret the amended Article 263(4) TFEU as allowing challenges to EU Regulations that are of direct concern and that do not entail implementing measures.

A narrower view, however, was that the provision distinguishes between regulatory and legislative acts, with the latter defined by Article 289(3) TFEU as 'legal acts adopted by legislative procedure' (i.e. the EU's ordinary or special legislative procedures set down in the Treaty).[156] By that reading, only acts of direct concern which do not entail implementing measures *and* have not been adopted by legislative procedure fall under this provision.

In *Inuit Tapiriit Kanatami*, which concerned a challenge to a Regulation on trade in seal products,[157] the General Court came down strongly in favour of this narrower meaning of 'regulatory act', holding that this term does not extend to all acts of general application, and in particular does not include legislative acts.[158] The General Court expressly rejected the applicants' argument that a broad interpretation of the term was necessitated by the Aarhus Convention.[159] On appeal, the CJEU upheld the judgment of the General Court, interpreting Article 263(4) TFEU in the light of its wording, objectives, and context, and the 'provisions of European law as a whole'.[160] In particular, the CJEU reasoned that interpreting the concept of 'regulatory acts' to include all legislative acts of general application would amount to nullifying the distinction made in Article 263 TFEU between 'acts' and 'regulatory acts'.[161] It followed that the concept of 'regulatory acts' excluded legislative acts (including Regulations and Directives).

---

[155] *Ibid.*

[156] Arts. 289(1) and (2) TFEU. See also the distinction between legislative and regulatory acts contained in Art. 207(6) TFEU.

[157] Regulation (EC) No. 1007/2009 of the European Parliament and of the Council of 16 September 2009 on trade in seal products, OJ 2009 L 286/36.

[158] Case T-18/10 *Inuit Tapiriit Kanatami and Others* v. *European Parliament and Council of the European Union*, Order of the General Court of 7 September 2011 ECLI:EU:T:2011:419. See para. 49, where the General Court relies in support of its interpretation on the history of negotiating what became Article 263(4) TFEU in the drafting of the Constitutional Treaty.

[159] *Ibid.*, para. 55. It is notable that the Aarhus Convention itself makes a fundamental distinction between decisions of public bodies acting in legislative and non-legislative capacities (with only the latter category falling within the scope of the duty to ensure access to review procedures for decisions, acts and omissions of a 'public authority' under that Convention). See Art. 2(2) of the Aarhus Convention and, for instance, the Compliance Committee's findings and recommendations in case ACCC/C/2008/32 (EC), 14 April 2011, para. 70.

[160] Case C-583/11 P ECLI:EU:C:2013:625, para. 50.

[161] *Ibid.*, para. 58. The CJEU supported this conclusion by reference to the travaux préparatoires when the amendment to Article 263 TFEU was being drafted.

The CJEU specifically rejected the argument that the standing requirements for private parties in Article 263 TFEU were in breach of the right to an effective remedy provided in Article 47 of the Charter of Fundamental Rights of the EU.[162]

Aside from the meaning of 'regulatory act', the question of the Article 263(4) TFEU requirement that such an act 'does not entail implementing measures' has also been considered by the General Court. In *Arcelor*, the General Court held a challenge by a steel producer to the EU Emissions Trading Scheme Directive to be inadmissible.[163] The Court ruled that the new Article 263(4) TFEU would not have an effect on the matter, because Member States had a 'broad discretion' with regard to the implementation of the Directive. It follows that, in the case of regulatory acts, only those acts which do not entail a 'broad discretion' for Member States will fall under the more relaxed standing requirements of the amended Article 263(4) TFEU.

In an interim report of 2011, the Aarhus Convention Compliance Committee questioned the compatibility with the Convention of the EU's own restrictive conditions of *locus standi* under Article 263 TFEU actions, and in particular the restrictive approach to the doctrine of 'individual concern' exemplified by the *WWF* judgment, which was handed down after the EU had approved the Aarhus Convention.[164] In a second report of 2016, the Compliance Committee confirmed its concerns, finding that there had been no intervening jurisprudence to justify amending its position.

Draft Findings of the Aarhus Convention Compliance Committee in Complaint No. ACCC/C/2008/32, part II (June 2016)

The Committee regrets that, while the ECJ has held that national courts are bound [pursuant to the Slovak Brown Bear judgment, discussed above] to interpret, to the fullest extent possible, procedural rules relating to the conditions to be met in order to bring administrative or judicial proceedings in accordance with the objectives of article 9, paragraph 3, it does not apply this principle to itself.

The Committee considers that if the EU Courts had been bound in the same way as the national courts, the EU might have moved towards compliance with article 9, paragraph 3.

Access to Justice by Means of Internal Review under Regulation 1367/2006

As noted above and as discussed in Chapter 5, in addition to Directives 2003/4 and 2003/35, the EU implemented the Aarhus Convention as regards EU

---

[162] *Ibid.*, para. 105.
[163] Case T-16/04 *Arcelor* v. *European Parliament and Council*, judgment of the General Court of 2 March 2010 ECLI:EU:T:2010:54 para. 23.
[164] See Case ACCC/C/2008/32, Findings and recommendations adopted on 14 April 2011.

institutions in Regulation 1367/2006.[165] Article 10 of that Regulation provides for a right to internal review of administrative acts under environmental law.

> **Article 10, Regulation 1367/2006**
>
> Request for internal review of administrative acts
>
> 1. Any non-governmental organisation which meets the criteria set out in Article 11[166] is entitled to make a request for internal review to the Community institution or body that has adopted an administrative act under environmental law or, in case of an alleged administrative omission, should have adopted such an act.
>   Such a request must be made in writing and within a time limit not exceeding six weeks after the administrative act was adopted, notified or published, whichever is the latest, or, in the case of an alleged omission, six weeks after the date when the administrative act was required. The request shall state the grounds for the review.
> 2. The Community institution or body referred to in paragraph 1 shall consider any such request, unless it is clearly unsubstantiated. The Community institution or body shall state its reasons in a written reply as soon as possible, but no later than 12 weeks after receipt of the request.
> 3. Where the Community institution or body is unable, despite exercising due diligence, to act in accordance with paragraph 2, it shall inform the non-governmental organisation which made the request as soon as possible and at the latest within the period mentioned in that paragraph, of the reasons for its failure to act and when it intends to do so.

In any event, the Community institution or body shall act within 18 weeks from receipt of the request.

Importantly, the concept of 'administrative act' is defined by Article 2(1)(g) of Regulation 1367/2006 as meaning 'any measure of individual scope under environmental law, taken by a Community institution or body, and having legally

---

[165] OJ 2006 L 264/13. A further distinct type of access to justice is contained in the Ship Recycling Regulation 1257/13, OJ 2013 L 330/1, Art. 22 of which enables a 'request for action' to be lodged with the Commission in relation to alleged breaches of the Regulation by non-EU recycling facilities. The procedure is similar in nature to that provided for in the Environmental Liability Directive vis-à-vis national authorities, discussed further in Chapter 6.

[166] Art. 11(1) provides, 'A non-governmental organisation shall be entitled to make a request for internal review in accordance with Article 10, provided that: (a) it is an independent non-profit-making legal person in accordance with a Member State's national law or practice; (b) it has the primary stated objective of promoting environmental protection in the context of environmental law; (c) it has existed for more than two years and is actively pursuing the objective referred to under (b); (d) the subject matter in respect of which the request for internal review is made is covered by its objective and activities.'

binding and external effects'. Measures taken by an EU institution or body as an 'administrative review body' are expressly excluded from the scope of an 'administrative act' for this purpose, including measures taken under the competition rules or in the context of Article 258/260 TFEU infringement proceedings.[167]

Article 12 of the Regulation provides,

1. The non-governmental organisation which made the request for internal review pursuant to Article 10 may institute proceedings before the Court of Justice in accordance with the relevant provisions of the Treaty.
2. Where the Community institution or body fails to act in accordance with Article 10(2) or (3) the non-governmental organisation may institute proceedings before the Court of Justice in accordance with the relevant provisions of the Treaty.

In its January 2015 judgment in *Council and Commission v. Stichting Natuur en Milieu and Pesticide Action Network Europe*,[168] the CJEU held that, contrary to the General Court's judgment at first instance, Article 9(3) of the Convention could not be relied upon to assess the legality of Article 10(1) of the Regulation. The CJEU reasoned that it could not be considered that the EU intended to 'implement' Article 9(3) of the Convention – which the CJEU held concerns *national* administrative or judicial procedures – by adopting the Regulation.[169] In so holding, the CJEU overturned the judgment of the General Court, which had held that Article 10(1) of Regulation 1367/2006 was illegal insofar as it limited the internal review of administrative acts to those of individual scope in a manner contrary to Article 9(3) of the Convention.[170] *Stichting Natuur en Milieu and Pesticide Action Network Europe* was confirmed on this point in another judgment of the Grand Chamber of January 2015, *Council v. Vereniging Milieudefensie Stichting Stop Luchtverontreiniging Utrecht*, in which the CJEU again refused to review the legality of Article 10(1) of Regulation 1367/2006 in the light of Article 9(3) of the Convention.[171]

In June 2016, the Aarhus Convention Compliance Committee published draft findings indicating that it considered Article 10 of Regulation 1367/2006 to be contrary to Article 9(3) of the Convention. The Compliance Committee reasoned, in particular, that Article 10's restriction to acts of individual scope, and

---

[167] Art. 2(2), Regulation 1367/2006.
[168] Joined Cases C-404/12 P and C-405/12 P *Council and Commission v. Stichting Natuur en Milieu and Pesticide Action Network Europe* ECLI:EU:C:2015:5.
[169] *Ibid.*, para. 52. In particular, the CJEU's jurisprudence holding that, where an EU measure makes an express reference to an international agreement, or specifically implements the provisions of such an agreement, its legality may be assessed in the light of that agreement: see C-70/87 *Fediol v. Commission* EU:C:1989:254 and C-69/89 *Nakajima v. Council* EU:C:1991:186.
[170] Case T-338/08 ECLI:EU:T:2012:300, para. 84.
[171] Joined Cases C-401/12 P, C-402/12 P and C-403/12 P *Council and Ors v. Vereniging Milieudefensie Stichting Stop Luchtverontreiniging Utrecht* ECLI:EU:C:2015:4.

the exceptions provided for 'administrative review' in Article 2(2) of the Regulation, contravened Article 9(3). However, it noted that it would be open to the CJEU to interpret Article 12 of the Regulation in a manner that ensured that judicial review would comprise an adequate and effective remedy.[172] The Compliance Committee also criticised the January 2015 judgments of the CJEU discussed above, noting that, if the CJEU had allowed itself to assess the legality of Article 10(1) of the Regulation in the light of Article 9(3) of the Convention, 'this could have assisted the [EU] to comply with its obligations under the Convention'.[173]

These draft findings amply illustrate the potential for jurisdictional conflict between the CJEU and the Compliance Committee. As discussed in Chapter 5, however, it should be recalled that the Committee is not a 'court' and its findings not formally binding on the Parties to the Convention.[174]

Other Means of Accessing Justice at EU Level

Mention should also be made of three means of accessing justice in environmental matters at EU level in other ways, namely (1) complaints to the EU Ombudsman; (2) petitions before the European Parliament; and (3) the European Citizens' Initiative.

Established in 1993, the European Ombudsman is tasked with investigating complaints of maladministration in the institutions and bodies of the European Union.

> **Article 228 TFEU**
>
> 1. A European Ombudsman, elected by the European Parliament, shall be empowered to receive complaints from any citizen of the Union or any natural or legal person residing or having its registered office in a Member State concerning instances of maladministration in the activities of the Union institutions, bodies, offices or agencies, with the exception of the Court of Justice of the European Union acting in its judicial role. He or she shall examine such complaints and report on them.

The Ombudsman is empowered to conduct inquiries further to complaints on her own initiative, 'except where the alleged facts are or have been the subject of

---

[172] Draft findings in Complaint ACCC/C/2008/32, part II, at para. 112.
[173] Ibid., para. 80.
[174] The compliance procedure pursuant to the Aarhus Convention is expressly *not* a judicial one, and the Compliance Committee is not a court (Art. 15, Aarhus Convention), but it nonetheless has jurisdiction to make findings on how the Convention applies to individual cases brought before it. However, it is the Meeting of the Parties that ultimately has the final say on the 'appropriate measures to bring about full compliance with the Convention'. See Report of the First Meeting of the Parties to the Aarhus Convention, Addendum, Decision 1/7 Review of Compliance, ECE/MP.PP/2/Add.8, setting out the structure and functions of the Compliance Committee (esp. paras. 36–37).

legal proceedings'. Where a case of maladministration is established, the Ombudsman refers the matter to the institution, body or agency concerned, which has three months to inform her of its views. The Ombudsman then forwards a report to the European Parliament and to the institution, body or agency concerned. While the concept of 'maladministration' is not defined in the Treaties, in 2012 the Ombudsman specified five public service principles which should guide EU civil servants, namely:

(a) commitment to the EU and its citizens;
(b) integrity;
(c) objectivity;
(d) respect for others; and
(e) transparency.

In 2001, the European Parliament first approved the European Code of Good Administrative Behaviour, which provides that EU officials must act in a lawful, proportionate, impartial, independent, objective, consistent, fair and courteous manner, in respect for the principle of equal treatment, and shall not abuse their power.[175] The Ombudsman has emphasised that the Code is now further supported by, and overlaps with, the right to good administration provided in Article 41 of the Charter of Fundamental Rights of the EU. In an empirical analysis of the work of the European Ombudsman to date in environmental cases, Tsadiras has noted that environmental complaints have had, on average, a higher success rate (at 35 per cent success rate) than complaints in general to the Ombudsman (at 20 per cent success rate).[176] An example of a blatant breach of the duty of maladministration in the environmental context concerned a complaint lodged by the residents of the Greek municipality of Parga. In that case, the Ombudsman upheld claims that DG Environment failed to handle a complaint about breach of the EIA Directive impartially and properly due to the fact that a senior Commission official held a party political position in Greece which was incompatible with his duty to ensure that the project in question complied with EU law.[177]

A further non-judicial means of accessing justice at EU level is by lodging a petition with the European Parliament. Pursuant to Article 227 TFEU,

> Any citizen of the Union, and any natural or legal person residing or having its registered office in a Member State, shall have the right to address, individually or in association with other citizens or persons, a petition to the European Parliament on

---

[175] See www.ombudsman.europa.eu.
[176] Alexandros Tsadiras, 'Environmental Protection through Extra-Judicial Means: The European Ombudsman's Contribution' (2013) 22(4) *European Energy and Environmental Law Review* 152.
[177] Decision of the European Ombudsman on complaint 1288/99/OV against the European Commission.

> a matter which comes within the Union's fields of activity and which affects him, her or it directly.

The Rules of Procedure of the European Parliament specify the manner in which petitions will be examined. Petitions are dealt with by the European Parliament's Committee on Petitions, which produces annual reports of its activities. As with complaints to the Commission under Article 258 TFEU, however, the Committee is not obliged to take action by reason of a complaint. The Petitions Committee may, however, if it wishes, investigate complaints by means of a hearing of the petitioner in person, a fact-finding mission by a delegation from the Committee, and/or a public hearing. The Annual Reports of the Committee on Petitions show that the Committee has made use of these possibilities on a variety of occasions to investigate environmental complaints.[178]

Finally, the European Citizens' Initiative (ECI) constitutes a further non-judicial mode of recourse potentially available to citizens at EU level in relation to environmental issues. Article 11(4) TEU, inserted by the Treaty of Lisbon, provides 'Not less than one million citizens who are nationals of a significant number of Member States may take the initiative of inviting the European Commission, within the framework of its powers, to submit any appropriate proposal on matters where citizens consider that a legal act of the Union is required for the purpose of implementing the Treaties.' The procedure for invoking the ECI was set out by Regulation in 2011.[179]

The first ECI which successfully met the criteria to be submitted to the Commission as such was in the environmental field, concerning the right to water, which received the support of more than 1.6 million citizens.[180] The ECI invited the Commission to propose legislation implementing the 'human right to water and sanitation as recognised by the United Nations, and promoting the provision of water and sanitation as essential public services for all'. The Commission replied by Communication in 2014,[181] stating that it intended to take a variety of measures, including reinforcing implementation of its water quality legislation, launching an EU-wide public consultation on the Drinking Water Directive, and improving transparency for urban waste water and drinking water data management. However, it did not commit to bringing forward a legislative Proposal in the terms advocated by the ECI.

---

[178] See, for instance, the fact-finding missions in relation to compliance in certain Italian regions with EU waste management rules, which resulted in recommendations to national authorities and to DG Environment: 2012 Annual Report of the Activities of the Committee on Petitions, 2013/2013(INI), 20.

[179] Regulation 211/2011 of the European Parliament and of the Council of 16 February 2011 on the citizens' initiative, OJ 2011 L 65/1.

[180] ECI(2012)000003 (date of registration 10 May 2012).   [181] COM(2014)177.

8

Climate Change

Introduction

Climate change is the world's greatest environmental challenge. It jeopardises long-term economic and political stability across the globe. It is the most encompassing and disruptive man-made threat ever confronted by societies past or present.

People may disagree about the intensity and distribution of climate change impacts but (in Europe at least) some things are now commonly accepted as fact. As confirmed in the 5th Report of the Intergovernmental Panel on Climate Change (IPCC),[1] there is a 95 per cent scientific consensus that man-made emissions of greenhouse gases (GHGs) are causing global temperatures to rise on an unprecedentedly steep incline. Under business as usual circumstances, the planet could heat up by more than 5 degrees Celsius by the end of the century. To reiterate but a handful of the more cataclysmic predicted consequences of the business as usual scenario: polar icecaps will melt; many island States will be wiped off the face of the earth; even more countries will lose significant land mass to rising sea levels; changed climatological conditions will exacerbate flooding and trigger more extreme weather events; and rising temperatures will have dramatic impacts on ecosystems, unleashing a stream of towering challenges to human habitation, biodiversity protection, agriculture, forestry and fisheries.

Climate change will leave no corner of the planet unaffected, but the impacts will be very unevenly distributed. In a cruel twist of fate, the poorest countries with the smallest carbon footprints are likely to be the most heavily affected. The 2007 'Stern Review' estimated that, in the event of the 5 degrees' temperature rise, climate change will result in global GDP loss of between 5 per cent and 10 per cent.[2] Recent reports suggest that this estimate may well be too conservative. Many of the cities that are expected to see the fastest increase in GDP over the coming decades, including Dhaka in Bangladesh and Mumbai in India, are at an extreme risk of climate change. As their proportion of global GDP rises, so will the impact of climate change on global GDP.[3]

---

[1] IPCC Working Group 1, 'Climate Change 2013: The Physical Science Basis': www.climatechange2013.org/.
[2] Nicholas Stern, *The Economics of Climate Change* (Cambridge University Press, 2006) ('The Stern Review').
[3] 'Countries at climate risk to hold more GDP', 30 October 2013: www.globalpost.com/dispatch/news/afp/131029/countries-at-climate-risk-hold-more-gdp.

Beyond a consensus about the existence and the seriousness of climate change, there is broad agreement within the European Union that law and regulation have an important part to play in mounting a response to this era-defining challenge. The EU has arguably been the most proactive governance regime in existence on the issue of climate change, with initiatives, recommendations and even legislation in pursuit of climate change mitigation going back to the late 1980s to early 1990s.[4] Over time, EU activity on climate change has generated a wealth of Regulations, Directives, decisions, soft law instruments and court rulings. A full discussion of the material could easily fill its own dedicated bookshelf. To keep the investigation focused, this chapter identifies key challenges confronting the EU as a climate change law- and policy-maker, and illustrates how provisions in EU climate change legislation and case law relate to these challenges. They are:

- leadership on climate change;
- the scope of climate change regulation;
- climate change as a multi-level governance challenge; and
- facilitating a regulation-based market.

Before investigating each of these challenges in detail, the next pages locate climate change within the EU's Treaty-based competences and identify the ways in which climate change competences are distinct from other EU environmental powers.

Mandate of the European Union with Regard to Climate Change

The EU's competence to regulate for climate change mitigation rests on stable foundations.[5] Climate change is, evidently, a major threat to the environment. A failure to respond will thoroughly derail the sustainable development of Europe which, according to Article 3(3) of the Treaty on European Union (TEU), must be based on 'balanced economic growth and price stability, a highly competitive social market economy, aiming at full employment and social progress, and a high level of protection and improvement of the quality of the environment'. Article 3(5) TEU adds that the EU should uphold its values and interests in its relations with the wider world, which include an aspiration to contribute to the sustainable development of the Earth. Moreover, in its provisions on EU environmental policy, Article 191 of the Treaty on the Functioning of the European Union (TFEU) singles out climate change and states that EU environmental policy should aim to contribute to 'promoting measures at international level to deal

[4] Kati Kulovesi, Elisa Morgera and Miquel Muñoz, 'Environmental Integration and Multifaceted International Dimensions of EU Law: Unpacking the EU's 2009 Climate and Energy Package' (2011) 48 *Common Market Law Review* 829–891, at 836.
[5] Krämer, *EU Environmental Law*, 308.

with regional or worldwide environmental problems, and in particular combating climate change'.

Many climate change initiatives have a direct impact on energy policy. The EU's formal competence in this field is of recent date: following the Lisbon Treaty amendments, Article 194 TFEU establishes a legal basis for an EU energy policy which, among other objectives, explicitly mandates the European Union to promote energy efficiency, energy saving, and the development of new and renewable energy sources. These missions directly correspond with two pillars of the EU's climate and energy package (see below). The new energy policy provision bolsters the EU's claim as the main architect of the European climate change strategy. However, it also illustrates that climate change compels policy-makers to wade into nationally highly sensitive areas. Article 194 TFEU affirms the EU's role in securing the smooth functioning, the sustainability and the security of the energy market, but at the same time it underlines the Member States' prerogative to determine the composition of the domestic energy portfolio and the conditions for the exploitation of national energy resources. In contrast to internal market measures and environmental policy measures, EU energy law is adopted pursuant to a special legislative procedure (the consultation procedure), which reduces the input of the European Parliament and reserves greater control for Member State governments. Hence, the EU's legal authority with regard to the energy-related aspects of its climate change policy may have strengthened, but the opportunities for the EU's key supranational players, the European Commission and the European Parliament, to set the legislative agenda for climate change may in some instances be fewer than in the pre-Lisbon era.

Both environmental and energy policy fall within the zone of shared competences. Legislative proposals on climate change must therefore pass the subsidiarity test.[6] As they address a global problem caused by diffuse emissions with a transboundary reach, climate change mitigation measures are unlikely to stumble over subsidiarity concerns. EU climate change adaptation initiatives, on the other hand, are on shakier ground. Whereas mitigation seeks to prevent or reduce temperature rises, adaptation measures aim to anticipate the impacts of climate change in order to contain the damage. EU Member States may have very different adaptation needs. With 7,600 kilometres of coastline, Italy is expected to face a set of climate-related challenges that landlocked Austria will not. Also, the prospect of longer droughts and potential desertification preoccupies Spain considerably more than it does Finland. This differentiation makes it harder to justify the added value of a harmonised EU approach. Moreover, regulating for adaptation is likely to have considerable distributive impacts and to touch on notoriously sensitive areas of domestic policy, such as strategic planning and security. These are areas in which the EU is wise to tread lightly.

Hence, it is unsurprising that the European Union's adaptation programme looks modest in comparison to its mitigation portfolio. The 2013 Adaptation Strategy emphasises the supplementary and supporting spirit in which it was

---

[6] See Chapter 4.

conceived.[7] The Strategy's main targets are to promote adaptation at the Member State level, to 'climate-proof' EU policies such as agriculture and transport by ensuring they take account of adaptation concerns, and to contribute to our knowledge about adaptation needs and solutions through research. This facilitating approach is undeniably attractive in the current political climate of widespread Euro-scepticism and nervousness about the fragility of economic recovery within and beyond the Eurozone. In the longer run, however, the EU will very likely face pressures to intensify its engagement with climate change adaptation. The 2015 Paris Agreement,[8] adopted in implementation of the United Nations Framework Convention on Climate Change (UNFCCC),[9] elevates climate change adaptation as a key goal of international climate law, alongside mitigation and climate finance. As a signatory and chief promoter of the Agreement, the EU will need to integrate adaptation more prominently in its climate change policies. Moreover, shortcomings in national adaptation regimes can cause major externalities. This is most evidently the case where neighbouring Member States share natural resources, such as river basins or mountain ranges, but local failings in adaptation can also impair biodiversity across the EU by, for instance, depriving migratory birds of breeding grounds. Potentially, locally uncontrolled impacts of climate change could constitute major health, safety and security risks that disrupt EU trade and jeopardise the Union's precarious financial stability. The adaptation question thus illustrates one of the perennial dilemmas that confront the EU as a governance regime: expanding the remit of EU policies towards domestically sensitive areas raises concerns of illegitimate 'competence creep'[10] and the erosion of national sovereignty beyond Treaty-based limits. However, not doing so could jeopardise the effectiveness with which the EU fulfils its core role of integrating the market and strengthening the Member States' economic development. This, too, could cast a shadow on the legitimacy of the EU. The EU, it seems, cannot avoid legitimacy challenges, but rather must carefully navigate between them.

High Stakes: The Challenge of Climate Change Leadership

The European Union is at the forefront of climate change law and policy. It is the main driver behind international efforts to maintain and enhance a binding international legal regime equipped to respond to ever more pressing global needs for climate change mitigation and adaptation. Internally, the EU has

---

[7] Commission Communication to the European Parliament, the Council, the European Economic and Social Committee and the Committee of the Regions, 'An EU Strategy on Adaptation to Climate Change', 16 April 2013, COM(2013)216, p. 5.
[8] Paris (France), 13 December 2015, in force November 2016, available at http://unfccc.int.
[9] New York (USA), 9 May 1992, in force 21 March 1994, available at: http://unfccc.int.
[10] Stephen Weatherill, 'Competence Creep and Competence Control' (2004) 23 *Yearbook of European Law* 1–55.

introduced a range of climate change laws and supporting measures that, in terms of scale and ambition, considerably exceed those adopted outside of the EU region. The European Union's progressive stance on climate change has made EU climate change law a model and a strong point of reference for law and policy development across the world.[11]

Climate change leadership offers the European Union considerable advantages.[12] The EU's central position in international climate change negotiations gives it opportunities to control the agenda, and thus contain the risk that any ensuing agreement would favour strategies or technologies that run counter to the EU's economic, environmental and technological interests. Symbolically, the European Union's role in climate change is a signpost of its maturity as a player in international politics and diplomacy, talked of in the same breath as world powers such as the USA, China and Germany. Its engagement with climate change science and its pursuit of an agenda that is crucial not only for European but also for global sustainability projects an image of the EU as a forward-thinking and humanitarian force.[13] This representation can be a welcome antidote to the familiar caricature of the EU as a bureaucrats' paradise concerned with the endless production of rules for rules' sake; a reputation that pursues the EU in both its internal and external relations.

Yet leadership comes with a hefty price tag. The failure of the international regime to deliver timely and credible instruments for global emissions reductions could undo instead of build the EU's reputation as a global power broker.[14] The mission of leading by example also exposes the EU to intense pressures on the home front. It is proving increasingly difficult to keep 28 Member States, which have widely varying commitments to the cause of climate change abatement and expect to be differently impacted by both climate change and climate change regulation, on message.[15] The longer third countries drag their feet, the greater the risk that the EU's efforts towards climate change abatement are cancelled out by rising emissions elsewhere and have as their only real effect a setback in European economic competitiveness. The interdependence between the external and internal pillars of climate change leadership could easily trap climate change policy in a vicious circle, since any signal that the EU is losing its battle with the Member States to stay committed to an ambitious climate change

---

[11] R. Daniel Kelemen, 'Globalizing European Union Environmental Policy' (2010) 17(3) *Journal of European Public Policy* 335–349, at 343–345.
[12] Sebastian Oberthür and Claire Roche Kelly, 'EU Leadership in International Climate Policy: Achievements and Challenges' (2008) 43(3) *The International Spectator: Italian Journal of International Affairs* 35–50.
[13] Kulovesi et al., 'Environmental Integration and Multifaceted International Dimensions of EU Law', 830.
[14] Alina Averchenkova and Samuela Bassi, 'Beyond the Targets: Assessing the Political Credibility of Pledges for the Paris Agreement' (Policy Brief of the Grantham Research Institute on Climate Change and the Environment, February 2016), available at: http://eprints.lse.ac.uk/65670/1/Averchenkova-and-Bassi-2016.pdf.
[15] See e.g. Wojciech Kość, 'Polish "No" to Higher EU Climate Ambition for 2030', *ENDS Europe*, 16 March 2016.

mitigation programme could harm the EU's already precarious international leadership position and, thus, jeopardise the adoption and implementation of meaningful global commitments.

The following three sections analyse the EU's role in forging an international legal framework for climate change, and offer a brief overview of the current state of play in international law. After examining the external dimension of the EU's climate change leadership, the section turns to the impact of climate change leadership on the relation between the different Member States, and identifies the legal strategies deployed to balance the need for a united, proactive stance on climate change with concerns about the effect on the EU's economic competitiveness and with calls for intra-EU differentiation. The final section illustrates both the external and internal dimension of the climate change leadership challenge through the controversy of emissions trading for aviation.

The External Dimension of Climate Change Leadership

Considering the scale of the challenge, the body of treaty law dedicated to climate change control is quite modest. It comprises two binding international agreements: the 1992 United Nations Framework Convention on Climate Change (UNFCCC) and the 1997 Kyoto Protocol (KP), and the decisions of the Conference of the Parties (COP) adopted under the auspices of the UNFCCC. The 2015 Paris Agreement (PA) joined this set of documents in November 2016.

The European Union as well as the Member States individually are signatories to the UNFCCC, the KP and the PA, and therefore subject to their provisions and the accompanying COP decisions. Portraying the EU as merely 'subject to' climate change law, however, significantly underplays the institution's formative role in its enactment. Climate change and global warming entered public consciousness around the mid-1980s, in large part thanks to awareness-raising campaigns by scientific organisations and epistemic communities, such as the World Meteorological Organisation (WMO).[16] Although quite a few scientific summits were held within EU territory, EU bodies kept a relatively low profile on climate change until the end of the decade. This is not surprising: in the wake of its successful negotiation of the Vienna Convention on Substances that Deplete the Ozone Layer,[17] countries looked to the USA for global environmental leadership. Moreover, we should recall that the European Union only achieved formal competence in environmental policy following the Single European Act, which entered into force in 1988.

The EU soon adopted a more assertive stance. A pivotal moment came by the turn of the decade, when it agreed on a (then) EC-wide goal of stabilising CO_2 emissions at 1990 levels by the year 2000. Having made the commitment

---

[16] Daniel Bodansky, 'The United Nations Framework Convention on Climate Change: A Commentary' (1993) 18 *Yale Journal of International Law* 451–558, at 458.

[17] Vienna Convention for the Protection of the Ozone Layer, Vienna, 22 March 1985, in force 22 September 1988, 1513 UNTS 293; (1988) ATS 26; 26 ILM 1529 (1987).

internally, the EU became an avid campaigner for the global adoption of binding emissions targets, which contravened the US preference for a more decentralised and flexible 'pledge and review' approach to emissions reductions. The growing divergence between EU and US approaches to climate change control did not scupper the UNFCCC (which in any event contains no binding targets for emissions reduction), but it most certainly affected the course of the Kyoto Protocol and the Paris Agreement negotiations.

EU insistence on and US resistance to quantified reduction targets for developed countries under Kyoto, and the absence of corresponding obligations for developing States, hung heavy over the five years of Kyoto Protocol negotiations (1992–1997). Several attempts were made to keep America on board, for instance through the introduction in the text of the Protocol of flexible mechanisms for emissions reduction, an approach that US negotiators strongly advocated. Nevertheless, the USA withdrew from Kyoto and thus, ironically, the champions of what may well be Kyoto's most enduring legacy, the proliferation of market-based approaches to environmental regulation, had no part in its implementation. The Kyoto Protocol, adopted in 1997, ultimately entered into effect in 2005, when Russia ratified the document. Russia's hard-won support was the result of intensive rounds of European diplomacy and persuasion. It was recognised at the time as a sign of the EU's arrival in the international arena.[18]

The provisions of the UNFCCC, the Kyoto Protocol and the Paris Agreement are expertly discussed in many publications, so a short summary suffices here. The UNFCCC has attracted near universal membership and calls on its signatories to take measures towards the stabilisation of greenhouse gases (GHGs) in the atmosphere at levels that would 'prevent dangerous anthropogenic interference in the climate system' (Art. 2), which since the 2010 Cancun Agreements is understood as a commitment to keep global temperature rise to below 2 degrees Celsius. Article 2(a) of the Paris Agreement restates this goal as:

> Holding the increase in the global average temperature to well below 2°C above pre-industrial levels and pursuing efforts to limit the temperature increase to 1.5°C above pre-industrial levels, recognising that this would significantly reduce the risks and impacts of climate change.

The UNFCCC maps out a broad range of tasks that member countries should undertake towards climate change mitigation, ranging from inventorying GHG domestic emissions and adopting national mitigation policies, to fostering education and awareness-raising campaigns. It operates on the principle of common but differentiated responsibilities, which resonates in the division between (developed) Annex I countries and (developing) Annex II countries and non-Annexed developing countries, as well as the expectation

---

[18] Charles F. Parker and Christer Karlsson, 'Climate Change and the European Union's Leadership Moment: An Inconvenient Truth?' (2010) 48(4) *Journal of Common Market Studies* 923–943, at 929.

that the former shoulder greater burdens in climate change mitigation, enable technology transfers and offer financial assistance to developing countries. Indeed, one of the most significant results of UNFCCC cooperation is the establishment of a Green Climate Fund. Developed countries pledged US$30 billion towards the fund for the period 2010–2013, with a long-term goal of US$100 billion per year by 2020. The UNFCCC is inclusive, expansive, aspirational and, predictably, largely toothless as a consequence; its provisions are not of a nature to bind its signatories to specific mitigation actions or emissions reduction results. Even if they were, the Convention contains no provisions on enforcement beyond the boilerplate Treaty provisions for dispute settlement between the parties. While weak on enforcement, the UNFCCC is, however, markedly strong on institution-building: its provisions secured the establishment of a stable infrastructure that has served as a forum for global climate change summits since 1992. Progress on mitigation and adaptation may be frustratingly slow, but the institutional stability provided by the UNFCCC has undoubtedly helped to keep climate change on the global agenda through periods of political insecurity and economic instability.

The Kyoto Protocol sets binding GHG emissions reduction targets, to be achieved in the period 2008–2012 ('Phase I') against a 1990 baseline. Targets are imposed on the countries listed in Annex B, which, in broad brushstrokes, covers Europe, North America,[19] Australia, New Zealand and Japan. Kyoto does not mandate how emissions reductions should be achieved, but it does provide a framework for implementation through flexible mechanisms: emissions trading, joint implementation and the clean development mechanism. Emissions trading is discussed more extensively further in the chapter. Joint implementation, briefly, refers to the option for Annex B countries to pool their total allowable emissions and achieve their respective caps jointly. The Clean Development Mechanism, in turn, enables Annex B countries to meet their targets by investing in clean technology in developing countries instead of through local abatement. Achievement of the targets is monitored and, in notable contrast to the UNFCCC, the Protocol establishes a non-compliance mechanism that has been actively used to support and compel Annex B countries to progress towards their emissions reduction targets.[20]

With its quantified maximum emissions percentages, specified timeline and provisions on implementation and enforcement, the Kyoto Protocol is a much more hard-nosed, 'hard law' document than the UNFCCC. Yet this strength proved simultaneously its greatest weakness. The EU encountered difficulty in getting the Protocol past the ratification threshold and the USA is notably absent from the Kyoto fold. The GHG emissions reduction targets were binding, but they were also very modest and, consequently, incommensurate to the degree of change

---

[19] The USA was never bound by its target since it did not ratify Kyoto. Australia ratified in 2007.
[20] Anna Huggins, 'The Desirability of Depoliticization: Compliance in the International Climate Regime' (2015) 4(1) *Transnational Environmental Law* 101–124.

required credibly to stay within the overall 2 degrees Celsius rise by 2100. Most damningly, Phase I of Kyoto expired at the end of 2012, without any agreement on a successor instrument or targets.[21] The infamous Copenhagen Conference of the Parties of 2009 was generally anticipated to be the forum for a global agreement on Kyoto II, but it ended in disarray.[22]

It took another six years before the international community agreed on a new binding instrument to fill the void left by the Copenhagen failure. As with the Kyoto Protocol, the EU played a very prominent role in bringing the Paris Agreement to fruition, but the differences between Paris and Kyoto far outweigh the similarities. Instead of imposing top-down emissions reduction commitments on developed countries, the Paris Agreement embraces a bottom-up strategy that requires all signatory parties, whether developed or developing, to make nationally determined contributions (NDCs) towards climate change control. The Paris Agreement is therefore more flexible in approach, and places greater emphasis on self-differentiation than on common but differentiated responsibilities (CBDRs) as expressed through differentiated emissions reduction targets. Most of the real 'bite' of the Paris Agreement resides in its procedural provisions: member countries must update and communicate NDCs every five years. The Agreement creates an expectation of progressive ambition in domestic climate change strategies, and introduces extensive information provisions for all parties to enable tracking of progress on NDCs and support offered to and received by developing countries.

The Paris Agreement arguably affirms the EU's continuing importance as a climate change leader, but its unexpectedly long and difficult gestation simultaneously underscores the fragility of leadership.[23] Moreover, the successful preservation of the international climate change architecture has come at the cost of a significant loss of control: decision-making on emissions reduction targets has essentially been reclaimed by national governments. If NDCs collectively fall short of delivering the level of mitigation commensurate with the aspirations of Article 2(a) of the Paris Agreement – as is presently the case[24] – the Paris Agreement may enable the international community to detect the shortfall, but it does not offer mechanisms to police or rectify the problem. The fragility may also impact on the EU's ability to maintain an ambitious, cohesive climate change policy internally. This is further explored in the section below.

---

[21] A number of Annex B countries have mutually agreed to unilaterally adopt a second generation of emissions reduction targets, which are applied in the interim between the expiry of Phase I and the entry into force of a new multilateral legal instrument. On average, participants in the interim phase have committed to an 18 per cent reduction by 2020, with the EU's share at 20 per cent. Canada, Australia, Russia and Japan, however, have declined to recommit.

[22] Radoslav S. Dimitrov, 'Inside Copenhagen: The State of Climate Governance' (2010) 10 (2) *Global Environmental Politics* 18–24.

[23] Krämer, *EU Environmental Law*, 311.

[24] Quirin Schiermeier, 'Combined Climate Pledges of 146 Nations Fall Short of 2 °C Target' *Nature News*, 30 October 2015.

The Internal Dimension of Climate Change Leadership

From the early 1990s, the European Union adopted a policy of 'leading by example' on climate change. Through its unilateral assumption of ambitious and proactive climate change targets, the EU hopes to lower the threshold for third countries to follow suit and, thus, to overcome the large-scale collective actions problems that delay global climate action.

Leading by example is a daring, arguably optimistic strategy that creates a range of particular challenges for the EU as a lawmaking and regulatory authority. Preliminarily, it is useful to remember that leading by example adds yet another target to the already crowded mission statement of EU environmental policy. Many EU environmental measures, covering issues from chemicals to endangered species, aspire both to achieve a high level of environmental protection and to facilitate the functioning of the internal market. The feasibility of effectively combining both objectives within a single regulatory framework has been called into question, for instance in writings suggesting that environmental protection may formally have equal footing but is practically subservient to the market rationale of EU regulation.[25] The mandate of leading by example adds a further layer of complexity to the already precarious balancing act between multiple public policy goals in EU regulation. Kulovesi, Morgera and Munoz identify the Carbon Capture and Storage (CCS) Directive as a pioneering framework designed to inspire the development of both international and domestic law.[26] They suggest that the Directive, which establishes a legal framework for the environmentally safe geological storage of carbon dioxide (CO_2), came into being not because of a demand for harmonised conditions to facilitate the development of the technology in Europe, but because fostering CCS in Europe would legitimise the EU's attempts to have CCS recognised under the Clean Development Mechanism, which would in turn enable the introduction of CCS in developing countries. If so, this could explain why the CCS Directive has been crippled by unusually long implementation delays and has resulted in precious little CCS innovation so far.[27] It has moreover been asserted that the CCS Directive offers a rare example of the goal of market harmonisation being undone by the pursuit of excessively demanding environmental conditions.[28] High regulatory hurdles arguably deter investment in CCS installations and, hence, the very formation of an internal market for CCS. Relatedly, the absence of actual examples of CCS regulation in action erodes the Directive's exemplary force.

---

[25] See Chapter 13.
[26] Kulovesi et al., 'Environmental Integration and Multifaceted International Dimensions of EU Law', 872.
[27] Peter Radgen, Robin Irons and Hans Schoenmakers, 'Too Early or Too Late For CCS – What Needs to Be Done to Overcome the Valley of Death For Carbon Capture and Storage in Europe?' (2013) 37 *Energy Procedia* 6189–6201, at 6199.
[28] Zen A. Makuch, Slavina Z. Georgieva and Behdeen Oraee-Mirzamani, 'Carbon Capture and Storage Liability' in Karen E. Mukuch and Ricardo Pereira (eds.), *Environmental and Energy Law* (Wiley-Blackwell, 2012), 273.

Leadership by example stands or falls with the credibility of the EU's internal climate change commitments. This means that the EU must persuade its Member States – all twenty-eight facing different economic circumstances, having different interests and different views on the best approach to the climate change challenge – to adopt harmonised, ambitious and potentially costly measures. A number of strategies have been developed to facilitate Member State allegiance to the EU's climate change agenda. First, to bridge the differences in wealth and fossil fuel dependency between Member States, EU climate change law deploys 'effort sharing'. In an arrangement akin to the individualised GHG emissions reduction goals for Annex B countries under the Kyoto Protocol, the 2009 Effort Sharing Decision lays down national emissions limits for the 2013–2020 period, ranging from a maximum increase of 20 per cent from a 2005 baseline for Bulgaria to a minimum reduction by 20 per cent for Denmark and Ireland.[29] The Effort Sharing Decision introduces differentiation but at the same time allows a degree of flexibility by allowing Member States to either carry forward or bank a percentage of their annual emissions allocation. At the time of writing, the Commission is drafting a proposal for a follow-up 'Effort Sharing Regulation', which will allocate emissions reduction targets between Member States for the 2020 to 2030 period.[30]

A second strategy to boost the acceptability of ambitious climate change targets vis-à-vis the Member States consists of identifying sectors at risk of carbon leakage, and introducing special arrangements to safeguard them. Carbon leakage occurs when emissions reductions in one region cause emissions elsewhere to increase.[31] For instance, CO_2 reduction targets imposed on the European steel sector make European steel costlier and cause construction companies to source their supplies increasingly from third country suppliers. This triggers a rise in third country steel production and, if CO_2 is less stringently regulated abroad, an increase in emissions that might even outstrip the carbon footprint of European steel manufacturers before the reduction targets took effect. Under the Emissions Trading Directive (ETD), sectors that are deemed 'at significant risk of carbon leakage' receive a higher proportion of emissions allowances, and can make greater use of carbon offsets.[32] Unsurprisingly, this provision made the term 'significant risk of carbon leakage' a hotly contested commodity. In response, the European Commission has drawn up a carbon list, which is currently in

---

[29] Decision No. 406/2009/EC of the European Parliament and of the Council of 23 April 2009 on the effort of Member States to reduce their greenhouse gas emissions to meet the Community's greenhouse gas emissions reduction commitments up to 2020, OJ 2009 L 140/136.
[30] European Commission Press Release, 'Climate Action: Europe readies next steps to implement the Paris Agreement', 2 March 2016, available at: http://europa.eu/rapid/press-release_IP-16-502_en.htm.
[31] Thomas Eichner and Ruediger Pethig, 'Carbon Leakage, the Green Paradox, and Perfect Future Markets' (2011) 52(3) *International Economic Review* 767–805, at 767–769.
[32] Art. 10a ETS 2009. See, further, below.

its second iteration and applies for the years 2015 to 2019.[33] In principle, an industrial sector is covered if the additional costs induced by the implementation of the ETD add at least 5 per cent to production costs, and the intensity of trade with third countries is above 10 per cent. In practice, carbon leakage sectors include many of the EU's more traditional industries, including mining, metal and cement manufacture, manufacture of electrical equipment and, to the relief of oenophiles everywhere, wine production.

Carbon leakage strategies compensate for reduced competitiveness as a result of climate change regulation, but at the same time EU documents are quick to emphasise the synergies between climate action and competitiveness. The European Commission, particularly, is prone to espouse a 'win–win' narrative that portrays climate policy as a catalyst to innovation and a chance to set the EU on a path towards sustainable growth and global green technological leadership.[34] '20 20 by 2020', the Commission's landmark climate policy paper, is tellingly subtitled 'Europe's Climate Change *Opportunity*'.[35] The adoption of a win–win framework, too, is a strategy deployed to cement allegiance to the EU's climate change agenda and, thus, consolidate its internal leadership.

Yet differentiation under effort sharing, compensation for carbon leakage and a positive account of the climate-economy dynamic may not be enough to safeguard the EU's leadership by example. In the first post-Kyoto period of 2013–2020, the EU committed itself to a 20 per cent emissions reduction and indicated its willingness to drop to 30 per cent if its efforts were matched by comparable emissions reduction commitments from other developed nations, and by adequate contributions from economically more advanced developing nations, 'according to their responsibilities and respective capabilities'.[36] The conditional nature of this commitment was already a step removed from a pure 'leadership by example' ethos. The Commission's 2013 Green Paper on climate and energy policy for 2030[37] confirms that the EU's climate package should be sufficiently ambitious to ensure that it is 'on track to meet longer term climate objectives', but immediately adds that it should reflect a number of important changes that have taken place since 2009, including the economic recession and the sovereign debt crisis; new developments on European and

---

[33] Commission Decision of 24 December 2009 determining, pursuant to Directive 2003/87/EC of the European Parliament and of the Council, a list of sectors and subsectors which are deemed to be exposed to a significant risk of carbon leakage, OJ 2010 L 1/10.

[34] Heyvaert, 'Governing Climate Change', 817. See also the 2030 Green Paper 'A 2030 Framework for Climate and Energy Policies', COM(2013)169 final.

[35] Communication From the Commission to the European Parliament, the Council, the European Economic and Social Committee and the Committee of the Regions, 20 20 by 2020 Europe's climate change opportunity, 23 January 2008, COM(2008)30 final.

[36] European Parliament and Council Decision 406/2009/EC on the effort of Member States to reduce their greenhouse gas emissions to meet the Community's greenhouse gas reduction commitments up to 2020, OJ 2009 L 140/136. See also *ibid.*, Commission Communication on 20 20 by 2020: Europe's climate change opportunity.

[37] Green Paper, 'A 2030 Framework for Climate and Energy Policies', COM(2013)169 final.

global energy markets; concerns over fuel poverty and the affordability of energy for business; and the varying levels of commitment and ambition of international partners in reducing GHG emissions. Subsequent Council Resolutions continue to endorse a progressive climate change policy, but their tone too is decidedly cautious. They place a strong emphasis on the overriding imperative of economic growth, on the need to afford Member States flexibility in achieving climate change targets, and on the importance of protecting European industries against the risk of carbon leakage. In a similar vein, the 2014 European Council Resolution on a Coherent European Union Energy and Climate Policy[38] underscores that EU policy should ensure affordable energy prices, industrial competitiveness, security of supply and achievement of our climate and environmental objectives. Climate and environmental concerns are present, but their last place position betrays a European Council disposition that appears more preoccupied with economic than climate leadership. The successful conclusion of the Paris Agreement at the end of 2015 caused some resurgence of enthusiasm for the EU to ramp up its climate change actions beyond established 2020 to 2030 targets,[39] but more coal-dependent Member States such as Poland have stated their firm intention not to go further than previously agreed.[40]

In concrete terms, the EU Council has endorsed a 2030 renewables target of 27 per cent, an energy efficiency goal of 30 per cent, and an overall emissions reduction target of 40 per cent, with 43 per cent reductions for sectors covered by emissions trading. Although relatively less path-breaking than the 2020 targets, this is still an ambitious agenda. Yet the rift on matters of climate change between the 'older' Member States and a number of post-2014 EU accession States is worrying. The latter typically express a strong preference for an uncompromising insistence on reciprocity in the international arena, for indicative over mandatory targets, high levels of national flexibility, and resolute, proactive intervention to avert carbon leakage. These circumstances do not necessarily spell the end for EU climate change leadership, but they certainly represent a considerable challenge.

The Challenge of Leadership Exemplified: The Case of Aviation

Aviation contributes approximately 3 per cent to global GHG emissions and its share is projected to rise over time. The sector was not included in the first stage of the Emissions Trading System (ETS), the EU's flagship CO_2 emissions reduction instrument, but was added in the 2009 amendment to the ETD, with effect from 2012. The ETD will be analysed in more detail further in the chapter but, for the purposes of this discussion, the key facts are the following. From 2012 onwards, any flight landing in or departing from the European Union was required to

---

[38] European Council Conclusions 20/21 March 2014, EUCO 7/1/14 REV 1 CO EUR 2 CONCL 1, 7.
[39] See European Parliament resolution of 23 June 2016 on the renewable energy progress report (2016/2041(INI)).
[40] Kość, 'Polish "No" to Higher EU Climate Ambition for 2030'.

submit emissions allowances at the rate of one allowance per tonne of CO_2 emitted during the journey. Significantly, allowances were levied for the entire flight, not only for the emissions that happened in European airspace. In the start-up years, up to 85 per cent of allowances would be handed to airlines free of charge, but over time an increasing percentage would need to be purchased. Airlines could be exempted if, according to the European Commission, they were already subject to third country restrictions of equivalent impact to the ETD.

The extension of the ETS to international aviation caused a global outcry. Non-EU countries vocally protested against what they saw as a move towards heavy-handed unilateralism by the European Union.[41] It was argued that aviation had purposely been left out of the Kyoto Protocol because it was agreed at the time that emissions reduction measures in the sector should be adopted internationally and by consensus under the auspices of the International Civil Aviation Organization (ICAO). The EU's actions had therefore usurped ICAO's prerogative. The EU, in turn, emphasised that the ICAO had failed to make any progress on this issue for years. In the absence of a multilateral solution, it was entitled to proceed unilaterally and adopt necessary measures to curb CO_2 emissions from high contributing sectors.

The aviation battle was fought on both diplomatic and legal fronts. The Air Transport Association of America challenged the planned implementation of the ETD aviation provisions before the British court, arguing that since the ETD provisions relating to aviation were unlawful, so were the forthcoming implementing measures. A preliminary reference to the European Court of Justice followed.[42] It addressed the legality of the ETD aviation provisions in Grand Chamber, resulting in one of the most anticipated CJEU rulings of the past decades.

> **Case C-366/10** *Air Transport Association of America and Others* v. *Secretary of State for Energy and Climate Change*
>
> Case C-366/10 affirmed the legality of the ETD aviation provisions. In reaching its decision, the Grand Chamber addressed the compatibility of the aviation provisions with the Chicago Convention on International Civil Aviation; the Kyoto Protocol; the Open Skies Agreement; and various norms of international customary law. The Chicago Convention, which mostly regulates access to airspace to support the global market for aviation, was held not to bind the European Union because its signatories are the Member States instead of the EU itself, and the Member States' powers in the context of the Convention had not been transferred in their entirety to the EU. The Kyoto Protocol was equally quickly dispensed with: although unequivocally binding on the EU, its

---

[41] Joanne Scott and Lavanya Rajamani, 'EU Climate Change Unilateralism' (2012) 23 *European Journal of International Law* 469–494.

[42] Case C-366/10 *Air Transport Association of America and Others* v. *Secretary of State for Energy and Climate Change* [2011] ECR I-13755.

provisions on implementation were held to be insufficiently precise and unconditional to garner direct effect.

The most fascinating parts of the judgment in C-266/10 relate to the Open Skies Agreement and the principles of customary international law. The former is a market liberalisation treaty between the EU and USA. It exempts aircraft fuel from 'taxes, duties, fees and charges'.[43] The Court considered that emissions allowances did not constitute a fuel consumption tax and were, therefore, not caught by the fuel tax prohibition. This is, arguably, a narrow reading of the prohibition, all the more so since historic fuel consumption constitutes the key factor in calculating the total allowances cap for the aviation sector and in determining allocation per airline. On the point of customary international law, the CJEU recognised the applicability of the principles that each State has complete and exclusive competence over its own airspace; that no State may subject any part of the High Seas to its Sovereignty; and the principle of freedom over the High Seas. However, given their general nature, judicial review was limited to a manifest error assessment. The ETD aviation provision easily cleared this hurdle. The Grand Chamber considered that the provision that aircraft must either land in or depart from an airport in the EU to be caught by the ETD, whereas planes crossing over through EU airspace are unaffected, constituted a sufficient connection to the EU territory to dispel concerns of extraterritoriality and infringement of third country sovereignty.

The ETD aviation provisions and their legal challenge proved a real treasure trove for scholarship. Commentators have pored over every aspect, resulting in lively streams of scholarship on issues ranging from the rules of primacy between EU and international law, the impact of the ECJ ruling on interpretations of sovereignty, the interaction between multilateral and unilateral approaches to climate action and the adequacy of differentiation under the ETD, to the compatibility of the ETD with World Trade Organization (WTO) law.[44] Yet in terms of settling the dispute between EU and non-EU countries, Case C-366/10 was far less effective. Initially buoyed by its victory, the European Commission saw the ECJ ruling as an opportunity to press its advantage on the international stage and call for reform under the ICAO. It added that any ensuing international agreement should go beyond the emissions reductions resulting from the ETS for the aviation provisions in the ETD to be suspended. Negotiations did indeed resume under the ICAO, but so did the campaigning against the ETS. Some governments,

---

[43] Articles 11(1) and 2(c) Air Transport (Open Skies) Agreement, OJ 2007 L 134/4.
[44] See e.g. Scott and Rajamani, 'Climate Change Unilateralism'; An Hertogen, 'Sovereignty as Decisional Independence over Domestic Affairs: The Dispute over Aviation in the EU Emissions Trading System' (2012) 1(2) *Transnational Environmental Law* 281–301; Sanja Bogojević, 'Legalising Environmental Leadership' (2012) 24 *Journal of Environmental Law* 345–356; Geert De Baere and Cedric Ryngaert, 'The ECJ's Judgment in Air Transport Association of America and the International Legal Context of the EU's Climate Change Policy' (2013) 3 *European Foreign Affairs Review* 389–410.

including the US White House and the Chinese government, cautioned their national airlines not to surrender allowances, and even prepared legislation to outlaw participation in the EU ETS. They approached Member States individually and emphasised the potentially damaging impact of the ETS on good trading relations between the countries. Within less than one year of the CJEU judgment, cracks had appeared in the EU's 'hard line' stance and, after rumoured lobbying by the UK, Germany and France, in late 2012 the European Commission proposed to 'stop the clock' on the implementation of the ETD aviation provisions vis-à-vis international flights, pending negotiations for an international agreement under the ICAO. More than three years later, an ICAO-sponsored deal has indeed emerged. It is, however, a pale shadow of the EU's initial stipulation that any international agreement should exceed the ETD aviation provisions in ambition. The proposed Carbon Offsetting Scheme for International Aviation (COSIA) will require airlines to offset CO_2 emissions from 2020.[45] However, preliminary concern has been raised regarding the stringency of the proposed regime, which could be hampered by an overly permissive interpretation of what amounts to 'offsetting' for the purposes of emissions reduction, and a generous approach to exemptions provided. Moreover, membership of COSIA may make it difficult for countries to prepare their own more ambitious regional measures to tackle emissions.[46]

The ETS aviation saga offers fascinating insights into the power and limits of climate change law. On the one hand, the EU's decision to regulate aviation emissions triggered a chain of events that rekindled the dormant ICAO negotiation structure and will probably result in an international agreement on aviation emissions. Its content may fall short of the EU's aspirations, but it could constitute a more sustainable basis for further development than were the EU's unilateral actions. The experience also shows that law needs more than judicial approbation; it needs to be recognised as lawful and legitimate in the broader community to survive. The CJEU ruling did little to change the hearts and minds of third country governments, and was ultimately unsuccessful in insulating the ETS aviation scheme from further attack. Finally, the developments of recent years vividly illustrate the complex dynamics between international and internal climate leadership. The EU's decision 'stop the clock' on the international application of the ETS rules appeased its international trading partners, but exposed it to the wrath of EU budget airlines which were still caught by the ETS rules and found themselves at a competitive disadvantage vis-à-vis third country airlines. In its climate change policy, the EU must navigate between the pitfalls of unilateralism on the one hand, and leading by example on the other.

---

[45] See ICAO Draft Assembly Resolution text on a Global Market-based Measure (GMBM) Scheme, as of 11 March 2016, available at: www.icao.int/Meetings/GLADs-2016/Documents/Draft%20Assembly%20Resolution%20text%20on%20GMBM%20for%202016%20GLADs.pdf.

[46] Simon Roach, 'International Veto Could Derail Use of EU ETS for Aviation', *ENDS Europe*, 16 May 2016.

The Scope of the Climate Change Challenge

Climate change is the child of a billion causes. Certain economic sectors (such as electricity generation, heavy industrial production, transport) are exceptionally heavy contributors, but carbon dependency characterises every aspect of our daily work, of how we spend our leisure time and organise our family life. Elevated GHG emissions are much more than a technological challenge; they are the consequence of an endless web of interconnected economic and cultural choices. Any sustainable regulatory response to the risks of climate change must therefore face up to both the unprecedented scale and the nearly boundless scope of the challenge.

The exceptional scale and scope explain a number of prominent features of the EU's governance regime for climate change. Institutionally, the Commission added the post of European Commissioner for Climate Action to the roster in 2010, and strengthened the Commission's administrative branch with the addition of a Directorate-General for Climate Action ('DG CLIMA'). They take the lead in the development of climate change proposals. However, given the diffuse impacts of climate change, their work requires extensive involvement with a broad range of other Commissioners and Directorates, including those responsible for environment, energy, internal market, transport, agriculture, fisheries and trade. The climate change mandate thus represents the Commission's greatest test of inter-departmental cooperation and orchestration.

The multi-causal nature of climate change is also reflected in the establishment of EU climate change targets and the range of legal instruments. The EU's climate change strategy for 2030 pursues mitigation on three fronts: 40 per cent reduction in CO_2 emissions; a shift towards 27 per cent of the EU's energy needs being met from renewable energy sources; and a 30 per cent enhancement in energy efficiency.[47] The binding instruments to secure these targets include the Climate and Energy Package (the very name of which alludes to the composite nature of mitigation), the Energy Efficiency Plan and a host of additional instruments covering monitoring and reporting of GHG emissions; transport and fuels; fluorinated gases; and forests and agriculture. The main components of EU climate change legislation are:

The Climate and Energy Package

The EU Emissions Trading System (ETS)
Directive 2003/87/EC establishing a scheme for greenhouse gas emission allowance trading within the Community OJ 2003 L 275/32 (ETD)
  Directive 2004/101/EC establishing a scheme for greenhouse gas emission allowance trading within the Community, in respect of the Kyoto Protocol's project mechanisms OJ 2004 L 338/18 (Linking Directive)

---

[47] European Council Conclusions 20/21 March 2014, EUCO 7/1/14 REV 1 CO EUR 2 CONCL 1, 7.

Directive 2008/101/EC amending Directive 2003/87/EC so as to include aviation activities OJ 2009 L 8/3

Directive 2009/29/EC amending Directive 2003/87/EC so as to improve and extend the trading scheme OJ 2009 L 140/63

Effort Sharing
Decision 406/2009/EC on the effort of Member States to reduce their greenhouse gas emissions to meet the Community's greenhouse gas emissions reduction commitments up to 2020 OJ 2009 L 140/136 (Effort Sharing Decision)

Renewable Energy
Directive 2009/28/EC on the promotion of the use of energy from renewable sources OJ 2009 L 140/16 (Renewable Energy Directive or RED)

Carbon Capture and Storage (CCS)
Directive 2009/30/EC on the geological storage of carbon dioxide OJ 2009 L 140/114 (CCS Directive)

Energy Efficiency

Directive 2012/27/EU on energy efficiency OJ 2012 L 315/1

Ghg Monitoring and Reporting

Regulation (EU) no 525/2013 on a mechanism for monitoring and reporting greenhouse gas emissions and for reporting other information at national and Union level relevant to climate change OJ 2013 L 165/13

Transport and Fuels

Directive 1999/94/EC relating to the availability of consumer information on fuel economy and CO_2 emissions in respect of the marketing of new passenger cars OJ 2000 L 12/16

Directive 2009/30/EC amending Directive 98/70/EC as regards the specification of petrol, diesel and gas-oil and introducing a mechanism to monitor and reduce greenhouse gas emissions OJ 2009 L 140/88

Fluorinated Gases

Regulation (EC) No. 842/2006 on certain fluorinated greenhouse gases OJ 2006 L 161/1

Forests and Agriculture

Decision No. 529/2013/EU on accounting rules on greenhouse gas emissions and removals resulting from activities relating to land use, land-use change and forestry and on information concerning actions relating to those activities OJ 2013 L 165/80

As mentioned earlier, a full discussion of EU climate change law within the confines of any one chapter has become a practical impossibility. This contribution focuses on the Renewable Energy Directive, which is examined in greater detail in the next section, and the ETS. The main purpose of the information boxes above is to offer a starting point for further inquiry and to convey a general sense of the enormity of the climate change agenda for law and regulation.

Climate Change as a Multi-Level Governance Challenge: The Example of Renewable Energy

Successful climate change abatement policies require fundamental social change. Conducting business as usual will not stabilise global GHG emissions, but will instead propel society towards dramatic temperature hikes of 4 to 6 degrees Celsius by 2100, far beyond the maximum 2 degrees' rise targeted by the Paris Agreement.[48] Hence, the mission of EU climate change mitigation law is not just to prevent deterioration but to foster large-scale conversion in how energy is sourced and deployed in business and at the domestic level across the EU. Climate change action requires governments to rethink *how* business is done and even *what* business is done. Successful implementation will have a deep impact on a wide range of domestic policies, from industrial policy and planning to tourism, trade and even defence. Indeed, the potential impact of EU climate change law is much more acute and intensive than it is in any other area of EU environmental governance. Unsurprisingly, the depth of the climate change challenge heightens concerns about the extent to which EU law erodes national sovereignty and limits governments' ability to represent and protect the countries' chief economic interests. EU climate change law must therefore perform a difficult balancing act of being proactive and resolute while at the same time flexible and respectful of national differences.

Renewable Energy Policy in the EU: Reconciling European Ambition with National Differentiation through Multi-Level Governance

EU law and policy regarding renewable energy sources aptly illustrate the depth of the climate change challenge and the political and legal tensions in its wake. The EU has committed to increase the share of renewable energy (RE) in the energy mix to 20 per cent by 2020, and 27 per cent by 2030. To compare, the overall RE share in the EU-27 was 8.1 per cent in 2005.[49] According to the

---

[48] Heyvaert, 'Governing Climate Change', 817.
[49] Manjola Banja, Nicolae Scarlat, Fabio Monforti-Ferrario and Jean-François Dallemand, 'Renewable Energy Progress in EU 27, 2005–2020', *Joint Research Centre Scientific and Policy*

most recent figures, it currently stands at approximately 15.9 per cent.[50] The commitment evidently represents a sizeable shift in energy provision: the share of RE has almost doubled in the past ten years, and it needs to expand further in the next ten years to keep the EU on track for its 2027 target. It also requires a significant degree of deliberate intervention in the market: under business-as-usual assumptions, the share of RE in gross final energy consumption would have been predicted to rise to 12.7 per cent by 2020.[51]

There is some cause for optimism regarding the prospects of RE in Europe. The EU is generally on track to meet its 2020 target.[52] Moreover, the expanding production and use of RE may serve more than Member States' environmental interests. Since the 1990s, the argument has been made repeatedly that, in addition to reducing GHG emissions, RE can harness energy security, lead to job creation in innovation technologies[53] and improve economic competitiveness.[54] These are highly attractive claims. The volatility in the global oil and gas markets, fuelled by intractable geo-political problems including the disputes between Ukraine and Russia and the political instability in the Middle East, have put the need for energy security foremost in Member States' minds.[55] The persistent after-effects of the global economic crash, the fragility of the Eurozone, the ever-present threat of the EU backsliding into recession and, now, the new and still very much uncertain challenges represented by the UK's intended departure from the EU, have made employment and competitiveness the incontrovertible priorities within and among EU States. Yet underneath the encouraging figures and the apparent synergy between RE, energy security and economic growth, lurks a more complex reality. Energy policy in the EU requires the careful orchestration of EU and national roles and responsibilities to be able to achieve its triple objective of climate change mitigation, energy security and economic competitiveness. It is an expressive example of multi-level governance in action, and illustrates both the strengths and challenges that complex regimes face.

An important consideration here, is that this push for innovation in energy sourcing happens in a market that was formerly a State monopoly and that still

---

Reports, Report EUR 26481 (EN), 2013, 7, available at: http://iet.jrc.ec.europa.eu/remea/sites/remea/files/re_progress_in_eu_27_2005–2020_online_final.pdf.

[50] EurObserv'ER, *The State of Renewable Energies in Europe* (2015 Edition), available at: www.eurobserv-er.org/15th-annual-overview-barometer/.

[51] Pantelis Capros, Leonidas Mantzos, Leonida Parousos, Nikolaos Tasios, Ger Klassen and Tom Van Ierland, 'Analysis of the EU Policy Package on Climate Change and Renewables' (2011) 39, *Energy Policy* 1476–1485, at 1477.

[52] Commission Renewable Energy Progress Report, 15 June 2015, COM(2015)293 final.

[53] Commission Energy Roadmap 2050, 15 December 2011, COM(2011)885 final, 9.

[54] Roger Hildingsson, Johannes Stripple and Andrew Jordan, 'Renewable Energies: A Continuing Balancing Act?' in Andrew Jordan, Dave Huitema, Harro van Asselt, Tim Rayner and Frans Berkhout (eds.), *Climate Change Policy in the European Union: Confronting the Dilemmas of Mitigation and Adaptation?* (Cambridge University Press, 2011), 108.

[55] Vanessa Mock, 'EU, Russia, Ukraine to Meet on Energy Security; Crisis in Ukraine has Sparked Fears about the Supply of Gas to Europe' *Wall Street Journal*, 29 April 2014.

retains monopolistic features.[56] Moreover, energy is a public good, the supply and consumption of which are pivotal to the functioning of each country's economy. These factors, together with the need for energy security, mean that the development of an internal market for energy, which is a key component of the EU's competitiveness and growth strategy, needs to be structured as a gradual and step-wise process.[57] Unfettered liberalisation may not threaten energy security from an EU perspective, but it certainly does so from a national point of view, as it entails the risk that domestic energy suppliers will be outcompeted by companies in neighbouring EU States. By the same token, the economic and strategic importance of the energy sector may suppress Member States' willingness to sign up to mandatory targets and harmonised approaches towards the promotion of RE.

Moreover, the implementation of RE targets is highly politically sensitive. Given the energy sector's centrality to the economy, and the concentrated interests at stake, shifts in energy policy represent tough political challenges for Member State governments. They need to balance the short-term and often localised disruption caused by changes in energy regulation and support against the long-term, general benefits of energy innovation. Unsustainable energy production may still be sustaining local communities, and there is often no obvious compensation for their losses in the pursuit of a greener economy. Similarly, local protests against the establishment of wind power installations might be brushed off as an exponent of a not-in-my-backyard mentality (NIMBYism), but they also represent serious and legitimate concerns about who bears the costs and who reaps the rewards of environmental innovation. From this perspective, EU renewable energy policy can have significant implications for environmental justice. This constitutes a further factor complicating the adoption of ambitious and harmonised RE targets at the EU level.

Finally, the quest for energy security may turn EU Member States away from excessive reliance on fossil fuel, but it does not necessarily lure them towards renewables. RE competes with other alternative energy sources, such as shale gas and nuclear energy, which represent a different combination of risks and benefits to society from an environmental perspective, an energy security perspective, as well as a growth perspective.[58] The attractiveness of RE, relative to that of non-renewable alternative fuel energy sources, depends on many factors, including national geography and availability of natural resources, the particular energy needs of the country's dominant industries and services, historical development and even cultural preferences. France, for example, is well known for looking

---

[56] For example, energy suppliers are dependent on access to the grid, a physical network of transmission lines, substations, transformers and more that deliver electricity from the power plant to enterprises and households, to conduct their business.

[57] Hildingsson et al., 'Renewable Energies', 103.

[58] Commission Energy Roadmap 2050 COM(2011)885 final; Lucy Finchett-Maddock, 'Responding to the Private Regulation of Dissent: Climate Change Action, Popular Justice and the Right to Protest' (2013) 25(2) *Journal of Environmental Law* 293–304, at 295.

favourably upon nuclear energy.[59] Germany, on the other hand, decided after the Fukushima disaster to discontinue its investment in nuclear energy production.[60] Hence, even though the goals of climate change mitigation, energy security and economic competitiveness are shared, Member States' views on the best mix of policies and tools towards their achievement differ.

The upshot is that, although there are strong drivers towards the liberalisation, harmonisation and promotion of RE at the EU level, legal developments are kept in check by national interests to retain a high degree of control over energy law and policy. The resulting need for balance between EU-wide objectives and Member State differentiation was readily apparent in the 2001 Renewable Electricity Directive,[61] a precursor to the present Renewable Energy Directive (RED).[62] The 2001 Directive exhorted Member States to 'take appropriate steps to encourage greater consumption of electricity produced from renewable energy'[63] and, to this end, called on the Member States to set national indicative targets. The key contribution of the Directive was to lay down a framework that structured and facilitated the development of RE strategies at the national level, but Member States remained in charge of setting the actual RE targets and selecting support schemes, such as feed-in tariffs, green certification and energy taxation. The 2009 RED introduces a comparatively higher degree of centralisation, but it still retains some key balancing features that characterise EU legislation in nationally sensitive areas. Moreover, the 2014 European Council conclusions on the 2030 Climate and Energy Policy Framework herald a return to more decentralised approaches after 2020.[64] Hence, for the foreseeable future, multi-level governance is set to remain a prominent feature of EU energy policy and regulation.

The 2009 Renewable Energy Directive (RED)

The RED[65] sets out a common framework for the production and promotion of 'energy from renewable non-fossil sources', by which the Directive means wind, solar, aerothermal, geothermal, hydrothermal and ocean energy, hydropower,

---

[59] Tuula Terävainen, Markku Lehtonen and Mari Martiskainen, 'Climate Change, Energy Security, and Risk – Debating Nuclear New Build in Finland, France and the UK' (2011) 39(6) *Energy Policy* 3434–3442.

[60] Miranda A. Schreurs, 'Climate Change, Energy Security, and Risk – Debating Nuclear New Build in Finland, France and the UK' (2013) 14(1) *Theoretical Inquiries in Law* 83–108.

[61] Directive 2001/77/EC, OJ 2001 L 283/33.

[62] The Commission was scheduled to prepare a proposal for a follow-up Renewable Energy Directive, covering the 2020 to 2030 period, by end 2016.

[63] Art. 3(1) RED.

[64] European Council (23 and 24 October 2014) Conclusions EUCO 169/14 CO EUR 13 CONCL 5.

[65] Directive 2009/28/EC of the European Parliament and of the Council of 23 April 2009 on the promotion of the use of energy from renewable sources and amending and subsequently repealing Directives 2001/77/EC and 2003/30/EC establishes a common framework for the production and promotion of energy from renewable sources (RED), OJ 2009 L 140/16.

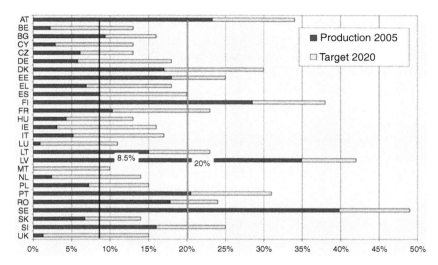

Figure 8.1 Renewable Energy Production 2005 and 2020 Targets
Source: Hans Bloem, Fabio Monforti-Ferrario, Marta Szabo and Arnulf Jäger-Waldau, 'Renewable Energy Snapshots 2010', Joint Research Centre Scientific and Technical Reports, European Union, 2010.

biomass, landfill gas, sewage treatment plant gas and biogases.[66] Article 3 and Annex I of the Directive assign each Member State a mandatory overall national target for the share of renewable energy in gross final consumption of energy by 2020 (Figure 8.1).[67] The targets encompass consumption through use of electricity, heating and cooling and transport, the last of which has a specific and uniform target of 10 per cent RE (mostly biofuel-sourced) by 2020. The targets are differentiated and range from 10 per cent (for Malta) to 49 per cent (for Sweden). Taken together, they secure the EU-wide 20 per cent target for 2020.[68]

The European Council affirmed in 2014 that national mandatory targets will be abandoned for the 2020–2030 period. Instead, the 27 per cent RE goal for 2030 will be achieved through 'Member States contributions guided by the need to deliver collectively the EU target without preventing Member States from setting their own more ambitious national targets and supporting them'. National targets will be indicative, and will be discussed and negotiated 'informally and bilaterally' between the Member States and the Commission.[69] This approach to EU policy implementation, which focuses on collective targets and de-formalises national implementation expectations, has been labelled the 'new governance

---

[66] Art. 2 RED.
[67] Pantelis et al., 'Analysis of the EU Policy Package on Climate Change and Renewables', 1477.
[68] The transport target is undifferentiated between the Member States. See *ibid.*, 1477–1478.
[69] 'Climate Governance Divides Countries, MEPs', *ENDS Europe*, 7 January 2015.

approach'.[70] It will considerably decrease the opportunities for the European Parliament to have an input on the development of EU RE policy, and reduce Member States' exposure to CJEU scrutiny. The new governance approach could therefore be said to represent a swing from supranational towards a more intergovernmental variant of multi-level governance. Moreover, in the wake of the European Council conclusions on climate change and energy targets for 2030, the new governance approach is now being mooted as a general strategy for EU energy policy.

The RED displays several characteristics of metaregulation.[71] Beyond the determination of (currently) compulsory national targets, the Directive leaves the Member States a broad degree of discretion in how to develop an implementation strategy.[72] Moreover, the RED does not mandate a harmonised approach towards the adoption of support schemes to bolster the competitiveness of RE on the energy market.[73] Instead, it 'governs the government' by focusing predominantly on harmonised procedural expectations and accountability standards to structure, support and legitimise domestic implementation.[74] Moreover, the RED contains a number of provisions that foster, but do not demand, cooperation between Member States towards the achievement of the mandatory targets. The paragraphs below zoom in on some of the RED's key provisions.

National Action Plans

The RED's main procedural expectation is that Member States draw up National Renewable Energy Action Plans (NREAPs), which map out each country's implementation strategy and include 'estimated trajectories'.[75] In accordance with the Commission template for NREAPS, estimated trajectories plot each Member State's anticipated RE deployment on a sectoral, yearly and a biannual

---

[70] Commission, 'A policy framework for climate and energy in the period from 2020 to 2030', 22 January 2014, COM(2014)015 final.

[71] Neil Gunningham, 'Environment Law, Regulation and Governance: Shifting Architectures' (2009) 21(2) *Journal of Environmental Law* 179–212.

[72] Art. 13 RED contains a limited number of minimum expectations, including the expectation that public buildings will play an exemplary role (Art. 13(5)) and that RE heating and cooling systems will be promoted in building regulations and codes (Art. 13(6)).

[73] The list of support schemes includes, but is not restricted to: 'investment aid, tax exemptions or reductions, tax refunds, renewable energy obligation support schemes including those using green certificates, and direct price support schemes including feed-in tariffs and premium payments' (Art. 2(k) RED). During the preparatory stages of the RED, the European Commission showed a preference for the development of an EU-wide system of renewable energy support through green certificates quota and trading, but this preference was not shared by the majority of the Member States. See Lee, *EU Environmental Law, Governance and Decision-Making*, 149.

[74] See e.g. Art. 5 RED, which lays down a harmonised methodology to calculate the share of RE in gross final energy consumption; Art. 13 RED, which lays down administrative governance standards for the authorisation, certification and licensing of RE enterprises; and Art. 14 RED, which calls on Member States to provide information and training.

[75] Art. 4(1) and Annex VI RED. All NREAPs are available at: http://ec.europa.eu/energy/node/71.

basis.[76] The trajectories constitute an important accountability mechanism. The 20 per cent RE by 2020 goal imbues Member State action with a long-term perspective, but it also defers accountability. The possibility of non-compliance litigation almost ten years into the future is unlikely to hold the government of the day in line. The trajectories counteract this responsiveness deficit. In combination with the biannual performance reports that each Member State must submit,[77] they constitute a means for the Commission (as well as other EU institutions and fellow Member States) to check in a somewhat timely manner whether Member States are on track towards 2020. It is, however, a fairly soft check: Article 3(4) RED provides that if Member States fail to meet their indicative targets in the two preceding years, they 'shall submit an amended national renewable energy action plan to the Commission by 30 June of the following year, setting out adequate and proportionate measures to re-join, within a reasonable timetable, the indicative trajectory'. The Commission may also issue recommendations on the basis of the NREAPs.[78] However, since the indicative trajectories are non-binding, it is highly unlikely that a failure to meet them could, in itself, constitute the basis for an infringement proceeding.

Cooperation between Member States
Articles 6 to 11 RED provide a framework that infuses the EU's renewable energy strategy with a degree of 'tradability'. To achieve national targets, Member States may stimulate the production and consumption of RE within their own borders, but they may also opt to exchange units of renewable energy through statistical transfers 'of a specified amount of energy from renewable sources from one Member State to another Member State'.[79] This provision enables Member States with more limited capacity in RE production to negotiate with Member States with greater RE capacity and 'buy' a segment of their performance. The approach is intended to boost both efficient allocation and economies of scale in RE production, which could potentially make RE more competitive with traditional energy sources and, thus, speed up market penetration.[80] On the other hand, if Member States can 'transfer away' any excess amount of renewable energy produced, they may have fewer incentives to overshoot the national target. Conversely, countries receiving the transfer may rely more on foreign production to meet their own national targets, and be less inclined to invest in long-term domestic RE production.[81]

Alternatively, national targets may be achieved through 'joint projects', either between EU Member States (Articles 7 and 8 RED) or in cooperation with third

---

[76] Commission Decision of 30 June 2009 establishing a template for National Renewable Energy Action Plans under Directive 2009/28/EC, C(2009)5174–1.
[77] Art. 23 RED The reports must indicate the RE share achieved in the preceding two years, as well as an explanation and evaluation of the domestic supports mechanisms put in place.
[78] Art. 3(5) RED.   [79] Art. 6(1) RED.   [80] See http://ec.europa.eu/energy/node/154.
[81] Gerd Winter, 'The Climate is No Commodity: Taking Stock of the Emissions Trading System' (2010) 22(1) *Journal of Environmental Law* 1–25.

countries (Articles 9 and 10 RED). To count towards the achievement of Member States' targets, the following conditions must be met:

- the electricity must be consumed in the EU;
- the electricity must be produced by a newly constructed installation (after June 2009); and
- the quantity of electricity produced and exported must not benefit from any other support.

So far, cooperative ventures between Member States, and Member States and third countries, remain a largely theoretical proposition. A clear majority of Member States confirmed in their NREAPs that they had no plans to introduce flexible mechanisms in the foreseeable future, and anticipated meeting their targets through domestic production and use.[82] Several Member States expressed their endorsement of cooperation in principle, and indicated a potential interest in cooperating, but so far little firm action has been undertaken to put the joint initiatives into practice. Of the countries that mentioned the prospect of engaging in statistical transfers, most anticipated to be able to export excess; only four Member States indicated that they might need to boost their domestic quota through imports.[83] If a market for transfers does emerge, it could be predominantly supply-driven.

One factor that arguably suppresses Member States' appetite for cooperation is the concern for energy security, and uncertainty about the impact of joint projects on national support schemes.[84] Moreover, the slow uptake of flexible mechanisms may illustrate that, in spite of earlier assumptions, market-based approaches need an extensive administrative infrastructure to flourish. As will be explored in the next section, this is a lesson that has vividly imposed itself in the context of EU emissions trading. Similarly, with regard to the flexible mechanisms for RE, several Member State NREAPs assert that, in the absence of a more detailed regulatory framework for statistical transfers and joint projects, it is difficult to go beyond generic expressions of approval.

Access to the Grid and Guarantees of Origin

Electric energy needs to be fed into 'the grid', a physical network of transmission and distribution lines operated by one or more control centres, to be delivered to

[82] See http://iet.jrc.ec.europa.eu/remea/national-renewable-energy-action-plans-nreaps. No plans for Austria, Croatia, Cyprus, the Czech Republic, Estonia, Finland, Germany, Greece, Latvia, Lithuania, Ireland, the Netherlands, Poland, Portugal, Romania, Slovakia, Spain, Sweden or the UK. France, Belgium, Denmark, Estonia and Hungary expressed a potential interest in flexible mechanisms but have no actual plans.
[83] France, Bulgaria, Denmark, Estonia, Germany, Ireland, Lithuania and Spain anticipate being in a position to sell. Italy, Luxembourg, Malta and Slovenia indicate they may need to import.
[84] Commission Communication on delivering the internal electricity market and making the most of public intervention, 5 November 2013, SWD (2013) 440 final, 4.

households and enterprises. Achievement of the 20 per cent RE final consumption target therefore hinges on RE producers obtaining effective access to the grid. This is the preoccupation of Article 16 RED, which calls for both the development and further enhancement of the grid to accommodate the production of electricity from RE sources, and mandates that Member States give priority or guaranteed access to RE producers.

Once energy enters the grid, its source becomes generally untraceable. To overcome this problem, Article 15 RED requires all Member States to ensure the issuance of a 'guarantee of origin', which attests renewable sourcing. The guarantee contains a standardised set of information,[85] and must be recognised by all Member States. Importantly though, the guarantee's function is simply that: proof of renewable sourcing. As confirmed in recent ECJ case law, it is not equivalent to any renewable or green certificate that a Member State may issue in the context of a national support scheme.[86]

The Difficult Question of Biofuels

Biofuels and bioliquids are among the renewable energy sources covered in the RED, but their regulation presents a number of special challenges. The Directive stipulates an across-the-board fixed target of 10 per cent RE use in the transport sector. Practically, this target will be met mostly through biofuels, which creates a specific and growing demand for this particular RE source.

Unfortunately, the green credentials of biofuels have proved questionable.[87] Conventional biofuels and bioliquids, which are produced from cereal and other starch-rich crops (such as maize), sugars and oil crops, do not necessarily achieve significant GHG savings compared to 'regular' fuels. Large-scale farming is typically a carbon-intensive industry, and is likely to take a significant toll on local biodiversity, soil, air and water resources. Moreover, the introduction of biofuel crops either results in additional land being claimed for farming, or in an intensification of farming practices to increase the yield. The expansion of farm land happens because land is newly cleared for biofuel production (direct land-use change), or because it displaces traditional food, feed and textile crops, triggering pressures for expansion or intensification elsewhere (indirect land-use change). Whether direct or indirect, land use changes are particularly problematic if the land being claimed is rich in biodiversity and/or a productive carbon sink. The upshot is that shifting from fossil fuels to biofuels may produce what Jolene Lin refers to as 'negative GHG savings',[88] as well as a significant deterioration of the natural environment.

---

[85] Art. 15(6) RED.
[86] C-573/12 *Ålands Vindkraft* ECLI:EU:C:2014:2037; Joined Cases of C-204/12 and C-208/12 *Essent Belgium* ECLI:EU:C:2014:2192.
[87] Annie Dufey, 'Biofuels Production, Trade and Sustainable Development: Emerging Issues', IIED Sustainable Markets Discussion Paper No. 2 (2006), 36–45.
[88] Jolene Lin, 'Governing Biofuels: A Principal–Agent Analysis of the European Union Biofuels Certification Regimes and the Clean Development Mechanism' (2011) 24(1) *Journal of Environmental Law* 48–49.

Biofuels are also more easily transportable than, say, wind or solar-powered energy. Consequently, in developing a regime for the environmentally sound deployment of biofuels, the EU must take into account international trade.[89] Since many of the negative carbon and environmental impacts of biofuels are a consequence of how they are produced, the EU finds itself in a difficult and legally precarious situation. The environmental soundness of production typically does not show up in the end product, which means that environmental regulation must target the process itself. But process standards are difficult to formulate and harder to monitor, especially when the production takes place outside EU jurisdiction. Moreover, standards that regulate production and processing methods (PPM) are at greater risk of violating international trade law than product standards.[90]

How, then, does EU law respond to the complexities of responsibly integrating biofuels into its renewable energy strategy? A pivotal provision is Article 17 RED, which lays down sustainability criteria for biofuels. The criteria correspond with those laid down in the 2009 Fuel Quality Directive,[91] which forms part of the energy efficiency pillar of the EU's climate change package and mandates a 6 per cent reduction in GHG emissions by 2020. To count towards the 20 per cent RE target, biofuels must meet the following minimum criteria:

- Biofuels must achieve greenhouse gas savings of at least 35 per cent in comparison to fossil fuels. This savings requirement rises to 50 per cent in 2017. In 2018, it rises again to 60 per cent for production plants installed after 2016. All life-cycle emissions are taken into account when calculating greenhouse gas savings. This includes emissions from cultivation, processing and transport.
- Biofuels production should not negatively impact the carbon capacity and environmental significance of the land. Hence, biofuel crops cannot be grown in areas converted from land with previously high carbon stock such as wetlands or forests, or from land enjoying a high biodiversity value, or from land that was formerly peatland.

---

[89] Hartmut Kahl, 'Trade Law Constraints to Renewable Regional Energy Support Schemes' in Marjan Peeters and Thomas Schomerus (eds.), *Renewable Energy Law in the EU Legal Perspectives on Bottom-up Approaches* (Edward Elgar, 2014), 43.

[90] William A Kerr and Laura Loppacher, 'Trading Biofuels – Will International Trade Law Be a Constraint?' (2005) 6 *Current Agriculture, Food and Resource Issues*, 50–62, at 59; Stephanie Switzer, 'International Trade Law and The Environment: Designing a Legal Framework to Curtail the Import of Unsustainably Produced Biofuels' (2007) 6(1) *Journal of International Trade Law and Policy* 30–44.

[91] Directive 2009/30/EC amending Directive 98/70/EC as regards the specification of petrol, diesel and gas-oil and introducing a mechanism to monitor and reduce greenhouse gas emissions, OJ 2009 L140/88, Art. 7(b).

The sustainability criteria for biofuels are further detailed in the 2015 Biofuels Directive,[92] which focuses on the climate change risks posed by indirect land use change (ILUC). The Biofuels Directive, *inter alia*, affirms the 60 per cent energy savings goal; introduces an indicative 0.5 per cent target for 'advanced biofuels', which are generated from non-food sources; and limits the share of biofuels from crops grown on agricultural land that can be counted towards the 2020 targets to 7 per cent. The latter cap is significantly more generous than the 5 per cent maximum in the original Commission proposal,[93] which exceeded the ambitions of the European Parliament (supporting a 6 per cent cap) and, particularly, those of the Council, which favoured 7 per cent.[94] The differences in ambition illustrate both the political sensitivity and path dependency of energy sourcing strategies: a relative drop in the amount of conventional biofuels that can count towards the RE target may further environmental objectives, but it may undermine investment choices made on the basis of the 2009 targets, and lead to an oversupply in biofuel crops, resulting in price volatility and increased pressure on the EU agricultural sector. Here again, the path towards 'win–wins' for climate change mitigation, energy security and competitiveness proves more winding and treacherous in practice than the theory suggests.

To assess compliance with the sustainability criteria, the EU relies on certification schemes. However, these schemes are not run by either the Commission or national regulatory authorities at the Member State level; they are managed by a variety of transnational actors such as intergovernmental organisations, NGOs and business associations. The Commission's job is to develop benchmarks for acceptable certification schemes and decide on requests for recognition submitted by certification scheme operators.[95] The biofuels sustainability regime therefore relies on the participation of public and private actors, which may operate at international, regional or (sub) national levels, to secure the effective implementation of its criteria. It represents an advanced form of transnational or 'hybrid' multi-level governance, which is no longer limited to the interaction between the European and the Member State level, but encompasses a broader range of transnational actors.[96]

---

[92] Directive (EU) 2015/1513 of the European Parliament and of the Council of 9 September 2015 amending Directive 98/70/EC relating to the quality of petrol and diesel fuels and amending Directive 2009/28/EC on the promotion of the use of energy from renewable sources, OJ 2015 L239/1.

[93] Proposal for a Directive of the European Parliament and of the Council amending Directive 98/70/EC relating to the quality of petrol and diesel fuels and amending Directive 2009/28/EC on the promotion of the use of energy from renewable sources COM(2012)595 final, 17 October 2012.

[94] 'Lead MEP Calls for Stronger Biofuel Reform', *ENDS Europe*, 5 January 2015.

[95] For further detail on the benchmarking and certification process, see Lin, 'Governing Biofuels', 53–58.

[96] Cf. Veerle Heyvaert, 'What's in a Name? The Covenant of Mayors as Transnational Environmental Regulation' (2013) 22(1) *Review of European, Comparative and International Environmental Law* 78–90.

A final question to consider is whether the 60 per cent savings required, combined with the sustainability criteria and certification requirements for biofuels that count towards the renewable energy target, are compatible with international trade law. The EU's biofuels policy remains, thus far, untested on this score, but a number of factors suggest that it may be vulnerable to challenge. As observed earlier, the WTO Dispute Settlement Bodies (DSB) traditionally take a firmer line with PPM-based restrictions than with product requirements.[97] The EU biofuels provisions by and large fall within the former category. If conventional biofuels are considered 'like products' to those biofuels that meet the GHG savings and sustainability criteria, it may be very difficult for the EU to justify its proposed cap.[98] Moreover, although existing case law suggests that the WTO DSB would probably accept climate change measures as justifiable exceptions to the GATT free trade prescriptions,[99] this is yet to be explicitly confirmed, and it may not salvage the EU's approach if it is considered arbitrarily to discriminate between 'sustainable' and 'regular' biofuels.

National Support Schemes

As observed in the RED, 'Member States have different renewable energy potentials and operate different schemes of support' for green energy.[100] For instance, Member States may boost renewable energy production through green energy certification. In this case, renewable energy producers receive certificates for every predetermined quantity of RE produced, which they may sell either together with the energy or separately. The scheme works in combination with domestically set quotas that require obligated parties (which may be the generators, the suppliers or the consumers) to submit green certificates to cover a proportion of their overall energy production, distribution or use. The certificate gets around the problem that, once fed into the grid, the provenance of energy is hard to trace, by creating recorded proof of its creation and making this proof tradable. Green certification was the approach to stimulating RE consumption championed by the European Commission, which in the early 2000s aspired to elevate it to the harmonised EU-approach to RE support.[101] However, the initiative did not find favour with a number of Member States, including Spain and Germany, which preferred alternative schemes such as feed-

---

[97] See nn. 93 and 94, above.

[98] Alan Swinbank and Carsten Daugbjerg, 'Improving EU Biofuels Policy? Greenhouse Gas Emissions, Policy Efficiency, and WTO Compatibility' (2013) 47(4) *Journal of World Trade* 813–834.

[99] Articles III and XX GATT. WTO Appellate Body Report, United States – Import Prohibition of Certain Shrimp and Shrimp Products (US – Shrimp), WT/DS58/AB/R, adopted 6 November 1998; WTO Appellate Body Report, United States – Standards for Reformulated and Conventional Gasoline (US – Gasoline), WT/DS2/AB/R, adopted 20 May 1996.

[100] RED, Preamble, 25.

[101] Electricity from renewable energy sources and the internal electricity market. Commission working document. SEC(99)470 final, 13 April 1999.

in tariffs.[102] Feed-in tariffs guarantee RE producers access to the grid at a fixed tariff, under fixed conditions, and for a fixed period of time. Feed-in tariffs are designed to facilitate market access in the transition period during which it is difficult for new market entrants to offer competitive prices compared to the incumbents.[103] Ultimately, attempts to harmonise national support schemes failed: the 2009 RED leaves the choice of scheme to the Member State and, instead, focuses on harmonising the general conditions for the implementation of such schemes. Thus, Article 13(2) requires that the technical specifications that facilities must meet to qualify for national support should be clearly defined and, where available, be expressed with reference to European standards.

Whichever support scheme is preferred at the national level, a few general points demand reflection. First, under business-as-usual conditions the EU is predicted to fall short of its 20 per cent RE target by 2020. Support schemes are, therefore, an intrinsic part of the EU's climate change policy. Secondly, established national support schemes will typically only support domestically produced renewable energy. The RED foresees the possibility of inter-State cooperation but, as discussed earlier, so far few Member States have shown an inclination to pursue cooperative ventures for renewable energy development. The overwhelmingly domestic focus of national support schemes puts national RE policies on a potential collision course with free movement principles, and uncovers the tension between competing conceptualisations of competitiveness and energy security as a national or, alternatively, a European mandate.

Free Movement of Renewable Energy: Navigating between the Goals of Trade Liberalisation, Environmental Protection and National Control over Energy Policy

The compatibility of domestic energy support schemes with the free movement prescriptions of Article 34 TFEU has been the subject of a compact but rich vein of CJEU case law. The first landmark case, *Campus Oil*,[104] concerned an Irish requirement that national oil companies source a proportion of their oil from an Irish refinery. Although the main driver behind the policy was to secure the economic viability of the refinery, and although economic justifications as a rule cannot be invoked to exculpate free movement restrictions, the CJEU permitted the requirement. In its submission, the Irish government emphasised that keeping the refinery operational was a matter of strategic importance and internal security for the Irish Republic. On this basis, the CJEU reasoned that the requirement fell within the public policy exception in Article 36 TFEU.

---

[102] Hildingsson et al., 'Renewable Energies', 109–110.
[103] Doerte Fouquet and Thomas B. Johansson, 'European Renewable Energy Policy at Crossroads – Focus on Electricity Support Mechanisms' (2008) 36(11) *Energy Policy* 4079–4092.
[104] C-72/83 ECLI:EU:C:1984:256.

Campus Oil shows a European Court that is arguably permissive in its understanding of the public policy exception as applied to energy policy, particularly considering the overtly discriminatory nature of the Irish scheme. Yet in assessing its relevance to determine the legality of national support schemes under the RED, two additional factors need to be considered. First, the Irish policy in *Campus Oil* was not justified on the basis of environmental considerations. Secondly, the decision precedes the ongoing (and still incomplete) EU programme towards the liberalisation of energy markets. To understand how these factors impact on the compatibility of national support schemes with Article 34 TFEU, we must turn to the decisions in *PreussenElektra*, *Ålands Vindkraft* and, most recently, *Essent*.[105]

In each case, the contested measure was part of a national strategy to promote RE production: a requirement that electricity retailers source a proportion of their electricity from wind farms in *PreussenElektra* and a requirement that energy distributors and major users submit green energy certificates in proportion to their energy sale and use in *Essent* and *Ålands Vindkraft*. Each policy overwhelmingly or exclusively favoured domestic RE producers: only German wind farms could supply electricity to retailers under the scheme in *PreussenElektra* and only certificates issued by the Swedish (*Ålands Vindkraft*) or Flemish (*Essent*) authorities counted towards the quotas. To qualify for the certificates, RE producers needed to be established respectively in Sweden or Norway (*Ålands Vindkraft*) or Belgium (*Essent*).

Notwithstanding the similarities, *PreussenElektra*, *Ålands Vindkraft* and *Essent* each have a distinctive feature. *PreussenElektra* was decided in 2001, when the liberalisation and integration of EU energy markets was far less advanced than it is now. The scheme in *Essent* was adopted under the predecessors of the 2009 RED (Directives 2001/77 and 2003/54), which asked Member States to develop indicative RE targets but did not impose mandatory national targets for RE as a proportion of final energy consumption. Finally, although the CJEU ruling precedes the decision in *Essent*, the measures under scrutiny in *Ålands Vindkraft*, in contrast, were the first to be reviewed in the context of the 2009 RED. Addressing the question whether national support schemes that favour and potentially disadvantage national production of renewable energy are caught by the prohibition on trade restrictions in Article 34 TFEU, the CJEU in each instance answered in the affirmative. This means that national support measures for renewable energy are not exempt from CJEU scrutiny. However, in each of the three cases the CJEU also found that the contested measures were 'useful for the protection of the environment inasmuch as [they contribute] to the reduction in greenhouse gas emissions, which are amongst the main causes of climate change that the European Union and its Member States have pledged to combat'.[106] What is more, the Court observed that an increased use of RE

---

[105] C-379/98 *PreussenElektra* ECLI:EU:C:2001:160; C-573/12 *Ålands Vindkraft* ECLI:EU:C:2014:2037; Joined Cases of C-204/12 and C-208/12 *Essent Belgium* ECLI:EU:C:2014:2192. For further discussion, see also Chapter 3.

[106] *Essent* at 91, referring to *Alands*, at 75.

contributes towards the protection of the health and life of humans, animals and plants, the policy grounds enshrined in Article 36 TFEU on the basis of which Member States may justify trade restrictive measures, even if they are discriminatory in design or impact, as the RE national support schemes were. Moreover, the decision to exclude foreign RE producers, or externally generated certificates in the case of *Essent*, from the scope of the support scheme was an acceptable way for a Member State to ensure that its RE strategy would effectively stimulate RE production as well as consumption within the Member State and to exercise a degree of control over the national energy mix. The contested measures were, therefore, in compliance with the proportionality principle.

The *PreussenElektra-Ålands Vindkraft-Essent* triptych settles the question of whether national RE strategies may favour local RE production. However, the endurance of the CJEU's vision may be less guaranteed than the high similarity of argumentation in the three judgments suggests. First, the creation of a European Energy Union, by pooling resources, combining infrastructures and uniting negotiating power vis-à-vis third countries, is a priority agenda point of the Juncker Commission.[107] It is questionable whether national understandings of energy security, which reduce willingness to rely on energy supply from other Member States, will continue to fit within a unified model that squarely frames energy security and efficiency as collective, European missions. Moreover, the environmental tenet of the CJEU's reasoning is weak. As emphasised in Advocate General Bot's Opinions in both *Ålands Vindkraft* and *Essent*, from a climate change perspective it does not matter where renewable energy is generated. Arguably, the inclusion of foreign producers in national support schemes could foster economies of scale and, thus, make the production of green energy more cost-effective, which could in turn speed up market penetration. Evidently, the CJEU decided differently, but the AG opinions serve as a question mark that continues to invite discussion and, potentially, reconsideration. Finally, the existence of mandatory national RE targets in *Ålands Vindkraft* played a significant part in explaining the need for Member States to keep a firm hand on domestic energy production and usage patterns. Yet mandatory targets will expire in 2020, and will not be reissued for the 2020–2030 period. It may not be a decisive element – the backdrop of indicative targets in *Essent* did not stop the Court from considering the exclusion of foreign certificates acceptable – but it is yet another factor that cautions us to keep a watchful eye on the renewable energy–energy security–market liberalisation nexus.

The Challenge of a Regulation-Based Market

Unquestionably the most famous tenet of the EU's Climate Change Package is the Emissions Trading System (ETS or EU ETS). The ETS was established in

---

[107] Jean-Claude Juncker, 'A New Start for Europe: My Agenda for Jobs, Growth, Fairness and Democratic Change. Political Guidelines for the Next European Commission', Opening Statement in the European Parliament Plenary Session (Strasbourg, 22 October 2014), available at: http://ec.europa.eu/priorities/docs/pg_en.pdf#page=6.

the 2003 Emissions Trading Directive (ETD)[108] and adopts a cap-and-trade approach to emissions control. Operators targeted in the ETD include GHG-intensive sectors such as power plants, steel mills and, controversially, commercial airlines (see above).[109] Covered enterprises must obtain emissions allowances, each of which conveys the right to emit one tonne of CO_2 (or its equivalent in nitrous oxide or perfluorocarbons) and annually surrender sufficient allowances to cover their emissions. The total number of allowances issued corresponds to an overall emissions cap which, as of Phase III of the ETD,[110] is determined centrally for all Member States and which decreases by 1.74 per cent annually.[111] The cap is fixed at a level that should guarantee that, by 2020, ETS sectors will have reduced their GHG emissions by at least 20 per cent compared to 2005. In accordance with the recently adopted 2020–2030 strategy for Phase IV, GHG emissions within the ETS sectors are to drop an additional 20 per cent by 2030.[112] To achieve this, the overall cap will need to come down by 2.2 per cent annually from 2021.[113] The Phase IV targets are confirmed in a 2015 Commission proposal to amend the ETD, and are yet to be agreed upon by the Council and European Parliament.[114]

The ETS as Market-Based Regulation

The EU ETS is a grand experiment in market-based regulation, significantly surpassing previous models (such as the US Acid Rain Program)[115] and alternative carbon markets in scope and scale. It is designed to harness market mechanisms in service of the efficient delivery of regulatory outcomes. Operators that own excess allowances can trade these on the open market, which should incentivise investment in green innovation. Through the Linking

---

[108] Directive 2003/87/EC of the European Parliament and of the Council of 13 October 2003 establishing a scheme for greenhouse gas emissions allowance trading within the Community and amending Council Directive 96/61/EC, OJ 2003 L 275/32.

[109] Annex 1, ETD.

[110] The implementation of the ETD is organised in different phases, the start and end dates of which coincide with key points in EU and international climate change policy. The initial period (Phase I) started at the entry into force of the ETD in 2005 and ran until 2008. Phase II covered the Kyoto compliance period between 2008 and 2012. We are currently in Phase III, which will expire in 2020.

[111] The total number of allowances for 2017 is 1,931,244,800. Assuming the continued inclusion of the UK in the EU ETS, this total will reduce by 38,264,264 allowances per year until 2020.

[112] See n. 39, above.   [113] See http://ec.europa.eu/clima/policies/ets/index_en.htm.

[114] Proposal for a Directive of the European Parliament and of the Council amending Directive 2003/87/EC to enhance cost-effective emissions reductions and low-carbon investments, COM(2015)337 final, 15 July 2015.

[115] A. Denny Ellerman, Paul L. Joskow, Richard Schmalensee, Juan-Pablo Montero and Elizabeth M. Bailey, *Markets for Clean Air: The US Acid Rain Program* (Cambridge University Press, 2000).

Directive,[116] Emission Reduction Units (ERUs) obtained via Joint Implementation under the Kyoto Protocol, and Certified Emission Reductions (CERs) issued by the Clean Development Mechanism (CDM), can be converted into allowances and offset against ETS emissions within the EU. The possibility of trading allowances, or balancing domestic emissions with emissions reductions achieved outside the EU, holds out the promise of emissions reductions happening more cost-effectively than under a command-and-control approach with uniform emissions reduction standards. Under market-based regulation, sectors that can innovate cheaply will make the greatest cuts in emissions. Those for whom emissions reductions are expensive will hold onto their allowances and, if necessary, purchase allowances freed up through emissions reductions elsewhere.

Emissions trading has become a part of the European regulatory landscape, yet its introduction was far from unproblematic and its future success remains highly precarious. The history of the EU ETS offers a wealth of lessons in the legal challenges that accompany the deliberate creation of a new market to support a regulatory strategy. They include, to name but a few: the legal tussles over acceptable national allocation of allowances in compliance with the overall cap;[117] the myriad challenges involved in the establishment of reliable, verifiable and compatible monitoring systems for emissions and registration regimes for allowances;[118] the scope for and need to combat fraud in allowances trade;[119] the questions surrounding the legal status of emissions allowances as a newly created commodity;[120] and so on. The EU ETS has also invigorated extensive debates about the pros and cons of incentive-based regulation compared to command-and-control and/or alternative regulatory approaches and about the extent and ethics of commodification.

The sections below highlight two important messages that emerge from the EU ETS experience but that also potentially transcend the context of GHG emissions trading. The ETS reveals that attempts to harness the market for regulation infuse a high degree of complexity into regulatory design and decision-making. First, they introduce a new and challenging narrative into effectiveness assessments. Secondly, the use of market-based regulation has resulted in the construction of a heavily regulation-based market. Keeping this market afloat

---

[116] Directive 2004/101/EC establishing a scheme for greenhouse gas emissions allowance trading within the Community, in respect of the Kyoto Protocol's project mechanisms, OJ 2004 L 338/18.
[117] E.g. Christoph Böhringer and Andreas Lange, 'Mission Impossible!? On the Harmonization of National Allocation Plans under the EU Emissions Trading Directive' (2005) 27(1) *Journal of Regulatory Economics* 81–94.
[118] See the literature review in Valentin Bellassen et al., 'Monitoring, Reporting and Verifying Emissions in the Climate Economy' (2015) 5 *Nature Climate Change* 319–328.
[119] Katherine Nield and Ricardo Pereira, 'Fraud on the European Union Emissions Trading Scheme: Effects, Vulnerabilities and Regulatory Reform' (2011) 20(6) *European Energy and Environmental Law Review* 255–289.
[120] Sabina Manea, 'Defining Emissions Entitlements in the Constitution of the EU Emissions Trading System' (2012) 1(2) *Transnational Environmental Law* 303–323.

demands the ongoing, dedicated investment of regulatory resources and ingenuity.

Gauging the Effectiveness of Market-Based Regulation

A first lesson regards the consequences of adopting incentive-based environmental strategies for the conceptualisation of regulatory effectiveness. The EU ETS experience shows that, when it comes to evaluating effectiveness, market performance and environmental performance have become deeply entangled. The most frequently used yardstick to gauge how well (or poorly) the ETS is working is the price per emissions allowance or 'carbon price'. There is some justification for this: economists estimate that carbon allowances, currently trading at approximately €4.7/unit,[121] would need to be priced at €30 or above to stimulate innovation.[122] At lower prices, it remains more efficient for operators to purchase extra allowances than to invest in change. Hence, market transactions can help speed up the rate of innovation and, potentially, enable the EU to commit to more ambitious reduction targets on an accelerated schedule. Moreover, the availability of a unit price as a quantified, straightforward benchmark of regulatory success is highly appealing to analysts of regulatory effectiveness, given the well-documented complexity of accurately assessing the impact of more traditional measures such as emissions limits and technical standards.[123]

The equation of market performance with environmental performance is, however, not unproblematic. Arguably, a focus on the 'trade' pillar of the cap and trade regime diverts attention away from the ETS's true engine for change, namely, the gradually tightening cap.[124] If the cap is effectively enforced, reduction targets will be met regardless of the carbon price. Indeed, it is possible to conceive of scenarios where the carbon price is low yet the environmental targets of the regime are being achieved, for example if operators offset their GHG emissions against reductions achieved in the developing world (see below). There is, therefore, a risk that a low carbon price could be used to discredit the effectiveness of EU climate change policies that, from an environmental perspective, are nonetheless delivering. Moreover, efforts to support the market in allowances may not necessarily be the most effective to achieve rapid GHG emissions reductions. Potentially, regulatory authorities could be led to prioritise salvaging the ailing carbon market over investing the limited regulatory resources at their disposal into alternative, perhaps more effective, approaches towards climate change mitigation. The 2011 disagreement between erstwhile Energy Commissioner Oettinger and Climate Change Commissioner Hedegaard over

---

[121] Data available at: www.eex.com/en#/en.
[122] Megan Darby, 'Economists Warn of "Lost Decade" Risk for EU Carbon Market', 18 February 2015, available at: www.rtcc.org/2015/02/18/economists-warn-of-lost-decade-risk-for-eu-carbon-market/.
[123] Cf. Daniel Bodansky, *The Art and Craft of International Environmental Law* (Harvard University Press, 2010), 252–253.
[124] Cf. Winter, 'The Climate is No Commodity'.

whether mandatory energy efficiency targets should be imposed on the ETS sectors, illustrates the tension. Although contributing to climate change mitigation, the concern was raised that efficiency standards would destabilise the market for emissions allowances and should therefore be avoided.[125] It appears that the choice for the market may have a severely restrictive impact on regulatory alternatives.

Managing a Regulation-Based Market

The latter observations link to the second, arguably most resounding lesson imparted after a decade of the EU ETS: markets established through regulation are high-maintenance constructions. From the outset, the EU carbon market has been plagued by deficiencies and underperformance. Pulling it back from the brink of collapse appears to be a constant regulatory endeavour. This is surprising since one of the much-vaunted benefits of market-based regulation over command-and-control is that the former produces less red tape: regulators are free to focus on the big picture while the market works out the technical details.[126] Several features of the ETS in its original design help to explain the puzzle.

The Allocation of Allowances

Many of the key causes of the sluggish EU carbon market are traceable to distributional choices made at the inception of the ETD. Most significantly, the decision was made to allocate the overwhelming majority of allowances for Phase I through grandfathering. The prospect of free allowances led the industries targeted by the ETD liberally to estimate existing emissions volumes, which affected the initial calculations for the overall cap and resulted in the over-allocation of allowances. Consequently, there was little pressure on the ETS sectors to either reduce emissions beyond business-as-usual predictions or to purchase additional allowances. In fact, many treated the receipt of this newly created asset as a windfall, the cost of which was passed on to the consumer.[127] The trade-suppressing impact of grandfathering was exacerbated by the regime in place for the EU-wide allocation of allowances during Phases I (2005–2007) and II (2008–2012) of the ETS. It was up to the Member States to draw up National Allocation Plans (NAPs) which set out both an overall estimate of emissions and the initial allocation of allowances per sector, down to the individual installations involved. In this task of estimation and allocation, global concerns of climate change and national concerns regarding the competitiveness of the ETS sectors intermingled. Consequently, NAPs tended to err on the side of generosity. This

---

[125] Heyvaert 'Governing Climate Change', 841.
[126] Bruce A. Ackerman and Richard B. Stewart, 'Reforming Environmental Law' (1985) 37 *Stanford Law Review* 1333–1365, at 1336–1337 and 1342–1343.
[127] Luca Rubini and Ingrid Jegou, 'Who'll Stop the Rain? Allocating Emissions Allowances for Free: Environmental Policy, Economics, and WTO Subsidy Law' (2012) 1(2) *Transnational Environmental Law* 325–354.

resulted, first, in acrimonious disputes between the Member States and the Commission, which was tasked with approving submitted NAPs and, on occasion, withheld this approval.[128] Secondly, the generous estimates further contributed to over-allocation.

Member State allocation has now been centralised and is, to a significant degree, systematised through the annual tightening of the overall cap by 1.74 per cent up to 2020. Grandfathering, in turn, is gradually replaced by auctioning, which forces the ETS sectors to internalise the costs of GHG emissions and, thus, provides a clearer market signal in support of emissions reduction and innovation. By 2013, slightly over 40 per cent of emissions allowances were auctioned.[129] However, a full switch to auctioning is proving contentious as Member States are nervous about the impact of cost internationalisation on the global competitiveness of the ETS sectors. Originally scheduled to be completed by 2027, the push towards auctioning now looks likely to be suspended: the October 2014 EU Council Resolution affirmed that:

> free allocation will not expire; existing measures will continue after 2020 to prevent the risk of carbon leakage due to climate policy, as long as no comparable efforts are undertaken in other major economies, with the objective of providing appropriate levels of support for sectors at risk of losing international competitiveness. The benchmarks for free allocations will be periodically reviewed in line with technological progress in the respective industry sectors. Both direct and indirect carbon costs will be taken into account, in line with the EU state aid rules so as to ensure a level-playing field. In order to maintain international competitiveness, the most efficient installations in these sectors should not face undue carbon costs leading to carbon leakage.[130]

The observations are an important reminder that regulatory choices are determined by more than considerations of efficiency. As during the start-up phase, the success of the EU ETS is vitally dependent on the willingness of the Member States to support the regime and of the energy-intensive sectors to comply with its prescriptions. In regulating and reforming the ETS, the EU must maintain a difficult balance between environmental effectiveness, economic efficiency, and political acceptability.[131]

Recession and Transnational Offsetting

Two additional factors that suppressed the carbon price were the availability of externally created credits and the economic recession. The latter negatively

---

[128] See e.g. Case C-267/11 P *Commission* v. *Latvia* ECLI:EU:C:2013:624; Case C-505/09 P *Commission* v. *Estonia* ECLI:EU:C:2012:179; Case C-504/09 P *Commission* v. *Poland* ECLI:EU:C:2012:178.

[129] See http://ec.europa.eu/clima/policies/ets/auctioning/index_en.htm.

[130] n. 39, above.

[131] Christopher Arup and Hao Zhang, 'Lessons From Regulating Carbon Offset Markets' (2015) 4(1) *Transnational Environmental Law* 69–100, at 80–88.

impacted growth in the ETS sector, producing the (admittedly very thin) silver lining that the already generously allocated allowances amply covered many operators' GHG emissions. As to the former, the option of converting CDM credits into allowances, and of using converted credits to cover EU-based emissions, increased the number of allowances in circulation, driving the carbon price down. In theory, the availability of CDM credits should not negatively affect either the push for innovation or climate change mitigation on a global scale, since the greater ease it affords to EU-based operators in meeting their obligations is offset against investment in green technology and GHG emissions reduction in the developing world. Unfortunately, it often proves extremely difficult to determine whether CDM projects create genuine 'additionality', that is, whether they reduce GHG emissions beyond the point that would have been reached under standard growth projections. Or, low-carbon projects might score well on GHG emissions, but perform poorly with regard to the broader yardstick of environmental sustainability.[132] Moreover, particularly during its start-up years, the CDM proved vulnerable to weaknesses in carbon accounting and corruption. One of the most vivid examples was the strategy adopted by a number of coolant factories in the developing world to ramp up the production of HCFC-22. HCFC-22 is a refrigerant and feedstock for certain plastics. Its production releases a by-product, HFC-23, a GHG that is 11,700 times more potent than CO_2. Companies deliberately created more HFC-23 in order to capture and destroy it, and claim the credit. The fact that, as Kaime and Glicksman report, 46 per cent of all CDM credits generated between the establishment of the CDM and 2012 were awarded to refrigerant producers,[133] suggests that this was by no means a rare occurrence.

ETS provisions regarding CDM offsetting have been considerably tightened to manage the above-described risks. Whereas the original Linking Directive imposed no maximum cap on use of international credits and instead left this matter to be determined by the Member States, the 2013 Regulation implementing the ETD stipulates that existing installations may offset to either the amount afforded them by the Member State under Phase II, or to 11 per cent of their freely allocated allowances.[134] New installations may only offset up to 4.5 per cent of their total emissions volume. The Commission has been granted greater authority to exclude problematic CDM projects from the remit of the EU ETS, and to ensure that CDM initiatives meet expectations of environmental sustainability.[135]

---

[132] Eva Lovbrand et al., 'Closing the Legitimacy Gap in Global Environmental Governance?: Lessons from the Emerging CDM Market' (2009) 9(2) *Global Environmental Politics* 74–100, at 100.

[133] Thoko Kaime and Robert L. Glicksman, 'A Comparative Analysis of Accountability Mechanisms for Ecosystem Services Markets in the United States and the European Union' (2013) 2(2), *Transnational Environmental Law* 259–283, at 269.

[134] Regulation (EC) No. 1123/2013 on Determining International Credit Entitlements pursuant to Directive 2003/87/EC of the European Parliament and of the Council, OJ 2013 L 299/32.

[135] Arup and Zhang, 'Lessons', 81–83.

Addressing the Burden of the Past: Backloading and the Market Stability Reserve

The changes in allowance allocation and in the approach to international offsetting may help to prevent future dips in the carbon market, but they do not address the existing surplus of approximately 2 billion allowances. To tackle this, the EU agreed to 'backload' allowances that were due to be auctioned in Phase III, postponing their introduction into the market until 2019–2020 by which time, it is hoped, demand will have picked up.[136]

Backloading is a one-off fix. As a more enduring, sustainable solution to the over-allocation challenge, the EU has now agreed to the establishment of a Market Stability Reserve, which will become operative in 2019.[137] The Reserve will act as a buffer to absorb market shocks, lending greater stability and predictability to the carbon price. It will, in the words of the Commission, 'operate entirely according to pre-defined rules which would leave no discretion to the Commission or Member States in its implementation'.[138]

If implemented effectively, backloading allowances and a Market Stability Reserve may help to stabilise the carbon market and keep carbon prices at a level that incentivises the ETS sectors to explore low carbon avenues. However, in the wake of the many adjustments and additional rules adopted to keep the carbon market afloat, one question becomes hard to ignore. To what extent will the resulting arrangements still resemble a genuine market? Will the supporting measures actually facilitate trade, or will they instead transform the carbon market into a centralised, sophisticated variant on an EU-wide GHG permitting regime? From a climate change perspective, the answer to this question may be of limited importance. As a test of the workability and resilience of large-scale market-based regulation, on the other hand, it could hardly be more crucial.

Concluding Remarks

Climate change has dramatically changed the landscape of EU environmental regulation. Most evidently, it has led the EU to adopt swathes of new legislation to confront this era-defining challenge. It has caused the European Union to test its leadership mettle in the international arena, and has invited the European executive to rethink its institutional organisation. It has unquestionably raised the profile of EU environmental policy, yet its high visibility may at the same time have cast a shadow on other, non-climate-related issues. Because of the diffuse

---

[136] Commission Regulation (EU) No. 176/2014 of 25 February 2014 amending Regulation (EU) No. 1031/2010 in particular to determine the volumes of greenhouse gas emissions allowances to be auctioned in 2013–20, OJ 2014 L56/11.

[137] Decision (EU) 2015/1814 of the European Parliament and of the Council of 6 October 2015 concerning the establishment and operation of a market stability reserve for the Union greenhouse gas emissions trading scheme and amending Directive 2003/87/EC, OJ 2015 No. 264/1.

[138] See http://ec.europa.eu/clima/policies/ets/reform/index_en.htm.

and global nature of the problem, the development and implementation of climate change policies have required much more advanced efforts of determining strategies, orchestration and coordination than any other policy area within or outside the environmental remit. The development of the ETS has converted the market-based approach from an optional side dish into a staple of environmental regulation. Leaving aside, through necessity, the tremendously thorny and globally conditional question of whether EU climate change law will be successful in containing global warming to the aspired to 2 degrees Celsius temperature rise, it is impossible to ignore the deep impact of climate change law on the EU's legal and regulatory heritage.

9

Air Pollution and Industrial Emissions

Air pollution regulation was a relative late bloomer on the European Union environmental policy agenda. The main building blocks for EU water and waste policy were laid down in a series of seminal 1970s Directives. By comparison, it took until approximately 1980 for the EU to develop a somewhat cohesive air pollution policy.

This is at first sight surprising because air pollution is a quintessentially transboundary problem.[1] The textbook example of Scandinavian acid rain and deforestation, caused by sulphur dioxide (SO_2) emitted from British industrial chimneys and blown across the North Sea, vividly illustrates the transnational nature of air pollution as an environmental challenge.[2] Yet it also provides a first clue to understanding an important contributory cause for any delay in action. The vision of SO_2 migrating across the North Sea is, after all, a mental image; there are no puffy, jaundiced clouds of pollutants genuinely to be perceived. It is also very difficult to discern air pollution on an experiential level: we rely on scientists to tell us that, for example, the ozone layer is thinning and that, somewhere down the line, this affects our well-being. Even more so than water pollution, air pollution as a political issue struggles with problems of visibility.[3] The low visibility of impacts may have also supported an assumption that, in contrast to water pollution and, say, the protection of wild birds, air pollution was reasonably well controlled at the national level and therefore less dependent on early EU intervention.[4]

Yet recent reports resoundingly affirm that any complacency with regard to the health and environmental effects of atmospheric emissions would be fatally misconceived. A European Environment Agency (EEA) Report of 2014 estimates that, over a five-year period (2008–2012), the costs of air pollution from industrial facilities amount to between €329 billion and €1,053 billion.[5] At the

---

[1] Tania Börzel, 'Pace-Setting, Foot-Dragging and Fence-Sitting: Member State Responses to Europeanization' (2002) 40(2) *Journal of Common Market Studies* 193–214, at 197.
[2] Amy A. Fraenkel, 'The Convention on Long-Range Transboundary Air Pollution: Meeting the Challenge of International Cooperation' (1989) 30(2) *Harvard International Law Journal* 452–453.
[3] B. Everard, B. Pontin, T. Appleby, C. Staddon, E. T Hayes, J. H Barnes and J. W. S. Longhurst, 'Air as a Common Good' (2013) 33 *Environmental Science and Policy* 354–368.
[4] S. Bell, D. McGillivray and O. W. Pedersen, *Environmental Law* (8th edn., Oxford University Press, 2013).
[5] EEA, 'Costs of Air Pollution from European Industrial Facilities 2008–2012: An Updated Assessment', EEA Technical Report No. 20/2014, Publications Office of the European Union.

same time, the United Nations Environment Programme's (UNEP) Sixth Global Environment Outlook Report identifies poor air quality as 'the single largest health risk to the population in Europe'.[6] The World Health Organization (WHO) Regional Office for Europe reported that 'Exposure to air pollution accounted for 7 million deaths worldwide in 2012, including almost 600,000 in the WHO European Region.'[7] In the United Kingdom alone, air pollution was associated with the premature death of 29,000 people in 2009[8] – a death toll second only to fatalities linked to smoking. These daunting figures affirm the vital importance of a well-developed EU air quality policy as well as an effective legal and regulatory framework for air pollution control.

Introduction: Key Themes of EU Air Pollution and Industrial Emissions Law

As is the case for many environmental policy fields, air pollution is effectively a group name that houses a diversity of environmental challenges. In its most high-profile form, air pollution happens through the emission of greenhouse gases (GHGs) that contribute to climate change. EU climate change law is rich and varied enough to merit its own chapter,[9] and is therefore not specifically covered in the present examination of EU air pollution legislation.[10] This chapter focuses, instead, on two other major air pollution challenges: ozone depletion and ambient air quality. Through an analysis of key EU legal instruments governing these issues, namely, the Ozone-Depleting Substances Regulation (ODS Regulation),[11] the Air Quality Framework Directive (AQFD),[12] the National Emissions Ceiling Directive (NECD)[13] and the Industrial Emissions Directive (IED),[14] the chapter offers an overview of the content and the main themes and pressure points of EU air pollution legislation.

---

[6] UNEP, 'Global Environment Outlook Assessment for the Pan-European Region (GEO-6) 2016', available at: www.ccacoalition.org/en/resources/geo-6-assessment-pan-european-region, p. 36.
[7] See www.euro.who.int/en/health-topics/environment-and-health/air-quality/news/news/2014/03/almost-600-000-deaths-due-to-air-pollution-in-europe-new-who-global-report.
[8] Public Health England, 'COMEAP [Committee on the Medical Effects of Air Pollutants]: Mortality Effects of Long Term Exposure to Particulate Air Pollution in the UK', 21 December 2010, available at: www.gov.uk/government/publications/comeap-mortality-effects-of-long-term-exposure-to-particulate-air-pollution-in-the-uk.
[9] See Chapter 8, above.
[10] Climate change challenges do, however, inevitably crop up during air pollution discussions because the objective of climate change abatement frames and, as the discussion will bear out, occasionally obstructs the pursuit of air quality goals.
[11] Regulation (EC) No. 1005/2009 on substances that deplete the ozone layer, OJ 2009 L 286/1.
[12] Directive 2008/50/EC on ambient air quality and cleaner air for Europe, OJ 2008 L 152/1.
[13] Directive 2001/81/EC on national emission ceilings for certain atmospheric pollutants, OJ 2001 L 309/22.
[14] Directive 2010/75/EU on industrial emissions, OJ 2010 L 334/17.

A first theme is the deeply transboundary nature of air pollution as an environmental problem. If noxious emissions do not stop at the national border, neither do they take the EU borders as a natural resting point. It is therefore not surprising that air pollution is governed not only by EU and national law, but is also the subject of a range of international treaties and protocols. The most famous – and arguably most successful – are the Vienna Convention for the Protection of the Ozone Layer[15] and its seminal Montreal Protocol.[16] The discussion on the EU ODS offers an opportunity to explore the dynamics between international and EU law and to reflect on the role of international law in harnessing the effectiveness of regional (and, potentially, national) instruments. In the same vein, it will be shown that international law on long-range transboundary air pollution had a formative influence on the structure and approaches in EU ambient air quality policy.

While ozone depletion regulation beautifully illustrates the multi-level structure of contemporary environmental governance, it is arguably atypical of another prominent feature of air pollution law and policy. Ozone depletion is tackled through the phasing out of an identifiable, discrete group of substances for which, fortuitously, replacements tend to exist on the market. The availability of such 'silver bullets' is a very rare phenomenon in air pollution policy. Indeed, the multiplicity of polluting sources constitutes one of the field's most intractable challenges. Harmful emissions are caused by activities as diverse as cattle farming, waste disposal, industrial production, painting the garden fence, transport, outdoor leisure activities, pesticide use and so on. Correspondingly, air quality regulation must engage with a very broad range of regulatory addressees, who may have different interests, abilities and inclinations to respond to regulatory communications. This fosters a need for variety in regulatory approaches and instruments.

EU air pollution legislation highlights this need for variety, both in terms of the range of legal instruments that deal with air pollution and in terms of the variety in approaches to standard setting. The AQFD and the NECD both determine maximum emissions levels, but they come at the problem from different angles. The AQFD focuses on measurement and quality targets; the NECD lays down annual overall maximum emissions quotas for specific substances. The IED, in turn, is both an example of a more targeted approach to air pollution control as it exclusively engages with large industrial facilities, and an example of a 'belt and braces' approach to standard setting which accommodates quality standards as well as quantified maximum levels. The IED is moreover an excellent entry point to study the use and evolution of the 'best available techniques' (BAT) standard, which traditionally relies on a combination of binding prescriptions and soft law to achieve a particular level of environmental quality within industrial

---

[15] Vienna Convention for the Protection of the Ozone Layer, Vienna, 22 March 1985, in force 22 September 1988, 1513 UNTS 293; (1988) ATS 26; 26 ILM 1529 (1987).
[16] Montreal Protocol on Substances that Deplete the Ozone Layer, Montreal, 16 September 1987, in force 1 January 1989, 1522 UNTS 3; 26 ILM 1550 (1987).

installations. As soft law is increasingly prominent within EU environmental law and beyond, its authority and legitimacy are urgent points of debate.

The diffuse nature of air pollution is also a key factor in explaining a third feature of EU air quality policy, namely, its heavy dependence on cooperation and implementation at the domestic level. It is one thing for the EU to prescribe overall objectives for maximum concentrations of particulate matter, but these remain purely aspirational unless a national strategy is in place to achieve the objectives through, for example, planning, industrial, consumer and road transport policies. Member States retain a broad range of discretion in determining how to implement EU air quality requirements. However, here as in other areas of EU environmental law, vigorous interpretation by the European Court of Justice (CJEU) of primary Treaty law and secondary air pollution provisions has both framed and constrained domestic air quality policy to a greater extent than the broad language of the AQFD and NECD would suggest.

A fourth and, for the purpose of this chapter, final feature to take into account when examining EU air pollution law and policy is the challenge of coherence. Member States must meet EU air quality standards, but they also need to comply with other aspects of EU environmental law, and EU law generally. Moreover, in respect of the integration principle (Art. 11 TFEU), environmental objectives, including air ozone protection and air quality objectives, should be taken into account in decision-making across and beyond EU environmental policy. The analysis below will show that such coherence cannot always be taken for granted.

Ozone-Depleting Substances

Ozone (O_3) assumes a particular, Janus-faced position in air quality and air pollution control policy. At the ambient or ground level, ozone is an air pollutant that is formed by the reaction of sunlight with air containing hydrocarbons and nitrogen oxides (found in, for instance, car exhaust emissions). Ozone concentrations are linked to significant risks to human health, including the increased incidence of asthma and other respiratory ailments, and risks to the environment, such as the inhibition of photosynthesis necessary for plant growth. It is also a powerful greenhouse gas (GHG) and can bind to certain other pollutants and amplify their negative effect. At the atmospheric level, the ozone layer acts as a protective shield against ultraviolet radiation from the sun. Depletion of the atmospheric ozone layer, caused by the use of man-made chemicals such as chlorofluorocarbons (CFCs), puts the planet at risk of overexposure to UV radiation. This can lead to sunburn, skin cancer and cataracts in humans. It also reduces the level of plankton in the oceans, negatively affecting fish stocks, and stunts plant growth. Ozone is, therefore, both an air pollution villain and hero.

In many ways, atmospheric ozone depletion is the archetype of the 'modern' environmental problem. Largely caused by the use of chemicals in products such as refrigerators, aerosols and air conditioners – appliances that epitomise the late twentieth-century post-industrial, convenience-oriented and consumerist society – ozone depletion is an entirely scientifically constructed problem. This qualification should not be read to dilute the seriousness or reality of the problem, but simply emphasises that our awareness of the threat that ozone depletion poses to human health and the environment is shaped through scientific discovery and analysis rather than experience. The corresponding calls for a policy to protect the ozone layer, before the harmful impacts of depletion were felt, represented a pivotal shift from harm-based to preventive and risk-oriented thinking in public decision-making, an approach that has since become a prominent feature of environmental policy and regulation.[17] Ozone depletion is also an early example of a truly global risk. Both in terms of its causes and its predicted impacts, ozone depletion presented itself from the outset as a matter of shared, transboundary concern.

Equally relevant, though much less typical of contemporary environmental problems, is the fact that ozone layer protection is widely seen as a global regulatory success story. The year 1985 saw the adoption of the Vienna Convention for the Protection of the Ozone Layer, which provided a general framework under the auspices of which signatory states would cooperate to halt and reverse ozone depletion through systematic observation, research, information exchange and domestic action.[18] Commitments for national regulatory action were further concretised in the 1987 Montreal Protocol on Substances that Deplete the Ozone Layer. The Protocol's keystone Article 2 introduces a timed schedule for the phase out or banning of the production and consumption of a wide range of ozone-depleting substances (ODS).[19] The schedule and targets have been expanded and tightened over time to reflect advances in scientific knowledge and industrial application; they are binding upon the signatory states and allow but few exceptions. In addition to possessing a degree of precision that is rarely found in international environmental law, the Montreal Protocol is an early example of an international instrument that aims to secure global engagement by differentiating the respective responsibilities of developed and developing countries.[20] The latter's participation is facilitated through a range of differentiation mechanisms, including provisions that offer longer transition periods and derogations, as well as the establishment of a financial mechanism to support treaty-developing States in capacity building and investment in compliance. Owing to the introduction of an active compliance mechanism, it

---

[17] Elizabeth DeSombre, 'The Experience of the Montreal Protocol: Particularly Remarkable, and Remarkably Particular' (2000) 19 *UCLA Journal of Environmental Law and Policy* 49–81, at 50.

[18] Art. 2 of the Vienna Convention.

[19] Art. 2 of the Montreal Protocol; CFCs; fully halogenated CFCs; carbon tetrachloride; 1,1,1-trichloroethane (methyl chloroform); HCFCs; hydrobromofluorocarbons; methyl bromide; bromochloromethane.

[20] Christopher Stone, 'Common but Differentiated Responsibilities in International Law' (2004) 98(2) *American Journal of International Law* 276–301, at 279.

enjoys a relatively high degree of enforcement credibility.[21] Most importantly, it shares with its parent Convention the unprecedented distinction of universal ratification: in September 2009, East Timor became the 196th and thereby final country to ratify the Protocol.[22]

The European Union is a signatory to the Vienna Convention and Montreal Protocol, and it has fully implemented and transcended its treaty-based commitments. Interestingly, the EU is said to have been initially a rather reluctant partner in international negotiations on ozone protection.[23] Instead, in a reversal of what has since become the standard dynamic, the USA was a lead driver towards international agreement. The EU's heavy commercial involvement in CFCs, which accounted for two-thirds of the global CFC production, was undeniably a factor in the EU's hesitancy regarding global action. Moreover, it is important to remember that the Vienna and Montreal negotiations preceded the Single European Act 1986, which formally recognised the then European Community's competence in environmental matters.[24] Absence of formal competence, as we know, had not held the Community back in developing environmental action plans and adopting some of the main building blocks of its environmental legal *patrimonium*, such as the Waste Framework Directive and the Wild Birds Directive,[25] but it certainly cannot have helped to push the EU towards a proactive role in international negotiations.

Notwithstanding its initial reluctance, the EU has since fully embraced the goal of a rigorous phase-out and control of ODS. Since the early 1990s, it has adopted and subsequently amended a succession of EU Regulations on the subject that meet and even overshoot the Montreal objectives. In its current incarnation, Regulation 1005/2009 on substances that deplete the ozone layer (ODS Regulation) lays down an extensive set of restrictions, covering the 'production, import, export, placing on the market, recovery, recycling, reclamation and destruction' of ODS.[26] Having already phased out the production and marketing of traditional ODS and equipment containing ODS, the main objectives of the 2009 version of the ODS Regulation are additionally to phase out hydro-chlorofluorocarbons (HCFCs) by 2020 and progressively ban the use of ODS in servicing old equipment that still contains ODS. Following the ODS

---

[21] Antonio Cardesa-Salzmann, 'Constitutionalising Secondary Rules in Global Environmental Regimes: Non-Compliance Procedures and the Enforcement of Multilateral Environmental Agreements' (2012) 24(10) *Journal of Environmental Law* 103–132, at 115.
[22] UNEP, 'Ozone Treaty Anniversary Gifts Big Birthday Present to Human Health and Combating of Climate Change' (16 September 2009), available at: www.unep.org/Documents.Multilingual/Default.asp?DocumentID=596&ArticleID=6305&l=en.
[23] Tom Naess, 'The Effectiveness of the EU's Ozone Policy' (2004) 4 *International Environmental Agreements: Politics, Law and Economics* 47–63, at 51.
[24] Single European Act 1986, OJ 1987 L 169.
[25] Directive 2008/98/EC on waste, OJ 2008 L 312/3; Directive 79/409/EEC on the conservation of wild birds, OJ 1979 L 103, amended and codified by Directive 2009/147/EC, OJ 2010 L 20/7. See also Chapters 12 and 14.
[26] Art. 1 ODS Regulation OJ 2009 L 286/1.

Regulation's prescriptions, the only ODS that should still persist on the EU market by 2020 are those used as feedstock, as process agents in industrial installations established before September 1997, in lab research, marketed for the purpose of controlled destruction or reclamation, or produced in trace quantities as unavoidable by-products of industrial processes.[27]

The ODS Regulation is not flawless (for example, its lack of definition of 'trace quantities' might create grounds for dispute regarding permissible industrial production), but the empirical data certainly support a favourable impression of its effectiveness. A 2013 EEA Report confirms a sharp decline in the production, import, export, destruction and consumption[28] of ODS between 2006 and 2013. Exports, for example, have dropped 85 per cent since 2006, and now mainly consist of HCFCs which are subject to a gradual phase-out to be completed by 2020.[29]

As environmental feel-good stories are thin on the ground, scholarly interest in ozone depletion regulation has unsurprisingly concentrated on attempts to uncover the secrets of its success. In a careful study of the Vienna Convention and Montreal Protocol, Elizabeth DeSombre identified the flexible structure of the international regime, with a broadly worded framework foundation and scope for ratcheting up more concrete ODS restrictions through the adoption over time of protocols and subsequent amendments, as a key ingredient of the regime's effectiveness.[30] Additionally, the adoption of an internationally binding instrument was strongly supported by US industry, which, having already had to accept the prospect of a phase-out as a matter of internal US policy, was keen to ensure that its international competitors, too, would face comparable regulatory restrictions.[31] Other factors that contributed to the effectiveness of the Convention and Protocol were the inclusion of developing countries, facilitated through the incorporation of common but differentiated responsibilities in the regime,[32] and the presence of the aforementioned compliance mechanism.[33] Turning to the EU level, the existence of a robust international 'backbone' certainly harnessed the credibility and effectiveness of the EU ODS regime. Moreover, researchers such as Tom Naess have argued that, even though EU Member States were already under an obligation to implement ODS phase-outs in their guise as signatories to the Montreal Protocol, the existence of EU

---

[27] *Ibid.*; Arts. 3(14); 7; 8; 9 and 10.
[28] 'Consumption' figures aggregate the numbers for import, export, production and destruction.
[29] 'Air Quality in Europe – 2013 Report', EEA Report No. 9/2013. Available at: www.eea.europa.eu/publications/air-quality-in-europe-2013.
[30] DeSombre, 'The Experience of the Montreal Protocol', 52–57.
[31] *Ibid.*, 57–69. On the 'ratcheting up' dynamic generally, see David Vogel, 'Trading Up and Governing Across: Transnational Governance and Environmental Protection' (1997) 4(4) *Journal of European Public Policy* 556–571.
[32] Veerle Heyvaert, 'Levelling Down, Levelling Up, and Governing Across: Three Responses to Hybridization in International Law' (2009) 20(3) *European Journal of International Law* 647–674.
[33] DeSombre, 'The Experience of the Montreal Protocol', 69–75.

regulation was instrumental in embedding and strengthening the commitment towards ozone layer protection. This particularly goes for Member States that, in the absence of EU law, might have been slow to comply with their international obligations. Hence, on the field of ozone layer protection, the triple-tiered, multi-level governance structure of ODS regulation apparently positively affected regulatory efficacy.[34]

The ODS example underscores the value of regulation beyond the State. The majority of writings on the subject concede that the problem would not have been addressed as proactively or as quickly in the absence of international and European regulation. At the same time, many caution against overstating or overgeneralising the lessons from the ozone saga. Although hampered by the 'invisibility factor' that generally makes air pollution problems difficult to convey and control, stratospheric ozone layer depletion does have particular features that make it amenable to resolution. Most importantly, it is caused by an identifiable and discrete group of substances. Many other environmental problems, within and outside the field of air pollution, are caused by a more diffuse and changeable constellation of inputs. Equally importantly, it proved possible to engineer affordable substitute substances that delivered the same qualities as ODS without the harmful ozone impact. In fact, the swift introduction of substitutes has led some commentators to present the phase-out of ODS as a consequence of industrial progress rather than regulatory intervention, suggesting that CFCs would have been discontinued with or without the Montreal Protocol.[35] DeSombre, however, sees ODS regulation as the driver rather than the consequence of change:

> The mere existence of the Vienna Convention, which promised abatement measures, followed by the negotiation of the Montreal Protocol, which required them, put industry on notice that it would not be able to continue profiting from ozone-depleting substances to the extent it previously had. In the same way that DuPont found substitute propellants for aerosol spray cans in anticipation of certain US regulation (and with the support of consumer demand), the ODS industry responded to the inevitability of international regulations.[36]

Qualifications notwithstanding, the ozone protection example remains an affirmation of the scope for international and transnational regulation to make a substantive contribution to environmental protection. At the same time, it is a reminder that many factors need to coalesce to generate such beneficial outcomes. The effectiveness of international and European environmental regulation, therefore, is a quality not to be taken for granted.

---

[34] Naess, 'The Effectiveness of the EU's Ozone Policy'.
[35] David L. Levy, 'Business and International Environmental Treaties: Ozone Depletion and Climate Change' (1997) 39(3) *California Management Review* 53–71, at 61.
[36] DeSombre, 'The Experience of the Montreal Protocol', 60.

Ambient Air Quality

Like ODS regulation, the EU legal framework for ambient air quality identifies a range of pollutants, such as sulphur dioxide (SO_2), oxides of nitrogen (NO_x) and particulate matter (PM), and lays down measures to curtail their emission and presence in the surrounding air. Most air pollutants are, essentially, airborne waste generated as a result of industrial or agricultural processes, machinery and vehicle use, or solid and liquid waste processing. The text box below gives an overview of the key air pollutants subject to EU regulation and their main impacts on human health and the environment.

> **Air Pollutants Covered in the AQFD and NECD**
>
> **Ground level ozone (O_3):** Typically emitted from industrial facilities and electric utilities, motor vehicle exhaust, gasoline vapours, and chemical solvents. Exposure to O_3 can trigger health problems including asthma, and can have harmful effects on sensitive vegetation and ecosystems. (AQFD)
>
> **Sulphur dioxide (SO_2):** Primarily emitted from fossil fuel combustion in industrial facilities and transport. SO_2 is a major precursor for acid rain, which causes destruction of vegetation, soil and eutrophication of water sources, and is linked to a range of health impacts, from airway inflammation to heart failure. (AQFD and NECD)
>
> **Oxides of nitrogen (NO_x):** NO_x form when fuel is burned at high temperatures. Main sources include motor vehicle exhausts and industrial boilers. Nitrogen oxides contribute to ozone formation and can significantly contribute to a number of environmental effects such as acid rain and eutrophication in coastal waters. (AQFD and NECD)
>
> **Nitrogen dioxide (NO_2):** Belongs to the family of NO_x. Nitrogen dioxide can irritate the lungs and lower resistance to respiratory infections such as influenza. (AQFD)
>
> **Particulate matter (PM10 and PM2.5):** PM is the term used for solid or liquid particles emitted to the air. Generally, any activity which involves burning of materials or any dust-generating activities are sources of PM. Some sources are natural, such as volcanoes and water mist. PM decreases visibility, which constitutes a safety risk, may harm plant life and poses health risks including lung disease and cancer. (AQFD)
>
> **Volatile organic compounds (VOCs):** carbon-based chemicals that easily evaporate at room temperature and that are capable of producing photochemical oxidants (e.g. O_3) by reactions with NO_x in the presence of sunlight. This group includes chemicals such as CFCs, benzene and methane. (AQFD, NECD)

Benzene: A highly volatile chemical that occurs in compounds such as crude oil and cigarette smoke, and in a range of materials from plastics to solvents and paints. It is a source of outdoor and indoor air pollution. It is toxic and a carcinogen. (AQFD)

Lead: A metal that, as an air pollutant, is typically emitted from petrol-driven vehicles or industrial facilities such as waste incinerators and metal processing plants. Lead is toxic and bio-accumulative. (AQFD)

Carbon monoxide (CO): Produced in the incomplete combustion of carbon-containing fuels. CO is toxic. (AQFD)

Ammonia (NH$_3$): A caustic gas typically stored under high pressure in liquid form, NH$_3$ is used in bleaching or cleaning, in the production of fertilisers, plastics, pharmaceuticals, rubber and petrochemicals and as an anti-fungal agent for foodstuffs. It can harm vegetation, contributes to acidification and is a corrosive and irritating substance. (NECD)

Methane (CH$_4$): A greenhouse gas emitted from natural, industrial and agricultural sources. (NECD proposal)

A second point of similarity between the EU ODS regime and ambient air quality regulation is its multi-level character: the EU and its Member States are signatories to the Convention on Long Range Transboundary Air Pollution (CLRTAP) and most of its implementing protocols.[37] Although the EU's ambient air quality policy and legal framework is more expansive and in certain respects more ambitious than international air pollution law, the CLRTAP has exercised considerable influence on the structure and regulatory approaches within EU air quality legislation.[38] This is most prominently the case for the establishment of national emissions ceilings (NECs), an approach mandated by the 1999 Gothenburg Protocol to the CLRTAP.[39] At the other end of the multi-level regulatory chain, the success of EU air quality policy depends heavily on Member State cooperation at the implementation and enforcement stages. Compliance with EU air quality standards cannot be achieved merely by cutting and pasting Directive provisions into national law. It requires considerably more initiative and planning on the part of the Member State, which needs to determine a combination of governance and legal strategies (ranging from product

---

[37] Geneva (Switzerland), 13 November 1979, in force 16 March 1983, 1302 UNTS 217; available at: www.unece.org/env/lrtap_h1.html.
[38] Adam Byrne, 'The 1979 Convention on Long-Range Transboundary Air Pollution: Assessing its Effectiveness as a Multilateral Environmental Regime after 35 Years' (2015) 4(1) *Transnational Environmental Law* 41–43.
[39] Protocol to Abate Acidification, Eutrophication and Ground-level Ozone, Gothenburg (Sweden), 30 November 1999, in force 15 May 2005, 1593 UNTS 287; available at: www.unece.org/env/lrtap/multi_h1.html.

standards to road planning) in order to bring and keep local air pollution down to the targets set in EU law.

What ambient air quality law does not share with ODS legislation, however, is the latter's relative structural and operational simplicity: EU law for the protection of the ozone layer is contained within a single legal instrument, and effectuated overwhelmingly through a single strategy: the phase-out and commercial substitution of a particular group of harmful chemicals by ozone-neutral alternatives. Improvements in ambient air quality, in contrast, are pursued through a plethora of instruments, some targeting particular products and appliances such as passenger vehicles,[40] others focusing on groups of installations such as medium or large combustion plants,[41] and yet others directly regulating the overall level or concentration of air pollutants emitted into or present in the ambient air. This chapter concentrates chiefly on the latter category of measures, which are contained in two landmark EU instruments: the 2008 Air Quality Framework Directive (AQFD) and the 2001 National Emissions Ceiling Directive (NECD). This analysis is supplemented in Part 4 with an exploration of the main features of the 2010 Industrial Emissions Directive (IED), which incorporates an installation-based approach. Air pollution is one of many environmental issues addressed under the IED; the Directive also tackles emissions into water and solid waste production, and maps out the requirements for Integrated Pollution Prevention and Control (IPPC) that are mandatory for those EU industrial sectors that are likely to have a heavy ecological footprint. The AQFD, NECD and IED are core instruments of the EU legal arsenal to combat air pollution. An understanding of their structure and implementation therefore offers valuable insights into the defining approaches, strengths and weaknesses of EU air pollution law generally. It remains, however, important to remember that they constitute a selection of a broader range of EU air pollution provisions.

The regulatory complexity of ambient air quality law also manifests itself in the variety of standard-setting approaches deployed to achieve air quality targets. The aspiration to reduce, say, levels of fine particulate matter (PM2.5) in the ambient atmosphere might be expressed through technological standards that regulate the processes through which PM2.5 is generated; through emissions standards that prescribe the maximum quantities and/or concentrations of PM2.5 that may be released into the air; or through quality standards that indicate the maximum concentration of PM2.5 that may be detected in the atmosphere at any given location. The paragraphs below discuss different standardisation choices in the context of EU law, and review the advantages and limitations of each method.

---

[40] Directive 99/94/EC on the reduction of CO_2 emissions from passenger vehicles, OJ 2000 L 12/16.
[41] Directive 2001/80/EC on the limitation of emissions of certain pollutants into the air from large combustion plants, OJ 2001 L 309/1.

Approaches to Standardisation

Air pollution control policies may be pursued through various regulatory strategies, each with different strengths and weaknesses. The introduction of technical standards that prescribe the use of specific equipment or processes, such as the installation of wet scrubbers to lower the amount of sulphur dioxide (SO_2) emitted into the air from industrial chimneys and exhausts, follows what has been labelled an 'instrumental approach'.[42] It directs the attention towards the means through which pollution abatement is pursued rather than to the end result of lower pollution levels, and leaves regulatory addressees limited choice of how to comply with legal requirements. The remoteness between the technical requirement as formulated and the ultimate goal of cleaner, healthier air is often flagged up as a weakness of the instrumental approach as it is seen to erect a barrier between the regulator and the public in whose interest the standard is adopted.[43] This regulatory distance may dent the legitimacy of technical prescriptions. Technical standards do not communicate well with outsiders to the regulatory process. On the flip side, they are highly eloquent in their conversations with regulatory addressees, and offer clear, precise instructions to their target audiences on what processes and techniques need to be implemented to stay within the limits of the law. They also tend to enable relatively straightforward compliance assessment, which further enhances the reliability and the security generated through technical standard setting. Yet, at the same time, the very certainty and predictability of technical standards affirms their lack of flexibility, which can impact negatively on their efficiency as the same technical prescription may not be the most cost-effective way of achieving pollution abatement across installations or industrial sectors.

At the other end of the spectrum, air quality standards afford more flexibility in implementation, as long as the ultimate goal of not exceeding legally determined maximum allowable amounts or concentrations of pollutants in the ambient air is achieved. There is a pleasing immediacy to this approach in that it draws public attention to what arguably matters most. This is particularly relevant when considering that, calculations and projections notwithstanding, compliance with technical prescriptions does not necessarily translate into better air quality. Quality standards are also much more informative of the level of regulatory ambition than technical prescriptions and are, in that regard, more publicly transparent than the latter.[44] 'Allowable nitrogen oxide levels exceeded by 30 per cent in Northern Spain' is a much more evocative message for the public to grasp than 'three Northern Spanish industrial plants found in breach of best available techniques for common waste water and waste gas treatment/

---

[42] Gertrude Lübbe-Wolff, 'Efficient and Environmental Legislation: On Different Philosophies of Pollution Control in Europe' (2001) 13(1), *Journal of Environmental Law* 79–87, at 82.
[43] Ibid.; Bruce A. Ackerman and Richard B. Stewart, 'Reforming Environmental Law' (1985) 37 *Stanford Law Review* 1333–1366, at 1345.
[44] Ibid.

management systems in the chemicals sector'. Yet quality standards, too, have shortcomings. Most obviously, they cannot be implemented without further instrumentalisation; at some point down the line, quality objectives need to be translated in more mundane and less flexible sets of emissions standards and even technical requirements. Air quality standards do not bypass instrumental approaches but devolve them to a less centralised level. This may be a virtue from a subsidiarity perspective, but it also creates a risk of uneven implementation, as it may foster the development of inconsistent, even counterproductive local approaches, and loss of efficiency. Furthermore, authors such as Lübbe-Wolff and Lee have identified the risk of pollution displacement as the Achilles heel of quality-based regulatory approaches.[45] A focus on local quality may incentivise regulatory addressees to export, rather than reduce, pollution to different media (e.g. shifting from incineration to solid waste disposal) or regions (the famous 'taller chimneys' phenomenon).

It should be noted that technical standards are not necessarily immune to displacement problems. Wet scrubbing to abate airborne SO_2 pollution, for example, can easily result in heightened levels of water pollution.[46] In fact, the risk of sectoral displacement needs to be taken into account in environmental decision-making regardless of whether a technical, emissions- or quality-oriented approach is adopted. Geographic displacement, on the other hand, is better controlled through fixed emissions standards than technical or quality-based requirements. Arguably, this makes emissions standards particularly attractive in a transnational context. As a regulatory technique, emissions standards are situated somewhere in between technical and quality standards. Whether they display more of the flexibility and generality of quality standards, or the rigidity and precision of technical standards, depends in the first place on their scope. Emission standards for designated industrial sectors can be virtually indistinguishable from technical standards; overall regional or national maximum emissions levels, on the other hand, leave considerable room for discretion and variety in implementation.

Since technical standards, emissions standards and quality standards have different strengths and weaknesses, any ranking in order of preference will depend on which regulatory qualities are most sought after. In general terms, the current regulatory climate tends to prize efficiency as the primary condition for effective regulation. Within an efficiency-oriented paradigm – which arguably constitutes the leading framework within which EU regulatory decision-making currently operates[47] – the initial assumption is that the most flexible approaches are to be preferred, starting with market-based

---

[45] Ibid., and Maria Lee, *EU Environmental Law Governance and Decision-Making* (2nd edn., Hart Publishing, 2014), 110.

[46] Alexandra Popescu, 'Sulphur Abatement Technology Poses Environment Risk', *ENDS Europe*, 13 March 2015.

[47] Commission Communication, 'Better Regulation for Better Results – An EU Agenda', COM(2015)215 final, 19 May 2015.

approaches[48] and quality standards[49] and dropping down towards emissions levels and technical prescriptions.[50]

In the EU context, the choice between different standard-setting approaches represents not only a tussle between efficiency-based and alternative (e.g. procedural or normative) understandings of regulatory legitimacy, but also one between different regulatory cultures.[51] The friction between Germany, which generally favours emissions-oriented approaches in both air and water policy, and the UK preference for more flexible quality targets, has been well documented in the literature.[52] In particular, the UK's reluctance to accept maximum air pollution emissions levels was a key factor contributing to its 1980s and 1990s reputation as the 'dirty man of Europe'.[53] Arguably, however, the controversy was more a disagreement about competence than one about the appropriate level of environmental protection.[54] Under an air quality approach, Member States retain the right to determine how – through which combination of planning strategies, industrial policies, detailed emissions standards, tax incentives and so on – the quality targets will be achieved. When emissions standards are adopted, national options narrow.

In answer to the question which culture prevailed in this regulatory battle, a first glance at EU air pollution legislation suggests that neither approach emerged victorious (or, adopting a glass half-full perspective, both were winners). The AQFD and the NECD, the two foundational instruments of EU air pollution law, embrace respectively a quality-based and an emissions-based perspective. In a similar vein, best available techniques adopted under the auspices of the IED typically comprise both quality and emissions standards. The more pertinent question, however, is whether the targets can be pursued alternatively, or must be met cumulatively. In the former scenario, the greater flexibility of the quality-based approaches is retained at the Member State level. In the latter, it is lost. Here, the clear message from the case law at both EU and national levels is that the standards must be met cumulatively.[55] Moreover, a recent, small but important set of CJEU rulings displays a clear attempt to concretise Member State obligations and, correspondingly, to rein in domestic discretion

---

[48] Ackerman and Stewart, 'Reforming Environmental Law'.
[49] David Popp, 'Pollution Control Innovations and the Clean Air Act of 1990', National Bureau of Economic Research Working Paper Series, WP 8593 (2001), available at: www.nber.org/papers/w8593.
[50] Scott E. Atkinson and Donald H. Lewis, 'A Cost-Effectiveness Analysis of Alternative Air Quality Control Strategies' (1974) 1 *Journal of Environmental Economics and Management* 237–250, at 237–238.
[51] Börzel, 'Pace-Setting, Foot-Dragging and Fence-Sitting', 194.
[52] See Lübbe-Wolff, 'Efficient Environmental Legislation'.
[53] Chris Rose, *The Dirty Man of Europe: Great British Pollution Scandal* (Simon & Schuster, 1991).
[54] Lübbe-Wolff, 'Efficient Environmental Legislation', 201–202.
[55] *R (Rockware Glass Ltd) v. Chester City Council* [2006] EWCA Civ 992.

in the implementation of air quality standards.[56] Overall, therefore, the presence of relatively fewer flexible emissions-based standards in the EU legal sphere arguably dilutes the flexibility of the quality-based instruments.

The EU Legal Framework

The three approaches to air pollution standardisation correlate with three keystone instruments of EU air pollution law: the 2001 NECD, which represents an emissions-oriented approach; the 2008 AQFD, which is organised around quality standards; and the 2010 IED, which incorporates BAT standards that are, essentially, a combination of technical, emissions-based and quality-oriented approaches.

The 2008 AQFD combines, extends and repeals earlier EU air quality legislation, specifically Council Directive 96/62/EC on ambient air quality assessment and management and three of its four 'daughter directives'.[57] The Fourth Daughter Directive, which focuses on arsenic, cadmium, mercury, nickel and polycyclic aromatic hydrocarbons (PAHs) in ambient air, is still in force. This is likely to remain the legal package for the foreseeable future; there are no immediate plans on the part of EU policy-makers to overhaul the air quality-oriented aspects of EU legislation. The same cannot be said of the 2001 NECD, which is currently in the final stages of renegotiation.[58] In all likelihood, it will be replaced by an updated instrument that contains emissions targets for the period up to 2030, in parallel with the timings of EU climate change legislation.[59]

The 2001 NECD

The NECD concentrates on pollutants responsible for acidification, eutrophication and ground-level ozone pollution (SO_2, NO_x, non-methane VOCs and ammonia) and for each of these sets overall emissions limits that Member States should not exceed as of 2010. Marine and aircraft emissions are excluded from the

---

[56] See e.g. Case C-237/07 *Janecek* ECLI:EU:C:2008:447, and Case C-404/13 *ClientEarth v. the Secretary of State for the Environment, Food and Rural Affairs* ECLI:EU:C:2013:805, both discussed further below.

[57] Directive 96/62/EC, OJ 1996 L 296/55. The four daughter directives are: Council Directive 1999/30/EC relating to limit values for sulphur dioxide, nitrogen dioxide and oxides of nitrogen, particulate matter and lead in ambient air (First Daughter Directive); Directive 2000/69/EC relating to limit values for benzene and carbon monoxide in ambient air, OJ 2000 L 313/12 (Second Daughter Directive); Directive 2002/3/EC relating to ozone in ambient air, OJ 2002 L 67/12 (Third Daughter Directive); and Directive 2004/107/EC relating to polyaromatic hydrocarbons, arsenic, nickel, cadmium and mercury in ambient air, OJ 2005 L 23/3 (Fourth Daughter Directive).

[58] José Rojo, 'EC Ramps Up Pressure in Final Push for NEC Deal', *ENDS Europe*, 20 June 2016.

[59] Susanna Williams, 'Air, Waste Proposals to be Replaced Next Year', *ENDS Europe*, 16 December 2014.

remit of the Directive. The NECD implements the emissions ceilings introduced in the 1999 Gothenburg Protocol under the auspices of the CLRTAP and, similar to the EU implementation of the Montreal Protocol, outstrips the Protocol in the stringency of ceilings imposed. This is a laudable accomplishment, but the impact should not be overstated: EU emissions ceilings remain insufficient to meet the WHO guideline values for the protection of human health and vegetation from photochemical pollution. The existing emissions limits are, therefore, technically, interim values that ought to be replaced by more robust limits for 2020/2030.[60] At the moment, however, there appears limited EU legislative appetite for ambition on this front, with the Council of Ministers particularly hesitant to complete the long-intended review process of the, by now, quite outdated limits in the NECD.

In addition to adhering to the overall emissions limits, Member States are required to prepare and update emissions inventories and projections annually.[61] Beyond that, it is up to the Member States to determine what measures to undertake to ensure respect of the national emissions ceilings;[62] the NECD does not prescribe specific emissions reduction actions and consequently leaves Member States a significant level of freedom in implementation.[63]

The 2008 AQFD

The AQFD's main objective is to 'lay down measures to define and establish ambient air quality objectives'[64] with regard to sulphur dioxide (SO_2), nitrogen dioxide (NO_2), oxides of nitrogen, particulate matter (PM10 and PM2.5), benzene, carbon monoxide (CO) and ozone. Vital steps towards this end are the production and disclosure of ambient air quality data in accordance with standardised measurement techniques, and the development of common criteria for the number and location of measuring stations.[65] The AQFD thus contains provisions to, first, enhance and standardise information about air quality and, secondly, to mandate the development of air pollution reduction strategies.

The basic organisation of the AQFD is as follows: pursuant to Article 4 AQFD, Member States must establish zones and agglomerations for air quality assessment.[66] The reasoning behind this requirement is that different areas within

---

[60] The European Parliament mooted the possibility of introducing an additional set of binding intermediate targets for 2025. See David Keating, 'MEPs Demand Binding 2025 Air Quality Targets', *ENDS Europe*, 15 July 2015.
[61] Art. 7 NECD.   [62] Art. 6 NECD.
[63] See Joined Cases C-165/09 to C-167/09 *Stichting Natuur en Milieu and Others* v. *College van Gedeputeerde Staten van Groningen and College van Gedeputeerde Staten van Zuid-Holland* ECLI: EU:C:2011:348, para. 75.
[64] Art. 1 AQFD.   [65] Ibid.
[66] Maps of the EU national territories divided into zones and agglomerations are available at: http://ec.europa.eu/environment/archives/air/pdf/zones/aq_zones_map1.pdf.

Member States are likely to face very different types and degrees of air pollution;[67] the air quality profile of Italy's industrial Treviso zone in the Northern Veneto is unlikely to resemble that of rural Umbria. Consequently, regulatory strategies and policy initiatives that are highly significant for one region may be inappropriate to govern the very distinctive air pollution problems faced 200 kilometres further south. Dividing the EU geographical area into zones and agglomerations enables the EU to match prescriptions, and the Member States to match policies, to local conditions.

Measurement of the registered pollutants (SO_2, PM2.5 and so on) happens within the zones and agglomerations. Which measurement techniques Member States are expected to use to carry out such measurement depends on the existing levels of pollution in the area: if pollution levels are above the 'upper assessment level', fixed measurements must be used. For pollution levels between the upper and lower, a combination of fixed measurements and modelling techniques may be relied on; and for zones and agglomerations below the assessment level, modelling or objective-estimation techniques suffice.

The same managerial strategy of linking mandated Member State responses to EU-established thresholds also characterises those AQFD provisions that concern the actual management and improvement of air quality. In addition to the aforementioned upper and lower assessment thresholds, Article 2 AQFD introduces a wealth of benchmarks, such as 'critical levels', and 'alert thresholds'. The first refer to pollution levels that are elevated enough to present risks to some environmental receptors (e.g. trees, grass) but not to humans. The overall objective for Member States is simply to keep registered pollutants below these critical levels, but no particular calls for action are attached.[68] Alert thresholds, in turn, indicate a level of pollution that is high enough to constitute a risk to human health or the environment even under conditions of brief exposure. Correspondingly, if alert thresholds are breached within a particular zone or agglomeration, a public information duty is triggered: Member States are obliged to inform the public via TV, radio, newspapers or the Internet.[69] Moreover, the breach of alert thresholds may necessitate the adoption of a short-term air quality plan (see below).

The pivotal reference points in the AQFD are the 'limit' and 'target values', referring to pollution levels, which, when exceeded, trigger a Member State duty to establish an air quality plan for the respective zone or agglomeration. Typically, target values are used in areas where scientific uncertainty or political disagreement between the Member States prevents firm determinations of a limit value.[70] The key provision is Article 23 AQFD which affirms that the exceeding of any limit or target value, plus any relevant margin of tolerance, compels the Member State to draft an air quality plan in order to

---

[67] Mark Wilde, 'The New Directive on Ambient Air Quality and Cleaner Air for Europe' (2010) 12 *Environmental Law Review* 282–290, at 285.
[68] Art. 14 AQFD.   [69] Art. 18 AQFD.
[70] Wilde, 'The New Directive on Ambient Air Quality and Cleaner Air for Europe', 285.

keep the period of exceedance as brief as possible. Additionally, the Directive introduces a requirement for short-term action plans when Member States are at risk of exceeding the alert thresholds (Article 24 AQFD), and lays down specific measures for nitrogen dioxide, benzene and PM10. As it was anticipated that a number of Member States might not manage to reach the air quality targets with respect to these pollutants by the 2010 deadline, a mechanism was provided in Article 22 through which Member States could apply for an extension of a maximum of five years. Since the time period for the five-year extension has now also elapsed, the mechanism in its current form can no longer be invoked. However, it is useful to be aware of the provisions under Article 22 AQFD because they are at issue in one of the landmark European Court rulings regarding the AQFD.[71]

What Articles 22, 23 and 24 AQFD have in common is that they require Member States to develop a considered strategy that identifies why and how pollution levels are being exceeded, and introduce a range of measures to tackle the problem. Such measures can go from supporting research into new vehicle emissions abatement technologies, lowering speed limits, temporarily closing off roads and introducing congestion charges, to tightening the conditions for planning permission. However, as is the case for the achievement of national emissions ceilings, the Directive refrains from specifying which particular measures Member States should adopt to reduce air pollution below limit, target or alert levels. There are minimum data requirements for air quality action plans: pursuant to Article 23 in combination with Annex XV, action plans must cover, *inter alia*, topographic and climatic conditions in the affected zone or agglomeration; pollution concentrations observed over previous years; a list of main emissions sources; and details of possible measures for improvement. Evidently, these conditions still leave Member States a wide range of choices how to develop and put into effect an air quality strategy. Moreover, it is important to remember that action plans are only required when regulatory limits are exceeded. Hence, the terms of the AQFD undeniably leave Member States considerable freedom in implementation.

Member State Implementation of EU Ambient Air Legislation

The programmatic approach and broad range of Member State discretion in the implementation of EU ambient air pollution legislation conforms to the legal principles of subsidiarity and proportionality, which instruct EU institutions to favour broadly formulated framework measures over more detailed prescriptions where possible.[72] It also responds to efficiency-driven considerations that prioritise flexible measures over more constraining command-and-control types of instruments as the former are presumed more cost-effective.[73] Moreover, in the

---

[71] *ClientEarth v. the Secretary of State for the Environment, Food and Rural Affairs* ECLI:EU:C:2013:805 (see below).
[72] See Chapter 4.   [73] Ackerman and Stewart, 'Reforming Environmental Law'.

context of air quality the focus on overall emissions and quality goals is deeply pragmatic. Air pollution is a global problem, but its causes are affected by quintessentially local conditions that differ from measuring station to measuring station, zone to zone, country to country. Contributing factors range from climatological and geographic conditions, the organisation and availability of public versus private transport, the makeup of regional industries, and the degree of urbanisation, to a wealth of less obvious but equally relevant elements (such as the existence or absence of school catchment policies and local practices for handling animal manure). The high degree of local differentiation underlies the zonal and agglomeration approach followed in the AQFD, as well as the reliance on national planning for implementation.

Yet it is important to qualify the discretion enjoyed by Member States. First, discretion should not be confused with a carte blanche. National air quality plans submitted pursuant to Articles 22 and 23 AQFD, which require Member States that did not meet the limit values for NO, benzene and PM10 by 2010 to apply for an exemption, are subject to Commission approval, which places an important constraint on discretion.[74] More generally, the CJEU has underlined that even though the requirements of the NECD and AQFD are too broad and programmatic to compel Member States to take (or avoid) a *specific* set of measures (for instance, Member States cannot be made to refuse planning permission for individual projects that will cause emissions of regulated pollutants to rise), there are limits to Member State discretion:

> Whilst the Member States thus have a discretion, Article 6 of the NEC Directive nevertheless involves limits on its exercise, which are capable of being relied upon before the national courts, relating to the appropriateness of the body of policies and measures adopted or envisaged within the framework of the respective national programmes to the objective of limiting, by the end of 2010 at the latest, emissions of the pollutants covered to amounts not exceeding the ceilings laid down for each Member State.[75]

Secondly, although flexibility in implementation is deemed to foster better and more cost-effective compliance, experience with EU ambient air pollution legislation indicates that it is by no means a panacea. National track records are not exactly exemplary: in 2015, the European Environment Agency (EEA) reported that ten Member States had exceeded at least one of their national emissions ceilings in 2013,[76] a narrow improvement over the preceding year

---

[74] Art. 22(4) AQFD. See also Case C-68/11 *Commission* v. *Italy* ECLI:EU:C:2012:815, paras. 24–26.
[75] See Joined Cases C-165/09 to C-167/09 *Stichting Natuur en Milieu and Others* ECLI:EU:C:2011:348, para. 103. For similar observations in the context of the AQFD, see Case C-237/07 *Janecek* ECLI:EU:C:2008:447, para. 46.
[76] EEA, NEC Directive Status Report 2014. Reporting by Member States under Directive 2001/81/EC on national emission ceilings for certain atmospheric pollutants, EEA

when 11 Member States were in breach.[77] The limit values in the AQFD, too, are proving a challenge for many EU countries: no fewer than 22 Member States needed to avail themselves of the option provided in Articles 22 and 23 of the AQFD to request an extension of the compliance deadline for the pollutants PM10 and NO_2.[78]

Given these well-documented compliance struggles and, in the case of emissions limits, outright compliance failures, the number of enforcement actions in this field is comparatively modest. So far, the Commission has initiated very few legal proceedings against Member States for failure to comply with the NECD.[79] The fact that Member States had until 2010 to meet the limits set in the Directive is undeniably a factor, but it hardly constitutes an exhaustive explanation. This is all the more so when we consider that, during the transitional period between the entry into force of the NECD and 2010, Member States already had significant and, according to the CJEU, justiciable commitments. During this period, Member States were under a general obligation to 'adopt or envisage, within the framework of national programmes, appropriate and coherent policies and measures capable of reducing, as a whole, emissions of the pollutants'.[80]

There has been some more action on the AQFD front. At the time of writing, infringement proceedings are pending against Poland for persistent failure to meet the AQFD's PM2.5 targets.[81] Additionally, there is already a good handful of court rulings on Member State compliance with either the AQFD, its predecessor Directive 96/62/EEC, or any of the daughter directives. Most consist of succinctly phrased and straightforward findings of non-compliance, but Case C-68/11, *Commission v. Italy*, merits a closer look. Italy sought to avail itself of the exemption procedure in Article 22 AQFD, which permits Member States to postpone air quality attainment deadlines for pollutants including PM10, subject to the production of an air quality plan to be reviewed by the European Commission.[82] The Commission did not approve of the Italian exemption requests and accompanying remediation strategies and, consequently, launched

---

Technical Report No. 7/2015, available at: www.eea.europa.eu/publications/nec-directive-status-report-2014.

[77] Ibid.

[78] Information available at: http://ec.europa.eu/environment/air/quality/legislation/time_extensions.htm.

[79] Only three cases involve implementation failures regarding the NECD: Case C-273/08 *Commission v. Luxembourg* [2008] ECR I-194; Case C-146/04 *Commission v. Netherlands* ECLI:EU:C:2005:236; and Case C-68/04 *Commission v. Greece* ECLI:EU:C:2005:347. They all involve a straightforward failure to notify implementing measures in a timely fashion.

[80] See Joined Cases C-165/09 to C-167/09, *Stichting Natuur en Milieu and Others*, ECLI:EU:C:2011:348, para. 103.

[81] Case C-48/12 *Commission v. Poland* ECLI:EU:C:2013:3 (pending). See also Robyn Lancaster, 'Poland Faces Court over Air Pollution', *ENDS Europe*, 11 December 2015.

[82] The allowable exemption period for PM10 lapsed on 11 June 2011.

proceedings against Italy for non-compliance with the AQFD. In its defence, Italy did not deny exceeding the limit values but instead asserted that the goals set in the AQFD were impossible to achieve and would have required 'drastic economic and social measures', which, in turn, would 'infringe fundamental rights and freedoms such as the free movement of goods and persons, private economic initiative and the right of citizens to public utility services'.[83] Its failure to meet PM10 targets, Italy asserted, was due to a combination of factors beyond its control:

> (i) the complexity of the process of PM10 formation,
> (ii) the impact of the weather on concentrations of PM10 in the atmosphere,
> (iii) insufficient technical knowledge of the process of PM10 formation which led to the imposition of time limits which were too short for compliance with those limit values,
> (iv) the fact that the various European Union policies to reduce PM10 precursors did not produce the results expected, and
> (v) the absence of a link between European Union policy concerning air quality and, *inter alia*, that aiming at reducing greenhouse gas emissions.[84]

In its reply, the CJEU decided that the five listed circumstances constituted no excuse for non-compliance. The Court pointed out that no Member State had challenged the legality of the AQFD on the basis of it being unworkable, and that factors beyond the Member State's control might justify temporary but not long-term and systemic breaches of EU environmental law. It is not exactly surprising that the Court should be unmoved by Italy's argumentation. To decide otherwise could be read as an acknowledgement that the binding nature of EU law is, to a degree, conditional, which would constitute a troublesome judicial precedent. It is, however, regrettable that the CJEU offers no further reflection on the challenges caused by the impacts of scientific uncertainty on national regulatory effectiveness. First, we might question whether the expiry of the deadline for a Member State to request the annulment of an EU legal instrument should necessarily mean that the validity of this instrument can no longer be called into question in infringement proceedings.[85] Arguably, the fact that Member States have not challenged the legality of a measure in time does not automatically render the measure legal, it simply forecloses judicial review as an avenue to assessment. This reasoning would appear all the more appropriate when the alleged illegality of the instrument may be obscured by conditions of scientific uncertainty and incomplete information. The Court is on firmer ground

---

[83] C-68/11, n. 69, para. 40. [84] *Ibid.*, para. 41
[85] Note that the deadline does not affect private litigants, who can challenge the legality of EU legal instruments in domestic proceedings, with the option of a preliminary reference to the CJEU. See C-314/85 *Foto-Frost* v. *Hauptzollamt Lübeck-Ost* ECLI:EU:C:1987:452; C-461/03 *Gaston Schul Douane-expediteur* ECLI:EU:C:2005:742.

with its second motivation. Although the uncertainties and coordination challenges that Italy refers to could very conceivably cause temporary effectiveness failures, recognising them as a justification for persistent and systemic underperformance would jeopardise the credibility of the entire regulatory framework. Still, Italy's arguments are a worthwhile reminder that attaining and maintaining a predetermined level of air quality is a highly difficult mission that is easily scuppered. The recent Volkswagen scandal illustrates the point: the company equipped its diesel engines with software that could detect when the vehicle was tested and, in such event, lower its emissions. This type of technology is what is called a 'defeat device'; it is purpose-built to undermine regulatory effectiveness. It is certainly arguable that national regulatory regimes should be robust enough to absorb a degree of private non-compliance and even fraud,[86] but it is equally evident that this demands a level of prescience and focus that today's resource-strapped and over-extended regulators may struggle to deliver.

If infringement actions have been used relatively sparingly in air pollution policy, the alternative avenue of private enforcement of EU law has proven unexpectedly productive in regulating Member State implementation. The CJEU has affirmed that the broad and programmatic nature of Member State responsibilities pursuant to the NECD and the AQFD does not stand in the way of certain provisions having direct effect. Under the NECD, the Member States' obligations to limit their annual national emissions under Article 4 afford too much discretion for private parties to deploy them as a basis to challenge the legal validity of specific measures that may have an impact on the overall level of regulated substances emitted.[87] However, Article 6 of the NECD, which requires the Member States to draw up and make publicly available national programmes for the progressive reduction of national emissions, was deemed unconditional and sufficiently precise to have direct effect.[88] It therefore appears that, if private parties cannot challenge the legality of specific measures, they might challenge 'the appropriateness of the *body of policies and measures* adopted or envisaged within the framework of the respective national programmes to the objective of limiting, by the end of 2010 at the latest, emissions of the pollutants covered to amounts not exceeding the ceilings laid down for each Member State'.[89]

Similar perspectives inform two preliminary reference rulings concerning the AQFD and its 1996 predecessor. In *Janecek*, the claimant lived in the Landshuter Allee district, a heavily polluted part of Munich.[90] The State of Bayern had

---

[86] Moreover, with regard to the Volkswagen emissions scandal, questions have been raised whether and to what extent the Commission and national governments were aware of the practice. See European Parliament (plenary sitting), 'Motion for a Resolution pursuant to Rule 133 of the Rules of Procedure on the Commission's role in the Volkswagen scandal', B8–1184/2015, 28 October 2015, available at: www.europarl.europa.eu/sides/getDoc.do?pubRef=-//EP//NONSGML+MOTION+B8-2015-1184+0+DOC+PDF+V0//EN.
[87] Joined Cases C-165/09 and C-167/09, n. 52, above, para. 88.   [88] *Ibid.*, para. 99.
[89] *Ibid.*, para. 103.   [90] Case C-237/07 *Janecek* ECLI:EU:C:2008:447.

adopted an air quality action plan for the city of Munich, but not a specific plan with short-term measures for the district. The CJEU decided that this ran counter to Bayern's obligations under EU air quality law (including Council Directive 96/62/EC) and that, where a risk exists that limit values or alert thresholds may be exceeded, individuals whose health is directly at risk because of this exceedance 'must be in a position to require the competent national authorities to draw up an action plan'.[91] When it comes to the content of the action plan, however, Member States are less constrained: there is a general expectation of 'adequacy', but Member States are not obliged to take measures to ensure that limit values or alert thresholds are never exceeded.[92]

The boundaries of Member State discretion are further explored in Case C-404/13, *ClientEarth* v. *the Secretary of State for the Environment, Food and Rural Affairs*.[93] ClientEarth challenged the legality of the UK government's decision not to apply for an extension under Article 22 AQFD for 16 zones or agglomerations in respect of which the air quality plans projected compliance with the limit values well beyond the 2010 deadline, namely, between 2015 and 2025. Applications under Article 22 AQFD may buy Member States extra time, but they do come with strings attached. In particular, Article 22 sets 2015 as the latest possible date for compliance, which was at least five years before the UK government anticipated being able to bring nitrogen dioxide (NO_2) emissions within the legal limits. Additionally, applications under Article 22 must be accompanied by an air quality action plan that must pass Commission scrutiny.

Both the national court proceedings and the preliminary ruling in *ClientEarth* constitute important decisions for several reasons. First, the case affirms that the right to rely on the direct effect of certain air quality legal provisions is not limited to individuals whose personal health is at stake, as was the case in *Janecek*, but also extends to non-governmental organisations acting on behalf of the environment. Secondly, the case has an interesting national backstory. Whereas both the domestic court of first instance and the Court of Appeal took a permissive approach to executive discretion in implementation, the UK Supreme Court decided, without a CJEU steer, that the government was incontrovertibly in breach of its obligation to respect the nitrogen dioxide limit values enshrined in the AQFD. Having already decided the case in favour of the plaintiff, the Supreme Court then turned to the CJEU to obtain further clarification on the scope and extent of the UK's non-compliance, asking whether Member States are obliged to avail themselves of the mechanism under Article 22 AQFD to seek a postponement of the deadline for zones and agglomerations where the limit values are not reached by the 2010 deadlines, and whether any exceptions to this obligation exist. The CJEU's reply was equally noteworthy: 'when it is objectively apparent, having regard to existing data, and notwithstanding the implementation by that Member State of appropriate pollution abatement measures, that conformity with those values cannot be achieved in a given zone or agglomeration by the specified deadline', Member States are indeed obliged to follow

---

[91] *Ibid.*, para. 42.   [92] *Ibid.*, paras. 44 and 46.   [93] ECLI:EU:C:2013:805.

the procedures and requirements in Article 22.[94] This obligation brooks no exception. On 17 December 2015, the UK Department for Environment, Food and Rural Affairs (DEFRA) released 40 new air quality plans to comply with the Supreme Court's and CJEU's judgments.[95]

As mentioned before, the practical relevance of the Court's stance with regard to Article 22 AQFD specifically will be limited since the five-year grace period has now lapsed and any further exceedances must be dealt with under Article 23 AQFD. However, two abiding messages flow from the CJEU's reasoning in this case. In the first place, the Court's discussion of Articles 22 and 23 AQFD sheds more light on the intended role of the respective mechanisms. Whereas Article 22 deals with a burden of the past and offers a longer leeway to reach agreed air quality targets, Article 23 is designed to enable Member States to cope with new rises in emissions that cause Member States to overshoot previously attained targets and therefore require a new set of responsive measures. An important message to take from this is that action undertaken pursuant to Article 23 must be designed to eliminate any exceedance as soon as possible. Secondly, the ruling clearly affirms that de facto or informal compliance does not suffice; Member States must follow the designated procedures to avoid a breach of EU law.

Regulating Industrial Emissions

In addition to cross-sectoral measures such as the AQFD and the NECD, air pollution regulation features in a range of EU instruments that target particular activities, processes or products. They include provisions affecting cars, vans and other vehicles, as well as non-mobile road machinery (e.g. hydraulic cranes).[96]

---

[94] *Ibid.*, para. 33.
[95] The air quality plans can be found at: www.gov.uk/government/policies/environmental-quality?page=2.
[96] Directive 2009/30/EC amending Directive 98/70/EC on the specification of petrol, diesel and gas-oil and introducing a mechanism to monitor and reduce greenhouse gas emissions and amending Directive 1999/32/EC on the specification of fuel used by inland waterway vessels and repealing Directive 93/12/EEC, OJ 2009 L 140/88; Regulation (EC) No. 715/2007 on type approval of motor vehicles with respect to emissions from light passenger and commercial vehicles (Euro 5 and Euro 6) and on access to vehicle repair and maintenance information, OJ 2007 L 171/1; Regulation (EC) No. 595/2009 on type-approval of motor vehicles and engines with respect to emissions from heavy-duty vehicles (Euro VI) and on access to vehicle repair and maintenance information and amending Regulation (EC) No. 715/2007 and Directive 2007/46/EC and repealing Directives 80/1269/EEC, 2005/55/EC and 2005/78/EC, OJ 2009 L 188/1; Directive 97/68/EC on the approximation of the laws of the Member States relating to measures against the emission of gaseous and particulate pollutants from internal combustion engines to be installed in non-road mobile machinery, as amended, OJ 1997 L 59/1. Directive 97/68/EC and its amendments are currently being revised, see Proposal for a Regulation of the European Parliament and of the Council on requirements relating to emissions limits and type-approval for internal combustion engines for non-road mobile machinery COM/2014/0581 final – 2014/0268 (COD).

This section examines one such instrument in greater detail, namely, the 2010 Industrial Emissions Directive (IED).

The main objective of the IED is to govern the environmental behaviour of society's heavy industrial polluters, from combustion plants, steel manufacturers and chemicals producers to waste treatment facilities and poultry farms.[97] To this end, the IED adopts an integrated approach that far exceeds emissions into the air; it is equally concerned with water pollution, soil treatment and the environmental risks associated with waste generation. Integrative thinking resonates in the Integrated Pollution Prevention and Control (IPPC) permitting approach, which constitutes the IED's core regulatory technique to ensure industrial compliance with environmental prescriptions. It is also reflected in the IED's genesis: the Directive is, itself, an updated and integrated version of no fewer than seven EU environmental measures, including the former IPPC Directive, a Directive on emissions from large combustion plants, measures on waste incineration, volatile organic compounds and waste from the titanium dioxide industry.[98]

In accordance with Article 4(1) IED, Member States must ensure that none of the industrial installations covered by the Directive operates without a permit. Member States may only issue such a permit to installations that live up to the environmental standards and prescriptions laid down in the Directive. The tasks of implementation are left chiefly to national regulatory authorities, who are charged to:

- establish and govern the permitting scheme,
- detail EU regulatory prescriptions and interpret them in the light of the local context where necessary,
- ensure the compatibility of individual permit applications with the Directive's objectives and expectations, and
- police compliance with the permitting conditions.

---

[97] See Annex I to the IED.
[98] IPPC: Directive 2008/1/EC concerning integrated pollution prevention and control, OJ 2008 L 24/8. LCPs: Directive 2001/80/EC on the limitation of emissions of certain pollutants into the air from large combustion plants, OJ 2001 L 309/1. Waste incineration: Directive 2000/76/EC on the incineration of waste, OJ 2000 L 332/91. VOCs: Council Directive 1999/13/EC on the limitation of emissions of volatile organic compounds due to the use of organic solvents in certain activities and installations, OJ 1999 L 85/1. 3. Directives on Titanium Dioxide waste: Directive 78/176/EEC on waste from the titanium dioxide industry, OJ 1978 L 54/19; Council Directive 82/883/EEC on procedures for the surveillance and monitoring of environments concerned by waste from the titanium dioxide industry, OJ 1982 L 378/1; and Council Directive 92/112/EEC on procedures for harmonising the programmes for the reduction and eventual elimination of pollution caused by waste from the titanium dioxide industry, OJ 1992 L 409/11.

The discussion below offers further insights into the IED as a model of integrated environmental governance, and then concentrates on the IED's distinctive approach to environmental standardisation – a combined approach organised around the concept of 'best available techniques' (BAT) and effectuated through an extensive body of reference documents that are situated in the penumbra between binding law and guidance document. The concluding paragraphs of this section reflect on the difficult, constantly evolving, yet persistent challenges of reconciling calls for flexibility in environmental regulatory decision-making with legal expectations of uniformity and predictability.[99]

Integrated Pollution Prevention and Control within the IED

The idea of integration occupies a variety of spaces within EU law. At Treaty level, the integration principle is chiefly associated with the requirement expressed in Article 11 TFEU to take environmental questions into account across Union policy fields and activities. On this account, the integration principle presents itself as a key tenet of sustainable development, which confirms environmental protection as an integral part of the development process rather than an external concern that irritates or potentially obstructs development.[100] Within the sphere of EU environmental legislation itself – as constituted by the body of directives, regulations and decisions that have as their goal the pursuit of a high level of environmental protection – the idea of integration more typically refers to a need to foster coherence between different environmental policy fields and to manage the risk of pollution displacement. It is in the latter guise that integration, or integrated control, has informed the regulation of industrial installations.

In this context, it is useful to remember that the IED is, itself, the product of a drive to merge, or integrate, different directives that all governed aspects or activities of large-scale industries. Prominent among the predecessor legal instruments of the IED is Directive 2008/1/EC concerning integrated pollution prevention and control (IPPC Directive), which was itself an updated version of the 1996 original.[101] The name may not have survived the 2010 merger and recasting exercise, but the idea of IPPC is alive and well within the IED. At the heart of IPPC is the premise that environmental protection can be more effectively achieved if policies and rules regarding soil, water, air and waste are not developed in isolation but instead crafted in a joined-up, coherent

---

[99] Themes discussed in this chapter are a selection of the many issues covered by the IED and the broad range of debates to which they connect. Matters such as soil and groundwater contamination, waste management, the specific provisions governing large combustion plants, the regulation of newly emerging techniques deployed in industrial settings, EU expectations regarding inspection, public participation in IPPC-related decision-making, and the establishment of a pollutant release and transfer register, remain outside the scope of this investigation.

[100] See Chapter 3, pp. 103–105.

[101] Council Directive 96/61/EC concerning integrated pollution prevention and control OJ 1996 L 257/26.

manner. To this end, decisions regarding industrial installations should be based on assessments of the polluting and consuming potential of the installation as a whole.[102] The approach was first advocated in the Fifth Environmental Action Programme, and was inspired by the UK Integrated Pollution Control (IPC) legislation of 1990.[103]

The IED espouses the ideal of integration at the level of conception, administration, application and decision-making. At the *conceptual* level, integration refers to the choice to address the environmental media of soil, air and water within a single instrument in order to pursue environmental protection as a whole. Indeed, the very first Article of the IED affirms that the Directive: 'lays down rules designed to prevent or, where that is not practicable, to reduce emissions into air, water and land and to prevent the generation of waste, in order to achieve a high level of protection of the environment taken as a whole'. *Organisationally*, the IED offers a one-stop-shop approach to the industrial installations under its remit. This may be effectuated by bundling all permitting competences within a single institution – the avenue followed in England and Wales where the Environment Agency receives and processes all aspects of environmental permitting applications. Alternatively, permitting applications may be processed by a combination of public authorities, as happens in Germany. In that case, Article 5(2) IED requires the process to be 'fully coordinated', in order to 'guarantee an effective integrated approach'.

In terms of *application*, the IED prescribes that applications for permits should include, as a minimum, a description of the various sources of emissions; the nature and quantities of foreseeable emissions from the installation into each medium; and the main alternatives to the proposed technology, techniques and measures studied by the applicant in outline. Finally, at the stage of *permitting*, competent authorities are, again, called to take a holistic approach in the determination of permitting conditions. Such conditions must cover, at least, emissions limit values for polluting substances, which must be determined with regard to the nature of the pollutants and their potential to transfer pollution from one medium to another (Article 14(1)(a) IED). Additionally, conditions should specify, *inter alia*, 'appropriate requirements ensuring protection of the soil and groundwater and measures concerning the monitoring and management of waste' (Article 14(1)(b) IED). Moreover, Article 14(4) IED generally requires permit conditions to be determined with reference to BAT conclusions. The aim of the BAT standard, which will be discussed in greater detail in the next section, is to support the development of conditions that are equipped to prevent or, where that is not possible, reduce the impacts of regulated installations on the environment

---

[102] Lee, *EU Environmental Law, Governance and Decision-Making*, 109.
[103] Michael Purdue, 'Integrated Pollution Control in the Environmental Protection Act 1990: A Coming of Age of Environmental Law?' (1991) *Modern Law Review* 534–551, at 544; Bell et al., *Environmental Law*, 519.

'*as a whole*'. Thus, the idea of integration permeates the IPPC approach from its institutional design to its case-by-case application.

Still, there are limits to the IED's drive to integration. As mentioned, permit applications do not necessarily need to be handled by one institution; it suffices that the application process is coordinated and that applicants only need to submit a single permit request. This arrangement arguably responds better to regulated parties' desire for cutting red tape than to the goal of avoiding displacement of pollution risks. Secondly, and most prominently, the IED addresses the environmental impacts of the side effects of production (emissions and waste), but not the production output itself. The best available techniques may, thus, still be put to work to produce a range of environmentally irresponsible goods and services. Finally, although a primary driver of integrated approaches is to avoid pollution displacement which may erode the effectiveness of environmental regulation, it should be noted that integrated approaches could create alternative erosion risks. Recently approved Commission conclusions on the best available techniques for the refining of mineral oil and gas endorse the use of environmental management systems that deploy a 'bubble approach', in which emissions limits are applied to the refinery as a whole rather than to each individual unit.[104] This infuses environmental permitting with a degree of flexibility that, while welcomed by industry as enabling regulatory standards to be met in a more cost-effective way, has raised concerns among environmental NGOs that this particular mode of integrated thinking may induce an unwarranted relaxation of emissions standards at the level of the individual units.[105]

'Best Available Techniques' (BAT)

The regulatory approach within the IPPC part of the IED is developed around the concept of 'best available techniques' (BAT). In the following paragraphs, we look, first, at the meaning of BAT in the IED, and we then explore how BAT is used to anchor the IPPC regime to a broad and general foundation of environmental principles and expectations.

BAT

'Best available techniques' (or BAT) is a term of art that refers to the combination of design, technology and operating procedures ('techniques') that are most effective and up to date in terms of preventing or minimising adverse environmental impacts, that are generally considered to be accessible and affordable for installations that are representative of the sector ('available') and that are capable of delivering a high level of environmental protection ('best').

---

[104] European Commission Joint Research Centre (JRC), 'Best Available Techniques (BAT)', Reference Document for the Refining of Mineral Oil and Gas (2015). See http://eippcb.jrc.ec.europa.eu/reference/BREF/REF_BREF_2015.pdf.

[105] 'Refineries Win "Bubble" Option for IED Compliance', *ENDS Europe*, 31 October 2014.

To appreciate the significance of the three key 'ingredients' of BAT, it is useful to compare the term to alternative and earlier iterations found in regulation and scholarship. Formerly, BAT was routinely translated as 'best available technology', which expresses a similar combination of state-of-the-art expectations with economic feasibility but is more narrowly focused on infrastructural technology rather than the more encompassing range of techniques and processes that industrial installations deploy. The 1980s and 1990s witnessed a preference for the term BATNEEC, signalling 'best available technology (or techniques) not entailing excessive cost', which could be taken as a reflection of the growing preoccupation with cost–benefit considerations in regulatory decision-making that characterised the era.[106] A third alternative is the 'best practicable environmental option' (BPEO) standard, which reflects the requirement that, for a given objective, the least environmentally harmful option will be chosen. Like BAT, BPEO infuses a dose of pragmatism into decision-making through its reference to 'practicability' (comparable to BAT's 'availability' disclaimer). However, it does not introduce an overarching expectation that a high level of environmental protection will be maintained. It merely requires the best practicable option *for the predetermined objective*, however environmentally damaging that objective may be. The IED's understanding of BAT, in contrast, does reflect such expectation and is therefore a less relativist standard than BPEO.

> **Article 3(10) IED**
>
> 'Best available techniques' means the most effective and advanced stage in the development of activities and their methods of operation, which indicates the practical suitability of particular techniques for providing the basis for emissions limit values (ELVs) and other permit conditions designed to prevent and, where that is not practicable, to reduce emissions and the impact on the environment as a whole:
>
> (a) 'techniques' includes both the technology used and the way in which the installation is designed, built, maintained, operated and decommissioned;
> (b) 'available techniques' means those developed on a scale which allows implementation in the relevant industrial sector, under economically and technically viable conditions, taking into consideration the costs and advantages, whether or not the techniques are used or produced inside the Member State in question, as long as they are reasonably accessible to the operator;
> (c) 'best' means most effective in achieving a high general level of protection of the environment as a whole.

---

[106] See e.g. David Pearce, 'Cost Benefit Analysis and Environmental Policy' (1998) 14(4) *Oxford Review of Economic Policy* 84–100.

Notwithstanding the fulsome definition in Article 3(10) IED, BAT is an essentially 'open' standard: its concrete meaning depends on where, when, and under which general economic circumstances it is applied. In principle, such openness lends itself well to decision-making in the EU context since it accommodates a degree of regional differentiation and discretion in implementation which, in turn, squares the IPPC approach with the demands of subsidiarity and which may help to smooth over differences in national preferences regarding environmental standardisation, such as the previously discussed clashes between the UK and the German approach. This discretion is, however, not unconstrained. First, a significant proportion of the sectors listed in the IED are covered by BAT reference documents or 'BREFs', which are guidelines that describe the applied techniques, present emissions and consumption levels, as well as the techniques considered for the determination of BAT within a specific sector. This data constitutes the basis for 'BAT conclusions', which are adopted by the European Commission and lay down the particular modes for determining BAT for defined activities or sectors. BAT conclusions also, importantly, indicate the ELVs associated with BAT for the respective sector or activity. BAT conclusions can moreover contain information on issues such as appropriate monitoring strategies and site remediation measures.

The presence of BAT conclusions does not obviate the role of national permitting authorities – they typically cannot simply be cut and pasted into individual permits but instead require further detailing and application. However, the BREFs and BAT conclusions incontrovertibly give a strong steer to the permitting process. Moreover, even if the activity for which permission is sought is not covered by a BREF, Member State authorities are required to follow a standardised set of 12 criteria in their determination of BAT, listed in Annex III to the IED. The criteria include requirements that BAT incorporate the use of low-waste technology and of less hazardous substances; that factors such as technological advances, changes in scientific knowledge and understanding, the need to prevent the overall impact of emissions and the length of time needed to introduce BAT are taken into account in decision-making; and that information published by public international organisations is used in the determination of BAT. Evidently, these are broadly formulated prescriptions, but they nonetheless frame the context in which regulatory authorities are expected to operate.

Finally, it is important to remember that the flexibility inherent in the BAT standard also has a temporal dimension. Since what is 'best' and what is 'available' change over time, BAT automatically updates itself without the need for continuous legal amendment. Some commentators have singled out this scope for 'dynamic tightening' as a key driver of technological innovation.[107] Others, however, have denounced BAT's orientation towards the 'best' for every

---

[107] David Williamson and Gary Lynch-Wood, 'Ecological Modernisation and the Regulation of Firms' (2012) 21(6) *Environmental Politics* 941–959, at 944; Martin Jänicke and Stefan Lindemann, 'Governing Environmental Innovations' (2010) 19(1) *Environmental Politics* 127–141.

installation in every regulated sector as a major source of regulatory inefficiency, since achieving the best may be far costlier in one sector than it is in others. Bruce Ackerman and Richard Stewart famously took aim at the BAT standard in their seminal 1985 article on 'Reforming Environmental Law', which unfavourably compares BAT approaches to market-based instruments in terms of their cost-effectiveness, impact on innovation and democratic legitimacy.[108] It is therefore interesting to contemplate how the EU's increasing reliance on market-based approaches, as evidenced in fields such as climate change and waste policy, impacts on the BAT ethos. One evident impact is the presence of Article 9 IED, pursuant to which the permitting conditions for installations that are also subject to the Emissions Trading Directive may not include ELVs for greenhouse gases. Furthermore, it is possible to discern within the IED as well as in its further implementation some seedling attempts to reconcile the installation-based focus in BAT with the promised greater efficiencies associated with overall capping in combination with (re)allocation at the individual level. Article 4(2) IED allows Member States to issue permits that cover 'two or more installations or parts of installations operated by the same operator on the same site', although the scope for efficiency-driven reallocation is severely limited by the ensuing requirement that each installation complies with the requirements of the IED. More significant may be the aforementioned recent inclusion of a 'bubble approach' in the determination of best available techniques for mineral oil and gas refinery. This move responds to stakeholder calls for flexibility, but also raises the question whether the best available outcomes are still being achieved, or whether instead the goalposts have shifted towards the most cost-effective available outcomes.

Standardisation in the IPPC Framework: The Anchoring Function of BAT

Recent market-based and alternative approaches to regulation may be influencing IPPC at the margins, but the core of the European Union's regulatory policy to control the environmental impacts of industrial installations remains firmly committed to standardisation generally and BAT in particular. References to BAT are woven into the fabric of IPPC at both the general level and within the more detailed permitting conditions that together make up the bulk of Chapter 1 of the IED. BAT thus anchors and gives a focal point to the complex and at times confusing alternative sets of conditions that Member States and installations must meet to secure compliance with European environmental law.

The overarching target of IPPC is set out in Article 15(4) IED, and demands that no significant pollution should be caused and a high level of environmental protection should be achieved. To that effect, the Member States'

---

[108] Ackerman and Stewart, 'Reforming Environmental Law'.

competent authorities must ensure that all covered installations are operated in compliance with general principles (Article 11 IED) as well as with applicable environmental quality standards (EQS) (Article 18 IED). Among the general principles listed in Article 11, some feature the requirement to apply best available techniques, which embeds the BAT standards as a general principle of IPPC. Article 11 further lists as general principles: taking all appropriate measures to prevent pollution; causing no significant pollution; using energy efficiently; and generating and treating waste in accordance with the prescriptions of the waste hierarchy.

The general targets and principles of IPPC are operationalised through a permitting approach, which can assume one of two different forms. For certain categories of installations, Member States may decide to adopt 'general binding rules', which create essentially a predetermined 'set menu' of standards and prescriptions that can be directly applied at the installation level (Articles 6 and 17 IED). Such general binding rules, the IED demands, must be based on BAT. The alternative and comparatively more 'bespoke' avenue is via the general permitting process. One very prominent permitting condition is that emissions limit values (ELVs) be fixed for all polluting substances listed in Annex II of the IED (which includes familiar air pollutants such as sulphur dioxide, oxides of nitrogen, volatile organic compounds and arsenic)[109] as well as for any other pollutants likely to be emitted in significant quantities, taking into account their nature and propensity for cross-media pollution transfer (Article 14(1) IED). The determination of ELVs, in turn, must be made on the basis of BAT conclusions or, if no such conclusions exist (yet), on the basis of BAT as determined by national competent authorities in compliance with the Annex III criteria. Finally, in their determination of ELVs with reference to BAT or BAT conclusions, national authorities once again face two main options. Either, they can espouse something akin to a 'cut and paste' approach whereby they express ELVs for the same or shorter periods and under the same reference conditions as those associated with BAT, or they follow a more tailored approach that stipulates different values, timeframes and/or reference conditions from those associated with BAT and potentially indicated in BAT conclusions. If the latter path is chosen, the permitted installation's emissions

---

[109] The full list of Annex II pollutants further contains: sulphur compounds, nitrogen compounds, carbon monoxide, metals and their compounds, dust including fine particulate matter, asbestos, chlorine and its compounds, fluorine and its compounds, arsenic compounds, cyanides, carcinogens, mutagens and reprotoxins (both airborne and aquatic), polychlorinated dibenzodioxins and polychlorinated dibenzofurans, organohalogen compounds and substances which may form such compounds in the aquatic environment, organophosphorus compounds, organotin compounds, persistent hydrocarbons and persistent and bioaccumulable organic toxic substances, biocides and plant protection products, materials in suspension, substances which contribute to eutrophication (in particular, nitrates and phosphates), substances which have an unfavourable influence on the oxygen balance (and can be measured using parameters such as BOD, COD, etc.), and substances listed in Annex X to Directive 2000/60/EC.

need to be monitored annually in order to ascertain compatibility with BAT under normal operating conditions (Article 15(3)).

The centrality of BAT is thus affirmed in every layer of IPPC decision-making. In deviation of the standard trajectory, Article 14(2) IED provides that ELVs may be supplemented or replaced by alternative parameters or technical measures that ensure an equivalent level of environmental protection. Yet here again, the technical or equivalent measures adopted in lieu of or alongside ELVs must still be based on BAT. Only in a few discrete scenarios will the permitting provisions lay down prescriptions that do not correspond to BAT. The first instance occurs when regulated installations must comply with environmental quality standards (EQS) and sheer adherence to BAT does not achieve this goal. Here, the Member States' national authorities will need to introduce conditions that go above and beyond BAT. At the other side of the spectrum, BAT expectations may be temporarily suspended if the installation wishes to apply new or emerging techniques. Additionally, it may be allowable to drop below the BAT threshold in the determination of ELVs if adherence to BAT, as described in the BAT conclusions, would entail disproportionately high costs on the installation compared to the environmental benefits. In the event, the IED imposes two 'failsafe' conditions: first, limit values may not drop below the ELVs included in the Annexes to the IED and, secondly, this relaxation of BAT cannot override the general requirement that no significant pollution be caused and a high level of environmental protection be maintained.

The Evolution of BREFs: A Hardening Attitude towards EU Soft Law

The BAT standard sets down a general benchmark for industrial installations covered by the IPPC regime, but its broadly formulated Annex III criteria, which call on national authorities to consider issues such as 'the use of low-waste technology' and to take into account 'information published by public international organisations', offer little by way of practical guidance. This is all the more so when we consider the diversity of industrial sectors subject to permitting requirements under the IED. Low-waste technologies in glass manufacturing are likely to be radically different from those used in animal slaughterhouses.

The early 1990s vision of the EU IPPC regime was that the practical elaboration and application of BAT in the permitting process should remain a Member State responsibility. This would enable differentiation depending on sectoral and regional variation and imbue the IPPC framework with a desirable degree of flexibility and responsiveness to local conditions. To assist national authorities in this task, the Commission resolved to facilitate the development of BAT reference documents or 'BREFs'. These were conceived as informal, non-binding guidelines to describe the applied techniques, present emissions and consumption levels, and the techniques considered for the determination of BAT within specific sectors. BREFs were developed in a multi-partite process, connecting Member State representatives, industry stakeholders and civil society organisations through the establishment of an Information Exchange Forum (IEF). The BREF development process was orchestrated by the IPPC Bureau, which forms part of the European Commission's Joint Research Centre (JRC) and is located in Seville (Spain). It correspondingly became known as the 'Seville process'.

The contemporary treatment of BREFs, enshrined in the 2010 IED, retains a number of key features of the earlier approach, yet there are marked differences. As before, BREFs are the product of a development process involving Member States, industry representatives, NGOs and the Commission. The process has, however, become more tightly structured and proceduralised over time. Article 13 IED calls on the Commission to 'establish and regularly convene' a forum composed of Member State representatives, the industries concerned and environmental NGOs. It thereby bestows a formal status and a degree of permanence on the IEF. The IEF is serviced by Technical Working Groups (TWGs), which consist of representatives of national environmental ministries and/or regulators, as well as trade association, industry and NGO representatives. The TWGs constitute the technocratic counterpart of the more politically oriented IEF, with data gathering and technical specification dominating in the former and review and negotiation characterising the latter.

A second key change is that the function and role of the IEF is much more clearly circumscribed now than it was before the entry into effect of the IED. Article 13(2) lists a minimum number of issues that information exchange must cover, such as the performance of installations and techniques in terms of emissions; raw materials, water and energy consumption; monitoring associated with the techniques used; cross-media effects; and the impact of emerging technologies on BAT. Article 13(3), in turn, requires that the Commission consult the IEF on a range of issues, including the latter's operating procedures and work programme, as well as, crucially, guidance on data collection and on the drawing up of BREFs.

The third and most important change introduced in the IED concerns the legal status of BREFs. Whereas the 1996 IPPC Directive afforded them no special status (in fact, it was silent on their subject), Articles 13(1), (4) and (5) IED charge the Commission to draw up and review BREFs, for the purpose of which it must 'obtain and make publicly available' the IEF's opinion on the proposed content of BREFs. The Commission must also take the IEF's opinion into account in its decisions on BAT conclusions, which contain the decisive parts of the BREF concerned. The BAT conclusions, we recall, function as a primary and, in principle, mandatory reference point for national authorities in their determination of ELVs. The legal significance of BAT conclusions is reflected in the choice of decision-making procedure: in accordance with Article 13(5) IED, BAT conclusions must be adopted following the regulatory comitology procedure, which essentially means that the Commission's enactment of BAT conclusions must be vetted by a committee of Member State representatives. In the absence of the committee's approval, the question is referred to the Council, which is thereby granted an opportunity to review and, if appropriate, reject the Commission proposal by qualified majority.

The most immediate impact of the IED reforms is that it is now much harder for national authorities to avoid applying BREF guidelines in the determination of ELVs and related standards. This change was very much intentional; one of the stated objectives of IPPC reform was to iron out unevenness in the interpretation of BAT, and thus to address the ensuing deficiencies in environmental protection at the national level.[110] The incorporation of BAT conclusions in Commission decisions may also enhance the procedural legitimacy of the Seville process. In contrast to BREFs, Commission decisions are binding EU acts adopted in accordance with the 1999 Comitology Decision.[111] They are subject to transparency requirements and to judicial review. This constitutes a potentially important accountability guarantee vis-à-vis parties that find themselves outside the 'inner circle' of the Seville process. However, it is important not to take for granted the significance of reviewability, especially when the entity that seeks to have an EU legal act annulled is a private party or, in EU terminology, a 'non-privileged applicant'. In spite of a relative relaxation in the Lisbon Treaty, the standing requirements for non-privileged applicants to challenge the legality of EU acts under Article 263 TFEU remain notoriously demanding.[112] The access to justice provisions under the Aarhus Regulation, which focus on measures governing environmental issues and enable environmental NGOs to request an internal review of administrative acts, thus far have brought only limited change, mostly because of the Commission's narrow interpretation of what constitute 'administrative acts'.[113] Alternatively, the legality of Commission decisions on BAT conclusions could be queried in national court proceedings in the context of a permitting process. This could trigger a preliminary reference to the European Court and, thus, offer third parties such as NGOs an indirect opportunity to challenge BAT conclusions. An opportunity to challenge, however, does not equate with an easy win: EU legal acts have proven resilient to review. The CJEU afford a broad margin of discretion to administrative and regulatory decision-makers and usually are loath to second guess decision-making on the substance. Hence, the firmer legal status of BREFs bestowed via Article 13 IED may ultimately serve to protect the outcomes of the Seville process, rather than to secure effective accountability.

The recognition of BREFs in Article 13 is an important step towards legally firming up the standards and methodology BREFs contain, but the full impact of

---

[110] Lee, *EU Environmental Law, Governance and Decision-Making*, 120.
[111] Council Decision 1999/468/EC, OJ 1999 L 184/23.
[112] Haakon Roer-Eide and Mariolina Eliantonio, 'The Meaning of Regulatory Act Explained: Are There Any Significant Improvements for the Standing of Non-Privileged Applicants in Annulment Actions?' (2013) 14 *German Law Journal* 1851–1865, answering the titular question largely in the negative.
[113] NGOs are listed under Title IV of the Aarhus Regulation 1367/2006, OJ 2006 L 264/13. Commission Decision 2008/50/EC, OJ 2008 L 13/24 further elucidates the rules that apply for an NGO requesting an internal review of administrative acts.

this development is still to be determined. For example, it is presently unclear whether BREFs are to be treated as an exhaustive source of information on BAT in a particular industrial sector. A 2009 CJEU judgment determined that the sheer fact that a BREF regarding poultry farming only covered laying hens, meat chickens, turkey, duck and guinea fowl did not imply that quail farming should be treated as outside the scope of the 1996 IPPC Directive. In its reasoning, the Court emphasised that 'such a document has no binding effect or interpretative value for Directive 96/61, as it is limited to providing an inventory of technical knowledge on the best available farming techniques'.[114] The reference to BREFs in Article 13 IED does not necessarily compel a change of course on this issue, but by the same token it opens the door for a change of judicial perspective on the relation between BREFs and the general provisions of the IED. Moreover, BREFs may be invoked in cases outside the remit of IPPC permitting. In *Saetti and Frediani*, for example, a BREF on oil and gas refining was pivotal in the CJEU's determination that the use of petroleum coke as fuel did not constitute a waste recovery process.[115] The evidentiary weight of authoritative but formally non-binding documents is a difficult matter for courts to settle. This is all the more so where, as in the case of BREFs, the document is at least partly the outcome of a negotiation process in which different interests are represented and from which winners and losers emerge.[116]

In sum, the reference to BREFs in Article 13 IED, and the incorporation of BAT conclusions in Commission decisions, will give BREFs a stronger footing in both administrative and judicial deliberations. The primary desired consequence is an improvement in the environmental quality of permitting decisions. As always, however, there are trade-offs to be considered. The elevated importance of BREFs transforms their development into a high stakes game, which could slow down consensus building and drain the process of environmental ambition. Also, the flip side of the higher level of uniformity that a mandatory reliance on BAT conclusions will bring is an inevitable loss of flexibility. The paragraphs below offer some concluding reflections on the difficulty of reconciling the theoretical virtues of flexibility with the pragmatism of technical standardisation.

Flexibility in the IED: An Assessment

The IPPC regime was designed with flexibility in mind. The very notion of BAT created scope for environmental regulators to vary the technical articulation of environmental standards depending on the local context: the question which

---

[114] Case C-473/07 *Association nationale pour la protection des eaux et rivières –TOS, Association OABA* v. *Ministère de l'Écologie, du Développement et de l'Aménagement durables* ECLI:EU:C:2009:30, para. 30.
[115] C-235/02, *Saetti and Frediani* ECLI:EU:C:2004:26.
[116] Bettina Lange, *Implementing EU Pollution Control: Law and Integration* (Cambridge University Press, 2008).

technologies and practices are 'available', and which are 'best' calls for a relative assessment that takes into account the time, location and socio-economic circumstances in which permit applications are made. BREF documents were intended to play a facilitating role;[117] to inform decisions-makers without constraining them. As a result of flexibility, decision-making would be both economically efficient and more democratic as determinations were made at a level closer to the parties affected.

The current regulatory regime as incorporated in the IED retains vestiges of flexibility, but its stronger emphasis on normalisation and centralisation is equally apparent. The assumption now is that national competent authorities determine permit conditions with reference to BAT conclusions based on BREFs. If they wish to deviate from this expectation, national authorities must show that following BAT conclusions would impose disproportionate costs compared to the environmental benefits.[118] This puts flexibility very much on the defensive. The regime still stops short of exhaustive and universal technical standardisation – BREFs typically need to be further interpreted to be applied within the context of a permit application or review – but it pursues a considerably higher degree of uniformity than the 1996 IPPC Directive did. Moreover, the IED enables Member States to opt out of the bespoke route and introduce 'generally binding rules' for certain categories of installations. In the UK, for example, operators of facilities such as recycling plants and low impact installations can apply for a set 'standard rules permit', which leaves no scope for installation-based tailoring but is both cheaper and faster than the full IPPC permitting route.[119]

Genuine flexibility appears desirable in theory but difficult to maintain in practice. One possible explanation might be that attempts at flexibility are dissonant within the EU legal ethos, which is geared towards 'ever closer union' and has always identified itself as deeply protective of the uniformity of EU law. Alternatively, the implementation of flexible approaches may demand more cognitive capacity and negotiating skill than national regulators or private operators possess. A recent study by Koutalakis, Buzogany and Börzel indicates that, in administratively weaker States particularly, the flexible and soft law aspects of the IPPC regime reduce the likelihood of compliance and risk 'hollowing out' the permitting regime.[120] From this vantage point, the higher degree of standardisation in decision-making within the IED may well represent a recalibration from an optimising to a satisficing approach in environmental regulation.

---

[117] Bell et al., *Environmental Law*, 519.   [118] Art. 15(4) IED.
[119] See www.gov.uk/government/collections/standard-rules-environmental-permitting#low-impact-installation.
[120] Charalampos Koutalakis, Aron Buzogany and Tanja A. Börzel, 'When Soft Regulation is Not Enough: The Integrated Pollution Prevention and Control Directive of the European Union' (2010) 4 *Regulation and Governance* 329–344.

Coherence in Air Pollution Law

Well-designed environmental policy regimes can reinforce each other. Energy efficiency, cleaner product design and robust waste prevention strategies may enhance the impact of water management and air quality frameworks; effective forest management can contribute to environmental policy targets from biodiversity protection and climate change mitigation to the reduction of noise pollution. In the field of air pollution and industrial emissions control, opportunities for synergy abound. For example, phasing out CFCs under the ODS Regulation enables the protection of the ozone layer and simultaneously helps to reduce GHG emissions. The implementation of zonal air quality plans under the AQFD can enhance a Member State's chances of meeting its targets under the NECD, as does the imposition of BAT-compliant ELVs. At other times, however, environmental regimes potentially undermine each other. For instance, the inclusion of CO_2 ELVs in the IED might negatively affect the workings of the EU Emissions Trading Regime. For this reason, the permitting conditions for installations covered by the Emissions Trading Directive exclude GHG emissions.

The coherence of air pollution policy and law internally, and of air pollution law with other segments of EU environmental law and EU law generally, can therefore not be taken for granted. The promotion of diesel fuel resulted in lower CO_2 emissions from cars, furthering climate change mitigation goals, but triggered a rise in particulate matter, one of the most harmful and persistent air pollutants of the age.[121] Commentators have observed that, at times, EU law explicitly limits the opportunities for coherence to be pursued and synergy to develop. In her discussion of case C-165/09, which relates to a review of the Dutch government's decision to issue environmental permits to three power stations initiated at the request of an environmental NGO (see above), Maria Lee critically observes that the CJEU dismissed the claimants' argument that the permits, and the ensuing operation of the power stations, would push emissions in the Netherlands beyond the limits for NO_x and SO_2 set in the NECD. In fact, the CJEU rejected any obligation to even *take account* of the NECs.[122] This, according to Lee, constitutes a failed opportunity to 'embed broader environmental standards in the permitting process' and, arguably, an impoverishment of the ideal of integrated decision-making.

Challenges of coherence have also materialised in the overlaps between EU environmental law and free movement law. Austria famously fell foul of the EU free movement of goods provisions by prohibiting heavy lorries from using the 'Inntalautobahn', a segment of the motorway that traverses the Inn river. In its

---

[121] Rob Swart, Markus Amann, Frank Raes and Willemijn Tuinstra, 'A Good Climate for Clean Air: Linkages between Climate Change and Air Pollution' (2004) 66 *Climatic Change* 263–269, at 265; Eric A. Mazzi and Hadi Dowlatabadi, 'Air Quality Impacts of Climate Mitigation: UK Policy and Passenger Vehicle Choice' (2007) 41(2) *Environmental Science and Technology* 387–392.

[122] Lee, *EU Environmental Law, Governance and Decision-Making*, 109–110.

defence, Austria argued that the prohibition was motivated by environmental protection concerns, and particularly the need to combat air pollution from transport in sensitive regions. However, the CJEU decided twice, first in 2005 and again in 2011,[123] that the prohibition constituted an unjustifiable restriction to trade. In the Court's view, excluding certain categories of transport vehicles from a stretch of the motorway was not the least restrictive means possible to achieve air quality improvements.

The *Inntalautobahn* cases arguably show the CJEU at its most intrusive. The relative effectiveness of different environmental regulatory schemes is notoriously difficult to measure, yet the Court showed little hesitation in wading into the thick of the matter and second guessing the policy choices made by the Austrian government. What is particularly remarkable about the most recent ruling, *Inntalautobahn II*, is that the Court maintained its view even though Austria had performed a thorough assessment of different policy options available in the wake of the 2005 judgment. Moreover, the prohibition formed part of Austria's plan to achieve a reduction in emissions from road traffic, so as to work towards compliance with Austria's air quality commitments under EU law.[124] It was not disputed that NO_x emissions in Austria exceeded the annual limit values set in in EU legislation. However, the CJEU firmly stated that obligations under EU environmental law do not absolve the Member State from their duty to comply with the Treaty provisions on free movement. For this reason, and in spite of a legally identified need to improve on its air quality record, Austria could not invoke EU air quality legislation in defence of its policy. *Inntalautobahn II* is, therefore, a complex ruling to evaluate. On the one hand, we can readily appreciate the concern that Member States might be tempted to deploy their failures to meet targets in EU environmental law as an excuse to introduce trade protectionist measures. On the other hand, we might question whether the Court's choice to adhere to a substantive and strict interpretation of the proportionality principle is warranted in a context where a clearly documented need exists for the Member State to up its level of environmental protection in order to comply with EU requirements.

Conclusion

The claim that air pollution abatement is a difficult goal to achieve will not raise eyebrows. All environmental protection goals pose challenges, and clean air is no exception. By the same token, the challenges of balancing general yet sufficiently instructive EU rules with national discretion in implementation will be familiar to readers versed in other aspects of EU environmental law and policy, from

---

[123] Case C-320/03 *Commission* v. *Austria* ('*Inntalautobahn I*') ECLI:EU:C:2005:684; and Case C-28/09 *Commission* v. *Austria* ('*Inntalautobahn II*') ECLI:EU:C:2011:854.

[124] As contained in the predecessors to the AQFD, namely, Directive 96/62/EC on ambient air quality assessment and management, OJ 1996 L 296/55 and Directive 1999/30/EC relating to limit values for sulphur dioxide, nitrogen dioxide and oxides of nitrogen, particulate matter and lead in ambient air, OJ 1999 L 163/41.

biodiversity protection to water quality management. Yet what the EU legal regimes explored in this chapter illustrate in a singularly exemplary fashion is that finding the balancing point between the EU and the Member State level, between standardised uniformity and local differentiation, is not a one-off exercise. In the context of ambient air legislation, the European Court has accepted the premise of both the National Emissions Ceiling Directive and the Air Quality Framework Directive as measures leaving a broad scope for discretion in implementation, yet it has signalled clearly that such discretion does not bestow immunity from scrutiny upon national governments. With regard to the Industrial Emissions Directive, the evolving status and role of BREFs could be interpreted as an attempt to recalibrate the relation between centralised rule-making and national regulatory discretion.

Since this ex-post renegotiation of the balance between EU law and national discretion has arguably favoured the former over the latter, it is tempting to view the case law on the AQFD and NECD, and the amendments to the IPPC regime, as yet more evidence of the inexorable 'pull towards the centre' to which policies within the field of shared competence are often said to fall victim. With every amendment and every ruling, more decision-making power is concentrated at the EU level, and national sovereignty is correspondingly hollowed out. Yet this portrayal is arguably both exaggerated and over-simplified. First, even with national discretion somewhat moderated by virtue of CJEU rulings, Member States remain firmly in control of the content of air quality plans. Secondly, identifying certain processes and documents, such as the Information Exchange Forum and BREFs, as the product of centralised decision-making may underplay the significant influence of Member States and national administrations in this context. Arguably, domestic authority is not so much diluted as reconfigured within soft lawmaking approaches. This is all the more so when we consider that the presence of BAT conclusions, validated in Commission decisions, can bolster the authority of national regulators in domestic permitting procedures.

A final reason not to jump to any premature conclusion that the field of air pollution abatement is on an unstoppable trajectory towards EU-level centralisation is possibly less felicitous. Presently, the European Commission has limited appetite to follow up on earlier air pollution initiatives, most notably illustrated by the significantly delayed review of the NECD. This gives cause for concern because we now know that air pollution may well be the most seriously underestimated environmental risk within the panoply of EU environmental policies. It is therefore to be hoped that, should the Commission's disinclination to promote the EU legal agenda with regard to the improvement of air quality persist, the Member States will pick up the baton instead. However, given the quintessentially transboundary nature of the problem, and the disincentives this creates for the adoption of effective responses at the national level, this hope might be more wish than realistic expectation.

10

EU Water Law

Introduction

Europe's Waters Interconnected

On the morning of 1 November 1986, residents in the Schweizerhalle industrial area near Basle in Switzerland were woken by sirens sounded by local authorities. They were told to stay indoors while firemen tackled a blaze at the Sandoz factory that had broken out in a storage building used for pesticides, mercury and other highly poisonous agricultural chemicals. By the end of the day, fourteen people, including one of the firemen fighting the blaze, were being treated in hospital after inhaling the fumes.

While the immediate toxicological effects were severe, the greatest impacts of the disaster were felt in the receiving aquatic environment. The water that flowed from the scene after the Swiss firemen had put out the blaze was contaminated with an estimated 10–30 tons of herbicides, insecticides and mercury compounds. Within ten days the pollution had travelled over a thousand kilometres along the length of the Rhine into the North Sea. The acute impact of the pesticides was estimated to have killed half a million fish, with some species wiped out completely. The chronic and bio-accumulative properties of mercury caused Dutch officials in the port of Rotterdam even greater concern where dredging brought up the heavy metal from the silt.[1] Dutch residents, meanwhile, feared for the quality of their drinking water.

The accident came ten years after the 1976 Dangerous Substances in Water Directive had been introduced to regulate intentional discharges into water and eleven years since the 1975 Drinking Water Directive had come into effect. Years of work had been undone in a single night both in Switzerland and the countries downstream. The incident vividly demonstrated the spatial connections between both Member States and countries outside the EU. While the immediate legislative response, the 1982 'Seveso Directive'[2] focused on the provision of information and notification in the case of an emergency, the concern felt by EU water regulators was even more significant in the long term. The incident

---

[1] 'A Pollution Watch on the Rhine', *Chemical Week*, 19 November 1986.
[2] Directive 82/501/EC on the major accident hazards of certain industrial activities, OJ 1982 L 230/1, amended by Council Directive 96/82/EC on the control of major-accident hazards involving dangerous substances, OJ 1997 L 10/13 (Seveso I and II Directives) and following further accidents in Romania, France and the Netherlands Directive 2003/105/EC amending Council Directive 96/82/EC on the control of major-accident hazards involving dangerous substances, OJ 2003 L 345/97.

emphasised the importance of an all-embracing EU system of water law, with a framework that regulates both deliberate and accidental emissions, from industrial point sources and diffuse agricultural run-off. In many ways, the repercussions of the Sandoz disaster paved the way for the 2000 Water Framework Directive[3] that became law in December of that year and now forms the basis of modern water regulation in the EU.

The History of EU Water Law

The regulation of water is a central pillar of Union environmental policy. It was an early arrival on the policy agenda, included in the first Environmental Action Programme in 1973 and has been a consistent strand of EU environmental activity since then. From the early 1970s onwards there has been a consistent political appetite to undertake water regulation to protect human and ecological health, manage water bodies as both consumer and economic resources, preserve aquatic ecosystems and, increasingly, conclude that water is 'heritage' within the EU.

While it is tempting to categorise the evolution of water law into distinct conceptual phases, focusing first, for example, on water quality and subsequently on restricting emissions, in practice, for all its fragmentation, the regulation of water has developed in an overlapping fashion, consistently aiming at higher environmental and health-based standards. It began by regulating drinking and bathing water, implementing its first programmatic directive in 1976, which focused on the emission of dangerous substances into water, before returning to a more focused approach regulating freshwater fish and shellfish waters. It addressed pollution from both point sources (under the integrated pollution prevention and control regulation and regulating urban waste water and industrial effluent) as well as non-point sources (controlling nitrate 'run-off' from agriculture). The development of water law has been an ongoing and reflexive process.

A new phase began with the entry into force of the Water Framework Directive in December 2000. This was, and still is, a self-consciously programmatic intervention. The Directive sets out the modern architecture for water law either linking with or incorporating the existing regulatory schemes for drinking water, bathing water, fish and shellfish water bodies, waste water and nitrates. Each of these regimes has needed legislative revision in light of its coming into force. The Water Framework Directive has also provided for two daughter Directives, on groundwater and priority substances respectively, both of which have since come into force. In 2008, the programmatic Marine Strategy Framework Directive was introduced, providing a framework to integrate the protection of coastal and marine waters into a similarly holistic structure.[4] This is

---

[3] Directive 2000/60/EC establishing a framework for Community action in the field of water policy, OJ 2000 L 327/1.

[4] Directive 2008/56/EC establishing a framework for community action in the field of marine environmental policy, OJ 2008 L 164/19.

both conceptually and procedurally modelled on the 2000 Water Framework Directive extending the holistic approach from inland waters out to sea.[5]

The Inter-Related Threads of EU and International Water Law

Overall, the development of EU water demonstrates more common threads than conceptual step changes and it is not possible convincingly to separate water law into different historical stages. One reason for this is that EU water law inevitably draws on international developments that pre-date the establishment of the Community. Given that politicians and civil servants responsible for water policy are active in both international and EU spheres of water policy, there is ample opportunity for cross-fertilisation of water law and policy.

This interaction is particularly noticeable in the common threads between the Conventions for the Protection of the Marine Environment in the North-East Atlantic concluded in 1972 and 1992 (generally now known as the Oslo–Paris or OSPAR Convention) and the Convention for the Protection of the Marine Environment of the Baltic Sea Area, concluded in 1974 and 1992 (the Helsinki Convention).[6] The 1976 Dangerous Substances into Water Directive[7] has, for example, continued the distinction between substances so dangerous that they must be phased out (the 'black list') and substances that despite their dangers should be controlled by prior authorisation and emissions limits (the 'grey list'). Similarly, the notions of 'best available technology' central to the 'combined approach' adopted in the Water Framework Directive and closely related to the 'best technical knowledge not entailing excessive costs' formula embedded in the 1991 Directive on Urban Waste Water[8] that was at the heart of the codified 2008 Integrated Pollution Prevention and Control Directive,[9] were also inspired by the OSPAR and Helsinki Conventions,[10] where they have long played a central role in characterising the compromise between industrial use and environmental concern that lies at the heart of much water policy. Indeed, following the practice of the international water commissions (notably the OSPAR Commission and HELCOM), the EU has incorporated an analogous longstanding and ongoing process of revision, refining methodologies in light of increasing scientific knowledge and understanding, encouraging scientists to

---

[5] The Marine Strategy Framework Directive 2008/56/EC is beyond the scope of this sample chapter.
[6] It is administered by the HELCOM Commission; see www.helcom.fi/.
[7] Directive 76/464/EC on pollution caused by certain dangerous substances discharged into the aquatic environment of the Community, OJ 1976 L 129/23.
[8] Directive 91/271/EEC concerning urban waste-water treatment, OJ 1991 L 135/40.
[9] Directive 2008/1/EC concerning integrated pollution prevention and control, OJ 2008 L 24/8.
[10] See Art. 2(3)(b)(i) and Appendix 1 of the 1992 OSPAR Convention and Arts. 3(3) and 6 and Annex II of the 1992 Helsinki Convention.

develop new techniques for reporting, measuring and indexing which have been integrated into legislation.[11]

Supplementing these common threads, however, has been the development of a distinctive EU approach to water law. While international law has focused primarily on transboundary and international waters, the EU has been able to look inwards, to regulate inland water at a more local or regional level. In particular, EU law has often proceeded on the basis of smaller water bodies, requiring Member States to identify waters by use (for drinking water, bathing, fishing and cultivating shellfish), which Member States are then required to regulate according to harmonised rules. The EU is also able to take a more holistic approach. This was particularly noticeable in the new 'macro-regional strategies' funded by cohesion money and beginning with the Baltic Sea Strategy.[12] Combining a geographical approach with an integrated mandate begins a new phase in water regulation in both EU and (if it is influential) possibly in future international water law.

Moreover, while EU water law has drawn on the international experience of revision and scientific verification, the EU institutions have applied their own distinctive style in introducing new forms of governance in this area. Coupled with the familiar pattern of reporting, publicising and monitoring results, they allow the institutions, national governments and 'civil society' to synthesise and analyse the data and findings and have created a different understanding of water law within the EU.

The 2000 Water Framework Directive

History of the Water Framework Directive (WFD)

While the Commission has noted simply that the 'preparation and the negotiations of the Directive were difficult',[13] more colourful descriptions of the events leading to the conclusion of the WFD reveal the political compromises and negotiations that underpinned it and ensured it did not, as it at one stage seemed it might, disappear from the policy agenda.[14] The negotiation of the WFD was marked by intense disagreement between the three institutional actors: the

---

[11] Including Directive 91/692/EEC standardising and rationalising reports on the implementation of certain Directives relating to the environment and Commission Decision 92/446/EEC concerning questionnaires relating to Directives in the water sector and Commission Decision concerning formats for the presentation of national programmes as foreseen by Art. 17 of Council Directive 91/271/EEC.

[12] Commission Communication to the European Parliament, the Council, the European Economic and Social Committee and the Committee of the Regions concerning the European Union strategy for the Baltic Sea Region COM/2009/0248 final, 6.

[13] SEC(2007)362 Accompanying Document to the Commission Report on Implementation (COM(2007)128 final).

[14] Chris Tydeman, 'Trying out the Conciliation Process on the Water Framework Directive' (2000) 2 *Environmental Law Review* 229.

Commission, the Council of Ministers and the Parliament, as well as between the multitude of lobbyists, environmental non-governmental organisations, chemical companies, water industry bodies and agriculturalists, to name but a few, each of which contributed to the negotiation process representing their own interests.[15] A delaying tactic by the European Parliament drawing out negotiations until after May 1999 ensured that the entry into force of the 1997 Amsterdam Treaty would require 'co-decision' procedures to be applied. This gave the European Parliament equal legislative power with the Council of Ministers, and effectively a temporary veto. Since no agreement could be reached between these two institutions, the conciliation procedures were invoked in order for the text to survive.[16] Consequently, 12 years after negotiations had begun, Directive 2006/60/EEC, the WFD, came into force on 22 December 2000. The WFD repealed several directives, some of which were repealed with effect from seven years after the date of entry into force of the WFD,[17] while some were repealed with effect from 13 years after the WFD's entry into force.[18]

Overview

The WFD has a broad reach both spatially and conceptually. Article 1 sets out the legislative purpose of the WFD as establishing a framework 'for the protection of inland surface waters, transitional waters, coastal waters and groundwater'. This holism is somewhat undermined by its continuation of the longstanding distinction between surface water and groundwater and by the fact that

---

[15] For lively descriptions of the negotiating process, see Maria Kaika, 'The Water Framework Directive: A New Directive for a Changing Social, Political and Economic European Framework' (2003) 11(3) *European Planning Studies* 299, at 305; Maria Kaika and Ben Page, 'The EU Water Framework Directive: Part I. European Policy-Making and the Changing Topography of Lobbying' (2003) 13 *European Environment* 314, at 317; Ben Page and Maria Kaika, 'The EU Water Framework Directive: Part 2. Policy Innovation and the Shifting Choreography of Governance' (2003) 13 *European Environment* 328.

[16] Under the WFD this took two phases in May 1999 and June 1999 respectively; see, generally, Kaika and Page, 'The EU Water Framework Directive: Part I', 317.

[17] Directive 75/440/EEC concerning the quality required of surface water intended for the abstraction of drinking water in the Member States, OJ 1975 L 194/26; Council Decision 77/795/EEC establishing a common procedure for the exchange of information on the quality of surface freshwater in the Community, OJ 1990 L 1/20; Council Directive 79/869/EEC concerning the methods of measurement and frequencies of sampling and analysis of surface water intended for the abstraction of drinking waters in the Member States, OJ 1979 L 271/44.

[18] Council Directive 78/659/EEC on the quality of freshwaters needing protection or improvement in order to support fish life, OJ 2006 L 264/20; Council Directive 79/923/EEC on the quality required of shellfish waters, OJ 1979 L 281/47; Council Directive 80/68/EEC on the protection of groundwater against pollution caused by certain dangerous substances, OJ 1980 L 20/43 and Directive 76/464/EEC (certain transitional periods were put in place for this directive), OJ 1976 L 129/23.

(due to the lack of consensus during the negotiation process) the key provisions on groundwater and priority substances have been left to the two 'daughter' directives, the 2006 Groundwater Directive[19] and the 2008 Priority Substances Directive[20] respectively.

Nevertheless, as a testament to its integrative approach, the Directive includes five environmental aims: addressing pollution, sustainable water use, protecting the aquatic environment, protecting groundwater and contributing to the mitigation of the effects of floods and droughts. Nested within these multiple objectives are two obligations that have become central to modern EU environmental law. The first is that as part of their administrative reporting obligations Member States must prepare a substantial programme of measures within their river basin monitoring plan. The second is that they must comply with the 'environmental objectives' that form the heart of the regulatory scheme. Overall, the WFD aims to simplify and to establish a binding architecture for water law, although it does not assume that it will always have the last word; at least in water chemical quality. In cases of a dispute caused by overlapping provisions included in other regulations, the 'combined approach' embedded in the WFD confirms that it is the most stringent provision that is to apply.

River Basin Management and the 'Programme of Measures'

One of the most striking features of the WFD is that it is administratively organised on a hydrological rather than a political scale. This was a widely supported feature of the initially proposed Directive, in part because many Member States already organise their national water management in administrative units corresponding to river catchments.[21] Article 3 requires Member States to coordinate their administrative arrangements within river basin districts. They are to identify the individual river basins lying within their national territory, assign them to individual river basin districts and identify a body (existing or newly created) as the relevant competent authority. Having undertaken this allocation, Member States are then required to ensure that their two primary tasks under the WFD, establishing a programme of measures and taking measures to achieve the environmental objectives set out in Article 4, are coordinated for the whole of the river basin district.

This is a novel, expansive approach. It reflects a sense that geography, not territory, should govern administrative regulation, and that watershed limits are

---

[19] Directive EC/2006/118 on the protection of groundwater against pollution and deterioration, OJ 2006 L 372/19.
[20] Directive EC/2008/105 on environmental quality standards in the field of water policy, OJ 2008 L 348/84. This Directive and the WFD were amended by Directive 2013/39/EU of the European Parliament and of the Council as regards priority substances in the field of water policy.
[21] For example, the Rhine (www.ccr-zkr.org) and the Danube (www.icpdr.org/).

preferable to political boundaries.[22] In practice, not all Member States have taken this line. Since there is no standard template to follow, Member States have exhibited different ways of identifying river basins.[23] However delineated, once the river basin district has been identified, Article 13 imposes an obligation to prepare a river basin management plan. This requires Member States to coordinate their administrative arrangements within river basin districts establishing a management plan at basin level.

The obligation to prepare a programme of measures for each River Basin District is set out at length in Article 11. While there is no clear legislative linkage between the river basin management plan and the programme of measures, in practice these are prepared together and as a result the requirement to prepare a six-yearly programme of measures lies at the very heart of the WFD. The programme of measures is an administrative requirement for Member States to outline the measures they have taken to ensure water quality. This takes a programmatic approach to requiring Member States to implement substantive provisions on water law. There is at least a backstop of non-deterioration: Article 11 confirms that, in implementing their 'basic measures', Member States' interventions 'may on no account lead, either directly or indirectly to increased pollution' (unless this would lead to increased pollution of the environment as a whole). This supplements a non-deterioration provision already included in the Directive's purpose as set out in Article 1. Yet, since Article 4 makes some provision for limited deterioration (for example, from 'high' to 'good' status surface water if certain conditions are met), it is still questionable how stringently this provision is applied.

The 'Environmental Objectives'

The second central, substantive strand of the WFD is the formulation of the 'environmental objectives' in Article 4. This provision imposes a series of obligations on Member States to preserve and protect water quality in respect of all waters, not just those within river basin districts (although it is applicable here as well). It distinguishes between surface waters, groundwater and 'protected areas' (that are to be listed in a register compiled under Article 6, listing areas requiring special protection under specific Community legislation for the protection of their surface or groundwater or for the conservation of habitats and species directly depending on water).[24] Article 4 imposes different obligations in respect

---

[22] See the implications of this approach in Corey Johnson, 'Toward Post-Sovereign Environmental Governance? Politics, Scale, and EU Water Framework Directive' (2012) 5(1) *Water Alternatives* 83–97.

[23] See more on http://ec.europa.eu/environment/water/participation/map_mc/map.htm.

[24] These are listed in Annex IV and include (i) areas designated for the abstraction of water intended for human consumption; (ii) areas designated for the protection of economically significant aquatic species; (iii) bodies of water designated as recreational waters, including areas designated as bathing waters; (iv) nutrient-sensitive areas, including areas designated as vulnerable zones and sensitive areas for nitrates; and (v) areas designated for the protection of

of each type of water, to have been achieved by 2015. Member States are required to 'aim' to achieve a carefully defined interpretation of 'good' surface water and 'good' groundwater status and to comply with relevant provisions for protected areas.

Surface Water

The objective of aiming to achieve 'good surface water status' by 2015 is both complex and innovative. It required Member States to achieve both 'good' chemical and ecological status referring to the definition in Article 2(18) that 'good surface water status' is 'the status achieved by a surface water body when both its ecological status and its chemical status are at least good'. While the chemical status of the water had previously been regulated under the 1976 Dangerous Substances in Water Directive, the introduction of a requirement of 'good ecclogical status' was an innovation building on the 2003 Commission proposal.[25] Underscoring this programmatic obligation is the non-deterioration provision also included in Article 4, under which Member States are to 'implement the necessary measures to prevent deterioration of the status of all bodies of surface water'. This provision is a legally binding obligation on Member States which 'involves an obligation on the Member States to act to that effect'.[26]

Chemical Quality

The WFD states that surface water will achieve good chemical water status when the body of water complies with quality standards established for chemical substances at European level. While initially these limits were set out as those contained in the daughter Directives to the 1976 Dangerous Substances in Water Directive (which were initially incorporated into Annex X of the Water Framework Directive), since the coming into force of the 2008 Priority Substances Directive[27] Member States must comply with the 33 standards set out in Annex II of that Directive and an additional 12 under the new Directive 2013/39/EU.[28] Both the 2008 Priority Substances Directive and the WFD maintain the distinction between pollutants that should be

---

habitats or species where the maintenance or improvement of the status of water is an important factor in their protection.

[25] Commission proposal for a Directive on the Ecological Quality of Water, COM(93)680 final.

[26] Case C-461/13 *Bund für Umwelt und Naturschutz Deutschland* ECLI:EU:C:2015:433, para. 31. The court stated that 'Member States are required – unless a derogation is granted – to refuse authorisation for an individual project where it may cause a deterioration of the status of a body of surface water or where it jeopardises the attainment of good surface water status or of good ecological potential and good surface water chemical status by the date laid down by the directive.'

[27] See, further, below, at 'Priority Substances Directive'.

[28] Directive 2013/39/EU of the European Parliament and of the Council of 12 August 2013 amending Directives 2000/60/EC and 2008/105/EC as regards priority substances in the field of water policy, OJ 2013 L 226/1.

progressively reduced ('priority substances') and pollutants that should be ceased or phased out ('priority hazardous substances'), although now the provision has been transformed into an aspiration rather than a requirement.[29] Article 16 of the WFD provides for the Commission at least to review the adopted list of priority substances every four years after the entry into force of this Directive and at least every six years thereafter as well as to put forward proposals for the progressive reduction of discharges. These provisions reflect an attempt to move the burden of listing from the Member States to the Commission.

Ecological Quality

While the requirement to achieve chemical quality builds on previous legislation, the focus on monitoring, maintaining and improving ecological quality is new. The WFD requires Members States to begin by undertaking an initial classification, dividing each body of water (fresh, ground, coastal and transitional) into water bodies, identifying its type, the significant pressures it faces and the impact of these pressures on its ecological, chemical and hydrological quality. One notable feature is the application of a quantitative dimension to ecological good status, rather than focusing exclusively on water quality as water law has conventionally done. Observers have praised this inclusive approach for recognising that the integrated management of water resources cannot be accomplished without attention to water quantity issues.[30] It is further developed in Annex V.

The process begins with an initial characterisation, where regulators assess the pressures and impacts on the water environment, such as pollution or overuse, and the risk of the water bodies failing to meet the Directive's objectives if no action is taken. Once this has taken place, water bodies can be classified by their current status (high, good, moderate or poor). Where a water body was found not to meet at least good status or if it was unlikely to reach this level by 2015 unless action was taken, it was deemed to be 'at risk' and required remedial action. The classification criteria are set out in Annex V, which also establishes the standards that must be achieved in order to qualify for 'good ecological status'. This sets out four levels of status for any given water body, including 'high status', 'good status', 'moderate status' and 'poor or bad status'. Annex V thus requires regulators to set out, for each kind of water, a series of ecological parameters that would be expected for a body of water to reach a given status. Good ecological status is defined in Annex V of the Water Framework Proposal in terms of the quality of the biological community, the hydrological characteristics and the chemical characteristics.

---

[29] This point is discussed further, below, at 'Listing Substances and Review of Adopted List of Priority Substances'.

[30] William Howarth, 'Accommodation without Resolution? Emission Controls and Environmental Quality Objectives in the Proposed EC Water Framework Directive' (1999) 1 *Environmental Law Review* 1, at 8.

Underpinning these characterisations is a baseline here of 'naturalness', with Annex V stipulating that high-water status is achieved when there are 'no, or only very minor, anthropogenic alterations' and good water status achieved when there are 'low levels of distortion resulting from human activity'. Where scientific certainty exists, data must be calibrated and these 'intercalibration exercises' form part of the information gathering and governance work of the Member States, the Union institutions and the Common Implementation Strategy body.[31] This reliance on a sense of 'minimal anthropogenic impact' as the ultimate ecological objective underlying the WFD, is conceptually familiar from the pollution context,[32] yet its application to ecology marks a turning point in EU law.

Despite their clear attraction, in practice these standards are extremely difficult to achieve for three reasons. First, the 'baseline' against which ecological quality standards need to be set is uncertain (this is conceptually more difficult than, for example, stating that water bodies should achieve contamination levels that are close to zero, since it is possible to identify this by quantitative measurement).[33] It is much more difficult to identify a water body's 'natural' state at a given point in time. Secondly, setting ecological quality standards to be achieved is scientifically difficult, entailing complex issues of ecological valuation and a recognition that the temporal and spatial variability of nature makes any given standard difficult to achieve.[34] Thirdly, the history of the negotiation of water law instruments demonstrates the contested political context in which these interventions take place. If standards are vaguely drafted or inconclusive, reluctant Member States will take full advantage of any legislative uncertainty.

Artificial and Heavily Modified Bodies of Water

Surface water bodies that are designated as 'artificial and heavily modified bodies of water' attract a lesser standard under Article 4. The Directive defines an 'artificial water body' as 'a body of surface water created by human activity';

---

[31] Commission Implementation Strategy, Guidance Document No. 6, 'Towards a Guidance on the Establishment of the Intercalibration Exercise' (2002). See more about the process and good practices in intercalibration in Sandra Poikane, Nikolaos Zampoukas, Angel Borja, Susan P. Davies, Wouter van de Bund and Sebastian Birk, 'Intercalibration of Aquatic Ecological Assessment Methods in the European Union: Lessons Learned and Way Forward' (2014) 44 *Environmental Science and Policy* 237–246.

[32] Notably the OSPAR Strategy on Hazardous Substances, which has the ultimate aim of achieving concentrations of naturally occurring substances in the environment near background, or natural, levels and close to zero for man-made synthetic substances.

[33] Howarth, 'The Progression Towards Ecological Quality Standards' (2005) 18(1) *Journal of Environmental Law* 3–35, at 33.

[34] Ibid.; Fred Bosselman and A. Dan Tarlock, 'The Introduction of Ecological Science on Environmental Law: An Introduction' (1994) 67 *Chicago-Kent Law Review* 847; Daniel Botkin, 'Adjusting Law to Nature's Discordant Harmonies' (1996) 7 *Duke Environmental Law and Policy Forum* 25, at 27; and Jonathan B. Wiener, 'Beyond the Balance of Nature' (1996) 7 *Duke Environmental Law and Policy Forum* 1, at 7.

this might include anything from a pond to a canal. A 'heavily modified water body' is understood as 'a body of surface water which as a result of physical alterations by human activity is substantially changed in character'; this might include a river deepened for reservation or a water source dammed to create a reservoir. Here Member States were required to 'protect and enhance' the water (rather than 'protect, enhance and restore') with the aim of achieving 'good ecological potential' (rather than reaching 'good ecological status') by 2015. The details are once again set out in Annex V. Member States are still required, however, to achieve 'good chemical status' for these bodies of surface water.

Groundwater

Groundwater under the Water Framework Directive (WFD)

The conventional characterisation of groundwater protection is the presumption that groundwater should not be polluted at all, since, once contaminated, groundwater is harder to clean than surface water and the consequences can last for decades. This is particularly problematic since groundwater is frequently used for the abstraction of drinking water, for industry and for agriculture as well as providing the base flow for many rivers (it can provide up to 90 per cent of the flow in some watercourses) and can thus affect the quality of surface water systems. Groundwater also acts as a buffer through dry periods and is essential for maintaining wetlands. As a result of these multiple functions, EU law has conventionally taken a more precautionary approach to groundwater than surface water,[35] with few specific groundwater standards established at EU level.[36]

The WFD defines 'good' groundwater in terms of its quantitative and chemical status.[37] The focus on quantity as well as quality has again been widely praised since excessive abstraction has its own impact on water quality; and water scarcity is a growing concern, particularly in the South of Europe.[38] The subject was contentious, particularly when linked to the issue of water pricing, and often interpreted as a North–South divide at the Water Framework Directive negotiations, although in practice issues of quality and quantity affect most Member States to some degree.[39] Increasingly contentious is the lack of any obligation to achieve good ecological status for groundwater,

---

[35] The purpose of the Groundwater Directive 1980/68/EEC, for instance, was 'to prevent the pollution of groundwater by [defined] substances ... and as far as possible to check or eliminate the consequences of pollution which has already occurred'.

[36] For exceptions, see the Nitrates Directive (96/676/EEC), OJ 1991 L 375/1, the Plant Protection Products Directive (91/414/EEC), OJ 1991 L 230/1 and the Biocides Directive (98/8/EC), OJ 1998 L 123/1.

[37] Art. 2(20) and 2(25).

[38] Commission Communication to the European Parliament and the Council addressing the challenge of water scarcity and droughts in the European Union, Brussels, COM(2007)414 final and COM/2012/0673 final.

[39] Page and Kaika, 'The EU Water Framework Directive: Part 1', 318.

despite ecologists' misgivings.[40] Member States are merely required to 'protect, enhance and restore all bodies of groundwater, ensure a balance between abstraction and recharge of groundwater, with the aim of achieving good groundwater status', in accordance with Annex V, by 2015.[41]

Article 4 requires Member States to implement the measures necessary to prevent or limit the input of pollutants into groundwater and to prevent the deterioration of the status of all bodies of groundwater subject to the applicable exceptions and exemptions (in particular, temporary derogations and the construction of new projects affecting groundwater). The system is supplemented by a frequent provision in groundwater legislation: the requirement to 'implement the measures necessary to reverse any significant and sustained upward trend in the concentration of any pollutant resulting from the impact of human activity in order progressively to reduce pollution of groundwater'.[42] While this backstop is a welcome inclusion, it is indicative of the general acceptance of at least some continued groundwater pollution. Again, however, underscoring this programmatic obligation is the non-deterioration provision included in Article 4, under which Member States are to 'implement the necessary measures to prevent deterioration of the status of all bodies of ground water'.

The 2006 Groundwater Directive

Directive 2006/118/EC on the protection of groundwater against pollution and deterioration (the 2006 Groundwater Directive) was introduced under Article 17 of the WFD as a 'daughter directive'. The WFD repealed the first groundwater directive, Directive 80/68/EEC on the protection of groundwater against pollution caused by certain dangerous substances with effect from 2013. Member States were required to comply with the 2006 Groundwater Directive by 2009, bringing into being the legislative and administrative framework to implement its provisions ready to achieve 'good groundwater status' as required by the WFD in 2015.

The 2006 Directive imposes three central obligations on Member States under Article 1. The first is to establish what constitutes 'good groundwater chemical status'. The second is to determine how to identify when there is a significant and sustained upward trend in contamination and then, if there is, to determine a starting point to reverse that trend. The third is to prevent or limit inputs of pollutants into groundwater through the programme of measures in accordance with Article 4 of the Water Framework Directive. These largely scientific objectives are supplemented by a qualified version of the non-deterioration objective in Article 1(2) where the directive 'aims to prevent the deterioration'

---

[40] The requirement is also excluded from the 2006 Groundwater Directive. For criticism of this omission, see Dan L. Danielopol et al., 'Incorporating Ecological Perspectives in European Groundwater Management Policy' (2004) 31 *Environmental Conservation* 185, at 188; and Christian Steube, Simone Richter and Christian Griebler, 'First Attempts Towards an Integrative Concept for the Ecological Assessment of Groundwater Ecosystems' (2009) 17 *Hydrogeology Journal* 23.
[41] Art. 4(1)(b)(ii). [42] Art. 4(1)(b)(iii).

of groundwater, a tentative provision that may not be entirely consistent with the non-deterioration provision in Article 4 of the WFD. Once again there is no obligation to achieve good ecological status for groundwater.

Establishing 'Good Groundwater Chemical Status'
Article 3 of the 2006 Groundwater Directive establishes a series of groundwater quality standards for Member States to use in the assessment of the chemical status of groundwater. The 'minimum list of pollutants and their indicators for which Member States have to consider establishing threshold values in accordance with Article 3' are: substances or ions or indicators – arsenic, cadmium, lead, mercury, ammonium, chloride, sulphate, nitrates and phosphorus/phosphates; man-made synthetic substances – trichloroethylene and tetrachloroethylene; and parameters indicative of saline or other intrusions – conductivity; listed in Part B of Annex II (as amended by Directive 2014/80/EU).

The factors Member States are to take into account when establishing these threshold values are set out in Part A of Annex II and are closely intertwined with the criteria set out in Annex V of the WFD. Part A requires that Member States establish threshold values for all pollutants and indicators of pollution which will then, pursuant to the river basin characterisation carried out in accordance with the WFD, identify those water bodies at risk of failing to achieve good groundwater chemical status. Member States are to establish the thresholds in such a way that if the monitoring results exceed the threshold this 'will indicate a risk that one or more of the conditions for good groundwater chemical status' are not being met. The monitoring under the 2006 Groundwater Directive thus assesses compliance with the obligation to achieve 'good groundwater status' under Article 4 of the WFD.

Significant and Sustained Upward Trends of Contamination
In addition to establishing and complying with these chemical thresholds, Member States are required under Article 5 to identify any significant and sustained upward trend in concentrations of pollutants or indicators of pollution found in bodies of groundwater identified as being at risk. Having done this, they should then define the starting point for reversing that trend, in accordance with Annex IV of the 2006 Groundwater Directive. Importantly, these analytical requirements are supplemented with a substantive one. Member States are required to 'reverse trends which present a significant risk of harm to the quality of aquatic ecosystems or terrestrial ecosystems, to human health, or to actual or potential legitimate uses of the water environment, through the programme of measures [under the WFD] … in order progressively to reduce pollution and prevent deterioration of groundwater'.[43] This is clearly a significant obligation, although calibration (carried out through the CIS, see below), is crucial here. Member States also have the further option of carrying out additional trend assessments for plumes of pollution in bodies of groundwater from point sources or contaminated land. In each case, these assessments are to be reported and explained in the Member States' river basin management plans under the WFD.

[43] Art. 5(2).

Prevent or Limit Inputs of Pollutants into Groundwater

In order to achieve the objective of preventing or limiting inputs of pollutants into groundwater in accordance with Article 4 of the WFD, Member States are to ensure that their programme of measures includes all measures necessary to prevent inputs into groundwater of any hazardous substances as specified in Annex VIII of the WFD. Under Article 6, Member States must also take these measures to prevent or limit inputs of non-hazardous pollutants if they present an existing or potential risk of pollution. They are to ensure that such inputs do not cause either deterioration or significant and sustained upward trends in the concentrations of pollutants in groundwater and should take account (where relevant) of established best practice, including the Best Environmental Practice and BAT. Even inputs from diffuse sources of pollution that impact on groundwater chemical status should be taken into account where technically possible.

Alternative Compliance

While not strictly derogations, Article 4 adjusts the first of the 2006 Directive's obligations by setting out the situations where 'good groundwater chemical status' might still be achieved even if the monitoring assessing the characterisation of good status under Annex V of the Water Framework Directive has not been achieved. These three 'alternative' methods of compliance are either situations where the emissions do not constitute 'a significant environmental risk', or the Member State complies with the conditions for good groundwater chemical status set out in Annex V and Article 7 (on water abstraction) of the Water Framework Directive, or (as a catch-all test) if 'the ability of the body of groundwater or of any of the bodies in the group of bodies of groundwater to support human uses has not been significantly impaired by pollution'. Other than these situations a failure to achieve 'good groundwater status' in accordance with Article 4 will be a breach of both the 2006 Groundwater Directive and also the Water Framework Directive itself since Member States will have failed to achieve 'good groundwater status'.

Similarly, Article 6 provides exemptions to the third of the 2006 Directive's requirements. It identifies six exemptions Member States can apply to their obligation to take 'all measures necessary' to prevent or limit inputs into groundwater of both hazardous and non-hazardous substances. These include criteria of cost and otherwise deleterious environmental effects. Any of these exemptions may only be used where the Member States have established efficient monitoring practices.

Assessment

The obligation to establish thresholds for groundwater pollutants is thus placed squarely on the Member States, which are required to set out these chemicals, their thresholds and the state of the groundwater bodies in their river basin management plan under the Water Framework Directive. This continues the approach that was so contentious under the 1976 Dangerous Substances in Water Directive and still patterns the 2008 Priority Substances Directive today. Indeed, it is clear that this obligation on Member States is to continue to be a part of the new architecture and the 2006 Directive explicitly links the monitoring, measuring and updating requirements into the WFD framework. In particular, the 2006 Groundwater Directive requires Member States to undertake six-yearly reviews (shadowing the river basin management scheme) and provides for amendments to the scheme to be made. Reflexivity is built into the system from the outset and it is here that the work of the Common Implementation Strategy has the potential to be so significant. For although the obligations are, on the face of the Directive, firmly imposed on the Member States, in practice it is for the working groups (in particular the groundwater working group) to flesh out both the detail and the practical application of these provisions.[44]

The Water Framework Directive's Derogations from the Environmental Objectives

The Water Framework Directive also contains significant potential derogations from the 'environmental objectives' in Article 4. These are in addition to the differential regime applied to artificial or heavily modified bodies of surface water discussed above, and all are limited to their immediate surroundings. Member States are not to allow the derogations to 'permanently exclude or compromise the achievement of the objectives of this Directive in other bodies of water within the same river basin district'.

The first of the four derogations (in Article 4(4)) is temporal. Deadlines may be extended if all necessary improvements in the status of bodies of water cannot reasonably be achieved due to technical feasibility, disproportionate cost or natural conditions. A second derogation (in Article 4(5)) enables Member States to 'aim to achieve less stringent environmental objectives' for water bodies so affected by human activity or their natural condition that 'the achievement of these objectives would be infeasible or disproportionately expensive' if there is no better means to achieve the environmental and socioeconomic needs (that themselves are a significantly better environmental option not entailing disproportionate costs), and Member States consider that the human activity still allows the highest possible environmental standards 'given impacts that could not reasonably have been avoided due to the nature of the human activity or pollution'. A third derogation (in Article 4(6)) excuses a temporary deterioration in a water body's status. This will be forgiven if it results from natural causes or force majeure, particularly unforeseeable floods, droughts or accidents, as long as all practicable steps are taken to prevent further deterioration in the status of these water bodies, and to ensure that other water bodies are not compromised.

A fourth derogation (in Article 4(7)) exists for new construction or other projects modifying water bodies. Here Member States need not achieve the appropriate objectives set out in Article 4 if they result from either 'new modifications to the physical characteristics of a surface water body or alterations to the level of bodies of groundwater' or they are the result of 'new sustainable

---

[44] CIS, Common Implementation Strategy for the Water Framework Directive (2000/60/EC): Guidance Document No. 15, Guidance on Groundwater Monitoring (2007). Other guidance documents on groundwater are available at: http://ec.europa.eu/environment/water/water-framework/groundwater/activities.htm.

human development activities' if the projects meet two requirements. The first of these is that these modifications or alterations are of overriding public interest and/or the benefits to the environment and to society of achieving the required objectives are outweighed by the benefits of the new modifications or alterations to human health, to the maintenance of human safety or to sustainable development.[45] The second is that the beneficial objectives served by those modifications or alterations of the water body cannot for reasons of technical feasibility or disproportionate cost be achieved by other means, which are a significantly better environmental option.[46] The effect of this provision is that while future developments affecting water are regulated by the Water Framework Directive, non-attainment of the environmental objectives at the start of Article 4 is permitted if Member States can draw on arguments of 'overriding public interest' (a provision drawn from the 1992 Habitats Directive)[47] or an assessment of the relative benefits or because of technical feasibility or disproportionate cost (a formula broadly drawn from the 2006 IPPC Directive).[48]

Clearly these derogations provide a significant limitation on the operation of the Water Framework Directive, particularly in regard to waters affected by human activity. Even though the central obligation in Article 4 is only expressed as 'aiming' to achieve good water status, these derogations provide further excuses for non-attainment primarily on the basis of cost and feasibility. These provisions are significantly broader than their equivalents under, in particular, the 2006 Dangerous Substances in Water Directive[49] and the 1998 Drinking Water Directive. If there is any conflict in the provisions (particularly in respect of chemical quality) then the more stringent obligation would bind. The combined approach set out in Article 10 (considered below) explicitly provides that wherever a quality objective or quality standard, wherever established, requires stricter conditions then the more stringent emissions controls will apply.

Combined Approach

Conventionally, pollution control has been seen as either focusing on emissions standards or on water quality. It is plausible that this dichotomy is not as fixed as is often supposed, particularly since the CJEU in *Commission* v. *Germany* in 1991[50] held that Germany was subject to both types of obligations under the 1976 Dangerous Substances in Water Directive. Nevertheless, Article 10 of the

---

[45] Art. 4(7)(c).   [46] Art. 4(7)(d).
[47] Directive 92/43/EEC on the conservation of natural habitats and of wild fauna and flora, OJ 1992 L 206/7. See, further, Chapter 12.
[48] Directive 2008/1/EC. See, further, Chapter 9. This derogation was recently discussed in Case C-461/13 *Bund* v. *Germany*.
[49] This Directive is repealed by the WFD as from the end of 2013.
[50] Case C-184/97 *Commission* v. *Germany* ECLI:EU:C:1999:546.

Water Framework Directive now explicitly adopts both methods in the 'combined approach'. This requires that Member States fulfil both their obligations under related water quality legislation, including the 2010 Industrial Emissions Directive,[51] the 2008 Waste Water Directive, the 1991 Nitrates Directive, the 2006 Groundwater Directive and the 2008 Priority Substances Directive. In doing this Member States must ensure the 'establishment and/or implementation of (a) the emissions controls based on best available techniques, or (b) the relevant emissions limit values, or (c) in the case of diffuse impacts the controls including, as appropriate, best environmental practices' as these other directives respectively require. This 'belt and braces' approach is supplemented with the provision in Article 10(3) stating that where 'a quality objective or quality standard' wherever established 'requires stricter conditions than those which would result from [applying the combined approach] more stringent emission controls shall be set accordingly'.

In effect, the combined approach suggests that whenever a higher standard is required for water quality, be it an emissions standard or an assessment of quality, the more stringent will apply. There is a certain opacity here in the balance between emissions standards and environmental quality objectives. Certainly, emissions controls are not the only way in which to achieve an environmental quality objective.[52] If an emissions standard is met yet the water quality is still unsatisfactory it seems only sensible to require its improvement. Conversely, it is difficult to imagine a situation (unless the standard has been significantly misconceived) where an emissions standard is not met and yet the water quality is judged good regardless. The combined approach is important, however, in that it applies a backstop of implementation preventing conflicts between different provisions wherever they exist and however they are applied.

Priority Substances

The regulation of 'priority substances' (the new terminology for those substances that were originally regulated under the 1976 Dangerous Substances in Water Directive) is limited under the Water Framework Directive. As agreement on these most contentious of issues could not be resolved during either the negotiation or the conciliation processes, binding provisions were ultimately left to the 'daughter' Directive concluded as the 2008 Priority Substances Directive and recently amended by Directive 2013/39/EU.[53] In its brief consideration of chemical concerns, the Water Framework Directive distinguishes between 'priority substances' and 'priority hazardous substances' (for which more stringent

---

[51] This Directive repealed and replaced Directive 2008/1/EC on integrated pollution prevention and control.
[52] Howarth, 'Accommodation without Resolution?', 13.
[53] Directive (EC) 2008/105 on environmental quality standards in the field of water policy, OJ 2008 L 348/84 and Directive 2013/39 of the European Parliament and the Council amending Directives 2000/60/EC and 2008/105/EC as regards substances in the field of water policy, OJ 2013 L 226.

environmental objectives apply because of their high persistence, bioaccumulation and toxicity).[54]

The Water Framework Directive does not appear to contain a substantive obligation to eliminate priority hazardous substances as some lobbyists had hoped at the time the Directive was concluded. While there are a number of provisions in the recitals that point to the phasing out of the most dangerous emissions and while the purpose of the Directive as set out in Article 1 'aims at enhanced protection and improvement of the aquatic environment, *inter alia*, through specific measures for the progressive reduction of discharges, emissions and losses of priority substances and the cessation or phasing-out of discharges, emissions and losses of the priority hazardous substances' these do not seem to amount to a coherent, binding obligation.

In practice, the most stringent obligations on the control of dangerous substances are not contained in the Water Framework Directive itself but in the range of existing EU measures aimed at controlling emissions of priority substances. These include the 2010 Industrial Emissions Directive, the Sustainable Use Directive 2009/128/EC[55] and the REACH Regulation on the regulation of chemicals policy.[56] Ultimately, these initiatives may have greater long-term beneficial effects on water quality than the WFD itself, since the focus of chemicals legislation is often to anticipate problems, restricting pollutants' availability and release before they enter water bodies. As a result, just as land use and farming policy is the key mechanism to control nitrate emissions under the 1991 Nitrates Directive, so life-cycle chemical regulations may yet be far more effective than 'end-of-the-pipe' controls.[57]

Economic Analysis

One of the striking features of the WFD is the introduction into water law of the idea of full-cost pricing for water, internalising the otherwise largely ignored social and environmental costs to 'take account of the principle of recovery of the costs of water services … in accordance in particular with the polluter pays principle' (as it was ultimately expressed in Article 9). This principle had been proposed by the Commission and championed by the British Government (although they had almost dropped the proposal in their desire to procure the conclusion of the Directive during the United Kingdom Presidency in 1998).[58]

---

[54] See Art. 16(1) WFD. [55] OJ 2009 L 309/71.
[56] Regulation (EC) No. 1907/2006 of the European Parliament and of the Council concerning the Registration, Evaluation, Authorisation and Restriction of Chemicals (REACH), OJ 2006 L 396/1.
[57] Howarth, 'Water Pollution: Improving the Legal Controls in Retrospect' (2008) 20 *Journal of Environmental Law* 3, at 4.
[58] Page and Kaika, 'The EU Water Framework Directive: Part 1', 318.

Under Article 9, Member States are required to include an 'economic analysis of water use' in their river basin management plans. In order to make this assessment, Member States are to rely on the provisions of Annex III which stipulates that the economic analysis is to contain sufficient information to make the relevant calculations under Article 9 and to make judgments about the most cost-effective combination of measures in respect of water uses to be included in the 'programme of measures'; based on estimates of the potential costs of such measures. While Member States are required by Annex III to take cost-effectiveness into account when selecting their programme of measures (and Article 4 itself makes frequent reference to disproportionate costs), this does not mean that such considerations are to predetermine their decisions. As the Common Implementation Strategy's first guidance document 'Economics and the Environment' stresses, 'economics is only there to inform decision makers'.[59] Article 9 itself confirms that cost-effectiveness cannot be an excuse for non-compliance: 'Nothing in this Article shall prevent the funding of particular preventive or remedial measures in order to achieve the objectives of this Directive'.

While the obligation is rather soft, Member States had, by 2010, to ensure that water-pricing policies provided adequate incentives for (industrial, household and agricultural) users to use water resources efficiently, thereby contributing to the environmental objectives of the Directive. Full cost pricing is ostensibly to be used as an implementation mechanism, the supply of water is to be calibrated with its cost. This is in keeping with the long-standing contribution economic instruments have made to the 'tool kit' of EU environmental law, even though the valuation difficulties remain complex. Ultimately, however, there is significant flexibility in the mitigation provision negotiated for by some Member States: when formulating their pricing policies they are to 'have regard to the social, environmental and economic effects of the recovery as well as the geographic and climatic conditions of the region or regions affected'. In the last paragraph of Article 9, the discretion appears repatriated even further, if a Member State can demonstrate 'established practices'.

Given the political compromises evident on the face of the text, it is perhaps unsurprising to see the slow progress in relation to water pricing. Although the water pricing should be consumption based taking into account the polluter-pays principle, very few Member States implemented a transparent recovery of environmental and resources cost.[60] Water efficiency is still not sufficiently increased as is best illustrated by the agricultural sector, which in many Member States is generally not required to pay the true price for the water it uses.[61]

---

[59] Common Implementation Strategy, 'Guidance Document No. 1: Economics and the Environment' (2003).
[60] SWD (2012) 393, 23 and 34.   [61] Ibid.

Public Involvement

Concluded after the 1998 Aarhus Convention[62] and the Commission's 2001 'White Paper on European Governance'[63] that set great store by the development of 'deliberative democracy', the provisions in the WFD that aimed to promote public participation in the Directive are perhaps to be expected. In particular, Article 14 establishes principles of public information, consultation and the 'active' involvement in the development of river basin management plans. Given the role of the Common Implementation Strategy (the CIS), discussed further below, there are certainly multiple publics here,[64] and expert publics supplement any involvement by 'civil society' as a whole.

Yet while the CIS encourages participation and the pooling of expertise at a thematic level, the participation envisaged under the Directive itself is more place based. This is significant in that while harmonised rules and scientific understandings are clearly developed, these must ultimately be implemented at the local level, in particular in the river basin district. Involving both expert and lay knowledges at the river basin level requires water law to pay increasing attention to land use patterns and to consider, and if necessary adjust, individual programmes' spatial fit.[65] These provisions for consultation and participation promote social learning at the river basin level itself,[66] rather than in working groups many miles away.

Governance

The WFD has become something of a celebrity in studies on EU governance.[67] Analysts who identify a trend away from formal lawmaking to governance

---

[62] Convention on Access to Information, Public Participation in Decision-Making and Access to Justice in Environmental Matters, Aarhus, 25 June 1998, in force 30 October 2001, 2161 UNTS 447. See, further, Chapter 5.

[63] Commission, 'White Paper on European Governance', COM(2001)428 final.

[64] Lee, 'Law and Governance of Water Protection Policy', 43. See more about the CIS's current structure and working methods in CIS's Work Programme 2016–2018, available at: https://circabc.europa.eu/faces/jsp/extension/wai/navigation/container.jsp.

[65] Tim Moss, 'The Governance of Land Use in River Basins: Prospects for Overcoming Problems of Institutional Interplay with the EU Water Framework Directive' (2004) 21 *Land Use Policy* 85; Pia Frederiksen, 'The Water Framework Directive: Spatial and Institutional Integration' (2008) 19 *Management of Environmental Quality* 100.

[66] Ilke Borowski and Claudia Pahl-Wostl, 'Where Can Social Learning be Improved in International River Basin Management in Europe?' (2008) 18 *European Environment* 216. See also about the role of Member States in encouraging public involvement in William Howarth, 'Aspirations and Realities under the Water Framework Directive: Proceduralisation, Participation and Practicalities' (2009) 21(3) *Journal of Environmental Law* 391

[67] The literature here is expanding, but notable contributions include: David M. Trubek and Louise G. Trubek, 'New Governance and Legal Regulation' (2007) 13 *Columbia Journal of European Law* 540; Charles Sabel and Jonathan Zeitl, 'Learning from Difference: The New Architecture of Experimentalist Governance in the EU' (2008) 14 *European Law Journal* 271; Joanne Scott and Jane Holder, 'Law and Environmental Governance in the European

see that much of the work done by the Directive, legal or otherwise, takes place below the surface. Here, in addition to the two established routes to implementation (the broader legislative framework and implementation by the Member States or their devolved equivalents), is a third implementation route that builds on the well-established Common Implementation Strategy (CIS).[68]

The Common Implementation Strategy (CIS)

The CIS was created in 2001 by the EU Water Directors to assist with filling out some of the open-textured principles and provisions of the Directive. It has developed into a hugely significant informal forum for open cooperation and information sharing, becoming an institution neither contemplated nor evident on the face of the directive itself. It is headed by the Water Directors who convene a meeting co-chaired by the Council Presidency and the European Commission (DG Environment) twice a year. This is overseen by the Strategic Coordination Group which also has oversight of a number of working and expert groups (including 'ecological status', 'groundwater' and 'chemical aspects').[69] The CIS has produced non-binding technical guidance documents, including 'Towards a Guidance on Establishment of the Intercalibration Network and the Process on the Intercalibration Exercise' and 'Monitoring under the WFD'.[70] This iterative process is intentionally reflexive and it is the focus on networks of experts, supplemented public participation, and continual innovation that marks the WFD to some observers as such a striking example of a new mode of collaborative governance.[71]

It is important to interpret the WFD in context. Despite its self-consciously programmatic nature, the most stringent obligations in EU water law are incorporated into the WFD through the requirement to achieve good chemical status. For environmental law, these are in many ways its legal core. Yet while under Article 4 the obligation is expressed as being one to 'aim' at to achieve this objective, under the 2006 Dangerous Substances in Water Directive and the 2008 Priority Substances Directive, actual compliance is required (albeit subject to derogations and applicable only to a small number of pollutants) and in

Union' in Gráinne de Búrca and Joanne Scott (eds.), *Law and New Governance in the EU and the US* (Hart Publishing, 2006); Neil Gunningham, 'Environment Law, Regulation and Governance: Shifting Architectures' (2009) 21 *Journal of Environmental Law* 179.

[68] Scott and Holder, 'Law and Environmental Governance in the European Union'.
[69] CIS, 'Common Implementation Strategy for the Water Framework Directive (2000/60/EC): Work Programme 2010–2012' (2009), 2.
[70] CIS, 'No. 6. Towards a Guidance on Establishment of the Intercalibration Network and the Process on the Intercalibration Exercise' (2003) Guidance Document Number 14: Guidance on the intercalibration process 2008–2011 (2011); CIS, 'No. 7. Monitoring under the Water Framework Directive' (2003) and CIS, 'No. 30. Procedure to fit new or updated classification methods to the results of a completed intercalibration exercise' (2015).
[71] See more in Lee, *EU Environmental Law, Governance and Decision-Making*, 89–90.

instances of conflict the 'combined approach' under the WFD means that the more stringent requirement is the one that binds.

Moreover, much of the flexibility attributed to the WFD concerns ecological, rather than chemical, good status. The inclusion of ecological quality in the WFD was an innovative development: it built on the 2003 Commission Proposal for a Directive on the Ecological Quality of Water.[72] Yet while the attainment of ecological good status is built on a widely applauded aim it remains politically contested, particularly when development decisions have to be made, balancing the protection of an aquatic habitat or species with a Member State's ability to authorise a new port or river project.[73] This is reflected in the drafting of both Article 4 and Annex V. The Court clarified its position in regard to surface waters and development projects, where it stated that the water management regime created by the WFD has primacy over any other EU legislation, provided that no derogations under the WFD apply.[74] The objective is also scientifically complex in its determination of 'naturalness' and its assessment of ecology's temporal and spatial variability.

Ultimately, given that this central substantive obligation in Article 4 is to 'aim' to achieve good water status, it is perhaps more likely that the networking and information strategies that pattern the implementation of the Directive come to resemble more closely the comparative and transparent strategies of the open method of coordination[75] in the social sphere promoting good practice rather than prohibiting bad. The Commission is taking an active role in providing guidance through the CIS to Member States on the correct approach to be taken in national practice. There is a pooling of expertise which seeks to override some of the structural difficulties in achieving water quality (including the striking disputes between Member States and the Commission over who was responsible for the listing of dangerous substances under the 1976 Dangerous Substances in Water Directive). This integrative approach facilitates the introduction of 'sustainability science', which recognises the limitations of reductionist disciplinary approaches to understanding systems.[76] This may be a significant development in pushing forward the development of water science and policy as a whole. Integrating

---

[72] Commission proposal for a Directive on the Ecological Quality of Water, COM(93)680 final.
[73] This conflict is evident also on land; see Art. 6(4) of the Directive 92/43/EC on the Conservation of natural habitats and of wild fauna and flora in Ludwig Kramer, 'The European Commission's Opinions under Article 6(4) of the Habitats Directive' (2009) *Journal of Environmental Law* 1.
[74] See Tiina Paloniitty, 'The Weser Case: Case C-461/13 BUND V GERMANY' (2016) 28 *Journal of Environmental Law* 156.
[75] The literature here is extensive and expanding. See Susana Borrás and Kerstin Jacobsson, 'The Open Method of Co-Ordination and New Governance Patterns in the EU' (2004) 11 *Journal of European Public Policy* 185; Sabrina Regent, 'The Open Method of Coordination: A New Supranational Method of Governance?' (2003) 9 *European Law Journal* 190; Paul Craig and Gráinne de Búrca, *EU Law: Text, Cases and Materials* (6th edn., Oxford University Press, 2015), 167–171.
[76] K. Blackstock and C. Carter, 'Operationalising Sustainability Science for a Sustainability Directive? Reflecting on Three Pilot Projects' (2007) 173, *Geographical Journal* 343.

science and policy is a notoriously complex challenge facing the scientific and policy-making communities. All too often, a lack of communication and clear coordination leads to research outputs being unavailable or even unknown to policy-makers. The CIS succeeded in providing one mechanism to communicate research and to facilitate knowledge sharing and exchange.[77]

Assessment

Ultimately the Water Framework Directive is innovative in many ways. It has a broad reach, including surface and groundwater, inland, transitional and coastal waters. It provides a framework for integrated proactive management of groundwater and surface water for the first time at European level. The directive is self-consciously programmatic, it coordinates and includes the regulation of environmental quality and sustainable water use, flood and drought management, and ecological and chemical quality integrating broader marine and international requirements. In its connection with the 2008 Marine Strategy Directive the Water Framework Directive provides a broad template for coordination, particularly in its spatial and inclusive understanding of water law. In focusing on ecological quality, the directive explicitly values these aspects of water law, providing a framework for calibration. Supplementing this with the combined approach confirms that no aspect of water protection is to have priority: quality and quantity, ecological and chemical statuses are all important. The CIS is in many ways a very different way of 'doing' environmental law.

There are caveats, however. The 'environmental objectives' set out in Article 4 are remarkably open textured;[78] and in terms of enforcement the Commission has a less central role than it does, for example, under the 2008 Marine Strategy Directive. The control of dangerous substances is less of a concern now with 12 new substances added and controlled with the WFD. Indeed, for all its holism and integration the WFD is remarkably fragmented, applying different obligations to surface and groundwater and protected areas. Its derogations also exempt a significant number of water bodies, particularly those modified by human use both historically and in the future. Ultimately, the directive reflects the political compromises that were necessary to reach agreement. These inevitably impact on both its holism and its innovation.

Drinking Water

History and Overview

Three drinking water directives have been introduced since 1975,[79] each setting higher standards than the last. This upward trend reflects greater scientific

---

[77] Philippe Quevauviller, 'Science-Policy Integration Needs in Support of the Implementation of the EU Water Framework Directive' (2005) 8 *Environmental Science & Policy* 203–211.
[78] See more about the achievement of environmental objectives in COM/2015/120 final.
[79] The earlier interventions were Directive 75/440/EC concerning the quality required of surface water intended for the abstraction of drinking water in the Member States and

understanding of chemical and microbiological parameters as well as greater political appetite for regulating the quality of drinking water. The focus is very much on water as a consumer resource and the central philosophy of Directive 98/83/EC on the quality of water intended for human consumption (the 1998 Drinking Water Directive) is that it is a 'tap water directive'. Article 6 establishes that the 'point of compliance' is where it emerges from the 'taps that are normally used for human consumption'. If the water is not supplied by a distribution network the point of compliance will be a tanker or where the water is bottled or used for food-production (subject to a *de minimis* exception). While previously water drawn from private supplies (such as wells) fell outside the scope of the 1980 Drinking Water Directive,[80] now the focal point is the water coming out of taps rather than its source.

Ensuring that Drinking Water is 'Wholesome and Clean'

The 1998 Drinking Water Directive's primary obligation is set out in Articles 1 and 4. These require Member States to take the measures necessary 'to protect human health from the adverse effects of any contamination of water intended for human consumption by ensuring that it is wholesome and clean'. Article 4 stipulates that water is 'wholesome and clean' if it is (a) free from any microorganisms and parasites and from any substances which, in numbers or concentrations, constitute a potential danger to human health, and (b) meets the minimum requirements set out in the Directive's Annex I for both microbiological and chemical parameters.

These standards set out in Annex I are mandatory[81] and are broadly similar to those set out in the earlier 1980 Drinking Water Directive. They list the very limited microbiological parameters Member States must test for (notably E. coli) in Table A, the 26 chemical parameters (including arsenic, benzene and mercury) in Table B, and the 20 indicator parameters (including radioactivity) in Table C. The 1998 Directive reduced the overall number of parameters to be assessed since some were no longer thought to be significant in determining water quality (although Member States are able to regulate additional substances or set higher standards as they see fit). The 1998 Directive also repatriated the setting of standards for aesthetic parameters (such as taste or smell) to Member States since these are believed to have no implications for health.[82] On the other hand the 1998 Directive strengthened some individual standards including those for boron, solvents trichloroethene and

---

Directive 80/778/EEC relating to the quality of water intended for human consumption.

[80] Case C-42/89 *Commisson* v. *Belgium* ECLI:EU:C:1990:285.

[81] In Annex I Part A and B respectively, see also Case C-316/00 *Commission* v. *Ireland* [2002] ECLI:EU:C:2002:657 where the CJEU upheld the Commission's action against Ireland for excess microbiological coliforms in the drinking water available at Ballycroy.

[82] Previously these were regulated in Annex I of the 1980 Directive alongside chemical parameters; now they are non-mandatory parameters set out in Annex I, Part C.

tetrachloroethene, and copper. Member States are required by Article 5 to set the values required to ensure that water in their territory meets the parameters set out in Annex I to ensure that the drinking water is fit for human consumption. This is a minimum standard and the initial extensions for implementation under the derogations have now expired. Member States are also, under Article 5(2), required to comply with an overarching obligation on non-deterioration. This is a familiar theme in EU water law. It had previously been included in the 1980 Drinking Water Directive.

Under Article 288 TFEU, all Directives are 'binding as to the result to be achieved'. In the context of drinking water, the CJEU has gone further still, specifically confirming that the standards contained in the 1980 Drinking Water Directive (and by implication now the 1998 Directive) are themselves individually and explicitly enforceable. It reached this conclusion in *Commission* v. *United Kingdom* in 1992 where it sought to remedy failures to comply with the 'maximum admissible concentrations' under the 1980 Drinking Water Directive (since 1998 these have been expressed as values to be set in accordance with parameters). The CJEU referred to the requirement in the Directive that Member States are 'to ensure that certain results are achieved' and held that, unless covered by derogations, Member States may not rely on special circumstances in order to justify a failure to discharge that obligation.[83] The Court rejected the United Kingdom's argument that it had taken 'all practicable steps to secure compliance' finding that this could not justify the United Kingdom's failure to comply with the Directive's requirement to ensure that water intended for human consumption met the appropriate standards.[84] The Court later confirmed that Member States must establish a 'specific legal framework' to implement the Drinking Water Directives. In 1999, it held that the United Kingdom's practice of accepting undertakings to improve from water companies which had been found to be supplying water that breached the standards on pesticides, again meant that the United Kingdom had failed to fulfil its obligations.

Providing for Hard Cases: Lead and Pesticides

One important change in the revised Directive has been to reduce the permitted level of lead from 50 μg/l to 10 μg/l to protect vulnerable consumers, including infants, young children and pregnant women, from its neurotoxic effects.[85] Compliance with this provision is extremely costly, often requiring the replacement of lead pipes and fittings and consequently, while the target was widely supported, the time frame for compliance, the method applied to obtain

---

[83] On this point, see also Case C-42/89 *Commission* v. *Belgium* ECLI:EU:C:1990:285 where the court held that financial or other practical problems could not justify a failure to implement the provisions of the 1980 Drinking Water Directive.
[84] Case C-337/89 *Commission* v. *United Kingdom* ECLI:EU:C:1992:456, paras. 24–25.
[85] Annex I, Part B.

a representative sample and the need to assess the scale of the lead problem on a regional basis, were all disputed.[86] This obligation has been staggered with an initial limit of 25 μg/l, which must have been met within five years of the Directive entering into force, and an ultimate limit of 10 μg/l, that was to be met within fifteen years of the Directive coming into force.[87] The thinking here is pragmatic: the initial requirement will already bring health benefits, while regulators recognise that the major lead pipe replacement programmes required to achieve the higher limits in some Member States will take several years to complete.

Moreover, the obligation is only on the Member State if the lead pipes are outside the home. If lead levels are exceeded 'due to the domestic distribution system or the maintenance thereof', then, under Article 6, the Member State is not in breach; and it will be up to the consumer to replace the pipework or take any other action required (unless the water concerned is being supplied to the public such as schools, hospitals and restaurants). A further area of controversy surrounds the decision of how best to control pesticides in drinking water. The parameters for individual pesticides (0.1 μg/l) and for total pesticides (0.5 μg/l) in Annex I of the 1998 Directive are not based on any scientific findings but on a (largely unarticulated) precautionary approach.[88] These limits differ from the WHO standards (which are generally used as a basis for standards in the Directive) in that the WHO has set guideline values for a large number of individual pesticides.[89] This decision not to assess levels of pesticides individually, implementing instead a statement of belief that pesticides simply should not be present in drinking water at all, has been criticised by representatives of the water industry.

Monitoring and Compliance

Article 7 requires Member States to undertake regular monitoring of drinking water at defined sampling points which are representative of the quality of the water consumed throughout the year. To that effect, they should develop monitoring programmes in accordance with Annexes II and III.[90] Article 13

---

[86] See more on early assessment of these changes in Ierotheos Papadopoulos, 'Revision of the Council Directive on the Quality of Water Intended for Human Consumption' (1999) 19 *The Environmentalist* 23, at 25.

[87] See Annex I, Part B.

[88] The only reference to the precautionary principle in any of the drinking water directives is in Recital (13) of Directive 98/83/EC which states simply that 'parametric values are based on the scientific knowledge available and the precautionary principle has also been taken into account'.

[89] See more in Tom Dolan, Peter Howsam, David J. Parsons and Mick J. Whelan, 'Is the EU Drinking Water Directive Standard for Pesticides in Drinking Water Consistent with the Precautionary Principle?' (2013) 47(10) *Environmental Science and Technology* 4999–5006.

[90] These Annexes have been recently updated by Directive (EU) 2015/1787 in the light of scientific and technical progress. This Directive introduces new EU rules to improve monitoring of drinking water leaving greater flexibility to Member States to conduct this process. It was a response to the first European Citizens' Initiative (ECI), after a Right2Water campaign.

requires Member States to publish a report every three years on the quality of water intended for human consumption with the objective of informing consumers and they must submit a copy of this report to the Commission.[91] This requirement has attracted criticism in that other EU water Directives require more frequent reports. The 2006 Bathing Water Directive, for example, requires annual reports in order to help consumers make choices about where to swim.

Ultimately monitoring is the key to compliance since if the water as sampled does not comply with the Directive's provisions, the Member State must act. It is required under Article 8 to investigate immediately the failure to meet the specified parametric values 'in order to identify the cause' and then take remedial action as soon as possible to restore its quality. Any drinking water identified as a potential danger to human health must, under Article 8, be either prohibited or immediately restricted, with consumers informed accordingly. Article 8, however, confirms that this need not necessarily involve interrupting the water supply if these risks would outweigh those of non-compliance with the Directive. The central test is whether there is a danger to human health. Unless an exceedance is a threat to health, Member States should continue to supply water to consumers whilst enforcement action is undertaken to produce a solution. If remedial action is taken, consumers should be notified by the competent authorities unless the non-compliance with the parametric value is considered to be trivial. Here, the Directive is clearly balancing the risks to consumers between supplying contaminated water and supplying no water at all. It expresses the conclusion that it is better to have water that is below the desired levels of water quality (as long as consumers are notified and can act accordingly) rather than allowing a Member State (or a water company) simply to shut off supplies.

One constant strand evident throughout the revision of the three drinking water Directives is that regulation has been profoundly influenced by the continued increase in scientific knowledge and understanding. The substantive obligations to meet water quality standards have been accompanied by a series of 'methodological' requirements, standardising testing and monitoring procedures across the EU.[92] In this way, EU water law is attempting to harmonise not only levels of pollutants but also the techniques used to assess contamination in the first place.

Assessment

As with other aspects of water law, there have been consistent problems with implementation and the Commission has brought legal action under Article 258

---

[91] These reports must also comply with Decision 95/337/EC concerning questionnaires relating to directives in the water sector and are now to be submitted as part of the Commission's 'Water Information System for Europe' (WISE); see http://water.europa.eu/.

[92] See Directive (EU) 2015/1787 introducing new EU rules to improve monitoring of drinking water.

TFEU against a number of Member States for failing adequately to implement the Directive.[93] The process is one of constant revision, particularly in order to ensure compliance with the Water Framework Directive. Ultimately in order to improve drinking water, more fundamental changes may be required.

Overall, however, as the European Environment Agency noted in *Europe's Environment: The Fourth Assessment* in 2015, most people in the European Union have continuous access to clean drinking water and take it for granted, while their counterparts elsewhere in Europe (particularly in the East), only have access to poor quality water; and sometimes even the supply of that is intermittent.[94] Still, smaller water supplies which serve some 22 per cent of the EU population have lower compliance with the quality standards.[95] Water scarcity and drought are issues of growing concern.[96]

Bathing Water

EU efforts at ensuring clean bathing waters were another early focus of regulation. Directive 76/160/EC concerning the quality of bathing water was introduced to protect both public health and the environment by keeping coastal and inland bathing waters free from pollution. While some technical amendments were introduced, the driving force behind the introduction of the revised Directive 2006/7/EEC concerning the management of bathing water quality was the need to incorporate bathing water law into both the managerial architecture and the integrative philosophy of the WFD.

Monitoring compliance with harmonised environmental limit values remains at the core of the 2006 Directive's regulatory spirit. Reflecting the influence of the WFD there is also now a greater emphasis on management including a fourfold classification system of bathing water as either poor, sufficient, good or excellent and an overarching requirement of improvement (requiring that by 2015 all bathing waters were at least 'sufficient').[97] There is also an increased emphasis on the provision of public information and the requirement for annual reporting by Member States.

Defining Bathing Waters

One striking feature of the Bathing Water Directives is their broad spatial reach. Given the longstanding use of rivers and lakes for bathing by many Member States (Sweden, for example, is estimated to have in excess of 100,000 lakes used for

---

[93] See Case C-122/02 *Commission v. Belgium* ECLI:EU:C:2003:39, Case C-63/02 *Commission v. United Kingdom* ECLI:EU:C:2003:38, Case C-29/02 *Commission v. Spain* ECLI:EU:C:2003:37, Case C-147/07 *Commission v. France* ECLI:EU:C:2008:67; some new infringements cases were launched in 2011 and 2010 against Spain (IP/11/728) and Luxembourg (IP/10/830).
[94] EEA, The European Environment: State and Outlook 2015: Synthesis Report (European Environment Agency, Copenhagen), 122.
[95] *Ibid.*   [96] *Ibid.*   [97] Art. 5.

bathing), the definition of bathing water under Article 1 of the 2006 Directive includes both coastal waters and inland waters in its application to 'any area of surface water' (although it excludes swimming pools and waters for therapeutic purposes). These surface waters are only included, however, 'where the competent authority expects a large number of people to bathe and has not imposed a permanent bathing prohibition, or issued permanent advice against bathing'.[98] According to the definitions set out in Article 2, a prohibition is 'permanent' if it extends beyond one 'bathing season'. There is plenty of scope for Member States to restrict the Directive's reach by their definitions of what are, and what are not, 'bathing waters'.

Indeed, in the past, Member States have used some innovative arguments to exclude waters from regulation. The United Kingdom's argument, for example, that it could identify locations where there were not 'large numbers of bathers' despite the presence of changing huts, lavatories, markers indicating bathing areas and lifeguards, consequently failed.[99] Similarly, Belgium declared bathing waters as insufficiently used simply because they were shallow, subject to unfavourable climatic decisions or (partially) used by kayaks.[100] In the event, both these arguments failed before the CJEU. Ultimately, however, these powers of designations provide an effective way to escape the Directive's obligations. Member States can simply prohibit bathing in certain, hard-to-protect locations thereby removing them from the Directive's definitional reach.

From Emissions Limit Values to Classification

The 1976 Bathing Water Directive required Member States as a minimum to comply with stated mandatory 'I', or imperative, and the 'G' guideline values that Member States were to 'endeavour' to observe within ten years (subject to temporal derogations, now since expired).[101] This approach was not continued in the 2006 Directive, which instead required Member States to monitor a set of parameters set out in Annex I. This has reduced the number of microbiological parameters assessed (from 19 to 2), since some were held to have little or no effect on the quality of the bathing water. The 2006 Directive also now sets differential standards for inland and coastal waters so that, for example, Annex I sets newly introduced standards of 200 E. Coli and 500 intestinal enterococci for inland waters while the equivalent limits are 100 E. Coli and 250 intestinal enterococci for coastal waters. Lastly, Articles 8 and 9 also require Member States to undertake 'appropriate monitoring' for cyanobacteria and macro-algae respectively if the bathing water profile indicates a potential for proliferation. Should the monitoring reveal health risks in either case, then measures 'shall be taken immediately to prevent exposure, including information to the public'.

---

[98] Art. 1(3).
[99] Case C-56/90 *Commission* v. *United Kingdom* ECLI:EU:C:1993:307, para. 34.
[100] Case C-307/98 *Commission* v. *Belgium* ECLI:EU:C:2000:284.   [101] Art. 3.

Most significantly, the 2006 Directive moves away from simply requiring Member States to monitor water quality, imposing an obligation to classify bathing water as either poor, sufficient, good or excellent. Once this analysis has been completed, Article 5 requires Member States to ensure that 'by the end of the 2015 bathing season, all bathing waters are at least "sufficient"' and that they 'take such realistic and proportionate measures as they consider appropriate with a view to increasing the number of bathing waters classified as "excellent" or "good"'. If waters are temporarily classified as 'poor', Article 5 provides that they may remain in compliance, but Member States are required to adopt adequate management measures. These include (under Article 5) either issuing a bathing prohibition or advice against bathing, as well as identifying the cause, taking 'adequate measures to prevent, reduce or eliminate the causes of pollution' and 'alerting the public by a clear and simple warning sign' advising them 'of the causes of the pollution and the measures taken'. If, however, bathing water is classified as 'poor' for five consecutive years (or if a Member State 'considers that the achievement of "sufficient" quality would be infeasible or disproportionately expensive'), then, under Article 5, a Member State may introduce a permanent bathing prohibition. In scientific terms, this breaks the pollution linkage, separating the 'target' (the swimmer) from the harmful substance (the sea). Prospective bathers, however, may find it less than convincing.

Monitoring and Assessment

Sampling is fundamental to both the 1976 and the 2006 Directives, although there has been a shift to a simpler sampling process in the revised Directive. Articles 4 and 5 of the 2006 Directive require Member States to assemble 'sets' of data to underpin the 'bathing water profile' for each relevant water body. Member States monitoring under the provisions of the 2006 Directive are to take one sample at each bathing place shortly before the start of the bathing season and continue sampling until the end of the season, with at least one sample each month. There is also a somewhat tautologous proactive requirement for timely and adequate management measures under Article 7 if Member States are aware of 'unexpected situations' that have, or could reasonably be expected to have, an adverse impact on bathing water quality and on bathers' health. Such measures are to include information to the public and, if necessary, a temporary bathing prohibition.

Public Participation

One significant new strand in the 2006 Directive is the emphasis in the Directive on public participation that is, according to Article 11, to 'ensure the provision of opportunities for the public concerned: to find out how to participate, and to formulate suggestions, remarks or complaints'. The influence of the Aarhus

Convention[102] is clear here: there is an attempt to go beyond the mere provision of information to actively facilitate a contribution to decision-making if not co-decision itself. As with the Water Framework Directive on which the 2006 Bathing Directive is so closely modelled, these provisions contain the kernel for increasing institutional water governance, particularly in Article 14, which sets out the reporting and review provisions within a framework for dialogue that ties in with provisions on technical adaptations under Article 15. Ultimately, however, this is (on the face of the directive) little more than a right to access information which is set out in Article 12.[103] At no stage does the directive envisage truly participatory decision-making.

Assessment

While there are then significant common strands between the 1976 and the 2006 Bathing Water Directives, particularly in the parameters assessed, the revised Directive is clearly modelled on the regulatory framework embodied in the WFD. One of the greatest differences between bathing water and the rest of the Water Framework system is the ability to exclude areas of 'poor' bathing water from the ambit of regulation entirely. There is no non-deterioration provision here requiring Member States to ensure that water quality does not get worse. The Directive is premised on the fact that if, after five years, bathing waters remain poor, then a permanent bathing prohibition or permanent advice against bathing 'shall' be introduced. Indeed, Article 5 states that a Member State may do this even earlier, if, as quoted above, before the end of the five-year period 'it considers that the achievement of "sufficient" quality would be infeasible or disproportionately expensive'. Such a provision has been understandably contentious since it has, in some Member States, led to a significant loss of bathing waters. Still, the 2006 Bathing Directive has contributed to the improvement of water quality in the EU. The vast majority of bathing water in the EU is considered to be good quality water. Indeed, in 2015, 84 per cent of bathing water sites satisfied the Directive's 'excellent' bathing water quality standards.[104]

Regulation of Dangerous Substances

Dangerous Substances in Water Directives

Toxic pollutants have been a longstanding concern in EU water law and, in the drafting of the original Directive 76/464/EC on pollution caused by certain

---

[102] 'Convention on Access to Information, Public Participation in Decision-Making and Access to Justice in Environmental Matters'. The trend towards encouraging participation is set out more fully in Chapter 1 and elaborated in Chapters 5 and 7.
[103] The public can view bathing water quality at more than 21,000 coastal beaches and inland sites across Europe at www.eea.europa.eu/themes/water/status-and-monitoring/state-of-bathing-water/state.
[104] EEA Report, *European Bathing Water Quality in 2015*, No. 9/2016, p. 4.

dangerous substances discharged into the aquatic environment of the Community (the 1976 Dangerous Substances in Water Directive), regulators drew liberally on the 1974 Paris Convention for the Prevention of Marine Pollution from Land-Based Sources.[105] The Community had signed this and was bound to implement its provisions, including the two-pronged distinction between chemicals that are so hazardous that they should be eliminated and those that are sufficiently dangerous that they should be strictly limited. It was this approach that formed the central basis for, first, the 1976 Dangerous Substances in Water Directive, and then its successor, Directive 2006/11/EC on pollution caused by certain dangerous substances discharged into the aquatic environment of the Community (the 2006 Dangerous Substances in Water Directive). The provisions of the 1976 Dangerous Substances Directive were later integrated into the WFD and this Directive was subsequently repealed.

Priority Substances Directive

Directive 2008/105/EC

It is against this background that Directive 2008/105/EC on environmental quality standards in the field of water policy (the 2008 Priority Substances Directive)[106] was introduced. It was prefigured by Article 16 of the WFD, which made specific provision for its introduction, given the failure to reach agreement on hazardous substance control during the negotiations and conciliation phase, particularly on the phasing out of emissions of the most dangerous hazardous substances into water.

Given its position as a daughter directive under the WFD, the 2008 Priority Substances Directive adopts the same legislative principles and institutional architecture. Its objective is to establish common quality rules for chemical analysis and monitoring of water, sediment and biota carried out by Member States; it aims to harmonise. In particular, it continues to distinguish between priority substances (where measures are to be aimed at progressive reduction) and priority hazardous substances (where the measures are to be aimed at the cessation or phasing-out of discharges, emissions and losses).[107] In this it follows the 1976 and 2006 Dangerous Substances in Water Directives in their distinctions between Lists I and II.

Listing Substances and Review of Adopted List of Priority Substances

As Article 1 makes clear, the aim of this Directive is to achieve good surface chemical water status in accordance with Article 4 of the WFD. As discussed, the

---

[105] Now replaced by the 1992 Paris Convention for the Protection of the Marine Environment of the North East Atlantic (the OSPAR Convention).
[106] Directive 2008/105 of the European Parliament and Council on environmental quality standards in the field of water policy, amending and subsequently repealing Council Directives 82/176/EEC, 83/513/EEC, 84/156/EEC, 84/419/EEC, 86/280/EEC and amending Directive 2000/60/EC, OJ 2008 L 348/84–97.
[107] Recital 6.

process of listing and standard setting are extraordinarily costly, labour-intensive and contentious and there has been only limited progress, with the 2008 Priority Substances Directive identifying 33 substances as environmental quality standards and listing a further 11 pollutants that had to be categorised as priority substances in Annex III. Still, the 2013 Directive specified another 12 substances and updated the environmental quality standards for seven of the 33 original priority substances as a result of newly available scientific and technical data (Article 3). These revised quality standards have to be included for the first time in river basin management plans, covering the period 2015 to 2021, while newly specified substances have to be taken into account 'in the establishment of supplementary monitoring programmes and in preliminary programmes of measures to be submitted by the end of 2018'.[108]

The 2008 Directive includes a substantive obligation as well as listing substances. In Article 3, it states that Member States 'shall' apply the environmental quality standards as set out in Annex I, though they may apply these to sediment or biota rather than water if they choose. The Directive also introduces a provision for 'mixing zones' and enables Member States to designate mixing zones adjacent to points of discharge. As a result, concentrations of one or more of the listed substances may exceed the relevant environmental quality standard if they do not affect the compliance of the rest of the body of surface water, or the concentrations in sediment and biota, as appropriate. To some extent, this mitigates the rigour of the spatial delineation at the heart of the 'river basin district' approach. The 2013 Directive introduces a 'watch list' of substances for which Union-wide monitoring data are to be gathered for the purpose of reviewing an adopted list of substances within prescribed deadlines.[109]

Assessment
On one view, the 2008 Priority Substances Directive is rather slight, listing and setting standards for just 33 priority and priority hazardous substances, containing no independent, substantive obligation to phase out or eliminate the most dangerous of pollutants entirely, as the 1976 Dangerous Substances in Water Directive had originally proposed. Directive 2013/39/EU, however, added new substances and reviewed quality standards for substances already on the list. Still, the tension at the heart of EU legislation on water pollution control remains. The desire to phase out or eliminate the most dangerous substances is often seen as unrealistic and is countered instead with the setting up of a system of programmes and prior authorisations based on emissions standards to ensure that discharges do not harm human health. Over time, the language has been watered down, beginning with a commitment in the 1976 Dangerous Substances in Water Directive[110] to no more than an ambition by the time of the Water Framework Directive[111] and 2008 Priority Substances Directive.[112]

---

[108] Recital 9 Directive 2013/39/EU. [109] Art. 8b. [110] Art. 2.
[111] Arts. 1(c), 2(30) and 4(1)(a)(iv). [112] Art. 5(5).

Nitrates

Regulating Non-Point Source Pollution

Directive 91/676/EEC concerning the protection of waters against pollution caused by nitrates from agricultural sources (the 1991 Nitrates Directive) aims both to reduce water pollution caused or induced by nitrates from agricultural sources and also to prevent any further pollution by nitrates. It marked the first concerted effort by the EU to control pollution from non-point sources. While point-sources, such as a pipe or a chimney, are generally straightforward to identify, non-point source pollution that contaminates water as a result of run-off (when soil is infiltrated to full capacity and excess water, from rain or melted snow, flows over the land) or where pollutants leach through the ground into the water below, have conventionally been harder to regulate (and even harder to enforce).

Non-point source pollution is caused both by atmospheric-borne pollutants and the application of chemicals, particularly fertilisers, directly to the land surface. Concerns about nitrates in particular first emerged over fears that elevated nitrate levels in drinking water led to methaemoglobinaemia, or 'blue baby syndrome', in infants; and the 1980 Drinking Water Directive introduced a 'maximum admissible concentration' of 50 mg/l for nitrates. More recently, a further concern is that nitrate pollution contributes to the eutrophication of waterways leading both to the deterioration in ecological quality (due to the destruction of natural habitats because of oxygen depletion) and the impairment of aesthetic qualities of water. The 1991 Nitrates Directive and the 1998 Urban Waste Water Treatment Directive both work towards the amelioration of eutrophication.

'Nitrogen Zones'

Article 3 of the 1991 Directive requires Member States to identify waters every four years that either already are, or could be, affected by agricultural nitrogen pollution. The waters are to be identified (under Annex I) on the basis that they are either surface freshwaters that have (or may have) excessive levels of nitrates for drinking waters or they are groundwaters that have (or may have) nitrate levels in excess of 50 mg/l or they may be natural freshwaters, estuaries, coastal or marine waters that are or may 'in the near future' be eutrophic. Having drawn on one of these three reasons to identify relevant waters, Member States are then required to designate as 'vulnerable zones' all known areas of land in their territories which drain into these identified waters and which contribute to pollution unless they establish and apply a nitrogen action programme throughout their national territory. The CJEU has confirmed that designation is a result of the presence of nitrogen, regardless of its cause. In 2005, the Court rejected Spain's argument that designation would only be required when the presence of nitrates is due to agricultural activity. Instead, it held that if waters are affected by pollution then Article 3 requires their designation, 'it is not necessary that nitrogen compounds of agricultural origin be the exclusive cause of the pollution. It is sufficient if they contribute to it significantly.'[113]

Once designated, Member States are required by Article 4 to establish a voluntary code or codes of good agricultural practice for farmers (including in Annex II restrictions on how and when to apply fertilisers and prescribed land management techniques). Where necessary, Member States are to supplement these codes with programmes of training and information. They are also required under Article 5 to set up 'action programmes' for all vulnerable zones in the territory of a Member State. These are to take into account both the available scientific and technical data and environmental conditions in the relevant regions of the Member State concerned and (under Annex III) 'shall include rules relating to' how and when farmers may use fertiliser on their land.

Improving Environmental Quality

In addition to these managerial objectives, the Directive includes the substantive obligation that Member States should 'aim' to achieve 'for all waters a general level of protection'.[114] This supplements the identification obligation in Article 3 which comes into effect if waters attain either excessive levels of nitrates for drinking waters or nitrate levels of 50 mg/l. This provision is coupled with the monitoring requirements set out in Article 5 which require Member States, in order to 'assess the effectiveness of the Directive's provisions', to draw up and implement suitable monitoring programmes either to assess the effectiveness of action programmes for individual nitrate vulnerable zones or at selected measuring points if they are applying the provisions throughout their national territory. In effect, these provisions treat all groundwater in 'nitrate zones' as potential drinking water and the elision has been criticised for adopting a single public health standard for all nitrogen zones, when the real objective in some water bodies will be to implement less tangible assessments of ecological quality.[115] The certainty, it is suggested, is perhaps ill-suited to the Directive's broader ecological aims.

Additional Measures and Derogations

Once again the Directive makes provision for reflexive learning, requiring Member States to submit four-yearly reports (followed by one by the Commission).[116] On the same four-yearly cycle, Member States are also required by Article 5 to take through their action programmes such additional measures 'as they consider necessary' if it appears that the voluntary code and the training

---

[113] Case C-416/02 *Commission* v. *Spain* ECLI:EU:C:2005:511, paras. 68–69. Here they relied also on Case C-293/97 *Standley and Others* ECLI:EU:C:1999:215, paras. 30 and 35.
[114] Art. 4.   [115] Howarth, 'The Progression Towards Ecological Quality Standards', 15.
[116] Art. 10.

programmes will not be sufficient to achieve the 'good level of protection' for the 'vulnerable zones' as required by Article 4.

Tucked away in Annex III paragraph 2 is a derogation. This permits Member States to exempt up to 170 kg nitrogen per hectare per year for livestock manure, provided that it is demonstrated that the Directive's objectives are still achieved; and that the derogation is based on objective criteria such as long growing seasons, crops with high nitrogen uptake, high net precipitation or soils with a high de-nitrification capacity. The derogation will only be granted if the Commission is satisfied that nitrate-vulnerable zones have been fully designated and if action programmes are fully in conformity with the Directive. The derogation is also time limited (though it may be extended).

Assessment

The 1991 Nitrates Directive is judged by the Commission to have been a success. While the use of fertilisers to replace or increase soil nutrients varies throughout the EU, overall agriculture's contribution to nitrogen loads that reach surface waters is decreasing in many Member States (although it still constitutes over 50 per cent of the total nitrogen discharge to surface waters in most Member States).[117] In groundwater quality, in EU-27 as a whole, and in many Member States, the latest Commission report covering 2008–2011 indicated improvement in monitoring of water quality.[118] Slight progress was identified for groundwater quality compared to the previous reporting period 2004–2007, while much better results were achieved regarding nitrate concentrations in fresh surface water.[119]

Urban and Industrial Waste Water

Directive 91/271/EEC concerning urban waste water treatment regulates the collection, treatment and discharge of urban waste water and the treatment and discharge of waste water by industry. It requires the collection and treatment of waste water in all settlement areas and areas of economic activity ('agglomerations') with a population of more than 2,000 (or in the case of discharges to coastal waters from agglomerations of less than 10,000). Any urban areas over this size will be regulated under the Directive. Since 2005, water receiving discharges from the smallest agglomerations of less than 2,000 population equivalent (p.e.) (or less than 10,000 p.e. in the case of discharges to coastal waters) must still receive 'appropriate treatment' to meet the relevant quality objectives both under this and other Community Directives under Article 7. In each case the Directive expresses the pollution load as a population-equivalent figure rather than the number of residents, as this reflects the assumed pollution experienced rather than the precise number of people themselves.

[117] SWD(2012) 393, 22.   [118] COM/2013/0683, final.   [119] *Ibid.*

Collection, Treatment and Disposal

Broadly, the Directive imposes a series of obligations on Member States with which all EU-15 States should by now have complied.[120] These are first that Member States are required to establish wastewater collection systems for all urban agglomerations that fall within the Directive in accordance with Article 3. Member States should ensure that the design, construction and maintenance of collecting systems is undertaken in accordance with the 'best technical knowledge not entailing excessive costs' as applied to the volume and characteristics of urban waste water, the prevention of leaks and the limitation of pollution of receiving waters due to storm water overflows as set out in Annex I(A).

Secondly, Member States must ensure under Article 4 that urban waste water entering collecting systems is subject to secondary treatment or an equivalent treatment (unless it discharges into less sensitive areas, as discussed below). The Directive defines secondary treatment as the treatment of urban waste water by a process generally involving biological treatment with a secondary settlement or other process that also complies with the standard it establishes for biochemical oxygen demand (BOD), chemical oxygen demand and total suspended solids.

Thirdly, under Article 12, Member States are required to reuse treated waste water whenever appropriate with disposal routes to be selected according to how they minimise the adverse effects on the environment. Member States are to establish a system of prior regulations and/or specific authorisation for the disposal of waste water from urban waste water treatment plants. Under Article 14, similar provisions are made for the reuse and regulation of sludge.

These requirements may be altered in what are designated as 'sensitive' or 'less-sensitive areas' by Member States under Articles 5 and 6 respectively. In areas designated as 'sensitive' by Member States, treatment standards will generally be higher requiring both secondary and tertiary treatment. In less-sensitive areas the standard of treatment may be lower.

Sensitive Areas

Article 5 requires that 'sensitive areas' are to be designated by Member States if they are water bodies either affected by eutrophication or used for the abstraction of drinking water or areas where waste water must be treated at a higher (tertiary) level in order to comply with other EU water Directives. The primary difference between secondary and tertiary treatment is the requirement to reduce emissions of nitrogen and phosphorus. While nitrogen has harmful effects on human health (notably it has been linked to methaemoglobinaemia), the primary reason for these requirements is that eutrophication continues to be an ongoing concern for

---

[120] For the EU-13 transitional periods will continue to expire with the last and final deadline expiring in 2018 (with the exception of the transitional period for Croatia). 7th Implementation Report COM/2016/0105, final.

regulators concerned with water quality in the rivers, lakes and seas of Europe.[121] Consequently, the Directive states that treatment standards 'shall be more stringent' in these sensitive areas although it leaves Member States some flexibility in establishing when precisely stricter standards relating primarily to nitrogen and phosphorus, the discharges that encourage eutrophication, should apply. If Member States can demonstrate that the minimum percentage of reduction of the overall load entering all urban waste water treatment plants in that area is at least 75 per cent for total phosphorus and at least 75 per cent for total nitrogen, then no stricter standards need be applied.[122]

Identifying Eutrophication

Given this focus on eutrophication and the cost of implementing tertiary treatment programmes, its definition has become central to the identification and designation of sensitive areas, particularly if Member States are to anticipate future problems as well as respond to existing concerns. The starting point has been the definition in the 1991 Urban Waste Water Directive where eutrophication is defined as 'the enrichment of water by nutrients, especially compounds of nitrogen and/or phosphorus, causing an accelerated growth of algae and higher forms of plant life to produce an undesirable disturbance to the balance of organisms present in the water and to the quality of the water concerned'.[123] Increasingly, however, the question is not simply whether eutrophication has occurred but rather whether unacceptable eutrophication has occurred. There is now broad scientific consensus that 'eutrophication' is more of a status than a trend and that the term describes the qualitative conditions of an aquatic environment that has been disrupted, rather than just its quantitative (biomass) productivity.[124]

This characterisation of eutrophication that requires intervention as more than simply a change, but an undesirable change, was set out by the CJEU in *Commission* v. *France* in 2004.[125] The Court upheld the Commission's claim stating that the core question of 'undesirability' in this context included significant harmful effects not only on flora and fauna but also on humans, the soil, water, air or landscape. In particular, they held that eutrophication includes effects as anthropocentric as a deterioration in the colour, appearance, taste or odour which prevents or limits water uses such as tourism, fishing, the abstraction of drinking water or the cooling of industrial installations.

More recently, however, in 2009, the CJEU returned to the definition of eutrophication in *Commission* v. *Finland* and *Commission* v. *United*

---

[121] See about the growing concerns of the impact of eutrophication on Europe's seas in EEA; 'State of Europe's Seas' Report No. 2/2015, 72–78.
[122] Art. 5(4) Urban Waste Directive. [123] Art. 2(11).
[124] 'Eutrophication and Health', WHO and Commission (2002), 13. See also Howarth, 'The Progression Towards Ecological Quality Standards', 3, at n. 50.
[125] Case C-280/02 *Commission* v. *France* [2004] ECR I8573, paras. 13–17.

Kingdom.[126] In both these cases it was prepared to adopt a less precautionary approach, imposing a stricter causal burden on the Commission. Rejecting the case against Finland, the Commission held that 'there must be an adequate causal link between discharges and pollution of sensitive areas'. In the absence of such a link, even though the water (here in the Baltic Sea) is undergoing eutrophication on account of nitrogen and other substances, then, as long as the Commission has not established that discharges of nitrogen from treatment plants of urban waste water from agglomerations of more than 10,000 p.e. which flow into the Baltic Sea properly contribute to eutrophication of that sea, 'it is not necessary to require tertiary treatment of nitrogen for each of those plants'.[127] No stricter sewage treatment was required.

Similarly, also finding in favour of the United Kingdom in 2009,[128] the Court held that 'proof of an accelerated growth of algae and higher forms of plant life cannot be considered, as such, to demonstrate undesirable disturbance to the balance of organisms present in the water and to the quality of the water'. Simply identifying change, as the Commission appeared to do, is insufficient to establish eutrophication, there needs to be an 'undesirable' disturbance to the balance of ecosystems. Still, this is almost certainly not the end of the Court's pronouncements on eutrophication since it is perhaps the most troubled aspect of the waste water regime.

Less-Sensitive Areas

Under Article 6, States may also designate areas as 'less sensitive' where the water must be collected but need only be subject to primary treatment, that is, by a physical and/or chemical process involving settlement of suspended solids. These less-sensitive areas are generally applicable in the case of smaller settlements (between 10,000 and 150,000 p.e. if the water is discharged into coastal waters, and smaller still between 2,000 and 10,000 p.e. if the discharge is into estuaries) and to settlements over 150,000 p.e. if there are 'exceptional circumstances' under Article 8; and it can be demonstrated that more advanced treatment will not produce any environmental benefits. These less-sensitive areas are likely to include open bays, estuaries and other coastal waters with a good water exchange that are unlikely to become eutrophic or oxygen depleted[129] and which 'comprehensive studies', provided by Member States to the Commission, indicate will not be adversely affected by the discharges. There are clear parallels here between the designation of less-sensitive areas and the

---

[126] Case C-335/07 *Commission* v. *Finland* ECLI:EU:C:2009:612 and Case C-390/07 *Commission* v. *United Kingdom* ECLI:EU:C:2009:765.
[127] Case C-335/07 *Commission* v. *Finland* ECLI:EU:C:2009:612.
[128] Case C-390/07 *Commission* v. *United Kingdom* ECLI:EU:C:2009:765.
[129] Annex II, para. B.

practice of granting derogations under the 1991 Nitrates Directive. In particular, both are premised on the principles and the practice of comitology.

Industrial Waste Water

As well as regulating urban waste water, Article 13 also requires Member States to regulate biodegradable industrial waste water from plants belonging to identified industrial sectors (including milk-processing, breweries and the meat industry) which does not enter urban waste water treatment plants before discharge. Such effluents must comply with conditions established in prior regulations and/or specific authorisation by the competent authority or appropriate body, in respect of all discharges from plants representing 4,000 p.e. or more. If the industrial discharges are not collected and treated as part of the existing waste water system, then they must be separately regulated.

Institutional Framework

In order to administer this regulatory scheme, Article 15 imposes monitoring requirements, obliging authorities to monitor discharges from urban waste water treatment plants and industrial plants. In less-sensitive areas and in the case of disposal of sludge to surface waters, Member States are to supplement this monitoring with 'relevant studies' to verify that the discharge or disposal does not adversely affect the environment. The biannual reports that Member States are required to publish under Article 16 are supplemented with the information on the implementation programme each Member State is required to establish and forward, again biannually, to the Commission under Article 17.[130]

All in all, the implementation of this Directive clearly represents a major financial challenge for the Member States, which is illustrated by a great number of infringement cases.[131] The provisions of the Directive have been significantly 'design-led' and influenced by the technologies perceived to be available. Further, given the cost of building sewage treatment plants, cohesion policy and regional funds have provided significant financial support to co-finance waste water treatment plants particularly within accession States to the EU.[132]

---

[130] See Commission Implementing Decision 2014/431/EU concerning formats for reporting on the national programmes for the implementation of Council Directive 91/271/EEC, OJ 2014 L 197/77.

[131] See Case C-233/07 *Commission v. Portugal* ECLI:EU:C:2008:271; Case C-438/07 *Commission v. Sweden* ECLI:EU:C:2009:613; Case C-390/07 *Commission v. United Kingdom* ECLI:EU:C:2009:765; Case C-301/10 *Commission v. United Kingdom* ECLI:EU:C:2012:633; Case C-526/09 *Commission v. Portugal* ECLI:EU:C:2010:734; Case C-23/13 *Commission v. France* ECLI:EU:C:2013:723; Case C-343/10 *Commission v. Spain* ECLI:EU:C:2011:260; Case C-565/10 *Commission v. Italy* ECLI:EU:C:2012:476; Case C-85/13 *Commission v. Italy* ECLI:EU:C:2014:251; Case C-395/13 *Commission v. Belgium* ECLI:EU:C:2014:2347.

[132] COM/2016/0105, final.

The full implementation of the Directive is a prerequisite for meeting the objective set out in the WFD, enabling Member States to ensure that all waters in the EU have achieved good ecological status by 2015 but also to maintain status quo in this policy area. As a result, it has an important place within EU water law and it is generally perceived as standing the test of time.[133]

---

[133] See SWD(2012) 393 and COM(2016)105, final.

11

Impact Assessment

Environmental impact assessment (EIA) has formed one of the principal horizontally applicable environmental regulatory techniques within the EU since 1985.[1] Within EU law, it is employed in two important Directives. First, the procedural requirement to carry out an EIA applies, by virtue of the EIA Directive, to projects likely to have significant effects on the environment.[2] Secondly, the Strategic Environmental Assessment (SEA) Directive requires an environmental impact assessment to be carried out at the higher level of policy formation, namely in the case of plans and programmes prepared by public authorities and likely to have significant environmental effects.[3] The requirements of each of these Directives, and their interpretation by the CJEU, are discussed further below.

Crucially, each of these Directives imposes purely procedural obligations, and does not require decision-makers to take whatever decision is best for the environment.[4] Thus, the CJEU has expressly confirmed that the EIA Directive does not lay down substantive rules on the balancing of the environmental effects of a project with other factors, or prohibit the completion of projects which are liable to have negative effects on the environment.[5] In that respect, the technique of impact assessment at the level of individual projects, plans and programmes is similar in nature to the technique of regulatory impact assessment imposed, in particular, as a result of the Article 11 TFEU integration obligation, and discussed in Chapter 3. Ultimately, neither technique ensures the achievement of any particular environmental quality level, or prohibits regulators from choosing a course which will seriously damage the environment.

History and International Context

> Environmental Impact Assessment can be described as a process for identifying the likely consequences for the biogeophysical environment, and for man's

---

[1] See, further, Chapter 4.
[2] The original EIA Directive dates from 1985, but is now codified in Directive 2011/92/EU of the European Parliament and of the Council of 13 December 2011 on the assessment of the effects of certain public and private projects on the environment, OJ 2012 L 26/1, as amended.
[3] Directive 2001/42/EC of the European Parliament and of the Council of 27 June 2001 on the assessment of the effects of certain plans and programmes on the environment, OJ 2001 L 197/30.
[4] On procedural techniques of environmental regulation, see, further, Chapter 4.
[5] Case C-420/11 *Leth* ECLI:EU:C:2013:166, para. 46.

> health and welfare, of implementing particular activities, and for conveying this information at a stage when it can materially affect their decision to those responsible for sanctioning the proposals.[6]

The technique of EIA was first formally incorporated in legislation in the USA, in the form of the National Environmental Policy Act (NEPA).[7] In the wake of the rise in scientific and broader social concern about the effects of human activity on the environment of the 1960s and 1970s,[8] NEPA required federal US agencies to produce a statement of environmental impacts and to make it available to the public, to show that these had been identified and addressed. In this way, EIA from its origins had the dual aim of incorporating substantive consideration of environmental considerations into administrative decision-making processes from an early stage, and ensuring accountability to the public.

Following its successful transposition at national level at an early stage in countries such as Australia, Canada, Ireland, Sweden and New Zealand,[9] EIA obligations have been introduced into numerous international treaties of regional and global scope, including the Espoo Convention on Transboundary Environmental Impact Assessment,[10] the Ramsar Convention on Wetlands of International Importance,[11] the Aarhus Convention on Access to Information, Public Participation in Decision-making and Access to Justice in Environmental Matters,[12] the United Nations Framework Convention on Climate Change[13] and the United Nations Convention on Biological Diversity.[14] The Espoo Convention, as an important European treaty specific to impact assessment extending beyond the EEA in geographic scope, is considered further below.

More broadly, the principle of EIA was incorporated into Principle 17 of the 1992 Rio Declaration on Environment and Development, which

---

[6] Peter Wathern (ed.), *Environmental Impact Assessment: Theory and Practice* (Routledge, 2013), chapter 1. For an overview of the development of EIA, see Richard Morgan, 'Environmental Impact Assessment: The State of the Art' (2012) 30(1) *Impact Assessment and Project Appraisal* 5–14.

[7] National Environmental Policy Act, 42 USC, chapter 55. See, further, Tim O'Riordan and W. Derrick Sewell (eds.), *Project Appraisal and Policy Review* (Wiley, 1981), chapter 1.

[8] See, further, the section on Environment, Philosophy and Ethics in Chapter 1.

[9] See O'Riordan and Sewell, 'Project Appraisal and Policy Review'.

[10] 1989 UNTS, 309 (25 February 1991).

[11] 996 UNTS, 245 (2 February 1971). See Art. 3(2).

[12] 2161 UNTS, 447 (25 June 1998). See, further, Chapters 5 and 6.

[13] 1771 UNTS, 107 (9 May 1992). See Art. 4(1)(f) (commitment to 'take climate change considerations into account, to the extent feasible, in their relevant social, economic and environmental policies and actions, and employ appropriate methods, for example impact assessments, formulated and determined nationally, with a view to minimizing adverse effects on the economy, on public health and on the quality of the environment, of projects or measures undertaken by them to mitigate or adapt to climate change').

[14] 1760 UNTS, 79 (5 June 1992), Art. 14.

provides, 'Environmental impact assessment, as a national instrument, shall be undertaken for proposed activities that are likely to have a significant adverse impact on the environment and are subject to a decision of a competent national authority.'

In its 2010 judgment in *Pulp Mills*, the International Court of Justice (ICJ) recognised the obligation to conduct an EIA as a principle of customary international law, in circumstances that the practice of EIA 'in recent years has gained so much acceptance among States that it may now be considered a requirement under general international law to undertake an environmental impact assessment where there is a risk that the proposed industrial activity may have a significant adverse impact in a transboundary context, in particular, on a shared resource'.[15]

It would seem, therefore, that the scope of EIA as a principle of international law is presently confined to the transboundary context, although its potential application in a purely national context has not yet been settled by the ICJ.[16] Nor, indeed, has the question whether or not the EIA principle in international law necessarily implies a duty to consult the public affected by the proposed project.[17] Rather, the nature of the obligation depends on its precise formulation in the international instrument at issue. At a practical level, the United Nations Environmental Programme Goals and Principles of Environmental Impact Assessment[18] and the World Bank Safeguard Policy on Environmental Assessment[19] represent two leading versions of the content and meaning of EIA at international level.

Despite its success as an environmental management technique at national and international levels, there is no clear consensus on the theoretical and conceptual foundations of EIA.[20]

Models of EIA

In the academic literature, six distinct models of EIA have been identified, each with their own distinctive conceptual basis justifying use of the EIA technique:[21]

---

[15] International Court of Justice, *Pulp Mills in the River Uruguay (Argentina v. Uruguay)*, Judgment, ICJ Reports 2010,14.
[16] See, similarly, the Advisory Opinion of the International Tribunal of the Law of the Sea, Responsibilities and Obligations of States sponsoring Persons and Entities with respect to Activities in the Area (Case No. 17, ITLOS (Seabed Dispute Chamber), Advisory Opinion, 1 February 2011), para. 148.
[17] See the discussion of *Pulp Mills* in Pierre-Marie Dupuy and Jorge Viñuales, *International Environmental Law* (Cambridge University Press, 2015), 70.
[18] UNEP Res. GC14/25, 17 June 1987, endorsed by the UN General Assembly (GA Res. 42/184, 11 December 1987).
[19] See the Operational Policy/Bank Procedure/4.01: Environmental Assessment, available at: http://web.worldbank.org.
[20] See David Lawrence, 'The Need for EIA Theory-Building' (1997) 17(2) *Environmental Impact Assessment Review* 79–107, at 79.
[21] See Robert Bartlett and Priya Kurian, 'The Theory of Environmental Impact Assessment: Implicit Models of Policy-Making' (1999) 27(4) *Policy and Politics* 415–433.

- the 'Information Processing' model, by which EIA is a rationalist mechanism of providing support for administrative decision-makers, guiding their choices from a range of alternatives based on an analysis of all relevant information;
- the 'Symbolic Politics' model, by which EIA is a mechanism to imply accordance with certain (environmental and social) values of society, but does not necessarily hold to those values in practice;
- the 'Political Economy' model, by which EIA is a mechanism for the private sector to reduce its financial risk and potentially increase financial opportunities, by internalising environmental externalities;[22]
- the 'Organisational Politics' model, by which EIA is a mechanism to bring about change in the internal politics of organisations subject to EIA obligations;
- the 'Pluralist Politics' model, by which EIA is a mechanism to bring about opportunities for discussion, negotiation and compromise between different interest groups within society; and
- the 'Institutionalist Politics' model, by which EIA is a mechanism to bring about change in (local, national and/or international) political institutions, by affecting their values and actions in the policy-making process.

As Richard Morgan observes,[23] the form of EIA that has emerged since the 1970s is still largely influenced by the rationalist model, whereby EIA is viewed as a tool for providing information to decision-makers to inform their choices. Nevertheless, elements of the other models discussed above are clearly evident in the developments in EIA which have occurred in EU law over recent years. For instance, the Pluralist Politics model is inherent in the changes brought about to the EIA Directive by the implementation of the Aarhus Convention with Directive 2003/35, discussed further below and in Chapter 7.

The 1991 UNECE Espoo Convention on Transboundary Environmental Impact Assessment

Overview

As with the Aarhus Convention discussed in Chapters 5 and 7, the Espoo Convention is a regional international treaty specific to Europe, signed under the auspices of the United Nations Economic Commission for Europe (UNECE). As noted in Chapter 5, the UNECE has a broader membership than the EU, with 56 member countries, extending for instance to the Russian Federation, Turkey, Tajikistan, Turkmenistan, Ukraine, Uzbekistan, and Western Balkan States such as Serbia. Perhaps counter-intuitively, the USA is also a member of the UNECE, and has signed, although not ratified, the Espoo

---

[22] On the concept of environmental externalities, see Chapter 4.
[23] Morgan, 'Environmental Impact Assessment: The State of the Art'.

Convention. At present, the Convention has 45 States Parties.[24] The European Union approved the Convention on 24 June 1997.

The Espoo Convention entered into force on 10 September 1997.[25] In 2003, the Kyiv Protocol on Strategic Environmental Assessment was signed. The Kyiv Protocol entered into force on 11 July 2010, and currently has 38 States Parties.

As with the Aarhus Convention, compliance with the Espoo Convention is monitored by an Implementation Committee, which supports the Meeting of the Parties of the Convention as well as that of the Protocol. By contrast to the Aarhus Convention, however, the Espoo Implementation Committee does not have the power to accept formal complaints from non-States Parties, although it may receive submissions from States Parties or take action on its own initiative (which action may, in turn, be inspired by communication from non-States Parties).[26] The Committee may, following investigation, choose to enter into correspondence on specific compliance issues with the relevant State Party, which correspondence and response thereto is published on its website.[27]

Obligations

The key obligations imposed by the Convention are as follows.

First, in terms of substantive obligations, the Convention requires Parties to take 'all appropriate and effective measures to prevent, reduce and control significant adverse transboundary environmental impact from proposed activities'.[28]

Secondly, Parties are obliged, in the case of a defined list of activities set out in Appendix I that are 'likely to cause significant adverse transboundary impact', to take the necessary measures to establish an environmental impact assessment procedure that permits public participation and preparation of specified environmental impact assessment documentation.[29] The minimum content of this documentation is specified in Appendix II, and the documentation must be distributed to the affected Party as well as to the public of the affected Party in

---

[24] Namely, States which have ratified, accepted, approved or acceded to the Convention.

[25] The Convention has been amended twice, in 2001 and 2004. The Second Amendment has not yet entered into force; the First Amendment entered into force in 2014, meaning that the Convention is now open to accession by UN Member States which are not members of the UNECE.

[26] See, for instance, the Committee Initiative EIA/IC/CI/5 on the United Kingdom, which was opened on the basis of information submitted by a German Member of the Parliament and the Irish NGO Friends of the Irish Environment, regarding the planned construction of the nuclear power plant Hinkley Point C by the United Kingdom.

[27] See www.unece.org/env/eia/implementation/implementation_committee.html.

[28] Art. 2(1) of the Convention. The Convention is expressed to be without prejudice of other international law obligations with regard to activities with transboundary impact: Art. 2(10).

[29] Art. 2(2).

the areas likely to be affected.[30] Where Parties cannot agree on whether or not there is likely to be a significant transboundary impact, there is provision for the creation of an ad hoc inquiry commission to advise on this issue, i.e. the 'screening' issue.[31]

The EIA must be undertaken prior to a decision to authorise or undertake the proposed activity.[32] EIAs must 'at a minimum' be undertaken at the project level of the proposed activity. There is no obligation to employ EIAs to policies, plans or programmes, although the Parties are to 'endeavour' to do so.[33] This element of the Convention is, however, to be read subject to the Kyiv Protocol to the Convention, which obliges Parties to ensure that a strategic environmental assessment (SEA) is carried out for plans and programmes falling within the Protocol's scope which are 'likely to have significant environmental, including health, effects'.[34] The affected State Party shall, if requested, provide the State of origin of the proposed activity with reasonably obtainable information necessary to prepare the EIA documentation.[35]

Thirdly, the Convention contains a number of obligations to notify. In particular, affected States Parties must be notified of the proposed activity in advance.[36] This must be done as 'early as possible' and no later than when the State of origin is informing its own public about the proposed activity.[37] Further, the public in the areas 'likely to be affected' must be provided by the Party of origin of the proposed activity with an opportunity to 'participate in' relevant EIA procedures regarding the activity, and to ensure that such opportunity is equivalent to that provided to the public in the Party of origin.[38] The concerned Parties must also ensure the public likely to be affected be 'informed of, and be provided with possibilities for making comments or objections on' the proposed activity, and for the transmittal of these comments to the competent authority in the Party of origin.[39] This must be possible 'within a reasonable time before the final decision is taken' on the proposed activity.[40] In the case of the SEA obligation in the Kyiv Protocol, specific provision for public participation is also provided for.[41]

Fourthly, after completion of the EIA documentation, the Party of origin must enter into consultations with the affected Party 'without undue delay' on, *inter alia*, 'the potential transboundary impact of the proposed activity and measures to

---

[30] Art. 4(1) and (2).   [31] Art. 3(7) and Appendix IV of the Convention.   [32] Art. 2(3).
[33] Art. 2(7).
[34] Kyiv Protocol to the Convention, Article 4(1). The matters to be subject to SEA are set out in Art. 4(2)–(4) read with Annexes I and II of the Protocol. 'Plans and programmes' are defined in Art. 2(5) as 'plans and programmes and any modifications to them that are: (a) required by legislative, regulatory or administrative provisions; and (b) subject to preparation and/or adoption by an authority or prepared by an authority for adoption, through a formal procedure, by a parliament or a government.' Plans and programmes for national defence, civil emergencies, and financial or budget purposes are excluded: Art. 4(5), Kyiv Protocol.
[35] Art. 3(6) of the Convention.
[36] Art. 2(4). The notification must contain the elements set out in Art. 3 of the Convention.
[37] Art. 3(1).   [38] Art. 2(6).   [39] Art. 3(8).   [40] Art. 4(2).   [41] Art. 8 of the Kyiv Protocol.

reduce or eliminate its impact'.[42] Such consultations may relate, for instance, to possible alternatives to the proposed activity.

Finally, the Parties must ensure that, in the final decision on the proposed activity, 'due account is taken of the outcome' of the EIA, including the EIA documentation, comments thereon, and consultations described above.[43] The final decision and reasoning must be provided to the affected Party.[44] There is provision for additional information, and post-project analysis, to be carried out where relevant.[45]

Overall, the conception of the EIA and SEA processes in the Espoo Convention and its Protocol contains certain similarities to that contained in EU law, but differs in a number of important respects. Most obviously, the Espoo process applies only to transboundary contexts. It is classically international in terms of its legal nature, in that the vast majority of its obligations adhere only to States Parties, although there is some provision for notification and consultation of the public likely to be affected by the proposed activity. Further, EIA is mandatory for certain listed activities, but, even for these, only where the proposed activity is 'likely to cause a significant adverse transboundary impact'. Unlike the situation under EU law, therefore, there is no category of activity for which an EIA is mandatory in all circumstances, without the need for a 'screening' of likely environmental impacts.

Nevertheless, the extended geographic reach of the Convention means that it forms an important additional aspect to understanding impact assessment law within Europe. As discussed below, the EU's EIA Directive was amended in 1997 to bring it into line with the Convention.[46]

The EIA Directive

The EIA Directive (Directive 85/337/EEC) entered into force in 1985,[47] and was amended three times, in 1997 (to implement the Espoo Convention), 2003 (to implement the Aarhus Convention) and 2009 (to account for carbon capture and storage projects).[48] The 1985 Directive was codified by Directive 2011/92/EU, which in turn was amended in 2014 to strengthen the EIA procedure, align it with the principles of smart regulation and improve coherence with other EU policy areas.[49] The 2014 amendment followed an official review of the EIA

---

[42] Art. 5 of the Convention. [43] Art. 6(1). [44] Art. 6(2). [45] Arts. 6(3) and 7.
[46] Directive 97/11/EC, OJ 1997 L 73/5.
[47] Directive 85/337/EEC on the assessment of the effects of certain public and private projects on the environment, OJ 1985 L 175/40.
[48] Directive 97/11/EC, OJ 1997 L 73/5; Directive 2003/35/EC providing for public participation in respect of the drawing up of certain plans and programmes relating to the environment, OJ 2003 L 156/17; Directive 2009/31/EC on the geological storage of carbon dioxide, OJ 2009 L 140/114.
[49] Directive 2011/92/EU of the European Parliament and of the Council of 13 December 2011 on the assessment of the effects of certain public and private projects on the environment, OJ 2012 L 26/1; Directive 2014/52/EU of the European Parliament and of the Council of 16 April 2014 amending Directive 2011/92/EU on the assessment of

Directive, which included a 2009 Commission report on the application and effectiveness of the EIA Directive[50] and a public consultation in 2010.

The Commission has issued a large number of guidance documents on aspects of the EIA Directive, some of which are discussed below. While not binding on the CJEU, these documents are useful indications of the Commission's own view on the interpretation of the Directive.

Scope and Purpose

Article 2(1) of the EIA Directive provides,

> 1. Member States shall adopt all measures necessary to ensure that, before development consent is given, projects likely to have significant effects on the environment by virtue, *inter alia*, of their nature, size or location are made subject to a requirement for development consent and an assessment with regard to their effects on the environment. Those projects are defined in Article 4.

The CJEU has held that Article 2(1) encapsulates the fundamental objective of the EIA Directive,[51] and sets the limits to the discretion left to Member States under the Directive, for instance in the screening process set out below.[52]

In interpreting Annex II of the Directive in the light of the Directive's purpose and general scheme in *Kraaijeveld*, the CJEU emphasised that the wording of the EIA directive 'indicates that it has a wide scope and a broad purpose'.[53] Nevertheless, the CJEU has also held that a purposive interpretation of the Directive 'cannot, in any event, disregard the clearly expressed intention of the legislature of the European Union'.[54] In *Leth*, the CJEU recalled that the purpose of the Directive was 'an assessment of the effects of public and private projects on the environment in order to attain one of the [Union's] objectives in the sphere of the protection of the environment and the quality of life'.[55] It followed that the information to be supplied by a developer in the developer's EIA report, and the criteria applied by the Member States in the screening process, each discussed below, must relate to that purpose.

---

the effects of certain public and private projects on the environment, OJ 2014 L 124/1. References to the 'EIA Directive' in this chapter refer to the consolidated version of the 2011 Directive.

[50] COM(2009)378.
[51] Case C-287/08 *Savia* ECLI:EU:C:2008:539, para. 52; Case C-486/04 *Commission v. Italy* ECLI:EU:C:2006:732, para. 36; Case C-215/06 *Commission v. Ireland* ECLI:EU:C:2008:380, para. 49.
[52] Case C-72/95 *Kraaijeveld* ECLI:EU:C:1996:404, para. 50; Case C-427/07 *Commission v. Ireland* ECLI:EU:C:2009:457, para. 41.
[53] Case C-72/95 *ibid.*, para. 31. See, further, Case C-2/07 *Abraham* ECLI:EU:C:2008:133, para. 32; Case C-142/07 *Ecologistas en Acción-CODA* ECLI:EU:C:2008:445, para. 28.
[54] Case C-275/09 *Brussels Hoofdstedelijk Gewest* ECLI:EU:C:2011:154, para. 29.
[55] Case C-420/11 *Leth*, cited above, para. 28.

What is an EIA?

The EIA Directive[56] defines an EIA as a process consisting of:

(i) The preparation of an EIA report by the developer pursuant to Article 5(1) and (2).
(ii) The carrying out of consultations pursuant to Articles 6 and, where relevant, 7.
(iii) The examination by the competent authority of the information presented in the EIA report and any supplementary information provided by the developer (pursuant to Article 5(3)) or received through consultations (under Articles 6/7).
(iv) The reasoned conclusion by the competent authority on the significant effects of the project of the environment, 'taking into account' the results of the examination under (iii) and, 'where appropriate, its own supplementary examination'.
(v) The integration of the competent authority's reasoned conclusion into any of the decisions referred to in Article 8a.

To this must be added, in the case of Annex II projects, the initial screening process described above, to determine whether or not an EIA is required.

The EIA must be carried out prior to grant of development consent,[57] defined as the 'decision of the competent authority or authorities which entitles the developer to proceed with the project'.[58] The CJEU has held that, where national law provides that the consent procedure is to be carried out in several stages, the EIA in respect of a project must, in principle, be carried out as soon as it is possible to identify and assess all the effects which the project may have on the environment.[59] Further, a national measure which provides that an EIA may be carried out only at the initial stage of the consent procedure, and not at a later stage in the procedure, is contrary to the Directive.[60]

Article 3 of the Directive provides that an EIA must 'identify, describe and assess in an appropriate manner, in the light of each individual case, the direct and indirect significant effects of a project' on:

- population and human health;

---

[56] Art. 1(2)(g).
[57] EIA Directive, Art. 2(1). See Case C-215/06 *Commission v. Ireland*, cited above, paras. 51–53.
[58] EIA Directive, Art. 1(2)(c).
[59] Case C-201/02 *Wells* ECLI:EU:C:2004:12, para. 53, and Case C-2/07 *Abraham and Others*, cited above, para. 26. See also Case C-290/03 *Barker* ECLI:EU:C:2006:286, para. 49.
[60] Case C-508/03 *Commission v. United Kingdom* ECLI:EU:C:2006:287, paras. 105 and 106.

- biodiversity, with particular attention to species and habitats protected by the habitats and birds directives;
- land, soil, water, air and climate;
- material assets, cultural heritage and the landscape; and
- the interaction between each of the above factors.[61]

These effects must include the 'expected effects deriving from the vulnerability of the project to risks of major accidents and/or disasters that are relevant to the project concerned'.

The CJEU has held that Article 3 is a fundamental provision of the EIA Directive, and requires not only the identification and description of the effects on the factors listed therein, but an assessment thereof in an appropriate manner.[62] This involves an examination of the substance of the information gathered as well as a consideration of whether or not it is necessary to supplement such information.[63] The assessment must include an overall assessment of the direct and indirect effects of the works envisaged, as well as the direct and indirect environmental impact liable to result from the use and exploitation of the end product of those works.[64] Further, the Article 3 assessment must include an analysis of the cumulative effects on the environment which the project may produce if considered jointly with other projects, insofar as this is necessary to ensure that the assessment includes examination of all the notable impacts on the environment of the project in question.[65]

The assessment under Article 3 of the Directive need not include an assessment of the effects of the project on the financial value of assets.[66] Nevertheless, the CJEU has recognised that a decrease in the financial value of an asset (in that case, a decrease in value of a house from noise pollution) is covered by the objective of the Directive in cases where it is a direct economic consequence of the environmental effects identified in the assessment.[67]

Crucially, however, Article 3 does not lay down substantive rules on the balancing of the environmental effects of a project with other factors, or prohibit the completion of projects which are liable to have negative effects on the environment.[68]

---

[61] Art. 3(1).
[62] Case C-50/09 *Commission* v. *Ireland* ECLI:EU:C:2011:109, paras. 35–41. This must be required by law, and cannot merely be done as a matter of administrative practice: Case C-332/04 *Commission* v. *Spain* ECLI:EU:C:2006:180, paras. 33–38; Case C-50/09 *Commission* v. *Ireland*, as above, para. 36.
[63] *Ibid.*
[64] Case C-2/07 *Abraham*, cited above, paras. 42–45; Case C-142/07 *Ecologistas en Acción-CODA*, cited above, para. 39; Case C-560/08 *Commission* v. *Spain* ECLI:EU:C:2011:835, para. 98.
[65] Case C-404/09 *Commission* v. *Spain* ECLI:EU:C:2011:768, para. 80.
[66] Case C-420/11 *Leth*, cited above, paras. 25–30.   [67] *Ibid.*, paras. 35–36.
[68] *Ibid.*, para. 46.

How can a competent national authority accurately predict the likely effects of a project on climate change and/or biodiversity?

In 2013, the Commission issued Guidance on Integrating Climate Change and Biodiversity into Environmental Impact Assessment, in which it recognised that the specific characteristics of climate change and biodiversity may pose significant challenges to addressing these issues in EIA.[69] Specifically, the Commission posited that the long-term and cumulative nature of effects on these areas, the complexity of the issues involved and of causal relationships, and the presence of uncertainty posed particular challenges in these fields.[70] The Commission issued a number of recommendations as to how such challenges may be met by, *inter alia*, avoiding 'snapshot' analyses taken only at a single point in time, working with worst-case and best-case scenarios, and basing recommendations on the precautionary principle.[71]

The 'Competent Authority'

As is evident from the above, the obligation to perform an EIA falls on the 'competent authority', defined by the Directive as the authority or authorities which the Member States designate as responsible for performing the duties under the Directive.[72] The competent authority performs its functions, however, without prejudice to limitations imposed by national laws, regulations, administrative provisions and 'accepted legal practices' concerning commercial and industrial confidentiality and the safeguarding of the public interest.[73] In *Commission* v. *Ireland*, the CJEU held that Member States are entitled to entrust the tasks under the Directive to several entities (in that case, to planning authorities as well as to the Irish Environmental Protection Agency) and the rules governing these entities must ensure that an EIA is carried out fully and in good time – that is, before consent is given.[74]

For their part, Member States are obliged to ensure that the competent authority performs its duties under the EIA Directive in an 'objective manner' and 'do not find themselves in a situation giving rise to a conflict of interest'.[75] In particular, where the competent authority is also the developer (for instance, in the case of a local authority which is the relevant planning authority and also the developer of a project), Member States are obliged to implement an 'appropriate separation between conflicting functions' when performing duties under the Directive.[76]

---

[69] Available at: http://ec.europa.eu/environment/eia/pdf/EIA%20Guidance.pdf.
[70] *Ibid.*, 16.   [71] *Ibid.*   [72] Art. 1(2)(e).
[73] Art. 10. This provision is, however, without prejudice to Directive 2003/4 on access to environmental information (discussed in Chapter 5). In the case of transboundary projects subject to Art. 7, discussed below, the transmission of information to another Member State is subject to the limitations in force in the Member State of origin of the project: *ibid.*
[74] Case C-50/09 *Commission* v. *Ireland*, cited above, paras. 77–85.   [75] Art. 9(a).   [76] *Ibid.*

Projects Subject to EIA

The concept of a 'project' is defined in Article 1(2) of the Directive as follows:

- the execution of construction works or of other installations or schemes,[77]
- other interventions in the natural surroundings and landscape including those involving the extraction of mineral resources.[78]

This does not include the renewal of an existing permit, in the absence of any works or interventions involving alterations to the physical features of a site.[79] However, the concept of 'construction' should be broadly interpreted, and may include, for instance, the refurbishment of an existing road.[80]

Annex I Projects: Mandatory EIA

For those projects listed in Annex I of the EIA Directive, an impact assessment is mandatory, subject only to the possibility of exemption on a case-by-case basis as described below. The CJEU has held that Annex I projects must be evaluated systematically, and that Member States have no discretion in this respect.[81]

Annex I Projects

Annex I contains a detailed and exhaustive list of the type of project which requires a mandatory EIA.[82] By way of illustration, this includes:

- crude-oil refineries;
- large thermal power stations and other combustion installations;
- nuclear power stations and nuclear reactors;
- works for the smelting of cast iron and steel, and for the production of non-ferrous crude metals;
- installations for the extraction of asbestos;
- integrated chemical installations;
- construction of long-distance railway lines and certain airport runways;
- construction and widening of certain roads;

---

[77] 'Other' works may include demolition works: see Case C-50/09 *Commission v. Ireland*, cited above, paras. 97–101.

[78] See, further, Case C-2/07 *Abraham*, cited above; Case C-275/09 *Brussels Hoofdstedelijk Gewest*, cited above, para. 20.

[79] Case C-275/09 *Brussels Hoofdstedelijk Gewest*, cited above, para. 24; Case C-121/11 *Pro-Braine* ECLI:EU:C:2012:225, para. 31.

[80] Case C-142/07 *Ecologistas en Acción-CODA*, cited above, para. 36. See also Case C-121/11 *Pro-Braine, ibid.*, para. 38.

[81] Case C-435/09 *Commission v. Belgium* ECLI:EU:C:2011:176, paras. 86 and 88. In May 2015, the Commission Guidance on the Interpretation of Project Categories of Annexes I and II of the EIA Directive, available at: http://ec.europa.eu/environment/eia/pdf/cover_2015_en.pdf.

[82] This summary does not purport to be exhaustive, and reference should be made to the full list for details.

- certain waste disposal installations;
- certain groundwater abstraction or recharge schemes;
- certain waste water treatment plants.

Changes to or extensions of projects listed in Annex I are also covered thereby to the extent that they satisfy the thresholds listed in the Annex.[83]

Annex II Projects: The Screening Process

For those projects listed in Annex II of the Directive, the Member State determines whether the project is likely to have significant effects on the environment (and therefore requires an EIA). This process is known as 'screening'.[84] Member States are required to screen projects by a case-by-case examination, and/or by thresholds or criteria set by the Member State.[85] Annex III of the Directive sets out the selection criteria which must be taken into account and evaluated in the screening process, whenever a request for development consent for an Annex II project is received.[86]

The CJEU has held that Member States must, in screening projects, take account of their cumulative effect with other projects.[87] Specifically, projects may not be 'split' such that they all escape the obligation to carry out an assessment when, taken together, they are likely to have significant effects on the environment within the meaning of Article 2(1) of the Directive.[88] Further, while Member States enjoy a measure of discretion in determining the method of screening to be used, the chosen method must not undermine the overall objective of the Directive, discussed above.[89] Thus, Member States may not exempt whole classes of projects in advance from the EIA obligation,[90] and may not establish thresholds or criteria which take into account only the size of projects,[91] or which are purely based on location.[92] The CJEU has held that even small-scale projects may have significant effects on the environment if they are in a location where the

---

[83] Annex I, at (24).   [84] *Ibid.*, Art. 4(2).   [85] Art. 4(2).

[86] See Case C-75/08 *Mellor* ECLI:EU:C:2009:279, para. 51; Case C-531/13 *Marktgemeinde Straßwalchen* ECLI:EU:C:2015:79, para. 42. The criteria to be taken into account are broken down in Annex III into considerations relating to the characteristics and location of the project, and the type and characteristics of the potential impact on the environment. See Case C-66/06 *Commission v. Ireland* ECLI:EU:C:2008:637, para. 62; Case C-435/09 *Commission v. Belgium*, cited above, para. 53.

[87] Case C-531/13 *Marktgemeinde Straßwalchen, ibid.*, para. 43.

[88] See Case C-392/96 *Commission v. Ireland* ECLI:EU:C:1999:431, paras. 76 and 82; C-2/07 *Abraham and Others*, cited above, para. 27; Case C-275/09 *Brussels Hoofdstedelijk Gewest*, cited above, para. 36.

[89] Case C-435/97 *WWF (Bolzano)* ECLI:EU:C:1999:418, paras. 42–45; Case C-244/12 *Salzburger Flughafen* ECLI:EU:C:2013:203, paras. 29–30.

[90] Case C-392/96 *Commission v. Ireland*, cited above, para. 73.

[91] *Ibid.*, paras. 65 and 72; Case C-435/09 *Commission v. Belgium*, cited above, paras. 52 and 55.

[92] Case C-332/04 *Commission v. Spain*, cited above, paras. 75–79.

environmental factors set out in Article 3 of the Directive are sensitive to the slightest alteration.[93]

> **Annex II Projects**
>
> Annex II contains detailed descriptions of the projects falling thereunder, broadly grouped under the following categories of projects relating to:
>
> - agriculture, silviculture and aquaculture;
> - the extractive (mining) industry;
> - the energy industry;
> - the production and processing of metals;
> - the mineral industry;
> - the chemical industry;
> - the food industry;
> - the textile, wood and paper industries;
> - the rubber industry;
> - infrastructure;
> - tourism and leisure.
>
> The Annex also extends to cover any change in or extension of projects listed in Annex I or Annex II, which are already executed or in the process of being executed, which may have significant adverse effects on the environment, but only to the extent that such change/extension is not covered by Annex I.[94]

In cases where Member States decide to require a screening determination for Annex II projects, the developer must provide information on the 'characteristics of the project and its likely significant effects on the environment'.[95] The developer must take into account, where relevant, the results of other relevant assessments of environmental effects carried out pursuant to other Union legislation, and may also describe features which might avoid or prevent what might otherwise have been significant adverse effects on the environment.

The competent Member State authority's screening determination must be made on the basis of the information provided by the developer, taking into account where relevant results of assessments of environmental effects carried out pursuant to other Union legislation.[96] The screening decision must be made available to the public, along with the reasons for the decision and, where the decision is that no EIA is required, a statement of features of the project and/or measures envisaged to avoid potential significant adverse effects on the

---

[93] Case C-392/96 *Commission* v. *Ireland*, cited above, para. 66.   [94] Annex II, at (13).
[95] Art. 4(4), and see the detailed list of information to be provided by the developer in Annex IIA.
[96] Art. 4(5).

environment.[97] Further, the screening decision must be taken 'as soon as possible' and at the most within 90 days from the date of submission of the relevant information by the developer (subject to extension in exceptional cases).[98] In *Gruber*, the CJEU confirmed that screening determinations fall within the access to justice provisions of Article 11 of the EIA Directive, considered below, such that the public concerned must be able to challenge them where the conditions set out in that Article are fulfilled.[99]

Exemptions from the EIA Requirement

The EIA Directive provides for a number of possible ways in which a Member State may seek to exempt a particular project, on a case-by-case basis, from the need to carry out an EIA. The CJEU has held that such exemptions must, however, be interpreted narrowly.[100]

Member States may decide, on a case-by-case basis, not to apply the Directive to projects or parts of projects having defence or civil emergencies as their sole purpose, where such application would have an 'adverse effect' on those purposes.[101] Article 2(4) of the EIA Directive provides for a further possibility of case-by-case exemption, subject to fulfilment of certain conditions.

Article 2(4) of the EIA Directive

Without prejudice to Article 7, Member States may, in exceptional cases, exempt a specific project from the provisions laid down in this Directive, where the application of those provisions would result in adversely affecting the purpose of the project, provided the objectives of this Directive are met.

In that event, the Member States shall:

(a) consider whether another form of assessment would be appropriate;
(b) make available to the public concerned the information obtained under other forms of assessment referred to in point (a), the information relating to the decision granting exemption and the reasons for granting it;
(c) inform the Commission, prior to granting consent, of the reasons justifying the exemption granted, and provide it with the information made available, where applicable, to their own nationals.

The Commission shall immediately forward the documents received to the other Member States.

Clearly, Article 2(4) does not define what is meant by an 'exceptional case'. It may be considered, however, that as a term of Union law it is ultimately

---

[97] See Case C-87/02 *Commission v. Italy* ECLI:EU:C:2004:363, para. 49 and Case C-75/08 *Mellor, ibid.*, paras. 61 and 66.
[98] Art. 4(6). [99] Case C-570/13 *Gruber* ECLI:EU:C:2015:231.
[100] Case C-435/97 *WWF (Bolzano)*, cited above; Case C-287/98 *Linster* ECLI:EU:C:2000:468, para. 49.
[101] Art. 1(3). See Case C-435/97 *WWF (Bolzano)*, cited above, paras. 65–67.

a concept for the CJEU, and not Member States, to define. In *Wells*, for instance, the CJEU held that the terms of a provision of Community law which makes no express reference to the law of the Member States for the purpose of determining its meaning and scope is normally to be given throughout the Community an autonomous and uniform interpretation which must take into account the context of the provision and the purpose of the legislation in question.[102]

In a 2006 Guidance document, the Commission noted that there had been 'very few cases' where the provision had been invoked, none of which provided sufficiently firm precedents on which to base clarifying guidance.[103]

Further, Member States may exempt projects adopted by a 'specific act of national legislation' from the provisions relating to public consultation contained in the EIA Directive, provided that the objectives of the EIA Directive are met.[104] The CJEU has held that, in order to benefit from this exemption, the wording of the legislative act must show that the Directive's aims have been achieved with regard to the project in question.[105] Further, a legislative act adopted in circumstances where the legislative body in question did not have the necessary information available to it on the likely environmental impacts of the project, but which merely ratified a pre-existing administrative act in the absence of this information, has been held not to fall under this exemption.[106]

The EIA Procedure

The Developer's EIA Report

Article 5 of the EIA Directive provides that, at the least, the developer's report must include:

- a description of the project and its likely significant effects on the environment;
- a description of the project's features and/or envisaged measures to avoid, prevent or reduce and, if possible, offset likely significant adverse effects on the environment;
- a non-technical summary of the above information;
- any additional information related to the specific characteristics of the project, as set out in Annex IV of the Directive.[107]

Where requested by the developer or where required by the Member State, the competent authority must provide an opinion on the scope and level of detail to

---

[102] Case C-201/02 *Wells*, cited above, para. 37
[103] Available at: http://ec.europa.eu/environment/eia/pdf/eia_art2_3.pdf.   [104] Art. 2(5).
[105] Case C-287/98 *Linster*, cited above, paras. 49–59; Case C-128/09 *Boxus* ECLI:EU:C:2011:667, paras. 39–43. See, further, Case C-43/10 *Nomarchiaki* ECLI:EU:C:2012:560.
[106] Case C-128/09 *Boxus, ibid.*, paras. 45–48 and 50; Case C-182/10 *Solvay* ECLI:EU:C:2012:82, para. 43. See also Case C-43/10 *Normarchiaki, ibid* and Joined Cases C-177–179/09 *Le Poumon vert de la Hulpe* ECLI:EU:C:2011:738.
[107] Art. 5(1).

be included in the developer's EIA report.[108] Where such an opinion is prepared, the developer's report must be based on it. The developer must take into account any available results of other relevant assessments under Union or national legislation when preparing the report.[109]

The developer is obliged to ensure that the EIA report is prepared by 'competent experts'. Further, the competent authority must ensure that it has access to sufficient expertise to examine the EIA report, and may seek supplementary information from the developer.[110]

Consultation and Public Participation

Member States must take the necessary measures to ensure that authorities likely to be concerned by the project by reason of their 'specific environmental responsibilities or local and regional competences' have an opportunity to express their opinion on the developer's EIA report and on the request for development consent.[111] The CJEU has held that such opinions are preparatory in nature, and are not generally subject to appeal.[112]

As discussed further in Chapters 5 and 7, the EU amended the EIA Directive in 2003 to implement the Aarhus Convention requirements of public participation and access to justice, meaning that stricter EU law requirements apply in this regard here than in other areas of EU environmental law. These requirements are set out in Article 6 of the EIA Directive, which provides that the public concerned must be informed 'electronically and by public notices or by other appropriate means'[113] of a range of details including the request for development consent, the fact that there is an EIA procedure, details of the competent decision-making authorities, the nature of the possible decision that may be made, an indication that information concerning the project will be made available and the time/place at which this will be done, and the arrangements for how public participation will occur. This must take place 'early' in the relevant environmental decision-making procedures and 'at the latest, as soon as information can reasonably be provided'.[114] The public concerned is defined as the public 'affected or likely to be affected by, or having an interest in', the relevant environmental decision-making procedures; in accordance with the requirements of the Aarhus Convention, ENGOs meeting any requirements under national law are deemed to have such an interest.[115]

---

[108] Art. 5(2). [109] Art. 5(1). [110] Art. 5(3). [111] Art. 6(1).
[112] Case C-332/04 *Commission* v. *Spain*, cited above, para. 54.
[113] Member States are left discretion to determine the detailed arrangements for informing the public: see Art. 6(5).
[114] Art. 6(2). Art. 6(3) further specifies the information which must be made available to the public concerned within 'reasonable time frames', including information gathered pursuant to Article 5, any reports issued to the competent authorities, and any other relevant information, in accordance with Directive 2003/4/EC (discussed further in Chapter 5).
[115] Art. 1(2)(e). On this, see Case C-263/08 *Djurgården* ECLI:EU:C:2009:631, discussed in Chapter 7, where the CJEU held that it was contrary to the Directive for a Member State to reserve the right of access to justice to ENGOs with at least 2,000 members.

The public concerned must be given 'early and effective opportunities to participate' in the relevant environmental decision-making procedures and shall 'for that purpose, be entitled to express comments and opinions when all options are open to the competent authority or authorities before the decision on the request for development consent is taken'.[116] Reasonable time frames must be provided for the different phases of the consultation and participation process, including at least 30 days for the public to be consulted on the developer's EIA report.[117] The CJEU has held that Member States may charge an administrative fee for participating in the consultation process, as long as it is not liable to constitute an obstacle to the exercise of participation rights.[118] In *Commission v. Ireland*, fees of €20 for participating in procedures before local authorities, and €45 for participating in planning appeals were held not to contravene the Directive.[119]

Transboundary Projects

Article 7 deals with transboundary projects and, as discussed above, implements the 1991 UNECE Espoo Convention. It obliges Member States which are aware that a project is 'likely to have significant effects on the environment in another Member State', or where a Member State likely to be significantly affected so requests, to send to the affected Member State 'as soon as possible and no later than when informing its own public' details including a description of the project and on the nature of the decision which may be taken.[120]

If the affected Member State wishes to participate in the relevant environmental decision-making procedures, it must be sent the necessary information.[121] The Member States concerned must then enter into consultations, including on the measures envisaged to reduce or eliminate transboundary effects, and shall agree detailed arrangements for those consultations.[122]

The Decision to Grant or Refuse Development Consent

A decision to grant development consent must contain a reasoned conclusion on the significant effects of the project on the environment, taking into account the competent authority's examination of the developer's EIA report and any supplementary information provided, as well as details of any environmental conditions attached to the decision, and a description of any features envisaged to avoid, prevent or reduce significant adverse environmental effects, and any monitoring measures.[123] The details of any monitoring must be 'proportionate to

---

[116] Art. 6(4).   [117] Art. 6(7).
[118] Case C-216/05 *Commission* v. *Ireland* ECLI:EU:C:2006:706, paras. 42–45.   [119] *Ibid*.
[120] Art. 7(1). See Case C-205/08 *Umweltanwalt von Kärnten* ECLI:EU:C:2009:767 and Case C-435/09 *Commission* v. *Belgium*, cited above, para. 92. See the Commission's 2013 Guidance on the Application of the EIA Procedure for Large-scale Transboundary Projects, available at: http://ec.europa.eu/environment/eia/pdf/Transboundry%20EIA%20Guide.pdf.
[121] Art. 7(2).   [122] Arts. 7(4) and (5).   [123] Arts. 8a(1) and 1(2)(g).

the nature, location and size of the project and the significance of its effect on the environment'.[124] In the case of a decision to refuse development consent, the main reasons must be stated.[125] In each case, the decision must be taken within a 'reasonable period of time' and in any event at a time when the competent authority's reasoned conclusion is still up to date.[126]

In each case, the information and consultations gathered under Articles 5–7 of the Directive (in particular, the developer's EIA report, as well as the results of the consultations and public participation described above) 'shall be duly taken into account'.[127]

Relationship with other Assessment Procedures
The EIA Directive does not require that an entirely new procedure for EIA be created by Member States: the EIA may be integrated into existing development consent procedures.[128] Where an appropriate assessment under the Habitats or Birds Directives must be carried out for the project also,[129] the Member State must 'where appropriate, ensure that coordinated and/or joint procedures' are provided for.

Where a requirement to assess environmental impacts also arises from other EU legislation in respect of that project (for instance, the Water Framework Directive or the Industrial Emissions Directive),[130] Member States 'may' provide for coordinated/joint procedures.[131]

EIA as a 'Bottleneck' for Strategic Energy Projects?

The so-called 'TEN-E' Regulation on trans-European energy networks[132] sets out a procedure to establish on a two-yearly basis Union-wide lists of Projects of Common Interest (PCIs) which will contribute to the development of energy infrastructure networks in the 12 strategic priority corridors for trans-European energy networks. Under the Regulation, PCI projects are to benefit from fast, more efficient permitting procedures, involving a pre-application procedure and statutory permit-granting procedure, the combined duration of which shall not (subject to certain exceptions) exceed 3½ years.[133] A one-stop-shop system is envisaged for the permitting process, in order to facilitate approval of PCIs.[134] As most energy infrastructure projects will fall under Annex I of the EIA Directive and will require a mandatory EIA, the potential for conflict with the requirements of the EIA Directive, including the public participation provisions

---

[124] Art. 8a(4).   [125] Art. 8a(2).   [126] Art. 8a(5) and (6).
[127] Art. 8. See Case C-50/09 *Commission* v. *Ireland*, cited above, para. 44.
[128] Art. 2(2). See also Art. 8a(3), Case C-50/09 *Commission* v. *Ireland*, paras. 73–75 and Case C-435/09 *Commission* v. *Belgium*, cited above, para. 62.
[129] See, further, Chapter 12.   [130] See, further, Chapters 9 and 10.   [131] Art. 2(3).
[132] Regulation 347/2013 of the European Parliament and of the Council of 17 April 2013 on guidelines for trans-European energy infrastructure, OJ 2013 L 115/39.
[133] *Ibid.*, Art. 10.   [134] *Ibid.*, Art. 8.

> thereof, are evident. For this reason, in 2013 the Commission issued Guidance on streamlining environmental assessment procedures for energy infrastructure projects of common interest, in which it stated that, without a strong coordinating authority or time limits on EIA procedures, they may become 'bottlenecks' holding up PCIs. The Commission has put forward a variety of recommendations for dealing with these potential 'bottlenecks', including early planning and scoping of assessments, early and effective integration of environmental assessments and of other environmental requirements, giving a competent authority strong coordinating competences, commencing data collection as soon as possible ensuring cross-border cooperation, and engaging in early and effective public participation.[135]
>
> The balance which the Guidance seeks to strike is a delicate one. On the one hand the Commission emphasises its aim of 'maintaining the highest possible standard of environmental assessment and protection'. At the same time the Commission's affirmation of the need to ensure the streamlining of these strategic energy projects, in a policy field of great European sensitivity, is clear. The pressure to short-circuit the EIA process in cases of important proposed PCIs is evident, and has already been highlighted by ENGOs in several case studies from across the EU.[136]

Communication of the Competent Authority's Decision

The competent authority is obliged to inform the public and any authorities likely to be concerned by the project by reason of their 'specific environmental responsibilities or local and regional competences'[137] of its decision, including any conditions attached thereto, the main reasons for it and information about the public participation process.[138] Any Member State consulted under the transboundary consultation process, discussed above, must also be informed, and Member States must ensure that this information is made available to the public concerned in its own territory.[139]

Remedies and Access to Justice

Pursuant to Article 10a of the EIA Directive, it is for Member States to lay down rules on penalties applicable to infringements of national laws transposing the Directive, as long as such penalties are 'effective, proportionate and dissuasive'.

---

[135] Available at: http://ec.europa.eu/environment/eia/pdf/PCI_guidance.pdf.
[136] See, for instance, Birdlife International, 'Projects of Common Interest? Case Studies of Environmentally Damaging and Controversial EU Energy Infrastructure "Projects of Common Interest" (PCIs)', October 2013, available at: www.birdlife.org (listing cases from Italy, Austria, Ireland, the Czech Republic and Estonia).
[137] Within the meaning of Art. 6(1).
[138] Art. 9(1). See Case C-332/04 *Commission* v. *Spain*, cited above, paras. 55–59 and Case C-182/10 *Solvay*, cited above, para. 64 (reasons may be made available to an interested party upon request).
[139] Art. 9(2).

As discussed in Chapter 6, in *Kraaijeveld*, the CJEU ruled that the *effet utile* of the Directive would be weakened if individuals were prevented from relying on it before their national courts, and if the latter were prevented from taking it into consideration as an element of EU law in order to rule whether the national legislature, in exercising the choice open to it as to the form and methods for implementation, has kept within the limits of its discretion.[140]

In *Wells*, the CJEU ruled that an individual may, where appropriate, rely on the duty to carry out an EIA under Article 2(1) of the Directive, read in conjunction with Articles 1(2) and 4 thereof.[141] The Directive, therefore, conferred on the individuals concerned a right to have the environmental effects of the project under examination assessed by the competent services and to be consulted in that respect. Further, the CJEU held that, under the principle of sincere cooperation laid down in Article 4(3) TEU, Member States must remedy the unlawful consequences of a breach of European Union law. However, the CJEU noted that, in order to remedy the failure to carry out an EIA of a project within the meaning of Article 2(1) of Directive 85/337, it is for the national court to determine whether it is possible under national law for a consent already granted to be revoked or suspended in order to subject the project in question to an assessment of its environmental impacts, in accordance with the requirements of Directive 85/337, or, alternatively, if the individual so agrees, whether it is possible for the latter to claim compensation for the harm suffered.[142]

In *Leth*, applying the doctrine of State liability in damages discussed in Chapter 6, the CJEU held that failure to carry out an EIA does not in principle in itself confer a right to compensation on an individual for pecuniary damage caused by a decrease in the value of property due to negative environmental effects.[143] However, it was ultimately for the national court to determine whether the requirements of EU law applicable to the right to compensation, in particular the existence of a direct causal link between the breach alleged and the damage sustained, had been satisfied.

In *Commission v. Ireland*, the CJEU held that, although it was permissible for national rules to allow, in certain cases, the regularisation of operations or measures which were contrary to the Directive, this must be on condition that it does not offer the persons concerned the opportunity to circumvent the Directive, and that it remains the exception.[144] Again, the Member State must take the necessary measures to remedy failure to carry out an EIA in conformity with Article 4(3) TEU, such as revoking or suspending development consent already granted in order to carry out an EIA.[145]

---

[140] Case C-72/95 *Kraaijeveld*, cited above, para. 56.
[141] Case C-201/02 *Wells*, cited above, para. 61. See also Case C-435/97 *WWF (Bolzano)*, cited above, para. 69; Case C-287/98 *Linster*, cited above, para. 32; Case C-201/02 *Wells* cited above, para. 57.
[142] C-201/02 *Wells*, cited above, paras. 66–69.   [143] Case C-420/11 *Leth*, cited above.
[144] Case C-215/06 *Commission v. Ireland*, cited above, paras. 57 and 59, concerning the Irish provisions on 'retention' planning permission.
[145] *Ibid.*

> Article 11(1) of the EIA Directive, inserted by Directive 2003/35, obliges Member States to ensure that, in accordance with the relevant national legal system, members of the public concerned:
>
> (a) having a sufficient interest, or alternatively;
> (b) maintaining the impairment of a right, where administrative procedural law of a Member State requires this as a precondition;
>
> have access to a review procedure before a court of law or another independent and impartial body established by law to challenge the substantive or procedural legality of decisions, acts or omissions subject to the public participation provisions of this Directive.

The CJEU's case law on the scope and nature of review required under this provision, including its judgments in *Altrip, Commission* v. *Ireland* and *Boxus*, is considered in Chapter 7.[146] It is not permissible for a Member State to restrict the pleas that may be put forward in an action pursuant to Article 11 of the Directive.[147] In particular, it is not permissible for a Member State to confine access to justice to those cases where no EIA at all was carried out.[148] Further, a Member State cannot require that a claimant show a causal link between any procedural defect and the ultimate outcome of the administrative decision.[149]

Member States shall determine:

- The stage at which the decisions, acts or omissions may be challenged.[150]
- What constitutes a 'sufficient interest and impairment of a right'. Such determination must, however, be consistent with the objective of 'giving the public concerned wide access to justice'.[151] Again, the interests of ENGOs meeting any requirements under national law shall be deemed to have such an interest and rights capable of being so impaired.[152]

The CJEU's case law interpreting the *locus standi* requirements of Article 11, including its judgments in *Trianel, Križan, Djurgården* and *Altrip*, are considered in Chapter 7.[153] In particular, it is not necessary to have participated in the prior public participation procedure in order to have *locus standi* under the access to

---

[146] Case C-72/12 *Altrip* ECLI:EU:C:2013:712, Case C-427/07 *Commission* v. *Ireland*, cited above, Joined Cases C-128/09 etc *Boxus*, cited above.

[147] However, restrictions on pleas made abusively or in bad faith are permissible: see Case C-137/14 *Commission* v. *Germany* ECLI:EU:C:2015:683, para. 81.

[148] Case C-72/12 *Altrip*, cited above, para. 36, Case C-137/14 *Commission* v. *Germany*, cited above, para. 47.

[149] Case C-72/12 *Altrip*, cited above, paras. 47 and 48, Case C-137/14 *Commission* v. *Germany*, cited above, paras. 55–67.

[150] Art. 11(2).   [151] Art. 11(3).   [152] Art. 11(3).

[153] Case 115/09 *Bund für Umwelt und Naturschutz Deutschland* ECLI:EU:C:2011:289, Case C-416/00 *Morellato* ECLI:EU:C:2003:475, Case C-263/08 *Djurgården*, cited above, Case C-72/12 *Altrip*, cited above.

justice provisions of the Directive.[154] Further, a Member State cannot set a minimum limit on the number of members which runs counter to the aim of facilitating judicial review of projects falling within the Directive's scope (in *Djurgården*, a minimum number of 2,000 members was held to be contrary to this aim).[155] In *Trianel*, the CJEU held that ENGOs may not be disqualified from access to justice pursuant to the EIA Directive on the ground that national procedural law only permits such actions to protect the interests of individuals, not the interests of the general public.[156] By contrast, in the case of claims brought by individuals, national law (in that case, German law) may validly require that, in order to have *locus standi*, the claimant must show that his/her 'rights have been infringed', which was held to be compatible with the Directive.[157]

Member States retain, however, the possibility of providing for a preliminary review procedure before an administrative authority, and may require administrative law procedures to be exhausted prior to judicial review procedures, where such a requirement exists in national law.[158] Procedures must be 'fair, equitable, timely and not prohibitively expensive'.[159] The CJEU's case law interpreting this phrase, including its judgments in *Commission v. Ireland*, *Edwards* and *Commission v. UK*, is considered in Chapter 7.[160] In particular, the CJEU has held that the persons covered by Article 11 'should not be prevented from seeking, or pursuing a claim for, a review by the courts that falls within the scope of those articles by reason of the financial burden that might arise as a result'.[161] While the CJEU has recognised that 'significant differences' remained between national laws as to costs, it has emphasised that an assessment of whether the costs of proceedings are prohibitively expensive cannot be carried out solely on the basis of the estimated financial resources of an 'average' applicant (an 'objective' assessment): the court must also have regard to the particular circumstances of the applicant at hand (a 'subjective' assessment).[162]

The CJEU has held that interim measures must also be available to applicants falling within the scope of the above access to justice provisions.[163]

More broadly, Member States are obliged to ensure that effective information is made available to the public on access to administrative and judicial review procedures.[164] In *Commission v. Ireland*, the CJEU held that Ireland had breached this obligation by failing adequately to make available information on its access to justice provisions on the internet and otherwise.[165]

---

[154] Case C-263/08 *Djurgården*, cited above, paras. 32–39.   [155] *Ibid*.
[156] Case C-115/09 *Bund für Umwelt und Naturschutz Deutschland*, cited above, para. 59.
[157] Case C-137/14 *Commission v. Germany*, cited above, paras. 30–35.
[158] Art. 11(4). On this, see the CJEU's judgment in C-416/10 *Križan* ECLI:EU:C:2013:8, discussed in Chapter 7.
[159] *Ibid*.
[160] Case C-427/07 *Commission v. Ireland*, cited above, Case C-260/11 *Edwards* ECLI:EU:C:2013:221, Case C-530/11 *Commission v. UK* ECLI:EU:C:2014:67.
[161] Case C-260/11 *Edwards, ibid*., para. 35.   [162] *Ibid*., paras. 37–38 and 42.
[163] C-416/10 *Križan*, cited above. See, further, Chapter 7.   [164] Art. 11(5).
[165] Case C-427/07 *Commission v. Ireland*, cited above.

The Strategic Environmental Assessment Directive

While the EIA Directive is concerned with the impact assessment of individual projects, the Strategic Environmental Assessment (SEA) Directive (Directive 2001/42)[166] is aimed at incorporating impact assessment at higher, 'upstream' tiers of decision-making, which the SEA Directive terms 'plans and programmes'.[167] The Preamble to the SEA Directive summarises the aim of incorporating impact assessment at this higher level of decision-making as follows: 'The adoption of environmental assessment procedures at the planning and programming level should benefit undertakings by providing a more consistent framework in which to operate by the inclusion of the relevant environmental information into decision-making. The inclusion of a wider set of factors in decision making should contribute to more sustainable and effective solutions.'[168]

As will be clear below, the SEA procedure is broadly similar to that provided for in the EIA Directive.[169] However, certain differences deserve mention. First, the SEA procedure requires the consultation of designated environmental authorities at the stage of screening of plans and programmes. Secondly, the scope and level of detail of the matters to be covered in the SEA report must in all cases be determined (the 'scoping' process). Thirdly, the SEA Directive requires an assessment of reasonable alternatives by the competent authority, whereas in the EIA Directive the developer selects the alternatives to be studied. Fourthly, under the SEA Directive, Member States must monitor significant environmental effects of implementation of plans and programmes. Fifthly, the SEA Directive requires Member States to ensure that environmental reports are of a sufficient quality. Sixthly, the provisions of the SEA Directive concerning public participation are phrased differently from those of the EIA Directive and the Aarhus Convention, and the SEA Directive contains no provisions on the third pillar of the Aarhus Convention: access to justice in environmental matters.

In its 2009 Review of the SEA Directive, the Commission noted that the Directive may require changes in the light of the entry into force of the Kyiv SEA Protocol to the Espoo Convention.[170] However, no such amendments have to date been made.

---

[166] Directive 2001/42/EC of the European Parliament and of the Council of 27 June 2001 on the assessment of the effects of certain plans and programmes on the environment, OJ 2001 L 197/30.
[167] See Thomas Fischer, *Theory and Practice of Strategic Environmental Assessment: Towards a More Systematic Approach* (Earthscan, 2007), chapter 1.
[168] Preamble, recital (5).
[169] The Commission considered and rejected the possibility of merging the SEA and EIA Directives in its 2009 Review of the SEA Directive: COM(2009)469.
[170] COM(2009)469.

Scope and Purpose of the SEA Directive

Article 2 of the SEA Directive defines 'plans and programmes' as plans and programmes (including those co-financed by the European Community, as well as any modifications to them),

- which are subject to preparation and/or adoption by an authority at national, regional or local levels or which are prepared by an authority for adoption, through a legislative procedure by Parliament or Government, and
- which are required by legislative, regulatory or administrative provisions.

In *Terre wallonne*, the CJEU held that action programmes under the Nitrates Directive[171] constituted a 'plan or programme' within the meaning of the SEA Directive.[172] In *Inter-Environnement Bruxelles*, the CJEU held that the concept of 'plan or programme' included a measure which defines criteria and detailed rules for the development of land and which subjects implementation of one or more projects to rules and procedures for scrutiny. This extended to land development plans which were provided for by national legislation, but whose adoption by the competent authority was not compulsory.[173] By contrast, the CJEU has held that a project for partial diversion of the waters of a river does not constitute a 'plan or programme' in the above sense.[174]

The Obligation to Carry Out an SEA

Article 3 of the SEA Directive contains the obligation to carry out an environmental assessment for certain plans and programmes which are likely to have significant effects. 'Environmental assessment' is defined as 'the preparation of an environmental report, the carrying out of consultations, the taking into account of the environmental report and the results of the consultations in decision-making and the provision of information on the decision in accordance with Articles 4 to 9'.

Plans and Programmes Subject to Mandatory SEA
Pursuant to Article 3(2), this obligation applies to:

- All plans and programmes prepared for agriculture, forestry, fisheries, energy, industry, transport, waste management, water management, telecommunications, tourism, town and country planning or land use and which set the

---

[171] Directive 91/676/EEC of 12 December 1991 concerning the protection of waters against pollution caused by nitrates from agricultural sources, OJ 1991 L 375/1.
[172] Case C-105/09 *Terre wallonne and Inter-Environnement Wallonie* ECLI:EU:C:2010:355, para. 42.
[173] Case C-567/10 *Inter-Environnement Bruxelles* ECLI:EU:C:2012:159, para. 30.
[174] Case C-43/10 *Nomarchiaki*, cited above.

framework for future development consent of projects listed in Annexes I and II to the EIA Directive; or
- which, in view of the likely effect on sites, have been determined to require an appropriate assessment under Articles 6 or 7 of the Habitats Directive.[175]

Within these categories, however, plans and programmes determining the use of 'small areas at local level' and 'minor modifications' to such plans and programmes only require an SEA where the Member States determine that they are likely to have significant environmental effects.[176]

Screening of other Projects

In a similar manner to the EIA Directive, provision is made for screening of other plans and programmes which set the framework for future development consent of projects. Thus, Article 3(3) of the SEA Directive provides that Member States must determine whether plans and programmes other than those referenced in Article 3(2), which set the framework for future development consent of projects, are likely to have significant environmental effects. The screening process may be carried out either through case-by-case examination or by specifying types of plans and programmes or by combining both approaches.[177] Further, during this process, Member States must 'in all cases' take into account the criteria set out in Annex II, 'in order to ensure that plans and programmes with likely significant effects on the environment are covered' by the Directive.[178]

The CJEU has held that, in carrying out the screening process, Member States may not provide in general terms that the assessment under the SEA Directive need not be carried out where mention is made of only one area of economic activity in local planning documents.[179]

Member States must ensure that the outcome of the screening process, including the reasons for not requiring an SEA, are made available to the public.[180]

Exemptions

The SEA Directive excludes plans and programmes with the sole purpose of serving national defence or civil emergency, and financial or budget plans and programmes, from its scope.[181] The CJEU has held that it is not permissible for a Member State to exempt a plan or programme from an SEA on the ground that it modifies and gives specific expression to another plan or programme which in itself was never subject to an SEA.[182]

---

[175] See, further, Chapter 12.   [176] Art. 3(3).   [177] Art. 3(5).
[178] Ibid. These criteria are grouped in Annex II into: the characteristics of plans and programmes, and the characteristics of the effects and of the area likely to be affected.
[179] Case C-295/10 REF. Where national legislation makes breach of a qualitative condition for exemption from SEA irrelevant to the legal validity of a plan, this is contrary to the SEA Directive: Case C-463/11 L v. M ECLI:EU:C:2013:247.
[180] Art. 3(7).   [181] Art. 3(8).
[182] Case C-473/14 Dimos Kropias Attikis ECLI:EU:C:2015:582.

The SEA Procedure

The SEA must be carried out during the preparation of a plan or programme, and before its adoption or submission to legislative procedure.[183]

Environmental Report

The SEA Directive requires that an 'environmental report' be prepared 'in which the likely significant effects on the environment of implementing the plan or programme, and reasonable alternatives taking into account the objectives and the geographical scope of the plan or programme, are identified, described and evaluated'.[184] The environmental report, 'shall include the information that may reasonably be required taking into account current knowledge and methods of assessment, the contents and level of detail in the plan or programme, its stage in the decision-making process and the extent to which certain matters are more appropriately assessed at different levels in that process in order to avoid duplication of the assessment'.[185]

A list of the information to be contained in such report is set out in Annex I, and includes:

- the likely significant effects on the environment,[186] including on issues such as biodiversity, population, human health, fauna, flora, soil, water, air, climatic factors, material assets, cultural heritage including architectural and archaeological heritage, landscape and the interrelationship between the above factors;
- the measures envisaged to prevent, reduce and as fully as possible offset any significant adverse effects on the environment of implementing the plan or programme;
- an outline of the reasons for selecting the alternatives dealt with, and a description of how the assessment was undertaken including any difficulties (including technical deficiencies or lack of know-how) encountered in compiling the required information.

Information obtained at other levels of decision-making or through other EU legislation may be used for compiling the report.

Consultation of Designated Authorities and of the Public Likely to be Affected

Article 6 of the SEA Directive provides for obligations to consult. Member States must designate authorities to be consulted which, by reason of their specific environmental responsibilities, are likely to be concerned by the environmental effects of implementing plans and programmes, and must consult these authorities in:[187]

---

[183] Art. 4(1).   [184] Art. 5(1).   [185] Art. 5(2).
[186] Including 'secondary, cumulative, synergistic, short, medium and long-term permanent and temporary, positive and negative effects'.
[187] Arts. 3(6); 5(3)–(4) and 6(3).

- the screening process; and
- deciding on the scope and level of detail to be contained in the environmental report.

Member States must also make available the draft plan or programme and the environmental report to these authorities, and must give these authorities an 'early and effective opportunity within appropriate time frames to express their opinion on the draft plan or programme and the accompanying environmental report before the adoption of the plan or programme or its submission to the legislative procedure'.[188]

In *Department for the Environment* v. *Seaport*, the CJEU held that the SEA Directive permitted 'internal' consultation within one and the same authority (in that case, the Northern Irish Department for the Environment) normally responsible for undertaking environmental consultation, and did not require the creation or designation of another authority to be consulted. However, this was only permissible if there was a functional separation between the two sections of the relevant authority, so that there was an internal administrative agency which had real autonomy, in the sense of its own administrative and human resources to enable it to fulfil the tasks of a designated authority under Article 6 of the SEA Directive.[189]

The 'public affected or likely to be affected by, or having an interest in' the decision, including 'relevant' NGOs 'such as those promoting environmental protection and other organisations concerned', must also be given such opportunity.[190]

Member States are left, however, discretion to determine the detailed arrangements for the information and consultation of the designated authorities and the public.[191] The CJEU has held that periods for consultation may be determined on a case-by-case basis, but must in all cases be sufficient to allow the consulted authorities and the public effective opportunities to express their opinions in good time on the draft plan or programme and on the environmental report.[192]

Transboundary Consultation

Article 7 of the SEA Directive provides for transboundary consultation where a Member State considers that the implementation of a plan or programme is likely to have significant effects on the environment in another Member State, or where a Member State likely to be so affected requests. In such cases, the Member State at issue is sent a copy of the draft plan or programme, and must indicate to the Member State of origin whether it wishes to enter into consultations before

---

[188] Art. 6(2).
[189] Case C-474/10 *Department of the Environment for Northern Ireland* v. *Seaport* ECLI:EU:C:2011:681.
[190] Art. 6(4). [191] Art. 6(5).
[192] Case C-474/10 *Department of the Environment for Northern Ireland* v. *Seaport*, cited above.

the adoption of the plan or programme.[193] Where such consultations take place, both Member States must agree on detailed arrangements to ensure that the designated authorities and the public likely to be affected, within the meaning of Article 6 of the Directive, are informed and given the opportunity to make their views known.

Relationship with Other Assessment Procedures
Member States may choose either to integrate the SEA procedures into pre-existing procedures, or establish new 'purpose-made' procedures.[194] Where a plan or programme forms part of a hierarchy, Member States must take into account the fact that an assessment will be carried out under the Directive at different levels of the hierarchy, with a view to avoiding duplication of the assessment.[195] SEAs are, however, without prejudice to any requirements under the EIA Directive and to any other EU law requirements, although coordinated or joint procedures may be provided for in order to avoid duplication of assessment.[196] The CJEU has held that, while an EIA does not dispense with the obligation to carry out an SEA, Member States may carry out a coordinated or joint procedure which means that there is no obligation to carry out a separate SEA.[197] However, there is no obligation to provide for coordinated or joint procedures in this sense.[198]

The Decision
Article 8 of the SEA Directive provides that the environmental report and the opinions expressed during the consultations 'shall be taken into account' during the preparation of the plan or programme and before its adoption or submission to the legislative procedure.

Information on the decision must be made available to the designated authorities, the public and any Member State consulted under Article 7. This includes the plan or programme as adopted, a statement summarising how environmental considerations have been integrated and how the environmental report and outcome of the consultations have been taken into account, the reasons for choosing the plan or programme, and any monitoring measures.[199] Member States are obliged to monitor the significant environmental effects of the implementation of plans and programmes, to be able to identify unforeseen adverse effects and undertake appropriate remedial action.[200]

Remedies

In *Inter-Environnement Wallonie*, the CJEU considered the question as to the effect of non-compliance with the SEA obligation, where applicable EU

---

[193] Art. 7(2).   [194] Art. 4(2).   [195] Art. 4(3).
[196] Art. 11. On the relationship between SEA and appropriate assessment under the Habitats Directive, see Case C-177/11 *Syllogos Ellinon Poleodomon* ECLI:EU:C:2012:378.
[197] Case C-295/10 *Valčiukienė* ECLI:EU:C:2011:608.   [198] *Ibid.*   [199] Art. 9.
[200] Art. 10.

legislation (in that case, the Nitrates Directive) had otherwise been complied with. Citing its EIA case law on the matter (namely, *Kraaijeveld, WWF* and *Wells*),[201] the CJEU ruled that,

> In the absence of provisions in that directive on the consequences of infringing the procedural provisions which it lays down, it is for the Member States to take, within the sphere of their competence, all the general or particular measures necessary to ensure that all 'plans' or 'programmes' likely to have 'significant environmental effects' within the meaning of [the SEA Directive] are subject to an environmental assessment prior to their adoption in accordance with the procedural requirements and the criteria laid down by that directive (see, by analogy, Case C-72/95 *Kraaijeveld and Others* [1996] ECR I-5403, para. 61; Case C-435/97 *WWF and Others* [1999] ECR I-5613, para. 70; and Case C-201/02 *Wells* [2004] ECR I-723, para. 65).
>
> It is clear from settled case law that, under the principle of cooperation in good faith laid down in Article 4(3) TEU, Member States are required to nullify the unlawful consequences of a breach of European Union law [...] Such an obligation is owed, within the sphere of its competence, by every organ of the Member State concerned.[202]

It follows that where a 'plan' or 'programme' should, prior to its adoption, have been subject to an assessment of its environmental effects in accordance with the requirements of Directive 2001/42, the competent authorities are obliged to take all general or particular measures for remedying the failure to carry out such an assessment (see, by analogy, *Wells*, para. 68). National courts before which an action against such a national measure has been brought are also under such an obligation, and, in that regard, it should be recalled that the detailed procedural rules applicable to such actions which may be brought against such 'plans' or 'programmes' are a matter for the domestic legal order of each Member State, under the principle of procedural autonomy of the Member States, provided that they are not less favourable than those governing similar domestic situations (principle of equivalence) and that they do not render impossible in practice or excessively difficult the exercise of rights conferred by the European Union legal order (principle of effectiveness) (see *Wells*, para. 67 and the case law cited). Consequently, courts before which actions are brought in that regard must adopt, on the basis of their national law, measures to suspend or annul the 'plan' or 'programme' adopted in breach of the obligation to carry out an environmental assessment (see, by analogy, *Wells*, para. 65). Nevertheless, in that particular case, the CJEU held that the Belgian referring court was entitled to maintain the effects of the national order at issue, which related to the use of nitrogen in vulnerable areas and was required by the Nitrates Directive, for a short period necessary to remedy the error. The CJEU reasoned that

---

[201] Cited above.
[202] Case C-41/11 *Inter-Environnement Wallonie* ECLI:EU:C:2012:103 paras. 42–46.

annulment of the order would in fact leave a legal vacuum which would be contrary to the Article 191 TFEU aim of achieving a high level of protection of the environment. In the CJEU's judgment, this constituted an 'overriding consideration relating to the protection of the environment' which exceptionally authorised Belgium to maintain the effect of the measure at issue.[203]

---

[203] *Ibid.*, paras. 48–63.

12

Nature and Biodiversity Protection

Introduction

The European Union is a region historically rich in biodiversity and wildlife.[1] However, this richness is under severe threat. The combined forces of (agro)industrialisation, urban sprawl, human mobility, climate change, consumerism and other environmental stress factors conspire against green spaces, forests, wetlands, breeding grounds, self-sustaining ecosystems and the species that populate them.[2] This chapter investigates the contribution of EU law as an instrument to halt and reverse the decline of nature and biodiversity in Europe. The discussion focuses on the two most prominent instruments in the EU's legal arsenal: the Birds Directive[3] and the Habitats Directive.[4] Additional measures, including the Regulation on Trade in Endangered Species (CITES Regulation)[5] and the more recent Regulation on Alien Invasive Species (AIS Regulation)[6] are flagged up in the final section but their analysis is outside the remit of this chapter.

The existence of a well-developed body of EU law on nature conservation and biodiversity may, at first sight, appear difficult to reconcile with subsidiarity and the doctrine of conferred competences. This is all the more so when we consider that the first piece of landmark legislation, the Birds Directive, was adopted well before the European Union acquired environmental policy competence in the Single European Act. The protection of nature and wildlife is intimately connected with decision-making on land use, development and the governance of property rights, which are all issues that are traditionally perceived as politically sensitive and therefore deeply domestic. Indeed, many considered that the focus on migratory (and therefore border-crossing) birds in the 1979 Birds Directive

---

[1] Commission Report on the State of Nature in the European Union, COM(2015)219 final, 20 May 2015.
[2] Charles-Hubert Born, An Cliquet, Hendrik Schoukens, Delphine Misonne and Geert Van Hoorick (eds.), *The Habitats Directive in its EU Environmental Law Context: European Nature's Best Hope?* (Routledge, 2000), 2.
[3] Directive 2009/147/EC of the European Parliament and of the Council of 30 November 2009 on the conservation of wild birds, OJ 2010 L 20/7.
[4] Council Directive 92/43/EEC on the conservation of natural habitats and of wild fauna and flora, OJ 1992 L 206/7.
[5] Regulation (EC) No. 338/97 on the protection of species of wild fauna and flora by regulating trade therein, OJ 1997 L 61/1.
[6] Regulation (EU) No. 1143/2014 on the prevention and management of the introduction and spread of invasive alien species, OJ 2014 L 317/35.

was but a thinly veiled justification for a major EU institutional over-reach.[7] Ultimately, the Directive has stood the test of time and, together with its younger sister Directive on the conservation of habitats, it is now much more solidly grounded in the Treaty's environmental protection provisions of Article 191 TFEU. A stronger awareness of the transnational interdependence of ecosystems has also helped to allay concerns about competence creep. A growing consensus now exists that uncoordinated national nature and biodiversity protection initiatives are highly unlikely to be effective in the fight against nature and biodiversity decline.[8]

Overt challenges to the EU's legitimacy as an environmental law- and policy-maker may be relegated to the past, yet the contested nature of EU competence still resonates in the rich case law on the Birds and Habitats Directives. This chapter starts with a discussion of the evolving meaning of nature and biodiversity protection within the EU and the impact of different narratives about nature on law and regulation. It then delves into the provisions of the Birds and Habitats Directives and, after a short overview of their key provisions and regulatory strategies, examines the seminal legal questions that have arisen in the implementation of both measures. Foremost among these questions is the extent to which Member States retain the discretion to take into account economic considerations in their pursuit and execution of the Directives' environmental protection goals. The preliminary references on this issue are not just queries about the correct interpretation of EU environmental law; they also constitute conscious and repeated interpellations on the institutional settlement between the European and national levels. The resulting formal arrangements and their practical implementation offer a vivid illustration of the power of the EU as a legal regime and of its simultaneous dependence on national cooperation to maintain credibility in the face of domestic challenges.

Nature conservation and biodiversity case law has also proved an unexpectedly fertile area for the development of a contextualised EU understanding of the precautionary principle. Since the precautionary principle relates to situations of scientific uncertainty, it was anticipated that precaution might play a formative role in those areas most directly associated with scientific and

---

[7] Susan Baker, 'The Dynamics of European Union Biodiversity Policy: Interactive, Functional and Institutional Logics' (2003) 12(3) *Environmental Politics* 23–41, at 31; Krämer, *EU Environmental Law*, 181.

[8] Marie Bonnin, Agnès Bruszik, Ben Delbaere, Hervé Lethier, Dominique Richard, Sandra Rientjes, Glynis van Uden and Andrew Terr, *The Pan-European Ecological Network: Taking Stock* (Council of Europe, 2007); Robert Brunner, 'Transboundary Cooperation: A European Challenge' in Andrew Terry, Karen Ullrich and Uwe Riecken (eds.), *The Green Belt of Europe: From Vision to Reality* (IUCN, 2006), 13–19; Marianne Kettunen, Andrew Terry, Graham Tucker and Andrew Jones, 'Guidance on the Maintenance of Landscape Connectivity Features of Major Importance for Wild Flora and Fauna: Guidance on the Implementation of Article 3 of the Birds Directive (79/409/EEC) and Article 10 of the Habitats Directive (92/43/EEC)', Institute for European Environmental Policy, 2007.

technological research and development, such as regulation regarding novel foods, chemicals and emerging technologies.[9] More surprising was its prominence in interpreting the requirements of the Habitats Directive. This chapter analyses the seminal CJEU preliminary rulings on this question and explores how precaution has come to be understood in the context of development planning and decision-making.

The provisions of the Habitats Directive also invite reflection on the extent to which it is feasible and acceptable to offset biodiversity losses. Offsetting is often presented as an alternative to regulation for nature and biodiversity protection,[10] yet the analysis will show that questions of trading off natural capital and compensating environmental damage equally emerge within the regulatory framework itself. The difficulty of offsetting is one of the many challenges that stand between the letter of nature conservation law and its effective implementation on the ground. Indeed, the presence of environmental law does not equate the existence of effective environmental protection. Many obstacles materialise on the path between lawmaking and real change, and nowhere is this more eloquently illustrated than in the area of nature and biodiversity protection. In one of the final sections, this chapter explores the effectiveness to date of the Birds and Habitats Directives. It goes without saying that the selection of themes in this chapter should not be taken to imply that other EU nature and biodiversity protection measures, which are listed briefly in the penultimate section, are unproblematic in terms of their implementation and enforcement. In fact, many of the effectiveness problems that characterise the implementation of the Birds and Habitats Directives have a broader resonance and are representative of challenges that cut across all of EU nature and biodiversity protection law, and even EU environmental law beyond the sphere of nature and biodiversity protection.

Changing Narratives: Nature Conservation, Biodiversity Protection and the Safeguarding of Natural Capital

The European Union's key objectives for a biodiversity strategy for 2020 and beyond are set out in the eponymous 2011 Commission Communication. By 2020, the loss of biodiversity – which is currently estimated to occur at a rate of 100 to 1,000 times the 'natural rate' – should be halted and restored insofar as feasible, as should the degradation of ecosystem services. By 2050, EU biodiversity and ecosystem services should be 'protected, valued and appropriately restored for biodiversity's intrinsic value and for their essential contribution

---

[9] See Chapter 13.
[10] See e.g. Natasha Affolder, 'Transnational Conservation Contracts' (2012) *Leiden Journal of International Law* 443–460; Colin T. Reid, 'Between Priceless and Worthless: Challenges in Using Market Mechanisms for Conserving Biodiversity' (2013) 2(1) *Transnational Environmental Law* 217–233.

to human well-being and economic prosperity, and so that catastrophic changes caused by the loss of biodiversity are avoided'.[11]

Grand aspirations as those formulated in the Communication are never the most informative, but a few things stand out. In the first place, the Communication sets a firm and concrete objective of halting biodiversity loss by 2020. Given the difficulty and complexity of protecting ecosystems against the plethora of environmental risks to which they are exposed, this is an encouragingly ambitious commitment. It should, however, be noted that halting biodiversity loss by 2020 is, in fact, a deferred goal, originally intended to have been achieved by 2010.[12] Moreover, the data gathered in the context of the 2015 Mid-term Review of the 2020 Biodiversity Strategy strongly indicates that the 2020 target, too, may prove beyond reach.[13] The failure of EU nature and biodiversity policy to hit its protection targets, and the role of law in this context, are discussed further, below.

A second point of note is that, in the formulation of objectives, the terms 'nature' and 'nature conservation' are conspicuous by their absence. The Communication emphasises the importance of biodiversity and ecosystem services, but it does not identify nature conservation as a related or separate goal of either the EU's medium- or long-term biodiversity strategy. This is surprising since the aim of protecting or conserving nature used to be prominent in the EU's environmental policies. Back in 1979, the preambles to the Birds Directive identified 'threat(s) to the conservation of the natural environment' as the primary justification for the EU to take action in this field. The aim of nature conservation is also expressly reflected in the establishment of 'Natura 2000'. Natura 2000 is a network of core breeding and resting sites for rare and threatened species, as well as some rare natural habitat types. Developed by the Member States under supervision of the European Commission, it now covers approximately 18 per cent of the EU's land mass and about 6 per cent of its marine territory, and constitutes a fundamental building block of the EU's 2020 biodiversity strategy. Areas within Natura 2000 are designated as 'special' and subjected to elevated environmental requirements, so as to ensure that the resident species and habitats types are protected and achieve a 'good *conservation* status'. The ideal of nature conservation echoes loudly within the construct of Natura 2000.

Yet, over time, the narrative deployed to convey the importance of the EU's initiatives in this area of environmental protection has shifted. In the 1990s, and at least partially under the influence of the 1992 Convention on Biological Diversity[14] to which the European Union is a signatory, the primary importance of managing the environmental risks confronting nature and wildlife was

---

[11] Commission Communication, 'Our Life Insurance, Our Natural Capital: An EU Biodiversity Strategy to 2020' (COM(2011)244), 2.
[12] Commission Communication, 'Options for an EU Vision and Target for Biodiversity Beyond 2010' (COM(2010)4 final), 19 January 2010.
[13] See pp. 443–444, below.
[14] Rio de Janeiro (Brazil), 5 June 1992, in force 29 December 1993, available at: www.cbd.int.

increasingly discussed in terms of biodiversity protection.[15] The 1992 Habitats Directive still affirms the 'preservation, protection and improvement of the quality of the environment, including the conservation of natural habitats and of wild fauna and flora' as an essential EU objective, but then continues that the Directive's main aim is to promote the maintenance of biodiversity,[16] which is typically understood as the variety among living organisms. More recently, the emphasis has shifted again towards a stronger preoccupation with maintaining the EU's 'natural capital'. Ecosystems are represented as precious resources that deliver a wealth of services on which humanity is vitally dependent to survive and to thrive. Ecosystem services are often grouped into four categories: supporting, provisioning, regulating and cultural services.[17] Supporting services are those that are fundamental for the maintenance of ecosystems. A tree, for example, delivers supporting services through soil formation and photosynthesis. If its fruit is harvested, if its bark is used to brew a medicinal poultice or its trunk is logged for timber, it renders its provisioning services. That same tree also provides shade and acts as a barrier to noise and as a carbon sink: all examples of key regulating services. When we marvel at its beauty, represent it in pictures or stories or even, simply, tie a swing onto its branches, we enjoy the tree's cultural services.

Undeniably, many of the strategies and regulatory measures adopted in the pursuit of nature conservation equally contribute to biodiversity protection and to the safeguarding of natural capital, and vice versa. Nevertheless, it would be a mistake to dismiss the difference between the three statements of objective as purely semantic. The concepts of nature, biodiversity, and ecosystem services represent sharply different ways of understanding the value of the environment and its relation to human society. The ideal of 'nature conservation' taps into bucolic imagery of green fields, imposing seascapes and mountainscapes, clear lakes brimming with fish and surrounded by thriving wildlife. Nature is valuable because it is beautiful, untouched and therefore special.[18] It contrasts to the greyness, the clanging sounds and concrete surfaces of our everyday urban experiences; it constitutes a form of otherness and a source of serenity that we must seek to preserve. Biodiversity, in contrast, comes to life not in the great outdoors but in laboratories and professional working spaces. Here, living organisms are broken down and reconstructed into species and subspecies, distinguishable not by their looks, habits or habitats, but by their genetic code. The concept of biodiversity locates value in the very existence of genetic variety. This value is derived at least partly from the economic opportunities that genetic variety represents: a newly identified sub-variant of a fern species may just hold

---

[15] 1998 EU strategy for biological diversity (COM(98)42).
[16] Cf. Jane Holder and Maria Lee, *Environmental Protection, Law and Policy* (Cambridge University Press, 2007), 634.
[17] Brendan Fisher, R. Kerry Turner and Paul Morling, 'Defining and Classifying Ecosystem Services for Decision-Making' (2009) 68 *Ecological Economics* 643–653, at 644.
[18] Cf. Holly Doremus, 'Biodiversity and the Challenge of Saving the Ordinary' (2001) 38 *Idaho Law Review* 325–354, at 327–329.

the 'golden' genetic material needed to develop a cure for arthritis.[19] Finally, the emphasis on nature's utility for human survival and well-being reaches its pinnacle in the representation of ecosystems as natural capital. The shift towards natural capital and ecosystem services transforms the question of environmental value from a predominantly aesthetic matter in the context of nature conservation and a chiefly scientific one in the sphere of biodiversity into an essentially economic assessment.

The point here is not to favour one narrative over others; all have appealing points and shortcomings. Nature conservation conveys a degree of awe and respect for the natural world that is difficult for 'biodiversity' and 'natural capital' to capture. On the other hand, it underlines human society's alienation from this natural world and is conducive to a selective appreciation that revolves around the rare, the charismatic[20] and the beautiful. It could be said to represent a 'museum approach' to the environment[21] that does little to dislodge our feelings of difference, distance and, ultimately, superiority. Biodiversity protection fosters a broader appreciation of ecosystems and their components, but also one that is shallower as it favours genetic code over context. With species preservation as the driving imperative, biodiversity protection easily becomes a matter of accounting; a Noah's ark strategy that is vulnerable to failure as it chases after the threatened and endangered, and is deaf to considerations of non-human welfare. The great merit of 'natural capital' approaches, in turn, is that they restate the relation between human society and the environment in much more interdependent terms, and thereby create greater scope for the acknowledgement and appreciation of non-human agency.[22] On the other hand, the emphasis on ecosystem services legitimises a degree of commodification of the natural world that some commentators find intellectually anaemic and morally compromised.[23]

The point is, however, that understanding the different narratives is important because they foster different policy and lawmaking priorities and support different regulatory strategies. The practice of carving up the landscape into ordinary and 'special' areas, which flows from the designation approaches adopted in the Birds and Habitats Directives, echoes nature conservation's sensitivity to special-ness, and also its vulnerability to alienation which might jeopardise long-term sustainability. By contrast, the prioritisation of special sites with sole reference to the occurrence of threatened or endangered species within the area, and

---

[19] Andreas Kotsakis, 'Change and Subjectivity in International Environmental Law: The Micro-Politics of the Transformation of Biodiversity into Genetic Gold' (2014) 3(1) *Transnational Environmental Law* 127–147.
[20] Doremus, 'Biodiversity and the Challenge of Saving the Ordinary'.
[21] Krämer, *EU Environmental Law*, 191.
[22] Susan Owens and Richard Cowell, *Land and Limits* (Routledge, 2002), 123.
[23] Jerneja Penca, 'Marketing the Market: The Ideology of Market Mechanisms for Biodiversity Conservation' (2013) 2(1) *Transnational Environmental Law* 235–257; Nicolás Kosoy and Esteve Corbera, 'Payments for Ecosystem Services as Commodity Fetishism' (2010) 69 *Ecological Economics* 1228–1236.

regardless of other ecological qualities that various special sites might possess, speaks of a clear preoccupation with the protection of genetic variety. The natural capital narrative, finally, resonates in those aspects of EU nature and biodiversity protection law that allow economic considerations to influence the degree of protection afforded to designated sites and to 'pay' for loss in natural capital through investment elsewhere. These are but a few of the features that have helped to define EU nature and biodiversity protection law over the years. The sections below explore the key legal regimes in greater detail.

The Birds Directive and Habitats Directive: The Twin Pillars of Natura 2000

The two main instruments of EU nature and biodiversity protection law are the Birds Directive and the Habitats Directive. Together, they constitute the first serious attempt legally to protect nature conservation sites across Western Europe. The Birds Directive, moreover, has the distinction of being the first piece of environmental legislation enacted at the EU level.[24] It was originally adopted in 1979, in response to public concern regarding the impact of customary hunting in Southern Europe and Northern Africa on the population of migratory birds.[25] This concern was bolstered by ornithological data which indicated a decline in the number of bird species in Europe. The Birds Directive put into place a range of protective measures to ensure the survival of Europe's migratory bird population. At present, Europe counts over 500 wild bird species, although for only 68 per cent of these 'good conservation status' is achieved. Some of the provisions of the 1979 Directive have been amended over time, some parts of the protective framework have merged with the provisions of the Habitats Directive, and ultimately the Directive and its amendment were codified into Directive 2009/147/EU on the Conservation of Wild Birds. Its core structure, however, is still very much that of the 1979 blueprint. The paragraphs below offer a short overview of the Birds Directive's main provisions.

The Birds Directive

The Birds Directive requires Member States to maintain and restore the population of wild bird species 'at a level which corresponds specifically to ecological and scientific requirements, while taking account of economic and recreational requirements' (Art. 2 BD). The Directive adopts a tiered approach to conservation. It introduces a general requirement for Member States to 'maintain or re-establish a sufficient diversity and area of habitats' for all wild bird species in Article 3, and a more stringent demand that Member States

---

[24] Wouter P. J. Wils, 'The Birds Directive 15 Years Later: A Survey of the Case Law and a Comparison with the Habitats Directive' (1994) 6(2) *Journal of Environmental Law* 219–241, at 219.

[25] Holder and Lee, *Environmental Protection, Law and Policy*, 627.

designate 'special protection areas' (SPAs) which are particularly relevant for wild bird conservation, and which must be notified to the European Commission.[26] SPAs now constitute part of the pan-European Natura 2000 network, along with sites notified under the Habitats Directive. With regard to SPAs, Member States must take appropriate measures to avoid pollution or deterioration of the site (Art. 4(4) BD). When it comes to the protection of bird species outside SPAs, Member States should 'strive to' avoid pollution or habitats degradation.[27] This, again, reflects the tiered approach to conservation, with broad but flexible expectations for the maintenance of habitats generally, and stricter standards at work within SPAs.

Designation-based protection is the most prominent conservation strategy embraced in both the Birds and the Habitats Directives. This is partly because of the pivotal role that designation plays in the establishment of the Natura 2000 network, and also because most of the extensive and high-profile European Court case law on nature and biodiversity protection relates to questions of designation and its consequences. Yet also important are the Bird Directive's stipulations with regard to particular practices that are likely adversely to affect wild bird populations, such as hunting, deliberate destruction of nests and eggs, and deliberate disturbance of breeding grounds.[28] Unless they are one of the 26 species listed in Annex III BD, the sale of live or dead wild birds is prohibited under the Directive.[29] Similarly, the Birds Directive prohibits the hunting of wild birds, except for the species listed in Annex II of the Directive. Any allowable hunting is moreover subject to restrictions, including a ban on hunting during the breeding and rearing season.[30] The Birds Directive also imposes a blanket ban on non-selective capture or killing.[31] Finally, it is possible for Member States to derogate from each of the restricted practices in the public interest. Importantly, however, economic development does not constitute a basis on which derogation can be justified; the public interests in Article 9 of the Birds Directive relate solely to the protection of health, safety and the environment, and to the support of research and education. All granted derogations, as well as a status report on trends in the bird population, must be reported to the European Commission.[32]

The Habitats Directive

The 1992 Habitats Directive follows a similar pattern to the Birds Directive, with some significant differences. Most obviously, the range of living organisms, ecosystems and ecosystem components covered by the Habitats Directive is much broader than the remit of the Birds Directive, as the former seeks to protect

---

[26] The notification requirement is set out in Art. 4(3) BD.
[27] The obligations under Article 4(4) BD are now subsumed under Articles 6(2) to (4) HD. See pp. 434–443, below.
[28] Art. 5 BD. [29] Art. 6 BD. [30] Art. 7 BD. [31] Art. 8 BD. [32] Art. 12 BD.

both sites of natural significance and a wide array of terrestrial and aquatic species. All together, the Habitats Directive covers over 1,000 animal and plant species,[33] and about 230 different habitat types.[34] Secondly, the Habitats Directive takes a more systematic approach to designation as the core foundation of the EU's nature and biodiversity protection strategy. The Directive enshrines the establishment of Natura 2000 as a legal goal to which each Member State must contribute 'in proportion to the representation within its territory of the natural habitat types and the habitats of species'[35] that are listed in the Directives' Annexes.[36] This contribution takes the form of the identification and designation, at the national level, of 'special areas of conservation' (SACs). Together, the SACs and the SPAs designated under the auspices of the Birds Directive constitute the pan-European ecological network of Natura 2000.

Because of its pivotal role within the EU's nature and biodiversity protection strategy, the ins and outs of designation deserve more detailed study. The sections below examine the legal provisions and case law governing the establishment and maintenance of Natura 2000. The creation of Natura 2000 remains a landmark case study of EU multi-level governance in action. It is also a cautionary tale of the many tensions that can flare up in the context of inter-institutional, multi-level cooperation between the Member States and the EU Commission. The sections also elucidate the consequences of designation and review the various Member State obligations vis-à-vis SACs. Such obligations fall into two main categories: those relating to the management of special sites and those pertaining to developments that might affect special sites. In both cases, effective implementation is highly challenging.

In addition to the provisions regarding designation, the Habitats Directive lays down a number of standards that are targeted at species rather than spaces. Similarly to the Birds Directive, these include prohibitions on the commercialisation of wild animals and plants as well as on deliberate capture and killing, deliberate disturbance of species and their breeding places, deliberate destruction or tampering with eggs, breeding sites and resting places, and deliberate collection or destruction of plants. Yet the approach in the respective instruments differs: whereas the Birds Directive introduces an across-the-board prohibition on such activities *unless* the species in question is explicitly exempted from the prohibition, the Habitats Directive limits its no-disturbance rules to those organisms listed in Annex IV, which contains the animal and plant species of Community interest in need of strict protection. This constitutes an exceptionalist regime rather than a default ban on the destruction or deliberate disturbance of wildlife in the EU, and is one of several factors supporting the view that, whereas the Habitats Directive is broader in its reach, it has less bite and is less environmentally ambitious than its older sibling, the Birds Directive.[37]

---

[33] Listed in Annexes II, IV and V HD.   [34] Annex I HD.   [35] Art. 3 HD.
[36] See Chapter 13.   [37] Wils, 'The Birds Directive 15 Years Later'.

Beyond the no-disturbance rules for species and plants in need of strict protection, the Habitats Directive demands that any taking and exploitation of species of Community interest (which are listed in Annex V HD) will be compatible with their being maintained at a favourable conservation status.[38] The fulfilment of this provision is, in turn, supported by Article 11 HD, which requires Member States to undertake surveillance of the conservation status of wild fauna and flora. Depending on the surveillance data, Member States may deem it necessary to intervene in order to safeguard Annex V species, and if so must adopt measures such as the restriction of roaming rights, a licensing and quota system for hunting and fishing, restrictions on sale, and so on.[39]

The rules regarding Annex V species give the Habitats Directive a broader reach, yet the qualifier '[i]f ... Member States deem it necessary' in the first sentence of Article 14 again underscores the scope for flexibility. By the same token, the Habitat Directive's approach to derogations is distinctly more permissive than its counterpart in the Birds Directive. Provided that no satisfactory alternative is available, and favourable conservation status is maintained, Member States may deviate from the protective regime for species for reasons of environmental protection, health, safety *and* 'for other imperative reasons of overriding public interest, including those of a social or economic nature' (Article 16 HD). The open-ended category of 'other imperative reasons' contrasts with the exhaustively enumerated grounds for derogation under the Birds Directive. Whereas the latter entails the imposition of a strict set of EU rules within a fairly narrow remit, the Habitats Directive represents more of a balancing act between EU and national decision-making authority. It also reflects a particular understanding of sustainable development: one that allows natural capital to be traded off against other social goods, provided that the overall quality of the stock is stable. This is known as 'weak sustainability'.[40] The Habitats Directive thus shifts the emphasis away from the well-being of individual animals and plants and towards the resilience of species. It also suggests a degree of fungibility of natural resources that is absent from the language of the Birds Directive.

Designation and its Consequences: The Legal Status of SPAS and SACS

The regulatory approach favoured in EU nature and biodiversity protection law is that of singling out particular areas of high importance to be governed by bespoke sets of nature and biodiversity protection rules that do not apply

---

[38] Art. 15 HD.   [39] Art. 14 HD.
[40] Robert Ayres, Jeroen van den Bergh and John Gowdy, 'Strong versus Weak Sustainability' (2001) 23(2) *Environmental Ethics* 155–168.

outside the designated area. The next paragraphs explore designation under Natura 2000 and its consequences.

The Designation Process

The Birds and the Habitats Directives leave the first step of the designation process to the Member States, although both instruments offer varying levels of instruction on how the Member States should proceed. For the purposes of the Birds Directive, an area should be designated as an SPA if it either features one (or several) of the vulnerable bird species listed in Annex I BD[41] or constitutes a breeding, moulting and wintering area or staging post along migration routes for regularly occurring migratory birds (Art. 4(2) BD). In this regard, Member States are expected to pay special consideration to wetlands, particularly those of international importance. Such sites are, in the first place, those listed under the 1971 Ramsar Convention on Wetlands,[42] to which EU Member States are signatory parties. In fact, the need to comply with the Ramsar Convention was a key factor steering the EU Member States towards early intra-EU cooperation on the issue of wild birds' protection.[43] The Birds Directive further requires Member States to notify the Commission of any designated areas. The Commission has developed a Standard Data Form for Member States to submit. The information therein helps the Commission to track progress in classification of SPAs across the EU[44] and to determine whether the designated sites are sufficient to form a coherent network of protection. The reported sites then become part of Natura 2000.

The Habitats Directive takes a more articulated approach to designation. The Directive requires Member States to list the habitats covered in Annex I HD (which includes areas such as sand dunes, freshwater habitats, bogs, mires and limestone pavements), as well as areas that host any of the species listed in Annex II HD (ranging from sea turtles to wild flowers, wolves to goby fish). To this end, Member States must apply the criteria listed in Annex III HD, which stipulate that a decision to select a site should be made on the basis of, *inter alia*, the representativeness of the site as one of the natural habitat types listed in Annex I; its size compared to the overall prevalence of the habitat type within the country; the number and density of the protected species population within the site; and the extent to which the habitat can sustain, or can be restored to sustain, the protected species dwelling within.[45]

---

[41] Annex I BD lists 194 bird species.
[42] Ramsar (Iran), 2 February 1971, entry into force 21 December 1975, available at: www.ramsar.org/sites/default/files/documents/library/current_convention_text_e.pdf.
[43] Born et al., *The Habitats Directive*, 3.
[44] This progress is summarised and updated in the Natura 2000 Barometer, which details, *inter alia*, the number of sites classified, the total area covered by these and what proportion. It also offers an evaluation of how complete is a Member State's network of protection.
[45] See Annex III HD for a full list of criteria.

The instructions on site selection are more detailed than those supplied under the Birds Directive, but it is at the stage of notification that the more regimented approach of the Habitats Directive really comes into focus. First, the Directive sets a deadline of three years for the Member States to complete the list of eligible sites and forward it to the Commission. Unfortunately (though perhaps not surprisingly), the deadline was royally missed by most Member States. Nonetheless, it constitutes a firmer basis for Member State accountability than would an open-ended obligation: in 2001, the ECJ found Ireland, Germany and France in breach of the time limits.[46] Secondly, the notification stage is followed by a moderation process in which the Commission, in consultation with the Member State, determines which of the eligible sites are 'sites of community importance' (SCIs) and should therefore be incorporated into Natura 2000. In this process, the Commission also indicates which among the SCIs are 'priority sites', which either host a natural habitat type or a species that is in danger of disappearance.[47] Within three years of Member State notification, and with Member State agreement, the Commission must decide upon a final list of SCIs. The Member States then have six years to designate all confirmed SCIs as SACs.

Following the deadlines in the Habitats Directive, and making allowances for the more recently acceded EU Member States, the Natura 2000 project and corresponding designation of SACs should have been completed by 2004 at the latest. Admittedly, the term 'completed' is slightly misleading: ecosystems are living entities that change and evolve over time. Of necessity, Natura 2000 must evolve with them. Nevertheless, a stable if fluid network should have been in place, and corresponding national protection regimes should have been established, by the early 2000s. In reality, it took substantially longer. Only around 2010 did the Commission conclude that, with approximately 26,000 sites designated across the EU, Natura 2000 could be considered as more or less maturely 'established'.[48] The adoption of adequate conservation measures at the national level to safeguard the ecosystems within the 26,000 designated sites is still very much a work in progress.[49]

The Consequences of Designation

The preceding overview of the EU designation process offers it is hoped a clear but admittedly quite placid account of EU-Member State cooperation. In reality,

---

[46] Case C-67/99 *Commission v. Ireland* ECLI:EU:C:2001:432; Case C-71/99 *Commission v. Germany* ECLI:EU:C:2001:433; and Case C-220/99 *Commission v. France* ECLI:EU:C:2001:434.

[47] Priority habitats and priority species are indicated with an asterisk in Annexes I and II HD respectively.

[48] Commission Communication, 'Options for an EU Vision and Target for Biodiversity Beyond 2010', COM(2010)4 final, 19 January 2010.

[49] Carlos Romão, 'The Added Value of the Habitats Directive: Is Biodiversity Better Protected since the Directive Entered Into Force?' in Born et al., *The Habitats Directive*, 23.

the classification of SCIs and the discretion enjoyed by Member States and the Commission in carrying out their respective tasks have been a hotbed of contention and are the basis of some of the most seminal environmental law rulings in the European Court's history. The crucial question revolved around whether Member States are free to take into account economic factors (such as the need for economic development to foster employment in depressed areas) in their selection of eligible sites, a question which the ECJ answered in the negative.[50] The case law on this and related issues is examined further in the next section, but in order to appreciate its relevance it is important first to have a sense of *why* control over the designation process was so hard fought. Ultimately, whether a classification as 'SPA' or 'SAC' matters, depends on the consequences attached. It is clear from the Birds and Habitats Directives that the consequences are, indeed, significant. Member States are obliged to develop and adopt special conservation regimes for protected areas, and they must take measures to avoid their disturbance and degradation. Crucially, the presence of an SCI, SAC or SPA complicates decision-making on development projects in the area, and may even outlaw certain projects altogether. The ramifications of designation are analysed in greater detail, below.

Designation and its Discontents

The Habitats Directive shows the European Union deeply committed to a designation (or 'enclave') strategy for nature and biodiversity protection. This is understandable, for designation has a number of strong assets. Most importantly, its focus on the physical habitats of undomesticated species directly engages with the greatest threat to biodiversity in the modern world, namely, habitats degradation and loss.[51] The selectiveness inherent in the approach also enables policy-makers to prioritise and to deploy special regulatory interventions that would be considered too intrusive to be publicly acceptable if applied in an indiscriminate manner. For example, the proposition that any industrial development, regardless of its location, would be conditional on a favourable environmental impact statement, would probably send 28 governments into a simultaneous tailspin. However, if developments are only affected when they happen in proximity to a 'special' area, the impacts are more tolerable and manageable. Moreover, while the tighter level of regulation within designated areas imposes certain costs, and conditionalises opportunities for development, the conveyance of a special status may by the same token enhance the appeal of particular regions and put them in a better position to secure public funding, attract eco-tourism and so on.

However, designation is not without its problems. Its static nature can limit its effectiveness: the European Commission may know where the boundaries of Nature 2000 are, but the species for the benefit of which the borders are drawn do not. When it comes to migratory birds, it is somewhat ironic that we have our

---

[50] See pp. 423–428, below. [51] Born et al., *The Habitats Directive*, 1.

gaze firmly fixed on the land while the object of our protection goes literally over our heads. Additionally, commentators have observed that a designation approach can backfire if it leads property owners and land managers to neglect or destroy features of interest on the basis that the land could have been designated, but was not.[52] This links back to the previously discussed dilemma of the nature conservation narrative that the elevation of select areas and species as 'special' generates a subtext that others are ordinary and not worth protecting. Yet, increasingly, the informed view is that the special cannot thrive in isolation, and that holistic approaches are essential to retain the conditions in which both the charismatic and the overlooked can thrive. Natura 2000's focus on coherence, on establishing corridors and interconnecting pathways, aims to mitigate the risks of isolation that are inherent in the designation approach. In the light of the delays incurred in establishing the network, it is still a little early to pass final verdict on the EU's designation strategy, but available data indicates that there is certainly much room for improvement.

Biodiversity and Sustainability: The Role of Economic Considerations in Natura 2000

As designation comes with serious responsibilities for both public authorities and private actors, the degree of discretion afforded to Member States in identifying and managing special sites is a point of great sensitivity. The assumption that, in carrying out their designation and associated management duties under the Birds Directive, Member States were free to factor in economic and social considerations initially appeared eminently plausible. After all, Article 2 BD states that 'Member States shall take the requisite measures to maintain the population of [wilds birds] at a level which corresponds in particular to ecological, scientific and cultural requirements, *while taking account of economic and recreational requirements*' (emphasis added). However, this expectation was dashed in a series of CJEU rulings in the late 1980s,[53] culminating in the 1991 *Leybucht* decision.[54] Here, the CJEU firmly asserted that, once an area is designated as an SPA under Article 4 BD, Member States cannot 'unilaterally escape from the obligations imposed on them by Article 4(4) [BD]'.[55] Instead, the power of the Member States to reduce the extent of SPAs can be justified only on exceptional grounds that relate to a general interest which is superior to the general interest represented by the ecological objective of the Directive.[56] The economic and recreational considerations mentioned in Article 2 BD, therefore, do not constitute an autonomous derogation from the general system of protection set up in the Directive. Hence, the CJEU treated Article 2 BD as, essentially, a default rule (*lex generalis*) which

---

[52] Holder and Lee, *Environmental Protection, Law and Policy*, 614.
[53] Case C-247/85 *Commission* v. *Belgium* ECLI:EU:C:1987:436 and Case C-262/85 *Commission* v. *Italy* ECLI:EU:C:1987:340.
[54] Case C-57/89 *Commission* v. *Germany* ECLI:EU:C:1991:89.   [55] *Ibid.*, para. 20.
[56] *Ibid.*, paras. 21–22.

does not apply to matters governed by more specific rules (*lex specialis*), such as those relating to SPAs in Article 4 BD.[57] By the same token, the deliberate disturbance, destruction, commercialisation and hunting restrictions in Articles 5 to 8 may only be deviated from on one of the grounds listed in Article 9, which exclude economic and recreational grounds.

The CJEU's decision in *Leybucht* has been called a 'bold and absolute approach'.[58] To some, it is a shining example of the CJEU stepping up to the plate and ensuring that Member State implementation does not under-deliver on the high level of environmental protection to which EU law should aspire (a goal, which, moreover, has been enshrined in EU Treaty law since 1987). To others, it is a vexing case of judicial activism in which the Court pushes Member States beyond negotiated boundaries and thereby disrupts the delicate balance between domestic and supranational authority. Either way, subsequent events suggest that the relation between the European Courts and the Member States is, and has always been, more evenly calibrated than the uncompromising tone of the Court rulings suggests. The *Leybucht* decision coincided with the negotiations on the legislative proposal for the Habitats Directive. Bearing in mind the Court's position on the relation between Articles 2 and 4 BD, the Member States agreed explicitly to include social and economic considerations as a ground for the justification of developments in spite of their adverse environmental impacts on an SAC.[59] Only priority sites benefit from a higher degree of protection. Moreover, the addition of Article 7 HD, which replaces the strict regime of Article 4(4) BD with the weaker sustainability approach of Articles 6(2)–(4) HD, took the sting out of the most forbidding consequences of the CJEU's stance in *Leybucht*.

In sum, the CJEU established a strict regime for the protection of SPAs, which triggered an ex-post legislative adjustment regarding the governance of both SACs and SPAs. However, *Leybucht* and Articles 6(2)–7 HD concern the management of sites that have *already* been recognised as special. What of the process leading up to designation: are Member States allowed to take into account economic factors when identifying candidates for Natura 2000? Is it admissible for Member States not to list a site that contains, say, migratory bird breeding grounds, or one that meets the criteria of Annex III HD, if plans are afoot to develop the area in order to alleviate extant high levels of unemployment in the region? Natura 2000 has now been established,[60] but the ECJ rulings regarding the interpretation of Articles 4(1) and (2) BD and Article 4 HD remain highly relevant. In the first place, habitats evolve. The boundaries of Natura 2000 may be rudimentarily in place, but Member States remain under a permanent obligation to review and modify. Secondly, certain Member States, including many of the more recent EU members, still need

---

[57] Cf. *Environmental Protection, Law and Policy*, 630. [58] *Ibid.*, 627.
[59] Krämer, *EU Environmental Law*, 186.
[60] Romão, 'The Added Value of the Habitats Directive', 23.

to extend existing sites or propose new sites.[61] Moreover, the Court rulings are highly relevant for any future accession States, such as Bosnia–Herzegovina and Kosovo. Finally, the case law illustrates some of the most abiding challenges that environmental law and policy face, namely, determining the appropriate role of expertise in judicial decision-making, and bridging the gap between a 'green judgment' and a 'green outcome'.

The European Court's approach towards Member State discretion in the designation process for wild birds is very much in line with its firmness regarding the management of SPAs. An early decision concerned the Spanish Santoña Marshes, one of the most important ecosystems of the Iberian peninsula, which hosts a variety of endangered and migratory birds. Although classified as a nature reserve under Spanish law, the Spanish government had neither identified nor notified the Santoña marshes pursuant to Article 4 BD. In its defence, the Spanish government argued, *inter alia*, that 'the ecological requirements laid down in that provision must be subordinate to other interests, such as social and economic interests, or must at the very least be balanced against them'.[62] With regard to its designation responsibilities specifically, Spain opined that 'national authorities have a margin of discretion with regard to the choice and delimitation of special protection areas and the timing of their classification as such'.[63] The CJEU, however, saw things decidedly differently. It reiterated its stance in *Leybucht* that the Article 2 BD considerations regarding economic and recreational requirements do not apply in the context of Article 4 BD.[64] As to the process of designation itself, the Court acknowledged that Member States have a margin of discretion regarding the choice of SPAs, but simultaneously limited Member State freedom in the matter and stated that the classification of SPAs is subject to ornithological criteria.[65] Precisely how much this constrained Member State discretion became evident a few years later in a CJEU judgment against the Netherlands. In Case C-3/96, the Court clarified that national discretion in choosing the most suitable territories as SPAs is discretion in the *application* of the ornithological criteria to identify the most suitable areas for classification. However, it does not enable Member States to pick and choose among the most suitable areas those which will be notified for classification: 'Member States are obliged to classify as SPAs *all* the sites which, applying ornithological criteria, appear to be the most suitable for conservation of the species in question' (emphasis added).[66]

The main reason for the Commission to bring action in *Commission* v. *Netherlands* was that, in its view, the Dutch State had excluded a large number of sites from classification even though they constituted the most suitable territories for conservation. This claim triggered an important evidentiary

---

[61] Hendrik Schoukens and Hans Erik Woldendorp, 'Site Selection and Designation under the Habitats and Birds Directives: A Sisyphean Task?' in Born et al., *The Habitats Directive*, 33.
[62] Case C-355/90 *Commission* v. *Spain (Santoña Marshes)* ECLI:EU:C:1993:331, para. 17.
[63] *Ibid.*, para. 25.   [64] *Ibid.*, paras. 18–19.   [65] *Ibid.*, para. 26.   [66] *Ibid.*, para. 62.

conundrum: on what basis could the Commission claim that the number of sites put forward by the State was insufficient; that more 'most suitable sites' existed than the Member State alleged? In its argumentation, the Commission relied heavily on the 1989 Important Bird Area inventory (IBA 89), which listed nearly twice as many sites as the Dutch authorities had notified. IBA 89 was prepared for the Commission by a civil society organisation in collaboration with the International Council of Bird Preservation and Commission experts. In its decision, the CJEU decided that the inventory, although not legally binding, could serve as a reference source to assess Dutch compliance with the Birds Directive. The potential for controversy is readily appreciated: the CJEU confirmed that an essentially informal document is a sufficient basis to hold Member States in breach of EU law. To buttress its decision, the Court clarified how the burden of proof should be allocated in cases involving scientific expertise:

> In the circumstances, IBA 89 has proved to be the only document containing scientific evidence making it possible to assess whether the defendant State has fulfilled its obligation to classify as SPAs the most suitable territories in number and area for conservation of the protected species. The situation would be different if the Kingdom of the Netherlands had produced scientific evidence in particular to show that the obligation in question could be fulfilled by classifying as SPAs territories whose number and total area were less than those resulting from IBA 89.[67]

Hence, the availability of (reputable) scientific evidence creates a rebuttable presumption in favour of the Commission[68] and reverses the burden of proof towards the Member State which then needs to supply evidence that, notwithstanding the expertise submitted, it complied with the provisions of the Directive. Over the years, this sequence has consolidated into the standard approach towards non-binding expert evidence in EU adjudication.

Another decision of note in the context of SPA designation is the *Lappel Bank* judgment.[69] It is not particularly revelatory in terms of ECJ reasoning as it follows the pattern established in Santoña Marshes, but as a preliminary ruling rather than an infringement proceeding it does differ from the preceding cases. The case was instigated by the UK Royal Society for the Protection of Birds (RSPB), which challenged the national competent authority's decision to exclude the Lappel Bank from the Medway estuary and marshes SPA. The exclusion, the RSPB argued, was economically motivated so as not to obstruct a planned port expansion and, for that reason, incompatible with the UK's responsibilities under the Birds Directive. In its ruling, the CJEU repeated that economic criteria have no role in the classification of SPAs, and thus implicitly decided the case in favour of

---

[67] Ibid., para. 69.
[68] Cf. Case C-418/04 *Commission v. Ireland* ECLI:EU:C:2007:780, para. 52.
[69] C-44/95 *Regina* v. *Secretary of State for the Environment, ex parte: Royal Society for the Protection of Birds* ECLI:EU:C:1996:297.

the RSPB. *Lappel Bank* is a vivid illustration of the opportunities that EU law creates for private actors to interpellate domestic policy choices. Like the seminal cases of *Kraaijeveld* (EIA),[70] *Janecek*[71] and *ClientEarth* (air pollution),[72] *Lappel Bank* confirms the important role that private actors and organisations have as guardians of EU environmental law. To a degree, *Lappel Bank* proved a pyrrhic victory: by the time the case was won, the marshes were lost to development.[73] Yet, on the other hand, the case was of great cautionary importance, since scenarios similar to *Lappel Bank* recurred throughout the country and across the EU. Hence, the contribution of private actors to the effectiveness of environmental law can be both smaller and much greater than the outcome of individual decisions.[74]

A final question to address is whether the CJEU's strict approach to Member State discretion with regard to designation carried over from the Birds to the Habitats Directive. In the light of the latter's weaker sustainability ethos, it would be plausible to assume more space for economic considerations in the Habitats Directive designation process than under the Birds Directive. However, the *First Corporate Shipping (FCS)* case established that the designation of SACs, too, must happen solely on the basis of ecological benchmarks; the exclusion of sites that meet the criteria of Annex III HD for economic, cultural or social reasons is in breach of the Habitats Directive. The Court explained its stance with reference to the overarching goal of establishing the Natura 2000 network:

> To produce a draft list of sites of Community importance, capable of leading to the creation of a coherent European ecological network of SACs, the Commission must have available an exhaustive list of the sites which, at national level, have an ecological interest which is relevant from the point of view of the Habitat Directive's objective of conservation of natural habitats and wild fauna and flora ... [Favourable] conservation status of a natural habitat or a species must be assessed in relation to the entire European territory of the Member States to which the Treaty applies. Having regard to the fact that, when a Member State draws up the national list of sites, it is not in a position to have precise detailed knowledge of the situation of habitats in the other Member States, it cannot of its own accord, whether because of economic, social or cultural requirements or because of regional and local characteristics, delete sites ... without jeopardising the realisation of that objective at Community level.[75]

---

[70] C-72/95 *Aannemersbedrijf P.K. Kraaijeveld BV e.a. v. Gedeputeerde Staten van Zuid-Holland* [1996] ECR I-5403.
[71] C-237/07 *Dieter Janecek v. Freistaat Bayern* [2008] ECR I-6221.
[72] C-404/13 *The Queen, on the application of ClientEarth v. The Secretary of State for the Environment, Food and Rural Affairs*, not yet reported.
[73] Holder and Lee, *Environmental Protection, Law and Policy*, 632.
[74] Cf. Reinhard Slepcevic, 'The Judicial Enforcement of EU Law through National Courts: Possibilities and Limits' (2009) 16(3) *Journal of European Public Policy* 378–394.
[75] Case C-371/98 *First Corporate Shipping* ECLI:EU:C:2000:600, paras. 22–23.

In its considerations, the CJEU arguably sought to moderate institutional tensions between the Commission and the Member States by representing the designation process more as a data-gathering exercise than a supranational imposition of regulatory authority. Member State discretion is curtailed not because Member States have limited competence, but because they have limited information and only the Commission is in possession of the panopticon view necessary to complete the task. This reasoning has a gloss of plausibility, but is arguably flimsy: the information on the Standard Data Forms could be (and typically is) made available to competent authorities of neighbouring States,[76] which enables them to situate their conservation assessments within a transboundary context. It also leaves open the question whether economic considerations might still enter the discussion at the moderation stage and affect Commission decision-making on SCIs. The reasoning in *FCS* certainly seemed to suggest so, and the view was explicitly espoused in Advocate General Léger's Opinion in the same case. Arguably, this approach tilted the scales in the Habitats Directive from weak sustainability to unsustainability, since it enabled future economic development of non-SCI areas without any particular consideration of its impact on conservation, even though such areas met the criteria of Annex III HD. The interpretation was heavily criticised by commentators such as Donald McGillivray,[77] and ultimately corrected by the CJEU in *Stadt Papenburg*.[78] Here, the Court confirmed that Member States may not withhold agreement to a Commission decision to designate an SCI on grounds other than environmental protection.[79] This still stops short of an unequivocal affirmation that economic, social and cultural considerations have no place at *any* point of the designation process, but it is undeniably more environmentally supportive than the approach in *FCS* was.

Protecting SCIs and the Role of the Precautionary Principle

Designation triggers a range of new managerial tasks for public authorities, and introduces an obligation to combat the deterioration and disturbance of protected sites. It may also interfere with domestic planning for industrial and economic development. The paragraphs below review the relation between the protective regimes in the Birds and Habitats Directives, the timing of protective measures, and then analyse the various Member State obligations following designation.

---

[76] In fact, most of the information submitted is publicly accessible on the European Environment Agency website; see www.eea.europa.eu/data-and-maps/data/natura-1.
[77] Donald McGillivray, 'Valuing Nature: Economic Value, Conservation Values and Sustainable Development' (2002) 14 *Journal of Environmental Law* 85–100, at 97.
[78] Case C-226/08 *Stadt Papenburg* ECLI:EU:C:2010:10.   [79] *Ibid*., para. 31.

Protective Regimes: The Relation between the Birds and Habitats Directives

The Birds Directive conveys the consequences of designation in a brief statement. Article 4(4) BD provides that in respect of SPAs 'Member States shall take appropriate steps to avoid pollution or deterioration of habitats or any disturbances affecting the birds, in so far as these would be significant having regard to the objectives of this Article. Outside these protection areas, Member States shall also strive to avoid pollution or deterioration of habitats.' However, this provision has been partially subsumed by the Habitats Directive, which holds in its Article 7 that 'any obligations arising under the first sentence of Article 4(4) [BD]' are replaced by the obligations set out in Articles 6(2) to 6(4) of the Habitats Directive. In the light of its pivotal importance, Article 6 HD is rendered in full below.

Article 6 Habitats Directive

1. For special areas of conservation, Member States shall establish the necessary conservation measures involving, if need be, appropriate management plans specifically designed for the sites or integrated into other development plans, and appropriate statutory, administrative or contractual measures which correspond to the ecological requirements of the natural habitat types in Annex I and the species in Annex II present on the sites.
2. Member States shall take appropriate steps to avoid, in the special areas of conservation, the deterioration of natural habitats and the habitats of species as well as disturbance of the species for which the areas have been designated, in so far as such disturbance could be significant in relation to the objectives of this Directive.
3. Any plan or project not directly connected with or necessary to the management of the site but likely to have a significant effect thereon, either individually or in combination with other plans or projects, shall be subject to appropriate assessment of its implications for the site in view of the site's conservation objectives. In the light of the conclusions of the assessment of the implications for the site and subject to the provisions of paragraph 4, the competent national authorities shall agree to the plan or project only after having ascertained that it will not adversely affect the integrity of the site concerned and, if appropriate, after having obtained the opinion of the general public.
4. If, in spite of a negative assessment of the implications for the site and in the absence of alternative solutions, a plan or project must nevertheless be carried out for imperative reasons of overriding public interest, including those of a social or economic nature, the Member State shall take all compensatory measures necessary to ensure that the overall coherence of Natura 2000 is protected. It shall inform the Commission of the compensatory measures adopted.

> Where the site concerned hosts a priority natural habitat type and/or a priority species, the only considerations which may be raised are those relating to human health or public safety, to beneficial consequences of primary importance for the environment or, further to an opinion from the Commission, to other imperative reasons of overriding public interest.

A combined reading of the provisions of Article 4(4) BD and Article 6 HD reveals the following composite picture:

- Article 6(1) HD requires Member States to take positive conservation measures for SACs, which may need to include the development of management plans specifically drawn up for the site. This is not an obligation that exists for SPAs as it is neither mentioned in Article 4(4) BD nor included in the cross-over provisions listed in Article 7 HD. Arguably however, it can be 'read into' Articles 4(1) and (2) BD, which require, in general terms, the adoption of special conservation measures for migratory birds.[80]
- In accordance with Articles 6(2) and 7 HD, Member States must take steps to avoid the deterioration of the areas and species within SACs and SPAs.
- Following Articles 6(3) and 7 HD, any development plan or project that could have a significant negative environmental impact on the integrity of an SPA or SAC must be assessed and can only be greenlit if it has been shown not to have a negative impact. The exception to this rule is laid out in Article 6(4) HD: developments with an adverse impact on SPAs or SACs may still go ahead if they respond to an overriding public interest need, and if compensatory measures are put in place. However, if the site hosts a priority habitat or species, the grounds for derogation are, in principle, more limited.
- Per Article 4(4) BD *in fine*, Member States should strive to avoid the pollution or deterioration of areas that are not classified as SPAs but do host wild bird habitats.

Article 7 HD streamlines the treatment of SPAs and SACs to an extent, but the resulting arrangements are not entirely coherent. First, the relation between conservation measures for SPAs and those governing SACs would benefit from clarification. Secondly, the absence of a softer requirement for Member States to strive to avoid pollution beyond the remit of SACs compares unfavourably to the framework for migratory birds. Moreover, the convergence between the Birds and Habitats Directives has effectively weakened the protection of wild birds under EU law. Although Articles 6(2) to (4) HD are more expansive, they embrace a more permissive approach to derogations than the Birds Directive allows. As the CJEU confirmed in *Leybucht*, the remit of an SPA protected under

---

[80] 'Commission Note on Establishing Conservation Measures for Natura 2000 Sites (Final version of 18 September 2013)', 1–2, available at: http://ec.europa.eu/environment/nature/natura2000/management/docs/commission_note/comNote%20conservation%20measures_EN.pdf.

Article 4(4) BD could not be reduced on the basis of 'economic and recreational requirements'.[81] Article 6(4) HD, by contrast, explicitly recognises social and economic considerations as a possible justification for actions likely to affect the environmental integrity of SACs. As it replaces the provisions of Article 4(4) BD, it moves the goalposts from absolute to relative protection. Final peculiarities of the present arrangements are that, since the last sentence of Article 4(4) BD (i.e. Member States should strive to avoid pollution in areas beyond SPAs) has not been supplanted, wild birds in some regards enjoy a stricter level of protection outside SPAs than within. On the one hand, Member States must only *strive* to avoid pollution and deterioration of non-SPA areas but, on the flip side, they cannot invoke economic or social justifications for not making such attempts. Moreover, bird habitats that have unlawfully not been classified as SPAs in spite of meeting the ornithological criteria, still must comply with the stricter regime of Article 4(4) BD.[82] In sum, the aspired coherence of the Natura 2000 network is arguably overshadowed by an apparent degree of unevenness in the level of nature and biodiversity protection.

Timing of Member State Obligations

The inclusion of an SCI under Natura 2000 compels the Member State concerned to designate the site as an SAC within six years at the latest.[83] However, sites are not wholly unprotected in the interval. As soon as a habitat has been confirmed as an SCI (or as a priority site in the case of vulnerable natural habitats or habitats hosting vulnerable species), Member States must comply with Articles 6(2) to (4) HD,[84] which essentially require that they must avoid the deterioration of SCIs and, subject to exceptions, disallow any development that could negatively affect the environmental integrity of the SCI. The provision of Article 4(5) HD thus aims to eliminate any perverse incentive for the Member State to treat the six-year deadline as the starting gun for eleventh-hour development, instead of a period in which to lay the foundation for a robust nature and biodiversity protection regime. To the extent that it aims to avert irreversible changes during periods of uncertainty and transition, Article 4(5) HD can be regarded as embodying a precautionary ethos. Note, however, that the extension of the protective regime to bridge the period between inclusion in Natura 2000 and domestic designation as an SAC does not cover the measures in Article 6(1) HD, which mandate the adoption of necessary conservation

---

[81] Case C-57/89 *Commission* v. *Germany* ECLI:EU:C:1991:89, para. 22.
[82] Case C-374/98 *Commission* v. *France* (*Basses Corbières*) ECLI:EU:C:2000:670.
[83] These arrangements for SPAs under the Birds Directive are less regimented than those governing SACs under the Habitats Directive. In particular, there is no Commission moderation stage and decision-making stage for SPAs; they acquire their status by virtue of a Member State decision which must be notified to the Commission.
[84] Article 4(5) HD. Cf. Case C-258/11 *Sweetman* v. *An Bord Pleanála* ECLI:EU:C:2013:220, para. 13.

measures, including management plans. Hence, up to the official SAC designation, Member States' obligations under the Habitats Directive are predominantly negative in that deterioration and development should be avoided. Once the SAC is in place, such measures must be complemented by an affirmative strategy capable of securing a good conservation status within the area.

Article 4(5) HD seeks to safeguard habitats from the point of their recognition as an SCI, but it does not cover the period between inclusion on the Member State list for notification and the Commission decision – which can take up to three years. What makes the issue particularly challenging is that, up to the point of the Commission decision, the status of the habitat is in limbo; conceivably the Commission might opt against inclusion in Natura 2000. However, the CJEU determined that in this period Member States must adopt 'appropriate protective measures'.[85] Interestingly, the CJEU's reasoning has less to do with avoiding perverse incentives and more with supporting the Commission moderation exercise. If the Commission is effectively to establish a coherent pan-European, ecological network, the information submitted by the Member States must remain reliable throughout the decision-making process: '[at] the time of the decision which the Commission is called upon to take, the sites identified by the Member States must reflect the situation on the basis of which the scientific evaluations of potential sites of Community importance have been carried out'.[86] This reasoning has stronger affinity with the principle of sincere cooperation[87] than with precautionary thinking. In a peculiar twist, it may also result in Member States being held to a higher standard of taking positive, protective measures to maintain the ecological conditions of a site during the stage of moderation than they are in the six-year period between SCI and SAC designation.

The Management of Protected Sites: Article 6(1) Habitats Directive

Article 6(1) of the Habitats Directive calls on the Member States to take 'the necessary conservation measures'. Such measures may include the adoption of management plans, legal provisions, administrative measures and contractual arrangements. This open formulation leaves Member States a very broad range of options to explore. Flexibility is commonplace in EU legal provisions, which must be responsive to the different legal and administrative cultures in which they find application. Still, the broad brushstrokes of EU environmental law are often refined in annexes; in delegated and implementing legislation; in case law and guidance notes. The body of further information on Article 6(1) HD, however, is noticeably sparse. No secondary legislation has been adopted. The case law on Article 6(1) HD, too, is on the minimalistic side: a few CJEU decisions confirm that

---

[85] Case C-244/05 *Bund Naturschutz in Bayern and others* ECLI:EU:C:2006:579, para. 44; C-117/03 *Dragaggi a.o.* ECLI:EU:C:2005:16, paras. 25–29.
[86] *Bund Naturschutz in Bayern and others*, para. 41.
[87] Art. 4 TEU. Cf. Schouken and Woldendorp, 'Site Selection and Designation', 50.

merely providing for the option of conservation measures to be adopted 'as need be' is not sufficient to meet the requirements of Article 6(1) HD;[88] and that commissioning the implementation of conservation measures to a separate entity is no excuse for non-implementation.[89] So far, no Court rulings have reviewed any particular set of national conservation measures to assess its compatibility with the Habitats Directive.

In the absence of legal sources, the most authoritative information on Article 6(1) HD comes in the form of Commission guidance. A collection of recent Commission documents[90] explains that conservation measures should be related to the conservation objectives of the site.[91] Hence, according to the Commission, to comply with Article 6(1) HD Member States should as a minimum define the conservation objectives of every protected site. This needs to happen in reference to species and habitats for which the site is designated, to the threats they face and with a view to maintaining or reaching a favourable status of conservation.[92] Commission guidance further reviews the range of conservation measures listed in Article 6(1) HD – management plans, statutory, administrative and contractual measures – but both the 2013 and 2014 documents remain inclusive in their approach: the choice and content of management plans, or of contractual arrangements between land owners and conservation authorities, is fully left to the Member State discretion.[93] Instead, the Commission emphasises the procedural qualities that nature conservation policy should embrace. Conservation measures should be developed on the basis of sound information, stakeholder participation and on an assessment of their costs and benefits. They should be precise, realistic and effectively implemented. These are familiar 'good governance' standards. Their constraining force, however, is highly questionable, primarily because the Commission 2013 Note and 2014 Guidance are non-binding documents, and secondly because listing procedural virtues only goes so far in supporting the messy reality of environmental policy-making. In sum, even with the value added of Commission guidance, the freedom that Member States enjoy

---

[88] Case C-508/04 *Commission v. Austria* [2007] ECLI:EU:C:2007:274, paras. 89–91.
[89] Case C-90/10 *Commission v. Spain* [2011] ECLI:EU:C:2011:606.
[90] European Commission, 'Establishing Conservation Measures for Natura 2000 Sites: A Review of the Provisions of Article 6.1 and their Practical Implementation in Different Member States' (2014), available at: http://ec.europa.eu/environment/nature/natura2000/management/docs/conservation%20measures.pdf; and 'Commission Note on Establishing Conservation Measures for Natura 2000 Sites'.
[91] Cf. Lucile Stahl, 'The Concept of "Conservation Objectives" in the Habitats Directive: A Need for a Better Definition?' in Born et al., *The Habitats Directive in its EU Environmental Law Context*, 57–58.
[92] Case C-127/02 *Landelijke Vereniging tot Behoud van de Waddenzee and Nederlandse Vereniging tot Bescherming van Vogels v. Staatssecretaris van Landbouw, Natuurbeheer en Visserij (Waddenzee)* ECLI:EU:C:2004:482, para. 54.
[93] The 2014 Commission guidance offers examples of management strategies in different Member States, including Denmark, France, Slovenia and the UK. 'Establishing Conservation Measures for Natura 2000 Sites', 9–11.

regarding the management of SCIs stands in clear contrast to the many supranational conditions that shape the designation process.

Avoiding Deterioration and Disturbance: Article 6(2) Habitats Directive

Article 6(2) of the Habitats Directive requires Member States to take steps to avoid the deterioration of natural habitats and species and to avoid any disturbance of species that could impact on the achievement of the site's conservation objectives. The requirement kicks in as soon as a habitat is confirmed as an SCI and applies to both SACs and SPAs. As with Article 6(1) HD, Member States can take a varied range of actions to comply with the non-deterioration and disturbance requirement. However, in contrast to the scarcity of judicial information regarding Article 6(1) HD, a richer body of European case law governs the interpretation of Article 6(2) HD. The Court judgments reveal that, to comply with the non-deterioration and non-disturbance requirements, Member States must adopt strategies that are expansive; specific; based on a case-by-case assessment; consistent and coherent; inclusive; residual; and precautionary. These qualities are further explained in Table 12.1.

Assessing Development: Article 6(3) Habitats Directive

Articles 6(1) and 6(2) of the Habitats Directive introduce important Member State responsibilities, but the most hotly debated provisions in EU nature and biodiversity protection law reside in the Directive's subsequent paragraph, which requires that any plan or project likely to have a significant environmental effect on a protected site should be subjected to an appropriate assessment, and should only go ahead if the development does not jeopardise the integrity of the site. Measures that directly impact upon local or regional development policies tend to have major economic and distributive consequences and are, therefore, highly politically sensitive. This impact is all the more significant since the territorial scope of Article 6(3) HD exceeds the boundaries of protected sites: any plan or project, regardless of whether it is designed to occur within, adjacent to or even far beyond the boundaries of a protected area, can fall within the remit of Article 6(3) HD. Finally, and importantly, the provisions of the Habitats Directive severely limit Member State discretion in response to a negative assessment. Whereas the Environmental Impact Assessment Directive (EIA Directive) binds the Member States as to the procedure to be performed but creates no expectation for public authorities to refuse development consent should an impact assessment prove negative,[94] Article 6(3) HD in principle demands that permission for environmentally harmful development be refused. Unless developments are justified with reference to overriding imperatives[95] and the

---

[94] See Chapter 11.
[95] See discussion of Article 6(4) HD below. Derogation may require a supportive opinion from the Commission in the case of priority sites.

Table 12.1 Habitats Non-Deterioration and Non-Disturbance Strategies

Article 6(2) of the Habitats Directive		
Interpretation	**Explanation**	**Case Law**
Expansive	Article 6(2) HD requires protective measures for all natural habitats and habitats of listed species, and must cover all types of disturbance	C-75/01, *Commission v. Luxembourg* [2003] ECR I-1585
Specific	Reliance on general legal provisions, such as criminal law provisions on trespass on private property, which are not specifically linked to habitats protection, do not constitute adequate implementation	C- 418/04, *Commission v. Ireland* [2007] ECR I-10947
Based on case-by-case assessment	Activities (e.g. hunting, fishing) may not categorically be qualified as activities that do not cause disturbance	C-241/08, *Commission v. France* [2010] ECR I-1697
Consistent and coherent	The application of heterogeneous legal standards to similar protected areas constitutes insufficient protection	C-293/07, *Commission v. Greece* [2008] ECR I-182
Inclusive	Protective measures include both measures aimed to address man-induced disturbance and those addressing natural developments that may impair the site's conservation status	C-6/04, *Commission v. UK* [2005] ECR I-9017
Residual	The requirements of Article 6(2) HD apply with regard to any unanticipated adverse impact of developments that have been duly authorised in accordance with Article 6(3) HD.	C-127/02, *Landelijke Vereniging tot Behoud van de Waddenzee and Nederlandse Vereniging tot Bescherming van Vogels v. Staatssecretaris van Landbouw, Natuurbeheer en Visserij* [2004] ECR I-7405
Precautionary	The obligations on Member States exist even before any reduction is observed in the number of birds or any risk of a protected species becoming extinct has materialised.	Case C-355/90, *Commission v. Spain (Santoña Marshes)* [1993] ECR I-4221

environmental losses are compensated, the Habitats Directive acts as a brake on development. At the very least, the requirements of Article 6(3) HD make economic development more costly, more time-consuming and less certain.

The seriousness of these ramifications makes it easy to understand why Member States battled to retain control over the designation process, resulting in the high-profile EU litigation reviewed above. By the same token, the interpretation of Article 6(3) HD became contested ground, resulting in yet another rich vein of CJEU nature and biodiversity protection case law.

Two seminal cases are the *Waddenzee*[96] and *Sweetman*[97] rulings, which clarified much of the key terminology surrounding nature conservation and development. They also helped to consolidate the remit and limits of Member State responsibilities under the Habitats Directive and, by extension, the Birds Directive. The following paragraphs highlight their significant contribution to EU nature and biodiversity protection law.

'Any Plan or Project'
The *Waddenzee* case concerned mechanical cockle fishing in the Dutch Waddenzee, one of the country's most valuable SPAs. Mechanical cockle fishing was not new to the area. Neither was it wholly unregulated: Dutch law required cockle fishing industries to renew their licence annually, which renewal was conditional upon an assessment of both the activity and of the site. A group of environmental NGOs, however, contended that, pursuant to the entry into force of the Habitats Directive, cockle fishing in the Waddenzee should be subjected to an appropriate assessment under Article 6(3) HD. To settle the dispute, it was first necessary to determine whether the notion 'plan or project', as referred to in Article 6(3) HD, was broad enough to include ongoing activities, or whether it strictly referred to new construction initiatives. The CJEU's reply on this matter gave a first clear indication of its expansive approach to Member State obligations under Article 6(3) HD. In the absence of a definition in the Habitats Directive, the Court turned to the EIA Directive, which includes both 'the execution of construction works or of other installations or schemes' and 'other interventions in the natural surroundings and landscape including those involving the extraction of mineral resources' within the remit of plan or project. The Court concluded that the fact that the activity at issue was both ongoing and periodically licensed was no obstacle to it constituting a plan or project for the purposes of the Habitats Directive.[98]

'Significant Effect' and 'Appropriate Assessment'
A second point of contention revolved around the meaning of the terms 'significant effect' and 'appropriate assessment'. The *Waddenzee* ruling asserted that significant effects need to be understood in connection with the conservation objectives for the site.[99] This view was again confirmed in *Sweetman*, which reviewed the legality of development consent granted for the construction of a bypass road in the vicinity of Galway (Ireland). A section of the proposed road was scheduled to cross the Lough Corrib area, an SCI hosting a variety of natural features including a natural limestone pavement, a priority habitat protected under Annex I HD. In its preliminary ruling, the Court in *Sweetman* held that 'Where

---

[96] Case C-127/02 *Landelijke Vereniging tot Behoud van de Waddenzee and Nederlandse Vereniging tot Bescherming van Vogels* v. *Staatssecretaris van Landbouw, Natuurbeheer en Visserij* (*Waddenzee*) ECLI:EU:C:2004:482.
[97] *Sweetman* v. *An Bord Pleanála* ECLI:EU:C:2013:220.   [98] *Waddenzee*, para. 28.
[99] Ibid., para. 45.

a plan or project ... is likely to undermine the site's conservation objectives, it must be considered likely to have a significant effect on that site'.[100] This triggers the requirement to perform an appropriate assessment, which the *Waddenzee* ruling had interpreted as a review of 'all the aspects of the plan or project which can, either individually or in combination with other plans or projects, affect those [conservation] objectives'.[101] Such review needs to be conducted in the light of the best scientific knowledge in the field.[102]

Thirdly and importantly, the *Waddenzee* ruling confronted and resolved the inherent circularity of the appropriate assessment requirement. Following Article 6(3) HD, an appropriate assessment is only required if a plan or project is likely to have a significant effect. However, the likelihood of a significant effect may only become apparent once the assessment is conducted. Hence, the conduct of an appropriate assessment is preconditioned on the availability of the very evidence that the mechanism is designed to produce. Circular constructions have the potential severely to undermine regulatory effectiveness. For example, the US requirement that chemicals should only be subjected to mandatory testing if they pose an unreasonable risk, which typically cannot be proven before testing has been done, notoriously paralysed the regulation of hazardous chemicals under the US Toxic Substances Control Act.[103] The CJEU averted a similar fate for Article 6(3) HD and decided instead that 'the triggering of the environmental protection mechanism' of Article 6(3) HD followed from the 'mere probability' that a plan or project would have significant effects.[104] This inevitably begged the question of the circumstances under which a mere probability of significant effects could be assumed. In formulating its answer, the Court overtly relied on the steering power of the precautionary principle and determined that:

> 44. In the light, in particular, of the precautionary principle, which is one of the foundations of the high level of protection pursued by Community policy on the environment, in accordance with the first subparagraph of Article 174(2) EC, and by reference to which the Habitats Directive must be interpreted, such a risk exists if it cannot be excluded on the basis of objective information that the plan or project will have significant effects on the site concerned ... Such an interpretation of the condition to which the assessment of the implications of a plan or project for a specific site is subject, which implies that in case of doubt as to the absence of significant effects such an assessment must be carried out, makes it possible to ensure effectively that plans or projects which adversely affect the integrity of the site concerned are not authorised, and thereby contributes to achieving, in accordance with the third recital in the

---

[100] *Sweetman*, para. 30; *Waddenzee*, para. 48.   [101] *Waddenzee*, para. 54.   [102] *Ibid.*
[103] See John S. Applegate, 'The Perils of Unreasonable Risk: Information, Regulatory Policy, and Toxic Substances Control' (1991) 91(2) *Columbia Law Review* 261–333.
[104] *Waddenzee*, para. 41.

> preamble to the Habitats Directive and Article 2(1) thereof, its main aim, namely, ensuring biodiversity through the conservation of natural habitats and of wild fauna and flora.
>
> 45. In the light of the foregoing, the answer to Question 3(a) must be that the first sentence of Article 6(3) of the Habitats Directive must be interpreted as meaning that any plan or project not directly connected with or necessary to the management of the site is to be subject to an appropriate assessment of its implications for the site in view of the site's conservation objectives if it cannot be excluded, on the basis of objective information, that it will have a significant effect on that site, either individually or in combination with other plans or projects.

The Court's dynamic reading of Article 6(3) HD through the lens of the precautionary principle introduced a partial reversal of the burden of proof: requests for development permission must deliver at least some 'objective information' that the plan or project is unlikely to have a significant effect on the protected site. In case of doubt, an appropriate assessment must take place. Moreover, the precautionary principle proved equally instructive at the tail end of the assessment process. In *Waddenzee*, the CJEU underlined that authorisation to carry out the assessed plan or project should only be granted if national competent authorities are *convinced* that such development will not negatively affect the integrity of the site.[105] And, according to the Court, such conviction can only exist where 'no reasonable scientific doubt' remains as to the absence of significant effects.[106] Where uncertainty remains, authorisation must be refused.[107]

'Integrity of the Site'

Finally, Article 6(3) HD indicates that not every negative environmental impact should result in development consent being withheld; only those affecting the 'integrity of the site' are caught by its restriction. The relation between significant effects and the integrity of the site was a pivotal point of the litigation in *Sweetman*. It was uncontested that the planned bypass would result in the loss of 1.47 hectares of limestone pavement from a distinctive ecological sub-area, which, in total, covers 85 hectares of limestone pavement. The sub-area, in turn, forms part of a broader area of 270 hectares of limestone pavement within the SCI as a whole.[108] According to Mr Sweetman, who had brought the action for judicial review before the Irish Supreme Court, the permanent loss of a part of a priority habitat of necessity compromised the integrity of the site. The Irish planning authorities, in contrast, contended that environmental damage to a site did not necessarily amount to an adverse effect on the site's integrity.[109]

---

[105] *Ibid.*, para. 56. [106] *Ibid.*, para. 58. [107] *Sweetman*, para. 41. [108] *Ibid.*, para. 13.
[109] *Ibid.*, para. 27.

In its response, the CJEU engaged in a teleological reading of the Directive's provisions and argued that, ultimately, the obligations under the Habitats Directive are geared towards maintaining or restoring favourable conservation status.[110] The conservation status of a habitat can be considered as favourable if, in accordance with Article 1 HD, 'its natural range and areas it covers within that range are stable or increasing and the specific structure and functions which are necessary for its long-term maintenance exist and are likely to continue to exist for the foreseeable future'. Any development that jeopardises this status should be construed as impairing the integrity of the site.[111] In the case at issue, the maintenance of a favourable conservation status required the preservation of the limestone pavement, a priority habitat which, 'once destroyed, cannot be replaced'.[112] The bypass therefore could not be authorised if, following an appropriate assessment and in the light of the precautionary principle, the competent authority concluded that it would lead to 'the lasting and irreparable loss of the whole or part of a priority natural habitat type'.[113] Significantly, *Sweetman* does not set a quantitative threshold for what constitutes a 'part of' a priority site. Hence, the ruling offers no reason to assume that 1.47 hectares is too small an area to enjoy the full protection of Article 6(3) HD.

Assessment

The Waddenzee and Sweetman rulings display an acute appreciation on the part of the CJEU that a permissive interpretation of evaluative concepts such as 'significant effect', 'appropriate assessment' and 'integrity of the site' easily devolves into an erosion of Member State responsibilities. Marshalling the precautionary principle, the Court's approach is designed to minimise the risk that the Natura 2000 network is gradually undermined by ill-considered and hastily approved development. Moreover, it shows a strong awareness of the typically incremental nature of habitats degradation[114] and seeks to avert decision-making patterns that repeatedly sacrifice small but irreplaceable environmental assets for 'the greater good'. The resulting case law imposes significant demands on developers and public authorities, but it has also been praised for its relative straightforwardness and clarity, which fosters both effective investment planning and consistent adjudication.[115]

Yet the proactive nature of the CJEU's interventions in this field should not blind us to its limitations. The parameters drawn by the Court are, themselves, open to a degree of interpretation: national competent authorities and judges may be far more easily satisfied, for example, that 'no reasonable scientific doubt' remains than the CJEU would envisage. Moreover, any development that

---

[110] *Ibid.*, para. 36.   [111] *Ibid.*, para. 39.   [112] *Ibid.*, para. 45.   [113] *Ibid.*, para. 46.
[114] Marc Clément, 'Global Objectives and Scope fo the Habitats Directive: What Does the Obligation of Result Mean in Practice? The European Hamster in Alsace' in Born et al., *The Habitats Directive*, 14.
[115] Veerle Heyvaert, Justine Thornton and Richard Drabble, 'With Reference to the Environment: The Preliminary Reference Procedure, Environmental Decisions and the Domestic Judiciary' (2014) 130 *Law Quarterly Review* 413–442, at 428.

stumbles over the appropriate assessment hurdle may still be allowed on the basis of Article 6(4) HD. Particularly for habitats other than priority sites, the provisions of Article 6(4) HD reintroduce a considerable margin of national regulatory discretion and, with it, an undeniable risk to the long-term environmental objectives of EU nature and biodiversity protection law.

Declassification

Inclusion in the Natura 2000 network conveys a permanent status upon SCIs; the Habitats Directive contains neither expiry dates nor renewal requirements for designated areas. The abiding nature of designation was moreover underlined in *Leybucht*,[116] which confirmed that, as long as a site continues to meet the designation criteria, Member States are not allowed to declassify, regardless of changing external circumstances.

It took another few decades, however, before the Court was invited to reflect on the consequences of a site no longer meeting the designation criteria. The 2014 *Tre Pini* litigation concerned a Lombardian SCI which had been heavily affected by the expansion of the Milano–Malpensa airport.[117] A local landowner asked for the boundaries of the site to be redrawn so that the existing property restrictions that accompanied the area's designation as a SAC could be lifted. In response to the question whether national competent authorities were allowed to grant such request, the CJEU held that if the criteria for inclusion can irretrievably no longer be met and the SCI is definitively incapable of contributing to the Directive's nature conservation objectives 'it is no longer warranted for the site to remain subject to the provisions of [the Habitats Directive]'.[118] Consequently, 'the Member State concerned is required to propose to the Commission that the site be declassified'.[119]

From an environmental perspective, the *Tre Pini* ruling could be considered a mixed blessing. On the one hand, it is helpful to avert the proliferation of 'dummy sites', which formally still count towards a Member State's designation quota in spite of no longer making a meaningful environmental contribution. Furthermore, it avoids that scarce conservation resources are dedicated to, essentially, hopeless causes.[120] On the other hand, notwithstanding the Court's insistence that a site should only be declassified if it is genuinely irretrievably unsuitable, the sheer possibility of declassification might tempt local authorities to throw in the towel and declare a site irreparably lost for conservation purposes sooner rather than later. Declassification could conceivably be a strategy to sidestep the obligations under Article 6(2) HD to adopt measures to avoid the deterioration of sites and to restore damage, including damage from development

---

[116] Case C-57/89 *Commission* v. *Germany* ECLI:EU:C:1991:89.
[117] Case C-301/12 *Cascina Tre Pini Ss* v. *Ministero dell'Ambiente e della Tutela del Territorio e del Mare and Others* ECLI:EU:C:2014:214.
[118] *Ibid.*, paras. 27–28. [119] *Ibid.*, para. 28. [120] *Ibid.*

that had not or had insufficiently been considered at the stage of development consent.[121]

Compensating Biodiversity Losses

In his seminal 1961 article, 'The Problem of Social Cost', Ronald Coase forcefully argued the proposition that socially harmful enterprise is intrinsically neither good nor bad.[122] Its desirability is determined solely by whether its contribution to society's overall level of welfare outweighs the associated costs. Applied in the field of environmental regulation, this founding tenet of the Coase theorem helped to entrench the assumption that protective measures should be pursued only if, and up to the point where, they generate greater environmental benefits than economic costs. Within this perspective – which resonates in Article 191(3) TFEU's stipulation that in preparing its environmental policy the Union shall take account of the potential benefits and costs of action or lack of action – environmental protection and economic growth are treated as fungible and tradable values. This is consistent with a weak sustainability approach.[123]

EU environmental law is richly stocked with weak sustainability provisions. They are present in, for example, the definition of 'best available techniques' in the Industrial Emissions Directive, which affirms that availability encompasses economic affordability and should be determined with reference to the respective costs and advantages.[124] Weak sustainability informs the decision-making process for chemicals of very high concern, which may be authorised for continued use if the socio-economic benefits outweigh the environmental risks.[125] The Birds and Habitats Directives, however, espouse a different understanding of the relation between economy and environment. EU nature and biodiversity protection law reflects the position that economic gains, although relevant and occasionally sufficiently important to override environmental objections, cannot wholly make up for environmental losses. Instead, natural capital losses can only be compensated with natural capital gains. This approach stops short of embracing the notion that natural capital should under no condition be expended for the benefit of human or financial capital, but it nudges the dial considerably closer to the strong sustainability side of the spectrum. This 'stronger sustainability' approach is most readily apparent in the provisions of Article 6(4) HD, which determine the conditions under which plans or projects likely to affect the integrity of an SCI, SPA or SAC may nonetheless be authorised. If social, economic or other overriding public imperatives prevail, Member States must

---

[121] *Waddenzee*, para. 37.
[122] Ronald Coase, 'The Problem of Social Cost' (1960) 3 *The Journal of Law and Economics* 1–40.
[123] Cf. Maité Cabeza Gutés, 'The Concept of Weak Sustainability' (1996) 17 *Ecological Economics* 147–156.
[124] Cf. Chapter 9.   [125] Cf. Chapter 13.

take 'all compensatory measures necessary to ensure that the overall coherence of Natura 2000 is protected'.

Compensating or 'offsetting' strategies are an exponent of the ecosystem services narrative, which fosters appreciation of both the importance and uniqueness of natural capital contributions to society, and emphasises the extent to which ecological resilience and human survival are intertwined. The notion of trading off biodiversity losses with biodiversity gains also meshes well with the contemporary appetite for flexible, market-based approaches to regulation.[126] Moreover, the focus on the stability of natural capital throughout the Natura 2000 network may help to avert some of the rigidity to which designation-based approaches are vulnerable. However, offsetting is a supremely challenging enterprise. In a recent study, Donald McGillivray reports that offsetting practices tend to be poor on delivering comparable ecological functionality; that compensation measures tend to be weak on follow-up (monitoring, review and enforcement); that natural capital losses are typically underestimated and compensatory gains overestimated; and that economic considerations, which should have no place in nature-for-nature trade-offs, all too frequently influence offsetting deliberations.[127] Crucially, his review of Commission opinions on Member State compensation proposals under Article 6(4) HD indicates that offsetting measures within the EU suffer from at least the latter two shortcomings. The data is insufficiently robust or transparent to make a firm determination as to ecological functionality and follow-up, but on both scores the author finds cause for concern.[128]

Even if the practical obstacles to effective compensation could be overcome, offsetting approaches are no panacea. For one, compensation provisions do not engage with well-being considerations and may even detract attention from the very real pain and suffering that animals experience when the boundaries of their habitats are 'redrawn' and development is 'accommodated'. Furthermore, as with the issue of declassification, the possibility of compensation may pose a moral hazard and may cause competent authorities to lower the threshold at which a plan or project is considered of overriding importance. Finally, even if environmental resources are traded off against other environmental resources rather than economic gains, they remain trapped within a transactional dynamic that thrives on commodification which arguably reframes rather than avoids the reductionism from which the ecosystem services narrative sought to escape.[129]

---

[126] See e.g. Neil Gunningham, 'Environment Law, Regulation and Governance: Shifting Architectures' (2009) 21(2) *Journal of Environmental Law* 179–212.

[127] Donald McGillivray, 'Compensatory Measures under Article 6(4) of the Habitats Directive: No Net Loss for Natura 2000?' in Born et al., *The Habitats Directive*, 101–118; and Donald McGillivray, 'Compensating Biodiversity Loss: The EU Commission's Approach to Compensation under Article 6 of the Habitats Directive' (2012) 24(3) *Journal of Environmental Law* 417–450. See also Colin T. Reid, 'Between Priceless and Worthless', 217–233.

[128] McGillivray, 'Compensatory Measures' and 'Compensating Biodiversity Loss'.

[129] Cf. Jerneja Penca, 'Marketing the Market: The Ideology of Market Mechanisms for Biodiversity Conservation' (2013) 2(1) *Transnational Environmental Law* 235–257.

The Effectiveness of the Birds and Habitats Directives

The Birds and Habitats Directives together constitute a legal regime that sets demanding expectations for Member State action on nature and biodiversity protection. In this endeavour, the EU legislature moreover has found a powerful backer in the CJEU, which through repeated judgments has sought to ensure that Member State implementation and enforcement match the Directives' ambition of securing a favourable conservation status of protected species and habitats. This is a key ingredient towards the achievement of the EU's strategic goals of halting biodiversity loss and restoring biodiversity and ecosystem services.

Yet the real force of EU law cannot be gleaned only from the terms of regulations and directives or even from the language of CJEU rulings. For genuine change to happen, national public authorities, courts, stakeholders and civil society must show a willingness to embrace and put into daily practice both the form and the spirit of EU legal provisions.[130] This is all the more so for policies such as nature and biodiversity protection, which heavily depend on drive and enthusiasm to succeed, and which are all too easily undermined by perfunctory compliance.

Attributes such as the level of true commitment by and within the Member States are extremely hard to measure, but the most recent data on the state of nature and biodiversity in Europe strongly indicates that such commitment is, at present, deeply insufficient to halt (and, where necessary, restore) biodiversity loss and ecosystem services degradation. EU nature and biodiversity law is currently reviewed under the Regulatory Fitness and Performance Programme (REFIT). REFIT is a Commission initiative to conduct an evidence-based investigation into the EU legal framework's fitness for purpose, aiming particularly to identify strategies to make EU law simpler and less costly.[131] As a foundational step in this investigation, the Commission in 2015 released a Mid-Term Review of the EU Biodiversity Strategy to 2020.[132] Together with the 2015 Report on the State of Nature in the EU,[133] published in compliance with the five-yearly reporting requirements under the Birds and Habitats Directives, the two documents offer the most up-to-date information on the EU's performance in this area.

The Mid-Term Review and State of Nature Report make for sobering reading. In 2010, up to 25 per cent of European animal species faced extinction, and 65 per cent of the Natura 2000 sites were in an unfavourable conservation

---

[130] Slepcevic, 'The Judicial Enforcement of EU Law through National Courts'.
[131] See Chapter 3.
[132] Report from the Commission to the European Parliament and the Council: The mid-term review of the EU biodiversity strategy to 2020, COM(2015)478 final, 2 October 2015.
[133] Report from the Commission to the Council and the European Parliament: The State of Nature in the European Union Report on the status of and trends for habitat types and species covered by the Birds and Habitats Directives for the 2007–2012 period as required under Article 17 of the Habitats Directive and Article 12 of the Birds Directive, COM(2015)219 final, 20 May 2015.

status. Basic ecosystem services were deteriorating. The Mid-Term Review confirms that, over the last few years, there has been a very slight improvement in the number of species and habitats with favourable conservation status, but, by and large, previously observed negative trends continue. Pressures on some ecosystem services, such as timber production, have somewhat abated, but they have intensified with respect to others, including pollination. There are major failings in enhancing the contribution of agriculture to biodiversity, and efforts with regard to forestry and fisheries fall well short of the mark. Some progress has been made in managing the risks of invasive alien species and in contributing to global biodiversity protection initiatives, but greater efforts are needed. Overall, the EU does not seem on track to meet its 2020 biodiversity targets.

There are no easy fixes for Member State underperformance on nature and biodiversity protection. Some commentators advocate greater toughness on the part of the EU and argue that the Commission, especially, should invigilate Member State implementation and enforcement far more closely and critically than it has done so far.[134] On the other hand, a perceived lack of flexibility or understanding for the difficulties which Member States face in putting the EU agenda into practice risks further to erode the already limited political willingness towards the EU's 2020 biodiversity strategy. Greater toughness is also difficult to reconcile with the current Commission's desire to focus strongly on competitiveness and to minimise regulatory burdens. This is the spirit in which REFIT was conceptualised. Its assessment of the Birds and Habitats Directives is therefore unlikely to result in recommendations in favour of closer Commission supervision, more intervention and increased infringement proceedings. Ultimately, the success of EU nature and biodiversity policy stands and falls with its Member States' willingness to engage.

Other Measures

The Birds and Habitats Directives are the gravitational point of EU nature and biodiversity protection law, but they are not the only instruments in the EU legal arsenal. Additionally, EU law includes regulatory measures covering issues from trade in endangered species to the keeping of animals in zoos. The most important instruments are listed in the text box below.

> **CITES Regulation:** Regulation (EC) No. 338/97 on the protection of species of wild fauna and flora by regulating trade therein (OJ 1997 L 61/1) implements the provisions of the CITES Convention.[135] The EU itself is not a party to

---

[134] Ludwig Krämer, 'Implementation and Enforcement of the Habitats Directive' in Born et al., *The Habitats Directive*, 244.
[135] Convention on International Trade in Endangered Species of Wild Fauna and Flora, Washington, DC (USA), 3 March 1973, in force 1 July 1975, available at: www.cites.org/eng/disc/text.php.

CITES, but its Member States are. Uniform implementation of the CITES provisions at EU level reconciles the Member States' international law commitments with the requirements of free trade within the single market.

Marine Strategy Framework Directive: Directive 2008/56/EC establishing a framework for community action in the field of marine environmental policy (OJ 2008 L 164/19) aims to achieve Good Environmental Status (GES) of the EU's marine waters by 2020 and to protect the resource base upon which marine-related economic and social activities depend.

Invasive Alien Species Regulation: Regulation (EU) No. 1143/2014 on the prevention and management of the introduction and spread of invasive alien species (OJ 2014 L 317/35) seeks to manage the risks of exposure to alien invasive species (such as the spread of zoonotic diseases and biodiversity loss) through preventive, early detection and response mechanisms.

Timber Regulation: Regulation (EU) No. 995/2010 laying down the obligations of operators who place timber and timber products on the market (OJ 2010 L 295/23) aims to reduce illegal logging by ensuring that no illegal timber or timber products can be sold in the EU.

Zoos Directive: Directive 1999/22/EC on the keeping of wild animals in zoos (OJ 1999 L 94/24) introduces a legal framework for biodiversity conservation in zoos, for implementation by the Member States through the adoption of a licensing and inspection system.

Leghold Traps Regulation: Council Regulation (EEC) No. 3254/91 prohibiting the use of leghold traps in the Community and the introduction into the Community of pelts and manufactured goods of certain wild animal species originating in countries which catch them by means of leghold traps or trapping methods which do not meet international humane trapping standards (OJ 1991 L 308/1).

Trade in Seal Products Regulation: Regulation (EC) No. 1007/2009 on trade in seal products (OJ 2009 L 286/36) bans trade in seal products manufactured or imported into the EU, with exceptions for the Inuit and other indigenous communities.

Conclusion: Overcoming Institutional and Systemic Dichotomy

Nature and biodiversity protection law exemplifies many of the most enduring challenges of EU environmental policy. Successful strategies are dependent on the development of coherent, interconnected and transboundary approaches, yet they also need broad national uptake truly to come to life. The chasm between the ambition of Natura 2000 and the EU's biodiversity strategy for 2020 on the one hand, and the actual state of nature in the EU on the other, strongly suggests that it remains difficult for EU policies, and the laws that put them into effect, to be fully embraced at the local level. It is also unclear which approach is most successful in fostering convergence between European and national environmental policy priorities: the 'iron fist' or the 'velvet glove'. In nature and biodiversity protection, the former is mostly associated with the CJEU's firm stance on matters such as the limited scope of Member State discretion in designation and development consent. The case law in this field has been praised for its ambition and clarity.[136] Yet litigation also turns EU and national authorities into adversaries, as if trapped in a zero-sum game, which may erode national willingness to comply. The Commission generally takes more of a velvet glove approach. For example, so far it has not issued a single negative opinion on Member State proposals for compensation (or offsetting) under Article 6(4) HD, in spite of their sometimes questionable quality.[137] This may lower the threshold for Member States duly to comply with notification requirements, but it has also been said to reduce the Commission's credibility and leverage in implementation matters.[138]

Judgments such as *Lappel Bank* and *First Corporate Shipping* reveal not only an institutional 'EU *versus* Member State' dichotomy, but also a systemic one. As so often in public policy, environment and the economy are pitted against each other: the subjects of a trade-off in which only one emerges victorious. The oft-lamented problem is that such trade-offs are typically made on the basis of incomplete and biased information, very much to the detriment of the environmental side of the equation. A strength of the ecosystem services narrative is that it can heighten awareness of our tendency to underestimate human reliance on a healthy environment and, conversely, of the risk that narrow and short-term perspectives on costs and benefits result in decisions that are neither environmentally nor economically responsible. Its prominence within the EU 2020 biodiversity strategy could, therefore, potentially, foster a less exceptionalist outlook on nature and biodiversity policy. However, it must be borne in mind that the ecosystem services narrative praises the environment by economising it. Conceivably, we might value the Alsatian hamster more as a 'cultural service provider' than as a rare species or a thing of beauty in nature. But it is hard to ignore the suspicion that something may be lost in translation.

---

[136] Heyvaert et al., 'With Reference to the Environment'.
[137] McGillivray, 'Compensatory Measures', 110.
[138] *Ibid.*, 118. See also Krämer, 'Implementation and Enforcement of the Habitats Directive', 244.

13

Technological Risk Regulation: Chemicals, Genetically Modified Organisms and Nanotechnology

Introduction

Many of the EU's most influential health and environmental provisions are embedded in product regulation. The adoption of harmonised standards for the manufacture and trade of goods is a fundamental pillar of the EU's market liberalisation strategy, so it is unsurprising that the European Union has a rich tradition in product regulation. To a significant degree, the first generations of EU health and environmental product standards represented an attempt to eliminate regulatory barriers to intra-EU trade that would otherwise result from differences in national attitudes towards technological risks. A very prominent area of early EU activity was the regulation of trade in chemicals: in 1967, the then European Economic Community adopted a landmark Directive to harmonise the classification, packaging and labelling of dangerous substances.[1] The Directive's primary goal was to facilitate the free circulation of chemical substances and preparations within the internal market.[2] In doing so, however, it simultaneously hammered out a skeleton approach towards the integration of health and environmental considerations, as the harmonisation exercise fostered the identification of a minimum set of 'dangerous characteristics' that would trigger classification and labelling requirements, and spurred the adoption of a minimum set of health, safety and, in due course, environmental packaging requirements.

Several factors explain the heavy focus on chemicals in EU product regulation. The chemicals sector was and continues to be a major pillar of the EU economy. Over time, it has also become a quintessentially European sector: a small majority of all chemicals produced in the EU are traded with other Member States. Moreover, chemicals are the very building blocks of our heavily technology-dependent consumer society: chemicals, and the products derived from them, constitute part of every single industrial production and service delivery cycle across the world. Think away a steady supply of chemical substances and mixtures, and the world as we know it comes to a grinding halt.[3]

---

[1] Council Directive 67/548/EEC of 27 June 1967 on the approximation of laws, regulations and administrative provisions regarding the classification, packaging and labelling of dangerous substances, OJ 1967 L 196/1.
[2] Elen Stokes and Steven Vaughan, 'Great Expectations: Reviewing 50 Years of Chemical Legislation in the EU' (2013) 25(3) *Journal of Environmental Law* 411–435, at 418.
[3] See data at: www.cefic.org/Facts-and-Figures/Chemicals-Industry-Profile/.

A third reason why chemicals are a hub of regulatory attention relates to the serious health and environmental risks associated with their production, trade and use. This rationale became more prominent as the EU matured into a fully fledged environmental regulator.[4] That chemicals pose health and environmental risks is hardly revelatory. In fact, many chemicals have been deliberately designed to have dangerous properties: lighter fluids would be pointless if they were not flammable; pesticides need to impair the health of target species to be effective. In these cases, the dangerous characteristics are known, but they still need to be controlled to avoid unintended harm, such as industrial accidents or harm to non-target species. These types of known dangers are often controlled through regulatory prescriptions, including packaging and labelling requirements. Yet the health and environmental risks posed by chemicals stretch leagues beyond those related to their known, dangerous properties. Chemicals can be toxic to human health and/or the environment. Chemicals can be 'CMRs', which stands for 'carcinogenic, mutagenic and reprotoxic'. Exposure to chemicals can trigger hormonal imbalances in recipient organisms, a process known as 'endocrine disruption'. Compounding their harmfulness is the fact that some chemicals are bioaccumulative and highly persistent: continuing exposure causes their presence to build up in the host environment and it takes, literally, centuries for these dangerous substances or compounds to degrade. Tragically, as these harmful properties are unintended, decades may pass before a particular chemical is credibly linked to an observed harmful impact. Industrial history is littered with examples of chemicals such as DDT, lead paint and PCBs,[5] which had become deeply entrenched in production and processing before evidence emerged that their catastrophic health and environmental effects far outweighed their benefits.

To comply with the EU legal principles of prevention, precaution and the achievement of a high level of health and environmental protection, the EU regulatory regime for chemicals must therefore respond not only to known and identifiable danger, but also to risk and uncertainty. A key mission of this chapter is to explore how EU regulation confronts this challenge. To this end, the analysis will chiefly concentrate on the regulation of chemicals, which must contend with both uncertainties related to exposure to chemicals that are already circulating on the market, and those of newly engineered chemicals. However, it is important to bear in mind that many of the most profound uncertainties in product regulation today are a consequence of the rapidly expanding deployment of new production technologies. Whereas we share an incomplete yet workable understanding of the typical range of risks that accompanies the synthesis of new substances and compounds through 'traditional' chemistry, this is not the case for processes that rely on biotechnology, nanotechnology, synthetic biology, cloning, etc. The range and scale of health and environmental risks that these advanced technologies represent, and the extent to which they can alter the industrial,

---

[4] Stokes and Vaughan, 'Great Expectations', 420.
[5] DDT (dichlorodiphenyltrichloroethane) is an insecticide; PCBs (polychlorinated biphenyls) were widely used as coolant fluids.

economic and even the political and social organisation of society, is shrouded in a fog of conjecture. The chapter therefore includes in its discussion reflections on regulation at the frontiers of science and technology. It focuses on genetically modified organisms (GMOs) and nanotechnology, both of which fields have given rise to particular regulatory challenges within the EU context.

The chapter starts with an exploration of the dual purpose of market harmonisation and environmental protection in EU product regulation, asking whether it is truly possible for a legal instrument to fulfil both goals at once and on an equal footing. The next section aims to convey a sense of the complexity and density of the regulatory regime governing chemicals. Many discussions on the topic focus predominantly, or exclusively, on the high-profile REACH Regulation, which entered into effect in 2007 and introduced a number of innovative risk management approaches into the EU regulatory landscape.[6] The emphasis on REACH is understandable and, for the most part, well-deserved: in terms of economic impact alone, REACH is arguably one of the most important instruments ever adopted at the EU level. It is a calling card for the EU's contemporary, precautionary approach to technological risk regulation, and several of its regulatory requirements are considered controversially, even radically, to push the boundaries in terms of the obligations they impose on the private sector. The discussion in this chapter, too, will pay careful attention to REACH. However, it is equally important to understand that the EU regulatory regime for chemicals control is the product of a multitude of regulations and directives, culminating in a dense, overlapping and at times dysfunctional regulatory network. GMO regulation, too, spans a complex set of regulatory instruments.

The third section of the chapter takes us into the heartland of risk regulation. Using chemicals, GMO and nanotechnology regulation as a reference point, the section explains that the adoption of a risk-based perspective fosters the conceptualisation of new legal mandates and the introduction of new legal requirements. It impacts on the position of regulators, regulatory addressees, advisers and third-party stakeholders alike and creates new institutional interdependencies. Concretely, one of the most significant consequences of the adoption of a risk-regulatory perspective is that it fuels the development of very lengthy, technically complex legal requirements that are further backed up by seemingly endless streams of guidance notes and other supporting material. This, it will be explained, poses not only a practical but also a serious legal challenge. Building on this discussion, the fourth section examines the various principles and techniques in EU chemicals, GMO and nanotechnology regulation that enable the regulator to cope with problems of scientific uncertainty and contestation. As will be shown, the insertion of requirements that respond to the inescapably preliminary nature of regulatory decisions adopted under conditions of uncertainty is a necessary but not necessarily sufficient step to ensure the legitimacy of risk regulation.

---

[6] Regulation (EC) No. 1907/2006 of the European Parliament and of the Council of 18 December 2006 concerning the Registration, Evaluation, Authorisation and Restriction of Chemicals (REACH), OJ 2006 L 396.

The last two sections focus on a typical challenge for GMO and nanotechnology regulation respectively. The GMO discussion tackles the problem of coexistence. Decades of regulatory turmoil, political stalemate and transnational dispute have taught us that the starkly different attitudes of Member States towards the acceptability of commercial GMOs are not a problem likely to fade over time or to be levelled by a stream of expert opinion. To become effective, EU regulation for GMOs must respond to a higher degree of national differentiation than is permissible in the context of 'mainstream' product regulation regimes. We will review the contribution and adequacy of the EU's most recent initiatives to ensure the coexistence of GMO-tolerant and GMO-sceptical regions. Finally, the sixth section takes as its point of departure the rapid development and commercialisation of nanotechnology to investigate the resilience of the EU's technological risk patrimonium. It analyses the openness of existing regulation to 'new' risks and discusses the pros and cons of introducing new requirements, or an entire new framework, in response to new scientific and technological developments.

Dual-Purpose Regulation: Reconciling Market Harmonisation with Health and Environmental Protection

Most regulations and directives governing chemicals, GMOs and nanotechnology are adopted on the basis of Article 114 TFEU, the internal market provision. Yet in EU product regulation, free movement of goods and environmental protection are explicitly intended to go hand-in-hand. The preambles to all the keystone instruments leave the reader in no doubt. REACH affirms the dual objectives of ensuring a 'high level of protection of health and the environment as well as the free movement of substances' in a single breath in its very first preamble, as does the 2008 Regulation on the Classification, Labelling and Packaging of Chemicals (the CLP Regulation).[7] The same perspective pervades legislation governing the commercialisation of GMOs.[8] The GMO Food and Feed Regulation (FFR), for example, emphasises that the 'free movement of safe and wholesome food and feed is an essential aspect of the internal market', and immediately continues that EU policies should pursue a high level of protection.[9]

---

[7] Regulation (EC) No. 1272/2008 of the European Parliament and of the Council of 16 December 2008 on classification, labelling and packaging of substances and mixtures, amending and repealing Directives 67/548/EEC and amending Regulation (EC) No. 1907/2006 OJ 2008 L 353/1.

[8] Laura Drott, Lukas Jochum, Frederik Lange, Isabel Skierka, Jonas Vach and Marjolein B.A. van Asselt, 'Accountability and Risk Governance: A Scenario-Informed Reflection on European Regulation of GMOs' (2013) 16(9), *Journal of Risk Research* 1123–1140, at 1127.

[9] Regulation (EC) No. 1829/2003 of the European Parliament and of the Council of 22 September 2003 on genetically modified food and feed, OJ 2003 L 268/1. Similar wording appears in the preambles of Council Directive 90/220/EEC of 23 April 1990 on the deliberate release into the environment of genetically modified organisms, OJ 1990 L 117/15 (referred to in successor Directive 2001/18/EC of the European Parliament and of the Council of 12 March 2001 on the deliberate release into the environment of genetically

The affirmations in the specific instruments are further backed up by the integration principle, which requires that 'environmental protection requirements must be integrated into the definition and implementation of the Union's policies and activities, in particular with a view to promoting sustainable development' (Article 11 TFEU).

The choice of the internal market legal basis should, therefore, not be read to sanction a subordination of the health and environmental protection goals in the EU's chemicals, GMO and nano policies. Until the entry into effect of the Amsterdam Treaty, the legal basis may have even had a beneficial effect on the level of environmental ambition, since internal market provisions were adopted following qualified majority voting (QMV) and with a stronger voice for the European Parliament than environmental measures. QMV creates an opportunity to escape lowest common denominator outcomes, and the European Parliament typically tends to adopt a greener perspective than the Council.

On the flip side, internal market measures are harder to deviate from than provisions adopted under the auspices of the Environmental Chapter of the TFEU. Moreover – and in contrast to the legislative procedures, which were streamlined as of 1999 – the Treaty-based differences regarding 'opt-ups' persist to this day.

Going beyond EU Environmental Standards

Article 193 TFEU allows Member States to maintain or introduce more-stringent protective measures, subject only to their compatibility with the Treaties. To opt up from market harmonisation measures under Article 114 TFEU, a far more exacting set of hurdles must be jumped, especially if a Member State wants newly to introduce, rather than maintain, environmental conditions after the adoption of a harmonisation measure. In many cases, such as those of GMO authorisation, it will be the very EU harmonisation measure that necessitates the adoption of a new national restriction in the first place. This places Member States in the difficult position of having to justify new measures, which requires the production of new scientific evidence relating to an environmental problem that is specific to the Member State and that arose after the adoption of the harmonisation measure (Article 114(5) TFEU). EU case law has affirmed that these provisions should be narrowly interpreted. For example, a reappraisal of existing test results does not meet the threshold of 'new scientific evidence'.[10] In the context of exemptions, the

---

modified organisms and repealing Council Directive 90/220/EEC, OJ 2001 L 106/1) and Regulation (EC) No. 1830/2003 of the European Parliament and of the Council of 22 September 2003 concerning the traceability and labelling of genetically modified organisms and the traceability of food and feed products produced from genetically modified organisms and amending Directive 2001/18/EC, OJ 2003 L 268/24.

[10] Case T-366/03 and 235/04 *Land Oberösterreich and Austria* v. *Commission* ECLI:EU:T:2005:347; confirmed on appeal in Case C-439/05 and 454/05 *Land Oberösterreich and*

> overriding market integration perspective undeniably limits options for the more environmentally ambitious Member States.

Moreover, the bias in favour of the internal market over health and environmental protection arguably pervades the regulatory framework.[11] However onerous specific data production, registration or approval procedures might be, EU regulation is ultimately adopted in support of a *market*.[12] Moreover, it is a market that, in accordance with EU aspirations, should be vibrant, competitive and an engine to innovation and growth. This vision implicitly puts a cap on how much restriction regulatory regimes can tolerate: allowances may be made to accommodate health and environmental concerns, but they should not come at the expense of the viability of the market itself. As the European Court confirmed in litigation regarding tobacco advertising, 'to justify recourse to Article 95 EC [now Article 114 TFEU] as the legal basis what matters is that the measure adopted on that basis must actually be intended to improve the conditions for the establishment and functioning of the internal market'.[13] Internal market legislation is therefore essentially facilitative and implies as well as demands the existence of a market.[14] This delegitimises the view that particular technologies should not be commercialised in the first place. Indeed, GMO regulation only engages with the possibility that individual releases of GMO products may be too harmful to be authorised; it contains little discursive space for the perspective that the technology as a whole should be abandoned. This is a potentially crucial factor in explaining the failure of repeated attempts to get the EU GMO authorisation regime running 'properly'. We will revisit this issue below.

The tensions between market facilitation and environmental protection may be less glaring in the case of EU chemicals regulation than they are with regard to GMOs, but it is certainly arguable that some of the regulatory choices made in, for example, the REACH Regulation are not those likely to yield the best environmental information. The Registration phase, which requires chemicals producers, importers and occasionally downstream users to create detailed technical dossiers to be submitted to the European Chemicals Agency (ECHA), is a one-time process resulting in the issuance of a registration number of unlimited validity. In contrast to the wealth of provisions and guidance documents written in support of this registration process, ex-post updating requirements are

---

Austria v. Commission ECLI:EU:C:2007:510. Floor Fleurke, 'What Use for Article 95(5) EC? An Analysis of *Land Oberösterreich and Austria v. Commission*' (2008) 20(2) *Journal of Environmental Law* 267–278.

[11] Elen Stokes, 'Nanotechnology and the Products of Inherited Regulation' (2012) 39(1) *Journal of Law and Society* 93–112, at 104.

[12] Ibid.

[13] Case C-380/03 *Germany v. European Parliament and Council of the European Union* (2006) ECR I-11573, para. 80.

[14] Paulette Kurzer and Alice Cooper, 'Consumer Activism, EU Institutions and Global Markets: The Struggle over Biotech Foods' (2007) 27(2) *Journal of Public Policy* 103–128.

summarily mentioned in the Regulation and comparatively under-specified. This reduces the likelihood that epidemiological data, which takes longer to collect but can be a more reliable indicator of environmental impact, will be adequately integrated into the regulatory process. The maximum scientific testing period provided under the standard registration provision is 28 days, which is a painfully brief window for ecotoxicological studies. Short-term and one-stop approaches do not always work well for the development of a reliable body of environmental risk information.[15] However, they are less likely to destabilise the market for chemical substances and products than long-term and cyclical regulatory obligations would do.

EU Chemicals Regulation as a Network

Chemicals regulation has a rich history in EU health and environmental law. The 1967 Directive laying down harmonised rules for the classification, packaging and labelling of dangerous substances was the starting shot for a steady stream of further legislation concerning packaging and labelling standards for dangerous preparations (now more commonly referred to as 'mixtures'); rules requiring data production and testing of new chemicals before their release on the European market (a process known as 'notification'); measures that sought to organise risk assessments for chemicals that had been circulating on the market since or before 1981 ('existing substances'); and restrictions on the marketing and use of certain dangerous chemicals. The collection of regulations and directives containing this broad variety of measures was thoroughly streamlined, amended and recast in the first decade of the twenty-first century into two key instruments: the 2006 REACH Regulation and the 2008 CLP Regulation. Together, REACH and the CLP constitute the backbone of the EU's approach to chemicals risk governance in the internal market.

Yet underneath the apparent simplicity of the current regulatory regime hides a more complex reality. First, the representation of REACH as a single instrument is arguably somewhat deceptive. REACH is perhaps better thought of as an umbrella regulation housing parallel pillars that relate to each other but function more or less independently. Secondly, to comprehend fully the impact of REACH and the CLP, we need to take into account the manifold linkages between them and legislation governing issues from worker safety to water quality. Finally, beyond the general measures contained in REACH and the CLP, EU law contains a wealth of instruments that address particular categories of commercial chemicals, or that regulate the use of chemicals in particular contexts or particular products. Together, this collection of regulations and directives forms an extensive and, it is argued, not always well-connected network of regulation.

---

[15] Benoît Ferrari et al., 'Environmental Risk Assessment of Six Human Pharmaceuticals: Are the Current Environmental Risk Assessment Procedures Sufficient for the Protection of the Aquatic Environment?' (2004) 23(5) *Environmental Toxicology and Chemistry* 1344–1354.

The REACH Regulation

REACH stands for the Registration, Evaluation and Authorisation of Chemicals. Additionally, overlooked in the acronym but equally important, are provisions regulating the adoption of restrictions for marketing and use of certain dangerous chemicals, and provisions governing the production of Safety Data Sheets for dangerous substances and products.

> **The REACH Registration process (Arts. 5–24 REACH)**
>
> Registration is the beating heart of REACH. It requires that manufacturers, importers and, under certain circumstances, downstream users of chemical substances in quantities of at least one tonne per year (1 t/y) create an extensive technical data file to be submitted to the European Chemicals Agency (ECHA). The registration dossier covers a wide range of information, including: the chemical's trading name and composition; its classification and applicable labelling requirements; use and exposure patterns; information about where the substance will ultimately end up after use and how it will be treated and disposed of; its physico-chemical properties such as density, flammability and viscosity; and toxicological and ecotoxicological data, which are mostly obtained through laboratory testing. Registrants of substances produced in high volumes (at least 10 t/y) must also submit a Chemical Safety Report, which contains a risk assessment of the chemical. Following a successful completeness check, ECHA assigns a registration number, which functions as proof of the registrant's right to continue producing, trading or using the substance on the European market.

Under current thresholds, registration affects approximately 60,000 substances, the overwhelming majority of which have been traded within the EU since before the 1980s. The registration regime thus encapsulates the EU's attempt to confront the 'burden of the past': to address the vast information deficit concerning 'old' or 'existing' chemicals, brought into circulation before the EU's data supply and notification requirements for new substances took effect. The lack of data regarding existing substances crippled the EU's – as well as Member States' – ability to devise an effective strategy to control chemical health and environmental risks. It also jeopardised innovation: confronted with a choice between continuing to produce old and lightly regulated chemicals or invest in the production of new, more heavily regulated alternatives, manufacturers were likely to favour the former. The failure to address the burden of the past was widely considered a significant weakness of the preceding regulatory regime.[16]

---

[16] Veerle Heyvaert, 'Guidance without Constraint: Assessing the Impact of the Precautionary Principle on the European Community's Chemicals Policy' (2006) 6 *Yearbook of European Environmental Law* 27–60, at 46.

The REACH Regulation aims to overcome the deficit through a combination of mandatory requirements, incentives and facilitation. Registration is mandatory and REACH famously operates under a motto of 'no data, no market' (Art. 5 REACH): after the lapse of a predetermined deadline, unregistered substances and products containing them must be withdrawn from circulation, regardless of indications of adverse health or environmental consequences. To spread the burden and expense of registration, the Regulation calls for the establishment of 'Substance Information Exchange Forums' (SIEFs), which group together prospective registrants of the same substance who can collaborate in the production of the registration dossier (Art. 28 REACH). The establishment of these substance-centred clubs, which accommodate the development of new cooperative arrangements between private actors competing within the same market, illustrates a persistent dilemma in technological risk regulation. The SIEFs exemplify the deeply privatised nature of chemical data production. On the one hand, this mode of organisation respects the polluter pays principle. It is also efficient as the most extensive and up-to-date knowledge regarding chemical hazards and risks will be held by those active in the sector. On the other hand, there are legitimate concerns about the wisdom of asking the chemicals sector to, essentially, write its own report card. Outright fraud may be an unappealingly high-risk strategy, but the temptation to dwell on the positives and gloss over the negatives may prove much harder to resist. An intriguing question is whether the peer pressure within the SIEFs will serve to discipline the process and enhance the fulsomeness and quality of registration data or whether it will instead foster collusion in attempts to spin the message. It is too early for conclusive answers, but early reports on the quality of registration dossiers give cause for some concern.[17] In 2016, the Commission adopted an implementing Regulation to establish common criteria for data sharing under REACH. However, the Regulation focuses on the transparency and fairness of data-sharing arrangements between SIEF members, and does not address data quality concerns.[18]

The Evaluation pillar (Arts. 40–54 REACH) organises the processing of chemical data with an eye to selecting priority chemicals for further scrutiny, to determine whether further risk control measures are needed under either the chemicals authorisation framework or the REACH provisions on restrictions, or under the auspices of alternative EU regulatory instruments. Evaluation includes both dossier evaluation (ECHA reviews of registrants' testing proposals and

---

[17] Out of 283 compliance check evaluations that ECHA performed in 2014, 111 (39 per cent) were concluded with no further action and 172 cases (61 per cent) led to a draft decision, indicating deficiencies in registration. These figures may overstate the problem since ECHA targets dossiers with a high risk of compliance deficits in its selection of sample cases. However, the numbers are undeniably too high to label compliance shortcomings as incidental. See ECHA, 'Evaluation Under REACH: Progress Report 2014', available at: http://echa.europa.eu/documents/10162/13628/evaluation_report_2014_en.pdf.

[18] Commission Implementing Regulation (EU) 2016/9 of 5 January 2016 on joint submission of data and data-sharing in accordance with Regulation (EC) No. 1907/2006, OJ 2016 L 3/41.

compliance checks of registrations) and, importantly, substance evaluation. ECHA draws up 'Commission rolling action plans' ('CoRAPs') that identify chemicals for further examination. The evaluation itself is performed by Member State authorities, which upon completion submit their recommendations for further action to ECHA.

One such recommendation for further action may be that the evaluated substance is placed on the candidate list of 'substances of very high concern' (SVHC), contained in Annex XIV to the REACH Regulation. Inclusion on the candidate list triggers the Authorisation phase of REACH (Arts. 55–66 REACH). By the expiry of a sunset date, indicated in Annex XIV of the Regulation, economic actors must discontinue the use of this substance unless it has been duly authorised by the Commission, which will adopt its decision on the basis of an opinion prepared by ECHA's Risk Assessment and Socio-Economic Analysis Committees. To obtain authorisation, applicants must show that the risks related to use are either adequately contained or outweighed by the socio-economic benefits of use, and that no less dangerous substitutes are available.

Separate from the authorisation process, REACH maps out the procedures for the adoption of restrictions on the marketing and/or use of dangerous chemicals (Arts. 67–73 REACH). Like authorisation decisions, restrictions are adopted by the European Commission. However, they are tailored according to a more 'classical' regulatory formula in which the regulatory authority gathers evidence and builds a case to justify its intervention in the interest of public health or environmental protection.[19] The balance of responsibilities is different in the authorisation regime, where the onus of making a positive case in favour of continued use rests on the applicant's shoulders. This explains why the authorisation procedure was far more heatedly contested during the REACH legislative negotiations, and why it has been asserted that authorisation 'reverses the burden of proof'.[20] This slightly oversimplifies matters because the substance's prior inclusion on the SVHC candidate list is probably the consequence of an intense and heavily evidence-based substance evaluation conducted by the designated Member State. Still, the authorisation pillar of REACH undeniably adopts an overtly precautionary approach to decision-making and displays distinctly different inter-party dynamics from the restriction process.

One question that the REACH Regulation does not settle is when recourse should be had to authorisation and when to restriction. Bergkamp and Herbatschek see this as indicative of a disjointedness in REACH; a telltale sign that REACH bears its own 'burden of the past' and is an amalgamation of new and pre-existing risk management approaches rather than an independent and

---

[19] See Case T-456/11 *International Cadmium Association* v. *Commission* ECLI:EU:T:2013:594; also discussed in Chapter 3.

[20] Cf. Veerle Heyvaert, 'No Data, No Market: The Future of EU Chemicals Control under the REACH Regulation' (2007) 9(3) *Environmental Law Review* 201–206, at 203.

coherent framework that fosters a rational and systematic consideration of various risk management alternatives.[21]

Similar reflections could be made regarding a third risk management measure contained in REACH: the requirement for chemical manufacturers and importers to furnish downstream users with Safety Data Sheets (SDS) (Art. 31 REACH). SDS offer essential information about the physical characteristics of the chemical, instructions on safe use and risk management protocols, and an overview of the applicable regulatory requirements. Often overlooked in discussions on chemical risk control, SDS are potentially the most powerful tool in REACH's risk management arsenal because they forge a direct line of communication between the supplier and chemicals user, and their use is widespread. SDS are mandatory for any substance that is classified as dangerous under the CLP Regulation, illustrating one of the many linkages between provisions in the EU chemicals regulation network. We will return to the CLP, and its many interactions with other regulatory instruments, in the next paragraph. As to SDS, beyond confirming that persistent, bioaccumulative and toxic or very persistent and very bioaccumulative substances require an SDS, as do substances on the candidate list (these affirmations are fairly superfluous since such substances are bound to be classified as dangerous), REACH is silent on the relation between SDS, authorisations and restrictions. This is less problematic than in the previous scenario as the approaches are not mutually exclusive, but it is nonetheless peculiar that the SDS stipulations on safe use instructions are seen to have no bearing on determinations whether risks are 'adequately controlled' under the authorisation pillar, or on decisions to adopt marketing and, especially, use restrictions.

The CLP Regulation

The second major EU instrument governing chemical risks is the CLP Regulation, which lays down harmonised requirements for the classification, packaging and labelling of chemical substances and mixtures. The default approach of the CLP is self-classification: manufacturers and importers apply the general criteria set out in the CLP and on this basis determine under which hazard classes their substance or mixture should be housed. For a minority of substances and mixtures, harmonised classifications have been adopted. The classification of the chemicals, in turn, determines applicable packaging and labelling requirements.

It is when analysing the CLP Regulation that the network structure of the EU chemicals regimes comes into sharp focus. The CLP and REACH feed into each other at various points: the information produced in the course of registration and

---

[21] Lucas Bergkamp and Nicolas Herbatschek, 'Regulating Chemical Substances under REACH: The Choice between Authorization and Restriction and the Case of Dipolar Aprotic Solvents' (2014) 23(2) *Review of European Community & International Environmental Law* 221–245, at 229.

testing under REACH may have an impact on classification, and conversely classification information needs to be included in a REACH registration dossier. The SDS requirement under Article 31 REACH applies to substances classified as dangerous, to be determined in accordance with the criteria set out in the CLP. The influence of CLP classifications moreover stretches far beyond REACH: CLP criteria are used to identify companies that, by virtue of the presence of dangerous substances on the site, must comply with the safety prescriptions to control major accident hazards under EU Directive 2012/18/EU.[22] In the context of the 2010 Industrial Emissions Directive, CLP hazard classifications serve to identify installations that are subject to particular emissions control and substitution requirements.[23] Following the Cosmetics Regulation,[24] CMRs identified in accordance with the classification criteria of the CLP are prohibited for use in cosmetics products. In a similar vein, CLP classifications function as reference points to determine employers' obligations under health and safety at work legislation.[25] CLP-based classifications, as well as risk assessments conducted in accordance with the EU legal provisions that preceded REACH, are used to identify hazardous substances and priority substances in the Water Framework Directive.[26]

Furthermore, the CLP is representative of cross-governance as well as cross-sectoral networking. The 2008 Regulation fully incorporates the standards contained in the Globally Harmonised System for Classification and Labelling of Chemicals (GHS), which regime was developed under the auspices of the United Nations.[27] GHS standards are the product of a lengthy, transnational multi-stakeholder negotiation and decision-making process, with active participation from the EU and its Member States, which resulted in the adoption of universally recognised classification and labelling standards aimed to facilitate global trade.[28] The GHS itself is not a binding instrument, but it has a high level of informal authority and creates strong incentives for chemicals producers across the world

---

[22] Directive 2012/18/EU on the control of major-accident hazards involving dangerous substances, OJ 2012 L 197/1.

[23] Directive 2010/75/EU on industrial emissions (integrated pollution prevention and control), OJ 2010 L 334/17, Art. 3(18) in combination with Arts. 58 and 59.

[24] Regulation (EC) No. 1223/2009 on cosmetics products, OJ 2009 L 342/59.

[25] See Art. 2(b) of Council Directive 98/24/EC on the protection of the health and safety of workers from the risks related to chemical agents at work (fourteenth individual Directive within the meaning of Article 16(1) of Directive 89/391/EEC), OJ 1998 L 131/11, as amended; and Art. 2(a) and (b) of Directive 2004/37/EC on the protection of workers from the risks related to exposure to carcinogens or mutagens at work (sixth individual Directive within the meaning of Article 16(1) of Council Directive 89/391/EEC), OJ 2004 L 158/50, as amended.

[26] Directive 2000/60/EC establishing a framework for Community action in the field of water policy, OJ 2000 L 327/1.

[27] Mary Frances Lowe, 'Toward a Globally Harmonized System: Negotiating to Promote Public Health, Environmental Protection and International Trade' (2003) 27(1) *Fletcher Forum of World Affairs* 195–204.

[28] Stokes and Vaughan, 'Great Expectations', 416.

to adhere to its classification and labelling rules. Within the EU, streamlining the CLP with the GHS has transformed the latter from a voluntary, soft law initiative into part and parcel of EU internal market law.

Further Measures

Chemical substances and mixtures may be subject to specialist regimes that either supplement or replace the general REACH and CLP requirements. In principle, all biocides and pesticides must obtain authorisation to be lawfully traded on the EU market, in accordance with requirements set out in, respectively, the 2012 Biocidal Products Regulation and the 2009 Regulation on Plant Protection Products.[29] For the purposes of REACH, chemicals that have been reviewed and assessed under the biocide or pesticide rules are exempt from further registration requirements.[30] Other frameworks, such as the Cosmetics Regulation, the Regulation on Ozone-Depleting Substances[31] and the EU pharmaceutical rules, do not obviate the REACH or CLP requirements but introduce additional, specific safety requirements for their respective product categories. Depending on the product and hazardous nature of the chemical concerned, requirements can range from targeted traceability and labelling provisions to across-the-board bans on manufacture and trade (for example, production and sale of chlorofluorocarbons (CFCs) is banned in the ODS Regulation).

A number of instruments regulate specific product categories that contain hazardous substances or mixtures, such as batteries and accumulators; electrical and electronic equipment; medical devices; thermometers and other measuring devices containing mercury; etc. Finally, EU provisions govern the use of chemicals in high-risk situations, such as the aforementioned legislation on the use of chemical agents at work and the Directive on waste electrical and electronic equipment (WEEE).[32]

The existence of a broad range of product- and use-specific chemicals regulation creates the possibility that a single substance or mixture is subjected to multiple risk management measures. Cosmetics mixtures may need to be notified under the Cosmetics Regulation and registered under REACH. Chemicals in the workplace may be subject to substitution requirements and maximum occupational exposure levels pursuant to the chemical agents at work rules, and may at the same time feature as an SVHC on the candidate list for authorisation under REACH. The multiple entry points for regulation to engage with chemical risks can reduce the likelihood that a dangerous substance or mixture slips through the mazes of the regulatory network. The chemicals sector has been vocal in its

---

[29] Art. 17 Biocidal Products Regulation (EU) No. 528/2012, OJ 2012 L 167/1 and Art. 4 Regulation on Plant Protection Products (EC) No. 1107/2009, OJ 2009 L 309/1.
[30] Art. 16 REACH.
[31] Regulation (EC) No. 1005/2009 on substances that deplete the ozone layer, OJ 2009 L 286/1.
[32] Directive 2012/19/EU on waste electrical and electronic equipment (WEEE) OJ 2012 L 197/38.

concern that overlapping requirements are inefficient, excessively burdensome and an exercise in 'regulatory overkill'. In March 2015, a coalition of major industries urged the Commission to rein in the 'authorisation' process for licensing use of restricted hazardous chemicals and, instead, to rely on the substitution and restriction requirements enacted in workplace legislation. In response, public interest groups asserted that workplace legislation, which shows variation in implementation between Member States, does not offer the same, uniform depth of protection as do the REACH provisions.[33] Evidently, what is a straitjacket to some is a safety net to others.

Chemicals, GMO and Nano Regulation as Technological Risk Regulation

The regulatory frameworks under scrutiny in this chapter are prime examples of EU technological risk regulation.[34] They tackle risks associated with the deployment of specialised, often advanced, technologies to create man-made substances and products for commercial purposes. The following paragraphs examine chemicals, GMO and nano provisions to understand how the core risk regulatory functions of risk identification, risk assessment and management[35] are organised in EU law.

Information Production

The adoption of a risk perspective has far-reaching ramifications for the design and implementation of regulatory regimes. As a product of the probability and the seriousness of negative consequences, risks are necessarily future-oriented. Information about what negative things may transpire if, say, the speed limit is raised by 5 mph or a new active ingredient is used in a pesticide, tends to be a scarce commodity. Entrepreneurs hardly have an incentive to disclose or even investigate risks, and consumers are typically insufficiently informed or organised effectively to demand reliable risk data. The threat of liability may stimulate some engagement by risk creators, but when it is difficult to establish a clear link between cause and effect (as will be the case for a claimant who argues that a traffic accident occurred because of a more permissive speed limit, or that a new pesticide used by a neighbouring farm has decimated the local bee population) or if a long time lag separates the risky activity from the harm, court action alone is insufficient to ensure that risks will be identified in a systematic and timely manner. Hence, the task falls to regulation.

The need for risk identification imbues regulation with an important new mandate, namely, to secure information production. Within the risk regulation paradigm, information production becomes a dominant preoccupation of market

---

[33] Valerie Flynn, 'Industries Ask Brussels to Ease Chemical Law Burden', *ENDS Europe*, 20 March 2015.
[34] Heyvaert, 'Governing Climate Change', 824.   [35] See Chapter 1, p. 26.

regulation, to the extent that it may come to be identified as the primary goal of the regulatory regime. Regulatory effectiveness, in turn, may be measured chiefly by the range and volume of information generated in compliance with regulatory prescriptions. The REACH Regulation offers a powerful example of the information-driven nature of technological risk regulation. Its dominant pillar is the registration procedure, the primary aim of which is to deal with the burden of the past and fill in the information deficit. In compliance with registration requirements, which are mapped out in the Regulation and further detailed in voluminous guidance documents, registrants produce prodigious amounts of technically complex hazard and risk data to be submitted to the European Chemicals Agency (ECHA). It is successful registration, rather than the more explicitly controlling stages of authorisation and restriction, that unlocks access to the market.[36] For the overwhelming majority of manufacturers and importers of the approximately 60,000 substances subject to registration, the regulatory reach of REACH begins and ends with data production. Only a small proportion of chemicals will be caught up in the evaluation, authorisation and/or restriction process.[37]

Beyond facilitating information production, risk regulation maps out standardised risk assessment conventions so that the relative probability and seriousness of hazards materialising can be measured in a predictable and comparable manner.[38] The REACH Regulation, the DRD and the FFR all contain risk assessment prescriptions.[39] The key difference between hazard assessments and risk assessments is that the latter take into account exposure information. Hence, a highly toxic chemical presents a significant hazard but could conceivably pose a relatively lower risk if, for example, it is only used in a closed system and ultimately is destroyed under controlled conditions by specially trained personnel. Commentators have observed that, from this perspective, the label of 'risk regulation' for REACH could be considered somewhat of a misnomer, because some regulatory consequences of REACH are triggered purely on the basis of the intrinsic hazards presented by the chemicals. Bergkamp and Herbatschek, notably, observe that decisions on which substances to place on the candidate list for authorisation do not take into account exposure.[40] However, exposure does become a factor when the subsequent authorisation decisions are taken.

Risk Management

The traditional understanding of risk regulation is that the hazard information produced and the risk assessments performed ultimately feed into risk management determinations. Risk management includes a host of strategies ranging from decisions to abstain from further intervention, requests for further information,

---

[36] Heyvaert, 'No Data, No Market', 201.
[37] Stokes and Vaughan, 'Great Expectations', 427.   [38] Ibid., 422.
[39] Art. 10(b) and Annex I REACH; Arts. 4(2)–4(4) DRD; Arts. 5(5)(a), 6(3)(b) and 6(3)(c) Food and Feed Regulation.
[40] Bergkamp and Herbatschek, 'Regulating Chemical Substances under REACH', 224.

labelling requirements, post-marketing monitoring demands and marketing and use restrictions, to outright refusals to authorise and product bans. In terms of institutional input, the conventional format is that the private sector supplies the data to the regulatory authority; the authority commissions an expert body (typically in the guise of an independent agency) to perform the assessment; and the regulator decides. The reality of risk regulation is, however, both more complex and more fluid.[41] First, for many substances under REACH, the stages of individual assessment and management are never triggered. Instead, it has been argued that the most important regulatory impetus from REACH does not derive from the risk management decisions adopted by the European Commission, but resides in the self-regulatory potential harnessed through data production.[42] Registration and the production of Safety Data Sheets constitute a learning process for chemical manufacturers and users, one that may help them to identify and respond to previously unknown hazards, as well as inefficiencies in use and dangerous practices that can be avoided through a change in protocol.

A second observation is that the responsibilities for risk assessment and management have shifted. Registrants of high production volume chemicals as well as applicants for authorisation under REACH – and applicants for authorisation under either the DRD or the FFR – will produce and submit extensive risk assessments, whether or not they are legally required. ECHA and the European Food Safety Authority (EFSA), the competent agencies for chemicals and GMOs respectively, do not so much perform as review the extensive risk assessment dossiers submitted by the private sector.[43] Paskalev describes ESFA as, essentially, a peer reviewer of GMO risk assessments.[44] On the flip side, the Agencies' role in risk management is arguably more pronounced than the terms of REACH, the DRD and the FFR suggest.[45] The Commission may formally impose, say, a maximum concentration limit for a particular hazardous substance, but it invariably acts on the basis of a risk management recommendation issued by ECHA or EFSA. Given the CJEU's insistence that risk-based and precautionary decisions must be taken on the basis of the best available evidence,[46] any Commission decision to deviate from the Agencies' recommendations is conditional and open to judicial review. As a rule of thumb, the Commission will typically follow the Agencies' advice, particularly on issues that are contentious between the Member States.

---

[41] Veerle Heyvaert, 'Regulating Chemical Risk: REACH in a Global Governance Perspective' in Johan Eriksson, Michael Gilek and Christina Ruden (eds.), *Regulating Chemical Risks: European and Global Challenges* (Springer, 2010).

[42] Martin Fuhr and Kilian Bizer, 'REACH as a Paradigm Shift in Chemical Policy: Responsive Regulation and Behavioural Models' (2007) 15 *Journal of Cleaner Production* 327.

[43] Marjolein B. A. van Asselt and Ellen Vos, 'Wrestling with Uncertain Risks: EU Regulation of GMOS and the Uncertainty Paradox' (2008) 11 *Journal of Risk Research* 281–300, at 284.

[44] Vesco Paskalev, 'Can Science Tame Politics: The Collapse of the New GMO Regime in the EU' (2012) 3(2) *European Journal of Risk Regulation* 190–201, at 194.

[45] Ibid.

[46] Case T-74/00 *Artegodan* [2002] ECR II-4945, paras. 197–200; Case C-77/09 *Gowan* [2010] ECR I-13533, para. 75; Case C-58/10 *Monsanto* [2011] ECR I-7765, para. 77.

Legitimacy and Effectiveness Challenges of Data-Driven Regimes

Risk regulation is highly proceduralised: legal frameworks and provisions contain little by way of substantive standards such as general marketing prohibitions (e.g. 'no toxics allowed for commercial purposes') or across-the-board maximum concentration levels.[47] Instead, risk regulation maps out the trajectory and rules that must be observed in order to arrive at individual determinations about the acceptability and the appropriate risk management measures for particular goods, services or projects. The data production and risk assessment provisions in chemicals and GMO legislation are a textbook example of this approach.

In the field of technological risk regulation, proceduralised approaches offer significant advantages over substantive standards. They are more responsive to conditions of uncertainty, enable a higher degree of individualisation and differentiation in decision-making, and they tend to emancipate regulatory addressees to a greater extent than substantive standards.[48] Less felicitously, and equally well demonstrated in the EU regimes governing chemicals and GMOs, proceduralised approaches typically find expression in very long and convoluted prescriptions. The REACH Regulation clocks in at an eye-watering 280 pages in the EU Official Journal. Yet this is only the tip of the iceberg: REACH is essentially a framework regulation:[49] it lays down a skeleton that is further fleshed out in towering stacks of guidance documents. By 2014, over a million words of guidance had been written to support the interpretation and application of REACH-based requirements, and the number is sure to grow.[50] The DRD and GMO Food and Feed Regulation are comparatively slender, but they too are further detailed by extensive and technically complex guidance documents.

The sheer volume and technical complexity of technological risk regulation poses serious legitimacy challenges. It practically means that the law is inaccessible to all but the most tenacious and technically well-versed reader. For example, the volume of the REACH Regulation and guidance documents together is such that even professionals working in the field of chemicals regulation and PhD students dedicating several years to its study would hesitate to declare themselves completely on top of all aspects of REACH. Size erodes opportunities for the public to engage meaningfully with the content of the regulation and to hold public authorities accountable for decisions adopted in implementation of regulatory requirements. Moreover, the real 'bite' of regulatory prescriptions will often only manifest when the latter are further detailed

---

[47] Karl-Heinz Ladeur, 'Zur Prozeduralisierung des Vorsorgebegriffs durch Risikovergleich und Prioritätensetzung' (1994) *Jahrbuch des Umwelt- und Techniksrechts* 297–331.
[48] Heyvaert, 'Governing Climate Change', 820.
[49] Emilia Korkea-aho, 'Laws in Progress? Reconceptualizing Accountability Strategies in the Era of Framework Norms' (2013) 2(2) *Transnational Environmental Law* 363–385.
[50] See Steven Vaughan, *EU Chemicals Regulation: New Governance, Hybridity and REACH* (Edward Elgar, 2015); Stokes and Vaughan, 'Great Expectations', 416–417.

and contextualised through copious amounts of recommendations and guidance documents. Increasingly, widespread reliance on these formally non-binding yet highly authoritative instructions raises urgent questions as to their legal status and challengeability. A smattering of case law from the CJEU reveals a willingness on the part of the Court to rely on 'post-legislative guidance'[51] to fill in and interpret REACH's framework provisions.[52] The case law further suggests that, under some circumstances, REACH guidance documents could be subject to judicial review, but much remains to be clarified on that score. To a degree, post-legislative guidance remains, in the words of Joanne Scott, 'in legal limbo'.[53]

Closely connected to questions of legitimacy are those of effectiveness: do the data production requirements in technological risk regulation actually succeed in generating the information needed to make responsible risk decisions?[54] To formulate a response, the quantity of data supplied is an important first indicator. The 1993 Existing Substances Regulation famously failed to stimulate more than a trickle of new information regarding old chemicals, and this failure was one of the key triggers for the REACH reform process.[55] By comparison, the REACH Regulation is proving far more effective: as of March 2015, 41,223 registration dossiers concerning 8,269 different substances had been submitted to ECHA.[56] Data quality, however, is a concern: Stokes and Vaughan report that 'the data produced to date has also been poor, a fact recognised by both ECHA and the Commission. Put simply, more information is not always better information.'[57] In fact, more information may paradoxically impede better risk management.[58] The authors also observe that, under REACH, a number of Safety Data Sheets have transformed from useable, if incomplete, brochures into labyrinthine compendia.[59] In the field of GMO regulation, the concern has been raised that the documentation submitted by applicants for authorisation is so overwhelming in scale and scope, and so technically specialised, that fully to review, test and evaluate the information exceeds the resources and skills of the

---

[51] Joanne Scott, 'In Legal Limbo: Post-Legislative Guidance as a Challenge for Administrative Law' (2011) 48(2) *Common Market Law Review* 329–355.
[52] See Case C-358/11 *Lapin elinkeino-, liikenne- ja ympäristökeskuksen liikenne ja infrastruktuuri – vastuualue* v. *Lapin luonnonsuojelupiiri ry* ECLI:EU:C:2013:142; and C-558/07, *The Queen, on the application of S.P.C.M. SA, C.H. Erblöh KG, Lake Chemicals and Minerals Ltd and Hercules Inc.* v. *Secretary of State for the Environment, Food and Rural Affairs* ECLI:EU:C:2009:430, as discussed in Korkea-aho, 'Laws in Progress?', 366–372.
[53] Scott, 'In Legal Limbo', 337–343.
[54] Wendy Wagner, 'Using Competition-Based Regulation to Bridge the Toxic Gap' (2008) 83 *Indiana Law Journal* 629–660, at 658.
[55] See European Commission, 'White Paper: Strategy for a Future Chemicals Policy', COM (2001)88 final.
[56] See statistics at: www.echa.europa.eu/web/guest/regulations/reach/registration/registration-statistics;jsessionid=9BE000937A29E6A84A6E7DB8F4FE6478.live1.
[57] Stokes and Vaughan, 'Great Expectations', 427.
[58] Lee, *EU Environmental Law, Governance and Decision-Making*, 210.
[59] Stokes and Vaughan, 'Great Expectations', 427.

regulator.[60] In such circumstances, authorisation processes begin to resemble wars of attrition as the burden of persuasion that applicants formally bear in practice collapses into a burden of production. Such dysfunctions are all the more likely to emerge when regulators operate in areas of scientific uncertainty, as is the case for chemicals and GMO regulation. The challenges of decision-making under conditions of uncertainty are further explored in the next section.

Regulating Uncertainty

Technological risk regulation is heavily data-driven. The lion's share of the information generated through the regulatory process is produced following scientific methodologies. The intimate involvement of the scientific community in risk regulation, and the close popular connotations of 'science' with concepts such as 'knowledge' and 'truth', can easily convey an impression of risk regulation as a factual and rational exercise. People in white coats test and identify the hazardous qualities of man-made materials; risk assessors calculate exactly how dangerous they are; and, armed with the 'facts', regulatory authorities decide whether and how to control their deployment in society. Yet this representation deeply underestimates the degree of uncertainty entrenched in risk-based decision-making processes. First, risks are not facts; they are predictions. Even under optimal circumstances, probabilistic assessments necessarily have a margin of error. Optimal circumstances, furthermore, rarely occur: even under the demanding REACH registration process, the range of risk data created is modest and correspondingly tentative. For example, the maximum test period to determine eco-toxicity under standard REACH testing requirements is 28 days. Considering that latency periods of months, even years, are not at all unusual in ecotoxicology, the risk of oversight is considerable. Moreover, even the most scrupulous scientist conducting the longest possible study will only test for those harmful effects that are on her radar. Adverse consequences that have not been contemplated, or 'unknown unknowns', are beyond the reaches of measurability.[61]

Secondly, risks are not merely an expression of the *likelihood* that harm will occur, but also of the *seriousness* of this harm. Questions of weight are intrinsically evaluative: reasonable people can disagree about how 'bad' a 7 per cent rise in mortality among non-target species is pursuant to the introduction of a new pesticide, especially if this pesticide proves more effective in eradicating target species, is cheaper than alternatives and/or more convenient in use. Our risk preferences are determined by much more than bare probabilities: we tend to

---

[60] Mihail Kritikos, 'Institutions and Science in the Authorization of GMO Releases in the European Union (1990–2007): The False Promise of Proceduralism', PhD thesis, London School of Economics (2007), available at: http://ethos.bl.uk/OrderDetails.do?uin=uk.bl.ethos.498143.

[61] See Elen Stokes' comments with regard to the lack of detection techniques and measurement methods for risks associated with nanotechnology. Stokes, 'Nanotechnology and the Products of Inherited Regulation', 97.

have a higher tolerance for mid- to high-probability, low to moderate impact risks (such as the risk associated with car travel), and a relatively higher dread of low-probability, high-impact risks (say, the risks associated with nuclear technology).[62] Finally, it is important to remember that scientific uncertainty is not a temporary state; a transitional phase to be muddled through until we 'know enough'.[63] In the context of GMO regulation, commentators have observed that the absence of experiential proof of harm does little to dispel uncertainty and concern.[64] Moreover, every further gain in consolidation of scientific convention reveals new unknowns – fact and uncertainty are co-produced in the epistemic process.

The upshot is that decisions adopted within risk regulatory regimes are discretionary. The degree of uncertainty may fluctuate depending on the field and the particulars of each case, but any form of risk decision-making inevitably requires the exercise of judgment.[65] Uncertainty as a regulatory challenge deeply affects the design and functionality of EU chemicals, GMO and nanotechnology regulation. The next paragraphs analyse and critically discuss the EU legal and regulatory provisions that aim to manage uncertainty at various levels of intensity in chemicals, GMO and nanotechnology regulation.

Legal Principles: The Requirement to Pursue a High Level of Environmental Protection (HLP) and the Precautionary Principle

A vital steer for EU risk regulatory authorities flows from the precautionary principle, in combination with the principle that the EU seeks to secure a high level of environmental protection.[66] Both environmental legal principles are enshrined in Article 191 TFEU, and applied across policy fields by virtue of the integration principle. Technological risk regulation, which is most frequently adopted under the internal market provisions of Article 114 TFEU, overtly acknowledges the formative role of both precaution and the HLP in the determination of the goals and ambition of chemicals, GMO and nanotechnology regulation. The very first Article of the REACH Regulation pronounces that its purpose is to 'ensure a high level of protection of human health and the environment' and that its provisions are 'underpinned by the precautionary principle'. Likewise, the DRD's first Article opens with the words 'In accordance with the

---

[62] Baldwin, Cave and Lodge, *Understanding Regulation*, 89–90.
[63] John S. Applegate, 'Bridging the Data Gap: Balancing the Supply and Demand for Chemical Information' (2007) 86(7) *Texas Law Review* 1365–1407.
[64] Drott et al., 'Accountability and Risk Governance', 1123–1124.
[65] ECHA, 'Guidance on Socio-Economic Analysis: Restrictions' (May 2008), available at: https://echa.europa.eu/documents/10162/13641/sea_restrictions_en.pdf; and ECHA, 'Guidance on the Preparation of Socio-Economic Analysis as Part of an Application for Authorisation' (January 2011), available at: http://echa.europa.eu/documents/10162/13637/sea_authorisation_en.pdf.
[66] Delphine Misonne, 'The Importance of Setting a Target: The EU Ambition of a High Level of Protection' (2015) 4(1) *Transnational Environmental Law* 11–36, at 13–17.

precautionary principle'. The precautionary language is less explicit in the FFR, but there is no doubt that, in this context too, the EU understands its mandate to be governed by both precautionary and HLP principles.[67] The very choice of an authorisation regime as the central engine of GMO regulation, which implies that no GMO or GMO product may be released into the European environment or placed upon the EU market without prior approval, regardless of pre-existing indications of potential harm, is widely seen as a precautionary strategy. As to nanotechnology, to the extent that nanoparticles are subject to general chemicals legislation, precautionary and HLP requirements necessarily apply. Moreover, a range of non-binding but authoritative instruments such as the Commission Code of Conduct on responsible research in nanosciences confirm the status of the precautionary principle as a guiding force in nanoscientific R&D.[68]

The impact of the precautionary principle is mostly evident in the design of regulatory procedures and the formulation of general criteria for decision-making. 'No data, no market' proactively engages with uncertainty by expanding the data set on the basis of which ensuing risk decisions can be adopted. Authorisation requirements, which apply to substances of very high concern (SVHCs) under REACH, as well as to GMOs, biocides, pesticides and pharmaceuticals, start from the default that certain goods should not be allowed on the market unless the regulator has been put in a position adequately to assess the health and environmental risks that would accompany such release and to impose conditions or, if appropriate, refuse authorisation. The substitution principle, which applies with regard to substances subject to authorisation under REACH, pesticides, biocides and chemical agents in the workplace, gives a dynamic impetus to risk regulatory decisions by stipulating that dangerous substances or mixtures should be tolerated only until safer alternatives are available, even if the socio-economic benefits of the former continue to outweigh the risks.[69]

Guided by the general language of EU risk regulation, we find ample evidence of precautionary thinking.[70] However, various commentators have questioned whether the precautionary spirit actually trickles down to the all-important level of application. The significance of the 'no data, no market' provision stands or falls with the quality of the information generated under the registration process. As discussed above, the first years of experience with REACH suggest that data quality is problematic. With respect to authorisation, it is important to remember that the existence of procedural hurdles does not

---

[67] Ibid., 11–24. Article 1(a) of the Food and Feed Regulation does explicitly refer to the HLP requirement.
[68] Commission Recommendation on a code of conduct for responsible nanosciences and nanotechnologies research, OJ 2008 L 116/46: http://ec.europa.eu/research/science-society/document_library/pdf_06/nanocode-apr09_en.pdf.
[69] Ragnar Lofstedt, 'The Substitution Principle in Chemical Regulation: A Constructive Critique' (2014) 17(5) *Journal of Risk Research* 543–564.
[70] Whether the lawfulness of requirements such as 'no data, no market', authorisation and substitution are dependent on the precautionary principle, is a different matter. See Heyvaert, 'Guidance without Constraint'.

automatically translate into substantive stringency. Within REACH, the ultimate degree of health and environmental protection that the authorisation regime affords – and hence the extent to which it meets the HLP requirement – will depend on how easily and frequently the Commission is persuaded that the risks of SVHCs are either adequately controlled or outweighed by socio-economic benefits, and that no alternatives are available. It is too early to draw firm conclusions regarding REACH authorisations,[71] but experience in the context of GMO authorisation gives pause. Vesco Paskalev's analysis of the authorisation process for Amflora, a genetically modified high-starch potato, finds no evidence of precautionary thinking. He suggests that, within the context of risk assessment, expert assessors are likely to fall back on the scientific method, which is more concerned with avoiding 'false positives' than 'false negatives'.[72] Unless a link is proven between a chemical agent, a genetically modified organism or a nanoparticle on the one hand, and a health or environmental impact on the other, it is deemed not to exist.[73] Maria Weimer reports a similar dynamic in the Commission's decision-making process concerning 'Herculex', a genetically modified corn variety.[74] The substitution principle, in turn, has proved exceedingly difficult to apply so as genuinely to lower chemical risks. In a careful study of three instances in which the substitution principle was applied, Ragnar Lofstedt concludes that only one case was incontrovertibly successful in reducing risk.[75]

Claims to Legitimacy: Expertise, Transparency and Participation

The heavy dependence of risk regulation on epistemic communities and expert advice is well documented in EU law. In its capacity as technological risk regulator, the European Commission relies on a wide range of expert advice. It obtains advice from its regulatory agencies (ECHA in the case of chemicals and nanoparticles; EFSA for GMOs), from expert advisory committees operating under the delegated or implementing decision-making procedures in Articles 290 and 291 TFEU, or under the earlier comitology procedures and through a range of informal channels. The expectation that environmental decisions will be taken with regard to 'available scientific and technical data' is incorporated in

---

[71] The first authorisations under REACH came through in late 2014.
[72] Paskalev, 'Can Science Tame Politics', 196.
[73] See also Maria Lee, *EU Regulation of GMOs: Law and Decision-Making for a New Technology* (Edward Elgar, 2008), 29.
[74] '[T]he Commission ultimately did not consider that the scientific uncertainty and limitations in the risk assessment of "Herculex" indicated in the EFSA opinions are sufficient to trigger the use of the precautionary principle. The Commission drafted a proposal authorizing maize relying on the EFSA's statement that there is no evidence of the adverse effects of maize 1507 on humans and the environment.' See Maria Weimer and Gaia Pisani, 'The EU Adventures of "Herculex": Report on the EU Authorization of the Genetically Modified Maize 1507' (2014) 5(2) *European Journal of Risk Regulation* 208–212, at 211.
[75] Lofstedt, 'The Substitution Principle in Chemical Regulation', 543–564.

Article 191(3) TFEU, and generations of CJEU jurisprudence have clarified that EU regulatory decisions should only deviate from expert advice in exceptional circumstances.[76]

Deference to expertise, however, can be as controversial as it is legitimacy-enhancing. Scientific uncertainty, and the application of the precautionary principle, do not absolve the regulator from taking into account the 'best available information', but they simultaneously problematise any approach that treats expert opinion as sacrosanct. The legitimacy of technological risk regulation therefore needs to be pursued through a broader arsenal of guarantees.

A key building block in the legitimation of risk regulatory decision-making is procedural fairness, which is primarily realised through transparency and participation requirements. Together, access to data and the ability to respond and engage with the decision-making process can serve to moderate and validate regulatory discretion. Regulatory inclusiveness through transparency and participation performs several functions. It is, in the first place, a mechanism for the regulator to explain its reasoning and, on this basis, foster acceptability of and compliance with regulatory decisions. Conversely, it enables public authorities to obtain better information regarding the concerns and risk preferences of the public in whose name and interest regulatory determinations are ultimately struck. Hence, it is simultaneously a mode of justifying and correcting risk regulation's heavy reliance on expert input and the bias this injects into decision-making.[77]

EU chemicals and GMO legislation duly lays down transparency requirements and creates opportunities for the public to express its opinion on questions of risk governance. In principle, information submitted in the process of REACH registration, evaluation, authorisation and restriction is accessible to the public, and various provisions require the inclusion of non-technical summaries aimed specifically at a readership beyond those professionally active in the chemicals sector.[78] The REACH authorisation and restriction processes provide a timeframe during which the public can review and comment on authorisation applications or draft restriction proposals, as do the GMO authorisation procedures under both the DRD and the FFR.[79] Doubts persist, however, regarding the meaningfulness of public participation in such deeply technical and complex fields as chemicals and GMO regulation.

---

[76] Case C-269/90 *TU München* v. *Hauptzollamt München Mitte* ECLI:EU:C:1991:438; Case T-13/99 *Pfizer Animal Health* v. *Council* ECLI:EU:T:2002:209.

[77] Cf. Maria Paola Ferretti, 'Why Public Participation in Risk Regulation? The Case of Authorizing GMO Products in the European Union' (2007) 16(4) *Science as Culture* 377–395, at 378.

[78] Confidential and commercially sensitive data may be kept away from the public gaze, although REACH does identify a minimum data set regarding which confidentiality exceptions may not be invoked. See Art. 119(2).

[79] Art. 58(4) REACH Regulation; Art. 18(7) GMO Food and Feed Regulation (EC) No 1829/2003, OJ 2003 L 268/1; Art. 9 Deliberate Release Directive (EC) 18/2001, OJ 2001 L 106/1.

A first concern regards the high threshold to public engagement: concerned citizens have limited time and resources to invest in public engagement. The highly specialised nature of information pertaining to technological risk, which easily pervades even 'non-expert summaries' and makes it difficult for the reader to relate technical data to their general concerns regarding public health and the state of the environment, exacerbates this problem. So does a lack of familiarity with the ins and outs of public consultation procedures, particularly when compared to special interest stakeholders who, in the chemicals, GMO and nano sectors, are highly professional and organised.[80] Most importantly, public misgivings regarding technology-dependence and technological innovation are not easily reducible to concerns about their health and environmental impacts. Especially in the context of GMOs and nanotechnology discussions, health and environmental concerns are often connected to broader themes such as the role of large companies in our society, the vulnerability of industrial society's faith in technology and technological innovation to fix social problems and generate welfare, the path dependency and long-term irreversibility of technological choices, the deep anthropocentrism of identifying and promoting 'superior' genetic variants of naturally occurring species, and the ethical consequences of 'playing God' by rearranging genetic code and tweaking molecular structures. Public participation provisions do not formally prohibit consultees from voicing such broader concerns, but, as they do not address any of the concrete grounds on which regulators adopt risk management decisions, it is argued that they float in the regulatory space untethered and do not translate into a discernible impact on decision-making.[81]

Claims to Legitimacy: Updating, Review and Monitoring

Alongside procedural fairness, procedural flexibility can boost the legitimacy of risk regulatory processes and decisions. Procedural flexibility responds to both the incomplete nature of information that is generated and processed through risk regulation and the changing context in which regulation takes place. Flexibility provisions assume various guises in EU technological risk regulation. The DRD, for example, lays down monitoring requirements, updating provisions and modification and review provisions. Consent for the cultivation of GMO crops is conditioned on, *inter alia*, the development of a monitoring plan to identify the effects of GMOs on the environment, which needs to be implemented and reported on throughout the life-cycle of the GMO or GMO product.[82] After the original cultivation consent, the DRD obliges the consent holder to report

---

[80] Maria Lee, 'GMOs in the Internal Market: New Legislation on National Flexibility' (2016) 79(2) *Modern Law Review* 317–340, at 334.

[81] Maria Weimer, 'Legitimacy through Precaution in European Regulation of GMOs' in Christian Joerges and Poul F. Kjaer (eds.), 'Transnational Standards of Social Protection Contrasting European and International Governance', 5 *ARENA Report* No. 5/08, *RECON Report* No. 4 2008, 159–197, at 162.

[82] Art. 5(2)(v), Art. 10, Art. 20 DRD.

any new information that might affect the risks of the GMO(s) to human health or the environment, which may in turn cause the regulatory authority to modify or withdraw consent.[83] The maximum period for the commercialisation of GMO and GMO-containing products, both in food and feed and in other forms (e.g. genetically modified decorative plants) is ten years, subject to renewal.

Flexibility provisions respond to the contingent nature of risk decision-making but, like procedural fairness requirements, they are not a panacea. Updating requirements are much less detailed, organised and supported in the regulatory framework than initial registration, notification or authorisation requirements, which dilutes their effectiveness. Moreover, regulatory and administrative decisions may be open to amendment, but their physical and economic impacts may endure. Once released into the environment, GMO material is difficult to contain, as attested by the acceptance in EU law of a 0.9 per cent contamination tolerance for the coexistence between GMO and non-GMO crops. Similar concerns plague the governance of nanotechnology: we have only a very tentative understanding of the controllability of nano-engineering, but know enough to realise that a simple requirement to report new information under REACH will hardly suffice to manage potential irreversibility challenges. Finally, even for old-fashioned, molecularly unadulterated chemicals, reversibility may prove elusive. Since risk-based decisions take into account more than just intrinsic hazard characteristics and include socio-economic factors, well-established products may prove hard to remove. By the time new health or environmental information becomes available, the chemical in question may have successfully settled into the market place, which strengthens the socio-economic case against their discontinuation.

GMO Regulation: A Fraught State of Coexistence

The internal market agenda is founded on a belief that open, integrated markets are good for the economy and enhance social welfare. The focus on regulatory harmonisation and mutual recognition as two drivers to bring about the qualities of openness and integration, moreover, reveals two underlying assumptions that energise the internal market project. Perhaps less clearly signposted and less frequently discussed than the acceptance of free trade regimes as economically virtuous, these assumptions are pivotal in determining the regulatory choices and the accompanying vulnerabilities that characterise the EU internal market. They are, first, that in the absence of transnational intervention, national regimes will display an inefficient degree of regulatory differentiation. The second assumption is that the differences between regulatory regimes are essentially bridgeable because, even if technicalities differ, Member States have broadly overlapping ideas about the scope and range of actions to be undertaken in pursuit of public interest objectives.

---

[83] Art. 15(4) DRD; Art. 7(5) FFR.

The understanding of regulatory differences as predominantly technical rather than normative finds its clearest expression in the famous *Cassis* formula that any good or product 'lawfully produced and marketed in one of the Member States' in principle meets the trading standards in all Member States.[84] Justifiable restrictions on the basis of mandatory requirements are cast as the exception and must, consequently, be proved by the Member State invoking them. It also resonates in the erstwhile New Approach to Harmonisation, a 1985 Commission initiative that sought to unblock and accelerate the adoption of EU market harmonisation legislation by shifting the Council and European Parliament's focus towards the general objectives of product and services regulation and away from the technical details, which were instead left to be worked out by EU standardisation bodies.[85] In both cases, there was thought to be a higher degree of convergence on values than on mode of implementation.

EU harmonisation legislation is well stocked with problem-solving techniques that help Member States to overcome 'bridgeable' regulatory differentiation; differentiation that is the product of broadly compatible values pursued through divergent technological choices and implementation strategies. Qualified majority voting simultaneously ensures that a lone Member State with divergent values cannot hold the decision-making process hostage and that any regulation adopted will echo the public interest perspectives shared by a large majority of States. Potential disagreements on the detail, in turn, are channelled to decision-making processes that combine a high degree of bureaucratic Member State involvement with a high concentration of residual decision-making power vested in the European Commission. This process creates space for Member States to iron out technical incompatibilities in committees and introduces a range of fall-back procedures that ensure that rare instances of Member State failure to reach a majoritarian decision do not block decision-making.

The fraught history of GMO regulation in the European Union eloquently illustrates the vulnerabilities of the EU internal market project when the assumptions do not hold up. Here, regulatory differentiation is the product of something much more deeply rooted, political and complex than a disagreement over technicalities. Member State views on whether a genetically modified soy bean is a benefit or a threat to the EU market are determined by more than their assessment of the health and environmental risks attached to the commercialisation of GMOs. Concerns about the impact of biotechnology on the organisation of agriculture and its wider ramifications on issues from changing farming practices to employment to national cultural identity, about the concentration of ownership of patented GMO seeds among a small group of supremely wealthy and powerful corporations, about the very long-term, inter-generational risks attached to creating more resilient variants of naturally occurring species, about

---

[84] Case 120/78 *Cassis de Dijon* ECLI:EU:C:1979:42, para. 14.
[85] Jacques Pelkmans, 'The New Approach to Technical Harmonization and Standardization' (1987) 25(3) *Journal of Common Market Studies* 249–269.

man's moral licence to tamper with the building blocks of creation,[86] to name but the most prominent debating points, all feed into national risk perceptions and are inextricably linked to the more mundane questions of marketability that are currently up for discussion within the EU regulatory sphere.

EU approximation instruments are arguably neither designed nor equipped to overcome the deep social, political and religious cleavages that complicate the governance of biotechnology. The gap between an EU regulatory authority operating on the premise that, as long as health and environmental risks are either negligible or adequately controlled, the circulation of GMOs should be facilitated within the EU, and the Hungarian Constitution which explicitly includes being 'GMO-free' as constitutive of the country's identity, is not one that can be overcome through the procedural ins and outs of risk regulation. This goes a long way towards explaining why, in spite of nearly 30 years of experience and several attempts at reform, EU GMO regulation is in a chronic state of dysfunction. Troubles crescendoed in the years between 1998 and 2004, when the EU 'essentially abandoned its regulatory framework' and maintained a de facto moratorium on GMO authorisations,[87] an action that fuelled antagonism between the USA and the EU trading blocks and was ultimately declared an infringement of WTO law.[88]

Yet even after the moratorium was lifted and additional GMO legislation had been put in place to harness the legitimacy of GMO authorisation processes, the introduction of genetically modified organisms into the European environment and on the European market remains fraught, highly controversial and cripplingly slow. A mere handful of food and feed products consisting of or containing GMOs have been accepted onto the EU market. The only GMOs ever to be approved for cultivation are MON810, a Bt expressing maize, and Amflora, the previously mentioned high-starch potato. It took 14 years for the Commission to authorise Amflora for cultivation and sale as animal feed in 2010. Within four years, the authorisation was annulled by the General Court which considered that, because the Commission only consulted the Member State Committees on its initial draft decision regarding Amflora but not on a subsequent amended draft decision taken in the light of new information and a newly released consolidated EFSA opinion, the Commission had failed to meet its procedural obligations under the GMO regulatory framework.[89] For GMO-sceptic Member States and civil society organisations, the General Court ruling was an important, if largely symbolic, victory. After all, BASF had already discontinued EU cultivation and withdrawn Amflora from the market, citing intractable opposition to the technology as the cause.[90]

---

[86] Lynn Frewer et al., 'Societal Aspects of Genetically Modified Foods' (2004) 42 *Food and Chemical Toxicology* 1181–1193.
[87] Lee, *EU Environmental Law, Governance and Decision-Making*, 224.
[88] European Communities – Measures Affecting the Approval and Marketing of Biotech Products, WT/DS291, WT/DS292, WT/DS293.
[89] Case T-240/10 *Hungary* v. *Commission* ECLI:EU:T:2013:645.
[90] Matt McGrath, 'Hot Potatoes! BASF Drops GM Spud Plans in EU', 2 February 2013: www.bbc.com/news/science-environment-21294487; 'EU Court Annuls GM Potato

The following paragraphs aim to shed some light on how the EU confronts the challenge of regulatory coexistence. Here, the term 'coexistence' is borrowed from the GMO field itself, where it is typically used to denote the need to secure that GMO and non-GMO agriculture, and GMO and non-GMO (containing) products remain, to the extent feasible, uncontaminated. The discussion briefly addresses issues attached to this more mainstream version of coexistence, but the dominant inquiry goes beyond agricultural and commercial coexistence. Instead, it poses the question whether and to what extent EU internal market law can accommodate sharply different regulatory traditions, fuelled by different beliefs, different values, different risk perceptions and different socio-economic circumstances. To this end, the paragraphs below offer a brief overview of the EU GMO licensing regimes and pinpoint where in the regulatory process the dysfunction materialises. We then evaluate the various accommodations towards regulatory coexistence and discuss future prospects for further reform.

The Regulatory Framework

The authorisation requirements of the 2011 DRD and the 2003 FFR constitute the central axis of the EU GMO governance regime. The specifics of authorisation differ depending on whether the applicant seeks to cultivate or import products, and on whether the marketed products are either human food or animal feed, or other products (for instance, genetically modified flowers or fabrics made from GMO cotton). Simply put, if the main goal of the application is to secure cultivation, then Member States' regulatory authorities will be more prominently involved in the early stages of authorisation and there will be a stronger focus on environmental risks in the authorisation process. If the emphasis is on sale and consumption, then the European Food Safety Authority (EFSA) plays the key role in the risk assessment process, and health risks will be foremost in consideration.

The key tenets of the authorisation process are listed in the text box below.

> Key features of the GMO authorisation process:
>
> - Data production is applicant-driven.
> - Applicants are required to generate their own risk assessments. The stage of regulatory authority and agency-led risk assessment is practically better understood as one of assessment peer review.
> - A formal separation distinguishes the risk assessment stage under the auspices of EFSA, charged with formulating a recommendation regarding the request for authorisation, and the risk management stage governed by the Commission, which officially adopts the draft decision.

Approval, Dealing Blow to Commission', 13 December 2013: www.euractiv.com/cap/eu-court-annuls-approval-basfs-a-news-532355.

- The Commission proposal is very unlikely to deviate from the EFSA recommendation.
- The regulatory framework incorporates expectations of transparency and creates scope for public consultation.
- The regime explicitly foresees consultation on ethical issues pertaining to the authorisation of GMOs for cultivation or consumption.
- The Commission adopts decisions on authorisation following a comitology procedure.

GMO authorisation embodies the main features of EU technological risk regulation; we discern similar structures, institutional arrangements and legal expectations in the context of, for instance, biocides, pesticides and pharmaceuticals authorisation. Arguably, the GMO regime is more inclusive than the chemicals authorisation framework as it explicitly calls for the consideration of concerns beyond the strictly health, environmental or socio-economic remit. Yet no other risk regulatory framework experiences legitimacy deficits that are as pervasive and persistent as those that beleaguer GMO regulation. Here is the crux: in order to adopt a GMO authorisation, the Commission draft decision must find the support of a qualified majority of Member State committee representatives. If it does not – a scenario that has played out time and again in the GMO authorisation saga – the matter is referred to the Council of the EU which must muster a qualified majority to either reject or adopt the decision. Unsurprisingly, the dividing lines that prevent agreement within the committee also create a deadlock within the Council, and no decision ensues. Consequently, decision-making power reverts back to the Commission, which will as a rule adopt its earlier draft decision.[91] Thus, the regulatory process succeeds in producing an outcome. However, it consistently fails to generate a result that is deemed legitimate and acceptable by at least a qualified majority of Member States, that is sufficiently efficient and reliable to satisfy the private sector and that, in the eyes of a significant proportion of the public, bears the telltale signs of a supranational bureaucracy riding roughshod over local, democratically rooted objections.

Scope for Post-Authorisation Differentiation

Once authorised, a GMO or GMO-containing product can be lawfully cultivated and marketed across the EU.[92] Predictably, this is perceived as deeply problematic in countries such as Hungary and Poland, which persistently object to GMO authorisation. Internal market regulation closes the door to regulatory

---

[91] Paskalev, 'Can Science Tame Politics', 192; Yves Thibergien, 'Competitive Governance and the Quest for Legitimacy in the EU: The Battle over the Regulation of GMOs since the mid-1990s' (2009) 31(3) *European Integration* 389–407, at 394–396.

[92] Art. 22 DRD; Art. 19(5) FFR.

differentiation. However, it does open some windows of opportunity for Member States either to contain the impact of GMO cultivation and use or to carve out a stance that effectively deviates from the EU position. The former goal is pursued through the adoption of 'coexistence measures'. As to opportunities for Member States to deny access to authorised GMOs, three key arrangements merit attention. EU internal market legislation typically includes a safeguard clause that enables Member States to take provisional measures to 'protect one or more of the non-economic needs' referred to in Article 36 TFEU.[93] Secondly, Member States may resort to Articles 114(4) or (5) TFEU in an attempt to maintain or introduce more stringent measures. Last, but by no means least, a revolutionary third avenue towards differentiation has recently been paved through the insertion of a new provision in the DRD. The amendment enables Member States to restrict or ban the cultivation of authorised GMOs on their territory, which effectively allows EU countries to suspend the workings of the internal market in this field. We discuss each in turn.

Coexistence Measures

GMO authorisation creates contamination risks. Once genetically modified seeds are sown, it is extremely difficult to contain them. Bees cross-pollinate indiscriminately; gusts of wind disperse GM and non-GM seeds alike. Unless GM and non-GM products are segregated with the utmost zeal, further opportunities for contamination occur during harvesting, treatment, storage and transport. Moreover, once a GMO product is placed on the market, contamination risks grow exponentially. The average consumer cannot tell a GMO and a non-GMO tomato apart. In sum, at every stage of the production process, contamination threatens product differentiation and consumer choice.

Managing the risks of contamination at the cultivation stage is largely left to the Member States. Article 26(a) DRD allows Member States to take measures to avoid the unintended presence of GMOs in alternative products. This particularly applies to avoiding the presence of GMOs in alternative produce, such as conventional or organic crops. Moreover, in accordance with the newly created entitlement for Member States to prohibit cultivation of authorised GMOs within (parts of) their territory (see below), GMO-cultivating Member States are required to take measures to avoid cross-border contamination into neighbouring States where GMO cultivation is banned.[94]

A number of Member States, such as Austria, Hungary, Poland, Luxembourg and the Slovak Republic, seized upon Article 26(a) to introduce stringent coexistence requirements that effectively limit the prospects for GMO farming in the region, such as a prohibition on GMO farming in designated areas and the

---

[93] Art. 114 (10) TFEU.
[94] Art. 1(1) of Directive (EU) 2015/412 of the European Parliament and of the Council amending Directive 2001/18/EC as regards the possibility for the Member States to restrict or prohibit the cultivation of genetically modified organisms (GMOs) in their territory, OJ 2015 L 68/1.

maintenance of generous buffer zones between traditional and GMO crops.[95] However, there are limits to the Member States' freedom to interpret Article 26(a) 'heroically'. The European Commission Recommendations and Guidelines on Coexistence (2010) prescribe a 0.9 per cent tolerance level for adventitious or technically unavoidable contamination. They furthermore require that more draconian interventions, in particular the designation of GMO-free zones, are treated as measures of last resort. Additionally, coexistence rules should be adopted in a transparent manner, with the involvement of all stakeholders, and in observance of the principle of proportionality. Moreover, even if the Guidelines adopted a highly permissive stance,[96] any Member State regulation must still pass the necessity and proportionality test of Articles 34 and 36 TFEU. In its 2011 *Pioneer* ruling, in which the Pioneer company successfully challenged the legality of Italy's decision to ban temporarily all GMO cultivation under Article 26(a) pending the adoption of detailed coexistence rules, the CJEU clearly signalled that the coexistence provision is not to be used as a carte blanche.[97]

In contrast, the management of contamination risks at the stages of marketing and use is centralised and organised predominantly through the imposition of traceability and labelling requirements.[98] We will not review the traceability and labelling arrangements in detail, but it is worthwhile to note that these measures, too, have come in for a fair share of criticism. Labelling provisions notwithstanding, GMOs can disappear down the food chain. Animal feed containing over 0.9 per cent of GMOs may be accurately labelled (though the information may be lost on the diner). However, the consumer of GMO feed may, at some point in its rather bleakly predictable history, end up on someone else's plate, without being labelled a 'GMO cut'.

Safeguard Clauses

Safeguard clauses usually lie dormant in EU legislation. Once harmonised measures are in place, Member States rarely ring the alarm bell. The derogation or 'opt-up' provisions in Article 114 TFEU generated comparatively more activity throughout the 1990s and early 2000s,[99] but over the past decade, and particularly since the economic recession, Member States have shown themselves wary of

---

[95] Volker Beckmann, Claudio Soregaroli and Justus Wesseler, 'Coexistence Rules and Regulations in the European Union' (2006) 88(5) *American Journal of Agricultural Economics* 1193–1199, at 1196.

[96] Maria Lee argues that the Commission Guidelines are, in fact, highly restrictive of national autonomy. See Maria Lee, 'The Governance of Coexistence between GMOs and other Forms of Agriculture: A Purely Economic Issue?' (2012) 20(2) *Journal of Environmental Law* 193–212 and Lee, *EU Environmental Law, Governance and Decision-Making*, 244–246.

[97] Case C-36/11 *Pioneer Hi Bred Italia* ECLI:EU:C:2012:534.

[98] Regulation (EC) No. 1830/2003 concerning the traceability and labelling of genetically modified organisms and the traceability of food and feed products produced from genetically modified organisms and amending Directive 2001/18/EC, OJ 2003 L 268/24.

[99] Nicholas De Sadeleer, 'Procedures for Derogations from the Principle of Approximation of Laws under Article 95 EC' (2003) 40 *Common Market Law Review* 889–915.

'goldplating' and are less inclined to spend political capital and financial resources campaigning for stricter domestic standards.[100] The exception to these developments is GMO regulation, where calls for post-harmonisation differentiation remain as ardent as ever. The continued opposition of certain Member States to EU-wide authorisations is a testament to the political and moral complexity of transnational GMO governance. Thus, GMO authorisations have become a key testing ground in which to explore the EU approach with regard to both safeguard and 'opt-up' clauses. Arguably, they have also become a testing ground for something more fundamental: they have opened up a space in which Member States challenge the boundaries of the trade liberalisation ethos and of the approach that, more than any others, embodies this ethos: the adoption of EU-wide product approvals under the auspices of the European Commission.

Both the DRD and the FFR contain a safeguard clause. Article 23(1) of the DRD allows Member States to take unilateral measures under the following circumstances:

> **Article 23(1) DRD**
>
> Where a Member State, as a result of new or additional information made available since the date of the consent and affecting the environmental risk assessment or reassessment of existing information on the basis of new or additional scientific knowledge, has detailed grounds for considering that a GMO as or in a product which has been properly notified and has received written consent under this Directive constitutes a risk to human health or the environment, that Member State may provisionally restrict and/or prohibit the use and/or sale of that GMO as or in a product on its territory.

The conditions are narrowly circumscribed. Member States can only resort to Article 23(1) if something has changed since the authorisation. The terms 'assessment or reassessment' and 'new or additional scientific knowledge' suggest a degree of flexibility as to the range of developments to which Member States may legitimately respond. For example, a new study that calls into question the robustness of the safety factors deployed in earlier GMO risk assessments might potentially meet the DRD's understanding of 'new or additional information', even if such a study does not, itself, provide new scientific information about formerly unknown health or environmental risks posed by the GMO in question.[101] By the same token, however, a reiteration of data supplied and concerns raised in the course of authorisation clearly does not suffice, regardless of how such information was treated during the decision-making process.

---

[100] J. H. Jans, L. Squintani, A. Aragão, R. Macrory and B. W. Wegener, '"Gold Plating" of European Environmental Measures?' (2009) 6(4) *Journal for European Environmental and Planning Law* 417–435.

[101] The safety factor is the margin of error deployed in risk assessment.

Secondly, the public interest justifications recognised in Article 23(1) DRD are distinctly fewer than 'one or more of the non-economic needs' of Article 36 TFEU: Member States may only take provisional measures to safeguard human health or the environment. The DRD safeguard clause pointedly does not engage with the broader objectives of public policy, public morality and public security protection, or the safeguarding of national treasures possessing artistic, historic or archaeological value. Reference to these grounds could potentially have opened up some scope for Member States to introduce information regarding the socio-economic, cultural, ethical and religious ramifications of commercialising GMOs. Instead, the wording of Article 23(1) clearly signals that the safeguard clause is conceived as a specific, temporary measure to be invoked in equally specific circumstances, not an opportunity for GMO-sceptic Member States to reopen a broader debate.

If the DRD safeguard clause is tightly drawn, its counterpart in the FFR is more restrictive still. Article 34 FFR provides the following regarding 'emergency measures':

> Where it is evident that products authorised by or in accordance with this Regulation are likely to constitute a serious risk to human health, animal health or the environment, or where, in the light of an opinion of the [EFSA] issued under Article 10 or Article 22, the need to suspend or modify an authorisation arises, measures shall be taken under the procedures provided for in Articles 53 and 54 of Regulation (EC) No. 178/2002.

Article 34 conditions action on evidence of *serious* risk to health or the environment; a higher threshold than in Article 23(1) DRD. Moreover, the procedures in Regulation 178/2002, the General Food Law,[102] only allow Member States to act unilaterally if and for as long as the Commission has not taken an EU-wide emergency measure. Such measure, again, needs to pass through a comitology procedure, which results in a re-enactment of the entrenchments, the unbridgeable differences and, consequently, the stalemate that bedevilled the authorisation procedure in the first place. In a display of regulatory déjà vu, the decision ultimately falls back to the Commission.

The upshot is that safeguard clauses are not suited to secure regulatory coexistence. Quite to the contrary, as the Court underlined in *Monsanto*, their purpose is to avoid long-term fragmentation.[103] National measures taken in accordance

---

[102] Regulation (EC) No. 178/2002 laying down the general principles and requirements of food law, establishing the European Food Safety Authority and laying down procedures in matters of food safety 2002 OJ L 31/1.

[103] Case C-236/01 *Monsanto Agricoltura Italia SpA* v. *Prezidenza del Consiglio dei Ministri* ECLI:EU:C:2003:431. In addition to underlining the essentially EU-wide ambit of the safeguard clause, the ECJ's ruling in *Monsanto* equally affirms that, although an expression of the precautionary principle, the safeguard clause can only be invoked on firmer evidence than a 'purely hypothetical risk'. Precisely how much data is required is difficult to gauge. See

with either Article 23(1) DRD or Article 34 FFR are temporary stopgaps to be replaced by a permanent and universally applicable EU decision.

Derogation or 'Opt-Ups' under Article 114(4)–(6) TFEU

At first sight, the opt-up provisions of Article 114(4) and (6) TFEU are more promising avenues towards regulatory coexistence than safeguard clauses because the former do envisage the possibility of a Member State deviating from the *acquis communautaire* on a permanent basis. If derogation is granted, the Commission may investigate the appropriateness of an EU-wide adaptation, but this does not jeopardise the status of the derogation itself.

However, the derogation procedure, too, imposes a range of evidentiary hurdles and constraints. In addition to the earlier discussed expectation that a Member State desirous to set aside a GMO authorisation furnish new scientific evidence in support of its request, and the strictness with which the ECJ has interpreted the concept of 'newness' in this context,[104] Article 114(5) limits the grounds for derogation to the protection of the environment or the working environment. The latter can be read to include concerns regarding the impact of GMO cultivation on traditional farming,[105] but many of the ethical, religious and socio-economic considerations that inform a Member State's position vis-à-vis GMOs are uncompromisingly outside the purview of the derogation clause. Moreover, any problem must be 'specific' to the Member State. It is difficult to determine clearly where the point of specificity lies beyond the rather obvious guideline that it is located somewhere between 'common to all' and 'unique to one', but the leading Court ruling on this issue indicates that, as with the requirement that new scientific information be produced, the evidentiary hurdles may be difficult to overcome.[106]

Article 26(b) DRD: Farewell Internal Market?

None of the pathways examined thus far offers a reliable, sustainable trajectory towards regulatory coexistence. The problem for GMO-sceptic Member States is obvious. They face the prospect of either mounting protracted and expensive legal battles with the odds of a favourable judgment stacked against them, or falling short of their public and, in some cases, constitutional mandate to resist the influx of genetically modified farming and products. However, and importantly, the absence of a space to address and, ideally, overcome the incommensurability between the risks that 'count' within the context of internal market legislation and the much more complex, historically, economically and culturally informed

---

Heyvaert, 'Facing the Consequences of the Precautionary Principle in European Community Law', 197–198.

[104] See pp. 451–452, above.

[105] See Commission Decision 2003/653 relating to national provisions on banning the use of genetically modified organisms in the region of Upper Austria notified by the Republic of Austria pursuant to Article 95(5) of the EC Treaty, OJ 2003 L 230/34.

[106] See *Austria* v. *Commission*, n. 10, above; Ludwig Krämer, 'Regional Ban of GMO – Admissibility under Art. 95(5) EC?' (2008) 5(1) *Journal for European Environmental and Planning Law* 117–118.

perspectives that crystallise into a stance of GMO opposition, is equally problematic for the European Union itself. In an environment of unresolved antagonism, any application for GMO authorisation is bound to turn into a war of attrition. The European Commission repeatedly confronts the unenviable choice of being perceived either to act in blunt disregard of national sensibilities or of caving in to Member State pressure. Neither is an image that the Commission is keen to cultivate.

In January 2015, the European Parliament and Council formally adopted an amendment to the Deliberate Release Directive. Directive 2015/412,[107] which entered into effect in April 2015, inserts a new provision in the DRD that enables Member States to ban the cultivation of EU authorised GMOs. It would be difficult to overestimate the significance of this development: for the first time in the history of the internal market, EU institutions have taken an overt step back from a fully harmonised sector and devolved a sizeable proportion of decision-making power back to the Member States. The 2015 Directive embodies an unprecedented acknowledgement that, the virtues of open markets notwithstanding, economies are geographically, historically and culturally embedded, and that economic and industrial choices are not – and, more to the point, should not be – dictated by GDP-maximising strategies.

The new Article 26(b) provides that, upon GMO authorisation or authorisation renewal, Member States may demand that the geographical scope of the authorisation be adjusted to exclude their territory or a part thereof. The choice of language is compelling: the term 'demand' places Member States firmly in the driving seat. The demand is communicated to the applicant, who may decide to adjust the scope of her application. In this manner, Article 26(b) creates scope for a direct settlement between applicant and Member State that bypasses Commission scrutiny. Although a concession, the prospect of a swift resolution may incentivise the applicant to 'cut her losses' and adjust the scope of the application.

If the applicant does not adjust the scope of the application, or if a Member State wishes to restrict or ban the cultivation of a GMO outside the context of a pending authorisation or renewal, it may adopt measures provided that they are 'in conformity with Union law, reasoned, proportional and non-discriminatory and, in addition, are based on compelling grounds'.[108] Intriguingly, whereas the 2010 Commission proposal excluded grounds 'related to the assessment of the adverse effect on health and environment', Article 26(b)(3) offers a non-exhaustive list of justifications, including land use, socio-economic impacts, agricultural policy, *and* environmental policy. However, the provision continues that adopted measures should in no case conflict with the health and environmental risk assessments carried out in pursuance of the DRD and FFR. Taken

---

[107] Directive (EU) 2015/412 amending Directive 2001/18/EC as regards the possibility for the Member States to restrict or prohibit the cultivation of genetically modified organisms (GMOs) in their territory, OJ 2015 L 68/1.

[108] Art. 26(b)(3) DRD.

together, the provisions may be indicative of an awareness that environmental policy is broader than the sum of case-by-case environmental risk management. Sustainable environmental policies, particularly when considered in combination with land use and socio-economic or other public policy factors, may point a Member State in the direction of a restriction even if an individual risk assessment does not.[109]

By October 2015, no fewer than fifteen Member States had notified the Commission of their intention to restrict or ban GMO cultivation in their territory.[110] Overwhelmingly, biotech companies chose to let their 30-day response period lapse without objection, which means the bans will be approved.[111] These developments mark the start of a new era of regulatory coexistence in the EU. However, it remains to be seen whether regulatory reform on the issue of GMO cultivation is indicative of a larger trend, or an aberration. A Commission proposal to introduce a similar arrangement with regard to the import and trade of GMO and GMO-containing products,[112] was roundly rejected by the European Parliament and the Council alike. Arguably, an importation or trade ban would undermine the principles underlying the internal market more aggressively than does a cultivation ban. Not only does a product ban call into question the soundness of harmonisation, it also undermines one of the key tropes of EU internal market policy: that of the informed and rational consumer. In a venerable line of case law, the Court has persistently favoured consumer emancipation through labelling over more paternalistic approaches such as 'recipe laws' and product bans.[113] Allowing Member States to ban traceable and labelled GMO products would require a drastic reinterpretation of what constitutes proportionate regulation in the pursuit of mandatory requirements.

The coming years are likely to be crucial for the fate of GMOs in Europe. Since Article 26(b) was conceived as, essentially, a tactical retreat, it is to be expected that efforts to secure cultivation authorisations for the 'coalition of the willing' Member States will intensify. So will controversies regarding the import and use of GM products. In the light of the continued divisions between the EU's political institutions on GMO questions, the CJEU role in settling these controversies is of key importance. A long line of cases attests to the Court's willingness to take seriously health and environmental protection in the face of free movement considerations.[114] On the other hand, an equally formidable body of judgments confirms its reputation as a staunch defender of EU authority against

---

[109] Heyvaert, 'Governing Climate Change', 817
[110] Simon Roach, 'Germany among 15 States Planning GMO Bans', *ENDS Europe*, 1 October 2015.
[111] Simon Roach, 'GM Cultivation Bans Set to be Approved', *ENDS Europe*, 5 November 2015.
[112] 'Brussels Mulls Nationalising GM Import Authorisations', *ENDS Europe*, 8 April 2015.
[113] Elen Stokes, 'You are What You Eat: Market Citizens and the Right to Know about Nano Foods' (2011) 2(2) *Journal of Human Rights and the Environment* 178–200, at 192.
[114] See cases discussed in Chapter 3, at 118–119.

Member State calls for exception.[115] In deciding whether a national GMO cultivation ban is adequately reasoned, proportionate and based on a compelling ground, the CJEU might well set high thresholds regarding the amount and quality of evidence that Member States must supply in support of the measure.[116] In *Commission v. Poland*, the latter sought to defend its breach of EU GMO legislation on the argument that, as a Catholic country, observance of GMO legislation would constitute a breach of public morality. The CJEU ducked the question of whether the argument was sound in principle, but ruled that

> [A]s regards, more specifically, the justification based on the protection of public morality [...] the relevant evidentiary burden is not discharged by statements as general as those put forward by that Member State during the pre-litigation procedure and consisting in references to fears regarding the environment and public health and to the strong opposition to GMOs manifested by the Polish people, or even to the fact that the administrative regional assemblies adopted resolutions declaring that the administrative regions are to be kept free of genetically modified cultures and GMOs.[117]

Precisely what does amount to sufficient evidence, however, remains for the time being shrouded in uncertainty.

Nanotechnology: New Rules for New Tools?

Nanotechnology enables the manipulation of matter at the molecular level.[118] The effectuated changes cause nanoparticles to display sometimes amplified, sometimes radically different physico-chemical properties from their bulk counterparts. Gold is a famously inert material, but nanogold is an effective conductor and catalyst for a range of chemical reactions. Nanosilver has powerful antimicrobial properties; nano carbon tubes are exponentially stronger than regular carbon; aluminium at the nano-scale becomes explosive. The potential for application is seemingly boundless: from the production of deodorising socks and lighter bicycle frames to enhancements in solar energy capture and chemotherapy treatments, nanotechnology has the potential dramatically to alter our environment and our conduct in every aspect of life.

If the promise of nanotechnology defies the imagination, then so do the risks. Concerns about the application of nanotechnology include but are by no means limited to those associated with traditional chemistry, such as the potential of

---

[115] See e.g. Case C-320/03 *Commission v. Austria* [2005] ECR I-9871; Case C-28/09 *Commission v. Austria* ECLI:EU:C:2011:854.
[116] Niamh Nic Shuibhne and Marsela Maci, 'Proving Public Interest: The Growing Impact of Evidence in Free Movement Case Law' (2013) 50(4) *Common Market Law Review* 965–1005, at 980–991.
[117] Case C-165/08 *Commission v. Poland* ECLI:EU:C:2009:473, at 54.
[118] R. Falkner and N. Jaspers, 'Regulating Nanotechnologies: Risk, Uncertainty and the Global Governance Gap' (2012) 12(1) *Global Environmental Politics* 30–55.

nanoparticles for toxicity, carcinogenicity, persistence and bioaccumulation. Moreover, nanotechnological applications could impact on human health and the environment in ways that are currently beyond the scope of contemplation. The example of endocrine disruption offers an instructive comparator: until the accidental discovery in 1978 of 'intersex' fish in the River Thames, the possibility that chemicals could trigger hormonal changes in recipient organisms was simply not on the map.[119] Moreover, as with biotechnology, concerns are not reducible to the direct input–output effects of individual applications. The stability of nanotechnological structures, and their potential for both self-replication and collapse, raises questions about their innate controllability and their systemic resilience. At worst, they summon nightmare scenarios of a post-industrial world dissolving into 'grey goo'.[120] At an ontological level, the 'transformative power of science', which involves 'the manipulation of both biological and non-biological materials and, thus, blur(s) the borders not only of scientific disciplines but also of what might constitute life',[121] challenges long-held assumptions about the distinction between the 'natural' and the 'man-made' and about the normative relevance of this divide.

For the EU, the governance of nanotechnology presents a formidable regulatory challenge. There are a number of compelling reasons why the EU may want to push ahead with regulating nanotechnology sooner rather than later. First, many of the environmental risks attached to the development and use of nanotechnology are transboundary. The EU therefore has a clear mandate to intervene. The uncertainty surrounding the range and scale of risks that are being created clamours for the development of a precautionary approach, in accordance with the general principles of EU law. Secondly, the EU may wish to pre-empt regulatory action at the national level to avoid the proliferation of incompatible standards and approaches that will later require streamlining through laborious harmonisation processes. Furthermore, the establishment of a structured and broadly applicable regulatory regime may foster nanotechnology in the EU because it stabilises expectations and enables entrepreneurs to develop strategies to identify and manage the risks attached to research, development and application of nanotechnological processes. As nanotechnology is generally considered a key growth sector of the European economy, the latter are crucial considerations.

On the other hand, the economic aspirations for nanotechnology in Europe are as frequently invoked by opponents of further regulation. There is a strong

---

[119] Charles R. Tyler and Susan Jobling, 'Roach, Sex, and Gender-Bending Chemicals: The Feminization of Wild Fish in English Rivers' (2008) 58(11) *Bioscience* 1051–1059; John P. Sumpter and Andrew C. Johnson, '10th Anniversary Perspective; Reflections on Endocrine Disruption in the Aquatic Environment: From Known Knowns to Unknown Unknowns (and Many Things in Between)' (2008) 10(12) *Journal of Environmental Monitoring* 1476–1485.

[120] Maria Lee, 'Risk and Beyond: EU Regulation of Nanotechnology' (2010) 32 *European Law Review* 799–821.

[121] Robert G. Lee, 'Look at Mother Nature on the Run in the 21st Century: Responsibility, Research, and Innovation' (2012) 1(1) *Transnational Environmental Law* 105–117, at 107.

concern that strict regulation will stifle innovation and reduce the EU's opportunities to compete against leaders in the field such as the USA and Japan.[122] Moreover, some might question whether new tools necessarily call for new rules. Nanotechnology is not maturing in a regulatory vacuum. Nanoparticles are, after all, chemicals, and are consequently subject to EU chemicals regulation. Many of the products in which nanotechnology finds application, such as cosmetics and medical devices, are already governed by product-specific EU regimes. Here it should also be remembered that the nature and variety of nanotechnological risks depend overwhelmingly on the context in which they are applied. The risks attached to using nano carbon in the production of golf clubs are leagues apart from those that materialise when nanotechnologically developed foams are used to absorb oil slicks in the wake of an environmental disaster. Hence, the feasibility of developing a singular regime or even a set of regimes to govern nanotechnological risk may be limited. Finally, as with biotechnology, public concerns regarding the proliferation of nanotechnology are not easily or fully captured under the heading of health or environmental risks. Nanoparticles may not be as emotive a matter as food, but their use nonetheless raises fundamental questions that regulatory regimes are not equipped to process. The EU's traumatic GMO history may serve as a cautionary tale for advocates of early and resolute EU intervention.

Thus far, the EU has resolved its regulatory dilemma by adopting a very gradual approach to nanotechnology regulation. Its initial stance was that REACH was the core regime for nano as well as bulk particles.[123] The combination of REACH with other measures, such as worker protection, environmental protection and product safety legislation, was, in principle, deemed sufficiently extensive and flexible to capture the particulars of nano.[124] Beyond regulation, the emphasis was on the development of supporting guidelines and recommendations, such as the 2008 Code of Conduct for Responsible Nanosciences and Nanotechnologies Research.[125]

In recent times, however, the adequacy of the existing regulatory network to respond to the challenges of nanotechnology is increasingly called into question. Supported by a number of NGOs and buoyed by examples of regulatory reform outside the EU region,[126] the European Parliament has repeatedly called for

---

[122] See information at: www.statnano.com/index.php?ctrl=news&action=news_view&id=41742&lang=2.
[123] Falkner and Jaspers, 'Regulating Nanotechnologies', 41.
[124] Commission Communication on the regulatory aspects of nanomaterials COM(2008)366, 17 June 2008; Elen Stokes and Diana Bowman, 'Looking Back to the Future of Regulating New Technologies: The Cases of Nanotechnology and Synthetic Biology' (2012) 2 *European Journal of Risk Regulation* 235–241, at 236.
[125] Commission Recommendation on a Code of Conduct for Responsible Nanosciences and Nanotechnologies Research and Council Conclusions for Responsible Nanosciences and Nanotechnologies Research (Luxembourg, 2009), at: http://ec.europa.eu/research/science-society/document_library/pdf_06/nanocode-apr09_en.pdf.
[126] Stokes and Bowman, 'Looking Back to the Future', 237; 'Greens, Consumer Groups Rap Commission for Nanomaterials Report', *Euractiv*, 4 October 2012.

further regulatory action on nanomaterials.[127] Even though a second regulatory review arrived at broadly similar conclusions regarding the adequacy of the existing regulatory network as its 2008 predecessor,[128] the Commission may not be able to stave off more through reform initiatives for much longer. Recent examinations of registrations under the REACH Regulation indicate that, theoretical compatibility notwithstanding, REACH may prove a very poor vehicle to address the health and environmental risks of nanomaterials, let alone the more complex social, economic, cultural and systemic issues that surround their proliferation. Azoulay and Buonsante report that, between 2008 and 2012, only one nanomaterial has been registered. For 12 additional substances, some information on the substance in nanoform was included in the dossier on the bulk chemical.[129] At the same time, the Project for Emerging nanotechnologies reports that 47 different nanomaterials (including gold, silver, titanium dioxide, cobalt, silicon) are being used in up to 1,824 consumer products,[130] from pregnancy tests to microchips.

Possibly, the risk-based approach adopted in the REACH Regulation may not be suited to the particular nature of nanotechnological risks. REACH deploys tonnage thresholds to determine registration requirements: if a chemical is produced in a quantity of less than one tonne per manufacturer and per year, it is exempt from registration. The tonnage threshold functions, essentially, as a proxy for exposure: if not much of the chemical is around, then the potential magnitude of harm is limited. Because of their generally much greater reactivity, however, the correlation between volume and potential magnitude of harm is less reliable for nanomaterials. This problem of 'fit' is a symptom of a more pervasive challenge that regulatory regimes increasingly confront as they mature: the challenge of path-dependency. Once enshrined, regulatory choices are difficult to dislodge, even if a new constellation of opportunities, problems and expectations could be better addressed through an alternative approach.

Recent developments in nanotechnology governance indeed raise the question whether old solutions are fit for new circumstances. A quick look at the first areas where nano-specific regulatory reform has been undertaken underscores the point. In response to a growing demand for EU regulation to enhance its responsiveness to nanotechnology, new 'nano' labelling requirements have

---

[127] European Parliament resolution of 24 April 2009 on regulatory aspects of nanomaterials (2008/2208(INI)); MEPs' letter to the Environment Commissioner urging a second regulatory review of nanomaterials, 6 July 2012, available at: www.endseurope.com/docs/120926a.pdf.

[128] Commission Communication on the second regulatory review on nanomaterials COM (2012)72, 3 October 2012.

[129] David Azoulay and Vito Buonsante, 'Regulation of Nanomaterials in the EU: Proposed Measures to Fill in the Gap' (2014) 2 *European Journal of Risk Regulation* 228–235, at 231.

[130] The reliability of the data is variable because, with exceptions (see below), manufacturers are not obliged to report on the presence of nanomaterials. Conversely, some manufacturers might boldly claim the use of nanotechnology to give their product a competitive edge. See www.nanotechproject.org/.

recently been incorporated in EU cosmetics and food law.[131] The EU's reliance on information disclosure as a key component of health, safety and consumer protection strategies is well established. Moreover, the CJEU has long favoured labelling as a proportionate response to mandatory requirements and the indicated first line of defence in consumer protection.[132] It is therefore not surprising that the first 'nano-regulation' actions focus on labelling. It is, however, questionable how informative the label 'nano' is. In contrast to chemical safety indications, which convey particular physical characteristics such as flammability or skin irritation, the word 'nano' does not clarify in the least whether the product in question poses particular risks, or what they are. Neither does it conjure up a set of fairly well understood connotations about how the product was manufactured and traded, as, for example, do 'fair trade' and 'organic' labels. As nanotechnology becomes an ever more important component of contemporary production as well as service delivery, the EU will need to make important choices about not only whether, but also *how*, it decides to regulate.

Conclusion

An overview of key issues in EU chemicals, GMO and nanotechnology law imparts important lessons not only about the legal treatment of environmental risks, but also about the nature of technological risk regulation as conceived and implemented within the EU.

It underlines the crucial role that risk regulation attributes to information as a fulcrum for health and environmental decision-making. In risk regulatory regimes, the ability to generate information becomes an important, arguably even the dominant, indicator of regulatory effectiveness. However, experience across the chemicals, GMO and nanotechnology spectrum also shows that introducing the right combination of regulatory requirements and incentives to stimulate copious data production is only part of the challenge of designing an information-driven risk regulation regime. The regulator also must address difficult questions of what 'counts' as information for regulatory purposes, how to guarantee quality in information production, and how to identify and correct biases in regulatory processes that favour particular categories of information over others. Moreover, the GMO saga suggests that, attempts at inclusiveness notwithstanding, there may be a limit to the extent to which information-driven regimes can generate acceptable outcomes in areas of high controversy. The prospect of a persistent gap between the rationale of risk regulation and the legitimacy of regulatory outcomes could, ultimately, force the EU to re-examine some of the fundamental assumptions upon which its regulatory edifice is built.

One vulnerable assumption may well be the body of preconceptions regarding the 'market' in EU risk regulation. The discussions in this chapter serve to

---

[131] Stokes and Bowman, 'Looking Back to the Future', 235.
[132] See e.g. Case C-120/78 *Rewe-Zentral AG* v. *Bundesmonopolverwaltung für Branntwein* (*Cassis de Dijon*) [1979] ECR-659; Case C-448/98 *Guimont* [2000] ECR I-10663.

illustrate the complexity of the relation between the market and regulation. In the first instance, the much-vaunted dual-purpose nature of internal market regulation may be a more elusive goal than countless preambles in harmonisation regulations and directives make it out to be. Moreover, the image of the EU market that appears through the cracks of controversy hatched in the canvas of GMO regulation is fascinating. The EU market is not a blank concept; it has texture and identity. The picture of the EU market that emerges from the rationale of EU technological risk regulation is of a space united by broadly compatible public interest aspirations and values but divided by technical choices. It is a space populated by informed consumers who are able to communicate their preferences. It is possible to characterise a number of the regulatory failures experienced in the context of chemicals and, particularly, GMO and nanotechnology regulation as the result of a disparity between the idea of the market and the political, socio-economic and cultural reality in which enterprise is conducted. The latest developments in GMO regulation suggest that, after decades of attempting to shoehorn reality into the ideal, EU law may be taking its first, tentative steps towards a reconceptualisation of the concept of the internal market.

14

Waste

EU Waste Policy

EU waste policy occupies an important place within the Union's environmental portfolio. This may be explained by the continuous rise of waste, which amounts, on average, to the disposal of half a tonne of household rubbish every year, per individual.[1] According to the European Environment Agency, 'the largest waste streams in Europe originate from construction and demolition, mining and quarrying, along with manufacturing activities'.[2] Though landfill used to be a traditional method of waste disposal, this is not sustainable in the long term as the primary source of waste disposal. Thus, the EU is continuously improving its waste management approach, which is now embodied in the waste hierarchy, with waste prevention as the preferred option. However, it is not only waste management that is central to the EU waste policy. Even more important is the fact that waste, due to its physical characteristics or method of disposal, represents a major source of pollution. As a result of economic and technological development we are facing different types of waste which require prevention to avoid adverse environmental or human health impacts. Yet, waste should not only be associated with environmental pollution but should be recognised as a valuable resource. The EU recognises its economic potential that may lead to wider economic and social benefits. One illustrative example is recycling as one waste management option which may boost employment, generate economic growth and foster innovation and a knowledge-based economy.

Waste policy has a long lineage in the EU, starting from the Commission's 1972 Communication on the EC Programme on Environment, where the focus was on reduction of waste generation and recycling.[3] Soon after, the Directive on waste oils and the Directive on waste were adopted in 1975, which paved the way for considerable legislative activism in this policy area.[4] The Directive on waste provided for the first time an appropriate legal framework for implementing EC waste policy. Although the essential objective of waste disposal was the protection of human health and the environment against any harmful effects, the preamble of the directive seemed to focus more on the need to regulate waste to avoid any distortion of competition in the common market. Still, the Directive set out

---

[1] Being Wise with Waste: The EU's Approach to Waste Management, European Commission (2010): http://ec.europa.eu/environment/waste/pdf/WASTE%20BROCHURE.pdf.
[2] See www.eea.europa.eu/themes/waste/intro.   [3] OJ 1972 C 52/12.
[4] The list of early legal acts adopted in the1970s, 1980s and 1990s is available in McCormick, *Environmental Policy in the European Union*, 172.

a definition of waste and introduced the waste hierarchy and polluter pays principles.[5]

Waste management was recognised as a priority area in all EU Environmental Action Programmes (EAPs). As was expected, the First EAP was less concerned with the prevention of waste generation but focused more on a remedial approach to problems of waste disposal.[6] The Second and Third EAPs emphasised the objective of the three-step waste hierarchy in the context of protection and management of natural resources.[7] In 1989, the Commission adopted the First Community Strategy on Waste Management which provided a comprehensive and strategic approach to the implementation of EC waste policy.[8] The Strategy sets out five actions which build upon the concept of waste hierarchy comprising prevention of waste generation and promotion of recycling and reuse.[9]

The same approach was endorsed in the Sixth EAP, which also established waste prevention and management as one of its key environmental priorities. This EAP also encouraged the development of thematic strategies[10] which resulted in the development of the Thematic Strategy on the Prevention and Recycling of Waste.[11] The Thematic Strategy emphasises the waste hierarchy as the centre of waste policy and addresses the issue of waste both as a valuable resource and as a source of pollution. In terms of opportunities that waste offers, the Strategy clearly indicates the connection between the waste policy and economic growth as the waste management and recycling industry offer great employment opportunities. As a way of main and first actions for improving the situation in the waste sector, the Strategy recommends the simplification of the waste legislation, in particular the Waste Framework Directive, which would entail a clarification of the definition of waste and the definition of recovery, disposal activities and recycling.[12] As a response, a revised Waste Framework Directive[13] (WFD) was adopted in 2008 introducing several new waste-related concepts, and tried to clarify the existing concepts.

An important turning point for further developments in the waste sector was the adoption of the Seventh EAP which pledges to 'turn the Union into a resource-efficient, green and competitive low-carbon economy'.[14] In the light of the financial crisis and slow economic growth, the EAP emphasises the waste sector as having great potential for boosting the EU economy and creating

---

[5] See, further, Chapter 3.   [6] OJ 1973 C 112/I.
[7] OJ 1977 C 139/I and OJ 1983 C 046/1.   [8] OJ 1973 C 112/I.   [9] SEC(89)934.
[10] Art. 4 of the Sixth EAP.
[11] Commission Communication to the Council, the European Parliament, the European Economic and Social Committee and the Committee of the Regions, 'Taking Sustainable Use of Resources Forward: A Thematic Strategy on the Prevention and Recycling of Waste', COM/2005/0666, final.
[12] COM/2005/0666, final.
[13] Directive 2008/98/EC of the European Parliament and of the Council of 19 November 2008 on waste and repealing certain Directives. Text with EEA relevance, OJ 2008 L 312/3.
[14] OJ 2013 L 354.

new jobs. One of the objectives of this new EAP is to encourage the use of market-based instruments that privilege prevention, recycling and reuse.[15]

EU waste law at the moment is one of the most extensively and comprehensively developed parts of the environmental *acquis* that attempts to cover all activities that may generate waste, as the text box below illustrates. It tends to be highly technical and requires Member States to invest in developing waste management infrastructure and waste treatment technologies. It also imposes an obligation to develop administrative capacities at all levels which will support the running of various waste treatment operations.

EU Waste Law

General Framework

- Directive 2008/98/EC of the European Parliament and of the Council on waste.
- Council Directive 1999/31/EC on the landfill of waste.
- Regulation (EC) No. 2150/2002 of the European Parliament and of the Council on waste statistics.
- Regulation (EC) No. 1013/2006 of the European Parliament and of the Council on shipments of waste.

Hazardous Waste

- Council Decision 93/98/EEC on the conclusion, on behalf of the Community, of the Convention on the control of transboundary movements of hazardous wastes and their disposal (Basel Convention).
- Council Decision 97/640/EC on the approval, on behalf of the Community, of the amendment to the Convention on the control of transboundary movements of hazardous wastes and their disposal (Basel Convention), as laid down in Decision III/1 of the Conference of the Parties.

Waste from Consumer Goods

- Council Directive 96/59/EC on the disposal of polychlorinated biphenyls and polychlorinated terphenyls.
- European Parliament and Council Directive 94/62/EC on packaging and packaging waste.
- Directive 2000/53/EC of the European Parliament and of the Council on end-of-life vehicles.
- Directive 2005/64/EC European Parliament and Council Directive on the type-approval of motor vehicles with regard to their reusability, recyclability and recoverability.

---

[15] *Ibid.*

- Directive 2006/66/EC of the European Parliament and of the Council on batteries and accumulators and waste batteries and accumulators.
- Directive 2011/65/EU of the European Parliament and of the Council on the restriction of the use of certain hazardous substances in electrical and electronic equipment.
- Directive 2012/19/EU of the European Parliament and of the Council on waste electrical and electronic equipment.
- Directive (EU) 2015/720 of the European Parliament and of the Council amending Directive 94/62/EC as regards reducing the consumption of lightweight plastic carrier bags.

Waste from Specific Activities

- Council Directive 86/278/EEC on the protection of the environment, and in particular of the soil, when sewage sludge is used in agriculture.
- Directive 2000/59/EC of the European Parliament and of the Council on port reception facilities for ship-generated waste and cargo residues.
- Directive 2006/21/EC of the European Parliament and of the Council on the management of waste from extractive industries.
- Directive 2010/75/EU of the European Parliament and of the Council on industrial emissions.
- A strategy for better ship dismantling practices, COM(2008) 767, final.

Radioactive Waste and Substances

- Council Regulation (Euratom) No. 1493/93 on shipments of radioactive substances between Member States.
- Council Directive 2006/117/Euratom on the supervision and control of shipments of radioactive waste and spent fuel.
- Council Directive 2011/70/Euratom establishing a Community framework for the responsible and safe management of spent fuel and radioactive waste.

Compliance with the waste *acquis*, however, continues to be a longstanding problem in the environmental sector. Waste is continuously recognised as one of the sectors with the highest number of infringement cases.[16] In its Communication on Implementing European Community Environmental Law in 2008, discussed further in Chapter 6, the European Commission identified the waste sector as challenging, in particular, 'the need in certain Member States to end illegal landfilling, put in place adequate networks of regulated waste facilities, prevent illegal waste shipments and intensify public awareness of the goals of

---

[16] See COM(2015)329, Part I: Monitoring application of EU law in EU policy areas, 66: http://ec.europa.eu/environment/legal/law/statistics.htm.

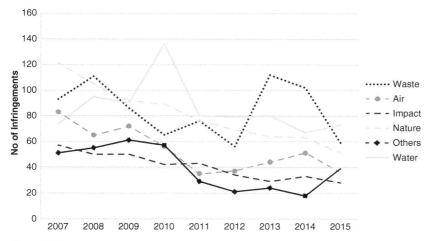

Figure 14.1 Infringements by Environmental Sector, 2007–2015
Source: DG Environment. The figure was compiled based on data available on the DG Environment website: http://ec.europa.eu/environment/legal/law/statistics.htm.

preventing, reusing and recycling waste'.[17] Although statistical data from 2007–2015 demonstrates notable improvements in regard to nature and water protection, the waste sector still remains an area of concern (Figure 14.1).

What explains this lack of compliance? Non-compliance as a preference seems like an obvious choice in this environmental sector as Member States are required to make legal, institutional and financial adjustments. This may be caused by constitutional factors, especially in Member States with decentralised governments or by the lack of resources for implementation and enforcement.[18] Further, certain Member States have refused to comply with the CJEU's judgments under Article 258 TFEU when the Court has found a failure to comply with the waste *acquis*, as it gives them more time to adjust to new rules and practices, which subsequently triggers the procedure under Article 260 TFEU.[19] Another tool to tackle certain types of infringements more effectively and in a more systematic manner is the doctrine of general and persistent (GAP) infringements, discussed further in Chapter 6. It was initially established in an environmental case, *Commission* v. *Ireland*,[20] when the Commission joined 12 individual complaints together in one case regarding the waste operators working without permits and the existence of illegal landfills.[21] This new strategy is especially valuable for the

---

[17] COM(2008)773 final.   [18] COM/2013/06, final.
[19] Pål Wennerås, 'A New Dawn for Commission Enforcement under Articles 226 and 228 EC' (2006) 43 *Common Market Law Review* 31–62, at 61. The Commission uses various preventive and coercive mechanisms within proceedings under Article 226 and 228. See more in Aleksandra Čavoški, 'An Assessment of Compliance Strategies in the Environmental Policy Area' (2016) 41(2) *European Law Review* 252–274.
[20] Case C-494/01 *Commission* v. *Ireland* ECLI:EU:C:2005:250.
[21] Wennerås, 'A New Dawn for Commission Enforcement', 33.

waste *acquis*, as it requires from Member States not only to put in place legal and administrative frameworks but also to ensure continuous application and enforcement of those provisions.

Waste Framework Directive (WFD)

Overview of the WFD

The Waste Framework Directive,[22] adopted in 2008, sets out a broad legislative framework for EU waste policy and represents an effort to modernise EU waste law and clarify existing concepts.[23] It repealed the previous Waste Framework Directive from 2006 and the two major pieces of waste legislation, namely the Directive on Waste Oils[24] and the Directive on Hazardous Waste,[25] which is often regarded as a major step in simplifying the complex and extensive EU waste law. Its main objective in protecting the environment and human health 'by preventing or reducing the adverse impacts of the generation and management of waste and by reducing overall impacts of resource use and improving the efficiency of such use' provides an overarching aspiration of the legislator when it comes to waste law. This objective was also recognised in the founding 1975 Council Directive on waste, though this first piece of waste legislation was primarily focused on preventing the distortion of competition in the common market. The WFD's objective sits comfortably with the EU's environmental policy objectives embodied in Article 191(2) of the TFEU, although there are justified concerns about raising even more tensions between waste prevention and waste regulation by minimising the adverse environmental and health impacts of resources generally.[26]

One of the main goals of the WFD is to clarify the main concepts of waste law, in particular the concept of waste as well as related concepts of recovery and disposal. The ambitious intention of the legislator stems from the main objective of the directive as well as the need to reduce the use of natural resources and implement the waste hierarchy.[27] In addition, the Directive tries to clarify the links with other related Directives and avoid overlapping provisions such as the Regulation on health rules concerning animal by-products not intended for human consumption.[28]

The WFD attempts to introduce a more comprehensive approach to waste prevention and more efficient and less harmful waste management as the long-term goal is to 'move the EU closer to a "recycling society", seeking to avoid waste generation and to use waste as a resource'.[29] The emphasis on waste prevention can be identified in several places in the Directive, most notably

---

[22] Directive 2008/98/EC of the European Parliament and of the Council of 19 November 2008 on waste and repealing certain Directives. Text with EEA relevance, OJ 2008 L 312/3.
[23] Recital 8 of the Directive 2008/98/EC.   [24] OJ 1975 L 194/23.
[25] Council Directive 91/689/EEC on hazardous waste, OJ 1991 L 377.
[26] Scotford, 'Trying to Do it All', 79.   [27] Recital 8 of the Directive 2008/98/EC.
[28] Regulation No. 1774/2002 of the European Parliament and of the Council laying down health rules concerning animal by-products not intended for human consumption, OJ 2002 L 273.
[29] Recital 28 of the Directive 2008/98/EC.

Figure 14.2 EU Waste Hierarchy
Source: 'Preparing a Waste Prevention Programme Guidance Document', 2012, figure 4.

through the obligation of Member States to draw waste prevention programmes which may be integrated within the waste management programmes or may function as separate ones.[30] The aim of these programmes, according to the Directive, is to break the link between economic growth and the environmental impacts associated with the generation of waste.[31] The Commission prepared guidelines for Member States in designing waste prevention programmes.[32] Likewise, Member States enjoy a variety of waste prevention measures that could become part of national waste management programmes such as raising awareness among businesses, voluntary agreements with consumers, producers, business and industry, use of economic instruments and eco-labelling.[33] The clarification of key concepts such as the definitions of waste, recovery and disposal is seen as an objective in the functioning of a wider goal of fostering waste prevention as a preferable option.[34] The Directive also tries to balance the focus on waste prevention by encouraging wider use of economic instruments that may also play a role in the achievement of waste prevention and management objectives.[35]

Waste prevention is part of a now extended five-step waste hierarchy (Figure 14.2) that represents a founding pillar of the EU and national waste management policies.[36] Prevention as the first step is regarded as the preferable solution, although technically prevention should not be considered as a part of waste management as it concerns substances before they became waste.[37] Still, there are concerns that defining prevention as measures to reduce the quantity of waste changes the primary objective of this concept which becomes the reduction rather than prevention.[38] Prevention is followed by a new concept, 'preparing for

---

[30] Art. 29 of the Directive 2008/98/EC.
[31] 'Preparing a Waste Prevention Programme Guidance Document', 2012, 14.
[32] See http://ec.europa.eu/environment/waste/prevention/index.htm.
[33] 'Guidance on the interpretation of key provisions of Directive 2008/98/EC on waste', 29.
[34] Recital 8 WFD.   [35] Recital 42 WFD.   [36] Art. 4 WFD.
[37] 'Guidance on the interpretation of key provisions of Directive 2008/98/EC on waste', 28.
[38] M. Gharfalkar, R. Court, C. Cambel, Z. Ali and G. Hiller, 'Analysis of Waste Hierarchy in the European Waste Directive 2008/98/EC' (2015) 39 *Waste Management* 308.

reuse', which is an important phase for identifying if material is considered to be waste. There is also a concept of 'reuse' defined as 'any operation by which products or components that are not waste are used again for the same purpose for which they were conceived'.[39] Unlike 'preparing for reuse' it does not feature in the waste hierarchy as it is regarded as a means for prevention.[40] This adds some confusion to the understanding of waste as it is not clear why the concept of 'reuse' only applies to non-waste and why it does not sit in its logical place after 'preparing for reuse'.[41]

The third phase of waste hierarchy is recycling and the Directive clearly indicates the EU's ambition to become a true recycling society. Yet, the targets set out in the Directive do not reflect this ambition and are considered to be very disappointing.[42] The Directive somewhat clarified the meaning and the distinction between the recovery and disposal as the two remaining stages of waste hierarchy. The Directive departs from a simplified approach of just listing the recovery and disposal operation and gives a comprehensive explanation of both operations supported by a non-exhaustive list of examples.[43] Although the waste hierarchy is a mandatory provision, the Member States enjoy some discretion in choosing the option that would deliver the best overall environmental outcome. However, they have to ensure that the development of waste legislation and policy is a fully transparent process involving the consultation of citizens and stakeholders.

The 2008 WFD to a large extent contains the same provisions as the 2006 Directive, and imposes several traditional obligations for Member States, including planning and supervisory and reporting functions obligations. National authorities must put in place a licensing system which requires each undertaking intending to carry out waste treatment to obtain a permit from the competent

---

[39] Art. 3(13).
[40] Guidance on the interpretation of key provisions of Directive 2008/98/EC on waste, 30.
[41] Gharfalkar et al., 'Analysis of Waste Hierarchy', 309
[42] Article 11(2) WFD: 'In order to comply with the objectives of this Directive, and move towards a European recycling society with a high level of resource efficiency, Member States shall take the necessary measures designed to achieve the following targets:

(a) by 2020, the preparing for reuse and the recycling of waste materials such as at least paper, metal, plastic and glass from households and possibly from other origins as far as these waste streams are similar to waste from households, shall be increased to a minimum of overall 50 per cent by weight;

(b) by 2020, the preparing for reuse, recycling and other material recovery, including backfilling operations using waste to substitute other materials, of non-hazardous construction and demolition waste excluding naturally occurring material defined in category 17 05 04 in the list of waste shall be increased to a minimum of 70 per cent by weight.'

[43] Art. 3 WFD: 'recovery' means any operation the principal result of which is waste serving a useful purpose by replacing other materials which would otherwise have been used to fulfil a particular function, or waste being prepared to fulfil that function, in the plant or in the wider economy; 'disposal' means any operation which is not recovery even where the operation has as a secondary consequence the reclamation of substances or energy.

authority.[44] The competent national authority must, *inter alia*, specify the quantity and type of waste treated as well as the duration of the issued permit. The WFD provides for certain exemptions from this rule, in which case the Member States must keep an appropriate register.

Member States must also develop waste management plans to cover the entire geographical territory of the Member State, though according to the new waste directive those waste management plans are much more detailed.[45] Besides information on type, quantity, origin and general technical requirements and disposal sites or installations, the new waste plans and programmes reveal a more strategic planning aspect, whereby they must contain evaluation of the development of waste streams in future as well as an assessment of the need for new collection schemes, closure of existing waste installations, additional waste installation structures and required investments in the future, as in Article 28(3)(a)(c). The overarching objective of preventing the adverse impact on human health and environment has also found its way into national plans and programmes, which must be drafted as to improve 'environmentally sound preparing for reuse, recycling, recovery and disposal of waste and ensure the fulfilment of objectives and provisions of WFD' (Article 28).

As a way of enforcing the polluter pays principle but also the waste hierarchy, the WFD introduces the concept of extended producer's responsibility: any natural or legal person who professionally develops, manufactures, processes, treats, sells or imports products (producer of the product) must carry out their treatment themselves or must employ someone else to carry out this task (Article 8). The 2015 Commission Proposal to amend the WFD introduces minimum operating conditions for extended producer responsibility which seeks to reduce costs, improve performance and ensure smooth functioning of the internal market.[46]

In line with the polluter pays principle, the costs of waste management are borne by the original waste producer or by the current or previous waste holders.[47] Member States are also encouraged to take appropriate measures which may prompt the environmentally friendly design of products that would contribute to the underpinning waste hierarchy principle. The WFD also reaffirms self-sufficiency and proximity principles, as a result of which, Member States shall 'in cooperation with other Member States where this is necessary or advisable ... establish an integrated and adequate network of waste disposal installations and of installations for the recovery of mixed municipal waste collected from private households ... taking into account best available techniques' (Article 16(1)). The proximity principle entails the disposal and recovery of waste 'in one of the nearest appropriate installations, by means of the most appropriate methods and technologies, in order to ensure a high level of protection for the environment and public health' Art. 16(3) WFD. This also indicates an

---

[44] Art. 23 WFD.   [45] Scotford, 'Trying to Do it All', 92.   [46] COM(2015)595, final.
[47] Art. 14, para. 1 WFD.

affinity with the rectification of damage at source principle (Article 191 TFEU) as it acts as a deterrent to any damage occurrence.

Current experiences of Member States in implementing the WFD are somewhat disappointing, and demonstrate significant problems in its implementation and enforcement. One significant concern is waste treatment, which often is not carried out in line with the waste hierarchy.[48] This relates in particular to the disposal of waste where most Member States rely heavily on landfills for the disposal of municipal waste, which is aggravated by a number of illegal landfills in certain Member States.[49] In some Member States, prevention, reuse and recycling are not efficient as there is no adequate infrastructure or the separate collection of waste, especially bio-waste, is not available or is not efficient.[50] As a result, in 2015, the Commission adopted a Proposal to amend the WFD that reviews recycling and other waste-related targets in the WFD by setting out more ambitious targets in line with the Seventh EAP and Resource Efficiency Roadmap.[51] With regard to reuse and recycling, the new proposal adds another target to be achieved by 2025 and 2030 as well as an early warning system to prevent any delays in meeting the targets.[52] The other major deficiencies are associated with the planning and implementation of waste management plans which are often outdated and do not reflect the collection and treatment facilities on the ground.[53] Finally, in some Member States, especially new Member States, the control and inspection of waste treatment facilities is lacking.

What is Waste?

The concept of waste is the subject of perennial debate by both academics and judges.[54] This is not surprising, as the subjective interpretation of waste differs from its legal and scientific meaning. An individual considers an object or substance waste based on its specific properties or its characteristics and does not care about the potential value that waste may have. The method of treatment or use of the substance would also signify for an individual that an object should

---

[48] Support to Member States in improving waste management based on assessment of Member States' performance, European Commission, 2013, 8–9: http://ec.europa.eu/environment/waste/framework/pdf/Final%20Report%20_130507.pdf.

[49] Support to Member States in improving waste management based on assessment of Member States' performance, European Commission, 2013, 8–9.

[50] Ibid., 9.   [51] COM(2015)595, final.

[52] COM(2015)595, final: '(c) by 2025, the preparing for reuse and the recycling of municipal waste shall be increased to a minimum of 60% by weight; (d) by 2030, the preparing for reuse and the recycling of municipal waste shall be increased to a minimum of 65% by weight.'

[53] Support to Member States in improving waste management based on assessment of Member States' performance, European Commission, 2013, 9.

[54] Ilona Cheyne, 'The Definition of Waste in EC Law' (2002) 14(1) *Journal of Environmental Law* 61; Eloise Scotford, 'Trash or Treasure: Policy Tensions in EC Waste Regulation' (2007) 19(3) *Journal of Environmental Law* 367; Robert Lee and Elen Stokes, 'Rehabilitating the Definition of Waste: Is it Fully Recovered?' in T. Etty and H. Somson (eds.), (2008) 8 *Yearbook of European Environmental Law* 162; Scotford, 'Trying to Do it All'.

be considered as waste.[55] Moreover, an individual is not concerned with the life-cycle of waste once he or she discards it, nor does he or she appreciate the subtle nuances between various stages of the waste hierarchy. Still, the definition of waste takes into account the intention of the holder of waste to discard the waste.

The concept of 'waste' is an autonomous concept of EU law.[56] It was originally defined in the 1975 Directive on waste as 'any substance or object which the holder disposes of or is required to dispose of'.[57] The definition of waste in the English version of the Directive was different in meaning from the French and German versions, as the term used in those languages referred to the action 'to discard' rather than 'to dispose of'.[58] This was one of the factors that prompted the terminological change in the definition, where the term 'dispose' was replaced by the current term 'discard' and the intention of the waste holder 'to discard' became part of the definition.

Waste is defined as 'any substance or object the holder discards or intends to discard or is required to discard' (Article 3 WFD). This definition differs slightly from the 2006 WFD, which provided in addition categories of substances or objects which a holder discards or intends to discard or is required to discard (Article 1(1)(a)).[59] The starting term in understanding the concept of waste is a 'waste holder', who is defined as the waste producer or the natural or legal person who is in possession of the waste, which indicates that the Directive embraces a broad definition of waste holder (Article 3 WFD). Though the notion of possession is not defined in the Directive, the term is often understood 'in the usual sense of the word', which, according to Advocate General Kokott, understands 'the actual physical control of an object, but does not presuppose ownership or a legal power of disposal'.[60] This has to be read in conjunction with Article 3(5) which defines the producer as 'anyone whose activities produce waste (original waste producer) or anyone who carries out pre-processing, mixing or other operations resulting in a change in the nature or composition of this waste'. In *Commune de Mesquer*, the concept of holder was discussed within the broader context of applying the polluter pays principle whereby it was held that the ship-owner may be regarded as having produced that waste (hydrocarbons spilled by accident at sea) within the meaning of Article 1(b) of Directive 75/442,

---

[55] However, in the *ARCO* case, it was held that 'the method of treatment or use of a substance does not determine conclusively whether or not it is to be classified as waste', Joined Cases C-418/97 and C-419/97 *ARCO Chemie* ECLI:EU:C:2000:318, para. 64.

[56] Opinion of AG Cruz Villalón ECLI:EU:C:2013:324, para. 42.

[57] Art. 1, OJ 1975 L 194/39.

[58] 'Lawmaking in the EU Multilingual Environment', European Commission Directorate-General for Translation (2010), 135. The French version, using the term 'déchet', refers to 'toute substance ou tout objet dont le détenteur se défait ou a l'obligation de se défaire en vertu des dispositions nationales en vigueur'.

[59] OJ 2006 L 114/9.

[60] Opinion of AG Kokott ECLI:EU:C:2004:67, para. 56. However, she further explains that for the purpose of the term waste holder, 'the notion of possession must therefore go beyond the narrow sense of the word to include a legal power of disposal over the waste, in addition to actual (direct or indirect) physical control'.

and on that basis may be considered as a 'holder' within the meaning of Article 1(c) of that Directive.[61]

This broad and flexible interpretation of the concept of waste also involves an understanding of the term 'discard', which is often regarded as the main concept in understanding the term waste as the 'scope of the term "waste" turns on the meaning of the term "discard"'.[62] As Scotford emphasises, the term 'discard' identifies waste as an action-based concept rather than substance based, as the Directive underlines the three alternatives in describing the action of the holder.[63] This includes an action of discarding, an intention to discard, and a situation when a holder is obliged to discard. Whether the holder intended to discard the object must be assessed based on all facts of the case, while ensuring compliance with the WFD objectives.[64] The legal obligation to discard may stem from EU or national legislation or may even be stipulated as the terms of the contract.[65]

While the CJEU has been asked on numerous occasions to interpret the concept of waste, the Court has never developed clear criteria of what is considered to be waste. In its first landmark case, the Court held that the concept of waste does not exclude substances and objects, which are capable of economic reutilisation.[66] Although the Advocate General in the *Tombesi* case recognised that imprecise and open-ended definition of waste in the Directive renders it difficult for Member States to apply it to various situations in practice,[67] the Court missed an opportunity to clarify the term 'discard' and indicated that subjecting a material to operations under Annex II B is good indication of it being regarded as waste.[68] The economic value of

---

[61] Case C-188/07 *Commune de Mesquer* v. *Total France SA and Total International Ltd* ECLI:EU:C:2008:359, para. 74.
[62] Case C-129/96, *Inter-Environnement Wallonie* ECLI:EU:C:1997:628, para. 26.
[63] Scotford, 'Trash or Treasure', 375.
[64] See the most recent case: Joined Cases C-241/12 and C-242/12, *Shell Nederland and Belgian Shell NV* ECLI:EU:C:2013:821, para. 48. See also Joined Cases C-418/97 and C-419/97 *ARCO Chemie* ECLI:EU:C:2000:318: 'The essential objective of all provisions relating to waste disposal must be the protection of human health and the environment against harmful effects caused by the collection, transport, treatment, storage and tipping of waste.' It should further be pointed out that, pursuant to Article 130r(2) of the EC Treaty (now, after amendment, Article 174(2) EC), Community policy on the environment is to aim at a high level of protection and is to be based, in particular, on the precautionary principle and the principle that preventive action should be taken. It follows that the concept of waste cannot be interpreted restrictively. See also Guidance on the interpretation of key provisions of Directive 2008/98/EC on waste, 10.
[65] UK 'Guidance on the legal definition of waste and its application', Department of the Environment, Food and Rural Affairs (August 2012), 31–32.
[66] Joined Cases C-206/88 and C-207/88 *Vessoso and Zanetti* ECLI:EU:C:1990:145, para. 9.
[67] Opinion of AG Jacobs ECLI:EU:C:1996:399, para. 56.
[68] Joined Cases C-304/94, C-330/94, C-342/94 and C-224/95 *Tombesi and others* ECLI:EU:C:1997:314, paras. 52–54. This interpretation was further clarified in *Inter-Environnement Wallonie* where the ECJ held that a substance is not excluded from the definition of waste in Article 1(a) of Council Directive 75/442, as amended, by the mere fact that it directly or indirectly forms an integral part of an industrial production process.

the waste was recognised in the *Walloon* case where the Court held that 'waste has an intrinsic commercial value' and 'whether recyclable or not, is to be regarded as "goods" the movement of which, in accordance with Article [28] of the Treaty, must in principle not be prevented'.[69]

The understanding of waste demonstrates how our subjective impression of what constitutes waste greatly differs from the legal implications of the term. This is not to say that physical characteristics of a substance or object are not important, but they cannot be considered to be the decisive factor in determining what is considered to be waste. This is best illustrated by the *Palin Granit* case, where the Court decided that leftover stone resulting from stone quarrying which was harmless and without any potential to be regarded as a source of pollution can constitute waste.[70] Similarly, the term 'discard' includes not only disposal but also recovery *of a substance or object*, regardless of whether discarding is intentional or involuntary.[71]

The Court recognised the need to have an open mind and flexible approach in interpreting the concept of waste as the term 'discard' can change its meaning in different situations. As the Court stated in *ARCO*, whether a substance or object is regarded as waste must be determined in the light of all circumstances, by comparison with the definition and the aim of the Directive, provided that its effectiveness is not undermined.[72] This indicates a teleological interpretation of the Directive which takes into account not only the negative impact on the environment and human health, but all environmental principles embedded in the Directive.[73] This flexible approach is seen in the Court's recognition that the 'directive would be undermined if the national legislature were to use modes of proof, such as statutory presumptions, which had the effect of restricting the scope of the directive'.[74] The reasoning in the *Avesta Polarit* case indicates that the scope of the 'term discard depends on a series of factors dictated in particular by the overriding requirement of environmental protection enshrined in the Directive'.[75] Some of those were put down in the *ARCO* case and expanded

---

[69] Case C-2/90 *Commission* v. *Belgium* ECLI:EU:C:1992:310, para. 28. This was later confirmed in Case C-444/00 *Mayer Parry* ECLI:EU:C:2003:356, 'First, obstacles to trade could arise if different concepts of recycling were applied in the Member States, so that the same material or product could be regarded as recycled in one Member State – and would accordingly have ceased to be classified as packaging waste and been freed from all waste-specific controls – while that would not be the case in another Member State.'

[70] Case C-9/00 *Palin Granit* ECLI:EU:C:2002:232. See also Case C-235/02 *Saetti and Frediani* ECLI:EU:C:2004:26; Joined Cases C-418/97 and C-419/97 *ARCO Chemie* ECLI:EU:C:2000:318.

[71] See Case C-129/96 *Inter-Environnement Wallonie ASBL* v. *Région wallonne*; ECLI:EU:C:1997:628, para. 27 and C-419/97.

[72] Joined Cases C-418/97 and C-419/97 *ARCO Chemie* ECLI:EU:C:2000:318, para. 97.

[73] See also Joined Cases C-241/12 and C-242/12 *Shell Nederland and Belgian Shell NV* ECLI:EU:C:2013:821.

[74] Joined Cases C-418/97 *ARCO Chemie* ECLI:EU:C:2000:318 and C-419/97 *Vereniging Dorpsbelang Hees* ECLI:EU:C:2000:318, para. 42. The Court also held that the concept of waste cannot be interpreted restrictively.

[75] Opinion of AG Jacobs ECLI:EU:C:2003:222, para. 41.

by subsequent case law.[76] These factors were also included in the Commission's Guidelines on the interpretation of key provisions of the WFD.[77]

The WFD definition of waste must be read in conjunction with several other provisions in the Directive. Several provisions of the Directive should be mentioned in that respect. Article 2 of the Directive sets out a slightly broader list of exemptions from the scope of the Directive, some based on previous CJEU case law. Article 5 of the Directive introduces the concept of by-product and sets out the list of requirements that need to be fulfilled for a substance or object to be classified as one. To some extent, the Directive provides more guidance as to when the waste ceases to be waste, by laying down guidelines for developing end-of-waste criteria (Article 6). This article needs to be read together with Article 3 of the WFD, which, unlike its predecessor, provides a more detailed explanation of the main stages of the waste hierarchy. Article 7 provides a basis for the compilation of the European list of waste, which plays an important role in the classification of hazardous waste.[78]

By-Product

Substances not produced as an end product are part of everyday manufacturing processes. Often they can be successfully reused or they can undergo some further treatment which ensures their future usage. However, they must be differentiated from products which are intentionally produced,[79] insofar as they represent something that was not intended to be the final outcome of the production process and which the producer wants to discard. As was stated in *ARCO*, 'the fact that the substance is a residue for which no use other than disposal can be envisaged may also be regarded as evidence of discarding'.[80] Still, this interpretation of waste would be too restrictive and is incompatible both with the CJEU

---

[76] The fact that that substance is commonly regarded as waste may be taken as evidence that the holder has discarded that substance or intends or is required to discard it (*ARCO Chemie*); Whether the use of a substance … is to be regarded as constituting discarding, it is irrelevant that that substance may be recovered in an environmentally responsible manner for use as fuel without substantial treatment (*ARCO Chemie*); The fact that a substance is the residue of the manufacturing process of another substance, that no use for that substance other than disposal can be envisaged, that the composition of the substance is not suitable for the use made of it or that special environmental precautions must be taken when it is used may be regarded as evidence that the holder has discarded that substance or intends or is required to discard it (*ARCO Chemie*); The place of storage of leftover stone, its composition and the fact, even if proven, that the stone does not pose any real risk to human health or the environment are not relevant criteria for determining whether the stone is to be regarded as waste (*Palin Granit*).

[77] Available at: http://ec.europa.eu/environment/waste/framework/pdf/guidance_doc.pdf.

[78] See Commission Decision (EU) No. 2014/955/EU and Commission Regulation (EU) No. 1357/2014.

[79] See Case C-9/00 *Palin Granit* and Case C-235/02 *Saetti and Frediani*. In the UK Guidelines on the legal definition of waste and its application, product is defined as 'something which is manufactured or produced with the intention of using or marketing', 44.

[80] Joined Cases C-418/97 and C-419/97 *ARCO Chemie* ECLI:EU:C:2000:318, para. 86.

understanding of waste, but also with any economic usage of residue deriving from a production process.

Production residue was defined in *Palin Granit* as a substance which is not, in itself, sought for a subsequent use,[81] while in the *Saetti* case it was clarified that product residue is not to be considered as 'the result of technical choice'.[82] If it is a production residue it must be determined whether it amounts to waste or if it can be regarded as a by-product. Although the determination of a by-product has to be assessed in each individual case, the WFD, based on the relevant CJEU case law,[83] lays down several cumulative requirements for a production residue not to be identified as waste:

Requirements for Production Residue not to be 'Waste': Article 5 WFD

- further use of the substance or object is certain;
- the substance or object can be used directly without any further processing other than normal industrial practice;
- the substance or object is produced as an integral part of a production process; and
- further use is lawful, i.e. the substance or object fulfils all relevant product, environmental and health-protection requirements for the specific use and will not lead to overall adverse environmental or human health impacts.

Certainty of use essentially indicates that there is some genuine usage for the production residue, not a mere possibility of that.[84] The CJEU has also introduced the concept of likelihood of use, *without any further processing prior to its reuse* as it may be very difficult always to identify the reuse of a substance or an object.[85] This will certainly be the case if it involves objects with potential market value[86] or objects having physical characteristics which offer the potential for further reuse, or there is a potential for a certain proportion of the material to be used.[87] When assessing the degree of certainty, the aim must be 'to exclude beyond all reasonable doubt any possibility that, owing to inappropriate treatment, the material which the holder purports to exploit as a by-product will ultimately be treated as waste which the holder discards in an improper manner'.[88]

The second criterion is a tricky criterion to apply as, in some cases, substances or objects need to be subjected to further processing in order to prepare them for further use. Activities such as washing and drying of a material or modification of

---

[81] Case C-9/00 *Palin Granit* ECLI:EU:C:2002:232, para. 32.
[82] Case C-235/02 *Saetti and Frediani* ECLI:EU:C:2004:26, para. 45.
[83] Cases C-9/00 and C-235/02.
[84] Case C-9/00 *Palin Granit*: 'the reasoning applicable to by-products should be confined to situations in which the reuse of the goods, materials or raw materials is not a mere possibility but a certainty, without any further processing prior to reuse and as an integral part of the production process.' See also Case C-188/07 *Commune de Mesquer*, para. 44.
[85] *Ibid.*, para. 37.   [86] *Palin Granit* emphasises the financial advantage, para. 37.
[87] COM(2007)59 final.   [88] Opinion of AG Cruz Villalón ECLI:EU:C:2013:324, para. 69.

size or shape by mechanical treatment do not restrict the concept of by-product.[89] However, in certain instances the assessment of any processing activity must be 'determined in the light of all the circumstances, account being taken of the aim of the directive'.[90]

The third requirement has to be assessed in each individual case and is highly dependent on the understanding of the concept of 'integral part of a production process'. It will normally depend on the type of the further processing activity to which a substance is subjected. Although there is no conclusive list of indicators for evaluating what constitutes an integral part of the production process, the Commission listed some facts that need to be taken into account such as 'the degree of readiness of the material for further use, the nature and extent of the tasks needed to prepare the material before further use, the integration of these tasks into the main production process and whether the tasks are being carried out by someone other than the manufacturer'.[91] The location of the processing activity may play a part in determining this requirement as it may be regarded that a change of location indicates two separate production processes. One has to be careful in interpreting this rule too narrowly as the production process may be run by two different operators at two different locations,[92] or the increasing specialisation of industrial processes may necessitate separate locations.[93]

The last requirement of 'lawful further use' for a production residue to be regarded as a by-product sits well with the WFD objective to minimise 'the negative effects of the generation and management of waste on human health and the environment'. Any activity that implies further use of a by-product must be in compliance with any product-related, environmental and health regulations. In *Avesta Polarit*, the holder of leftover rock and residual sand could use them lawfully for the necessary filling in of the galleries of that mine.[94]

End-of-Waste

Another important concept is the end-of-waste which applies to cases when a waste may be successfully transformed into a product. Thus, the end-of-waste concept is highly dependent on the understanding of the completion of a recovery operation[95] as certain waste shall cease to be waste 'when it had undergone a recovery, including recycling, provided it complies with certain criteria to be developed in accordance with the following conditions:

- the substance or object is commonly used for specific purposes;
- there is an existing market or demand for the substance or object;

---

[89] Guidelines on the interpretation of key provisions of Directive on waste, p. 18.
[90] Joined Cases C-418/97 and C-419/97 *ARCO Chemie* ECLI:EU:C:2000:318, para. 88.
[91] COM(2007)59 final.
[92] UK 'Guidelines on the legal definition of waste and its application', p. 48.
[93] COM(2007)59 final, p. 8.
[94] Case C-114/01 *Avesta Polarit Chrome* ECLI:EU:C:2003:448, para. 43.
[95] Guidance on the interpretation of Directive 2008/98/EC on waste, p. 22.

- the use is lawful (substance or object fulfils the technical requirements for the specific purposes and meets the existing legislation and standards applicable to products);
- use will not lead to overall adverse environmental or human health impacts.[96]

Although the intention of the legislator is to clarify further the concept of waste, there are still practical difficulties surrounding the requirements underpinning this concept. One of the difficulties results from the practical application of the definition of 'recovery', as not all operations necessarily meet the definition of 'recovery' set out in the WFD.[97] At the same time, subjecting waste to a recovery operation does not necessarily mean that the object cannot be regarded as waste.[98] In its recent *Lapin luonnonsuojelupiiri* judgment, the CJEU has provided some guidelines in regard to hazardous waste by indicating that REACH, 'in particular Annex XVII in so far as it authorises the use of certain chemicals, may be relevant for the purpose of determining whether hazardous waste ceases to be waste'.[99] This obliges Member States to develop a quite practical approach in dealing with individual cases.[100] The other difficulty may come from the above listed conditions that will be used for developing criteria for certain types of waste. The first two conditions are regarded as complementary conditions that should 'preclude the establishment of end-of-waste criteria for material for which uses and demand are not yet developed',[101] which raises concerns about disadvantageous effects of this approach to 'emerging or volatile markets involving recycled products'.[102] This also undermines the knowledge-based approach to waste management which is central to the waste management policies.[103] The evaluation of the adverse human health or environmental impacts also requires a holistic approach that brings together several elements of the recovery chain, including input materials; processes and techniques; quality control procedures; product quality; and potential applications or uses.[104]

Hazardous Waste

Although non-hazardous waste is more prevalent in everyday life, the regulation of hazardous waste occupies an important place in EU waste policy due to its potential adverse effects on human health and environment. Hazardous waste includes waste that contains substances or properties harmful for humans and the environment, though some waste may contain both hazardous and

---

[96] Art. 6 WFD.
[97] See Joined Cases C-418/97 and C-419/97 *ARCO Chemie* ECLI:EU:C:2000:318, para. 45.
[98] *Ibid.*, para. 51. [99] Case C-358/11 ECLI:EU:C:2013:142.
[100] UK 'Guidelines on the legal definition of waste and its application', 51.
[101] See End-of-Waste Criteria, Methodology and Case Studies Report, http://ipts.jrc.ec.europa.eu/publications/pub.cfm?id=2619, at 17.
[102] Scotford, 'Trying to Do it All', 82.
[103] Report from the Commission to the European Parliament, the Council, the European Economic and Social Committee and the Committee of the Regions on the Thematic Strategy on the Prevention and Recycling of Waste SEC(2011)70 final/COM/2011/0013 final.
[104] End-of-Waste Criteria, Methodology and Case Studies Report, at 18.

non-hazardous properties. The interface of science and law is especially important for the regulation of hazardous waste as it is highly dependent on scientific findings and the development of relevant technologies. The dissemination of this knowledge is also an important factor in treating the hazardous waste. An illustrative example is asbestos, where the regulators in all Member States together with the environmental civil society successfully raised awareness of the potential risk involved. Given the potential harm for humans and the environment, hazardous waste was one of the first areas regulated in the European Community, starting with the Council Directive 78/319 on toxic and dangerous waste,[105] which was later amended and replaced by Directive 91/689 on hazardous waste.[106]

As an attempt to simplify Union legislation and provide more clarity, the provisions on hazardous waste were incorporated in the WFD. Hazardous waste is defined as 'waste which displays one or more of the hazardous properties listed in Annex III' (Article 3 WFD). This Annex was recently amended to reflect technical and scientific progress concerning chemicals since classification of waste as hazardous is based, *inter alia*, on the Union legislation on chemicals. The amended Annex III still recognises 15 hazardous categories, but they are renamed so as to align the definitions of the hazardous properties with Regulation (EC) No. 1272/2008.[107] Test methods required to generate information on intrinsic properties of substances are specified in Council Regulation (EC) No. 440/2008.[108]

In addition to Annex III and for better understanding of the concept, the WFD makes reference to a list of waste, which is also important for the classification of hazardous waste (Article 7 WFD). It is binding in determining waste which is to be considered as hazardous waste (Article 7(1)).[109] Article 7 leaves discretion to Member States to consider waste as hazardous waste where, 'even though it does not appear as such on the list of waste, it displays one or more of the properties listed in Annex III'. Likewise, a Member State may demonstrate, based on evidence, that specific waste that appears on the list as hazardous waste does not display any of the properties listed in Annex III and it may be regarded as non-hazardous waste.[110] WFD also contains provisions on control of hazardous waste that impose obligation on Member States to undertake necessary measures concerning production, collection, transportation, storage and treatment of hazardous waste.[111] In addition, hazardous waste must be labelled in accordance with relevant international and Union standards.[112]

Shipment of Waste

Any shipment of waste, regardless of the modes of transport, may potentially have devastating effects on humans and the environment.[113] This risk is even more

---

[105] OJ 1978 L 84/21/43.   [106] OJ 1991 L 377/34/20.
[107] Recital 6 of the Commission Regulation (EU) No. 1357/2014.   [108] OJ 2008 L 142/1.
[109] See Commission Decision 2014/955/EU amending Decision 2000/532/EC on the list of waste pursuant to Directive 2008/98/EC of the European Parliament and of the Council, OJ 2014 L 370.
[110] Article 7, para. 3 WFD.   [111] Article 17 WFD.   [112] Article 19 WFD.
[113] The movement of the dioxin drums from the Seveso incident to France in 1982.

prominent today when the transport of waste is more intensive both within the EU and to countries outside the EU. In 2009 alone, 'the total amount of all notified waste shipped out of the EU Member States (EU-27) was about 11.4 million tonnes, of which about 7.2 million tonnes was hazardous waste'.[114] The necessity of regulating this area was recognised very early in the EU with the adoption of Directive 78/319 which addressed the transport of toxic and dangerous waste.[115] Since the shipment of waste is an issue of international importance, the development of EU law in this field is under the constant influence of international law and international agreements. This is reflected in Regulation 1013/2006, on shipment of waste, whose scope is quite broad and includes shipments of waste between Member States, within the EU, or with transit through third countries; imported into the EU from third countries; and exported from the EU to third countries and in transit through the EU, on the way from and to third countries.[116]

Shipment is defined as 'any transport of waste destined for recovery or disposal which is planned, or takes place', including any means of transport.[117] The Regulation applies to all waste, with limited exceptions such as radioactive waste.[118] It sets out two waste shipment control procedures within the EU, depending on the waste treatment and properties of waste, i.e. procedure of prior written notification that applies to all shipments of waste destined for disposal operations and waste listed in Annex IV (Amber Listed Waste) destined for recovery as well as the general information requirement procedure that applies to Green listed non-hazardous waste destined for recovery (Art. 3(1)).[119] The aim of the prior notification procedure is to ensure optimum supervision and control by duly informing the competent authorities about the shipment and enabling them to take all necessary measures for the protection of human health and the environment.[120] Under the notification procedure, the sender of a shipment has to notify the competent authority of dispatch by providing required information, evidence of a contract with the consignee for the recovery or disposal and financial guarantees.[121] The competent authority of dispatch must transmit the notification to the competent authority of destination with copies to any competent authority of transit within three working days, while the competent authority of destination has 30 days to give its consent with or without conditions or to express its objections.[122]

In line with the Basel Convention and international agreements, special provisions are put in place concerning the export and import of waste to and from non-EU countries. Hence, the export of waste from the EU destined for disposal is prohibited, except to EFTA countries which are party to the

---

[114] COM/2012/448, final.
[115] Council Directive 78/319/EEC on toxic and dangerous waste, OJ 1978 L 84.
[116] Art. 1 WSR OJ 2006 L 190.   [117] Art. 2 WSR.   [118] Art. 1, para. 3 WSR.
[119] Applies to Green listed waste.   [120] Recital 14 WSR.   [121] Art. 4 WSR.
[122] Art. 9 WSR.

convention.[123] Export from the EU of hazardous wastes destined for recovery is prohibited to countries to which the OECD Decision[124] does not apply. Finally, imports from third countries of waste destined for disposal or recovery are prohibited, with limited exceptions.[125]

Thus far, the Regulation provides an appropriate legal framework for the shipment of waste. However, recent amendments adopted in 2014 should improve the enforcement and inspection in Member States.[126] The lack thereof is seen primarily in illegal shipments of waste which may result from uncontrolled collection, sorting and storage of waste. Likewise, divergent inspection rules between Member States raise concerns about the proper classification of waste; and this may affect the subsequent shipment of waste. These problems should be addressed through adequate planning of inspections of shipments of waste and development of inspection plans based on risk assessment.[127] Interpretation of the main concepts prescribed by the regulations as well as types of waste that fall under the scope of this legislation are continuously provided by the CJEU in the preliminary reference procedure. Concepts of notifier and notifier's obligations were further interpreted in *Marius Pedersen A/S* v. *Miljøstyrelsen*,[128] together with further clarifications on the obligation of confidentiality and how it applies also to those involved in the shipment process.[129] In *Omni Metal Service*, the Court clarified the green list of waste as well as discretion left to Member States in relation to waste that does not appear on the green list.[130]

Waste Operations

Landfills

The Landfill Directive[131] was adopted in 1999 with the purpose of achieving several ambitious goals. Reduction of adverse environmental impacts on the environment and on human health undoubtedly is seen as its primary objective.[132] Attainment of this objective demonstrates the interconnectedness of waste policy with other environmental sectors, since the disposal at landfills significantly impacts other EU environmental policies, such as protection of

---

[123] Art. 34 WSR.
[124] Decision C (2001)107/Final of the OECD Council concerning the revision of Decision C (92)39/Final on the control of transboundary movements of wastes destined for recovery operations.
[125] Arts. 41 and 43 WSR.
[126] Regulation (EU) No. 660/2014 of the European Parliament and of the Council amending Regulation (EC) No. 1013/2006 on shipments of waste, OJ 2014 L 189.
[127] Art. 50 of the Regulation (EU) No. 660/2014.
[128] Case C-215/04 *Marius Pedersen A/S* v. *Miljøstyrelsen* ECLI:EU:C:2006:108.
[129] Case C-1/11 *Interseroh Scrap and Metals Trading* ECLI:EU:C:2012:194.
[130] Case C-259/05 *Omni Metal Service* ECLI:EU:C:2007:363.
[131] Council Directive 1999/31/EC of 26 April 1999 on the landfill of waste OJ 1999 L 182.
[132] Art. 1.

water and soil and climate change.[133] The Landfill Directive also plays an important role in encouraging the waste management hierarchy and diversion of waste from landfills. In this regard, the Directive sets out targets for the progressive reduction of biodegradable municipal waste disposed at landfills.[134] Beside its environmental agenda, the EU attempts to harmonise technical and methodological standards in waste policy across the EU by setting standards for the disposal of waste at landfills.

The Landfill Directive imposes several obligations on Member States. As the Directive divides landfills into three classes, national authorities must first classify landfill sites according to different categories of waste, which also includes the review of existing landfill sites.[135] National authorities are responsible throughout the whole life-cycle of the landfill, including the choice of siting, its construction, operation and closure and after-care. This is attained by establishing a permitting system which lays down conditions and elements of the permit (Articles 7, 8 and 9). Yet, the permitting system has to be accompanied by vigorous monitoring, inspection and enforcement mechanisms in each Member State (Articles 12 and 13). National authorities have an obligation to set up a national strategy for the implementation of the reduction of biodegradable waste disposed at landfills that will contain measures to achieve set targets for this type of waste (Art. 5). An important obligation for Member States is to ensure that the price charged by the operator for the disposal of any type of waste covers all costs involved in the setting up and operation of a landfill site (Article 10).

The Landfill Directive had some positive impact on national waste policies.[136] Most Member States successfully put in place the administrative structure and procedures responsible for authorising landfills, monitoring and inspecting of sites as well as preparing national strategies for the reduction of biodegradable waste. Technical requirements are correctly transposed in most Member States.[137] Statistical data demonstrates the reduction of biodegradable waste that is disposed at landfills which was due to short- and medium-term

---

[133] Art. 1. See also Directive 2011/92/EU of the European Parliament and of the Council on the assessment of the effects of certain public and private projects on the environment, OJ 2012 L 26.

[134] Article 5(2): 75 per cent by 16 July 2006; 50 per cent by 16 July 2009 and 35 per cent by 16 July 2016.

[135] Art. 4: landfills for hazardous waste; landfills for non-hazardous waste and landfills for inert waste.

[136] See more about experiences in implementing the landfill directive in C. Fischer, 'The Development and Achievements of EU Waste Policy' (2011) 13 *Journal of Material Cycles and Waste Management* 2; M. Dreyfus et al., 'Comparative Study of a Local Service: Waste Management in France, Germany, Italy and the UK' in H. Wolmann and G. Marcou (eds.), *The Provision of Public Services in Europe* (Edward Elgar, 2012); H. Scharff, 'Landfill Reduction Experience in The Netherlands' (2014) 34 *Waste Management* 2218; M. Calaf-Forn et al., 'Cap and Trade Schemes on Waste Management: A Case Study of the Landfill Allowance Trading Scheme (LATS) in England' (2014) 34 *Waste Management* 919–928.

[137] COM/2013/06 final.

deadlines set out in the directive.[138] There are still great variations between Member States in the quantity of generated waste and ways of collecting and managing waste.[139] Yet, disposal at landfills is still a preferred and most commonly used method of waste treatment, especially in newer Member States.[140] Landfilling remains the cheapest option. Likewise, illegal dumping is still widespread, which indicates a lack of proper enforcement and inspection in some Member States. The 2015 Commission proposal which is a part of the new Circular Economy Strategy[141] aims at phasing out the disposal of recyclable waste at landfills, including plastics, metals, glass, paper, cardboard and other biodegradable waste as a way of recovering economically valuable waste.[142] The new proposal should also bring more coherence to waste legislation as it aims to align main waste concepts from the Landfill Directive with the 2008 WFD as well as to simplify reporting obligations.[143]

Incineration of Waste

Incineration of waste is a relatively new waste treatment operation which still raises concerns about its impact on the environment and human health, and involves significant costs. The receptiveness of this waste treatment in some Member States is often constrained by the opposition of the wider public to waste incineration installations in their locality. Until recently, the use of this waste treatment option was primarily regulated by the Waste Incineration Directive[144] adopted in 2000 which repealed previous Directives on the incineration of hazardous waste[145] and municipal waste.[146] However, as a part of the review of EU *acquis* on industrial emissions, the EU regulator decided to undertake a horizontal recasting of the relevant legislation, by bringing together several acts covering related subjects and incorporating them into a single new act. As a result, the Industrial Emissions Directive (IED),[147] discussed further in Chapter 9, combined the seven following Directives with effect from 7 January 2014:

---

[138] Eurostat http://ec.europa.eu/eurostat/statistics-explained/index.php/Municipal_waste_statistics.

[139] *Ibid*.

[140] Malta (98 per cent), Bulgaria (97 per cent) Cyprus (95 per cent), Lithuania (91 per cent) and Poland (88 per cent).

[141] COM(2015)594, final. According to the proposal, it is estimated that an additional 600 million tons of waste could be recycled or reused. The proposal seeks to achieve a gradual limitation of the landfilling of municipal waste to 10 per cent by 2030.

[142] COM/2014/0397 final; total amount of this waste should not exceed 25 per cent of the total amount of municipal waste generated in the previous year, from 1 January 2025.

[143] COM(2015)594, final.

[144] Directive 2000/76/EC of the European Parliament and of the Council on the incineration of waste, OJ 2000 L 332.

[145] Council Directive 94/67/EC on the incineration of hazardous waste, OJ 1994 L 365.

[146] Directives 89/369/EEC (OJ 1989 L 163) and 89/429/EEC (OJ 1989 L 203).

[147] Directive 2010/75/EU of the European Parliament and of the Council on industrial emissions (integrated pollution prevention and control) (Recast) OJ 2010 L 334.

- Directive 78/176/EEC on titanium dioxide industrial waste.
- Directive 82/883/EEC on the surveillance and monitoring of titanium dioxide waste.
- Directive 92/112/EEC on the reduction of titanium dioxide industrial waste.
- Directive 1999/13/EC on reducing emissions of volatile organic compounds (VOCs).
- Directive 2000/76/EC on waste incineration.
- Directive 2008/1/EC concerning integrated pollution prevention and control. And, with effect from 1 January 2016
- Directive 2001/80/EC on the limitation of emissions of certain pollutants from large combustion plants.

By bringing the seven directives together, the IED firmly embraces an integrated approach to controlling emissions into air, water or soil, to waste management, to energy efficiency and to accident prevention. It also tries to simplify and clarify the existing provisions, as well as to reduce any unnecessary administrative burden.[148] At the same time, the IED leaves a great deal of flexibility to Member States in implementing this Directive.[149]

Besides the legislator's intention to clarify and simplify legislation on industrial installation and reduce unnecessary administrative burden, one of the reasons for incorporating provisions on waste incineration was to ensure a 'high level of environmental and human health protection and to avoid transboundary movements of waste to plants operating at lower environmental standards'.[150] The IED contains special provisions that apply to waste incineration and co-incineration plants of solid and liquid waste, with the exception of plants listed in Article 42(2). The main onus is on the operator who is responsible for the safe operation of the plant, including operation of the plant, cases of breakdown, delivery and reception of waste and collection of required data. In cases of breakdown, the operator has promptly to reduce the scope of operations or close down operations. The part of the operator's responsibility is to ensure the safe delivery and reception of waste as to limit as far as possible pollution of 'air, soil, surface water and groundwater as well as other negative effects on the environment, odours and noise, and direct risks to human health' (Art. 52(1)).

Member States must put in place a permitting system, including provision in cases of substantial change of operation of a waste incineration plant, and are responsible for monitoring, inspection and enforcement. The Directive also sets out elements to be included in the application for a permit, as well as a list of permit conditions together with special conditions of permit requirements for plants using hazardous waste.[151] Applications for new permits for waste incineration plants and waste co-incineration plants have to be available to the public before the competent

---

[148] Recital 4.
[149] This refers to discretion of Member States to determine the approach for assigning responsibilities to operators of installations provided that compliance with this Directive is ensured and setting emissions limit values.
[150] Recital 34.   [151] Art. 44.

authority passes its decision.[152] Member States are also responsible for monitoring the emissions in line with emissions limit values (ELVs) set down for discharges into the air and the aquatic environment (Annex VI).

Waste Streams

The waste stream is the journey a piece of waste takes from generation to an appropriate waste treatment. The regulation of waste streams in the EU has a long lineage. The first Directive adopted in the waste sector was Directive 75/439 on the disposal of waste oils which established requirements on their collection and disposal.[153] Just a year later, another Directive on the disposal of polychlorinated biphenyls and polychlorinated terphenyls was adopted.[154] Today, the breadth of the subject matter covered by the EU waste legislation on specific waste streams is very wide, including end-of-life vehicles;[155] batteries and accumulators;[156] electrical and electronic equipment;[157] packaging and packaging waste;[158] polychlorinated biphenyls and polychlorinated terphenyls;[159] agricultural use of sewage sludge;[160] waste oils; mining waste;[161] animal waste; biodegradable waste; and construction and demolition waste.

In recent years, the EU has been particularly interested in addressing waste from consumer goods and raising awareness of certain waste streams that are generating an increasing amount of waste. Most of the consumer waste streams share a common cause. Protection of environmental and human health by promoting waste hierarchy or restricting hazardous substances emerges as a main objective with the Packaging and Packaging Waste Directive, Batteries Directive, End-of-life Directive and Waste of Electrical and Electronic Equipment Directive. Likewise, the aim is also to improve environmental performance of all involved in the life-cycle of a product, partly by implementing the

---

[152] Art. 55(1).
[153] See more about the history of the EU waste policy in McCormick, *Environmental Policy in the European Union*, 155–168.
[154] Council Directive 76/403/EEC on the disposal of polychorinated biphenyls and poly-chlorinated terphenyls, OJ 1976 L 108.
[155] Directive 2000/53/EC of the European Parliament and of the Council on end-of-life vehicles, OJ 2000 L 269.
[156] Directive 2006/66/EC of the European Parliament and of the Council on batteries and accumulators and waste batteries and accumulators and repealing Directive 91/157/EEC, OJ 2006 L 266/1.
[157] Directive 2012/19/EU of the European Parliament and of the Council on waste electrical and electronic equipment, OJ 2012 L 197/38.
[158] European Parliament and Council Directive 94/62/EC on packaging and packaging waste, OJ 1994 L 365.
[159] Council Directive 96/59/EC on the disposal of polychlorinated biphenyls and polychlorinated terphenyls (PCB/PCT), OJ 1996 L 243.
[160] Council Directive 86/278/EEC on the protection of the environment, and in particular of the soil, when sewage sludge is used in agriculture, OJ 1986 L 181.
[161] Directive 2006/21/EC of the European Parliament and of the Council on the management of waste from extractive industries and amending Directive 2004/35/EC, OJ 2006 L 102.

producer responsibility, which is crucial for waste stream recycling directives, and partly by encouraging development of research and new technologies and products with a high recovery rate. As most of the waste stream legislation has been in force for over a decade, the Commission recently assessed its effectiveness and coherence so as to be in a position to propose amendments that will give new life to directives and align them with the Waste Directive.[162] With the exception of the Directive on Sewage Sludge, the Commission found the Directives assessed to be 'examples of meaningful European law making'. However, the assessment calls for further aligning of waste concepts in EU waste legislation, removal of obsolete legal requirements as well as more ambitious recycling targets especially concerning the recycling and preparing for reuse of packaging waste.[163]

Packaging

Packaging waste was recognised as one of the most important waste streams quite early, even though the first Directive had limited scope by only regulating liquid beverage containers for human consumption.[164] The Packaging and Packaging Waste Directive was adopted in 1994 with three broad objectives in mind – to protect or reduce the adverse impact of packaging and packaging waste on the environment in Member States and third countries; to ensure the functioning of the internal market; and to avoid obstacles to trade and distortion and restriction of competition within the Community.[165] The Directive applies to all packaging placed on the European market and all packaging waste, 'whether it is used or released at industrial, commercial, office, shop, service, household or any other level, regardless of the material used.'[166]

This is to be attained by preventing the generation of packaging waste and encouraging reuse, recycling and other forms of waste recovery (Articles 4, 5 and 6).[167] To that effect, Member States have an obligation to ensure that return, collection and recovery systems are put in place and functioning (Article 7). The Directive leaves discretion to Member States either to entrust this task to public authorities or to outsource private operators to provide the service. In order to facilitate the environmentally sound treatment of packaging waste, packaging should be properly marked and Member States have to ensure the compliance of Member States with essential packaging requirements (Annex II). Likewise, the requirement to develop databases on packaging and packaging waste provided in

---

[162] SWD(2014) 209. The assessment involved the examination of five waste stream directives: the packaging and packaging waste Directive, the Directive on sewage sludge, Directive on PCB/PCT, Directive on end-of-life vehicles and Directive on batteries and accumulators and waste batteries and accumulators.
[163] SWD(2014) 209; see COM(2015)596, final and http://ec.europa.eu/environment/waste/target_review.htm.
[164] Council Directive 85/339/EEC on containers of liquids for human consumption, OJ 1985 L 176.
[165] Directive 94/62/EC, Art. 1.   [166] Ibid., Art. 2.
[167] New and more specific targets were adopted in 2004. See Directive 2004/12/EC of the European Parliament and of the Council amending Directive 94/62/EC on packaging and packaging waste, OJ 2004 L 47.

the Directive assists the Commission and Member States to strengthen the monitoring of compliance with packaging directive provision (Article 12).

Most of the environmental objectives have been met so far. Recycling and recovering targets are attained in most of the Member States, and the Directive made significant contributions in reducing greenhouse gas emissions and ensuring access to raw materials.[168] However, the attainment of internal market requirements is still problematic as market operators have to adapt their packaging to requirements specific to each Member State.[169] The Directive only imposes an obligation for Member States to ensure that packaging meets essential requirements listed in Annex II, while the Commission should promote the development of European standards. Nevertheless, a recent study demonstrated the unwillingness of most Member States to enforce implementation of the essential requirements, while the industry is quite in favour of those requirements.[170] The Packaging and Packaging Waste Directive needs to be aligned with the WFD, which will entail the amendments of certain definitions; and more clarity is needed regarding the waste recycling targets in the PPW Directive and the household waste targets in the Waste Framework Directive.[171]

Batteries and Accumulators

The Batteries Directive[172] adopted in 2006 has a twofold objective. One is to reduce the adverse impact of 'batteries and accumulators and waste batteries and accumulators' on the environment, and the other to harmonise requirements concerning the heavy metal content and labelling of batteries and accumulators so to ensure the smooth functioning of the internal market and avoid distortion of competition within the Community.[173] The Directive applies to all types of batteries and accumulators, except those used in 'equipment connected with the protection of Member States' essential security interests, arms, munitions and war material or designed to be sent into space' (Art. 2). In order to achieve its environmental aims, the Directive lays down rules on the placing on the market of batteries and accumulators, in particular rules prohibiting selling batteries and accumulators containing cadmium and mercury above certain thresholds; as well as rules for the collection, treatment, recycling and disposal of waste batteries and accumulators. As a part of its environmental objectives, the Directive promotes high collection and recycling targets (Arts. 10 and 12)[174] but

---

[168] SWD/2014/209, 22. [169] *Ibid.*, 23.
[170] See http://ec.europa.eu/environment/waste/packaging/pdf/report_essential_requirements.pdf.
[171] SWD/2014/209, 65.
[172] Directive 2006/66/EC of the European Parliament and of the Council on batteries and accumulators and waste batteries and accumulators and repealing Directive 91/157/EEC, OJ 2006 L 266/1–14. It was recently amended by Directive 2013/56/EU of the European Parliament and of the Council amending Directive 2006/66/EC of the European Parliament and of the Council on batteries and accumulators and waste batteries and accumulators as regards the placing on the market of portable batteries and accumulators containing cadmium intended for use in cordless power tools, and of button cells with low mercury content, and repealing Commission Decision 2009/603/EC, OJ 2009 L 329.
[173] Recital 1. [174] Recycling by using best available techniques.

also gives emphasis to the development of new recycling and treatment technologies and research in this field. Member States must reach collection rates of at least 25 per cent by 26 September 2012 and 45 per cent by 26 September 2016.

All actors involved in the life-cycle of batteries and accumulators have a role to play in this process, whereby producers bear the costs of the collection, treatment, recycling and public information campaigns (Art. 16),[175] distributors have an obligation to take back waste portable batteries and accumulators (Art. 8) and to inform end-users about the options of discarding at sales points (Art. 20) and end-users are encouraged to deliver waste to designated points (Art. 8). In its last amendment, the EU regulator imposed some additional obligations on manufacturers who are encouraged to design appliances in such a way that waste batteries and accumulators can be readily removed or to include instructions on their removal for appliances in which batteries and accumulators are incorporated.[176]

Thus far, the Directive has proven to be a valuable instrument in addressing this waste stream. An especially significant result is the high level of consumer awareness about the separate collection of batteries. Another example is the mental association many consumers make with the now widely known EU sign of crossed-out wheeled bin which indicates 'separate collection' for all batteries and accumulators. The latest fitness check report indicates high collection rates for automotive and industrial batteries, though less positive results for collection of portable batteries.[177] Some environmental benefits outweigh the costs of its implementation; as is the case with substance labelling and the restriction on the use of heavy metals, the benefits exceed the costs.[178] Still, this Directive needs to be aligned with the WFD as it pre-dates the WFD. This will entail the inclusion of concepts such as the five-step waste hierarchy, life-cycle thinking and resource efficiency.[179]

End-of-Life Vehicles

'Every year, end-of-life vehicles (ELVs) generate between 8 and 9 million tonnes of waste in the European Union.'[180] The EU's response has been the adoption of the End-of-life Directive which focuses primarily on achieving environmental objectives, in particular the prevention of waste from vehicles and the increase of reuse, recycling and other forms of recovery of end-of-life vehicles and their components so as to reduce the disposal of waste (Article 1).[181] It applies to vehicles and end-of-life vehicles, including their components and materials. As a way of promoting waste prevention, this Directive places the primary onus on vehicle producers who

---

[175] There is an exemption for small producers.
[176] Directive 2013/56/EU. See also the new Commission proposal COM(2015)593 final, which tries to improve monitoring and compliance as well as to reduce administrative burdens on Member States.
[177] SWD/2014/209, 29.   [178] Ibid., 46.   [179] Ibid., 68.
[180] See http://ec.europa.eu/eurostat/web/waste/key-waste-streams/elvs.
[181] Directive 2000/53/EC of the European Parliament and of the Council on end-of-life vehicles. A related act is Directive 2005/64/EC of the European Parliament and of the Council on the type-approval of motor vehicles with regard to their reusability, recyclability and recoverability and amending Council Directive 70/156/EEC.

are encouraged to limit the use of hazardous substances in their new vehicles, design and produce vehicles which enable reuse and recycling and integrate an increasing quantity of recycled material in vehicles and other products (Article 4(1)). Nevertheless, the Directive also imposes responsibilities on other entities in the waste chain, including various economic operators involved in waste collection and treatment of waste, reuse and recovery. An important feature of the Directive is the obligation of Member States to ensure that economic operators use material coding standards that simplify the dismantling process (Article 8) and publish progress reports (Article 9(2)).

The Directive lived up to its expectations. According to the latest fitness check, four hazardous substances listed in the Directive (lead, mercury, cadmium and hexavalent chromium) had almost been phased out, while lead emissions have been reduced by 99.6 per cent, cadmium by 96 per cent and hexavalent chromium nearly completely (99.99 per cent).[182] Reuse and recycling targets from 2006 have been achieved by almost all Member States, and the number of waste treatment facilities is on the rise.[183] However, there are concerns that 2015 targets may not be achievable, which is dependent on the fluctuation of raw material prices in the future, but also the changing composition of vehicles.[184] The implementation of the directive resulted in some positive examples of how manufacturers are prone to change their behaviour provided environmental and economic benefits of the ELV Directive outweigh the costs of its implementation, especially in regard to the car industry. One of the successful examples is car manufacturer Nissan, which achieved possible recovery rates of 95 per cent, corresponding to the 2015 recovery target set by the Directive.[185]

Waste Electrical and Electronic Equipment (WEEE)

Waste generated by electrical and electronic equipment represents one of the fastest growing streams in the EU, with significant environmental and health implications for humans and the environment.[186] Initially this area was regulated by the first WEEE Directive adopted in 2002,[187] accompanied by the Directive on the restriction of the use of certain hazardous substances in electrical and electronic equipment.[188] The Directive sets up a general framework for the collection, treatment and recovery of waste electrical and electronic equipment, while imposing extensive financial responsibilities on producers. The Directive was revised in 2012 to tackle some of the difficulties experienced in its implementation, including unintended administrative and other costs, lack of environmentally sound collection and treatment of waste and unsatisfactory collection and recycling rates.[189]

---

[182] Ex-post evaluation of certain waste stream Directives Final Report, 18 April 2014, 149, http://ec.europa.eu/environment/waste/pdf/target_review/Final%20Report%20Ex-Post.pdf.
[183] Ibid., 117. [184] Ibid., 114. [185] Ibid. [186] Recital 5 of the WEEE Directive.
[187] OJ 2003 L 37.
[188] Directive 2002/95/EC of the European Parliament and of the Council on the restriction of the use of certain hazardous substances in electrical and electronic equipment, OJ 2002 L 37.
[189] Directive 2012/19/EU, OJ 2012 L 197/38; see Commission implementation reports available at: http://ec.europa.eu/environment/waste/weee/reports_en.htm. The Directive on the

The main purpose of this legislation is to contribute to sustainable production and consumption by prevention of WEEE generation, the promotion of reuse, recycling and other forms of recovery of such wastes and to contribute to the environmentally sound performance of all operators involved in the life-cycle of WEEE (Article 1). Unlike its predecessor, the new Directive applies to all electrical and electronic equipment, with very few exceptions (Article 2). In order to improve unsatisfactory collection rates, the new Directive lays down minimum collection targets from 2016, with a gradual increase,[190] and recovery and recycling targets to be met in phases.[191] As with all recycling Directives, special responsibilities are imposed on producers. The producer responsibility principle is implemented both through encouragement of design and production of electrical and electronic equipment and by imposing obligations on producers to finance the costs of waste management of their products (Articles 4 and 13).

Future Challenges

EU waste law and policy has a long lineage. It started with the well-known 1975 Directive on waste and grew into one of the most comprehensive environmental portfolios. The upward trend in generation of waste and the need to address and treat new types of waste prompted EU waste policy. However, the diversity of issues covered within this area, as well as a high dependence on the development of technologies and scientific advances, necessitate frequent review and amendment of the EU waste law. Very often this requires Member States to change their institutional, administrative and technical practices and heavily invest in this policy area. This often impedes or slows down the implementation and enforcement which proved over the years to be one of the most important challenges regarding waste. Likewise, implementation of the waste *acquis* occurs at the regional and local levels which requires strong partnership between local authorities, private providers and citizens. No less important is raising public awareness and addressing public concerns regarding various waste treatment operations at the local level. Finally, one of the challenges is fully to embrace waste not only as a hazard but as a resource that can render national economies greener. Although this approach is firmly stipulated in the 7th EAP, given the difficult economic situation for many Member States, their appetite for such a change in perspective has been reduced.

restriction of the use of certain hazardous substances in electrical and electronic equipment was recast in 2011 – Directive 2011/65/EU of the European Parliament and of the Council on the restriction of the use of certain hazardous substances in electrical and electronic equipment, OJ 2011 L 174.

[190] Art. 7(1): From 2016, the minimum collection rate shall be 45 per cent calculated on the basis of the total weight of WEEE collected in accordance with Articles 5 and 6 in a given year in the Member State concerned, expressed as a percentage of the average weight of EEE placed on the market in the three preceding years in that Member State. From 2019, the minimum collection rate to be achieved annually shall be 65 per cent of the average weight of EEE placed on the market in the three preceding years in the Member State concerned, or alternatively 85 per cent of WEEE generated on the territory of that Member State.

[191] Annex V.

Index

Aarhus Convention
　about, 168
　access to information, 172
　access to justice
　　about, 176, 237
　　access to environmental justice in general, 239
　　conditions of access, 240
　　effectiveness and equivalence of remedies for breach, 240
　　as to environmental information decisions, 238
　　EU implementation, 237, 240
　　harmonisation measures, 241
　　legal aid, 240
　　national procedural autonomy as to, 240
　　provisions, 238
　　public information, 240
　　as to public participation, 238
　compliance, 171
　content of, 171
　environmental governance, 42
　environmental information, 238, 240
　environmental rights approach, 169
　implementation in EU law, 179
　public information, access to justice as to, 240
　public participation
　　access to justice as to, 238
　　decisions on 'specific activities', 173
　　environmental plans, programmes and policies, 175
　　preparation of regulations or legislation, 176
　ratification, 170
　voluntary regulation schemes, 148
Aarhus Convention on Access to Environmental Information, Public Participation and Access to Justice in Environmental Matters. see Aarhus Convention
access to information, 172
access to justice
　Aarhus Convention. see Aarhus Convention
　complaints to EU Ombudsman, 254
　EIA Directive, 400
　EU courts, 246
　EU legislation on national level access, 237
　European Citizens' Initiative (ECI), 256
　internal review of administrative acts, 251
　non-judicial means of, 254
　petitions to European Parliament, 255
accession to EU. see enlargement of EU
accountability principle of governance, 42
Action programmes, 3
administration. see EU institutions
administrative feasibility of regulation, 125
Agricultural Fund for Rural Development, 87
agricultural land use
　climate change, 274
　water pollution from nitrates. see water law
air pollution
　about, 298
　air pollutants subject to regulation, 306
　Air Quality Framework Directive (AQFD)
　　about, 313
　　importance, 308
　　quality-based approach, 311, 312
　　repeal of previous Directives, 312
　ammonia (NH$_3$), 307
　benzene, 307
　carbon monoxide (CO), 307
　EU legal framework for ambient air quality, 306, 312
　EU/Member State balance, 336
　ground level ozone (O$_3$), 306
　industrial emissions. see industrial emissions
　key themes of EU air pollution law, 299
　lead, 307
　Member State implementation of EU ambient air legislation, 315
　methane (CH$_4$), 307
　National Emissions Ceiling Directive (NECD)
　　about, 312

Best Available Techniques (BAT) standards, 312
　importance, 308, 311
　nitrogen dioxide (NO$_2$), 306
　oxides of nitrogen (NO$_x$), 306
　ozone depleting substances, 301
　particulate matter (PM10 and PM2.5), 306
　standardisation of air pollution control policies, 309
　sulphur dioxide (SO$_2$), 306
　volatile organic compounds (VOCs), 306
ammonia (NH$_3$), air pollution from, 307
Amsterdam Treaty, 6
anthropocentrism. see philosophy

bathing water. see water law
Batteries Directive, 514
benzene, air pollution from, 307
Best Available Techniques (BAT) standards
　Industrial Emissions Directive (IED). see industrial emissions
　National Emissions Ceiling Directive (NECD), 312
biocentrism. see philosophy
biodiversity. see nature and biodiversity protection
biofuels and bioliquids. see energy
Birds Directive. see nature and biodiversity protection
business interest groups. see interest groups
by-products. see waste policy

carbon emissions. see climate change
carbon monoxide (CO), air pollution from, 307
cars. see road transport
central European countries, accession of, 48
CHAP central registry for complaints and enquiries, 191
charges and taxes. see taxation
Charter of Fundamental Rights, 8, 165
chemicals. see technological risk regulation

CITES Regulation, 444
civil society. *see* interest groups
climate change
   about, 257
   agricultural land use, 274
   Carbon Capture and Storage (CCS) Directive, 274
   challenge of, 273, 296
   climate and energy legislation package, 273
   competence of EU, 258
   consumer information on fuel economy and CO_2 emissions, 274
   Effort Sharing Decision, 274
   Emissions Trading System (ETS), 273
      allocation of allowances, 293
      approach to emission control, 289
      backloading of allowances, 296
      CDM credits and offsetting, 294
      economic recession, effects of, 294
      effectiveness of, 292
      market management issues, 293
      Market Stability Reserve, 296
      as market-based regulation, 290
   Energy Efficiency Directive (EED), 274
   Fluorinated Greenhouse Gases Regulation, 274
   forestry, 274
   greenhouse gas (GHG) emissions monitoring and reporting, 274
   leadership by EU
      aviation and emissions trading as example of, 269
      carbon leakage measures, 267
      challenges for, 260
      emission reduction targets, 268
      international agreements, 262
      'leading by example' policy, 266
   renewable energy. *see* energy
CLP Regulation, 457
Coase, Ronald, 441
coherence principle of governance, 42
Cohesion Fund, 86, 87
'command and control' regulation. *see* regulation
Commission White Paper on environmental governance. *see* governance
Committee of the Regions (COR), 69
Common Agricultural Policy (CAP), sustainability and, 88
Communications. *see* instruments
competence, environmental
   competences generally, 22

competent authorities
   EIA decisions, communication of, 398
   EIA obligation, 389
   Environmental Liability Directive powers and duties, 211
   SEA decisions, communication of, 407
complaints handling by European Commission. *see* enforcement
compliance
   Aarhus Convention, 171
   bathing water Directives, 367
   drinking water Directives, 363
   groundwater Directive 2006, 351
   urban waste water Directive, 377
consultation
   between Directorates General, 58
   EIA public consultation and participation, 395
   SEA procedure
      consultation of designated authorities, 405
      consultation of public affected or likely to be affected, 406
      transboundary consultation, 406
consumer information, car fuel economy and CO_2 emissions, 274
corporate social responsibility (CSR), 145
Council of the EU
   Environment Council, 60
   environmental policy role, 60
Court of Justice
   defences, 193
   environmental policy role, 67
   European Commission referral to, 192
   general, persistent or systemic breaches of EU law, 192
   penalties, 195
Court of Justice of the European Union (CJEU)
   Court of Justice. *see* Court of Justice
   General Court. *see* General Court
courts
   access to justice. *see* access to justice
   Court of Justice. *see* Court of Justice
   enforcement by. *see* enforcement
   General Court. *see* General Court
   legal aid, access to, 240
criminal penalties. *see* enforcement

damage to environment. *see* environmental damage
damages, State liability, 236

decent environment, no automatic right to, 153
decentred governance. *see* governance
decision-making, science-based, 35
Decisions. *see* instruments
derogations
   Birds Directive, 419
   Habitats Directive, 419
   technological risk regulation, 480
   Water Framework Directive (WFD) 2000, 352
direct effect. *see* effect of EU law
direct regulation. *see* regulation
Directives
   about, 78
   'horizontal' direct effect
      of 'general principle' of EU law, 235
   'incidental' effect, 234
   reliance on Directives against private parties, 229
   reliance on
      against private parties, 229
      against State and 'emanations of the State', 226
   transposition at accession, 50
   'vertical' direct effect
      concept of the 'State', 228
      prior to expiry of transposition period, 228
      reliance on Directives against the State and 'emanations of the State', 226
'discard', meaning of, 500
drinking water. *see* water law

eastern European countries, accession of, 48
EC Treaty, 1
eco-labelling schemes, 148
economic efficiency as regulatory factor, 124
economic law and policy. *see* integration with economic law and policy
effect of EU law
   direct effect
      about, 217
      bodies which must apply directly effective provisions, 222
      Decisions, 223
      Directives, 226
      international environmental agreements, 224
      must a directly effective provision confer a right on an individual?, 219
      Regulations, 223
      Treaty provisions, 222

effect of EU law (cont.)
 'horizontal' direct effect
  environmental impact assessment (EIA), 379
  of 'general principle' of EU law, 235
  'incidental' effect, 234
  reliance on Directives against private parties, 229
 indirect effect, duty of consistent interpretation, 230
 'vertical' direct effect
  concept of the 'State', 228
  direct effect of Directives prior to expiry of transposition period, 228
  reliance on Directives against the State and 'emanations of the State', 226
effectiveness principle of governance, 42
EIA Directive. see environmental impact assessment (EIA)
electrical and electronic equipment waste (WEEE). see waste policy
emissions. see climate change; industrial emissions
end-of-life vehicles (ELV). see waste policy
end-of-waste. see waste policy
energy
 climate and energy legislation package, 273
 Energy Efficiency Directive (EED), 274
 national measures for green energy, 112
 renewable energy
  EU/Member State balance, 275
  free movement of, 287
  multi-level governance, 275
  Sources (RES) Directive, 113
 Renewable Energy Directive (RED)
  about, 274, 278
  access to grid, 282
  biofuels and bioliquids, 283
  cooperation between Member States, 281
  guarantees of origin, 282
  National Renewable Energy Action Plans (NREAPs), 280
enforcement
 criminal penalties, 212
 effectiveness and equivalence of remedies, principles of, 240
 EIA Directive remedies, 398

Environmental Liability Directive. see Environmental Liability Directive
European Commission
 administrative phase, 188
 CHAP central registry for complaints and enquiries, 191
 defences, 193
 enforcement improvement initiatives, 199
 enforcement role, 186
 general, persistent or systemic breaches of EU law, 192
 interim measures, 194
 litigation phase, 192
 Maltese bird-hunting case as example, 195
 overview of procedure, 186
 penalties, 195
 Pilot scheme for complaints handling, 191
 prioritisation of cases, 189
interim measures, 194
national authorities
 IMPEL. see European Union Network for the Implementation and Enforcement of Environmental Law (IMPEL)
 principles, 200
nature and biodiversity protection, 444
penalties
 criminal penalties, 212
 European Commission, 195
private enforcement. see private enforcement
public enforcement, 184
SEA Directive remedies, 407
enlargement of EU
 central and eastern European countries, 48
 common difficulties in accession process, 50
 environmental benefits from, 49
 environmental challenges of, 47, 53
 environmental chapter, complexity of, 49
 EU financial assistance, 52
 institutional adjustments, 50
 political constraints on implementation process, 52
 transitional periods, 52
 transposition of environmental Directives, 50
Environment Council. see Council of the EU

environmental action programmes (EAPs)
 about, 82
 adoption of, 64
 Commission's competence to propose, 59
 first (1973–1982), 82
 second (1973–1982), 82
 third (1982–1986), 82
 fourth (1987–1992), 82
 fifth (1992–1999), 73, 83, 138
 sixth (2002–2012), 83, 490
 seventh (2013–2020), 15, 73, 83, 106, 107, 117, 129, 490, 517
 green economy, 129
 green public procurement, 117
 IMPEL, 73
 low-carbon economy, 86
 sustainability, 107, 138
 sustainable development, 15
 waste management, 490, 517
environmental ethics. see ethics
environmental governance. see governance
environmental governance generally. see governance
environmental guarantee provisions, 18
environmental impact assessment (EIA)
 conceptual foundations of, 381
 definition of, 379, 387
 direct horizontal application, 379
 EIA Directive
  access to justice, 400
  amendments, 385
  Annex I projects (mandatory EIA), 390
  Annex II projects (project screening), 392
  'competent authority', 389
  EIA process, 387
  entry into force, 385
  exemption generally, 393
  exemption of specific project, 393
  guidance documents, 386
  mandatory EIA, 390
  procedural requirements, 379
  project screening process, 391
  projects subject to EIA, 390
  purpose and scope, 386
  refusal of development consent, 434
  remedies, 398
  SEA Directive compared, 402
 Espoo Convention
  entry into force, 383
  Europe-wide application, 382

Implementation Committee, 383
obligations, 383
protocols, 383
signatories, 382
UNECE and, 382
if 'bottleneck' for strategic energy projects, 397
'Information Processing' model, 382
'Institutionalist Politics' model, 382
international environmental treaties, 380
as international law principle, 381
international spread of, 379
national applicability, 381
'Organisational Politics' model, 382
'Pluralist Politics' model, 382
'Political Economy' model, 382
procedure
  communication of competent authority decision, 398
  developer's EIA report, 394
  development consent decision, 396
  public consultation and participation, 395
  relationship between assessment procedures, 397
  transboundary projects, 396
public participation, 381
Pulp Mills judgment, 381
rationalist model, 382
Rio Declaration, 380
SEA procedure
  communication of competent authority decision, 407
  consultation of designated authorities, 405
  consultation of public affected or likely to be affected, 406
  environmental report, 405
  requirement for, 405
  transboundary consultation, 406
Strategic Environmental Assessment (SEA) Directive
  EIA Directive compared, 402
  exemptions, 404
  higher level of decision-making, 402
  mandatory SEA, 403
  obligation to carry out SEA, 403
  project screening process, 404
  purpose and scope, 403
  remedies, 407
  SEA procedure, 405
'Symbolic Politics' model, 382

environmental information. *see* Aarhus Convention
environmental integration principle
  about, 103
  treaty basis, 91
environmental law
  actors and institutions, overview of, 54
  competence. *see* competence
  contextual understanding of, 25
  effect of. *see* effect of EU law
  enforcement. *see* enforcement
  environmental policy. *see* environmental policy
  environmental protection. *see* environmental protection
  foundations of, 1
  general legal bases of, 17
  harmonisation. *see* harmonisation
  instruments. *see* instruments
  international law. *see* international environmental law
  legal bases of, 16
  legislation. *see* instruments
  principles. *see* principles
  regulation. *see* regulation
  treaty provision, historical development, 1
Environmental Liability Directive
  about, 204
  applicability, 205
  causation, 207
  competent authorities' powers and duties, 211
  duties imposed on operators, 209
  observations or 'requests for action', lodging of, 212
  transboundary damage, 212
environmental philosophy. *see* philosophy
environmental policy
  actors and institutions, overview of, 54
  aims of, 8
  contextual understanding of, 25
  environmental competences, 22
  ethics. *see* ethics
  and EU enlargement. *see* enlargement of EU
  EU/Member State balance. *see* State
  geography and. *see* enlargement of EU
  governance. *see* governance
  hierarchy of policy goals, 128
  'high level of environmental protection', aim of, 9
  historical development of, 1

overarching aim of, 8
philosophy. *see* philosophy
principle objectives of, 8
public participation right. *see* Aarhus Convention
risk. *see* risk
science and. *see* scientific evidence
and sustainable development, 12
environmental protection, aim of 'high level of', 9
environmental safeguard provision, 18
Espoo Convention. *see* environmental impact assessment (EIA)
ethics
  compatibility of regulation with, 127
  emergence of environmental ethics, 44
  moral perspective on environmental policy, 43
EU external action programme, 55
EU institutions
  internal review of administrative acts, 251
  Ombudsman, complaints to, 254
Europe
  Aarhus Convention. *see* Aarhus Convention
  Espoo Convention. *see* environmental impact assessment (EIA)
  United Nations Economic Commission for Europe (UNECE), 382
European Agricultural Fund for Rural Development, 86
European Citizens' Initiative (ECI), 256
European Commission
  'citizens' initiative' mechanism, 58
  competences, 57
  consultation between DGs, 58
  DG Environment, 57
  directorates general (DG), 55
  enforcement role. *see* enforcement
  environmental action programmes (EAPs), 59
  environmental policy role, 54
  international representation role, 59
  legislative programme, 59
  portfolios in environmental policy area, 56
  Regulatory Fitness and Performance Programme (REFIT), 108, 443
  size of, 55
  soft law instruments, 59
  supervisory initiatives, 59

Index

European Convention on Human
Rights (ECHR)
about, 153
no right to healthy or decent
environment, 153
right to fair trial (Article 6(1)), 161
right to property (Article 1 of
Protocol No. 1), 162
right to respect for private and family
life (Article 8)
development of ECtHR's
approach, 154
margin of appreciation, 158
European Council, 65
European Economic and Social
Committee (EESC), 68
European Environment Agency, 70
European Investment Bank (EIB), 72
European Maritime and Fisheries Fund,
86, 87
European Parliament
environmental policy role, 62
petitions to, 255
European Regional Development
Fund, 86, 87
European Social Charter (ESC). *see*
human rights
European Social Fund, 86, 87
European Structural Fund, 86
European Union Network for the
Implementation and
Enforcement of Environmental
Law (IMPEL)
aims of, 203
environmental policy role, 73
establishment of, 203
EU Seventh Environmental Action
Programme, 204
eutrophication, 375
expert advice, technological risk
regulation, 468

fair trial, right to. *see* human rights
financial assistance to accession
countries, 52
financial instruments. *see* instruments
flexibility of regulation, 126
flexible governance. *see* governance
forestry, climate change and, 274
free movement, renewable energy
and, 287
fundamental rights. *see* human rights
funds, structural and investment. *see*
instruments

General Court, 67
genetically modified organisms (GMOs).
see technological risk regulation

geography. *see* enlargement of EU
good governance. *see* governance
governance
Aarhus Convention, 42
accountability principle, 42
coherence principle, 42
Commission White Paper, 41
effectiveness principle, 42
environmental governance
generally, 36
flexible and decentred
governance, 40
good governance, principles
of, 41
hierarchy and, 39
multilevel governance
about, 39
renewable energy, 275
openness principle, 41
participation principle, 42
strategic environmental governance,
historical development, 37
transnational governance, 39
Water Framework Directive (WFD)
2000, 357
green energy. *see* energy
green public procurement. *see* public
procurement
greenhouse gases. *see* climate
change
ground level ozone (O_3), air pollution
from, 306
groundwater. *see* water law
Guidelines. *see* instruments

Habitats Directive. *see* nature and
biodiversity protection
harmonisation
access to justice, 241
environmental measures
generally, 18
technological risk regulation,
449, 450
hazardous waste. *see* waste policy
healthy environment, no automatic
right to, 153
hierarchy
governance and, 39
hierarchical regulation, 120, 121,
129
of policy goals, 128
'high level of environmental
protection', aim of, 9
'horizontal' direct effect. *see* effect of
EU law
human rights
Aarhus Convention. *see* Aarhus
Convention

about, 150
Charter of Fundamental Rights,
8, 165
ECHR. *see* European Convention
on Human Rights (ECHR)
European Social Charter (ESC),
163
international human rights law, 182

ideology. *see* ethics; philosophy
impact assessment. *see* environmental
impact assessment (EIA)
incineration. *see* waste policy
indirect effect. *see* effect of EU law
industrial emissions
Best Available Techniques (BAT)
standards
BAT reference documents
(BREFs), 330
flexibility of, 333
IED provision, 300, 325
standardisation function of, 328
costs of air pollution from, 298
Directive (IED)
analysis of, 299
Best Available Techniques (BAT)
standards, 300, 325
flexibility of, 333
focus on large industrial
facilities, 300
integrated pollution prevention
and control (IPPC), 323
standardisation within IPPC
framework, 328
regulation of, 321
industrial waste water. *see* water law
information
access to. *see* Aarhus Convention
consumer. *see* consumer information
institutional compatibility of
regulation, 126
instruments
Communications, 84
Decisions, 80
Directives. *see* Directives
EAPs. *see* environmental action
programmes (EAPs)
effect of. *see* effect of EU law
financial instruments, 84
flexibility in use of, 76
Guidelines, 84
LIFE (Financial Instrument for the
Environment Regulation), 84
Recommendations, 83
Regulations, 77
Regulatory Fitness and
Performance Programme
(REFIT), 108, 443

Index

Resolutions, 84
soft law, 83
structural and investment
    funds, 86
integrated pollution prevention and
    control (IPPC), 323
integration principle. *see*
    environmental integration
    principle
integration with economic law and
    policy
    about, 105
    green public procurement, 116
    internal market provisions, 109
    national measures for green
        energy, 112
    Renewable Energy Sources (RES)
        Directive, 113
interest groups
    business interest groups, 76
    enforcement by. *see* private
        enforcement
    European Citizens' Initiative
        (ECI), 256
    growth in, 74
    'horizontal' direct effect of Directives
        upon, 229
    involvement in regulation, 122
    observations or 'requests for action',
        lodging of, 212
    public interest groups (NGOs),
        74
    public participation right. *see* Aarhus
        Convention
    regulatory techniques associated
        with, 122
    voluntary regulation schemes. *see*
        regulation
internal review of EU administrative
    acts, 251
International Court of Justice (ICJ),
    Pulp Mills judgment, 381
international environmental law
    direct effect, 224
    environmental impact assessment
        (EIA), 380, 381
    EU leadership on climate
        change, 262
    EU water law in relation, 340
international human rights law.
    see human rights
Invasive Alien Species
    Regulation, 445
investment funds, structural and.
    see instruments

justice. *see* courts

labelling. *see* eco-labelling schemes
Landfill Directive, 508
lead
    air pollution, 307
    drinking water, 362
legal bases of environmental law, 16
legal proceedings. *see* courts
Leghold Traps Regulation, 445
legislation. *see* instruments
liability, State liability in damages, 236
LIFE (Financial Instrument for the
    Environment Regulation).
    see instruments
Lisbon Treaty, 7, 8
litigation. *see* courts

Maastricht Treaty, 6
Maltese bird-hunting case, 195
Marine Strategy Framework
    Directive, 445
market-based regulation. *see* regulation
Member States. *see* State
methane (CH_4), air pollution
    from, 307
morality. *see* ethics; philosophy
motor vehicles. *see* road transport
multilevel governance. *see* governance

nanotechnology regulation, 483
National Renewable Energy Action
    Plans (NREAPs). *see* energy
nature and biodiversity protection
    about, 410
    biodiversity protection
        Commission Communication
            2011, 412
        commitment to, 413
        concept of, 414, 415
        shift towards, 413
    Birds Directive
        adoption of, 410, 416
        derogations, 419
        designation process, 420
        designation-based protection, 417
        economic considerations, 423
        effectiveness of, 443
        Important Bird Area inventory
            1989 (IBA 89) and, 426
        Member State discretion, 425
        prohibitions, 418
        special protection areas (SPAs),
            416, 423
        tiered approach to
            conservation, 416
        challenges for, 445
        CITES Regulation, 444
        Coase theorem, 441

competence
    conferral, 410
    controversies, 411
conceptual changes, 412
conceptual differences, 414
Convention on Biological
    Diversity, 413
declassification of protected
    sites, 440
designation of protected sites
    advantages and disadvantages
        of, 422
    consequences of, 421
    declassification process, 440
    economic considerations, 423
    importance of, 418
    Lappel Bank case, 426
    Leybucht case, 423
    Member State discretion, 423
    process of, 420
    protective regimes compared, 428
    site selection, 420
development on protected sites
    'any plan or project', 436
    'appropriate assessment', 434
    assessment of proposals, 434
    case law, assessment of, 439
    'integrity of the site', 438
    'significant effect', 436
economic considerations, 423
ecosystem services, 414, 415
enforcement, calls for stricter, 444
EU/national policy balancing, 445
Habitats Directive
    adoption of, 416
    biodiversity protection, 413
    coverage, 417
    declassification process, 440
    derogations, 419
    designation process, 420, 428
    deterioration and disturbance of
        habitats and species, avoidance
        of, 434
    development on protected sites,
        assessment of proposals, 434
    effectiveness of, 443
    First Corporate Shipping (FCS)
        case, 427
    management of protected
        sites, 432
    Member State discretion, 427
    nature conservation, 414
    precautionary principle, 431, 432,
        434, 437, 439
    prohibitions, 418
    sincere cooperation, principle
        of, 432

Index

nature and biodiversity (cont.)
   site selection, 421
   sites of community importance (SCIs), 421, 428
   special areas of conservation (SACs), 418, 421, 427
   species of Community interest (Annex V species), 419
   sustainable development, 47
   timing of Member State obligations, 431
   Invasive Alien Species Regulation, 445
   Leghold Traps Regulation, 445
   Marine Strategy Framework Directive, 445
   Mid-Term Review of the EU Biodiversity Strategy to 2020 (2015), 443
   Natura 2000, 413, 417, 418, 420, 421, 424
   natural capital
     concept of, 415, 416
     emphasis on, 414
   nature conservation
     concept of, 414, 415
     shift from, 413
   offsetting of biodiversity losses, 412, 441
   precautionary principle, 411, 431, 432, 434, 437, 439
   Regulatory Fitness and Performance Programme (REFIT) and, 443
   sincere cooperation, principle of, 432
   State of Nature Report (2015), 443
   subsidiarity, 410
   threats to, 410
   Timber Regulation, 445
   Trade in Seal Products Regulation, 445
   weak sustainability, 441
   Zoos Directive, 445
nitrates. *see* water law
nitrogen dioxide (NO_2), air pollution from, 306
non-governmental organisations (NGOs). *see* interest groups

observations, lodging of, 212
Ombudsman, complaints to, 254
openness principle of governance, 41
oxides of nitrogen (NO_x), air pollution from, 306
ozone. *see* air pollution

packaging waste. *see* waste policy
participation principle of governance, 42

particulate matter (PM-10 and PM 2.5), air pollution from, 306
penalties. *see* enforcement
philosophy
   anthropocentrism, 44, 46
   biocentrism, 45
   compatibility of regulation with, 127
   environmental law and policy, 45
   environmental philosophy, historical development, 43
   moral perspective on environmental policy, 43
   sentientism, 45
   sustainable development, 46
   theories of value, 44
pilot scheme for complaints handling, 191
political feasibility of regulation, 125
polluter pays principle
   about, 100
   applicability to national legislation, 432, 93
   causation and, 208
   economic efficiency and, 124
   Environmental Liability Directive, 205, 209, 210
   introduction of, 489
   REACH Regulation, 455
   risk regulation, 29
   Single European Act (SEA), 5, 497
   treaty basis, 91
   Waste Framework Directive, 497
   Water Framework Directive, 355
   water pricing and, 356
pollution control and prevention
   Groundwater Directive 2006, 351
   integrated pollution prevention and control (IPPC), 323
   'priority substances'. *see* water law
precautionary principle
   about, 94
   science-based decision-making, 33
   technological risk regulation, 466
   treaty basis, 91
preventive principle
   about, 99
   Single European Act (SEA), 5, 497
   Third EAP, 82
   treaty basis, 91
principles
   in EU Environmental Law, 90
   as 'general' principles of EU law, 91
   integration principle. *see* environmental integration principle

integration with economic law and policy. *see* integration with economic law and policy
   legal status and effect of, 92
   polluter pays principle. *see* polluter pays principle
   preventive principle. *see* preventive principle
   proximity principle, 497
   source principle. *see* rectification at source principle
private enforcement
   about, 217
   access to justice. *see* access to justice
   direct effect of EU environmental law
     about, 217
     bodies which must apply directly effective provisions, 222
     Decisions, 223
     Directives, 226
     international environmental agreements, 224
     must a directly effective provision confer a right on an individual?, 219
     Regulations, 223
     Treaty provisions, 222
   duty of consistent interpretation ('indirect effect'), 230
   EU level, 246
   'horizontal' direct effect
     of 'general principle' of EU law, 235
     'incidental' effect, 234
     reliance on Directives against private parties, 229
   national level, 217
   state liability in damages, 236
   'triangular' cases, 233
   'vertical' direct effect
     concept of the 'State', 228
     direct effect of Directives prior to expiry of transposition period, 228
     reliance on Directives against the State and 'emanations of the State', 226
private sector. *see* interest groups
procedural fairness, technological risk regulation, 469
production residue. *see* waste policy
property, right to. *see* human rights
proximity principle, 497
public enforcement. *see* enforcement
public information. *see* Aarhus Convention

public interest groups (NGOs).
    see interest groups
public participation
    Aarhus Convention. see Aarhus
        Convention
    bathing water Directives, 367
    environmental impact assessment
        (EIA), 381
    technological risk regulation, 469
    Water Framework Directive (WFD)
        2000, 357
public procurement, 'greening' of, 116
public sector. see interest groups
Pulp Mills judgment, 381

radioactive waste and substances.
    see waste policy
REACH Regulation, 454
Recommendations. see instruments
rectification at source principle, 100
    implementation of, 92
    proximity principle and, 497
    Single European Act (SEA), 5,
        497
    treaty basis, 91
regulation
    changes in approach to, 120
    choice of regulatory technique
        administrative feasibility
            factor, 125
        economic efficiency factor, 124
        environmental effectiveness
            factor, 123
        factors and philosophies
            influencing, 123
        flexibility factor, 126
        ideological compatibility
            factor, 127
        institutional compatibility
            factor, 126
        political feasibility factor, 125
    direct (hierarchical or 'command and
            control') techniques
        about, 129
        advantages and disadvantages
            of, 133
        flexible direct regulation
            (framework Directives), 132
        proceduralised direct
            regulation, 133
    interest groups
        involvement in regulation, 122
        regulatory techniques associated
            with, 122
    market-based instruments
        about, 135
        environmental charges and
            taxes, 142

as policy tools, 137
tradable permit schemes, 139
public participation right. see Aarhus
    Convention
voluntary instruments
    Aarhus Convention
        provision, 148
    about, 143
    corporate social responsibility
        (CSR), 145
    eco-labelling, 148
Regulations. see instruments
Regulatory Fitness and Performance
    Programme (REFIT), 108,
    443
remedies. see enforcement
renewable energy. see energy
reporting
    developer's EIA report, 394
    greenhouse gas (GHG)
        emissions, 274
    SEA environmental report, 405
    'requests for action', lodging
        of, 212
Resolutions. see instruments
respect for private and family life, right
    to. see human rights
Rhine, River, Sandoz factory
    fire, 338
rights. see human rights
Rio Declaration
    environmental impact assessment
        (EIA), 380
    sustainable development, 46
risk
    EU risk regulation regimes, 27
    risk and science generally, 26
    risk regulation, critique of, 29
    risk regulation regimes, functions
        of, 26
    technological risk. see technological
        risk regulation
    uncertainty, regulation of. see
        technological risk regulation
rivers. see water law
road transport, consumer information
    on fuel economy and CO2
    emissions, 274
Rome, Treaty of. see EC Treaty

safeguard clauses, 477
Sandoz factory fire, 338
scientific evidence
    discretionary decision-making, 35
    precautionary principle, 33
    risk and science generally, 26
    scientific uncertainty, precautionary
        action, 33

Treaty provisions on, 31
sentientism. see philosophy
shipment of waste. see waste policy
Single European Act (SEA), 4
society sectors. see interest groups
source principle. see rectification at
    source principle
State
    concept of the 'State', 228
    EIA applicability, 381
    implementation of EU ambient air
        legislation, 315
    liability in damages, 236
    measures exceeding EU
        standards, 451
    policy balancing with EU
        air pollution, 336
        aviation emissions, 269
        nature and biodiversity
            protection, 445
        renewable energy, 275
    procedural autonomy on access to
        justice, 240
strategic environmental assessment
    (SEA). see environmental
    impact assessment (EIA)
strategic environmental governance. see
    governance
structural and investment funds. see
    instruments
sulphur dioxide (SO$_2$), air pollution
    from, 306
surface water. see water law
sustainability
    biofuels, 284
    CDM initiatives, 295
    Common Agricultural Policy
        (CAP), 88
    EAPs, 107, 138
    European Investment Bank
        (EIB), 72
    European Maritime and Fisheries
        Fund, 88
    Habitats Directive, 419
    integrated pollution prevention and
        control (IPPC) and, 323
    Maastricht Treaty, 6
    nature and biodiversity protection,
        weak sustainability, 423, 428,
        441, 443
    renewable energy, 32
    SEA Directive, 402
    'sustainability science', 359
    Sustainable Use Directive, 355
    waste electrical and electronic
        equipment (WEEE), 517
    Water Framework Directive (WFD),
        343, 352

Index

sustainable development
  Amsterdam Treaty, 7
  Charter of Fundamental Rights, 8, 167
  climate change and, 258, 261
  Cohesion Fund, 86
  corporate social responsibility (CSR) and, 143
  environmental action programmes (EAPs), 15
  environmental integration principle and, 103
  Environmental Liability Directive, 205
  environmental philosophy and, 46
  environmental policy and, 12
  environmental protection and, 103
  EU external action programme, 55
  Fifth Environmental Action Programme (1992–1999), 83, 138
  Habitats Directive, 47
  human rights and, 183
  LIFE (Financial Instrument for the Environment Regulation), 85
  Lisbon Treaty, 8, 9
  overarching principle of, 69
  policy conformity with, 74
  policy paradigm, 128
  promotion of, 93, 450
  Public Procurement Directive, 117
  Rio Declaration, 46
  scope of, 107
  Single European Act (SEA), 6
  strategic environmental governance, 38
  Sustainable Development Strategy (SDS), 105, 107

taxation, regulation proposals, 142
technological risk regulation
  chemicals
    CLP Regulation, 457
    REACH Regulation, 454
    regulatory focus on, 447
    regulatory regime, 448, 453
    risks from, 448
    supplementary measures, 459
    trade regulation, 447
  complexity, 463
  dual purpose regulation, 449, 450
  effectiveness of, 464
  environmental protection objective, 449, 450
  genetically modified organisms (GMOs)
    ban on cultivation, 481
    coexistence with non-GMO areas, 450, 471, 476
    derogations, 480
    post-authorisation differentiation, 475
    regulatory framework, 474
    safeguard clauses, 477
  harmonisation objective, 449, 450
  information, importance for decision-making, 487
  legitimacy challenges, 463
  market and regulation in relation, 487
  Member State measures exceeding EU standards, 451
  nanotechnology, 483
  proceduralised approach, 463
  regulatory functions, 460
  risk identification, 460
  risk management, 461
  risk-based perspective, 449
  uncertainty, regulation of
    decision-making, risk considerations, 465
    expert advice, 468
    high level of environmental protection (HLP) principle, 466
    precautionary principle, 466
    procedural fairness, 469
    procedural flexibility, 470
    public participation, 469
    transparency, 469
Timber Regulation, 445
tradable permit schemes, 139
Trade in Seal Products Regulation, 445
transboundary damage. *see* environmental damage
transitional periods, accession to EU, 52
transnational governance. *see* governance
transparency, technological risk regulation, 469
treaty provision, historical development, 1

uncertainty, regulation of. *see* technological risk regulation
United Kingdom
  polluter pays principle, 355
  SPA designation (*Lappel Bank* case), 426
United Nations Economic Commission for Europe (UNECE), 382
United States
  environmental impact assessment (EIA), 380
  toxic substances control, 437
  UNECE membership, 382
urban waste water. *see* water law

value, theories of. *see* philosophy
vehicles. *see* road transport
'vertical' direct effect. *see* effect of EU law
volatile organic compounds (VOCs), air pollution from, 306
voluntary regulation. *see* regulation

waste policy
  Batteries Directive, 514
  by-products, 502
  Community Strategy on Waste Management, 490
  compliance, lack of, 493
  comprehensiveness of, 491
  concept of waste, 498
  consumer goods, waste from, 491
  definition of waste, 499
  'discard', meaning of, 500
  economic benefits of, 490
  End-of-life Directive, 515
  end-of-waste, 504
  Environmental Action Programmes (EAPs), 490, 517
  future challenges, 517
  general regulatory framework, 491
  hazardous waste
    policy, 505
    regulatory framework, 491
  historical development of, 489
  importance of, 489
  incineration of waste, 510
  Landfill Directive, 508
  non-compliance, reasons for, 493
  packaging waste, 513
  polluter pays principle, 489
  production residue as 'waste', 503
  radioactive waste and substances, regulatory framework, 492
  'recycling society' objective, 496
  shipment of waste, 506
  Thematic Strategy on the Prevention and Recycling of Waste, 490
  waste electrical and electronic equipment (WEEE), 516
  Waste Framework Directive
    adoption of, 490, 494
    disposal phase, 496
    extended producer's responsibility, 497
    goals of, 494
    obligations under, 496
    'preparing for reuse' principle, 494

prevention principle, 495
recovery phase, 496
'recycling society' objective, 496
'reuse' principle, 496
waste hierarchy, 495
waste hierarchy principle, 489
waste streams
 about, 512
 batteries and accumulators, 514
 end-of-life vehicles (ELVs), 515
 packaging waste, 513
 waste electrical and electronic equipment (WEEE), 516
waste water. see water law
water law
 bathing water
  classification of waters, 367
  compliance and monitoring, 367
  definition of, 365
  Directives, 365
  implementation assessment and review, 368
  microbiological parameters, 366
  public participation, 367
 Common Implementation Strategy (CIS), 358
 dangerous substances
  Directives of 1976 and 2006, 368
  Priority Substances Directive 2008, 369
 Directives, 338
 drinking water
  compliance and monitoring, 363
  Directives, 360
  implementation assessment and review, 364
  lead levels, 362
  pesticide levels, 363
  'wholesome and clean', 361

EU and international water law in relation, 340
Groundwater Directive 2006
 about, 349
 alternative methods of compliance, 351
 'good groundwater chemical status', 350
 implementation assessment and review, 351
 pollution prevention or limitation, 351
 significant and sustained upward trends of contamination, 350
historical development of, 339
industrial waste water, 377
interconnectedness of European waterways, 338
Nitrates Directive
 additional measures, requirement for, 372
 'general level of protection', 372
 non-point source pollution, 371
 success of, 373
 'vulnerable zones' designation, 371
pollution control, combined approach to, 353
'priority substances', 354
Priority Substances Directive 2008
 about, 369
 listing and standard setting, 369
 quality assessment, 370
Sandoz factory fire, effect on Rhine, 338
urban waste water
 collection, 374

compliance and monitoring, 377
Directive, 373
disposal, 374
eutrophication, 375
less sensitive areas, 376
reuse, 374
secondary treatment, 374
sensitive areas, 374
success of Directive, 377
Water Framework Directive (WFD) 2000
 'artificial and heavily modified bodies of water', 347
 chemical quality of water, 345
 Common Implementation Strategy (CIS) and, 358
 content of, 342
 derogations from 'environmental objectives', 352
 drafting of, 341
 ecological quality of water, 346
 'economic analysis of water use', 355
 'environmental objectives', 344
 'good surface water status', 345
 governance, 357
 groundwater protection, 348
 innovative regulatory approach, 343, 360
 'priority substances', 354
 programmes of measures, 344
 public participation, 357
 river basin management approach, 343
 river basin management plans, 344, 351, 356

Zoos Directive, 445

For EU product safety concerns, contact us at Calle de José Abascal, 56–1°, 28003 Madrid, Spain or eugpsr@cambridge.org.

www.ingramcontent.com/pod-product-compliance
Ingram Content Group UK Ltd.
Pitfield, Milton Keynes, MK11 3LW, UK
UKHW030700060825
461487UK00010B/866